A GENERAL INDEX

TO THE

PHILOSOPHICAL TRANSACTIONS,

FROM THE FIRST TO THE END OF THE SEVENTIETH VOLUME.

By PAUL HENRY MATY, M.A. F.R.S.
UNDER LIBRARIAN TO THE BRITISH MUSEUM.

LONDON:
PRINTED FOR LOCKYER DAVIS AND PETER ELMSLY,
PRINTERS TO THE ROYAL SOCIETY.

MDCCLXXXVII.

AN

ALPHABETICAL INDEX

OF THE

MATTER

CONTAINED IN THE

PHILOSOPHICAL TRANSACTIONS.

AN ALPHABETICAL INDEX TO THE PHILOSOPHICAL TRANSACTIONS.

The first column refers to the Transactions at large, and the other to the Abridgment. The Roman numbers denote the volume, and the Arabic figures the page.

A B C A B D

	Transf.	Abridg.
ABCESS. Anatomical observations of an abcess in the liver; a great number of stones in the gall-bag and bilious vessels; an unusual conformation of the emulgents and pelvis; a strange conjunction of both kidneys and a great dilatation of the vena cava - - - *Tyson*	XII 1035	III 81
ABDOMEN. An account of the dissection of a bitch whose cornua uteri, being filled with the bones and flesh of a former conception, had, after a second conception, the ova affixed to several parts of the abdomen - - -	XIII 183	II 904
—— An account of a great quantity of hydatides found in the abdomen *Anhorn ab Hartwiss Thorpe*	XXXII 17	
—— An account of a dropsy in the left ovary of a woman aged 58, cured by a large incision made in the side of the abdomen - *Houston*	XXXIII 8	VII 541
—— Extract of two uncommon cases of tumours in the abdomen, from a Latin tract published at Strasburg, anno 1728, and intitled Boecleri etc. ad Exteros Medicos Epistola - *Rutty*	XXXV 562	—— 522
—— Case of a woman who had a foetus in her abdomen for nine years - - *Bromfield*	XLI 697	IX 191

	Trans.	Abridg.
—— Case of a large quantity of matter or water contained in cystis's or bags adhering to the peritonæum, and not communicating with the cavity of the abdomen - - *Graham*	XLI 708	IX 187
—— An improvement on the practice of tapping, whereby that operation, instead of a relief for symptoms, becomes an absolute cure for an ascites, exemplified in the case of Jane Roman *Warrick*	XLIII 12 (n. 472.)	XI 1030
—— A Method of conveying liquors into the abdomen, during the operation of tapping *Hales*	— 20	— 1034
—— Further accounts of the success of injecting medicated liquors into the abdomen, in the case of an ascites - - - *Warrick*	(n. 473.) — 47	
—— Account of a child being taken out of the abdomen after having lain there upwards of 16 years - - *Myddleton*	XLIV 617	XI 1017
—— A farther account of some experiments of injecting claret, &c. into the abdomen, after tapping - - *Warrick*	XLIX 485	
—— Account of an extraordinary steatomatous tumour in the abdomen of a woman - *Hanley*	LXI 131	
Aberration of the light of the fixed stars discovered - - - *Bradley*	XXXV 637	IV 149
—— Of light refracted at spherical surfaces and lenses - - - *Klingenstierna*	LI 944	
—— Theorem of the aberration of the rays of light refracted through a lens on account of the spherical figure - *Maskelyne*	LII 17	
—— Phases of the transit of Venus, supposed to be retarded by the aberration of light *Winthrop*	LX 358	
—— On the effect of the aberration of light on the time of a transit of Venus over the sun - *Price*	— 536	
Absorbent (Earth's). An observation of the immoderate and fatal use of crab-stones, and such like absorbent earths, from whence have proceeded stones in the stomach and kidnies *Breynius*	XLI 557	IX 171
Academy of Sciences. Part of a letter, giving an account of the new regulations of the Royal Academy of Sciences at Paris - *Geoffroy*	XXI 144	II 252
Acceleration. A letter concerning the acceleration of the moon - - *Dunthorne* (Accounts, see the next page)	XLVI 162	X 84
Acemella. An account of the acemella and its stone-dissolving faculty - *Hotton* (see Ahmella)	XXII 760	IV 2 322
Acephalous. An account of a monstrous acephalous birth - - *Cooke*	LXV 311	
Acid (Medical). A confirmation of the experiments		

made

bruzzo. Account of a journey into the Province of Abruzzo. Hamilton. 76:368.

Acids. Experiments on the transmission of the vapour of Acids trough an hot Earthen tube. Priestley. 79: 289

Experiments and observations on the dissolution of metals in acids, and their precipitations. Keir. 80: 359

On the nature of the salts termed triple Prussiates, and an Acid formed by the union of certain bodies with the elements of the Prussic Acid. Porrett. 1814: 5

Acids (Mineral) see Salts, Cold (Chemistry)

Acid of Fat. Experimenta ad penitiorem Acidi e Pinguedine bruti cognitionem. Crell. 72: 8.

Acid (Fluoric) An account of some experiments on different combinations of Fluoric Acid — — — Davy. 1812: 352

An account of some new experiments on the fluoric compounds — — — 1814: 62.

Acid (Vitriolic) Experiments on its congelation. — — — — Keir. 77: 267.

Acid (Muriatic) Account of a series of experiments, undertaken with the view of decomposing the Muriatic Acid. Henry. 1800: 188

Observations and experiments upon oxygenized and hyperoxygenized muriatic acid, and upon some combinations of the muriatic acid in its three states. Chenevix. 1802: 126

~~Researches on the elements of the muriatic acid~~ — — — — Davy. 1810: 2

Acidity (Principle of) Experiments and observations relating to — Priestley. 78: 147, 79: 7.

Additional experiments on the Muriatic and Oxymuriatic Acids. Henry. 1812: 238

Acid (Purpuric) Description of an acid principle prepared from the lithic or uric Acid. Prout. 1818: 420

Acid (Sorbic). On the nature and combinations of a newly discovered vegetable Acid; with observations on the malic Acid, and suggestions on the state in which Acid may have previously existed in vegetables. Donovan. 1815: 2

Aerostates. Sur un moyen de donner la direction aux machines aerostatiques. Galvez. 74: 4

	Tranf.	Abridg.
made by Sig. Fracaffati in Italy, by injecting acid liquors into the blood - *Boyle*	II 551	III 232
—— The cure of a total fuppreffion of urine, not caufed by the ftone, by the ufe of acids *Baynard*	XIX 19	III 148
—— Experiments on the diftillation of acids, volatile alkalies, &c. fhewing how they may be condenfed without lofs, and how thereby we may avoid difagreeable and noxious fumes *Woulfe*	LVII 517	
ACID (ANIMAL). Account of an infect likely to yield an acid liquor - *Lifter*	V 2067	II 792
—— Some experiments on a new animal acid *Crellius*	LXX 109	
ACID (NITROUS). Actual fire in detonation, produced by the contact of tin-foil, with the falt compofed of copper and the nitrous acid *Higgins*	LXIII 137	
ACIDULAE. Continuation of an experimental inquiry concerning the nature of the mineral elaftic fpirit or air contained in the Pouhon water, and other acidulae - *Brownrigg*	LXIV 357	
Acmella see Acemella & Ahmella		
ACOMACK. Relation of the effects of a violent ftorm at Acomack in America, Oct. 19, 1692, on the rivers of that country - *Scarburgh*	XIX 659	II 104
ACORNS. A letter on the fuccefs of experiments for preferving acorns for a whole year, without planting them, fo as to be in a ftate fit for vegetation, with a view to bring over fome of the moft valuable feeds from the Eaft Indies, to plant for the benefit of our American Colonies - - - *Ellis*	LVIII 75	
ACCOUNTS. Rules for correcting the ufual methods of computing amounts and prefent values, by compound as well as fimple intereft; and of ftating intereft accounts - - *Watkins*	XXIX 3	V P 2 243
ACRES. A demonftration of the number of acres contained in England, or South Britain; and the ufe which may be made of it - *Grew*	XXVII 266	IV 449
ACTINIA SOCIATA. An account of the actinia fociata, or cluftered animal flower, lately found on the fea-coafts of the new ceded iflands - *Ellis*	LVII ~~482~~ 428	
ADAMANT. ~~On the particles and ftructure of adamant~~ see Diamond - - ~~*Leeuwenhoek*~~	~~XXXII 199~~	~~VI 2 226~~
ADITS. An account how adits and mines are worked at Liege without air-fhafts - *Moray*	I 79	II 372
ÆTNA. A chronological account of the feveral eruptions of Mount Ætna - *Anon.*	IV 967	— 386
—— An anfwer to fome inquiries concerning the eruptions of Mount Ætna in 1669	— 1028	— 387

	Tranf.	Abridg.
—— A particular account of divers minerals, fent from the lately burning Mount Ætna - *Anon.*	IV 1041	II 390
—— An extract of a letter concerning a late eruption of Mount Ætna, 1755 - - *By the Magiftrates of Mafcali*	XLIX 209	
—— An account of a journey to Mount Ætna, 1769 - - *Sir William Hamilton*	LX 1	
AFRICA. An account of a journey into, from the Cape of Good Hope - *Sparrman* (See Cape of good hope Cape town)	LXVII 38	
AGARIC OF OAK. Experiments concerning the ufe of the agaric of oak in ftopping hæmorrhages - - *Sharp, Warner*	XLVIII 588	
—— Some obfervations upon the agaric, lately applied after amputations, with regard to determining its fpecies - - *W. Watfon*	— 811	
—— Two letters concerning the ufe of agaric as a ftyptic - - *Warner, Gooch*	— 813	
—— An account of a fpecies of plant, from which the agaric, ufed as a ftyptic, is prepared *W. Watfon*	XLIX 28	
—— Extracts of two letters concerning the effects of the agaric of the oak, after fome of the moft capital operations in furgery - *Latterman*	— 36	
—— An account of the fuccefs of agaric, and the fungus vinofus, in amputations - *Ford*	— 93	
—— An account of the fuccefs of agaric in amputations - - *Thornhill*	— 264	
—— See *Styptic* and *Lycoperdon.*		
AGE. Part of a letter concerning a perfon who had a new fett of teeth after 80 years of age; with fome obfervations upon the virtues and properties of fugar - - *Slare*	I 380	V 353
—— Two cafes of perfons cutting teeth in their old age - - - *Colepreffe*	XXVIII 273	III 297
AGITATION. An account of an unufual agitation of the fea at Ildfarcombe in Devonfhire, Feb. 27, 1756 - - *Prince*	XLIX 642	
AGNUS SCYTHICUS. An account of the Scythian vegetable Lamb, called Borametz - *Breynius*	XXXIII 353	VI 2 317
AGRICULTURE. Enquiries, propofed to be made concerning agriculture *Committee of the Royal Society*	I 91	II 752
—— An account of a voyage to Chufan in China, with a defcription of the ifland, of the feveral forts of tea, of the fifhing, agriculture of the Chinefe, &c. with feveral obfervations not hitherto taken notice of - *Cunningham*	XXIII 1201	V 2 171
—— A letter concerning the manuring of land with foffil-fhells - - *Pickering*	XLIII 191	X 796

Affinities (Chemical) see Attractions

Air. Experiments on Air — — — — — — — — — — Cavendish 74: 119
Remarks on Mr Cavendish's experiments on Air — — — Kirwan — 154
Answer to Mr Kirwan's remarks upon the experiments on Air. Cavendish — 170
Reply to Mr Cavendish's answer — — — — — Kirwan — 178
Experiments and observations relating to Air — — — Priestley 75: 279.
On the conversion of a mixture of dephlogisticated and phlogisticated air into nitrous acid, by the electric spark. — — — Cavendish 78: 261
Experiments on the affinities of the phlogisticated and light inflammable airs — — — — — — Austin — 379
Experiments and observations on the aërial fluids extricated from animal substances by distillation and putrefaction, with some remarks on sulphureous hepatic air — — — — Crawford 80: 391
Farther experiments relating to the decomposition of dephlogisticated and inflammable air — — — — — — — Priestley 81: 213.

	Tranſ.	Abridg.
Agues. An account of the ſucceſs of the bark of the willow in the cure of agues - *Stone*	LIII 195	
Ahmella. Letter concerning Swammerdam's treatiſe de Apibus; the Ahmella Ceylonenſibus, and the Faba S. Ignatii - *Hotton*	XXI 365	II 648
Air (In general). Some trials about the air uſually harboured and concealed in the pores of water - - - *Boyle*	V 2019	
—— Some experiments ſhewing the difference of ice made without air, from that which is produced with air - *Rinaldini*	VI 2169	II 164
—— An account of the increaſe of weight in oil of vitriol expoſed to the air - *Gould*	XIV 496	— 534
—— An experiment, of a ſurprizing change of colour from a pale tranſparent, or clear liquor, to a blue ceruleous one, and that in an inſtant, by the admiſſion of air only; applied to illuſtrate ſome changes of colour, and other effects on the blood of reſpiring animals - *Slare*	XVII 898	
—— Experiments concerning the effects of air paſſed through red-hot metals - *Haukſbee*	XXVII 199	IV 2 182
—— An experiment concerning the nitrous particles in the air - - *Clayton*	XLI 62	VIII 465
—— A ſuppoſition how the white matter is produced which floats about in the air in autumn *Arderon*	XLIV 428	
—— A diſſertation on the nature of evaporation and ſeveral phænomena of air, water, and boiling liquors - - *Hamilton*	LV 146	
—— Obſervations on different kinds of air *Prieſtley*	LXII 147	
—— A continuation of an experimental enquiry concerning the nature of the mineral elaſtic ſpirit, or air, contained in the Pouhon water, and other acidulae - *Brownrigg*	LXIV 3517	
—— An account of further diſcoveries in air *Prieſtley*	LXV 384	
—— Experiments upon air, and the effects of different kinds of effluvia upon it - *White*	LXVIII 194	
Air (Appearances obſerved in the). An account of the appearance of ſeveral unuſual parhelia, or mock ſuns; together with ſeveral circular arches lately ſeen in the air - *Halley*	XXIII 1127	IV 228
—— A letter from Annapolis in Maryland, containing an account of an exploſion in the air *Lewis*	XXXVIII 119	VIII 685
—— Two obſervations of exploſions in the air, one heard at Halſted in Eſſex, the other at Springfield in the ſame county *Vievar and Shepheard*	XLI 288	VIII 526
—— An account of a meteor ſeen in the air in the day time on Dec. 8, 1733 - *Crocker*	— 346	VIII 517

	Tranſ.	Abridg.
—— An account of a fire-ball ſeen in the air, and of an exploſion heard Dec. 11, 1741, near London - - - *Lord Beauchamp*	XLI 870	VIII 523
—— ———— in Suſſex - *Fuller*	— 871	— —
—— ———— in Kent - *Goſtlin*	— 872	— 524
—— Account of a fiery meteor ſeen in the air July 14, 1745 - - *Coſtard*	XLIII 522	
—— ———— Dec. 16, 1742 - *Moſtines*	— 524	
—— Letter concerning an exploſion in the air, heard at Norwich in Jan. 7, 1750 - *Arderon*	XLVI 698	X 513
—— An account of a fire-ball ſeen in the air July 22, 1750 - - *Stukeley*	XLVII 1	
—— Another account - - *Baker*	— 3	
AIR (Damp).——An account of the damp air in a coal-pit of Sir James Lowther, Bart. ſunk within 20 yards of the ſea *Lowther*	XXXVIII 109	VIII 656
—— An experiment to ſhew, that ſome damps in mines may be occaſioned only by the burning of candles under ground, without the addition of any noxious vapours, even when the bottom of the pit has a communication with the outward air, unleſs the outward air be forcibly driven in at the ſaid communication or pipe - - - *Deſaguliers*	XXXIX 281	— 657
—— A letter containing a ſhort account of an exploſion of air in a coal-pit at Middleton, near Leeds in Yorkſhire - *Bernard*	LXIII 217	
AIR (Denſity of the).——An account of an experiment touching the different denſities of the air, from the greateſt natural heat to the greateſt natural cold in this climate *Haukſbee*	XXVI 93	IV 2 181
AIR (Effects of the, on animals)		
—— A compariſon of the times, wherein animals may be killed by drowning in air, or withdrawing it - - *Boyle*	V 2028	
—— Of the accidents that happen to animals in air brought to a conſiderable degree, but not near the utmoſt one of rarefaction. - *Boyle*	V 2036	IV 225
—— Of the obſervations produced in an animal in changes as to rarity and denſity made in the ſelf-ſame air - - *Boyle*	V 2039	IV 225
—— Experiments on the neceſſity of air to the motion of ants and mites - - *Boyle*	V 2054	
—— A letter containing ſome conſiderations about the ſwimming bladders in fiſhes - *Ray*	X 349	II 846
—— A conjecture concerning the bladders of air that are found in fiſhes, illuſtrated by an experiment ſuggeſted by the Hon. Robert Boyle	X 310	— —

	Transf.	Abridg.
—— The art of living under water; or a difcourfe concerning the means of furnifhing air at the bottom of the fea, in any ordinary depths - - - *Halley*	XXIX 492	IV 2 188
—— Obfervations on a cafe publifhed in the laft volume of the Medical Effays, &c. of recovering a man dead in appearance, by diftending the lungs with air - *Fothergill*	XLIII 275	XI 969
—— On the degree of falubrity of the common air at fea, compared with that of the fea-fhore, and that of places far removed from the fea - - - *Ingen Houfz*	LXX 354	
AIR (Effects of the air when condenfed or rarefied by the air-pump and condenfing engine).—Propofals to try the effects of the pneumatick engine exhaufted, on plants, feeds, eggs of filk-worms - - *Beale*	II 424	II 656
—— Various experiments made in the exhaufted receiver - - *Boyle*	V 2011, 2013, 2015, 2017, 2023, 2024, 2026, 2027, 2040, 2049, 2051, 2052	II 215
—— Some experiments made in the air pump at Paris by Papin, directed by Huygens - *Papin*	X 443	— 239
—— Some experiments made in the air pump upon plants, together with a way of taking exhaufted receivers away from off the faid engine. - - *Papin and Huygens*	— 477	— 205
—— A continuation of the above experiments on the prefervation of bodies *Papin and Huygens*	— 492	— 245
—— Some experiments touching animals, made in the air pump - *Huygens and Papin*	— 542	II 250
—— Promifcuous experiments made in the air-pump - - - *Huygens and Papin*	— 544	
—— An account of an experiment of fhooting by the rarefaction of the air - *Papin*	XVI 21	I 456
——— A demonftration of the velocity wherewith the air rufhes into an exhaufted receiver *Papin*	XVI 193	— 497
——— Concerning the application of an air-pump to cupping-glaffes - *Luffkin*	XXI 287	III 265
——— Letter concerning the application of the pneumatick engine to cupping-glaffes *Luffkin*	— 408	— —
—— Experiments on the refilition of bodies in common air, in vacuo, and in air condenfed - - - *Haukfbee*	XXIV 1946	IV 2 181

—— An

		Transf.	Abridg.
—— An experiment on the descent of malt-dust in an evacuated receiver — *Hauksbee*		XXIV 1948	IV 2 173
—— An experiment shewing, that the seemingly spontaneous ascent of water in small tubes, open at both ends, is the same in vacuo as in the open air — — *Hauksbee*		XXV 2223	— - 181
—— An account of an experiment, touching the difficulty of separating two hemispheres, upon the injecting of an atmosphere of air on their outward surfaces, without withdrawing the included air — — *Hauksbee*		XXV 2415	— - 180
—— An account of the success of an attempt to continue several atmospheres of air condensed in the space of one, for a considerable time — — — *Hauksbee*		XXVI 217	— - 181
—— Experiments on animal fluids in the exhausted receiver — *Darwin*		LXIV 344	
AIR (Elasticity and mechanical observations concerning)—— An account how adits and mines are wrought at Liege without air-shafts *Moray*		I 79	— 372
—— Experiments shewing that air, become unfit for respiration, may retain its wonted pressure — — — *Boyle*		V 2046	
—— Of its use to elevate the steams of bodies *Boyle*		V 2048	— 297
—— A table shewing to what degree air is compressible in sea-water, from the depth of 1 foot to 1947 feet; useful to divers. — — *Members of the Royal Society*		VI 2192	II 201
—— Considerations touching the compressure of the air — — *Leewenhoeck*		IX 21	III 683
—— Ten new experiments about the weakened spring, and some unobserved effects of the air *Boyle*		X 467	II 235
—— A full description, with the use of a new contrivance for raising water — *Papin*		XV 1274	I 540
—— Answer to several objections made by Mr. Nevis against his engine for raising water by the rarefaction of the air — *Papin*		XVI 263	— 542
—— A discourse concerning the measure of the air's resistance to bodies moved in it — *Wallis*		XVI 269	I 484
—— An experiment shewing, that the springs or constituent parts of air are capable to suffer such disorder by a violent impulse, as to require time to recover their natural state *Hauksbee*		XXV 2412	IV 2 181
There are two pages of this No. in this vol. and this is the second.			
—— Experiments concerning the time required in the descent of different bodies of different magnitudes			

	Tranſ.	Abridg.
tudes and weights in common air, from the ſame height - - *Haukſbee*	XXVII 196	IV 2 182
—— Barometrical experiments for diſcovering the various elaſticity of the air in different parts of Switzerland - *Scheuchzer*	XXIX 266	IV 2 16
—— An account of ſome experiments made on the 27th of April, 1719, to find how much the reſiſtance of the air retards falling bodies - - *Deſaguliers*	XXX 1071	IV 2 175
—— Further experiments - *Deſaguliers*	— 1075	— - 178
—— An account of ſeveral experiments concerning the running of water in pipes, as it is retarded by friction and intermediate air, with a deſcription of a new machine, whereby pipes may be cleared of air, as the water runs along, without hand-pipes, or the help of any hand *Deſaguliers*	XXXIV 77	VI 347
—— An attempt made to ſhew how damps or foul air may be drawn out of any ſort of mines, &c. by an engine - *Deſaguliers*	XXXV 353	VI 2 193
—— An account of an inſtrument or machine for changing the air of the room of ſick people in a little time, by either drawing out the foul air, or forcing in freſh air; or doing both ſucceſſively, without opening doors or windows - - - *Deſaguliers*	XXXIX 41	VIII 270
—— A calculation of the velocity of the air moved by a new-invented centrifugal bellows of 7 feet in diameter, and 1 foot thick within, which a man can keep in motion with very little labour, at the rate of two revolutions in one ſecond - - - *Deſaguliers*	XXXIX 44	VIII 271
—— The uſes of the foregoing machine	— 47	— 273
—— An account of an invention and method of changing the air in the hold, and other cloſe parts of a ſhip - *Sutton*	XLII 42	— 628
—— Obſervations upon Mr. Sutton's invention to extract foul and ſtinking air out of ſhips, with critical remarks upon the uſe of windſails - - - *Watſon*	XLII 62	— 630
—— An account of the great benefit of blowing ſhowers of freſh air up through diſtilling liquors - - *Hales*	XLIV 312	
—— Thoughts on Dr. Hales's new method of diſtilling by the force of air and fire *Brownrigg*	XLIX 534	
AIR (Electricity of the). Obſervations upon the electricity of the air, made at the Chateau de		

		Transf.	Abridg.
Maintenon in June, July, and October 1753 - - -	*Mazeas*	XLVIII 377	
AIR (Fixed). A Letter on the solubility of iron in simple water, by the intervention of fixed air - - -	*Lane*	LIX 216	
—— The description of an apparatus for impregnating water with fixed air, and of the manner of conducting that process -	*Nooth*	LXV 59	
AIR (Gravity and temperature of the). Letter containing particulars of a philosophical nature, viz. a narrative of the strange effects of thunder upon a magnetic card; some remarks concerning the gradual alteration of the temperature of the air in divers countries; a contrivance of an uncommon hygroscope; the musky scent of certain parts of the animal called the musk-quash - - -	*Anon.*	XI 647	II 42 43
—— A discourse concerning the air's gravity - - -	*Wallis*	XV 1002	III 122
—— A letter giving an account of several observations in Virginia and in his voyage thither, more particularly concerning the air	*Clayton*	XVII 781	III 575
—— Second letter of farther observations on Virginia - - -	*Clayton*	— 790	
—— An account of an experiment, touching the proportion of the weight of air, to the weight of a like bulk of water, without knowing the quantity of either -	*Haukſbee*	XXV 2221	IV 2 180
—— An observation of extraordinary warmth of the air in January 1741 -	*Miles*	XLII 20	III 469
—— On the correspondence of the barometer with the air and weather -	*Holman*	XLVI 101	X 428
—— Remarks on the heat of the air in July 1757 - - -	*Huxham*	L 428	
—— Additional remarks -	*Watson*	— 429	
—— An account of the extraordinary heat of the weather in July 1757, and of the effects of it - - -	*Huxham*	— 523	
—— Remarks on the different temperature of the air at Eddystone, from that observed at Plymouth, between the 7th and 14th of July 1757 - - -	*Smeaton*	— 488	
—— An investigation of the difference between the present temperature of the air in Italy and some other countries, and what it was seventeen centuries ago -	*Barrington*	LVIII 58	
—— An account of a most extraordinary degree of			

cold

-(Fixed) On the decomposition of fixed Air. - - - - - - Tennant. 81:182.

[e]xperiments made with the view of decompounding fixed air, or carbonic acid Pearson. 1792:289.

Air (Dephlogisticated) Thoughts on its constituent parts - - - - Watt 74: 329, 35
Experiments on the production of it from water, with various substances. Thompson 77: 84

Air (Hepatic) Experiments on hepatic air - - - - - Kirwan 76: 118.
Sur les Gas Hepatiques - - - - - - - Hassenfratz 77: 305

Air (Inflammable) Experiments on the analysis of the heavy inflammable air.
Austin. 80: 51.

AIR

	Tranf.	Abridg.
cold at Glaſgow in January 1780; together with ſome new experiments and obſervations on the comparative temperature of hoar-froſt, and the air near to it, made at Glaſgow - *Wilſon*	LXX 451	
AIR (Hiſtory of the). A phyſical hiſtory of the earth and air for the year 1732 - *Cyrillus*	XXXVIII 184	VIII 625
AIR (Inflammable). A chemical experiment, ſerving to illuſtrate the phænomenon of inflammable air, ſhewn to the Royal Society by Sir James Lowther, and deſcribed in the Tranſactions, Nº 429 - - *Mau.*	XXXIX 282	IX 396
——— Account of a new kind of inflammable air or gas, which can be made in a moment without apparatus, and is as fit for exploſion as other inflammable gaſſes in uſe for that purpoſe; together with a new theory of gunpowder - *Ingen-Houſz*	LXIX 376	
——— Experiments and obſervations on the inflammable air breathed by various animals - - - - *Fontana*	— 337	
AIR (Nitrous). Eaſy methods of meaſuring the diminution of bulk taking place upon the mixture of common air and nitrous air; together with experiments on platina *Ingen-Houſz*	LXVI 257	
AIR (Production of). An account of an experiment to try the quality of air produced from gunpowder, fired in vacuo Boyliano *Haukſbee*	XXIV 1807	IV 2 172
——— An account of an experiment touching the quantity of air produced from a certain quantity of gunpowder fired in common air - - - *Haukſbee*	XXV 2409	IV 2 181
——— Three papers containing experiments on factitious air - - *Cavendiſh*	LVI 141	
——— Account of the airs extracted from different kinds of waters; with thoughts on the ſalubrity of the air at different places - *Fontana*	LXIX 432	
AIR (Promiſcuous properties of). Obſervations on ſeveral paſſages in the Tranſactions, relating to ſome unobſerved qualities of the air; to the mixing fermenting liquors in vacuo; to the hiſtory of birds; the anatomy of the trunks of vegetables, baroſcopes, &c. - *Anon.*	X 533	
——— An experiment touching the freezing of common water, and water purged of air *Haukſbee*	XXVI 302	IV 2 182
——— An experiment touching the weighing of bodies of the ſame ſpecies, but of very unequal ſur-

	Tranſ.	Abridg.
faces in common water, being of an equal weight in common air - *Haukſbee*	— 306	— - 181
AIR (Refraction of the). An experiment of the refraction of the air, made at the command of the Royal Society - *Lowthorp*	XXI 339	I 228
—— Some allowances to be made in aſtronomical obſervations for the refraction of the air, with an accurate table of refractions - *Halley*	XXXI 169	VI 167
AIR-PUMP. An account of ſome improvements in the air-pump - *Smeaton*	XLVII 415	
——— An account of ſome experiments made with an air-pump on Mr. Smeaton's principle; together with ſome experiments with a common air-pump - - *Nairne*	LXVII 614	
ALBATENIUS. Emendations and notes upon the antient aſtronomical tables of Albatenius, with the reſtoration of his luni-ſolar tables *Halley*	XVII 913	III 522
ALCALI. Two letters, giving an account of a red colour produced by mixture of a ſulphureous ſpirit with a volatile alcali - *Gibbon*	XIX 542	— 367
ALCALINE SALTS. A diſſertation on fixed alcaline ſalts - - *Neuman*	XXXIV 3	VII 700
——— Continued - *Neuman*	— 45	— 717
—— A chemical experiment of the effect of quick lime upon volatile alcaline - *Schloſſer*	XLIX 222	
—— Experiments on the diſtillation of acids, volatile alkalies, &c. ſhewing how they may be condenſed without loſs, and how thereby to avoid diſagreeable and noxious fumes *Woulfe*	LVII 517	
—— See *Salt.*		
ALCANNA. Concerning ruſma and alcanna - - *Phil. Soc. Oxf.*	XX 295	II 645
ALDEBARAN. An obſervation of the moon's tranſit by Aldebaran, Apr. 3, 1736 - *Bevis*	XL 90	VIII 133
—— An occultation of Aldebaran by the Moon, Dec. 12, 1738 - - *Graham*	XLI 632	— 135
ALEPPO. A relation of a voyage from Aleppo to Palmyra in Syria - *Hallifax*	XIX 83	III 503
ALGA. Obſervations on the ſea alga with broad leaves - - - *Peyſſonel*	L 631	
ALGEBRA. Thoughts about ſome defects in algebra - - - *Collins*	XIV 575	
—— A treatiſe of algebra, both hiſtorical and practical - - *Wallis*	XV 1095	
—— A correction of the 109th chapter of Wallis's algebra - - *Wallis*	XIX 729	
—— An inſtance of the excellence of the modern al-		

gebra

tir-Pump. Description of an improved Air-pump. Cavallo 73:435.
On a new construction of a Condensor and Air-pump.
Austin 1813:138.

tir Vane of great sensibility. - - - - - - . Bennet. 1792:

lbumen. see (Animal) Fluids.

lburnum. On the origin and office of the Alburnum of trees. Wright. 1808:313.

lcaline salts. Experiments on the formation of Volatile Alkali. Austin. 78:379.
On some new phenomena of chemical changes produced by Electricity, particularly the decomposition of the fixed Alkalies, and the exhibition of the new substances which constitute their bases; and on the general nature of Alkaline bodies. Davy. 1808:1.

Alcohol. see Spirit.
Algohol of Sulphur. Experiments on the Alcohol of Sulphur or Sulphuret of Carbon. Marcet & Berzelius. 1813:171.
Algæ. On the fructification of the submersed Algæ. Correa. 1796:494.

Algebra. On finding the value of Algebraical Quantities by converging serieses, and demonstrating and extending propositions given by Pappus and others. Waring 77:

Algol. Observations on, and Discovery of the period of variation of the light of the bright star in the head of Medusa, called Algol. Goodricke 73:474

Observations of the variation of light in the star Algol. - - - Englefield 74:1.

Palitch —4,5.

On the period of the changes of light in the star Algol - - - Goodricke —287.

Almanachs. An Account of three Hindoo Almanachs, belonging to C. Wilkins Esq: Cavendish. 1792:38

	Tranf.	Abridg.
gebra in the refolution of the problem of finding the foci of optick-glaffes univerfally *Halley*	XVII 960	I 183
—— A fecond letter concerning the roots of equations, with the demonftration of other rules in algebra - - *Maclaurin*	XXXVI 59	VI 25
—— An algebraic problem, and of the evolution of a certain mechanic curve amongft infinite hypermechanical ones, which refolve a certain equation (Lat.) - - *Fantoni*	LVII 358	
—— Obfervations on the limits of algebraical equations; and a general demonftration of Des Cartes's rule for finding their number of affirmative and negative roots - *Milner*	LXVIII 380	
———— On the general refolution of algebraical equations - *Waring*	LXIX 86	
—— See *Equations.*		
—— See *Opticks.*		
Alhazen. Letters between M. Slufius and M. Hugenius relative to an optic problem of Alhazen, - - -	VIII 6119 — 6139	I 172 — 174
Alicant. See *Soap.*		
Aliment. An account of the bones of animals being changed to a red colour by aliment only *Belchier*	XXXIX 287	IX 102
—— A further account of the bones of animals being made red by aliment only - *Belchier*	— 299	— 103
Allantois. The humane allantois fully difcovered, and the reafons affigned why it has not hitherto been found out, even by thofe who believed its exiftence; with an anfwer to their objections who deny it ftill - *Hale*	XXII 835	V 314
Alligator. An account of the foffile bones of an alligator, found on the fea-fhore near Whitby in Yorkfhire - *Chapman*	L 688	
—— Another account of the fame - *Wooller*	— 786	
Aloe Americana Serrati-folia. An experiment on Aloe Americana Serrati-folia weighed, feeming to import a circulation of the fap in plants - - - *Merret*	II 455	— 645
Alum. A defcription of a Swedifh ftone, which affords fulphur, vitriol, allum, and minium *Talbot*	I 375	II 531
—— A continuation of the difcourfe concerning vitriol, fhewing, that vitriol is ufually produced by fulphur, acting on, and coagulating with, a metal; and then making out, that alum is likewife the refult of the faid fulphur, as alfo evincing, that vitriol, fulphur, and alum, do agree in the faline principles: and, laftly, de-		

claring

	Tranf.	Abridg.
claring the nature of the falt in brimftone, and whence it is derived - *Anon.*	IX 66	II 544
ALUM-WORKS. An account of the Englifh alum-works - - *Colwall*	XII 1052	— 538
ALPHABET. An effay towards a univerfal alphabet, and new primer - *Lodwick*	XVI 126	III 373
—— A letter containing fome remarks on Mr. Lodwick's alphabet - *Byrom*	XLV 401	XI 1386
—— Further remarks upon M. l'Abbé Barthelemy's Memoir on the Phœnician letters; containing his reflections on certain Phœnician monuments, and the alphabets refulting from them - - - *Swinton*	LIV 393	
ALPINE MOUSE. The anatomy of the Alpine moufe - - - *Scheuchzer*	XXXIV 237	VII 452
———— A fhort natural hiftory of the Alpine moufe (Lat.) - - *Klein*	XLV 180	XI 900
ALTAR (ROMAN). Account of a Roman altar found at Chefter - - *Halley*	XIX 316	III 425
—— An account of two Roman altars lately found in the North of England, with notes, by Tho. Gale - - *Thorefby*	— 663	— 424
—— An attempt to explain two Roman infcriptions, cut upon two altars, which were dug up fome time fince at Bath - *Ward*	XLIV 285	
—— The infcription upon a Roman altar found near Stanhope, in the bifhoprick of Durham *Birch*	XLV 173	XI 1272
—— An account of a Roman altar, with an infcription upon it, found in April laft at York, and communicated to the Society of Antiquaries by F. Drake; as alfo a brief explication of the infcription by John Ward	XLVIII 33	
ALTERNATIONS. The doctrine of combinations and alternations improved and compleated - - - *Thornycroft*	XXIV 1961	IV 60
ALTITUDE. Table of the barometrical altitudes at Zurich in Switzerland, in the year 1708, by Scheuchzer; and at Upminfter in England, by Derham; as alfo the rain at Pifa in Italy, in 1707 and 1708, by Tilli; and at Zurich in 1708; and at Upminfter in all that time: with remarks on the fame tables; as alfo on the winds, heats, colds, and divers other matters occurring in thofe three parts of Europe *Derham*	XXVI 342	
ALTITUDES. The defcription of a new quadrant for taking altitudes, without an horizon, either at fea or land - - *Elton*	XXXVII 273

ALT AMB

	Tranf.	Abridg.
——— Account of a spirit-level to be fixed to a quadrant for taking a meridional altitude at sea, when the horizon is not visible - *Hadley*	XXXVIII 167	VIII 357
——— A description of a water-level to be fixed to Davis's quadrant for taking the sun's altitude at sea in thick and hazy weather without an horizon - - *Leigh*	XL 413	— 360
——— The description and use of an apparatus, added as an improvement to Davis's quadrant, consisting of a mercurial level, for taking the co-altitude of sun or star at sea, without the usual assistance of the sensible horizon, which frequently is obscured - *Leigh*	XL 417	— 362
——— A new method of finding time by equal altitudes - - *Aubert*	LXVI 92	
——— An account of the apparatus applied to the equatorial instrument, for correcting the errors arising from the refraction in altitude *Dollond*	LXIX 332	
AMALGAM. On the use of an amalgam of zinc, for the purpose of electrical excitation - - - *Higgins*	LXVIII 861	
AMAND (ST).-MINERAL WATERS. Letter concerning the mineral waters of St. Amand, near Tournay and Valenciennes - *Geoffry*	XX 430	II 334
AMBE. The ambe of Hippocrates, for reducing luxations of the arm with the shoulder, rectified - - - *M. le Cat*	XLII 387	IX 257
AMBER. Account of a curious piece of *Hevelius*	V 2061	II 490
——— An observation about white amber *Kirkby*	VII 4069	— 491
——— A compendious history and demonstration of the Prussian amber - *Hartmann*	XXI 5	— 473
——— An account of several curiosities relating to amber - - *Hartmann*	— 49	— 599
——— A Treatise on amber (*ambergris*) *Camel*	XXIV 1591	IV 2 278
——— Experiments on the luminous qualities of amber, diamonds, and gumlac - *Wall*	XXVI 69	— — 275
——— An observation of a piece of amber with a leaf of a plant impressed on it — *Breynius*	XXXIV 154	VI 2 232
——— An extract from a letter on the nature of amber - - - *Beurer*	XLII 322	VIII 734
——— Extract from an essay on the origin of amber - - - *Fothergill*	XLIII 21	X 774
AMBERGRISE. Letter concerning ambergrease, and its being a vegetable production *Boyle*	VIII 6113	II 492
——— An account of a great piece of ambergrise, thrown on the island of Jamaica *Tredway*	XIX 711	— —
——— Found in whales - - *Boylston*	XXXIII 193	VII 423
——— *Tractatulus de Ambaro* - - - *Camel*	XXIV 1591	IV 2 278

		Tranſ.	Abridg.
—— An eſſay upon the natural hiſtory of whales, with a particular account of the ambergreaſe found in the ſpermaceti whales	*Dudley*	XXXIII 256	VII 424
—— A treatiſe on ambergreaſe, Par. I -	*Neumann*	XXXVIII 344	IX 339
—— ———— Par. II -	*Neumann*	— 371	— 346
—— ———— Par. III -	*Neumann*	— 417	— 358
—— A review of the experiments on ambergreaſe made by Meſſrs. Browne and Hanckewits, by Dr. Martine, with Mr. Neumann's vindication of his own experiment -	*Neumann*	— 437	— 366
AMERICA. A narrative of ſome obſervations made upon ſeveral voyages to find a way for ſailing about the North to the Eaſt Indies, and for returning the ſame way from thence hither; together with the inſtruction given by the Dutch Eaſt India Company for the diſcovery of Jeſſo, near Japan. To which is added, a relation of ſailing through the northern America to the Eaſt Indies -	*Van Nierop*	IX 197	
—— Some obſervations concerning a poſſible paſſage to the Eaſt Indies by the Northern America, Weſtward - -	*Anon.*	— 207	
—— An account of that part of America which is neareſt to the land of Kamtchatka; extracted from the deſcription of Kamtchatka, by profeſſor Kraſhennikoff -	*Dumareſque*	LI 477	
—— A diſſertation on the bones and teeth of elephants, and other beaſts, found in North America, and other Northern regions; by which it appears they are the bones of indigenous beaſts - -	*Raſpe*	LIX 126	
—— Obſervations of eclipſes of Jupiter's firſt ſatellite at Greenwich, compared with obſervations of the ſame made by Samuel Holland in North America, and the longitudes of places thence deduced - -	*Maſkelyne*	LXIV 184	
—— Immerſions and emerſions of Jupiter's firſt ſatellites obſerved at Jupiter's inlet, on the iſland of Anticoſti, North America, and the longitude of the place deduced from compariſon with obſervations made at the Royal Obſervatory at Greenwich, by the Aſtronomer Royal	*Wright*	— 190	
AMIANTHUS. A curious relation, taken out of the third Venetian journal de Letterati, of a ſubſtance found in great quantities in ſome mines of Italy; out of which is made a kind of incombuſtible ſubſtance, both ſkin, paper, and			

candle-

Ambergrise. Account of — Schwediauer 73: 226.
On the production of Ambergris. - — — - - 81: 43.

Ambuscade. An account of the sinking of the Dutch Frigate Ambuscade near the great Nore, with the mode used in recovering her. Whidbey. 1803. 321.

America. A memoir on the geography of the north-eastern part of Asia, and on the question whether Asia and America are contiguous, or are separated by the sea. Burney, 1818.9.

Ammonia. On the production of an amalgam from Ammonia, and on its nature and properties. Davy. 1808: 35.

Experiments on Ammonia, and an account of a new method of analyzing it, by combustion with Oxygen and other gases. Henry. 1809: 43

+Amphibia. Observations on the class of animals called, by Linnaeus, Amphibia. Gray. 79: 21.

On the urinary organs and secretions of some of the Amphibia. Davy. 1818: 303.

+Analysis. On a method of analyzing stones containing fixed Alkali, by means of the Boracic acid. Davy. 1805: 231.

An account of some new analytical researches on the nature of certain bodies, particularly the Alkalies, Phosphorus, Sulphur, Carbonaceous matter, and the acids hitherto undecompounded; with some general observations on chemical theory. —— 1809: 39.

New analytical researches on the nature of certain bodies, being an appendix to the Bakerian Lecture for 1808. —— —— 450.

A synoptic scale of chemical equivalents. Wollaston. 1814: 1.

	Tranſ.	Abridg.
candle-wick, together with ſome experiments made therewith - *Caſtagna*	VI 2167	II 548
AMIANTHUS. See *Aſbeſtus*.		
AMLWCH WATERS. An account of the vitriolic waters of Amlwch, in the iſle of Angleſey *Rutty*	LI 470	
AMMONITÆ. A letter concerning ſome vertebræ of ammonitæ, or cornua ammonis *Miles*	XLVI 37	X 641
AMNII LIQUOR. Some obſervations, proving that the fœtus is in part nouriſhed by the liquor Amnii - - - *Fleming*	XLIX 254	
AMOMUM. A deſcription and figure of the true Amomum, or Tugus of the Philippines *Camelli*	XXI 2	II 646
AMOUNTS. Rules for correcting the uſual methods of computing amounts and preſent values by compound, as well as ſimple intereſt; and of ſtating intereſt-accounts - *Watkins*	XXIX 111	V 2 243
AMPHIBIOUS ANIMALS. An account of an amphibious bipes - - *Ellis*	LVI 189	
—— —— A ſupplement to the account of an amphibious bipes, being the anatomical deſcription of the ſaid animal - *Ellis*	— 307	
—— Obſervations upon animals, commonly called amphibious by authors - *Parſons*	— 193	
—— An account of the lymphatic ſyſtem in amphibious animals - - *Hewſon*	LIX 198	
AMPUTATION. A letter concerning the uſe of lycoperdon in ſtopping blood after amputation *Parſons*	XLIX 38	
—— An account of the ſucceſs of Agaric, and Fungus Vinoſus, upon amputations - *Ford*	— 93	
—— Remarks and conſiderations relative to the performance of amputation above the knee, by the ſingle circular inciſion - *Gooch*	LXV 373	
—— See *Agaric*, *Fungus Vinoſus*, *Lycoperdon* and *Styptic*.		
ANALYSIS. Experiments by way of analyſis upon the water of the dead ſea, upon the hot ſprings near Tiberiades, and upon Hamman Pharoan water - - - *Perry*	XLII 48	VIII 643
ANALYTICAL. Univerſal ſolution for quadratic and biquadratic equations, viz. analytical, geometrical, and mechanical - *Colſon*	XXV 2353	IV 66
—— Analytical ſolution of certain infiniteſimal equations - - *De Moivre*	— 2368	— 77
ANASTOMOSES. An account of ſome uncommon anaſtomoſes of the ſpermatic veſſels in a woman - - - *Mortimer*	XXXVI 373	VII 553
ANATOMY. Obſervations of milk found in the veins inſtead of blood - *Boyle*	I 100	III 239

	Tranſ.	Abridg.
Anatomy. An account of ſome chemical, medicinal, and anatomical particulars - *Behm*	III 650	— 84 351
—— Some anatomical inventions and obſervations, particularly the origin of the injection into veins, the tranſfuſion of blood, and the parts of generation - *Clarck*	III 672	III 290
—— Anatomical obſervations made at Venice *Grandi*	V 1188	— 84 301
—— Account of two new anatomical diſcoveries made in France - - *Anon.*	— 2083	— 78
—— Account of ſome anatomical engagements *Bellini*	— 2093	I 366
—— Anatomical obſervations on the ſtructure of the noſe - - *Vernay*	XII 976	III 56
—— Anatomical obſervation on the body of a woman, about fifty years of age, who died hydropical, in her left teſticle - *Sampſon*	— 1000	- 206 218
—— The anatomy of a monſtrous pig -	XIII 183	II 904
—— The anatomy of the Mexico muſk-hog *Tyſon*	— 359	— 873
—— Obſervations of what did præternaturally occur in the opening of the body of Mr. Smith of Highgate - - *Tyſon*	XVI 332	III 347
—— Obſervations made in the heads of fowls at ſeveral times - - *Moulen*	XVII 711	II 860
—— An anatomical account of ſome remarkable things found on the diſſection of a woman who died of a dropſy after the paracenteſis was performed; with a ſmall reflection on the cauſes of the dropſy - *Preſton*	XIX 330	III 141
—— A letter, giving an account of ſome anatomical obſervations made on a body diſſected at Padua, by John Ray - - *Dale*	XXV 2282	V 184
—— An anatomical deſcription of the heart of land tortoiſes from America - *Buſſiere*	XXVII 170	— 74
—— Some anatomical obſervations - *Cheſelden*	XXVIII 281	- 233 257
—— The anatomy of a decrepid old man of 109 years old - *Scheuchzer*	XXXII 313	VII 689
—— The anatomy of the poiſonous apparatus of a rattle-ſnake, with an account of the quick effects of its poiſon - *Ranby*	XXXV 377	— 416
—— Two anotomico-practical obſervations; one of an infant born with a bag full of water hanging from the Os Sacrum to the ankles (Lat.) - - - *Baſter*	XLII 277	IX 235
—— An account of glaſſes of a new contrivance; for preſerving pieces of anatomy or natural hiſtory in ſpirituous liquors - *Le Cat*	XLVI 6	XI 1349
Additions - - *Le Cat*	— 88	— —
—— Anatomico medical obſervations of a monſtrous		

double-

Analysis (Mathematical) Consideration of various points of Analysis
[illegible] the [illegible] between the Herschel, 1814 1840.
[illegible] of functions and other branches of Analysis.
Babbage. 1817. 197.

+ Anatomy. Account of a remarkable transposition of the viscera. Baillie. 78: 350.
Account of two instances of uncommon formation, in the viscera of the human body. Abernethy. 1793: 59.

ANA***tomy*** ANE

	Tranf.	Abridg.
double-bodied child, born Oct. 26, 1701, in Pannonia, and who died Feb. 23, 1723 (Lat.) - - - *Torkos*	L 311	
Another account - *Burnet*	— 315	
Another account - *Du Pleſſis*	— 317	
Another account (Lat.) - *Drieſchius*	— 318	
—— An uncommon anatomical obſervation of a defect in the right lobe of the lungs *Paitoni*	LV 79	
—— Anatomical obſervations on the torpedo - - - *John Hunter*	LXIII 481	
—— See *Diſſection.*		
ANATOMY OF VEGETABLES. Obſervations on ſeveral paſſages in the two laſt months Tranſactions, relating to ſome unobſerved qualities of the air; to mixing and fermenting liquors in vacuo; to the hiſtory of birds; the anatomy of the trunks of vegetables; baroſcopes, &c. *Anon.*	X 533	
—— The anatomical preparation of vegetables *Seba*	XXXVI 441	VI 2 338
ANCIENTS. Experiments concerning the encauſtic paintings of the ancients - *Colebrooke*	LI 40	
—— A letter concerning the ſucceſs of the former experiments - - *Colebrooke*	— 53	
—— Some obſervations concerning the lyncurium of the ancients - *William Watſon*	— 394	
—— Some attempts to aſcertain the utmoſt extent of the knowledge of the ancients in the Eaſt-Indies - - - *Caverhill*	LVII 155	
ANDERIDA. An accurate account of a teſſellated pavement, bath, and other Roman antiquities, lately diſcovered at Eaſt Bourne, in Suſſex - - - *Tabor*	XXX 549	V 2 63
—— The reſt of the treatiſe concerning the ſite of the ancient city of Anderida, and other remains of antiquity in the county of Suſſex - - - *Tabor*	— 783	— 2 71
ANDRACHNE. A deſcription of the andrachne and its botanical characters - *Ehret*	LVII 114	
ANEMONIES (SEA). An eſſay towards elucidating the hiſtory of the ſea-anemonies *Dicquemare*	LXIII 361	
—— A ſecond eſſay on the natural ſea-anemonies - - - *Dicquemare*	LXV 207	
—— A third eſſay on - *Dicquemare*	LXVII 1 56	
ANEMOSCOPE. Deſcription of the anemoſcope - - - *Pickering*	XLIII 9	
ANEURISM. An account of an extraordinary aneuriſm of the arteria aorta near the baſis of		

	Trans.	Abridg.
the heart, with the symptoms thereof - - - *Lesage*	XXII 666	
—— An account of an aneurism of the aorta *Dod.*	XXXV 430	VII 566
—— Some observations on aneurisms in general, and in particular on the foregoing *Nicholls*	— 440	— 569
—— A remarkable case of an aneurism, or disease of the principal artery of the thigh, occasioned by a fall. To which is prefixed, a short account of the uncertainty of the distinguishing symptoms. - - *Warner*	L 363	
—— Concerning aneurisms in the thigh *Gooch*	LXV 378	
ANGLE. A direct and geometrical method by which the aphelia, excentricities, and proportion of the orbs of the primary planets, may be investigated without supposing the equality of the angle of motion at the other focus of the planet's ellipsis - *Halley*	(see Planets) ~~XI 683~~	~~I 258~~
—— An account of an experiment concerning the angle required to suspend a drop of oil of oranges, at certain stations, between two glass planes, placed in the form of a wedge - - - *Hauksbee*	XXVII 473	IV 2 182
—— A new universal method of describing all curves of every order mechanically, by the assistance of angles and right lines - *Maclaurin*	~~XXX 939~~	~~57~~
—— Solution of the problem relating to the invention of curves, which, disposed in a certain manner in an inverse situation, may cut each other in a given angle - *Anon.*	(see Curves) XXXII ~~106~~	~~VI 85~~
—— Of the section of an angle *De Moivre*	— 228	— 65
—— A description of a new instrument for taking angles - - *Hadley*	XXXVII 147	— ~~139~~
—— An account of observations made on board the Chatham yacht August 30-1, and September 1, 1732, for the trial of an instrument for taking angles - *Hadley*	— 341	— 428
—— A description of a contrivance for measuring small angles - - *Dollond*	XLVIII 178	
—— An explanation of a new instrument made for measuring small angles - *Dollond*	— 551	
—— Account of a new instrument for measuring small angles, called the Prismatic Micrometer - - - *Maskelyne*	LXVII 799	
—— See *Micrometer*.		
ANGLESEY. See *Population*.		
ANIMALS (in General). Description of a microscope, by the means whereof there has been		

seen

Angle. A general theory for the mensuration of the Angle subtended by two objects, of which one is observed by rays after two reflections from plane surfaces, and the other by rays coming directly to the spectators eye. Atwood 71: 395.

Animals. Description of a new marine Animal.	Home	75: 333
Anatomical remarks on the same animal	Hunter	— 340

	Tranſ.	Abridg.
ſeen an animal leſſer than any of thoſe hitherto ſeen - - *Divini*	III 842	I 207
—— Obſervations of ſome animals, and of a ſtrange plant, made in a voyage into the kingdom of Congo. *M. Ang. de Guattini*, and *Dionyſius of Placenza*.	XII 977	III 57
—— Microſcopical obſervations about animals in the ſcurf of the teeth; the ſubſtance called worms in the noſe; the cuticula conſiſting of ſcales - - - *Leeuwenhoek*	XIV 568	— 684
—— Lumbricus Hydropicus; or an eſſay to prove, that the hydatides, often met with in morbid animal bodies, are a ſpecies of worms, or imperfect animals - - *Tyſon*	XVII 506	— 133
—— Letters concerning the ſeeds of plants, with obſervations on the manner of the propagation of plants and animals - *Leeuwenhoek*	XVII 700	III 685
—— An account of an animal reſembling a whelp voided per anum by a male greyhound *Halley*	XIX 316	II 904
—— Remarks on ſome animals, plants, &c. ſent from Maryland - - *Petiver*	XX 393	— 253
—— An account of ſome animals ſent from the Eaſt Indies, with remarks by J. Petiver *Brown*	XXII 859	
—— Account of more animals - *Brown*	— 1023	V 183
—— Account of more animals obſerved in the Philippine Iſlands - *Camelli*	XXIII 1065	— —
—— A new diviſion of terreſtrial brute animals, particularly of thoſe that have their feet formed like hands; where an account is given of ſome animals not yet deſcribed *Tyſon*	XXIV 1565	- 177, 178
—— An account of animals and ſhells ſent from Carolina - - *Petiver*	— 1952	IV 2 325
—— An account of the animals in the Philippine Iſlands - - *Camelli*	XXVI 241	V 183
—— Obſervations on the mouths of the eels in vinegar, and alſo a ſtrange aquatic animal *Baker*	XLII 416	IX 38
—— A deſcription of the female muſk animal, by the jeſuits at Pekin -	XLVII 321	
—— An account of worms in animal bodies *Nicholls*	XLIX 246	
—— Obſervations on corallines, and the polypus, and other ſea animals - *Baſter*	L 258	
Remarks on the above obſervations *Ellis*	— 280	
—— Obſervations on noxious animals in England - - - *Forſter*	LII 475	
Animal Flowers. An account of the urtica marina (animal flowers) - *Gaertner*	— 75	

	Transf.	Abridg.
—— Letter on the animal nature of the genus of zoophytes, called corallina *Ellis*	LVII 404	
—— On the nature of gorgonia; that it is a real marine animal, and not of a mixed nature, between animal and vegetable *Ellis*	LXI 1	
ANIMALS (Parts of). An observation about the epiploon, or the double membrane, which covers the entrails of animals, and is filled with fat *Malpighi and Fracassati*	II 553	II 658
—— An account of some animals that, having lungs, are yet found to be without the arterious vein; together with some other curious particulars *Swammerdam*	VIII 6040	III 256
—— An abstract of a letter concerning the parts of brain of several animals, the chalk-stones of the gout, the leprosy, and the scales of eels *Leewenhoek*	XV 883	— 684
—— An extract of a letter containing several observations on the texture of the bones of animals, compared with that of wood *Leewenhoek*	XVII 838	II 685
—— Observations on the muscular fibres of different animals *Leewenhoek*	XXXI 134	VI 2 336
Continued. *Leewenhoek*	XXXII 12	VII 468
—— An essay upon the use of the bile in the animal œconomy, founded on an observation of a wound in the gall-bladder *Stuart*	XXXVI 341	VII 572
—— Explanation of an essay on the use of the bile in the animal œconomy *Stuart*	XXXVIII 5	IX 195
ANIMALS (Experiments on).—An experiment of preserving animals alive, by blowing through their lungs with bellows *Hook*	II 539	III 66
—— Account of two animals included with large wounds in the abdomen in the pneumatical receiver *Boyle*	V 2026	
—— Of the motion of the separated heart of a cold animal in the exhausted receiver *Boyle*	— 2027	I 250
—— A comparison of the times wherein animals may be killed by drowning, or withdrawing of the air *Boyle*	— 2028	II 490
—— Of the accidents that happen to them in air brought to a considerable degree, but not near the utmost one, of rarefaction *Boyle*	— 2036	— 225
—— Of the observations produced in an animal in changes, as to rarity and density made in the self-same air *Boyle*	— 2039	
—— Of an unsuccessful attempt to prevent the necessity of respiration by the production or growth of animals in our vacuum *Boyle*	— 2040

Animals, Experiments on

Experiments on the power that Animals, when placed in certain circumstances, possess of producing cold. Crawford 71:479.

On some physiological researches, respecting the influence of the brain on the action of the heart, and on the generation of animal heat. — — — — — Brodie. 1811.36.

Further experiments and observations on the influence of the brain on the generation of animal heat. — — Brodie. 1812:378.

An account of some experiments on animal heat. — Davy. 1814:590.

Experiments and observations to prove that the beneficial effects of many medicines are produced through the medium of the circulating blood, more particularly that of the colchicum autumnale upon the gout. — — Home. 1816:257.

(An appendix to a paper on the effects of the colchicum autumnale on gout. — — — — — — — 262,

	Tranſ.	Abridg.
—— Of the power of aſſuefaction to enable animals to hold out in air by rarefaction made unfit for reſpiration - *Boyle*	V 2045	
—— Some experiments, touching animals, made in the air-pump - *Huygens and Papin*	X 542	II 250
—— Obſervations on the manner of propagation of animals and plants - *Leewenhoek*	XVII 700	III 685
—— Letter on the generation of animals - - *Joſephus de Aromatariis*	XVIII 150	
—— Experiments and obſervations on the effects of ſeveral ſorts of poiſons upon animals, made at Montpellier in 1678 and 1679. *Cowper*	XXVII 485	V 38
—— Letter on the generation of animals *Leewenhoek*	XXXII 438	VII 473
—— An account of the bones of animals being changed to a red colour by aliment only - - - *Belchier*	XXXIX 287	IX 102
—— A further account - *Belchier*	— 299	— 105
—— Obſervations and experiments with madder roots, which has the faculty of tinging the bones of living animals of a red colour *Du Monceau*	XLI 390	IX 103
—— Letter concerning the natural heat of animals - - - *Mortimer*	XLIII 473	XI 901
—— Part of two letters concerning the ſparkling of flannel, and the hair of animals in the dark - - *Cooke*	XLV 394	X 343
—— Experiments made on a great number of animals with the poiſon of Lama's and of Ticunas - - - *Heriſſant*	XLVII 75	
—— An account of ſome experiments on the ſenſibility and irritability of the ſeveral parts of animals - - *Brocklesby*	XLIX 240	
—— The effects of the opuntia, or prickly pear, and of the Indigo plant, in colouring the juices of living animals - *Baker*	L 296	
—— Experiments on animal fluids in the exhauſted receiver - - *Darwin*	LXIV 344	
—— Experiments on animals and vegetables, with reſpect to the power of producing heat - - - *John Hunter*	LXV 446	
—— Of the heat of animals and vegetables - - - *John Hunter*	LXVIII 7	
—— Experiments and obſervations on the inflammable air breathed by ſeveral animals *Fontana*	LXIX 337	
ANIMALS (Diſorders of).—Some obſervations on the motion of diſeaſes, and on the births and deaths of men, and other animals in different times of the Νοχθήμερον - *Paſchall*	XVII 815	III 311

	Transf.	Abridg.
—— Of an obstruction of the biliary ducts, and an impostumation of the gall-bladder, discharging upwards of 18 quarts of bilious matter in 25 days, without any apparent defect in the animal functions - *Amyand*	XL 317	VIII 503
ANIMAL (Fossile).—An account of the impression of the almost entire skeleton of a large animal in a very hard stone found at Elston, near Newark, Nottinghamshire - *Stukeley*	XXX 963	V 2 272
—— An account of a pair of very extraordinary large horns found in Wapping some years since; with a probable account whence they came, and to what animal they belonged *Sloane*	XXXIV 222	VII 441
—— An account of a fossile thigh-bone of a large animal dug up at Stone's-field, near Woodstock, in Oxfordshire - *Platt*	L 524	
—— See *Fossile*, *Generation*.		
ANIMAL JUICES. See *Juices*.		
ANIMALCULA. Observations concerning some little animals observed in rain, well, sea, and snow-water; as also in water where pepper had lain infused - - *Leewenhoek*	XII 821	III 683
—— ———————— *Leewenhoek*	— 844	— —
—— Observed in Semine Humano *Leewenhoek*	— 1040	
Leewenhoek answered by *Oldenburg*	— 1045	
Oldenburg answered by *Leewenhoek*	— 1044	
Extracts from other letters of *Leewenhoek*	— 1045	
—— Concerning animalcula found in the teeth - - - *Leewenhoek*	XVII 646	— 684
—— Several observations and experiments on the animalcula in pepper-water *Sir Edmund King*	XVII 861	— 654
—— Some microscopical observations of vast numbers of animalcula seen in water *Harris*	XIX 254	— 652
—— Answer to the objections made to Leewenhoek's opinions concerning the animalcula in semine in masculino - *Leewenhoek*	XXI 270	— 686
—— Concerning the animalcula in semine humano - - - *Leewenhoek*	— 301	— —
—— Further observations on the animalcula in semine masculino - *Leewenhoek*	XXII 739	
—— Several microscopical observations and experiments concerning the animalcula in semine masculino of cocks and spiders *Leewenhoek*	XXIII 1137	V 2 264
—— Letter concerning green weeds growing in water, and animalcula found about them - - - *Leewenhoek*	— 1304	

	Transf.	Abridg.
ANIMALCULA. Two letters from a gentleman in the country relating to	XXIII 1494	V 2 225
—— Observations on some animalcula in water - - - *Leewenhoek*	— 1430	- - 226
—— A letter concerning animalcula, on the roots of duck-weed - *Leewenhoek*	XXIV 1784	- - 267
—— Part of a letter concerning some microscopical observations upon the animalcula in semine of young rams - *Leewenhoek*	XXVII 316	- - —
—— A letter containing some further microscopical observations on the animalcula found upon duck-weed - *Leewenhoek*	XXVIII 160	- - —
—— Observations on a particular manner of increase in the animalcula of vegetable infusions, with the discovery of an indissoluble salt arising from hemp-seed put into water till it becomes putrid - - *Ellis*	LIX 138	
ANNUITIES. An estimate of the degrees of the mortality of mankind, drawn from curious tables of the births and funerals at the city of Breslaw; with an attempt to ascertain the price of annuities upon lives - *Halley*	XVII 596	
—— The easiest method of calculating the value of annuities upon lives from tables of observations - - - *De Moivre*	XLIII 65	
—— A letter concerning the value of an annuity for life, and the probability of survivorship - - - *Dodson*	XLVIII 487	
—— A letter concerning the method of constructing a table for the probabilities of life at London - - - *Brakenridge*	XLIX 167	
—— A letter with a table of the value of annuities on lives - - *Dodson*	— 891	
—— A letter concerning the term and period of human life: in which the inequalities in constructing, and the false conclusions drawn from Dr. Halley's Breslaw table, are fully proved; the supposed extraordinary healthfulness of that place is particularly examined, and confuted; and its real state shewn to be equalled by divers places in England; the imperfection of all the tables formed upon 1000 lives shewn; and a method proposed to obtain one much better - - - *T. W.*	LII 46	
—— Observations on the expectations of lives, the increase of mankind, the influence of great

	Transf.	Abridg.
towns on population, and particularly the state of London with respect to healthfulness and number of inhabitants - *Price*	LIX 89	
ANNUITIES. Short and easy theorems for finding, in all cases, the differences between the values of annuities payable yearly, and of the same annuities payable half-yearly, quarterly, or monthly - - *Price* (see Survivorship.)	LXVI 109	
ANNULUS. See *Saturn*.		
ANOMALIES. Considerations concerning Mercator's geometric and direct method for finding the apogees, excentricities, and anomalies of the planets - - *Mercator*	V 1168	I 253
ANOMALY. See *Planet*.		
ANTHELIUM. Observation on an anthelium seen at Witemberg Jan. 17-8, 1738 (Lat.) - - - *Weidler*	XLI 221	VIII 516
—— An account of an anthelium observed near Oxford July 24, 1760 - *Swinton*	LII 94	
ANTICOSTI. Immersions and emersions of Jupiter's first satellite, observed at Jupiter's inlet on the island of Anticosti, North America, and the longitude of the place deduced from comparison, with observations made at the Royal Observatory at Greenwich, by the Astronomer Royal - - *Wright*	LXIV 190	
ANTIENT SHRINE. An account of an antient shrine formerly belonging to the abbey of Croyland - - - *Stukeley*	XLV 579	XI 1313
ANTILLES. See *Currents*.		
ANTIMONY. On the virtue of antimony *Anon.*	III 774	II 56
—— Experiments of refining gold with antimony - - - *Godaard*	XII 953	II 595, 597, 598
—— Observations on the effects of the vitrum antimonii ceratum - *Geoffroy*	XLVII 273	
—— Medical and chemical observations upon antimony - - *Huxham*	XLVIII 832	
ANTIQUITIES. An account of a Roman monument found in the bishoprick of Durham, and of some Roman antiquities at York *Lister*	XIII 70	III 423
—— Some observations upon the ruins of a piece of a Roman wall and Multangular tower at York - - *Lister*	— 238	— 419
—— An account of an antient mantle-tree in Northamptonshire, on which the date of it (for the year of our Lord 1133) is expressed by the nu-		

	Transf.	Abridg.
meral figures, which shews the great antiquity of those figures in England	XIII 399	I 107
—— An account of some antiquities found at Kirkbythore, in Westmoreland - *Machel*	XIV 555	II 430
—— An account of an earthen vessel lately found near York - - *Anon.*	XV 1017	III 419
—— The figures of some antiquities explained *Anon.*	— 1159	— 446
—— An explanation of the figures of several antiquities - - *Anon.*	— 1201	— —
—— A discovery of some antiquities made upon the inundation of the Tiber - *Anon.*	XVI 227	— 448
—— Account of some Roman antiquities found in Yorkshire - *Thoresby*	XIX 738	— 421
—— Letter concerning some Roman antiquities lately found in Yorkshire - *Thoresby*	XX 310	— —
—— Letter concerning a piece of antiquity lately found in Somersetshire - *Musgrave*	— 441	— 441
—— Letter concerning the Saxon antiquity mentioned in Vol. XX, p. 441 - *Hickes*	XXII 467	— 442
—— Letter concerning some Roman antiquities in Lincolnshire - *De la Pryme*	— 561	— 428
—— Letter concerning several Roman antiquities found near the Devizes in Wiltshire *Clark*	— 758	V 2 31
—— An account of some Roman, French, and Irish inscriptions and antiquities lately found in Scotland and Ireland - *Llwyd*	— 768	IV 2 322
—— Letter concerning several Roman inscriptions, and other antiquities, in Yorkshire - - *Christopher Hunter*	XXIII 1129	V 2 44
—— Letter concerning a leaden coffin taken out of a Roman burying-place near York *Thoresby*	XXIV 1864	V 2 41
—— Part of a letter concerning some Roman antiquities found in Yorkshire *Thoresby*	XXVI 289	- - 40
—— A letter concerning some Roman antiquities observed in Yorkshire - *Thoresby*	— 314	- - 40
—— A letter concerning some antient brass instruments found in Yorkshire *Thoresby*	— 393	- - 98
—— A letter occasioned by some antiquities lately discovered near Bramham Moor, in Yorkshire - - - *Hearne*	— 395	
—— A letter giving an account of antiquities lately found at Corbridge, in Northumberland *Todd*	XXVII 291	- - 47
—— A letter giving a further account of what Mr. Lhwyd met with remarkable, in natural history and antiquities, in his travels through Wales - - *Lhwyd*	— 500	- - 120

	Tranſ.	Abridg.
—— Several obſervations relating to the antiquities and natural hiſtory of Ireland, in his travels through that kingdom - *Lhwyd*	XXVII 503	IV 2 182 V 2 125
- - - *Lhwyd*	— 524	V 2 126
—— Extracts of letters containing obſervations in natural hiſtory and antiquities, in his travels through Wales and Scotland - *Lhwyd*	XXVIII 93	- - 120, 123
—— Part of a letter containing a relation of ſeveral urns and ſepulchral monuments lately found in Ireland - - *Nevill*	— 252	- - 95
—— An account of ſome ancient trumpets, and other pieces of antiquity, found in the county of Tyrone in Ireland - *Nevill*	— 270	
—— An accurate account of a teſſellated pavement bath, and other Roman antiquities lately diſcovered at Eaſt Bourne in Suſſex *Tabor*	XXX 549	- - 63
The reſt of the treatiſe concerning the ſite of the ancient city of Anderida, and other remains of antiquity in the county of Suſſex - - - *Tabor*	— 783	- - 71
—— Some amendments and additions to the account of things found under ground in Lincolnſhire - - - *Thoreſby*	XXXII 344	VII 4 22
—— Ex veterum Pruſſorum re Antiquaria Schediaſma - - - *Klein*	XLI 384	IX 414
—— An attempt to explain ſome remains of antiquity lately found in Hertfordſhire *Ward*	XLIII 349	XI 1298
—— Extract of a letter concerning an antique obeliſk in Rudſtone church-yard *Knowlton*	XLIV 101	
—— A letter concerning an antique-ſhoe found in the iſle of Axholm, in Lincolnſhire - - - *Stovin*	— 571	
—— Letter concerning the antiquities dug up from the antient Herculaneum *Paderni*	XLVIII 71, 490	
- - - *Spence*	— 488	
- - - *Paderni*	L 49	
- - - *Nixon*	— 88	
- - - *Paderni*	— 619	
—— An account of ſome antiquities found in Cornwall - - *Borlaſe*	LI 13	
—— Account of ſeveral antiquities lately diſcovered in Italy - - *Venuti*	— 201	
—— Account of ſeveral antiquities in Italy *Venuti*	— 636	
With remarks - *Nixon*	— 639	
—— See *Herculaneum, Coin, Inſcription, Lamps, Rome.*		
ANTISEPTIC. Part of a letter on the antiſeptical regimen of the natives of Ruſſia *Guthrie*	LXVIII 622	

✝ Ants. Observations on the Sugar Ants - - - - - - Castles 80: 346.

	Tranſ.	Abridg.
ANT. Obſervations concerning emmets, or ants; their eggs, production, progreſs, coming to maturity, uſe, &c. - *King*	II 425	II 789
—— Experiments on the neceſſity of air to the motion of ants - - *Boyle*	V 2054	
—— Uncommon obſervations and experiments made with an acid juice; to be found in ants *Wray*	— 2063	— 791
- - - *Liſter*	— 2067	— 792
—— An abſtract of the Rev. Mr. Gould's account of Engliſh ants - - *Miles*	XLIV 357	IX 833
ANT-BEAR. An account of the ant-bear in the iſland of Ceilan - - *Strachan*	XXIII 1094	V 2 179
ANUS. An account of an animal reſembling a whelp voided per anum by a male greyhound *Halley*	XIX 316	II 904
—— Bones of a fœtus voided by anum ſome years after conception - *Morley*	— 486	
—— The head and ribs of a fœtus brought forth by the anus - *Lindelſtolpe*	XXXIII 171	VII 557
—— An account of a fork put up the anus, that was afterwards drawn out through the buttock - - - *Payne*	— 408	— 521
—— Account of the preternatural delivery of a fœtus at the anus - *Nourſe*	XXXVI 435	— 559
—— Caſe of the bones of a fœtus coming away by the anus - - *Winthorp*	XLIII 304	XI 1015
- - - *Simon*	— 529	— 1016
—— A letter concerning a child born with an extraordinary tumour near the anus, containing ſome rudiments of an embryo in it *Huxham*	XLV 525	— 1020
—— An account of a ſuppreſſion of urine cured by a puncture made in the bladder through the anus - *Robert Hamilton*	LXVI 578	
AORTA. An account of an extraordinary aneuriſma of the arteria aorta near the baſis of the heart, with the ſymptoms thereof - *Leſage*	XXII 666	
—— An account of an aneuriſm of the heart *Dod*	XXXV 436	— 566
Obſervations on the above *Nicholls*	— 440	— 569
APER MEXICANUS MOSCHIFERUS. The anatomy of the Mexico Muſk Hog - *Tyſon*	XIII 359	II 873
APHELIA. A direct and geometrical method by which the aphelia excentricities, and proportion of the orbs of the principal planets, may be found without ſuppoſing the equality of the angle of motion at the other focus of the planet's ellipſis - - - *Halley*	XI 683	I 258
APHIDES. Obſervations on the aphides of Linnæus - - - *Richardſon*	LXI 182	

APHYL-

	Tranſ.	Abridg.
APHYLLON. An account of aphyllon and dentaria heptaphylos of Cluſius, omitted by Mr. Ray - - - *William Watſon*	XLVII 428	
APOGEE. Conſiderations concerning Mercator's geometric and direct method for finding the apogees, excentricities and anomalies of the planets - - - *Mercator*	V 1168	I 253
—— A letter concerning the mean motion of the moon's apogee - *Murdoch*	XLVII 62	
APOGEE. See *Planet.*		
APONENSIAN. An account of the Aponenſian baths near Padua - *Doddington*	VII 4067	II 344
APOPLEXY. Phenomenon obſerved in the body of a noble Woman who died of an apoplexy *Cole*	XV 1068	III 29
APOSTEM. Cure of one who ſwallowed a knife, which lay in his ſtomach a year and 7 months, and then worked out at an apoſthem on his breaſt - - *Sloane*	XIX 120	
APOSTEMATION. A letter concerning the cure of an apoſtemation of the lungs - *Wright*	XXIII 1379	
—— ———— *Cowper*	— 1386	V 227
APPLEBY. See *Water.*		
APPLES. Of an excellent liquor made with cyder-apples and mulberries - *Colepreſs*	II 502	
—— Obſervations on inſects bred in rain-water, in apples, cheeſe, &c. - *Leewenhoek*	XVIII 194	III 685
—— An account of a new ſort of moloſſes made of apples - - *Dudley*	XXXII 231	VI 2 379
—— The effects which the farina of the bloſſoms of different ſorts of apple-trees had on the fruit of a neighbouring tree - *Cook*	XLIII 525	X 751
—— A letter concerning a mixed breed of apples from the mixture of the farina *Cooke*	XLV 602	X 752
—— Part of a letter concerning the effects of the mixture of the farina of apple-trees *Cooke*	XLVI 205	X 752
—— Singular obſervations upon the Manchenille apple - - *Peyſſonel*	L 772	
APPLES. See *Cyder.*		
APPROXIMATION. An attempt towards the improvement of the method of approximations, in the extraction of the roots of equations in numbers - - *Taylor*	XXX 610	IV 80
—— Conciſe rules for computing the effects of refraction and parallax, in varying the apparent diſtance of the moon from the ſun or a ſtar: alſo an eaſy rule of approximation for computing the diſtance of the moon from a ſtar,		

	Transf.	Abridg.
the longitudes and latitudes of both being given, with demonstrations of the same - - - *Maskelyne*	LIV 263	
Appulses. Appulses of the moon to Saturn, and the fixed stars observable in the year 1671 foretold, and reduced to the meridian and latitude of London - - *Flamstead*	V 2029	I 453
—— Letters concerning the appulses of the moon for 1673, and the other planets to the fixed stars, together with an observation of the planet Mars - - - *Flamstead*	VII 5118	- 265,424
—— The appulses of the moon, and other planets to the fixed stars, predicted for 1674 *Flamstead*	VIII 6155	III 149
—— An advertisement to astronomers, of the advantages that may accrue from the observations of the moon's frequent appulses to the Hyades, during the course of the three next ensuing years - - -	XXX 692	IV 298
—— On the method of determining the places of the planets, by observing their next appulses to the fixed stars - - *Halley*	XXXI 209	VI 170
—— A new method of calculating eclipses, particuly of the earth, and of any appulses of the moon to planets and fixed stars *Gersten*	XLIII 22	
—— An account of an appulse of the moon to Jupiter, observed at Chelsea - *Dunn*	LIII 31	
Aquafortis. A letter containing some microscopical observations upon the chrystallized particles of silver dissolved in aquafortis *Leewenhoek*	XXVII 20	V 2 267
—— Sequel to the case of Mr. Butler of Moscow, who was strangely affected by mixing verdigrease and false leaf-gold with aquafortis *Baker*	LIV 15	
Aquatic Animal. Account of a strange aquatic animal as viewed in the microscope *Baker*	XLII 416	IX 38
Aquatic Insect. A description of a very remarkable aquatic insect, found in a ditch of standing water near Norwich - *King*	LVII 72	
Aqueduct. An account of an aqueduct designed for carrying the river Eure to Versailles.	XV 1016	I 594
—— A farther account of the aqueduct near Versailles - -	— 1206	— —
—— See *Silver.*		
Arabian Figures. An account of an antient date in Arabian figures upon the north front of the parish church of Rumney in Hampshire - - - *Barlow*	XLI 652	IX 432
—— A brief inquiry into the reading of two dates in		

	Tranſ.	Abridg.
Arabian figures cut upon ſtones, which were found in Ireland - *Ward*	XLIII 283	XI 1260
—— A deſcription of an antient date in Arabian figures at Walling, near Aldermarſton, Berkſhire - - *Ward*	XLV 603	— 1267
—— See *Date*.		
ARALIASTRUM. Account of a new genus of plants called Araliaſtrum, of which the famous Nin-Zin, or Gin-ſeng of the Chineſe, is a ſpecies - - - *Vaillant*	XXX 705	IV 2 319
ARC. An inveſtigation of a general theorem for finding the length of any arc of any conic hyperbola by means of two elliptic arcs, with ſome other new and uſeful theorems deduced therefrom - - *Landen*	LXV 283	
ARCH. Extracts of ſeveral letters concerning the appearance of ſeveral arches of colours contiguous to the inner edge of the common rainbow at Petworth - *Langarth*	XXXII 241	VI 122
Another letter, with ſome reflections on the ſame ſubject - *Pemberton*	— 245	— 123
ARCHES. An account of the appearance of ſeveral unuſual parhelia, or mock ſuns, together with ſeveral circular arches lately ſeen in the air *Halley*	XXIII 1127	IV 228
—— Account of a luminous arch, Feb. 16, 1749 - - - *Cooper*	XLVI 647	X 507
ARCHIMEDES. Extract of a letter concerning Mr. de Buffon's re-invention of Archimedes's burning ſpecula - - *Buffon*	XLV 504	— 195
—— Obſervations upon father Kircher's opinion concerning the burning of the fleet of Marcellus by Archimedes - *Parſons*	XLVIII 626	
ARCHIPELAGO. A relation of the raining of aſhes in the Archipelago, upon the eruption of mount Veſuvius, ſome years ago *Robinſon*	I 377	II 143
—— Obſervations in travels from Venice through Iſtria, Dalmatia, Greece, and the Archipelago, to Smyrna - - *Vernon*	XI 573	
ARCTURUS. An enquiry into the quantity and direction of the proper motion of Arcturus; with ſome remarks on the diminution of the obliquity of the ecliptic - *Hornſby*	LXIII 93	
ARCUTIO. Extract of a letter concerning the arcutio to lay children in, to preſerve them from being overlaid - - *St. John*	XXXVII 256	VII 4 46
AREA. A ſpecimen of a new method of obſerving curvilineal areas; by which many ſuch areas		

	Transf.	Abridg.
may be compared, as have not yet appeared to be comparable by any other method *Landen*	LVIII 174	
—— Theorems concerning the greatest and least areas of polygons inscribing and circumscribing the circle - - *Horsley*	LXV 301	
—— Some new theorems for computing the areas of certain curved lines - *Landen*	LX 441	
—— See *Curve*.		
AREOMETER. Description and use of a new areometer - - *Fahrenheit*	XXXII 140	VI 326
AREOMETRY. An essay on pyrometry, and areometry, and on physical measures in general - - - *De Luc*	LXVIII 419	
ARITHMETICK. An extract of two essays in political arithmetick concerning the comparative magnitude of London and Paris *Petty*	XVI 152, 237	
—— An arithmetical paradox concerning the chances of lotteries - - *Roberts*	XVII 677	III 679
—— An account of a person who can neither read nor write, yet will reckon sums with great exactness - - *Locke*	XXII 893	V 2 219
—— A short account of negativo-affirmative arithmetick - - *Colson*	XXXIV 161	VI 1
—— The description and use of an arithmetical machine invented by - *Gersten*	XXXIX 79	VIII 16
—— On the arithmetic of impossible quantities - - - *Playfair*	LXVIII 318	
ARM. An account of the cure of two sinuous ulcers possessing the whole arm, with the extraordinary supply of a callus which fully answers the purposes of the Os Humeri lost in time of cure - - - *Fawler*	XXV 2466	V 388
—— An account of the man whose arm, with the shoulder-bone, was torn off by a mill, Aug. 15, 1737 - - *Belchier*	XL 313	IX 266
—— The case of Mary Howell, who had a needle run into her arm and came out at her breast - - - *Anon.*	XLI 767	— 238
—— An extraordinary case of a fracture of the arm - - - *Freke*	XLVI 397	XI 1108
—— An account of a cure of a paralytic arm by electricity - - *Hart*	XLIX 558	
—— An account of a remarkable operation on a broken arm - - *White*	LI 657	
—— An account of the extraction of three inches and ten lines of the bone of the upper arm, which was followed by a regeneration of the

	Tranſ.	Abridg.
bony matter; with a deſcription of a machine made uſe of to keep the upper and lower pieces of the bone at their proper diſtances, during the time that the regeneration was taking place; and which may alſo be of ſervice in fractures happening near the head of that bone - - - *Le Cat*	LVI 270	
—— Account of a woman enjoying the uſe of her right arm after the head of the Os Humeri was cut away - - *Bent*	LXIV 353	
ARMADILLA. An account of an American armadilla - - *W. Watſon*	LIV 57	
ARMENUS. Of an Hungarian Bolus of the ſame effects with the Bolus Armenus *Anon.*	I 11	II 457
AROMATIC. An account of an inſect feeding upon henbane, the horrid ſmell of which is in that creature ſo qualified thereby, as to become in ſome meaſure aromatical; together with the colour yielded by the eggs of the ſame *Liſter*	VI 2176	— 783
ARSENIC. Letter concerning cobalt, and the preparations of ſmalt and arſenic *Kreig*	XXIV 1754	V 420
ARTERIES. An account of ſome animals that, having lungs, are yet found to be without the arterious vein; together with ſome other curious particulars - - *Swammerdam*	VIII 6040	III 256
—— Some probable thoughts of the whiteneſs of the chyle, and what it is after it is conveyed within the arteries - - *Liſter*	XIII 242	— 106
—— An account of divers ſchemes of arteries and veins, diſſected from adult human bodies by J. Evelyn. To which are ſubjoined a deſcription of the extremities of thoſe veſſels, and the manner the blood is ſeen by the microſcope to paſs from the arteries to the veins in quadrupeds when living: with ſome chirurgical obſervations and figures after the life - - - *Cowper*	XXIII 1177	V 134
—— Of oſſifications or petrefactions in the coats of arteries, particularly in the valves of the great artery - - *Cowper*	XXIV 1970	— 347
—— A letter concerning the oſſification of the crural artery - - *Naiſh*	XXXI 226	VII 511
—— Two newly-diſcovered arteries in women going to the Ovaria - *Ranby*	XXXIV 159	— 541
—— Extract of a letter concerning ſome remarkable experiments made upon the arteries of horſes,		

with

Arseniates. Description of the Arseniates of Copper, and of Iron, from the county of Cornwall. Bournon. 1801: 169.
Analysis of the Arseniates of Copper and of Iron, described in the preceding paper. Chenevix. —— 193.
On a native Arseniate of Lead. Gregor. 1809: 195.

+ Arteries. Account of a peculiarity in the distribution of the arteries sent to the limbs of slow-moving animals. Carlisle. 1800: 98.
1804: 17.

On the functions of the Arteries. — — — — Young. 1809: 1.

On the influence of the nerves upon the action of the Arteries. 1814: 583.

Asa foetida. Description of a plant yielding Asa foetida. Hope 75: 36.

		Tranſ.	Abridg.
with the powder of lycoperdon, or lupi-crepitus, by Monſieur La Foſſe	*Latterman*	XLIX 37	
ARTERIES OF LEAVES. See *Leaves*.			
ARTERIES. See particular ones in their places.			
ARTICULATING CARTILAGES. Account of the Structure and diſeaſes of	*William Hunter*	XLII 514	IX 267
ARTS. A letter concerning ſome obſervations on the Mechanic arts of the Indians	*Papin*	XXVIII 225	V 2 182
ASBESTUS. An account of a ſort of paper made of linum aſbeſtinum. found in Wales	*Lloyd*	XIV 823	II 529
—— A letter concerning ſome incombuſtible cloth - - -	*Waite*	XV 1049	II 549, 550
Another on the above -	*Plot*	— 1051	— —
—— Letter concerning the aſbeſtus, and manner of ſpinning, and making an incombuſtible cloth thereof - -	*Ciampini*	XXII 911	IV 2 282
—— An account of the lapis amianthus, aſbeſtus or linum incombuſtibile, lately found in Scotland - - -	*Wilſon*	— 1004	— - 283
—— Part of a letter giving an account of the aſbeſtus, or lapis amiantus, found in the Highlands of Scotland - -	*Blair*	XXVII 434	- - 285
—— An account of a late diſcovery of aſbeſtos in France - -	*Needham*	LI 837	
ASCENSION. Some remarks upon the method of obſerving the differences of right aſcenſion and declination by croſs hairs in a teleſcope - - -	*Halley*	XXXI 113	VI 165
—— Deſcription of a method of meaſuring differences of right aſcenſion and declination, with Dollond's micrometer, together with other new applications of the ſame	*Maſkelyne*	LXI 536	
ASCENT. Several experiments touching the ſeeming ſpontaneous aſcent of water	*Haukſbee*	XXVI 258	- 2 181
- - -	*Haukſbee*	— 265	
ASCITES. Remarks taken upon diſſecting the body of a maid about 30 years of age, who died of an aſcites - -	*Anon.*	XVIII 15	III 140
—— Cured by tapping -	*Banyer*	XLII 628	IX 151
—— An improvement on the practice of tapping, whereby that operation, inſtead of a relief for ſymptoms, becomes an abſolute cure for an aſcites, exemplified in the caſe of Jane Roman - - -	*Warwick*	XLIII 12	XI 1030
A method of conveying liquors into the abdomen during the operation of tapping	*Hales*	— 20	— 1034

	Trans.	Abridg.
—— Further accounts of the success of injecting medicated liquors into the abdomen in the case of an ascites - *Il arren*	XLIII 47	
ASHES. A relation of the raining of ashes in the Archipelago, upon the eruption of Mount Vesuvius, some years ago - *Robinson*	I 377	II 143
—— A letter concerning tobacco-ashes *Leewenhoek*	XXIV 1740	V 2 267
ASH TREES. An account of insects in the barks of decaying elms and ashes - *Dudley*	— 1859	V 13
ASHFORD. Vide *Monument*.		
ASIA. Observations concerning some of the most considerable parts of Asia from Tavernier's voyages - - *Oldenburg*	XI 711	
More observations of M. Tavernier's voyages - - - *Oldenburg*	— 751	
—— Extract of a letter concerning the discoveries of the Russians on the north-east coast of Asia - - - *Euler*	XLIV 421	X 251
—— A letter concerning the distances between Asia and America - *Dobbs*	— 471	X 252
—— A short account of some new astronomical and physical observations made in Asia *Porter*	XLIX 251	
ASPERIÆ ARTERIÆ. An account of some particular advantages in the structure of the asperiæ arteriæ, or wind-pipes of several birds, and in the land tortoise - -	LVI 204	
ASSAYING. A new method of assaying copper ore - - - *Fordyce*	LXX 30	
ASTERISMS. See *Sphere*.		
ASTHMA. Observations on shortness of breath - - - *Leewenhoek*	XXIII 1137	V 2 264
—— Observations concerning shortness of breath - - - *Leewenhoek*	— 1143	
—— An account of what appeared on opening the body of —— St. Johns, Esq. who died of an asthma July 2, 1705, aged 72 years - - - *Cowper*	XXVII 534	
—— A letter giving an account of a polypus, resembling a branch of the pulmonary vein coughed up by an asthmatic person - *Nicholls*	XXXVII 123	VII 504
—— An account of what appeared on opening the body of an asthmatic person *W. Watson*	LIV 239	
ASTRONOMY. An account of such of the more notable celestial phænomena of the year 1670 as will be conspicuous in the English horizon - - - *Flamstead*	IV 1099	I 453

Asia. A memoir on the geography of the north-eastern part of Asia and on the question whether Asia and America are contiguous — — Burney. 1818:9

Astringent vegetables. An account of some experiments and observations on the constituent parts of certain astringent vegetables. Substance Davy. 1803:233.

Observations on an astringent vegetable from China Brande. 1817:37.

4 Recherches sur les principaux problemes de l'Astronomie nautique. Mendoza y Rios. 1797: 43.

An improved solution of a problem in physical astronomy, by which swiftly converging series are obtained, which are useful in computing the perturbations of the motions of the earth, Mars and Venus by their mutual attraction. — — Hellins 1798: 527. 1800: 86.

Demonstrations of the late Dr. Maskelyne's formulæ for finding the longitude and latitude of a celestial object from its right ascension and declination; and for finding its right ascension and declination from its longitude and latitude, the obliquity of the ecliptic being given in both cases. - - - 1816: 138.

better to enter it under Instruments

Astronomical Instruments. Observations on their graduation, with an explanation of the method invented by the late Mr. Hindley to divide Circles into any given number of parts. Smeaton 76: 1.

	Transf.	Abridg.
—— Emendations and notes upon the ancient astronomical tables of Albatenius, with the restoration of his luni-solar tables - *Halley*	XVII 913	III 522
—— An advertisement to astronomers, of the advantages that may accrue from the observation of the moon's frequent appulses to the Hyades, during the three next ensuing years	XXX 692	IV 298
—— Of great and small things which occur in the motion of the heavenly bodies	— 952	
—— Some allowances to be made in astronomical observations for the refraction of the air, with an accurate table of refractions - *Halley*	XXXI 169	VI 167
—— A letter concerning the Chinese chronology and astronomy - - *Costard*	XLIV 476	XI 1232
—— Remarks upon the solar and lunar years, the cycle of 19 years, commonly called the Golden Number, the Epact, and a method of finding the time of Easter, as it is now observed in most parts of Europe *Earl of Macclesfield*	XLVI 417	X 131
—— Essay on the precession of the equinoxes and the nutation of the earth's axis *Walmesley*	XLIX 704	
—— A theory of the irregularities that may be occasioned in the annual motion of the earth by the actions of Jupiter and Saturn *Walmesley*	— 737	
—— Introduction to two papers of Mr. John Smeaton - - *Maskelyne*	LVIII 154	
—— A discourse concerning the menstrual parallax, arising from the mutual gravitation of the earth and moon: its influence on the observation of the sun and planets; with a method of observing it - *Smeaton*	— 156	
Description of a new method of observing the heavenly bodies out of the meridian - - - *Smeaton*	— 170	
—— Geometrical solutions of three celebrated astronomical problems - *Pemberton*	LXII 434	
—— A proposal for measuring the attraction of some hills in this kingdom by astronomical observations. - - *Maskelyne*	LXV 495	
ASTRONOMICAL OBSERVATIONS. An account of some observations made in Spain by the Earl of Sandwich - -	I 390	I 562 II 185
—— Astronomical observations partly already made, partly to be made - *Flamstead*	VII 5034	I 348, 385, 424
—— The use of telescopic sights in astronomical observations - - *Hevelius*	IX 27	— 221
—— An astronomical dissertation on the visible conjunction		

	Tranſ.	Abridg.
junction of the interior planets with the ſun - - - *Halley*	XVII 511	I 427
—— Aſtronomical obſervations at China *Jeſuits*	XX 53	
—— Letter relating to ſome aſtronomical obſervations at China - - *Caſſini*	— 371	— 427, 569
—— Obſervations at Greenwich in 1711, 1712 - - - - *Flamſtead*	XXVIII 65	IV 281
—— Britiſh aſtronomical obſervations made at Greenwich in 1713 - *Flamſtead*	XXIX 285	— 291
—— Some late curious aſtronomical obſervations made at Wanſted - *Pound*	— 401	— 303
—— Accurate aſtronomical obſervations made in the laſt and the current year - *Anon.*	XXX 847	
—— Aſtronomical obſervations communicated to the Royal Society - - *Anon.*	— 1109	— 336
—— Aſtronomical obſervations made at Southwick, Northamptonſhire, with a 13 foot teleſcope, by apparent time - *Lynn*	XXXIV 66	VI 223, 240
—— Aſtronomical obſervations at Liſbon in 1725 and 1726 - - *Carbone*	— 90	VI 240
—— Aſtronomical obſervations made at Toulon *Laval*	— 100	— 241
—— Aſtronomical obſervations made at Vera Cruz by Mr. Harris; reviſed and communicated by - - - *Halley*	XXXV 388	— 147 VII 4 102
—— Aſtronomical obſervations made at Liſbon in 1726 - - *Carbone*	— 408	VI 241
—— Aſtronomical obſervations made at Liſbon *Carbone*	— 471	— 177
—— Aſtronomical obſervations made at Bologna - - - *Manfredi*	— 534	— 244
—— Aſtronomical obſervations made at Pekin, 1724 - - - *Kogler*	— 553	— 199, 239, 251 VII 4 101
—— Aſtronomical obſervations made at Ingolſtad, 1726 - - *Jeſuits*	— 556	VI 176, 242, 251, 252
—— Aſtronomical obſervations made at Pekin from Nov. 1727 to Nov. 1728 *Miſſionaries*	XXXVI 366	— 210, 218, 245
—— Aſtronomical obſervations made at Pekin in 1728 and 1729 - *Miſſionaries*	— 455	— 218, 222, 246
—— Aſtronomical, phyſical, and meteorological obſervations in 1733 at Witemberg *Weidler*	XXXIX 238	VIII 178
—— Aſtronomical obſervations made at Pekin by the jeſuits, from Nov. 1740 to Oct. 1741 *Hodgſon*	XLII 306	— 183, 186, 208
—— Aſtronomica obſervations made at Paraguay, in South America, from 1706 to 1730 - - - *De Caſtro Sarmento*	XLV 667	X 118

—— Aſtro-

	Tranſ.	Abridg.
—— Aſtronomical obſervations made at Paraguay - - - *Suarez*	XLVI 8	X 123
—— Aſtronomical obſervations made at Pekin in China, 1747 and 1748 - *Hallerſtein*	— 305	— 124
—— Aſtronomical obſervations at Pekin in 1746 and 1747 - - *Jeſuits*	XLVII 319	
—— Extracts from the aſtronomical obſervations made at Pekin in 1744 and 1747, by the jeſuits - - *Bevis*	— 376	
—— Aſtronomical obſervations in London - - - *Bevis and Short*	XLVIII 301	
—— An account of ſome aſtronomical obſervations made at Liſbon, 1753 - *Chevalier*	— 548	
—— A letter on the advantage of taking the mean of a number of obſervations in practical aſtronomy - - *Simpſon*	XLIX 82	
—— A ſhort account of new aſtronomical and phyſical obſervations made in Aſia *Porter*	— 251	
—— Remarks on a paſſage of the editor of the Connoiſſance des Mouvements Céleſtes pour l'Année 1762 - - *Raper*	LII 366	
—— Aſtronomical obſervations at Swelzingen *Mayer*	LIV 165	
—— Aſtronomical obſervations made at the Iſland of St. Helena - - *Maſkelyne*	— 348	
—— Aſtronomical obſervations made at the Iſland of Barbadoes; at Willoughby Fort, and at the Obſervatory on Conſtitution Hill, both adjoining to Bridge Town - *Maſkelyne*	— 389	
—— Aſtronomical obſervations made at Vienna *Bevis*	LV 130	
—— Aſtronomical obſervations made in ſeveral parts of the kingdom of Naples and Sicily *Zannoni*	LVIII 196	
—— Aſtronomical obſervations made in the forks of the river Brandiwine in Pennſylvania, for determining the going of a clock ſent thither by the Royal Society, in order to find the difference of gravity between the Royal Obſervatory at Greenwich, and the place where the clock was ſet up in Pennſylvania *Maſon and Dixon*	— 329	
—— Aſtronomical obſervations made at Swetzingen, 1767 and 1768 - *Mayer*	— 345	
—— Aſtronomical obſervations made by Samuel Holland, Eſq. and others, in North America	LIX 247	
—— Aſtronomical obſervations made at the North Cape for the Royal Society - *Bayley*	— 262	
—— Aſtronomical obſervations made by order of the Royal Society, at Prince of Wales's Fort, on		

Astronomical observations

		Transf.	Abridg.
the north-west coast of Hudson's Bay - - -	*Wales and Dymond*	LIX 467	
—— Astronomical observations made at Cavan, near Strabane, in the county of Donegal, Ireland, by appointment of the Royal Society, 1769 - - -	*Mason*	LX 454	
—— Astronomical observations in America	*Pingre*	— 497	
—— Astronomical observations at King George's Island, in the South Seas -	*Green*	LXI 397	
—— Several astronomical observations made at Portsmouth - -	*Wichell*	LXII 33	
—— Astronomical observations made at Chislehurst in Kent, 1772 -	*Wollaston*	LXIII 67	
—— Astronomical observations by the missionaries at Pekin - -	*Cipolla*	LXIV 31	
—— Astronomical observations for ascertaining the longitude of several places in the North district of North America	*Holland*	— 182	
—— Astronomical observations made at Chislehurst, in Kent, ~~1773~~ 1774 -	*Wollaston*	~~— 329~~ LXV 294	
—— Astronomical observations made at Leicester for determining the latitude of the place	*Ludlam*	LXV 366	
—— Astronomical observations made in the Austrian Netherlands in 1772 and 1773	*Pigott*	LXVI 182	
—— Astronomical observations made in the Austrian Netherlands in the years 1773, 1774, and 1775 - -	*Pigott*	LXVIII 637	
—— Extracts of three letters containing some astronomical observations; together with the longitude of Cork deduced from the said observations - -	*Longfield*	LXIX 163	
—— Astronomical observations relating to the Mountains of the Moon -	*Herschel*	LXX 507	
ATMOSPHERE. A new experiment concerning an effect of the varying weight of the atmosphere upon some bodies in the water	*Boyle*	VII 5156	II 204
—— The barometrical method of measuring the heights of mountains, with two new tables shewing the height of the atmosphere at given altitudes of Mercury -	*Scheuchzer*	XXXV 537	VI 2 30
—— An astronomical dissertation on the lunar atmosphere - -	*De Fouchy*	XLI 261	VIII 172
—— Some observations of the planet Venus, on the disk of the sun, June 6, 1761; with a preceding account of the method taken for verifying the time of that phænomenon; and certain			

+ Astronomical observations made by Nath. Pigott 71: 347.
made at Chislehurst in Kent, 1775–1783 – – Wollaston 74: 190.
Lyons and Marseilles – – – – – de Zach 75: 137.
York, 1781–1785 – – – – – – Edw. Pigott 76: 423.
Miscellaneous observations – – – – – – Herschel 1792: 23.
Astronomical observations relating to the construction of the heavens. – – – – – – Herschel. 1811. 269
Astronomical observations relating to the sidereal part of the heavens and its connection with the nebulous part, arranged for the purpose of a critical examination. – – – 1814: 248
Astronomical observations and experiments tending to investigate the local arrangement of the celestial bodies in space, and to determine the extent and condition of the milky way. —— 1817: 302.
Astronomical observations and experiments, selected for the purpose of ascertaining the relative distances of clusters of stars, and of investigating how far the power of our telescopes may be expected to reach into space, when directed to ambiguous celestial objects. – – —— 1818: 429.

Atmosphere. On the dispersive power of the Atmosphere, and its effect on astronomical observations. — — Lee. 1815: 375.

Attraction. On the grounds of the method which Laplace has given in the second chapter of the third book of his mecanique celeste for computing the attractions of spheroids of every description — Ivory. 1812: 1.

On the attraction of an extensive class of spheroids. — Ivory — — 46.

On the attraction of such solids as are terminated by planes and of solids of greatest attraction — Knight. 1812: 247.

	Transf.	Abridg.
reasons for believing there is an atmosphere about Venus - - *Dunn*	LII 184	
—— Certain reasons for a lunar atmosphere *Dunn*	— 578	
—— Theorems concerning the electrical atmosphere - - - *Beccaria*	LX 277	
—— A letter inclosing an account of some observations on atmospherical electricity; in regard to fog, mists, &c. with some remarks *Ronayne*	LXII 137	
—— Extraordinary electricity of the atmosphere observed at Islington in October 1775 *Cavallo*	LXVI 407	
—— Observations on the annual evaporation at Liverpool, in Lancashire, and on evaporation considered as a test of the moisture or dryness of the atmosphere - *Dobson*	LXVII 244	
—— Observations made in Savoy in order to ascertain the height of mountains by means of the barometer; being an examination of Mr. de Luc's rules, delivered in his "Recherches sur les Modifications de l'Atmosphere" *Shuckburgh*	— 513	
—— See *Air*.		
ATTRACTION, A letter in which the laws of attraction, and other principles of physic, are shewn - - *Keill*	XXVI 97	IV 353
—— A vindication of Dr. Freind's chemical lectures, wherein the objections (in Actis Lipsiensibus, Sept. 1710) brought against the attractive force of matter are removed - *Freind*	XXVII 330	V 428
—— An account of an experiment in order to discover the law of the magnetical attraction - - - *Taylor and Hauksbee*	XXIX 294	IV 2 297
—— Experiments and observations upon the light that is produced by communicating electrical attraction to animal or inanimate bodies, together with some of its most surprising effects - - - *Gray*	XXXIX 16	VIII 397
—— Ivestigations to prove that the figure of the earth nearly approaches to an ellipsis, according to the laws of attraction, in an inverse ratio of the square of the distances - *Clairault*	XL 19	— 392
—— A resolution of a general proposition for determining the horary alteration of the position of the terrestrial equator from the attraction of the sun and moon, with some remarks on the solutions given by other authors to that difficult and important problem *Simpson*	L 416	
—— Of the irregularities in the planetary motions,		

 caused

On the resolution of attractive powers. 79: 185

On the attraction of homogeneous Ellipsoids. Ivory. Waring 1809: 345.

	Tranſ.	Abridg.
cauſed by the mutual attraction of the planets - - - *Walmeſley*	LII 275	
—— A propoſal for meaſuring the attraction of ſome hills in this kingdom by aſtronomical obſervations - - *Maſkelyne*	LXV 495	
—— An account of obſervations made on the mountain Schehallien for finding its attraction *Maſkelyne*	— 500	
—— On the preceſſion of the equinoxes produced by the ſun's attraction - *Milner*	LXIX 505	
—— Calculations to determine at what point in the ſide of a hill its attraction will be the greateſt - - - *Hutton*	LXX 1	
ATTRITION. Several experiments on the attrition of bodies in vacuo - *Haukſbee*	XXIV 2165	IV 2 180
—— An account of an experiment touching the extraordinary electricity of glaſs produceable on a ſmart attrition of it; with a continuation of experiments on the ſame ſubject, and other phænomena - - *Haukſbee*	XXV 2327	— - —
- - - *Haukſbee*	— 2332	— - —
—— Several experiments ſhewing the ſtrange effects of the effluvia of glaſs, produceable on the motion and attrition of it - *Haukſbee*	— 2372	— - —
—— An account of ſome experiments touching the electricity and light produceable in the attrition of ſeveral bodies - *Haukſbee*	XXVI 87	
—— An account of an experiment ſhewing, that an object may become viſible through ſuch an opake body as pitch in the dark, while it is under the circumſtances of attrition and a vacuum - - *Haukſbee*	— 391	— - —
AURORA AUSTRALIS. An account of an Aurora Auſtralis obſerved at Rome Jan. 27, 1740. (Lat.) - - *Revillas*	XLI 744	VIII 554
—— —— An obſervation of the lights ſeen in the air, an Aurora Auſtralis, March 18, 1738-9, at London - - *Mortimer*	— 839	— 553
Another account of - *Martyn*	— 840	— 552
Another obſervation of, at Peterborough *Neve*	— 843	— 554
—— —— Seen at Chelſea January 23, 1749-50 - - *Martyn*	XLVI 319	X 488
AURORA BOREALIS. An account of two late northern Aurora's, obſerved at Sutton, and Hone in Kent, on Feb. 5, 1716-7, and March 30, 1716 - - *Barrel*	XXX 584	IV 2 153
An account of that ſeen 30th of March at London - - *Folkes*	— 586	— - 154

—— —— An

Attraction (Chemistry)

Attractive powers of various saline substances. R. Kirwan. 71: 7. 72:179. 73:15.

Observations on the affinities of substances in spirit of wine. Elliot. — 76:155.

A numerical table of elective attractions; with remarks on the sequences of double decompositions. Young. 1809:148.

	Tranſ.	Abridg.
—— —— An account of a very extraordinary Aurora Borealis ſeen at London Nov. 10, 1719, both morning and evening - *Halley*	XXX 1099	IV 2 163
Another account of the above ſeen at Cruwys Morchard in Devonſhire - *Maunder*	— 1101	— - 164
Seen at Dublin - -	— 1104	— - 165
Another ſeen Dec. 11, at Streatham, Surrey - - - *Hearne*	— 1107	— - 167
—— —— An account of an Aurora Borealis, Feb. 6, 1720-1, obſerved at Dublin *J. W*	XXXI 180	VI - 86
Another ſeen the ſame day at Cruwys Morehard, in Devonſhire; with an account of the weather both before and after it *Cruwys*	— 186	— - 89
—— —— Obſervations on Auroræ Boreales made for four years, at Lynn in Norfolk *Anon.*	XXXII 300	— - 92
—— —— Obſervations on a northern light, ſeen Sept. 20, 1717, near Upſal - *Burman*	XXXIII 175	— - 84
—— —— An account of an Aurora Borealis ſeen Sept. 1725, in Ireland - *Dobbs*	XXXIV 128	— - 93
—— —— ———— Petworth, Suſſex, Oct. 8, 1726 - - *Langwith*	— 132	— - 95
—— —— ———— Plymouth, Oct. 8, 1726 - - - *Huxham*	— 137	— - 97
—— —— ———— Exon, Oct. 8, 1726 *Hallet*	— 143	— - 100
- - - *Hadley*	— 146	— - 102
—— —— ———— Geneva, Oct. 8, 1726 - - - *Calandrini*	— 150	— - 104
—— —— Obſervations on the Lumen Boreale, or ſtreaming, on Oct. 8, 1726 *Derham*	— 245	— - 105
Southwick, in Northamptonſhire, Oct. 8, 1726 - - - *Lynn*	— 253	— - 109
A regiſter of obſervations of the northern lights for four years - *Raſtrick*	— 255	— - 113
—— —— An account of the Lumen Boreale, as ſeen at ſeveral times, Jan. 4, 1726-7 *Langwith*	XXXV 301	— - 111
Another deſcription of an Aurora Borealis, Jan. 4, 1726-7 - *Anon.*	— 304	— - 112
—— —— Extract of ſeveral letters, &c. from different parts of Europe relating to the Aurora Borealis ſeen Oct. 19, 1726, N. S.	— 453	— 292
—— —— A letter containing a deſcription of ſome uncommon appearances obſerved in an Aurora Borealis - - *Derham*	XXXVI 137	— 2 113
—— —— An account of an Aurora Borealis, attended with unuſual appearances *Cramer*	— 279	— - 114
—— —— An account of an Aurora Borealis ſeen in New England Oct. 22, 1730 *Greenwood*	XXXVII 55	— - 115

At.

	Tranf.	Abridg.
At Annapolis, in Maryland, Oct. 22, 1730 - - - *Lewis*	XXXVII 69	VI 2 122
—— —— A defcription of the Aurora Borealis feen at Wirtemberg 1732 - *Weidler*	XXXVIII 291	VIII 574
—— —— Obfervations on an Aurora Borealis at London, Sept. 13, 1735, and Oct. 4. *Celfius*	XXXIX 241	— 548
—— —— Obfervations on feveral Auroræ Boreales - - - *Weidler*	— 266	— 550
—— —— Obfervations of one Dec. 11, 1735 *Neve*	XL 52	— 508, 551
—— —— Letter from Edinburgh giving an account of an Aurora Borealis - *Short*	XLI 368	— 552
—— —— A collection of the obfervations of the remarkable red lights feen in the air Dec. 5, 1737, at Naples - *Prince of Cafino*	— 583	— 527
Padua - *Marq. Poleni*	— 587	— 529
Bononia - *Zanotti*	— 593	— 532
Rome - *Revillas*	— 601	— 536
Edinburgh - *Short*	— 605	— 538
Suffex - *Fuller*	— 606	— 539
—— —— Obferved at Chelfea Feb. 16, 1749-50 - - - *Martyn*	XLVI 345	X 484
Obferved at Tooting Jan. 23, 1750-1 *Miles*	— 346	— —
—— —— Obfervations on the northern lights feen Feb. 15 and 16, 1749-50 - *Huxham*	— 472	— 485
—— —— Abftracts of feveral obfervations of Auroræ Boreales lately feen - *Baker*	— 499	— —
—— —— An account of an Aurora Borealis obferved at the Hague Feb. 27, 1750 *Gabrias*	XLVII 39	
—— —— An attempt to account for the regular diurnal variation of the horizontal magnetic needle, and alfo for its irregular variation at the time of an Aurora Borealis *Canton*	LI 398	
—— —— Extract of a letter relating to a remarkable Aurora Borealis at Philadelphia, and at London, Nov. 12, 1757 - *Bartram*	LII 474	
—— —— Obfervations on an Aurora Borealis in Sweden - - *Bergman*	— 479	
—— —— An account of a remarkable Aurora Borealis obferved at Paris Aug. 6, 1768 *M. Meffier*	LIX 86	
—— —— An account of two Auroræ Boreales obferved at Oxford Feb. 26, 1769, and Sept 9, 1769 - - *Swinton*	— 367	
—— —— Obfervations of two Auroræ Boreales feen Aug. 6, and Dec. 5, 1768 *M. Meffier*	— 454	
—— —— Remarks on the Aurora Borealis in Sept. 1769 - - *Winn*	LXIV 128	
—— —— See *Lights in the Air*, *Meteor*.		

Averrhoa Carambola. Account of its sensitive quality. Bruce. 75:356.

	Trans.	Abridg.
AURUM MOSAICUM. Experiments to shew the nature of Aurum Mosaicum - *Woulfe*	LXI 114	
AVERDUPOISE. An account of a comparison lately made by some gentlemen of the Royal Society of the standard of a yard, and the several weights lately made for their use, with the original standards of measures and weights in the Exchequer, and some others kept for public use, at Guildhall, Founders-hall, the Tower, &c. - - *Graham*	XLII 541	IX 491
—— A state of the English weights and measures of capacity, as they appear from the laws, as well antient as modern, with some considerations thereon; being an attempt to prove that the present averdupoise weight is the legal and antient standard for the weights and measures of this kingdom - *Reynardson*	XLVI 54	XI 1356
—— Short and easy methods for finding the number of troy pounds, contained in any given number of averdupoise pounds, and vice versa - - - *Ferguson*	LV 61	
AVERNI. En extract of an essay entitled, 'On the uses of a knowledge of mineral exhalations when applied to discover the principles and properties of mineral waters, the nature of burning fountains, and of those poisonous lakes which the antients called Averni' - *Brownrigg*	-- 236	
AUSTRIA. Directions and enquiries, with their answers, concerning the mines, minerals, baths, &c. of Austria *Oldenburg and Brown*	V 1189	II 523, 585 III 631
AUTHORS. Letter on judging of the age of learned authors by the style - *Wanley*	XXIV 1993	V 2 1
AXIS. Of a permanent spot in Jupiter: by which is manifested the conversion of Jupiter about his own axis *Hooke, Cassini, and Oldenburg*	I 143	I 383,400
—— Description and uses of an instrument for finding the distances of Jupiter's satellits from his axis, with the help of the table of parallaxes and catalogue of eclipses, printed in the preceding transactions - *Flamstead*	XV 1262	— 404
—— The dimensions of the solid generated by the conversion of Hippocrates Lunula, and its parts about several axes, with the surfaces generated by that conversion - *Demoivre*	XXII 624	— 29
—— An examination of a new-invented axis in Pe-		

ritrochio,

	Transf.	Abridg.
ritrochio, said to be void of friction; with an experiment to confirm the reasoning made upon an axis in Peritrochio, first used in M. Perault's manner, then in the common way - - - *Desaguliers*	XXXVI 222	VI 317
A farther examination of the above *Desaguliers*	— 228	— 320
—— An enquiry concerning the figure of such planets as revolve about an axis, supposing the density continually to vary from the center to the surface - - *Clairault*	XL 277	VIII 90
—— Two letters concerning the rotatory motion of glass tubes about their axes, when placed in a certain manner before the fire *Wheeler*	XLIII 341	X 551
—— Essay on the precession of the equinoxes and the nutation of the earth's axis *Walmesley*	XLIX 704	
A theory of the irregularities that may be occasioned in the annual motion of the earth, by the actions of Jupiter and Saturn *Walmesley*	— 737	
Azimuth. The use of a new azimuth compass for finding the variation of the compass, or magnetic needle, at sea, with greater ease and exactness than by any yet calculated for that purpose - - *Middleton*	XL 395	VIII 374
Azimuth Compass. See *Compass.*		

B.

BACK. A case of an extraordinary exostosis on the back of a boy - *Freke*	XLI 369	IX 253
Back-Bone. An account of a stone fastened to the back-bone of a horse *Giornale de Letterati*	VII 4094	III 164
Bagford. An essay on the invention of printing by John Bagford; with an account of his collections for the same - *Wanley*	XXV 2397	V 2 18
Bahama. Account of a poisonous fish in one of the Bahama Islands - - *Locke*	X 312	II 842
Balances. An invention for estimating the weight of water in water, by ordinary balances and weights - - *Boyle*	IV 1001	I 520
—— A proposition on the balance, not taken notice of by mechanical writers, explained and confirmed by an experiment *Desaguliers*	XXXVI 128	
—— An account of an experiment explaining a mechanical paradox, viz. that two bodies of equal weight, suspended on a certain sort of balance, do not lose their equilibrium, by being re-		

[illegible]

Balaena mysticetus. An account of some peculiarities in the structure of the organ of hearing in the Balaena mysticetus of Linnæus. — — Home. 1812: 83.

		Transf.	Abridg.
moved one farther from, the other nearer to the center *Desaguliers*		XXXVII 125	VII 310
—— A letter shewing, that the electricity of glass disturbs the mariner's compass, and also nice balances *Robins*		XLIX 242	X 328
—— An account of a balance of a new construction, supposed to be of use in the woolen manufacture *Ludlam*		LV 205	
BALCARRAS. Observables in the body of the earl of Balcarras *Anon.*		I 86	III 158
BALL. Account of a ball extracted from a person who had suffered by it 30 years, in which was a plumb-stone *Young*		XXIII 1279	V 261
—— An extract of a letter concerning a ball voided by stool *Thoresby*		XXIV 1595	—— 281
—— Account of a large ball voided by stool *Thoresby*		—— 2164	—— 365
—— An account of balls of hair taken from the uterus and ovaria of several women *Younge*		XXV 2387	
—— An account of balls made at Liege *Hanbury*		XLI 672	IX 501
—— Account of vegetable balls which grow in a lake near the Humber in Yorkshire; with remarks by W. Watson *Dixon*		XLVII 498	
BALSAM. An observation and experiment concerning a mineral balsam found in a mine in Italy *Castagna*		VI 3059	II 460
BARBADOES. Extract of a letter containing some observations made at Barbadoes *Lister*		X 399	III 560
BARBARY. An account of the Moorish way of dressing their meat (with some remarks) in West Barbary, from Cape Spartel to Cape de Geer *Jones*		XXI 248	—— 626
BARK (MEDICINE). A letter concerning the jesuits bark *Oliver*		XXIV 1596	IV 2 323
—— Microscopical observations on the Cortex Peruvianus *Leewenhoek*		XXV 2446	V 2 267
—— An abstract of a book entitled, A short account of mortifications, and of the surprising effect of the bark, in putting a stop to its progress *Douglas*		XXXVII 429	—— 35
—— Of the use of the Peruvian bark to a gangrene *Shipton*		—— 434	VII 647
—— An account of the Peruvian, or jesuits bark, by Mr. John Gray; extracted from some papers given him by William Arrot, who had gathered it in Peru		XL 81	VIII 776
—— Extract of a letter concerning the bark preventing catching cold *Salter*		XLIV 1	X 762

	Trans.	Abridg.
—— A letter concerning the use of the Peruvian bark in the small-pox - *Wilmot*	XLIV 583	XI 1035
—— Of the use of the bark in the small-pox *Bayly*	XLVII 27	
—— Case of the efficacy of bark in a mortification - - - *Grindall*	L 379	
—— Case of the efficacy of the bark in the delirium of a fever - *Munckley*	— 609	
Willow bark —— An account of the success of the bark of the willow in the cure of agues - *Stone*	LIII 195	
—— Experiments on the Peruvian bark *Lee*	LVI 95	
—— Experiments on the Peruvian bark *Percival*	LVII 221	
—— Description of the jesuits bark-tree of Jamaica and the Caribbees - *Wright*	LXVII 504	
BARK OF TREES. Observations concerning the uniting of barks of trees cut, to the tree itself *Merret*	II 453	III 706
—— A letter concerning the barks of trees *Leewenhoek*	XXIV 1843	V 2 267
—— ~~An account of~~ insects ~~in the barks of decaying elms and ashes - *Dudley*~~	~~— 1859~~	~~— 13~~
Cabbage bark tree —— Description and use of the cabbage-bark tree of Jamaica - - *Wright*	LXVII 507	
BARNACLES. A relation concerning barnacles *Moray*	XII 925	II 849
—— Some observations on the Scotch barnacle - - - *Robinson*	XV 1036	— 850
—— An account of several rare species of barnacles - - - *Romilly*	L 845	
BAROMETER (Construction of the). A new contrivance of a wheel-barometer much more easy to be prepared, than that which is described in the micrography - *Hook*	I 218	— 252
—— An account of a new kind of baroscope, which may be called statical; and of some advantages and conveniences it hath above the mercurial - - - *Boyle*	— 231	— 28
—— Observations on several passages in the two last months Transactions relating to baroscopes - - - *Anon.*	X 533	
—— A description of an invention, whereby the divisions of the barometer may be enlarged in any given proportions - *Hook*	XVI 241	— 10
—— An account of some experiments about the height of the Mercury in the barometer at the top and bottom of the monument; and also about portable barometers - *Derham*	XX 2	-10,12,14
—— A letter about a contrivance to measure the height of the Mercury in the barometer, by a circle on one of the weather-plates, with		

a re-

+ Bark (Jesuits) Account of a new species of the Bark-tree, found in the Island of St. Lucia. Davidson. 74:4

+ On the formation of the bark of trees. — — — — — — — Knight. 1807:1
On the inconvertibility of Bark into Alburnum — — — — — — 1808:10

Barometer, Description of a Thermometrical barometer for measuring altitudes. — — — Wollaston 1817

BAR

		Tranf.	Abridg.
— a register of the weather, &c. for 1697 *Derham*		XX 45	II 12
—— A way of measuring the height of Mercury in the barometer more exactly *Gray*		— 176	— —
—— An account of Dr. R. Hook's invention of the marine barometer, with its description and uses *Halley*		XXII 791	IV 2 4
—— Part of a letter giving an account of a new baroscope invented by *Caswell*		XXIV 1597	— 2 6
—— A proposal for measuring heights of places, by help of the barometer of Mr. Patrick, in which the scale is greatly enlarged *Halley*		XXXI 116	VI 2 28
—— A description of a new barometer *Fahrenheit*		XXXIII 179	— — —
—— A description of a barometer, wherein the scale of variation may be encreased at pleasure *Rowning*		XXXVIII 39	VIII 445
—— The imperfections of the common barometers, and the improvement made in them by Charles Orme, of Ashby-de-la-Zouch, with some observations, remarks and rules for their use *Beighton*		XL 248	— 455
—— A description of a new thermometer and barometer *Fitzgerald*		LII 146	
—— An account of a new improvement of the portable barometer *Spry*		LV 83	
—— An account of some improvements made in a new wheel-barometer, invented by *Fitzgerald*		LX 74	
BAROMETER (General observations on the). Observations continued upon the barometer, or rather balance of the air *Boyle*		I 163	II 4
—— Observations of the sealed weather-glass, and the barometer, both upon the phænomenon, and in general *Wallis*		— 166	— 6
—— Some observations and directions about the barometer *Boyle*		— 181	— 5, 8
—— Some observations concerning the baroscope and thermoscope *Wallis and Beale*		IV 1113	— 5
—— An attempt to render the cause of that odd phænomenon of the quicksilver's remaining suspended far above the usual height in the Torricellian experiment *Hugens*		VII 5027	— 23
—— Concerning the suspension of quicksilver well purged of air, much higher than the ordinary standard of the Torricellian experiment *Wallis*		— 5160	— 24
—— A discourse concerning the rising and falling of the quicksilver in the barometer; and what

	Tranſ.	Abridg.
may be gathered from its great riſe in froſty weather, as to a healthy or ſickly ſeaſon *Liſter*	XIV 790	II 18
—— Letter concerning the Torricellian experiment, tried on the top of Snowdon Hill, and the ſucceſs of it - - *Halley*	XIX 582	— 13
—— An experiment to ſhew the cauſe of the deſcent of the Mercury in the barometer in a ſtorm - - - *Haukſbee*	XXIV 1629	IV 2 181
—— Remarks on the ſecond paper in the hiſtory of the Royal Academy of Sciences for 1711, concerning the cauſe of the variation of the barometer; to ſhew that the way of accounting for it in that paper is inſufficient, and that the experiment made uſe of to prove what is there aſſerted, does no way prove it *Deſaguliers*	XXX 570	— - 10
—— Obſervation of an extraordinary height of the barometer, Dec. 21, 1721 *Graham*	XXXI 222	VI - 28
—— The middle height of the barometer for a year - - - *Cruquius*	XXXIII 4	
—— An experiment made in a ſilver mine at Sala about the aſcent of Mercury in the barometer - - - *Celſius*	— 313	— - 48
—— Obſervations of the difference of the heights of barometers. (Lat.) - *Hollman*	XLII 116	VIII 452
—— Letters concerning the cauſe of the aſcent of vapour and exhalation, and thoſe of winds; and of the general phænomena of the weather and barometer - - *Eeles*	XLIX 124	
BAROMETER (Obſervations on it at different places).		
Obſervations on the barometer at Jamaica *Beeſton*	XIX 225	II 9
—— Part of a letter accompanying his obſervations of the height of the Mercury in the barometer, rains, winds, &c. for the year 1698, at Upminſter, in Eſſex - *Derham*	XXI 45	— 73, 102
—— Some obſervations of the Mercury's altitude, with the changes of the weather at Emay in China - - *Cunningham*	XXI 323	II 86
—— A proſpect of the weather, winds, and height of the Mercury in the barometer on the firſt day of the month, and of the whole rain in every month in 1703 and beginning of 1704, at Townley in Lancaſhire, by R. Townley, and at Upminſter by W. Derham	XXIV 1877	
—— Tables of the barometrical altitudes at Zurich in Switzerland, in the year 1708, by Scheuchzer; and at Upminſter, in England, by Derham; and alſo the rain at Piſa, in Italy, in		

Barometer. Abstract of observations on a diurnal variation of the Barometer between the tropics. Horsburgh. 1805: 177.

Observations upon the Marine Barometer, made during the examination of the coasts of New Holland and New South Wales, in the years 1801, 1802, and 1803. Flinders. 1806: 239.

	Tranſ.	Abridg.
1707 and 1708, by Tilli; and at Zurich in 1708; and at Upminſter in that time; with remarks on the ſame tables; as alſo on the winds, heats and colds, and divers other matters occurring in thoſe three different parts of Europe - - *Derham*	XXVI 342	
—— Experiments for diſcovering the various elaſticity of the air, in different parts of Switzerland - - *Scheuchzerus*	XXIX 266	IV 2 16
—— A meteorological, barometrical, thermometrical epidemical diary kept at Utrecht, 1729, 1730, and 1731 - *Van Muſchenbrock*	XXXVII 357, 406	VII 4 71, 86, 90
—— On the correſpondence of the barometer with the air and weather - *Holman*	XLVI 101	X 428
—— An account of the barometer, and the ſtate of the weather at Dublin, from Mar. 7, 1752, to Feb. 28, 1753 - *Simon*	XLVIII 320	
—— Obſervations on the barometer, thermometer, and rain in 1767, at Plymouth *Farr*	LVIII 136	
—— Extract of a regiſter of the barometer, thermometer, and rain, at Lyndon in Rutland, 1772 - - - *Barker*	LXIII 221	
—— Extract of a regiſter of the barometer, thermometer, and rain, at Lyndon in Rutland, 1773 - - - *Barker*	LXIV 202	
—— Meteorological journal for 1774 at Briſtol *Anon.*	LXV 194	
—— Extract of a regiſter of the barometer, thermometer, and rain, at Lyndon in Rutland, 1774 - - - *Barker*	— 199	
—— Extract of a regiſter of the barometer, thermometer, and rain, at Lyndon in Rutland, 1775 - - - *Barker*	LXVI 370	
—— Extract of a regiſter of the barometer, thermometer, and rain, at Lyndon in Rutland, 1776 - - - *Barker*	LXVII 350	
—— An abſtract of a regiſter of the barometer, thermometer, and rain, at Lyndon in Rutland, 1777 - - *Barker*	LXVIII 554	
—— Abſtract of a regiſter of the barometer, thermometer, and rain, at Lyndon in Rutland, 1778 - - - *Barker*	LXIX 547	
—— Regiſter of the barometer, thermometer, and rain, at Lyndon in Rutland, 1779 *Barker*	LXX 474	
Barometer (Applied to the meaſurement of heights). Obſervations concerning the height of the barometer, at different elevations above the ſurface of the earth - *Nettleton*	XXXIII 308	VI 2 44

	Transf.	Abridg.
—— M. de Luc's rule for measuring heights by the barometer, reduced to the English measure of length, and adapted to Fahrenheit's thermometer, and other scales of heat, and reduced to a more convenient expression *Maskelyne*	LXIV 158	
—— M. de Luc's rules for measurement of heights by the barometer, compared with theory, and reduced to English measures of length, and adapted to Fahrenheit's scale of the thermometer; with tables and precepts for expediting the practical application of them *Horsley*	— 214	
—— Observations on the depth of the mines in the Hartz - - *De Luc*	LXVII 401	
—— Observations made in Savoy, in order to ascertain the height of mountains by means of the barometer being an examination of Mr. De Luc's rules, delivered in his "Recherches sur les Modifications de l'Atmosphere" *Shuckburgh*	— 513	
—— Experiments and observations made in Britain in order to obtain a rule for measuring heights with the barometer - *Roy*	— 653	
—— Comparison between Sir George Shuckburgh and colonel Roy's rules, for the measurement of heights with the barometer *Shuckburgh*	LXVIII 681	
—— A second paper concerning some barometrical measures in the mines of the Hartz *De Luc*	LXIX 485	
Barrenness. An abstract of a letter giving an instance of the bath curing the palsy and barrenness - - *Peirce*	XV 944	II 399
Barrows. An attempt to examine the barrows in Cornwall - - *Williams*	XLI 465	IX 445
Basalt Hills. A letter containing a short account of some Basalt Hills in Hessia *Raspe*	LXI 580	
—— An account of two giants causeways, or groups of prismatic basaltine columns, and other curious volcanic concretions, in the Venetian state in Italy, with some remarks on the characters of these and other similar bodies, and of the physical geography of the countries in which they are found - *Strange*	LXV 5	
Bath. An accurate account of a tessellated pavement bath, and other Roman antiquities, lately discovered at East Bourne, in Sussex *Tabor*	XXX 549	V 2 63
—— See *Antiquities*, *Inscriptions.*		
Baths (Aponensian). An account of the Aponensian baths near Padua - *Dodington*	VII 4067	II 344

+ Basalt columns. Remarks on the stones in the country of Nassau, and the territories of Cleves and Colen, resembling those of the Giants Causeway in Ireland. Trembley. 49: 581.

Basaltes. Observations on the affinity between Basaltes and Granite. Beddoes. 81: 48.

Observations on Basalt, and on the transition from the vitreous to the stony texture, which occurs in the gradual refrigeration of melted Basalt. Watt. 1804: 279.

On the alterations that have taken place in the structure of rocks, on the surface of the Basaltic country in the Counties of Derry and Antrim. Richardson. 1808: 187

	Tranf.	Abridg.
Baths (Of Bath). Obfervations concerning the Bath fprings - - *Glanvill*	IV 977	II 336
—— An abftract of a letter giving an inftance of the bath in curing the palfy and barrennefs - - - *Peirce*	XV 944	— 339
—— —— Some obfervations on the heat of the waters at Bath - *Howard*	LVII 201	
Other obfervations on Bath waters *Canton*	— 203	
—— (Of Carlfbad). Part of a letter concerning the baths at Carlfbad - *Mounfey*	XLVI 217	X 569
—— (Of Germany, &c.). Directions and enquiries, with their anfwers, concerning the mines, minerals, baths, &c. of Hungary, Tranfylvania, Auftria, and other countries neighbouring to thofe *Oldenburgh and Brown*	V 1189	III 631
- - - *Brown*	— 1044	II 339 III 605
—— (Of Jamaica). Obfervations of a hot-bath in the ifland of Jamaica - *Keefton*	XIX 225	II 344
—— (Of Vinadio). An account of the hot-baths of Vinadio, in the province of Coni, in Piedmont - - *Bruni*	LI 839	
Bay Tree. The figure and characters of that elegant American evergreen, called by the gardeners Loblolly Bay, taken from bloffoms blown near London - - *Ellis*	LX 518	
Bayles (John). An account of the death and diffection of John Bayles, of Northampton, reputed to have been 130 years old *Keil*	XXV 2247	V 351
Beans. An account of four forts of ftrange beans frequently caft on fhore on the Orkney Iflands, with fome conjectures about the way of their being brought thither from Jamaica, where three forts of them grow - *Sloane*	XIX 298	III 540
Beasts. A differtation on the bones and teeth of elephants, and other beafts found in America, and other northern regions, by which it appears they are the bones of indigenous beafts *Rafpe*	LIX 126	
Beatification. Letter declaring that Dr. Watfon, as well as many others, have not been able to make odours pafs through glafs by means of electricity; and giving a particular account of profeffor Bon; his experiment of beatification, or caufing a glory to appear round a man's head by electricity - *W. Watfon*	XLVI 348	X 410
Beaucastle. See *Infcription*.		

	Tranf.	Abridg.
Beaver. The anatomy of a female beaver, and an account of caftor found in her *Mortimer*	XXXVIII 172	IX 78
Beech Tree. Account of letters found in the middle of a beech tree - *Klein*	XLI 231	VIII 845
Bees. Some communications about an early fwarm of bees - - *Reed*	VI 2128	
—— Some confiderations on an apiary, or difcipline of bees - - *Beal*	— 2144	
—— An account of the hatching of a kind of bee lodged in old willows - *Willughby*	— 2221	II 174
—— A defcription of a bee-houfe, ufeful for preventing the fwarming of bees, ufed in Scotland - - *Anon.*	VIII 6097	
—— Account of bees breeding in cafes made of leaves - - - *Lifter*	XIV 592	
—— An account of a ftrange fort of bees in the Weft Indies - - *M. I.*	XV 1030	— 775
—— Extract of a letter concerning the probofcis of bees - - *Garden*	— 1148	
—— Letter concerning the late Swammerdam's treatife De Apibus - *Holton*	XXI 365	
—— An account of a method lately found out in New England, for difcovering where the bees hive in the woods, in order to get their honey - - - *Dudley*	XXXI 148	VII 403
—— Of the bafes of the cells wherein the bees depofit their honey - *Maclaurin*	XLII 565	IX 2
—— Letter concerning bees, and their method of gathering wax and honey - *Dobbs*	XLVI 536	XI 841
—— An account of a fpecimen of the labour of a kind of bees, which lay up their young in cafes of leaves, which they bury in rotten wood - - *Styles*	LI 844	
—— Difcoveries on the fex of bees, explaining the manner in which their fpecies is propagated; with an account of the utility that may be derived from thofe difcoveries by the actual application of them to practice *Debraw*	LXVII 15	
—— A letter on Mr. Debraw's improvements in the culture of bees - *Polhill*	LXVIII 107	
Beetle. Curious experiments and obfervations on a beetle that lived three years without food - - - *Baker*	XLI 441	IX 8
—— An account of a Capricorn beetle found alive in a cavity, within a found piece of wood - - - *Mortimer*	— 861	— 11

Bees Observations on Bees. — — — — — — — Hunter. 1792: 121
On the economy of Bees. — — — — — — — — — Knight. 1807: 23

		Transf.	Abridg.
Belemnites. A differtation on thofe foffil-figured ftones called belemnites	*Mendez da Cofta*	XLIV 397	X 628
—— A letter containing confiderations on two extraordinary belemnitæ	*David Erfkin Baker*	XLV 598	— 639
—— A differtation on the belemnites	*Brander*	XLVIII 803	
—— An attempt to account for the origin and formation of the extraneous foffil commonly called the belemnite -	*Platt*	LIV 38	
Bell. The art of living under water; or, a difcourfe concerning the means of furnifhing air at the bottom of the fea, in any ordinary depth - - -	*Halley*	XXIX 492	IV 2 188
—— A letter concerning an improvement of the diving-bell - -	*Triewald*	XXXIX 377	VIII 634
Bella Donna. A brief botanical and medical hiftory of the folanum lethale, bella-donna, or deadly nightfhade -	*W. Watfon*	L 62	
Bellows. An experiment of preferving animals alive by blowing through their lungs with bellows - -	*Hook*	II 539	III 66
—— Letter concerning an improvement of the Heffian bellows - -	*Papin*	XXIV 1990	IV 447
—— A calculation of the velocity of the air moved by a new-invented centrifugal bellows of 7 feet in diameter, and 1 foot thick within, which a man can keep in motion with very little labour, at the rate of two revolutions in one fecond -	*Defaguliers*	XXXIX 44	VIII 271
The ufes of the foregoing machine -		— 47	— 23
—— A defcription of a new invention of bellows called water-bellows -	*Triewald*	XL 231	— 272
Belluga Stone. Some obfervations on the Belluga ftone - -	*Collinfon*	XLIV 451	XI 266
Belly. Relation of a child that remained 26 years in the mother's belly -	*Bayle*	XII 979	III 127
—— An account of a fœtus lying without the uterus in the belly - -	*Savard*	XIX 314	— 214
—— The hiftory of a tumor in the lower part of the belly - -	*Giles*	— 420	
—— A cafe concerning a child born with the bowels hanging out of its belly -	*Amyand*	XXXVII 258	VII 516
Belt. See *Jupiter* and *Saturn.*			
Bengal. An account of the heat of the climate at Bengal - -	*Martin*	LVII 217	
—— Two letters of a voyage to Bengal, with obfervations made there -	*Rofe*	LX 444	

Benjamin. Botanical description of the Benjamin Tree of Sumatra. Dryander 77: 307.

	Tranſ.	Abridg.
Bermudas. Inquiries for Virginia and the Bermudas - - *Royal Society*	II 420	III 631
—— An account of the courſe of the tides at Bermudas; of wells, both ſalt and ſweet, digged near the ſea; and of the whale-fiſhing there practiſed anew, and of ſuch whales as have the ſpermaceti in them - *Norwood*	— 565	II 268, 298, 844
—— Letter concerning the tides at the Bermudas; as alſo whales, ſpermaceti, ſtrange ſpider's webbs, and the longevity of the inhabitants - - - *Stafford*	III 792	- 268,845 III 561
Bernoulli. A ſolution of two mathematical problems propoſed by John Bernoulli *Anon.*	XIX 384	I 33, 463
—— A ſolution of the problem propoſed in the French Diary by J. Bernoulli - *Craig*	XXIV 1527	IV 35
—— Apology againſt J. Bernoulli's objections *Taylor*	XXX 955	V 244
Berries. An account of a new die from the berries of a weed in South Carolina *Lindo*	LIII 238	
Bezoar. A letter concerning the Pietra de Mombazza, or the rhinoceros Bezoar *Sloane*	XLVI 118	XI 910
Bianchini. The phænomena of Venus repreſented in an orrery made by Mr. James Ferguſon, agreeable to the obſervations of Signior Bianchini - -	XLIV 127	X 95
Bile. Anatomical obſervations of an abſceſs in the liver; a great number of ſtones in the gall-bag and bilious veſſels; an unuſual conformation of the emulgents and pelvis; a ſtrange conjunction of both kidnies, and a great dilatation of the Vena Cava *Tyſon*	XII 1035	III 81
—— Extract of a letter concerning an experiment made with the bile of perſons dead of the plague - - *Deidier*	XXXII 105	VII 600
—— An eſſay upon the uſe of the bile in the animal œconomy, founded on an obſervation of a wound in the gall-bladder - *Stuart*	XXXVI 341	— 572
—— Explanation of an eſſay on the uſe of the bile in the animal œconomy - *Stuart*	XXXVIII 5	IX 195
—— Of an obſtruction of the biliary ducts, and an impoſtumation of the gall-bladder, diſcharging upwards of 18 quarts of bilious matter in 25 days, without any apparent defect in the animal functions - *Amyand*	XL 317	VIII 503
—— Obſervations on the caſe of Mr. Le Grange - - - *Stuart*	— 325	IX 146
Bills of Mortality. See *Annuity*, *Mortality*, and *Population*. Birth.		

Binomial Theorem. Note respecting the demonstration of the binomial theorem inserted in the last volume of the Philos. Transact. Knight. 1817: 245.

Binomial Theorem demonstrated by the principles of multiplication. Robertson 1795: 298.
legally demonstrated by Algebra. Sewell. 1796: 382.
A new demonstration of the binomial theorem, when the exponent is a positive or negative fraction. Robertson. 1806: 305.

A new demonstration of the binomial theorem. Knight. 1816: 331.

		Trans.	Abridg.
BIQUADRATIC. Cubic and biquadratic equations constructed by one single parabola and a circle - - -	*Halley*	XVI 335	
—— Universal solution of quadratic and biquadratic equations, viz. analytical, geometrical, and mechanical - -	*Colson*	XXV 2353	IV 66
BIRCH. Ways of ordering birch-water	*Tonge*	V 2070	II 684
BIRDS. A way of preserving birds taken out of the egg, and other small fœtus's	*Boyle*	I 199	III 650
—— Observations on several passages in the two last months Transactions relating to the history of birds - -	*Anon.*	X 533	
—— Letter to Mr. Ray, concerning some particulars that might be added to the ornithology - - -	*Lister*	XV 1159	II 849, 853
—— Anatomical observations made on the heads of fowl at several times -	*Moulen*	XVII 711	— 860
—— Observations on the birds of the Philippine islands - -	*Camelli*	XXIII 1394	V 183
—— Part of a letter concerning the migration of birds - -	*Derham*	XXVI 123	— 33
—— A letter containing several observations in the natural history of birds, made in travels through Wales -	*Lhwyd*	XXVII 462	— 34
- - -	*Lhwyd*	— 466	— —
- - -	*Lhwyd*	— 467	V 2 118
—— An account of birds of passage	*Catesby*	XLIV 435	XI 886
—— Divers means for preserving from corruption dead birds, intended to be sent to remote countries, so that they may arrive there in good condition. Some of the same means may be employed for preserving quadrupeds, reptiles, fishes, and insects -	*Reaumur*	XLV 309	— 891
—— An account of a bird supposed to have been bred between a turkey and a pheasant	*Edwards*	LI 833	
—— An account of the different species of the birds called pinguins -	*Pennant*	LVIII 91	
—— An account of the lymphatic system in birds - - -	*Hewson*	— 217	
—— Method of preparing birds for preservation - - -	*Davies*	LX 184	
—— Four letters on the preservation of dead birds - - -	*Kuckahn*	— 302	
—— A description of a bird from the East Indies - - -	*Edwards*	LXI 55	
—— A letter containing a technical description of an uncommon bird from Malacca	*Badenach*	LXII 1	

—— An

	Tranſ.	Abridg.
—— An eſſay on the periodical appearing and diſappearing of certain birds, at different times of the year - - *Barrington*	— 265	
—— An account of birds ſent from Hudſon's Bay; with obſervations relative to their natural hiſtory; and Latin deſcriptions of ſome of the moſt uncommon - - *Forſter*	— 382	
—— Experiments and obſervations on the ſinging of birds - - *Barrington*	LXIII 249	
—— An account of certain receptacles of air in birds, which communicate with the lungs, and are lodged both among the fleſhy parts and in the hollow bones of thoſe animals *John Hunter*	LXIV 205	
See particular birds in their places.		
Birth. An account of an extraordinary birth in Staffordſhire - - *Birch*	XIII 281	III 221
- - - *Tyſon*	— —	— —
—— Some obſervations on the motion of diſeaſes, and on the births and deaths of men and other animals, in different times of the Νυχθήμερον - - - *Paſchall*	XVII 815	— 311
—— An argument for Divine Providence; taken from the conſtant regularity obſerved in the births of both ſexes - *Arbuthnott*	XXVII 186	V 2 240
~~—— An account of an extraordinary acephalous birth~~ (see monster) - ~~*Cooper*~~	~~LXV 311~~	
—— See *Child*, *Monſter*.		
Bitch. An account of the diſſection of a bitch, whoſe cornua uteri, being filled with the bones and fleſh of a former conception, had, after a ſecond conception, the ova affixed to ſeveral parts of the abdomen - *Anon.*	XIII 183	II 904
—— An account of the cutting out the cæcum of a bitch - - *Muſgrave*	— 324	III 112
Bite. Relation of a man, bitten with a mad dog, and dying of the diſeaſe, called hydrophobia - - - *Liſter*	— 162	II 276
—— Letter concerning the cure of the bitings of mad creatures, with a remark on the ſame by Hans Sloane - *Dampier*	XX 49	III 284, 285
—— Letter concerning the bitings of mad dogs, &c. - - - *De La Pryme*	XXIII 1073	IV 2 218
—— Part of a letter concerning the viper-catchers, and their remedy for the bite of a viper *Burton*	XXXIX 312	IX 61
—— A narration of the experiments made by the viper-catchers June 1734, before the Royal		

Do. An account of an appendix to the small intestines in birds. Macartney. 1811: 257

On the different structures and situations of the solvent glands in the digestive organs of birds, according to the nature of their food and particular modes of life. Home. 1812: 394.

Births. Calculations of the proportion of male to female children, as well as of Twins, monstrous productions, and children that are dead-born. Bland. 71: 355.

A remarkable case of numerous Births, with observations. Garthshore 77: 344.

Bitumen.
Observations on the change of some of the proximate principles of vegetables into Bitumen, with analytical experiments on a peculiar substance which is found with the Bovey coal. Hatchett. 1804: 385.

Black Wadd. Some experiments upon the Ochra friabilis nigro fusca of Da Costa, called by the Miners of Derbyshire, Black Wadd. Wedgwood 73: 284.

	Transf.	Abridg.
Society; and some remarks on the bite of a mad dog - *Mortimer*	XXXIX 313	IX 221
—— The case of a lad bitten by a mad dog *Nourse*	XL 5	— 222
—— The effects of Dampier's powder in curing the bite of a mad dog - *Fuller*	— 272	— 224
Another case drawn up by *Hartley and Sandys*	— 274	— —
—— Letter concerning the virtues of the star of the earth, coronopus, or buck's horn plantain, in the cure of the bite of a mad dog *Steward*	— 449	VIII 83
—— Case of a person bit by a mad dog *Peters*	XLIII 257	
—— A letter containing an account of what Mr. Breintal felt after being bit by a rattle-snake - - - *Breintal*	XLIV 147	XI 856
—— An account of a horse bit by a mad dog *Starr*	XLVI 474	— 913
—— An account of the successful application of salt to wounds made by the bite of rattle-snakes - - - *Gale*	LV 244	
—— See *Dog*.		
Bivalve Insects. Observations on some bivalve insects found in common water *Muller*	LXI 230	
Black. Experiments on dying black *Clegg*	LXIV 48	
Black Assize. An account of the black assize at Oxford in 1577, from the register of Merton College - - *Ward*	L 699	
- - - *Birch*	— 702	
Black Dust. An account of an extraordinary shower of black dust that fell in the island of Zetland Oct. 20, 1755 - *Mitchell*	— 297	
Black Lead. Observations concerning the substance commonly called black lead - *Plot*	XX 183	II 462
Black Vomit. An extract of so much of A. de Ulloa's account of his voyage to South America, as relates to the distemper called the Vomito Priero, or black vomit *William Watson*	XLVI 134	XI 1063
Blackness. An account of an unusual blackness of the face - - *Yonge*	XXVI 424	V 199
- - - *Yonge*	— 432	— —
Bladder. Account of a great number of stones found in the bladder - *Goodrick*	II 482	II 382
—— An account of an human body opened at Dantzick, and 38 stones found in the bladder thereof - - *Kirkby*	VIII 6155	III 149
—— Letter concerning a triple bladder *Bussiere*	XXII 752	V 289
—— A relation of the cutting an ivory bodkin out of the bladder of a young woman in Dublin - - - *Proby*	— 455	III 162

	Tranſ.	Abridg.
—— An account of a pin taken out of the bladder of a child - - *Gregory*	XL 367	IX 185
—— Account of a ſhuttle-ſpire taken out of the bladder of a boy - *Arderon*	XLIII 194	XI 1006
—— A propoſal to bring ſmall paſſable ſtones with eaſe out of the bladder - *Hales*	— 502	— 990
—— The caſe of a tumour growing on the inſide of the bladder, ſucceſsfully extirpated *Warner*	XLVI 414	— 1006
—— Obſervations on fungous excreſcences of the bladder; a cutting forceps for extirpating theſe excreſcences; a canula for treating theſe diſeaſes - - *Le Cat*	XLVII 292	
—— A deſcription of the lymphatics of the urethra and neck of the bladder *Henry Watſon*	LIX 392	
—— An account of a ſuppreſſion of urine cured by a puncture made in the bladder through the anus - *Robert Hamilton*	LXVI 578	
—— See *Stone.*		
Bladders (Natural Hiſtory). A conjecture concerning the bladders of air that are found in fiſhes, by A. J. illuſtrated by an experiment ſuggeſted by the Hon. Robert Boyle	X 310	II 846
—— Conſiderations on the ſwimming-bladders in fiſhes - - *Ray*	— 319	I 846
Blemish. An obſervation concerning a blemiſh in an horſe's eye, not hitherto diſcovered by any author - - *Lower*	II 613	II 864
Blindness. Philoſophic ſolution of the cure of a young man who grew blind in the evening - - - *Briggs*	XIV 804	III 39
—— An account of ſome obſervations made by a young gentleman who was born blind, or loſt his ſight ſo early that he had no remembrance that he had ever ſeen, and was couched between 13 and 14 years of age *Cheſelden*	XXXV 447	VII 491
Blister. A diſcourſe of the operation of a bliſter when it cures a fever - *Cockburne*	XXI 161	III 260
—— Caſes of the remarkable effects of bliſters in leſſening the quickneſs of the pulſe in coughs attended with an infarction of the lungs and fever - - *Whytt*	L 569	
Blood. Anatomical obſervations of milk found in the veins inſtead of blood - *Boyle*	I 100	— 239
A farther account of an obſervation about white blood - - *Boyle*	— 117	— —
—— A further account concerning the exiſtence of veins in all kind of plants; together with a		

diſcovery

	Transf.	Abridg.
discovery of the membraneous substance of those veins, and of some acts in plants resembling those of sense; and also of the agreement of the venal juice in vegetables with the blood of animals - *Lister*	VII 5131	II 693
—— Notice of an admirable liquor, instantly stopping the blood of arteries pricked or cut, without any suppuration, or without leaving any scar or cicatrice - *Denys*	VIII 6039	III 252
Experiments made with the liquor at London - *Needham and Wiseman*	— 6052	— 253
———————— At Paris - *Denis*	— 6054	— 291
An addition to the experiments - *Anon.*	— 6074	— 254
Experiments in St. Thomas's Hospital *Anon.*	— 6078	— —
Further success in the Fleet - *Anon.*	— 6115	— 255
—— Microscopical observations concerning blood, &c. - - *Leewenhoek*	IX 121	— 683
—— A relation concerning a strange kind of bleeding in a little child - *Gard*	— 193	— 251
—— Microscopical observations concerning the texture of the blood - *Leewenhoek*	X 380	— 683
—— An account of a periodical evacuation of blood at the end of one of the fingers. - - - *Dublin Society*	XV 989	— 252
—— Letter concerning the circulation of the blood as seen by the help of a microscope, in the lacerta aquatica - *Molyneux*	— 1236	II 133 III 225
—— A conjecture of the quantity of blood in men, together with an estimate of the celerity of its circulation - - *Moulin*	XVI 433	— —
—— An account of an experiment of the injection of mercury into the blood, and its ill effect on the lungs - - *Moulin*	XVII 486	— 233
—— An experiment of a surprizing change of colour, from a pale transparent, or clear liquor, to a very blue ceruleus one, and that in an instant, by the admission of air only, applied to illustrate some changes of colour, and other effects on the blood of respiring animals - - - *Slare*	— 898	
—— Letter on the human blood - *Vieussens*	XX 224	— 220
—— Letter concerning the circulation and stagnation of the blood in tadpoles -	XXII 447	— 685
—— Answer of the College of Physicians at Rome to the letter of M. Vieussens, on the existence of acid salt in the blood, and its proportion	— 599	— 247

—— An

	Transf.	Abridg.
—— An account of divers ſchemes of arteries and veins diſſected from adult human bodies, by J. Evelyn. To which is ſubjoined a deſcription of the extremities of thoſe veſſels, and the manner the blood is ſeen by the microſcope, to paſs from the arteries to the veins in quadrupeds when living: with ſome chirurgical obſervations and figures after the life - - - *Cowper*	XXIII 1177	V 334
—— An account of an eruption of blood from almoſt every part of the body *Meſaporitus*	XXIV 2144	
—— Microſcopical obſervations on the blood-veſſels and membranes of the inteſtines - - - *Leewenhoek*	XXVI 53	V 2 267
—— A letter concerning the circulation of the blood in fiſhes - *Leewenhoek*	— 250	— - —
—— Manner of obſerving the circulation of blood in an eel - - *Leewenhoek*	— 444	— - 398
—— A letter containing obſervations upon the ſeminal veſſels, muſcular fibres, and blood of whales - - - *Leewenhoek*	XXVII 438	— - 267
—— An account of ſome experiments relating to the ſpecifick gravity of human blood *Iurin*	XXX 1000	— 326
—— Part of a letter concerning a new experiment made with the blood of a perſon dead of the plague - - *Couzier*	XXXII 103	VII 601
—— Of the magnitude of the globules of the blood - - - *Leewenhoek*	— 341	— 562
—— An account of an extraordinary flux of the blood by the penis - *Howman*	— 418	— 539
—— Of the globules in the blood, and in dreggs of wine - - *Leewenhoek*	— 436	— 562
—— Obſervations on a treatiſe of Mr. Hevelius; deſigned to prove that the lungs do not divide and expand the blood, but on the contrary cool and condenſe it - *Nicholls*	XXXVI 163	— 500
—— An account of a perſon vomiting blood, cured by drinking exceſſive cold liquors in water - - - *Michelotti*	XXXVII 129	— 508
—— An obſervation of a white liquor reſembling milk, which appeared inſtead of ſerum ſeparated from the blood after it had ſtood ſome time - - *Stuart*	XXXIX 289	IX 193
—— Some remarks concerning the circulation of the blood, as ſeen in the tail of a water eft through a ſolar microſcope - *Miles*	XLI 725	— 69

—— Mi-

+. Blood. Observations on the changes which blood undergoes, when extravasated into the urinary bladder, and retained for some time in that viscus, mixed with the urine. Home. 1796: 486.

Observations and experiments on the colour of blood. Wells. 1797: 416.

On the non-existence of sugar in the blood of persons labouring under diabetes mellitus. [illegible] Wollaston. 1811: 96

Reply of Dr Marcet to Dr Wollaston on the same subject. — 106

The Croonian lecture.

On the changes the blood undergoes in the act of coagulation Home. 1818: 172

Some additions to the Croonian lecture on the changes the blood undergoes in the act of coagulation. — — 185

Circulation of the Blood.

Account of the dissection of a human foetus, in which the circulation of the blood was carried on without a heart. Brodie. 1809: 161.

An account of the circulation of the blood in the class Vermes of Linnæus, and the principle explained in which it differs from that in the higher classes. — — Home. 1817: [illegible]

	Tranf.	Abridg.
—— Microfcopic obfervations on the human blood - - - *Styles and Torre*	LV 252	
—— Experiments on the blood, with fome remarks on its morbid appearances *Hewfon*	LX 368	
—— On the degree of heat which coagulates the limph and the ferum of the blood, with an enquiry into the caufes of the inflammatory cruft or fize, as it is called - *Hewfon*	— 384	
—— Further remarks on the properties of the coagutable limph, on the ftopping of hæmorrhages, and on the effects of cold upon the blood - - - *Hewfon*	— 398	
—— On the figure and compofition of the red particles of the blood, commonly called the Red Globules - - *Hewfon*	LXIII 303	
—— Obfervations on refpiration, and the ufes of the blood - - *Prieftley*	LXVI 226	
Blood (The transfufion of). Account of the rife and attempts of a way to convey liquors immediately into the mafs of blood *Oldenburgh*	I 128	III 364
—— The fuccefs of the experiment of transfufing the blood of one animal into another *Lewis*	-- 352	— 226
—— The method obferved in transfufing the blood out of one animal into another *Boyle*	— 353	— —
—— Trials propofed to be made for the improvement of the experiment of transfufing blood out of one live animal into another *Boyle*	— 385	
—— An account of an eafier and fafer way of transfufing blood, viz. by the veins only *King*	II 441	
—— An experiment of bleeding a mangy into a found dog - - *Coxe*	— 451	— 229
—— Letter touching the transfufion of blood *Denis*	— 453	— —
—— An account of fome effects of the transfufion of blood at Paris - *Anon.*	— 479	— 229
—— An advertifement concerning the invention of the transfufion of blood *Oldenburgh*	— 489	
—— Some experiments of injecting liquors into the veins of animals - *Fracaffati*	— 490	— 232
—— An experiment upon blood grown cold *Fracaffati*	— 493	— 456
—— An account of more trials of transfufion, accompanied with fome confiderations thereon, chiefly in reference to its circumfpect practice on man; together with a further vindication of this invention from ufurpers *Oldenburg*	— 517	— 230
—— A confirmation of the experiments made by Sign. Fracaffati in Italy, by injecting acid liquors into the blood - *Boyle*	— 551	— 332

	Trans.	Abridg.
—— An account of an experiment of transfusion, practised upon a man in London - - - *Lower and King*	II 557	III 231
—— A relation of some trials of the same operation lately made in France - *Denis*	— 559	— 230
—— An account of the cure of an inveterate phrenzy, by the transfusion of blood at Paris *Denis*	— 617	— 291
—— Some anatomical inquiries and observations, particularly on the origin of the injection into veins, the transfusion of blood, and the parts of generation - - *Clarck*	III 672	— 290
—— An extract of a printed letter touching differences risen about the transfusion of blood *Denis*	— 710	— 292
—— An account out of the Giornale de Letterati, about two considerable experiments of the transfusion of blood -	— 840	— 230
—— Of the antiquity of the transfusion of blood from one animal to another *Oldenburg*	— 731	— 291
—— A letter from Paris concerning some transactions there, relating to the experiment of the transfusion of blood - - *Anon.*	IV 1075	— —
—— Experiment concerning the expansion of blood, and other animal juices - *Boyle*	V 2043	
Blossoms. The effects which the farina of the blossoms of different sorts of apple-trees had on the fruit of a neighbouring tree *Cook*	XLIII 525	X 751
Blow. An account of a blow upon the heart, and its effects - - *Akenside*	LIII 353	
Blue. An experiment of a surprizing change of colour, from a pale transparent or clear liquor, to a very blue or ceruleous one, and that in an instant, by admission of air only: applied to illustrate some changes of colour, and other effects on the blood of respiring animals - - *Slare*	XVII 898	
—— Letter concerning powdered-blue passing the lacteal veins - - *Lister*	XXII 819	V 259
—— An experiment made for the transmitting a blue-coloured liquor into the lacteals *Musgrave*	— 996	— —
—— Account of the preparation of the Prussian blue - - *Anon.*	XXXIII 15	VII 748
—— Observations and experiments on the foregoing preparation - - *Brown*	— 17	— —
—— A letter concerning the blue well near Newcastle upon Tyne - *Durant*	XLIV 221	X 588
—— Experiments and observations on a blue sub-		

stance;

	Tranſ.	Abridg.
ſtance; found in the Peat Moſs in Scotland - - - *Douglas*	LVIII 181	
Bodies (Human). Obſervables in the body of the earl of Balcarras - - - *Anon.*	I 86	III 158
—— —— Some obſervables of odd conſtitutions of bodies - - *Oldenburg*	— 138	— 10
—— Some conſiderations touching the parenchymous parts of the body - *King*	— 318	— 17
—— Obſervations on a human body, dead of odd diſeaſes - - *Fairfax*	II 546	— 76
—— A narrative of two petrifactions in human bodies - - *Kirkby*	VI 2158	— 150, 158
—— A new way of orthographically delineating by paralled viſual rays the poſtures and actions of an human body, exactly obſerving the ſymmetry and proportion of the parts *Saint-Clare*	VIII 6079	I 599
—— Anatomical obſervations in the body of a woman about 50 years of age, who died hydropical in her left teſticle - *Sampſon*	XII 1000	III 206, 218
—— An anatomical obſervation of four uterers in an infant - - *Tyſon*	— 1039	— 146
—— Account of a kidney of an unuſual ſhape and texture taken out of the body of a man; with obſervations on horns and glandules in general - - - *Malpighius*	XIV 601	— 682
—— An account of a girl in Ireland, who had ſeveral horns growing on her body *Aſh*	XV 1202	— 12
—— Letter concerning worms found in the tongue, and other parts of the body *Dent*	XVIII 219	— 137
Letter concerning the ſame operation *Lewis*	— 222	— —
—— An account of the opening of the body of a boy who died ſuddenly, and what obſervables were found therein - *Preſton*	XIX 362	— 62
—— A relation of a ſtrange ſymptom attending a hydrops pectoris, and the reaſon of it, as it appeared on the diſſection of the body *Doudy*	— 390	— 77
—— Extract of a letter giving an account of Mr. Malpighi; the circumſtances of his death, and what was found remarkable at the opening of his body - - *Lanciſi*	— 467	— 31
—— An account of a negro-boy that is dappled in ſeveral parts of his body with white ſpots *Byrd*	— 781	II 8
—— Some uncommon obſervations on the diſſection of morbid bodies - *Vaughan*	XXIII 1244	V 272, 291
—— Obſervations concerning the worms of human bodies - - *Bonomo*	— 1296	— 199

	Transf.	Abrigd.
—— A letter giving an account of some anatomical observations made on a body dissected at Padua by John Ray - - *Dale*	XXV 2282	V 184
—— Account of several solid bodies voided by urine - - - *Yonge*	XXVI 420	— 286
—— An account of what appeared on the dissection of the body of Mr. Dove - *Cowper*	XXVII 512	— 325
—— Account of a fœtus that continued 46 years in the mother's body - *Steigerthal*	XXXI 128	
—— Account of an extra-uterine fœtus, taken out of a woman after death, that had continued five years and a half in the belly *Howston*	XXXII 387	VII 555
—— Part of a letter concerning the difference of the height of a human body, between morning and night - - *Wasse*	XXXIII 87	
Some remarks on the above *Beckett*	— 89	VI 680
—— An account of an human body found in a copper mine - - *Legel*	— 136	— 2 204
—— An account of what appeared most remarkable in opening the body of Anne Edwards, who died Jan. 1729-30, having a large umbilical rupture - - *Ranby*	XXXVII 221	VII 516
—— An account of the dead bodies of a man and woman, who were preserved 49 years in the Moors of Derbyshire - *Balguy*	XXXVIII 423	VIII 706
—— An account of what was observed upon opening the corpse of a person who had taken several ounces of crude mercury internally; and of a plumb-stone lodged in the coats of the rectum - - - *Madden*	XXXIX 291	IX 152
—— Two observations of a diseased conformation in bodies - - *Haller*	XLIV 527	XI 1062
—— A letter concerning the body of a woman found in a morass in the isle of Axholm, in Lincolnshire - - *Stovin*	— 571	— 1326
—— Extract of several letters concerning a body found in a vault in the church of Staverton, in Devonshire, entire, after having been buried upwards of 80 years *Huxham and Tripe*	XLVII 253	
—— An account of a very remarkable case of a boy, who, notwithstanding that a considerable part of his intestines were forced out by the fall of a cart upon him, and afterwards cut off, recovered, and continues well *Needham*	XLIX 238	
—— Anatomico-medical observations of a monstrous double-bodied child born Oct. 26, 1701, in		

Pannonia,

		Tranſ.	Abridg.
Pannonia, who died Feb. 23, 1723 (Lat.) - - -	*Torkos*	L 311	
Another account -	*Burnet*	— 315	
Another account -	*Du Pleſſis*	— 317	
Another account (Lat.) -	*Dieſchius*	— 318	
—— Obſervations concerning the body of his late majeſty, Oct. 26, 1760 -	*Nicholls*	— 265	
—— Caſe of a boy who died of a gun-ſhot wound - - -	*Woolcomb*	LX 94	
—— Some account of a body lately found in uncommon preſervation, under the ruins of the abbey, at St. Edmund's Bury, Suffolk; with ſome reflections upon the ſubject	*Collignon*	LXII 465	
—— A ſhort account of Dr. Maty's illneſs, and of the appearances in the dead body - -	*Hunter and Henry Watſon*	LXVII 608	
—— See *Death*.			
BODIES (Animal). Lumbricus Hydropicus; or an eſſay to prove that hydatides, often met with in morbid animal bodies, are a ſpecies of worms, or imperfect animals -	*Tyſon*	XVII 506	III 133
—— An account of worms found in animal bodies - - -	*Nicholls*	XLIX 246	
BODIES (Natural philoſophy in general). Mr. Hook's treatiſe, entitled, an account of micrographia; or the phyſiological deſcription of minute bodies made in magnifying glaſſes	*Oldenburg*	I 27	
—— Several experiments on the attrition of bodies in vacuo - -	*Haukſbee*	XXIV 2165	IV 2. 180
—— An account of an experiment to ſhew by a new proof, that bodies of the ſame bulk do not contain equal quantities of matter, and therefore that there is an interſperſed vacuum - - -	*Deſaguliers*	XXXI 81	VI - 157
—— A courſe of experiments to aſcertain the ſpecific buoyancy of cork in different waters: the reſpective weight and buoyancy of ſalt water and freſh water: and for determining the exact weight of human and other bodies in fluids - - -	*Wilkinſon*	LV 95	
—— Experiments on ignited bodies	*Roebuck*	LXVI 509	
—— Experiments on ignited ſubſtances	*Whitehurſt*	— 575	
BODIES (Electrical). An account of ſome experiments touching the electricity and light produceable on the attrition of ſeveral bodies	*Haukſbee*	XXVI 87	
—— Experiments and obſervations upon the light			

	Transf.	Abridg.
that is produced by communicating electrical attraction to animal or inanimate bodies; together with some of its most surprising effects - - - *Gray*	XXXIX 16	VIII 397
—— A letter concerning the revolutions which small pendulous bodies will, by electricity, make round larger ones from east to west, as the planets do round the sun - - *Gray*	— 220	
—— Some electrical experiments chiefly regarding the repulsive force of electrical bodies *Wheler*	XLI 98	— 406
—— Observations of luminous emanations from human bodies and from brutes; with some remarks on electricity - *Miles*	XLIII 441	X 278
Bodies (Natural history). Account of sundry experiments made upon a chrystal-like body sent from Ireland - - *Bartholin*	V 2039	
—— An account of some uncommon fossil bodies - - - *Baker*	XLVIII 117	
—— An account of some fossile fruits, and other bodies found in the island of Shepey *Parsons*	L 396	
—— Case of an extraordinary body forced into the lungs - - *Martin*	LV 39	
Bodies (In motion). A discourse concerning gravity, and its properties, wherein the descent of heavy bodies, and the motion of projects is briefly, but fully handled; together with the solution of a problem of great use in gunnery *Halley*	XVI 3	I 472,473
—— Experiment concerning the time required in the descent of different bodies, of different magnitudes and weights, in common air from a certain height - *Hauksbee*	XXVII 196	IV 2 182
—— A letter concerning an experiment, whereby it has been attempted to shew the falsity of the common opinion, in relation to the force of bodies in motion - *Pemberton*	XXXII 57	VI 276
—— An account of some experiments made to prove that the force of moving bodies is proportionable to their velocities - *Desaguliers*	— 269	— 281
—— Animadversions upon some new experiments relating to the force of moving bodies; with two new experiments on the same subject - - - *Desaguliers*	— 285	— 285
—— A remark upon the new opinion relating to the force of moving bodies, in the case of the collision of non-elastic bodies *Eames*	XXXIV 183	— 287
—— Remarks upon a supposed demonstration, that the moving forces of the same body are not as		

the

	Trans.	Abridg.
the velocities, but as the ſquares of the velocities - - *Eames*	XXXIV 188	VI 289
—— Remarks upon ſome experiments in hydraulics, which ſeem to prove, that the forces of equal moving bodies are as the ſquares of their velocities - - *Eames*	XXXV 343	— 292
—— A letter occaſioned by the preſent controverſy among mathematicians, concerning the proportion of velocity and force in bodies in motion - - - *Samuel Clarke*	— 381	— 291
—— An account of an experiment explaining a mechanical paradox, viz. that two bodies of equal weights, ſuſpended on a certain ſort of balances, do not loſe their equilibrium, by being removed one farther from, the other nearer to the center - *Deſaguliers*	XXXVII 125	— 310
—— An account of an experiment contrived by G. J. s'Graveſande, relating to the force of moving bodies; ſhewn to the Royal Society by - - - *Deſaguliers*	XXXVIII 143	VIII 235
—— An inquiry into the meaſure of the force of bodies in motion: with a propoſal of an experimentum crucis, to decide the controverſy about it - - - *Jurin*	XLIII 423	X 174
—— A letter containing a demonſtration of a law of motion in the caſe of a body deflected by two forces tending conſtantly to two fixed points - - - *Robertſon*	LIX 74	
—— An experimental examination of the quantity and proportion of mechanic power, neceſſary to be employed in giving different degrees of velocity to heavy bodies from a ſtate of reſt - - - *Smeaton*	LXVI 450	
—— A new theory of the rotatory motion of bodies affected by forces diſturbing ſuch motion - - - *Landen*	LXVII 266	
BODIES (Gravity of). Of the weight of a cubic foot of divers grains, &c. - *Anon.*	XV 926	I 522
—— A further liſt of ſpecific gravities of bodies *Anon.*	— 927	— 523
—— A diſcourſe on this problem; why bodies diſſolved in menſtrua ſpecifically lighter than themſelves ſwim therein *W. Molyneux*	XVI 88	— 535
With ſome reflections *T. Molyneux*	— 93	— 537
—— Obſervations on the comparative, intenſive, or ſpecific gravities of various bodies *I. C.*	XVII 694	— 524
—— An experiment touching the weighing of bo-		

	Tranſ.	Abridg.
dies of the ſame ſpecies, but of very unequal ſurfaces in common water, being of an equal weight in common air - *Haukſbee*	XXVI 306	IV 2 181
Bogs. Of the bogs and loughs of Ireland *King*	XV 948	II 732
—— An account of a moving bog in Ireland *Anon.*	XIX 714	— 737
—— A true deſcription of the bog of Kapanihane in the county of Limerick; with an account of the motion thereof, June 7, 1697 - - - *Molyneux*	— —	— —
Boiling Fountains. Some obſervations on boiling fountains and ſubterraneous ſteams *Robinſon*	XV 922	— 349
—— —— An account of boiling and other fountains - - *Robinſon*	— 1036	— 320, 349
Boiling Water. Experiments about the degree of heat of ſome boiling liquors *Fahrenheit*	XXXIII 1	VI 2 49
—— —— A propoſal for warming rooms by the ſteam of boiling water conveyed in pipes along the walls - - *Cook*	XLIII 370	XI 1391
—— —— A diſſertation on the nature of evaporation, and ſeveral phænomena of air, water, and boiling liquors - - *Hamilton*	LV 146	
—— —— The ſuppoſed effect of boiling upon water, in diſpoſing it to freeze more readily, aſcertained by experiment - *Black*	LXV 124	
—— —— On the variation of the temperature of boiling water - *Shuckburgh*	LXIX 362	
Bologna Bottles. An account of the Bologna bottles - - *Bruni*	XLIII 272	XI 1343
Bolognian Stone. A relation of the loſs of the way to prepare the Bolognian ſtone for ſhining - - - *Anon.*	I 375	III 346
—— —— An account of a factitious ſtony matter or paſte, ſhining in the dark like a glowing coal, after it hath been a little while expoſed to the day or candle-light - *Baldwin*	XI 788	
An improvement of the Bolognian ſtone - - - *Malpighi*	XII 842	XI 1059
—— An eaſy method of making a phoſphorous, that will imbibe and emit light like the Bolognian ſtone; with experiments and obſervations - - *Canton*	LVIII 337	
—— See *Phoſphorus.*		
Bolognini. A ſhort hiſtory of the diſeaſe of which Joſeph Bolognini died *De Camillis*	XLIII 40	— —
Bones. Microſcopical obſervations concerning bones - - - *Leewenhoek*	IX 121	III 683

—— Mi-

	Tranſ.	Abridg.
—— Microſcopical obſervations of the ſtructure of teeth and other bones - *Leewenhoek*	XII 1002	III 684
—— Part of two letters concerning a prodigious Os Frontis in the Medicine School at Leyden - - - *Molyneux*	XV 880	— 2
—— An extract of a letter containing ſeveral obſervations on the texture of the bones of animals compared with that of wood *Leewenhoek*	XVII 838	II 685
—— Oſteographia Elephantina; or a full and exact deſcription of all the bones of an elephant, with their ſeveral dimenſions: to which are premiſed, an hiſtorical account of the natural endowments and ſeveral wonderful performances of elephants, with the manner of taking and taming them. An anatomical account of their parts, &c. - - *Blair*	XXVII 53	V 82
- - - *Blair*	— 117	
—— Obſervations upon the bones and the perioſteum - - - *Leewenhoek*	XXXI 91	VII 672
—— An account of a præter-natural bony ſubſtance found in the cavity of the thorax *Rutty*	XXXIV 152	— 505
—— An account of a large bony ſubſtance found in the womb, 1733 - *Hody*	XXXIX 189	IX 191
—— An account of the bones of animals being changed to a red colour by aliment only *Belchier*	— 287	— 102
—— A further account of the bones of animals being made red by aliment only *Belchier*	— 299	— 105
—— A picture of the ſize of a gigantic bone; with a problem for determining the ſize of the giant according to the rules of the art of drawing - - - *Klein*	XLI 308	XI 311
—— Obſervations and experiments with madder root, which has the faculty of tinging the bones of living animals of a red colour - - - *Du-Monceau*	— 390	IX 103
—— —— An account of tumours which rendered the bones ſoft - - *Pott*	— 616	XI 247
—— An account of a large piece of the thigh-bone, which was taken out and its place ſupplied by a callus - - *Richardſon*	— 761	
—— An account of an extraordinary caſe of the bones of a woman growing ſoft and flexible - - - *Bevan*	XLII 488	X 251
—— The caſe of a young child at Houghton, in Huntingdonſhire, born with all its bones diſplaced - - *Davis*	XLIV 539	XI 1110

	Transf.	Abridg.
—— Cafe of Anne-Elizabeth Queriot of Paris, whofe bones were diftorted and foftened *Hofty*	XLVIII 26	
—— A remarkable cafe of fragility, flexibility, and diffolution of the bones - *Pringle*	— 297	
—— Cafe of William Carey, aged 19, whofe tendons and mufcles were turned into bones *Henry*	LI 89	
Further account - *Henry*	— 92	
—— An account of a bone found in the pelvis of a man at Bruffels - *Brady*	— 660	
—— A further account of the cafe of William Carey, whofe mufcles began to be offified *Henry*	LII 143	
—— A account of the extraction of three inches and ten lines of the bone of the upper arm, which was followed by a regeneration of the bony matter; with a defcription of a machine made ufe of to keep the upper and lower pieces of the bone at their proper diftances, during the time that the regeneration was taking place; and which may alfo be of fervice in fractures happening near the head of that bone *Le Cat*	LVI 370	
Bones (Foffil). Chartham news: or a brief relation of fome ftrange bones lately digged up in fome grounds of Mr. John Somner's in Canterbury - - - *Wallis*	XXII 882	IV 2 222
Second letter relating to Mr. Somner's treatife of Chartham News - *Wallis*	— 1022	
—— Account of fome large bones lately found in a gravel-pit near Colchefter *Luffkin*	— 924	IV 2 1
—— The dimenfions of fome human bones of an extraordinary fize, which were dug up near St. Alban's, in Hertfordfhire *Chefelden*	XXVII 436	V 2 267
—— An account of elephants teeth and bones found under ground - - *Sloane*	XXXV 457	VI 2 205
Part fecond - - - *Sloane*	— 497	— - 211
—— An account of feveral bones of an elephant found at Leyfdown, in the ifle of Shepey - - - *Jacob*	XLVIII 626	
—— Obfervations on the bones, commonly fuppofed to be elephants bones, which have been found near the river Ohio in America *William Hunter*	LVIII 34	
—— Account of fome bones found in the rock of Gibraltar; with remarks by Dr. Hunter - - - *Boddington*	LX 414	
Bones (Incrufted). An account of fome human bones incrufted with ftone, now in the Villa Ludovifia at Rome - *Folkes*	XLIII 557	X 598
Bones (Of fœtus's). Account of the bones of a fœtus		

voided

Bones. Experiments and observations on Shell and Bone. Hatchett. 1799: 315.

Bones (Fossil) Account of some remarkable Caves in the Principality of Bayreuth,
and of the fossil bones found therein. - - - - - - 1794: 402.
Observations on the fossil bones presented by the Margrave of Anspach. Hunter —— 407.

Borax. Some particulars relative to the production of Borax. Blane. 77:297.
Rovato — 301.

On the decomposition of the acid of Borax, or sedative salt. Crell. 1799, 56.

	Tranf.	Abridg.
voided by anum some years after conception *Mosley*	XIX 486	
—— Account of a woman who voided the bones of a fœtus above the os-pubis, and by other extraordinary ways. *Philosophic Society at Oxford*	XX 292	III 219
—— Bones of a human fœtus voided through an imposthume in the groin - *Skippon*	XXIV 2077	V 306
—— Bones of a dead fœtus taken out of the uterus of a cow - - *Sherman*	XXVI 450	— 54
—— Case of the bones of a fœtus coming away by the anus - - *Winthrop*	XLIII 304	XI 1015
- - - *Simon*	— 524	
—— Letter concerning the bones of a fœtus being discharged through an ulcer near the navel - - - *Drake*	XLV 121	IX 1019
—— Case of a woman from whom the bones of a fœtus were extracted - *Debenham*	XLVII 92	
BOOKS. Copy of a letter concerning the books and antient writings dug out of the ruins of an edifice near the site of the old city of Herculaneum to Monsignor Cerati of Pisa; with a translation by - *Locke*	XLIX 112	
BORAMETZ. A short account of the Scythian vegetable Lamb, called borametz *Breynius*	XXXIII 353	VI 2 317
BOSE. See *Electricity*.		
BOTANY. Account of the physic garden at Amsterdam - - *Ellis*	XXIII 1416	V 2 11, 134
—— A letter attempting to ascertain the tree that yields the common varnish used in China and Japan; to promote its propagation in our American colonies, and to set right some mistakes which botanists appear to have entertained concerning it - *Ellis*	XLIX 866	
—— A brief botanical and medical history of the solanum lethale, bella-donna, or deadly nightshade - - *W. Watson*	L 62	
—— A letter upon the early cultivation of botany in England; and some particulars about John Tradescant, a great promoter of that science, as well as natural history, in the last century, and gardener to king Charles I. *Ducarel*	LXIII 79	
BOTTLE. An extract of a letter given an account of an experiment made in the Bay of Biscay of sinking a bottle, close corked, under various depths of water - *Oliver*	XVII 908	I 521
BOVEY COAL. Remarks on the Bovey coal *Miller*	LI 534	

	Transf.	Abridg.
—— —— A farther account of some experiments made on the Bovey coal	LI 941	
BOVILLUS. See *Cycloid*.		
BOULIMIA. Letter concerning a boulimia *Burrough*	XXII 598	III 111
—— An account of the surprizing quantities of food devoured by a boy 12 years old in six succesive days *Mortimer*	XLIII 366	XI 1066
Another account *Cookson*	— 380	— 1086
Bow (MARINER's). An account of Mr. Thomas Godfrey's improvement of Davis's quadrant transferred to the mariner's bow *Logan*	XXXVIII 441	VIII 366
BOWELS. An observation made of a man anatomised, whose bowels were found inverted *Sampson*	IX 146	III 111
—— A case concerning a child born with the bowels hanging out of its belly *Amyand*	XXXVII 258	VII 516
—— See *Monstrous Birth*.		
Box. Account of the number of pores on the leaves of box *Leewenhoek*	XXXI 231	VI 2 327
Boy. An account of a negro-boy that is dappelled in several parts of his body with white spots *Byrd*	XIX 781	II 8
—— An account of the Friesland boy with letters in his eye *Ellis*	XXIII 1416	
—— Account of a monstrous boy *Cantwell*	XLI 137	IX 314
—— Some account of the gigantic boy at Willingham, near Cambridge *Anon.*	XLIII 249	XI 1205
Another account *Almond and Dawkes*	— 251	
—— Observations on the history of the Norfolk boy	L 836	
BRADLEY. An account of the case of the late Rev. Mr. James Bradley *Lysons*	LII 635	
BRAHE. Letter concerning the remains of the observatory of the famous Tycho Brahe *Gourdon*	XXII 691	I 216
BRAIN. Some discoveries concerning the brain *Malpighi*	II 491	III 23
—— Microscopical observations concerning blood, milk, bones, the brain, spittle, and cuticula, &c. *Leewenhoek*	IX 121	— 683
—— Observations of the cortical and medular part of the brain *Leewenhoek*	XII 899	— 684
—— An abstract of a letter concerning the parts of the brain of several animals *Leewenhoek*	XV 883	— —
—— A relation of a petrified glandula pinealis, lately found in the dissection of a brain *King*	XVI 228	— 157
—— An account of a child born alive without a brain, and the observables in it on dissection *Preston*	XIX 457	— 24

Boutan. see Thibet.

Brain. The croonian lecture on some physiological researches, respecting the influence of the brain on the action of the heart, and on the generation of animal heat. Brodie. 1811:3.

Further experiments and observations on the influence of the brain on the generation of animal heat. —— 1812:3.

Branchial artery. Observations on the structure of the Branchial artery. Home. 1813:227.

	Tranf.	Abridg.
—— An obfervation of an infant, where the brain was depreffed into the hollow of the vertebræ of the neck - - *Tyfon*	XIX 533	III 26
—— An obfervation of one hemifphere of the brain fphacelated, and of a ftone found in the fubftance of the brain itfelf - *Tyfon*	— 535	— 27
—— An anatomical account of a child's head, born without a brain, 1698 - *Buffiere*	XXI 141	— 26
—— Obfervations of remarkable appearances in the brain of three perfons who died of epilepfies - - *Rhætus*	XXXV 315	VII 486
—— Hiftory of a fœtus born with a very imperfect brain; to which is fubjoined a fupplement of the effay on the ufe of ganglions *Johnfton*	LVII 118	
—— See *Dura Mater*.		
BRAMHAM MOOR. See *Antiquities*.		
BRAMINES. An account of the religion, rites, notions, cuftoms, manners of the heathen priefts, commonly called bramines *Marfhal*	XXII 729	V 2 165
—— An account of the Bramins obfervatory at Benares - - *Barker*	LXVII 598	
BRANDY. Differtation on a falfe but common method of trying French fpirit of wine *Neuman*	XXXIII 398	VII 739
BRASIL. Inquiries for Guaiana and Brafil - - - *Royal Society*	II 422	III 632
BRASS. The method, manner, and order of the tranfmutation of copper into brafs *Povey*	XVII 735	II 565
—— Letters concerning feveral copper-mines, in anfwer to fome queries of Dr. Lifter *Davies*	— 737	— 563
—— A further account - *Davies*	— 741	— —
—— The method, manner, and order of the tranfmuting of copper into brafs *Povey*	XXII 474	— 565
—— An hiftorico-phyfical obfervation on the brafs waters of Neofolis, commonly called Cement-Watzer, changing iron to brafs *Belius*	XL 351	VIII 645
—— Extract of a letter on giving magnetifm and polarity to brafs - *Arderon*	L 774	
—— See *Antiquities*.		
BRASS WIRE. Cafe of a young man who had loft the ufe of his hands by cleanfing brafs-wire *More*	LI 936	
BREAD. An abftract of a letter concerning the making of turnep-bread in Effex *Dale*	XVII 971	II 667
BREAD FRUIT. Account of the bread-fruit trees, and the fruits of them *Thunberg*	LXIX 462	
BREASTS (Animal). An account of two young turkies joined together by their breafts *Floyer*	XXI 434	— 898

	Tranf.	Abridg.
BREASTS (Human). An account of a very fudden and exceffive fwelling of a woman's breafts - - - *Durfton*	IV 1047	III 78
—— A letter concerning the death of the big-breafted woman, together with what was obferved on her body - *Durfton*	— 1068	— 79
—— Letter giving an account why the big-breafted woman was not opened after her death *Durfton*	— 1077	— 80
—— Cafe of one who fwallowed a knife, which lay in his ftomach a year and 7 months, and then wafhed out at an apofthem on his breaft *Sloane*	XIX 180	— 91
—— Account of a child born with a large wound in the breaft, fuppofed to arife from the force of imagination - *Cyprianus*	— 291	— 222
—— The cafe of Mary Howell, who had a needle run into her arm, which came out at her breaft - - - *Anon.*	XLI 767	IX 238
BREATHING. Letter concerning the caufe of the neceffity of breathing - *Mufgrave*	XX 178	III 67
BREEDING. Part of a letter concerning a child born with the jaundice upon it, received from its father; and of the mother taking the fame diftemper from her hufband the next time of being with child - *Cooke*	XLVI 205	XI 1963
BRESLAW. An eftimate of the degrees of the mortality of mankind, drawn from curious tables of the births and funerals at the city of Breflaw, with an attempt to afcertain the price of annuities upon lives - *Halley*	XVII 596	III 669
BREWING. See *Sap.*		
BRIDEKIRK. See *Infcription.*		
BRIDEWELL AT NORWICH. Extract of a letter concerning the antient bridewell at Norwich - - - *Baker*	XLIII 520	— 1304
BRIDGE. Letter concerning the bridge of St. Efprit in France - - *Robinfon*	XIV 584	I 293
—— A further account, with a parallel hiftory of fome other bridges at Rome *Robinfon*	— 712	— 593
—— Defcription of a bridge that may be built 70 feet long, without any pillar under it *Anon.*	— 714	— 594
—— Problems concerning the fall of water under bridges; applied to the falls under London and Weftminfter bridges - *Robertfon*	L 492	
BRIDGNORTH. An extract of a topographical account of Bridgnorth, in the county of Salop - - - *Stackhoufe*	XLII 127	VIII 347

	Transf.	Abridg.
Bright. Letter concerning Mr. Bright, the extraordinary fat man at Malden, in Essex *Anon.*	XLVII 188	
Brimstone. Of the mineral of Liege, yielding both brimstone and vitriol, and the way of extracting them out of it, used at Liege *Anon.*	I 45	II 530
—— A continuation of the discourse concerning vitriol, shewing, that vitriol is usually produced by sulphur, acting on, and coagulating with, a metal; and then making out, that allum is likewise the result of the said sulphur; as also evincing, that vitriol, sulphur, and allum, do agree in the saline principles; and, lastly, declaring the nature of the salt in brimstone, and whence it is derived - *Anon.*	IX 66	— 544
—— Extract of two letters concerning the effects of a cane of black sealing-wax and a cane of brimstone in electrical experiment *Miles*	XLIV 27	X 317
—— Observations made on the brimstone-hill in the island of Guadeloupe - *Peyssonel*	XLIX 564	
Bristle. An account of a bristle that was lodged in a gentleman's foot, and caused a violent inflammation - *Arderon*	XLIV 192	XI 1114
Bristol Water. Observations on the heat of Bristol waters - - *Canton*	LVII 203	
Britain. A discourse tending to prove at what time and place Julius Cæsar made his first descent upon Britain - - *Halley*	XVII 495	III 412
—— A dissertation on Britain being formerly a peninsula - *Musgrave*	XXX 589	IV 469
Bronchotome. The postscript of a letter giving an account of the operation of bronchotome - - - *Græme*	XXXVI 448	VII 496
Brontiæ. An account of certain transparent pebbles, mostly of the shape of the ombriæ, or brontiæ - - *Lister*	XVII 778	II 467
Bronze. An attempt to explain an antient Greek inscription, engraven upon a curious bronze cup with two handles, and published with a draught of the cup by Dr. Pocock in his description of the East, vol. II. part II. pag. 207 *Ward*	XLVI 488	XI 1278
Broughton. Letter concerning Broughton in Lincolnshire, with observations on the shell-fish observed in the quarries about that place - - - *De La Pryme*	XXII 677	II 428 III 429
Brownææ. A description of a rare American plant of the brownææ kind; with some remarks on this genus - - *Bergius*	LXIII 173	

	Transf.	Abridg.
Brutes. Divers inftances of peculiarities of nature, both in men and brutes - *Fairfax*	II 549	III 191, 287
—— Obfervations of luminous emanations from human bodies and from brutes, with fome remarks on electricity - - *Miles*	XLIII 441	X 278
Bubonocele. Of a bubonocele, or rupture in the groin, and the operation made upon it - - - *Amyand*	XL 361	IX 161
Bucks-horn Plantain. Letter concerning the virtues of the ftar of the earth, coronopus, or bucks-horn plantain, in the cure of the bite of a mad dog - - *Steward*	— 449	VIII 83
Buenos Ayres. The longitude of Buenos Ayres determined from an obfervation made by - - - *Pere Feuillée*	XXXII 2	
Buffon. A view of the relation between Dr. Halley's tables and the notions of Mr. de Buffon, for eftablifhing a rule for the probable duration of the life of man - *Kerffeboom*	XLVIII 239	
Building. Directions for inquiries concerning ftones and other materials for the ufe of building; together with a fuggeftion for retrieving the art of hardening and tempering fteel for cutting porphyry and other hard marbles *Oldenburg*	VIII 6010	I 588 III 419
—— An account of the advantage of Virginia for building fhips - -	— 6015	II 566
—— Defcription of a moft effectual method of fecuring buildings againft fire *Lord Mahon*	LXVIII 884	
Bulbous Roots. A letter giving an account of tulips, and fuch bulbous plants, flowering much fooner when their bulbs are placed upon bottles filled with water, than when planted in the ground - - *Triewald*	XXXVII 79	VI 2 54
An account of the fame experiments tried the next year by - *Miller*	— 81	— - 355
—— —— Experiments and obfervations on bulbous roots, plants, and feeds growing in water - - - *Curteis*	XXXVIII 267	VIII 525
Bulk. Specific gravity of feveral metalline cubes, in comparifon with their like bulks of water - - - *Haukfbee*	XXVII 511	IV 2 182
—— An account of an experiment to fhew by a new proof, that bodies of the fame bulk do not contain equal quantities of matter, and therefore that there is an interfperfed vacuum - - - *Defaguliers*	XXXI 81	VI 2 157

Buds. On the reproduction of Buds. — — — — — — — - - — Knight 1805: 257.

	Tranf.	Abridg.
BULK. Extract of a letter concerning two men of an extraordinary bulk and weight *Knowlton*	XLIV 100	XI 1245
BULLET. Account of a bullet voided by urine *Fairfax*	III 803	III 160
—— A brief narrative of the shot of Dr. Robert Fielding with a musket-bullet, and its strange manner of coming out of his head, where it had lain near 30 years; written by himself *Fielding*	XXVI 317	V 205
—— An account of a wound which the late lord Carpenter received at Brihuega, whereby a bullet remained near his gullet for a year wanting a few days *Carpenter*	XL 316	
BULLOCK. An account of a very extraordinary effect of lightening on a bullock at Swanborow, in the parish of Iford, near Lewes in Sussex *Lambert and Green*	LXVI 493	
BUOYANCY. A course of experiments to ascertain the specific buoyancy of Cork in different waters: the respective weights and buoyancies of salt water and fresh water; and for determining the exact weight of human and other bodies in fluids *Wilkinson*	LV 95	
BURDETT. See *Serpent*.		
BURNING. An account of the burning of several hay-ricks by a fiery exhalation or damp: and of the infectious quality of the grass of several grounds *Floya*	XVIII 49	II 181
—— An account of a woman accidentally burnt to death at Coventry *Wilmer*	LXIV 340	
BURNING FOUNTAINS. An extract of an essay entitled, On the uses of a knowledge of mineral exhalations when applied to discover the principles and properties of mineral waters, the nature of burning fountains, and of those poisonous lakes which the antients called Averni *Brownrigg*	LV 236	
BURNING GLASSES. An account of a not ordinary burning concave lately made at Lyons, and compared with several others made formerly *Vilette*	I 95	I 211
—— —— An account of the invention of grinding optick and burning glasses of a figure not spherical *Smethwick*	III 631	— 194
—— —— An account of the making an extraordinary burning glass at Milan *Anon.*	— 795	— —
—— —— An account from Paris concerning a great		

metalline

	Tranſ.	Abridg.
metalline burning concave, and ſome of the moſt conſiderable effects of it *Anon.*	IV 986	I 242
—— —— Two obſervations made by F. Lana concerning ſome of the effects of the burning concave made at Lions - *Lana*	VI 3060	III 325
—— —— A relation of the great effects of a new ſort of burning ſpeculum lately made in Germany - *Acta Eruditorum and Hook*	XVI 352	I 213
—— —— Experiments upon metals, made with the burning glaſs of the duke of Orleans *Geoffroy*	XXVI 374	IV 190
—— —— An account of ſome experiments tried with Monſ. Vilette's burning concave in June 1718 - *Harris and Deſaguliers*	XXX 976	— 198
—— Part of a letter giving an account of a new mirror, which burns at 66 feet diſtance; invented by M. de Buffon - *Needham*	XLIV 493	X 194
Concerning the ſame mirror burning at 150 feet diſtance - *Nicolini*	— 495	— 195
—— Extract of a letter concerning M. de Buffon's re-invention of Archimedes's burning ſpecula *Buffon*	XLV 504	— 195
—— —— Obſervations upon father Kircher's opinion concerning the burning of the fleet of Marcellus by Archimedes *Parſons*	XLVIII 626	
—— —— A ſhort narrative of the ſtructure and effect of parabolic burning glaſſes made by M. Hoeſen of Dreſden; and an account of experiments made with them on the fuſion of different ſubſtances - *Wolfe*	LIX 4	
Burning Mountain. An account of the upper part of the burning mountain in the iſle of Ternata, according to the view taken thereof *Witzen*	XIX 42	II 392
—— —— A further relation of the horrible burning of ſome mountains of the Molucco iſlands - - *Witzen*	— 529	— 394
—— See *Volcano.*		
Burning Rock. Extract of a letter from Calcutta concerning a burning rock and a burning well - - - *Wood*	LII 415	
Burning Spring. A letter giving an account of the eruption of a burning ſpring at Broſeley in Shropſhire - - *Hopton*	XXVII 475	IV 2 195
Burning Well. A letter concerning a burning well at Broſeley - - *Maſon*	XLIV 370	X 586
Butler. Sequel to the caſe of Mr. Butler of Moſcow, who was ſtrangely affected by mixing verdigreaſe and falſe leaf-gold with aquafortis. See *Aquafortis* - - *Baker*	LIV 15	

Burrampooter (River) Account of — Rennell 71: 87.

+ Calamine. A chemical analysis of some Calamines. - - - - - Smithson. 1803. 12.

	Tranf.	Abridg.
BUTTER. Account of an extraordinary meteor, or kind of dew refembling butter, that fell in Ireland - - *Vans*	XIX 223	
- - - *Bifhop of Cloyne*	— —	
BUTTS. Letter concerning the circulation of the blood in butts - *Leewenhoek*	XXII 552	III 686
BUXTON WATER. Experiments and obfervations on the water of Buxton and Matlock in Derbyfhire - - *Percival*	LXII 455	

C.

CABBAGES. An account of fome trials to cure the ill tafte of milk, which is occafioned by the food of cows, either from turnips, cabbages, or autumnal leaves, &c; alfo to fweeten ftinking water - - *Hales*	XLIV 339	
CABBAGE-BARK TREE. Defcription and ufe of the cabbage-bark tree in Jamaica *Wright*	LXVII 507	
CACAO-TREE. An accurate defcription of the cacao-tree, and the way of its curing and hufbandry, &c. - - *Anon.*	VIII 6007	II 662
CACHALOT. Defcription of the blunt-headed cachalot - - *Robertfon*	LX 321	
CACTUS OPUNTIA. An account of the male and female cochineal infects, that breed on the cactus opuntia, or Indian fig, in South Carolina and Georgia - - *Ellis*	LII 661	
CAERLEON. See *Infcription.*		
CÆSAR. A difcourfe tending to prove at what time and place Julius Cæfar made his firft defcent upon Britain - *Halley*	XVII 495	III 412
CÆSARIAN OPERATION. An account of the Cæfarian operation performed by an ignorant butcher - - *Copping*	XLI 814	IX 239
CAIRO. An account of E. W. Montague's journey from Cairo in Egypt, to the Written Mountain in the Defart of Sinai *Montague*	LVI 40	
CALAIS. Letter relating to that ifthmus, or neck of land, which is fuppofed to have joined England and France in former times, where now is the paffage between Dover and Calais *Wallis*	XXII 967	IV 2 227
CALAMINARIS. An account of digging and preparing the lapis calaminaris *Pooley*	XVII 672	II 554
CALCINATION. A retractation of the 7th and laft paragraph of Mr. W. Molyneux's letter, vol.		

 XIX.

	Tranſ.	Abridg.
XIX. p. 552, concerning Lough Neagh ſtone, and its non-application to the magnet upon calcination - - *Molyneux*	XIV 820	II 323
See *Lake*.		
CALCULUS. See *Stone*.		
CALEDONIA. Part of a journal kept from Scotland to New Caledonia in Darien; with a ſhort account of that country - *Wallace*	XXII 536	III 561
CALENDAR. Remarks upon the ſolar and lunar years, the cycle of 19 years, commonly called the Golden Number, the Epact, and a method of finding the time of Eaſter, as it is now obſerved in moſt parts of Europe - - *Earl of Macclesfield*	XLVI 417	X 131
—— See *Style*.		
CALENTURE. A letter concerning a calenture *Oliver*	XXIV 1562	V 364
CALESH. Part of a letter concerning a new ſort of caleſh - - *R. B.*	XV 1028	I 504
CALF. An account of a very odd monſtrous calf - - - *Boyle*	I 10	II 899
An obſervation touching ſome particulars further conſiderable in the monſtrous calf *Thomas*	— 20	— —
—— Account of a monſtrous calf with two heads - - - *Southwell*	XX 79	— —
—— Part of a letter concerning a monſtrous calf - - - *Adams*	XXV 2414	V 34
—— A deſcription of the head of a monſtrous calf - - - *Craig*	XXVII 429	— 35
—— An account of double fœtus's of calves *Le Cat*	XLV 497	XI 1216
—— See *Fœtus*.		
CALF (SEA). Some account of the phoca, vitulus marinus, or ſea calf, ſhewn in London in 1743 - - *Parſons*	XLII 383	IX 74
CALIFORNIA. An extract of a memoir concerning the diſcovery of a paſſage by land to California; with a map and deſcription of that country - - *Picolo*	XXVI 232	V 2 191
CALLUS. An account of the cure of two ſinuous ulcers poſſeſſing the ſpace of the whole arm; with the extraordinary ſupply of a callus, which fully anſwers the purpoſes of the Os Humeri, loſt in time of cure *Fawler*	XXV 2466	— 388
—— Obſervations upon the callus of the hands and feet - - *Leewenhoek*	XXXII 156	VII 480
—— An account of a large piece of the thigh-bone, which was taken out, and its place ſupplied by a callus - - *Richardſon*	XLI 761	

Camels. On the rate of travelling as performed by Camels, and its application, as a scale, to the purposes of Geography. Rennell. 81:129.

Observations on the Camel's stomach respecting the water it contains, and the reservoirs in which that fluid is inclosed; with an account of some peculiarities in the urine. Home 1806: 357.

Camera obscura. On a periscopic camera obscura and microscope. Wollaston. 1812:3[illegible]

+Cancer. Experiments and observations on the matter of Cancer . . . Crawford. 80:391.

		Tranf.	Abridg.
Camden. An account of fome obfervables in Lincolnfhire, not taken notice of by Camden, or any other author -	*Merret*	XIX 343	II 267 III 533
Cameleon. Some obfervations on a cameleon - - -	*Goddard*	XII 930	II 816
—— An account of a particular fpecies of cameleon - - -	*Parfons*	LVIII 192	
Camelopardalis. A letter on a camelopardalis about the Cape of Good Hope	*Carteret*	LX 27	
Camp. A letter concerning two ancient camps in Hampfhire - -	*Wright*	XLIII 273	XI 1295
—— A letter giving an account of the prefent condition of the Roman camp at Caftor in Norfolk, with a plan of it -	*Baker*	XLVI 196	— 1295
Camphire. An account of camphire	*Neuman*	XXXIII 321	VII 692
- - -	*Brown*	— 361	— 697
—— A letter touching the efficacy of camphire in maniacal diforders -	*Kinnier*	XXXV 347	— 632
—— Differtation on the camphire of Thyme	*Neuman*	XXXVIII 202	IX 382
—— Experiments with camphire	*Alexander*	LVII 65	
Canals. Treatife on rivers and canals	*Mann*	LXIX 555	
Canary Seed. The hufbandry of canary feed - - -	*Tenifon*	XXVIII 91	IV 2 309
Cancer. Letter concerning a ftrange cancer of which his father died -	*Kay*	XXIII 1069	V 217
—— Two hiftories of internal cancers, and of what appeared upon diffection -	*Burton*	XLII 99	IX 225
—— A differtation upon the cancer of the eye-lids, nofe, great angle of the eye, and its neighbouring parts, commonly called the noli-me-tangere, deemed hitherto incureable by both antients and moderns, but now fhewn to be as cureable as other diftempers	*Daviel*	XLIX 186	
—— An account of a cafe [fwellings in the breafts or cancer] in which green hemlock was applied - - -	*Colebrook*	LIII 346	
Cancer-major. Some obfervations on the cancer-major - -	*Collinfon*	LXIV 70	X 864
Further obfervations -	*Collinfon*	XLVII 40	
—— See *Crab.*			
Candle. A ready way of lighting a candle by a very fmall electrical fpark	*Ingenboufz*	LXVIII 1022	
Canella. A difcourfe on the cinnamon, caffia, or canella - -	*White*	L 860	
—— Letter on cinnamon -	*Comber*	— 873	
Canker Worm. A narrative of the deftruction of the canker-worms and locufts which deftroyed			

the

	Tranſ.	Abridg.
the fields near Witemberg for ſeveral years - - - *Weidler*	XXXVIII 294	
CANNARA. An explanation of the figures of a Pagan temple, and unknown characters, at Cannara in Salſet - *Stuart*	XXVI 372	V 2 60
CANNON BALLS. The force of fired gunpowder, and the initial velocities of cannon-balls, determined by experiments: from which is alſo deduced the relation of the initial velocity to the weight of the ſhot and the quantity of powder - - *Hutton*	LXVIII 50	
CANON. A queſtion in muſick lately propoſed to Dr. Wallis concerning the diviſion of the monochord or ſection of the muſical canon, with his anſwer to it - *Wallis*	XX 80	I 610
CANTHARIDES. Letter concerning the internal uſe of cantharides - *Yonge*	XXIII 1210	V 405
CANTON. New electrical experiments and obſervations, with an improvement of Mr. Canton's electrometer - - *Cavallo*	LXVII 388	
CANULA. Obſervations on fungous excreſcences of the bladder; a cutting-forceps for extirpating theſe excreſcences; and canulæ for treating theſe diſeaſes - *Le Cat*	— 292	
CAPE CORSE. Two letters giving an account of the cuſtoms of the inhabitants, the air, &c. of Cape Corſe; with an account of the weather there from Nov. 24, 1686, to Nov. 24, 1687 - - - *Hillier*	XIX 687	II 53
CAPE OF GOOD HOPE. An account of two plants lately brought from the Cape of Good Hope - - - - *Sloane* (See Africa)	XVII 664	II 672
——— An account of the Cape of Good Hope - - *Maxwell*	XXV 2423	
——— An obſervation of the end of the total lunar eclipſe Mar. 5, 1718, obſerved near the Cape of Good Hope, ſerving to determine the longitude thereof; with remarks thereon - - - *Halley*	XXX 992	IV 451
CAPE TOWN. An account of three journies from the Cape Town into the ſouthern parts of Africa; undertaken for the diſcovery of new plants, towards the improvement of the Royal Botanical Gardens at Kew - *Maſſon*	LXVI 268	
CAPILLARY TUBES. See *Water*.		
CARD. A deſcription of a mariner's compaſs, contrived by - *Gowen Knight*	XLVI 505	X 689

—— An

Carbon. Experiments on carbonated hydrogenous Gas, with a view to determine whether Carbon be a simple or a compound substance. Henry. 1797: 401.

On the quantity of Carbon in carbonic acid. Allen & Pepys. 1807: 267.

	Tranſ.	Abridg.
— An account of ſome improvements of the mariner's compaſs, in order to render the card and needle, propoſed by Dr. Knight, of general uſe - - *Smeaton*	XLVI 513	X 474
CARDAN. A method of extending Cardan's rule for reſolving one caſe of a cubic equation $x^3 - qx = r$ to the other caſe of the ſame equation, which it is not naturally fitted to ſolve, and which is therefore called the irreducible caſe - - - *Maſeres*	LXVIII 912	
- - -	LXX 85	
CARDOIDE. Of a cardoide curve, and of the figure ſo called - *Caſtilioneus*	XLI 778	VIII 108
CAREY (WILLIAM). The caſe of William Carey, whoſe tendons and muſcles were oſſified *Henry*	LI 89	
Further account - *Henry*	— 92	
Further account - *Henry*	LII 143	
CARIBBEE ISLANDS. Obſervations made by a curious and learned perſon ſailing from England to the Caribbee Iſlands - *Stubbes*	II 494	III 546
With an enlargement of the obſervations *Stubbes*	III 699	— 551
And other obſervations in the ſame voyage - - - *Stubbes*	— 717	— 557
— — Enquiries and directions to be made in the Caribbee Iſlands -	— 634	— 631
CARGUEYA. Account of the anatomy of an opoſſum - - - *Tyſon*	XX 105	II 881
CARLSBAD (WATERS). An account of the Carlsbad mineral waters in Bohemia - *Milles*	L 25	
— — Obſervations on the lithontriptic virtues of Carlsbad water - *Whytt*	— 386	
CARNATION. A way to make two clear ſpiritous inflammable liquors, which differ very little in taſte and ſmell; and being mixed together, do give a fine carnation colour, without either ſenſible fermentation or alteration *Geoffroy*	XXI 43	III 367
CAROLINA. An account of animals and ſhells ſent from Carolina - *Petiver*	XXIV 1592	
— An account of Mr. Mark Cateſby's eſſay towards the natural hiſtory of Carolina and the Bahama Iſlands, with ſome extracts out of the firſt three ſets by - *Mortimer*	XXXVI 425	VII 480
Continued, with extracts out of the fourth ſet - - *Mortimer*	XXXVII 174	
Continued, with extracts out of the fifth ſet - - - *Mortimer*	— 447	

Continued,

	Trans.	Abridg.
Continued, with extracts out of the sixth set - - - *Mortimer*	XXXVIII 315	
Continued, with extracts out of the seventh set - - *Mortimer*	XXXIX 112	
Continued, with extracts out of the eighth set - - *Mortimer*	— 251	
Continued, with extracts out of the ninth set - - *Mortimer*	XL 343	
Continued, with extracts out of the tenth set - - - *Mortimer*	XLIV 599	XI 925
Continued, with extracts out of the appendix - - - *Mortimer*	XLV 157	— 926
CARP. Observations upon a pleasant way of catching carp - - *Templer*	VIII 6066	II 837
—— A letter on the management of carp in Polish Prussia - - *Forster*	LXI 310	
CARPENTER (LORD). See *Wound.*		
CARRIAGE. Experiments to be made relating to land-carriage - - *Petty*	XIV 666	I 514
CARTEIA. A discourse tending to shew the situation of the antient Carteia, and some other Roman towns near it - *Conduitt*	XXX 903	V 83
CARTRAGES. Observations on cartrages lodging themselves in old willows *Willoughby*	V 2100	II 773
CASSIA. An extract of a letter containing microscopical observations on Cassia, &c. *Leewenhoek*	XVII 949	III 685
—— A discourse on the cinnamon, cassia, or canella - - - *White*	L 860	
Letter on cinnamon - *Comber*	— 873	
CASSINI. Considerations concerning his geometric and direct method for finding the apogees, excentricities and anomalies of the planets - - - *Mercator*	V 1168	I 253
—— Extract of two letters, the one concerning an instrument to shew the moon's true place to a minute or two; as also the writer's design of correcting the hitherto-assigned motions of the sun: the other touching the necessity of making new solar numbers; together with an expedient of making trial, whether the refractions in Signor Cassini's table be just - *Flamstead*	IX 219	
—— The curve assigned by Cassini to planets as their orbit, considered and rejected *Gregory*	XXIV 1704	IV 206
CASTELLIONE. Remarks upon a paper in Castellione's life of Sir Isaac Newton *Winthorp*	XLIV 153	
CASTLE-LEOD (Waters.) An account of the sulphureous mineral waters of Castle-Leod and		

Fairburn,

Carotids. On a case of nervous affection cured by the pressure of the carotids, with some physiological remarks. Parry. 1811: 89.

+Cat. Tiger-cat of the Cape of Good Hope described by J. R. Forster. 71: 1.

	Tranſ.	Abridg.
Fairburn, in the county of Roſs; and of the ſalt purging water of Pitkeatly, in the county of Perth in Scotland - *Monro*	LXII 15	
CASTOR. A receipt for the curing of caſtorium, according to the cuſtom uſed in Ruſſia *Anon.*	XVII 501	
—— Letter concerning the Ruſſia caſtor *Mounſey*	XLVI 217	
—— See *Camp.*		
CASTRATION. An account of Mr. Tull's method of caſtrating fiſh - *Watſon*	XLVIII 870	
CAT. A diſcourſe on the diſſection of a monſtrous double cat - - *Mullen*	XV 1135	II 901
—— An account of an animal of the cat kind ſent from the Eaſt Indies by general Clive to the duke of Cumberland - *Parſons*	LI 648	
CATACOMBS. Letter concerning the catacombs of Rome and Naples - *Monro*	XXII 643	III 448
CATADIOPTRICAL TELESCOPES. An account of a new catadioptrical teleſcope invented by Mr. Newton - - *Anon.*	VII 4004	I 197
—— Further ſuggeſtions about Mr. Newton's reflecting teleſcopes; together with his table of apertures and charges for the ſeveral lengths of that inſtrument - *Newton*	— 4032	— 200
—— Anſwer to ſome objections made by an ingenious French philoſopher, to the new reflecting teleſcopes - - *Newton*	— 4034	— 201
—— Some conſiderations upon part of a letter of M. de Bercé concerning the catadioptrical teleſcope, pretended to be improved and refined by Mr. Caſſegrain - *Newton*	— 4056	— 204
—— An account of a catadioptrick teleſcope made by John Hadley, Eſq. with the deſcription of a machine contrived for applying it to uſe - - - *Hadley*	XXXII 303	
—— A new method of improving and perfecting catadioptrical teleſcopes, by forming the ſpeculums of glaſs inſtead of metal *Smith*	XLI 326	VIII 113
CATALEPSY. Caſe of a cataleptick woman *Reynell*	XXXIX 49	IX 216
CATARACT (Of the eye). An account of two obſervations upon the cataract of the eye - - - *Benevoli*	XXXII 194	VII 489
—— An account of the diſſection of an eye with a cataract - - *Ranby*	XXXIII 36	— 488
—— Hiſtory of the ſubſtance of a cataract *Rhætus*	XXXV 315	— 486
—— An explication of the inſtruments uſed in a new operation on the eyes - *Cheſelden*	— 451	— 493

	Tranf.	Abridg.
—— Extract of two letters concerning M. Daviel's method of couching a cataract *Hope*	XLVII 530	
—— A defcription of a new method of opening the cornea, in order to extract the cryftalline humour - - *Sharp*	XLVIII 161	
—— A fecond account of a new method of opening the cornea for taking away the cataract *Sharp*	— 322	
—— An account of the fuccefs of Monf. Daviel's method of extracting cataracts *Cantwell*	LII 519	
CATARACT (Fall of water.) Letter concerning a cataract near Gottenburg - *Gourdon*	XXII 691	II 325
CATARRHAL DISORDER. Extract of a letter containing fome remarks upon the catarrhal diforder, which was very frequent in London and in its neighbourhood in May 1762; and upon the dyfentery which prevailed in the following autumn - - *Watfon*	LII 646	
CATENARIA. Account of the curve called catenaria - - - *Gregory*	XIX 637	I 39
—— Anfwer to the animadverfions on Dr. Gregory's curva catenaria made in the Leipfick acts - - - *Gregory*	XXI 419	— 50
—— An eafy mechanical way to divide the nautical meridian line in Mercator's projection; with an account of the relation of the fame meridian line to the curva catenaria *Perks*	XXIX 331	IV 456
CATERPILLARS. Letter concerning caterpillars that deftroy fruit - - *Garden*	XX 54	II 759
—— An account of the cornel caterpillar - - - *Skelton*	XLV 281	
—— An abftract of Mr. Bonnet's memoirs concerning caterpillars; drawn up in French by Mr. Abraham Trembley, here tranflated into Englifh - - *Anon.*	— 300	IX 831
CATHARTICUM. Obfervations and experiments on the Sal Catharticum Amarum, commonly called the Epfom falt - *Brown*	XXXII 348	VII 729
Further obfervations - *Brown*	— 372	— 732
CATOPTRICKS. An univerfal fpherico-catoptrick theorem - - *Dutton*	XXIV 1810	IV 184
—— Account of a catoptrick microfcope - - - *Robert Barker*	XXXIX 259	VIII 120
CATTLE. Account of a pond in Somerfetfhire, to which pigeons refort, but cattle will not drink at - - *Beale*	I 323	II 332
Further account of this pond, with fome particulars touching water - *Beale*	— 359	— —

—— An

+Caterpillars. Account of the Black Canker Caterpillar, which destroys the Turnips in Norfolk. Marshall 73:217.

	Trans.	Abridg.
—— An account of a murrain in Switzerland, and the method of its cure - *Wincler*	XIII 93	II 869
- - - *Slare*	— 94	— 870
—— A dissertation concerning the dreadful contagious distemper seizing the black cattle in the Venetian territories, and especially about Padua - - *Ramazzini*	XXIX 46	V 183
Recipe for the disorder amongst the cattle; sent from Holland - *Anon.*	— 50	
—— A brief account of the contagious disease which raged among the milch-cows near London in 1714; and of the methods that were taken for suppressing it - *Bates*	XXX 872	— 48
—— An account of the distemper raging among the cow-kind in the neighbourhood of London; together with some remarks proposed for their recovery - - *Mortimer*	XLIII 532	XI 916
Further observations - *Mortimer*	— 549	— 917
—— A third account of the distemper among the cows - - - *Mortimer*	XLIV 4	— 921
—— Concerning the burying of cows dead of the present reigning distemper, in lime or not - - - *Milner*	— 224	— 925
—— A discourse of the usefulness of inoculation of the horned-cattle, to prevent the contagious distemper among them - *Layard*	L 528	
—— Letter relative to the distemper among the horned-cattle - - *Layard*	LXX 536	
CAVERNS. A description of the cave of Killarny, in the barony of Burren in Ireland *Lucas*	XLI 360	VIII 668
—— A letter concerning a subterraneous cavern in Weredale - - *Durant*	XLIV 221	X 588
—— An account of large subterraneous caverns in the Chalk Hills near Norwich *Arderon*	XLV 244	— 593
—— A letter containing an account of the cavern of Dunmore Park, near Kilkenny in Ireland - - - *Walker*	LXIII 16	
CAUL. Observations on a large omentum *Huxham*	XXXIII 60	VII 518
CAUMONT (MARQUIS). See *Stone.*		
CAUSWAY. See *Giants Causway.*		
CAYLUS. Extract of a letter concerning an antient method of painting, revived by Count Caylus - - - *Mazeas*	XLIX 652	
—— Observations on the Abbé Mazeas's letter on the Count de Caylus's method of imitating the antient painting in burnt ware *Parsons* See *Encaustick*	— 655	

	Tranſ.	Abridg.
CEILAN. Method of catching fowl and deer in the Iſland of Ceilan, with an account of the cinnamon - - *Strachan*	XXIII 1094	V 2 179
—— Some obſervations made in Ceilan *Strachan*	— 1248	— - 181
CELANDINE. A letter concerning the tubes or canals that convey the yellow ſap in the herb called Chelidonium Majus, or Celandine - - - *Leewenhoek*	XXIV 1730	— - 267
CEMENT WASZSER. An hiſtorico-phyſical obſervation of the braſs waters of Neoſolis, commonly called Cement Waſzſer, changing iron to braſs - - - *Belius*	XL 351	VIII 645
CENTER. On the finding of the center of oſcillation - - - *Taylor*	XXVIII 2	IV 384
—— An account of an experiment explaining a mechanical paradox, viz. that two bodies of equal weight, ſuſpended on a certain ſort of balances, do not loſe their equilibrium, by being removed one farther from the other nearer to the center - - - *Deſaguliers*	XXXVII 125	VI 310
CENTRIFUGAL FORCE. A commentary of ſome new obſervations to diſcover whether pendulums are obſtructed by any centrifugal force *Polenus*	XLII 299	VIII 250
CENTRIFUGAL BELLOWS. See *Bellows*.		
CENTRIPETAL. On the laws of the centripetal forces - - - - *Keill*	XXVI 174	IV 359
—— Obſervations on the phyſico-mathematical commentaries of J. Bernoulli on centripetal force - - - *Keill*	XXIX 91	— 367
CEPPHUS. A deſcription of the cepphus *Lyſons*	LII 135	
CEREBELLUM. An obſervation on a ſchirrus of the cerebellum - - *Haller*	XLIII 100	
CEREUS. A deſcription of the Cereus Peruvianus, which flowered at Norimberg in 1730 - - - *Steigertahl*	XXXVI 462	VI 2 330
CERUSS. A relation of the making of ceruſs *Vernatti*	XII 935	II 576
CHAFFE. A way of preſerving ice and ſnow by chaffe - - *Ball*	I 139	III 240
CHALK. A letter containing certain chalky tubulous concretions called malm - *Needham*	XLII 634	VIII 732
—— An account of large ſubterraneous caverns in the chalk-hills near Norwich *Arderon*	XLV 244	X 593
—— Remarks upon a petrified echinus of a ſingular kind, found on Bunnan's land, in the pariſh of Bovingdon in Hertfordſhire, which is a clay, and ſuppoſed to have been brought with the chalk dug out of a pit in the field *Parſons*	XLIX 155	

CHALK-

+On Centripetal forces - - - - - - - - - Waring 78: 67.

4 Channel. On the effect of westerly winds in raising the level of the British Channel. Rennell. 1809: 400.

	Transf.	Abridg.
CHALK-STONES. On the chalk-stones of the gout — — — *Leewenhoek*	XV 883	III 684
CHALYBEATE. A short account of the nature and virtues of the Pyrmont waters, with some observations on their chalybeate qualities *Slare*	XXX 564	IV 2 201
CHANCE. An arithmetical paradox concerning the chances of lotteries — *Roberts*	XVII 677	III 679
—— The laws of chance in a set of problems — — — *De Moivre*	XXVII 213	V 2 266
—— A solution of the 15th general problem, proposed by De Moivre in his treatise de Mensura Sortis — *Bernoulli*	XXIX 133	— — 255
Another general solution of the preceding problem, with the assistance of combined and infinite series — *De Moivre*	— 145	— — 266
—— An essay towards solving a problem in the doctrine of chances — *Bayes*	LIII 370	
—— A demonstration of the second rule in the essay towards the solution of a problem in the doctrine of chances, published in vol. LIII. — — — *Price*	LIV 296	
CHANNEL. An advertisement necessary for all navigators bound up the channel of England — — — *Anon.*	XXII 725	I 585
CHARACTERS. A letter containing the exact draughts of several unknown characters, taken from the ruins at Persepolis — *Flowers*	XVII 775	III 526
—— A paper containing some unknown antient characters, with remarks thereon, by Francis Aston, Esq. — — *Flowers*	— 872	— 530
—— An explanation of the figures of a Pagan temple, and unknown characters, at Cannara in Salset — — *Stuart*	XXVI 372	V 2 60
—— An explanation of the Runic characters of Kelsingland — — *Celsius*	XL 7	IX 438
—— Extract of a letter concerning a supposed connection between the hieroglyphical writing of antient Egypt, and the characteristic writing which is in use at this day among the Chinese — — — *Morton*	LIX 489	
—— See *China*.		
CHARCOAL. Experiments and observations on charcoal — — *Priestley*	LX 211	
—— Extract of a letter on some electrical experiments made with charcoal *Kinnersley*	LXIII 38	
—— Account of the manner in which the Russians		

treat

	Tranf.	Abridg.
treat perfons affected by the fumes of burning charcoal, and other effluvia of the fame nature - - *Guthrie*	LXIX 325	
CHARM. Conjectures on the charming or fafcinating power attributed to the rattle-fnake; grounded on credible accounts, experiments, and obfervations - - *Sloane*	XXXVIII 321	IX 55
CHARR-FISH. Some account of the charr-fifh, as found in North Wales *Farringdon*	XLIX 210	
CHARTS. Some remarks on the variation of the magnetical compafs, publifhed in the memoirs of the Academy of Sciences, with regard to the general chart of thofe variations made by E. Halley; as alfo concerning the true longitude of the Magellan Straights -	XXIX 165	IV 453
—— A fhort differtation on maps and charts - - - - *Mountaine*	L 563	
—— Remarks on the cenfure of Mercator's chart, in a pofthumous work of Mr. Weft of Exeter - - - *Dunn*	LIII 66	
—— A defence of Mercator's chart againft the cenfure of Mr. Weft - *Mountaine*	— 69	
—— A letter concerning a new chart of the Red Sea, with two draughts of the roads of Mocha and Judda, and feveral obfervations made during a voyage on that fea - *Newland*	LXII 77	
—— Particulars of the country of Labradore; extracted from the papers of Lieut. Roger Clarke, of his majefty's floop the Otter, with a plane chart of the coaft - *Curtis*	LXIV 372	
CHARTHAM. See *Bones.*		
CHEEK. An account of an extraordinary tumour or wen lately cut off the cheek of a perfon in Scotland - - *Bower*	XXX 713	V 217
—— Account of a rottennefs of the cheek-bone, occafioned by a vaft quantity of matter flowing from the mouth of a boy for three years - - - - *Hardifway*	XXXV 374	VII 494
CHEESE. Obfervations on infects bred in cheefe, &c. by - - *Leewenhoek*	XVIII 194	III 685
CHELIDONIUM MAJUS. A letter concerning the tubes or canals that convey the yellow fap in the herb called Chelidonium Majus, or Celandine - - *Leewenhoek*	XXIV 1730	V 2 267
CHERRY TREES. An experiment of making cherry-trees, that have withered fruit, to bear full		

Chermes Lacca. see Lacca.

Entry	Author	Transf.	Abridg.
and good fruit; and of recovering the almoſt-withered fruit -	*Merret*	II 455	II 652
CHESHIRE. Obſervations on the Roman colonies and ſtations in Cheſhire and Lancaſhire	*Percival*	XLVII 216	
CHESNUT TREES. A letter concerning cheſnut-trees - - -	*Ducarel*	LXI 136	
Another letter on cheſnut-trees	*Thorpe*	— 152	
Another - -	*Haſted*	— 160	
Another - -	*Barrington*	— 167	
CHESTER. Obſervations on the population and diſeaſes of Cheſter in the year 1774	*Haygarth*	LXVIII 131	
—— See *Altar.*			
CHICHESTER. See *Inſcription.*			
CHICKENS. Manner of hatching chickens at Cairo - - -	*Graves*	XII 923	— 581
CHILD. An account of two monſtrous births at Paris - -	*Anon.*	II 479	III 301
—— An account of two monſtrous births in Devonſhire - -	*Colepreſſe*	— 480	— —
—— An account of two odd births	*Grandi*	V 1188	— —
—— Anatomical obſervations on a monſtrous birth at Plymouth - -	*Durſton*	— 2098	— —
—— Extract of a letter containing ſome relations concerning ſome odd worms vomitted by children - -	*Liſter*	X 391	— 135
—— A relation of a monſtrous birth	*Morris*	XII 961	— 302
—— Relation of a child that remained 26 years in the mother's belly -	*Bayle*	— 979	— 127
—— An account of an extraordinary birth in Staffordſhire - -	*Birch*	XIII 281	— 221
With reflections thereon -	*Tyſon*	— —	— —
—— The deſcription of a monſtrous child born in South Jutland -	*Krabe*	XIV 599	— 304
—— Relation of an extraordinary child of ſix years old, who in face, &c. was as large as a full-grown woman; and of what appeared on the diſſection of the body -	*Sampſon*	XIX 80	— 20
—— An account of a child born with a large wound in the breaſt, ſuppoſed to proceed from the force of imagination -	*Cyprianus*	— 291	— 222
—— Letter concerning a child who had its inteſtines, meſentery, &c. in the cavity of the thorax - - -	*Holt*	XXII 992	V 269
—— Part of a letter concerning a monſtrous birth - - -	*Taylor*	XXV 2345	— 309
—— Account of ſome monſtrous births in Ireland in 1708 - -	*Derham*	XXVI 308	— —

		Tranſ.	Abridg.
—— Account of a child crying in the womb	*Derham*	XXVI 485	V 310
—— A ſhort diſſertation on a child's crying in the womb - -	*Derham*	— 487	— —
—— An account of a monſtrous double birth in Lorrain - -	*Maclaurin*	XXXII 346	VII 688
—— Two extraordinary caſes of a large ſtone in the urethra, brought on by the venereal infection, and a child born with a remarkable tumour on the loins -	*Huxham*	XXXVI 257	— 560
—— A caſe concerning a child born with the bowels hanging out of its belly -	*Amyand*	XXXVII 258	— 516
—— Account of a monſtrous boy	*Cantwell*	XLI 137	IX 314
—— Account of a monſtrous child born of a woman under ſentence of tranſportation	*Sheldrake*	— 341	— 313
—— An account of a monſtrous fœtus reſembling an hooded monkey -	*Gregory*	— 764	— 315
—— Caſe of the heart of a child turned upſide down - - -	*Torres*	— 776	— 135
—— A remarkable conformation, or luſus naturæ, in a child - -	*Warwick*	XLII 152	— 316
—— Part of a letter concerning a child of a monſtrous ſize - -	*Geoffroy*	— 627	— 317
—— Account of a child's being taken out of the abdomen after having lain there upwards of 16 years - -	*Myddleton*	XLIV 617	XI 807
—— A letter concerning a child born with an extraordinary tumour near the anus, containing ſome rudiments of an embryo in it	*Huxham*	XLV 325	— 1020
—— An account of a præternatural conjunction of two female children -	*Parſons*	— 526	— 1209
—— Part of a letter concerning a child born with the jaundice upon it, received from its father; and of the mother taking the ſame diſtemper from her huſband the next time of being with child - -	*Cooke*	XLVI 205	— 1063
—— An account of a monſtrous fœtus without any mark of ſex - -	*Baſter*	— 469	— 1208
—— An account of a double child born at Hebus, near Middleton in Lancaſhire	*Percival*	XLVII 360	
—— An account of an extraordinary caſe of a child - - -	*Guy*	XLIX 34	
—— Anatomico-medical obſervations of a monſtrous double child born Oct. 26, 1701, in Pannonia, and died Feb. 23, 1723. (Lat.)	*Torkos*	L 311	
Another account -	*Burnet*	— 315	
Another account -	*Du Pleſſis*	— 317	
Another account (Lat.)	*Drieſchius*	— 318	

—— An

	Tranſ.	Abridg.
—— An account of a monſtrous human fœtus, having neither head, heart, lungs, ſtomach, ſpleen, pancreas, liver nor kidnies *Le Cat*	LVII 1	
—— An account of a very ſmall fœtus brought into the world at the ſame time with a child in its full growth - *Warner*	LX 453	
—— An account of an extraordinary acephalous birth - - *Cooper*	LXV 311	
CHILD-BED. Diſſection of a woman who died in child-bed - *Silveſtre*	XXII 787	V 303
CHILD-BIRTH. See *Fœtus, Monſter, Parturition.*		
CHILTENHAM (Mineral water of). An examination of the Chiltenham mineral water; which may ſerve as a method in general for examining mineral waters - *Senckenberg*	XLI 380	VIII 650
CHIMNEY-PIECES. An account of two large ſtone chimney-pieces, with a peculiar ſort of arch-work thereon - *Wallis*	XIV 800	I 595
CHINA. A voyage of the emperor of China into the Eaſtern Tartary, 1682 - *Anon.*	XVI 39	III 632
—— A voyage of the emperor of China into the Weſtern Tartary, 1683 - *Anon.*	— 52	— —
An explanation neceſſary to juſtify the geography ſuppoſed in theſe letters *Anon.*	— 62	— —
—— Obſervations and conjectures concerning the Chineſe characters - *R. H.*	— 63	— —
—— An account of a voyage to Chuſan in China; with a deſcription of the iſland, of the ſeveral ſorts of tea, of the fiſhing, agriculture, &c. of the Chineſe, &c. with ſeveral obſervations not hitherto taken notice of *Cunningham*	XXIII 1201	V 2 171
—— An account of ſome plants collected at Chuſan in China, by - *James Petiver*	— 1419	IV - 286
—— An explanation of the new chronological table of the Chineſe hiſtory; tranſlated into Latin from the original Chineſe by father John Fr. Foucquet - *Dereham and Foucquet*	XXXVI 397	VII 4 13
—— A letter concerning the Chineſe chronology and aſtronomy - - *Coſtard*	XLIV 476	XI 1232
—— Account of the knowledge of geography amongſt the Chineſe - *Gaubil*	XLVI 327	X 255
—— Some account of the paper money current among the Chineſe - *Gaubil*	— —	XI 1364
—— A letter giving an account of ſeveral of the natural and artificial productions of China - - - *D'Incarville*	XLVIII 253	

N —— Two

	Tranf.	Abridg.
—— Two letters concerning the Chinefe chronol gy and aftronomy - *Gaubil*	XLVIII 309	
—— On the fuppofed connection between the hieroglyphical writing of antient Egypt, and the characteriftic writing which is in ufe at this time among the Chinefe *Morton*	LIX 489	
CHINA CABINET. An account of a China cabinet filled with feveral inftruments, fruits, &c. ufed in China - - *Buckley*	XX 390	II 252
Further account - *Sloane*	— 461	— —
Further account - *Sloane*	XXI 44	— 646
Further account - *Sloane*	— 70	— 252
CHINA DISHES. An intimation of a way found in Europe to make China difhes *Anon.*	I 127	III 658
CHINA STOVES. A letter containing an account of the manner in which the Chinefe heat thei rooms - - *De Vifme*	LXI 59	
An account of the Kang, or Chinefe ftoves - - - *Gramont*	— 61	
CHINA VARNISH. The way of making feveral China varnifhes; fent from the Jefuits in China to the great duke of Tufcany *Sherard*	XXII 725	I 585
CHIRURGERY. An argument for the more frequent ufe of laryngotomy, urged from a remarkable cafe in chirurgery - *Mufgrave*	XXI 398	III 61
—— A relation of a deaf and dumb perfon who recovered his hearing and fpeech after a violent fever: with fome other medical and chirurgical obfervations - *Martin*	XXV 2469	V [357] V 2 127
—— Part of a letter concerning a cafe in chirurgery, which is commonly miftaken for a fracture of the patella - *Devere.*	XXXI 44	VII 678
—— Two medico-chirurgical obfervations on the hydatides and confequences of an incomplete hernia, and on the functions of the inteftines expofed to fight - *Le Cat*	XLI 712	IX 189
—— Various medico-chirurgical obfervations (Lat.) - - - *Schlichling*	XLII 270	— 232
CHOROEIDES. Anfwer to Mr. Pecquet about the opinion, that it is the principal organ of fight with other confiderable experiments *Marriot*	V 1023	
CHOROGRAPHY. A folution of a chorographical problem, propofed by Richard Townley *Collins*	VI 2093	I 366
—— The folutions of three chorographical problems - - *Anon.*	XV 1231	— 222
CHRONOLOGY. Remarks upon the obfervations made upon a chronological index of Sir Ifaac Newton;		

Chloranthus, a new genus of plants described. — Swartz. — 77: 359.

Chlorine. On a gaseous compound of carbonic oxide and Chlorine — Davy. — 1812: 144.

An account of some experiments on the combinations of different metals and Chlorine etc. — ——— — 1812: 169.

On a new detonating compound. — ——— — 1813. 1.

Further observations on the same — ——— — ——— 242.

On the failure of the experiments in which water is said to have been found by the decomposition of Chlorine. — ——— — 1818: 169.

+ Chronology. On the chronology of the Hindoos — — — — Marsden [illegible]9: 560. [80 written above]
On the Civil Year of the Hindoos, and its divisions — — — Cavendish 1792: 383.

Chrystalline Lens. On its structure in fishes and quadrupeds, as ascertained by its action on polarised light. — Brewster. [illegible]

	Tranſ.	Abridg.
ton; tranſlated into French by the obſervator and publiſhed at Paris - *Newton*	XXXIII 316	
—— Remarks upon ſome diſſertations lately publiſhed at Paris by the Rev. P. Souciet, againſt Sir Iſaac Newton's chronology *Halley*	XXXIV 205	VII 4 7
—— Some farther remarks on P. Souciet's diſſertations againſt Sir Iſaac Newton's chronology - - - *Halley*	XXXV 296	— - 11
—— An explanation of the new chronological table of the Chineſe hiſtory; tranſlated into Latin from the original Chineſe by father John Fr. Foucquet *Dereham and Foucquet*	XXXVI 397	— - 13
—— A letter concerning the Chineſe chronology and aſtronomy - - *Coſtard*	XLIV 476	XI 1232
—— The application of Dr. Saunderſon's theorem for ſolving unlimited equations to a curious queſtion in chronology *Horſefall*	LVIII 100	
CHRYSTALLINE HUMOUR. Obſervations about the chryſtalline humour of the eye *Leewenhoek*	XIV 790	
—— Letter concerning the chryſtalline humour in the eye of whales, fiſh, and other creatures and of the uſe of the eye-lids *Leewenhoek*	XXIV 1723	V 2 267
CHUSAN. An account of a voyage to Chuſan in China, with a deſcription of the iſland, of the ſeveral ſorts of tea, of the fiſhing, agriculture of the Chineſe, &c. with ſeveral obſervations not hitherto taken notice of - - - *Cunningham*	XXIII 1201	— - 171
—— An account of ſome plants collected at Chuſan in China, by - *James Petiver*	— 1419	IV - 286
CHURCHIL RIVER. Journal of a voyage made by order of the Royal Society to Churchil River, on the north-weſt coaſt of Hudſon's Bay; of thirteen months reſidence in that country; and of the voyage back to England in 1768, 1769 - - - *Wales*	LX 100	
CHYLE. Some anatomical obſervations and experiments concerning the unalterable character of the whiteneſs of the chyle within the lacteous veins; together with divers particulars obſerved in the guts, eſpecially ſome ſorts of worms found in them - *Liſter*	VIII 6060	III 101
—— An account of an experiment made for altering the colour of the chyle in the lacteal veins - - - *Liſter*	XIII 6	— 102
—— Some probable thoughts of the whiteneſs of the		

Subject	Author	Transf.	Abridg.
chyle, and what it is after it is conveyed within the arteries - -	*Lister*	XIII 242	III 106
—— An account of chylification	*Cowper*	XIX 231	— —
CHYMISTRY. An account of some chymical, medical, and anatomical particulars	*Behm*	III 650	— 351
—— Some reflections made on the enlarged account of Dr. Wittie's answer to hydrologia chymica, chiefly concerning the cause of the sudden loss of the virtues of mineral waters	*Foot*	IV 1050	II 365
—— Observations on these three chymical operations, digestion, fermentation, and triture or grinding (hitherto in the author's opinion not sufficiently regarded) by which many things of admirable use may be performed	*Langelot*	VII 5052	III 315
—— The chymical touch-stone of Mr. John Kuncle, De acido & urinoso sale calido & frigido, contra Doctor. Voight's spirit. vini vindicatum - - -	*Kuncle*	XV 896	
—— Two propositions in chymistry desired to be answered in a year and a half by any person; if they are not in that time, the proposer promises he will do it himself -	*Anon.*	XXI 186	II 752
—— Observations on the class of sweet tastes, made by comparing the tastes of sweet plants with Mr. L'Emery's chymical analysis of them in his treatise of drugs -	*Floyer*	XXIII 1160	V 406
—— A vindication of Dr. Freind's chymical lectures, wherein the objections (in the Leipsic Transactions, Sept. 1710) brought against the attractive force of matter are removed	*Freind*	XXVII 330	— 428
—— A discourse concerning the usefulness of thermometers in chymical experiments, and concerning the principles on which the thermometers now in use have been constructed; together with the description and uses of a metalline thermometer newly invented by - - -	*C. Mortimer*	XLIV 672	X 435
—— A chymical experiment of the effect of quicklime on alcaline sal volatile	*Schlosser*	XLIX 222	
see Analysis. —— ~~Experiments and observations on~~ see lead-ore - - -	~~*Richard Watson*~~	~~LXVIII 863~~	
CICADA. Observations on the cicada or locusts of North America -	*Collinson*	LIV 65	
—— See *Locust*.			
CICINDELA VOLANS. Observations on the cicindella volans, or flying glow-worm with the figure - -	*Waller*	XV 841	II 761

Oxym. spec. On some combinations of Phosphorus and Sulphur, and on some other subjects of chemical inquiry. Davy. 1812: 405.

Circle, (Astronomical) On an improved Reflecting Circle. Mendoza Rios. 1801: 363.

Description of an astronomical circle, and some remarks on the construction of circular instruments. Pond. 1806. 424.

	Trans.	Abridg.
CICUTA. See *Hemlock.*		
CINNABAR. Extract of a letter containing several observations on cinnabar and gunpowder - - - *Leewenhoek*	XVII 754	III 685
CINNAMON. A description of the cortex Winteranus, or wild cinnamon tree - *Sloane*	— 462	II 663
—— An account of the cinnamon in the island of Ceilan - - *Strachan*	XXIII 1094	V 2 179
—— An account of the cinnamon-tree in Ceylon, and its several sorts; communicated by the chief inspector of the cinnamon trade and manufacture in that island to Albertus Seba *Anon.*	XXXVI 97	VI 2 321
Some additions to the foregoing account *Seba*	— 106	
—— An account of the cinnamon-tree *W. Watson*	XLVII 301	
—— A discourse on the cinnamon, cassia, or canella - - *White*	L 860	
Letter on the cinnamon - *Combes*	— 873	
CIRCLE (ASTRONOMY). An observation of an extraordinary lunar circle, and of two paraselenes made at Paris Oct. 20, 1747 *Greschow*	XLV 524	X 483
CIRCLE (GEOMETRY). Answer to the animadversions of Mr Hugenius upon Dr. Gregory's book, De vera Circuli & Hyperbolæ Quadratura, as published in the Journal des Scavans *Gregory*	III 732	
—— Some considerations on Mr Huygens's letter, printed in vindication of his Examen of the book intitled, De vera Circuli & Hyperbolæ Quadratura - - *Gregory*	— 882	
—— The quantity of a degree of a great circle in English measures - *Oldenburg*	XI 636	I 587
—— Cubic and biquadratic equations constructed by a parabola and circle - *Halley*	XVI 335	— 63
—— The construction of a quadratrix to the circle, being the curve described by its equable evolution - - *Anon.*	XXII 445	— 56
—— An investigation of some theorems which suggest some remarkable properties of the circle, and are of use in resolving fractions, whose denominators are certain multinomials, into more simple ones - *Landen*	XLVIII 566	
—— Of triangles described in circles and about them - - *Stedman*	LXV 296	
—— Theorems concerning polygons of greatest and least areas and perimeters inscribing and circumscribing the circle - *Horsley*	— 301	
—— A new and general method of finding simple and quickly converging series; by which the		

propor-

	Transſ.	Abridg.
proportion of a diameter of a circle to its circumference may eaſily be computed to a great number of places of figures *Hutton*	LXVI 476	
CITRON. Some hortulan communications about the curious engrafting of oranges and lemons, or citrons, upon one another's trees; and of one individual fruit, half orange and half lemon, growing on ſuch trees, &c. - *Anon.*	II 553	II 685
CIVITA TURCHINO. An account of ſome ſubterraneous apartments with Etruſcan inſcriptions and paintings, diſcovered at Civita Turchino in Italy - - *Wilcox*	LIII 127	
CLARET. A further account of ſome experiments of injecting claret, &c. into the abdomen, after cupping - - *Warrick*	XLIX 485	
CLAYS. An ingenious propoſal for a new ſort of maps of countries; together with tables of ſands and clays, ſuch chiefly as are found in the north parts of England - *Liſter*	XIV 739	— 450
—— An account of curious waſps neſts made of clay in Pennſylvania - *Bartram*	XLIII 363	XI 847
—— Remarks on a petrified echinus of a ſingular kind, found at Bunnan's Land, in the pariſh of Bovingdon in Hertfordſhire, which is a clay, and ſuppoſed to have been brought with the chalk dug out of a pit in the field *Parſons*	XLIX 155	
CLEPSYDRA. A deſcription of a clepſydra, or water-clock - - *Hamilton*	XLIV 171	X 428
CLIFFS. Extract of a letter containing obſervations on the precipices and cliffs on the north-eaſt coaſt of Norfolk - *Arderon*	— 275	— 589
CLIMATE. An eſſay upon the cauſes of the different colours of people in different climates *Mitchell*	XLIII 102	XI 926
CLIFTON. See *Coins.*		
CIRCULATION OF THE BLOOD. See *Blood.*		
CLOCK. A new invention of a clock aſcendant on a plane inclined - *De Gennes*	XII 1006	I 468
—— A letter wherein Mr. Williamſon aſſerts his right to the curious and uſeful invention of making clocks to keep time with the ſun's apparent motion - *Williamſon*	XXX 1080	IV 394
—— A contrivance to avoid the irregularities in a clock's motion, occaſioned by the action of heat and cold upon the rod of the pendulum - - - *Graham*	XXXIV 40	VI 297
—— An account of ſome obſervations made in London by Mr. Graham, and at Black River, in		

circle. Propositions containing some properties of tangents to circles; and of trapeziums inscribed in circles, and non-inscribed. Together with propositions on the elliptic representations of circles, upon a plane surface, by perspective. —Rev. 1814, 348.

		Transf.	Abridg.
Jamaica, by Colin Campbell, concerning the going of a clock, in order to determine the difference between the lengths of isochronal pendulums in those places	*Bradley*	XXXVIII 302	VII 238
—— An account of the influence which two pendulum-clocks were obferved to have upon each other - -	*Ellicott*	XLI 126	VIII 246
Subject continued -	*Ellicott*	— 128	
—— A defcription of a clepfydra, or water-clock - - -	*Hamilton*	XLIV 171	X 428
—— Two methods by which the irregularity of the motion of a clock, arifing from the influence of heat and cold upon the rod of the pendulum, may be prevented -	*Ellicott*	XLVII 479	
—— Letter concerning the inventor of the contrivance in the pendulum of a clock to prevent the irregularities of its motion by heat and cold - -	*Short*	— 517	
—— Obfervations on a clock of Mr. John Shelton, made at St. Helena -	*Mafkelyne*	LII 434	
—— Obfervations for proving the going of Mr. Ellicott's clock at St. Helena	*Mafon*	— 534	
—— An account of Mr. Mafon's paper concerning the going of Mr. Ellicott's clock at St. Helena - - -	*Short*	— 540	
—— Remarks on the foregoing account	*Mafkelyne*	LIV 380	
—— Aftronomical obfervations made in the Forks of the river Brandivine in Pennfylvania, for determining the going of a clock fent thither by the Royal Society, in order to find the difference of gravity between the Royal Obfervatory at Greenwich, and the place where the clock was fet up in Pennfylvania - - -	*Mafon and Dixon*	LVIII 329	
—— An account of the going of an aftronomical clock - -	*Wollafton*	LXI 559	
—— See *Pendulum, Watches*.			
CLOGHER. An account of the fubfiding or finking down of a hill near Clogher in Ireland - - -	*Bifhop of Clogher*	XXVIII 267	IV 2 250
CLOTH. A new engine to make linen-cloth without the help of an artificer	*De Gennes*	XII 1007	I 501
CLOUDS. An attempt to folve the phænomenon of the rife of vapours, formation of clouds, and defcent of rain -	*Defaguliers*	XXXVI 6	VI 2 61
—— Extracts of two letters relating to the extracting electricity from the clouds	*Nollet*	XLVII 553	

	Tranſ.	Abridg.
Clouds. Another letter relating to the extracting electricity from the clouds - *Mylius*	XLVII 559	
Cloves. An extract of a letter containing microſcopical obſervations on cloves *Leewenhoek*	XLII 949	III 685
Clustered Animal-Flower. An account of the actinia ſociata, or cluſtered animal flower, lately found on the ſea-coaſts of the new-ceded iſlands - *Ellis*	LVII 428	
Cluster Polype. Letter concerning a cluſter polype, found in the ſea near the coaſt of Greenland - - *Ellis*	XLVIII 305	
Coal. Obſervations and trials about the differences between a burning coal and ſhining wood *Boyle*	II 605	— 646
—— An account of two uncommon mineral ſubſtances found in ſome coal and iron mines in England - - *Jeſſop*	VIII 6179	II 458, 459
—— Obſervations on a ſubterranean fire in a coal mine near Newcaſtle - *Hodgſon*	XI 762	— 383
—— A relation of ſome ſtrange phænomena, accompanied with miſchievous effects, in a coal-work in Flintſhire - *Moſtyn*	XII 895	— 378
—— The different ſtrata obſerved in boring for coals in ſeveral parts of Yorkſhire, with the expence of the ſame - *Maleverer*	XXI 73	— 599
—— A letter concerning a colliery that took fire, and was blown up near Newcaſtle, killing 69 perſons, on Auguſt 18, 1708 *Charlett*	XXVI 215	IV 2 206
—— A deſcription of the ſeveral ſtrata of earth, ſtone, coal, &c. found in a coal-pit at the weſt end of Dudley, Staffordſhire. To which is added, a table of the ſpecifick gravity of each ſtratum *Fettiplace and Haukſbee*	XXVII 541	— - 182
—— A curious deſcription of the ſtrata obſerved in the coal-mines of Mendip in Somerſetſhire *Strachey*	XXX 968	— - 260
—— An account of the ſtrata in coal-mines *Strachey*	XXXIII 395	VI - 222
—— An account of the damp air in a coal pit of Sir James Lowther, Bart. ſunk within 20 yards of the ſea - *Lowther*	XXXVIII 109	VIII 656
—— An experiment concerning the ſpirit of coals - - - *Clayton*	XLI 59	IX 395
—— An account of coal-balls made at Liege *Hanbury*	— 672	— 501
—— A letter concerning a coal-mine taking fire near Newcaſtle upon Tine *Durant*	XLIV 221	X 588
—— A letter concerning ſpelter melting iron with pit-coal - - *Maſon*	— 370	— 671
—— An account of the impreſſions of plants on the ſlates of coals - *Da Coſta*	L 228	

—— Re-

+ Coal. Some remarks on Coal — — — — — — — — — Hatchett. 1806: 109

Cobra de Capello. Remarks on the voluntary expansion of the skin of the neck, in the Cobra de Capello or hooded Snake of the East Indies — Russell. 1804: 346.
Description of the structure of the parts which perform that office — — Home. — 347.

		Transf.	Abridg.
—— Remarks on the Bovey coal	*Milles*	LI 534	
—— An account of a case of a young man stupified by the smoke of sea-coal	*Frewen*	LII 454	
—— A letter containing a short account of an explosion of air in a coal-pit at Middleton, near Leeds in Yorkshire -	*Bernard*	LXIII 217	
—— See *Bovey, Damp.*			
Coati Mondi. A letter concerning the Coati Mondi of Brasil -	*Mackenzie*	XXXII 317	VII 449
Cobalt. Part of a letter concerning cobalt, and the preparations of smalt and arsenic	*Kreig*	XXIV 1754	V 420
—— Commentary on cobalt -	*Linckius*	XXXIV 192	VI 2 236
Coccus Radicum. Some corrections and amendments concerning the generation of the insect called coccus radicum -	*Breynius*	XXXVII 444	VII 466
Cocherel. See *Sepulchre.*			
Cochineal. Observations concerning cochineal, accompanied with some suggestions for finding out and preparing such like substances out of other vegetables -	*Anon.*	III 796	II 784
—— Letter enlarging and correcting his former notes upon Kermes; and withal insinuating his conjectures of cochineal's being a sort of Kermes - -	*Lister*	VII 5059	
—— Observations on the making of cochineal, according to the relation had from an old Spaniard at Jamaica -	*Anon.*	XVII 502	— 785
—— A letter concerning cochineal	*Leewenhoek*	XXIV 1614	V 2 266
—— The natural history of cochineal	*Rutty*	XXXVI 264	VII 478
—— An account of the male and female cochineal insects, that breed on the cactus opuntia, or Indian fig, in South Carolina and Georgia - - -	*Ellis*	LII 661	
—— An account of the Polish cochineal	*Wolfe*	LIV 91	
Further account -	*Wolfe*	— 95	
—— A further account of the Polish cochineal	*Wolfe*	LVI 184	
Cochlea. A description of the organ of hearing in the elephant, with the figures and situation of the ossicles, labyrinth, and cochlea, in the ear of that animal -	*Blair*	XXX 885	V 82
Cocks. Microscopical observations and experiments concerning the animalcula in semine-masculino of cocks and spiders, shortness of breath, &c. - -	*Leewenhoek*	XXIII 1137	— 2 264
Cod Fish. Letter concerning the spawn of cod-fish - - -	*Leewenhoek*	XXII 821	— - 266
Cod (Of the seed of plants). Instances shewing the			

		Tranſ.	Abridg.
correſpondence of the pith and timber with the ſeed of the plant; as alſo of the bark or ſap in the bark with the pulp of the fruit, or ſome encompaſſing coat or cod containing the ſeed - -	*Beal*	IV 919	II 710
COECUM. An account of the cutting out of the cœcum of a bitch -	*Muſgrave*	XIII 524	III 112
—— A letter in anſwer to Mr. Oldenburgh, wherein he deſired an explanation of a paragraph, touching the uſe of the inteſtinum cœcum	*Lyſter*	XIV 457	— 425
—— Of an inguinal rupture, with a pin in the appendix cœci incruſted with a ſtone, and ſome obſervations on wounds in the guts	*Amyand*	XXXIX 329	IX 153
COFFEE. An account of the coffee-ſhrub	*Sloane*	XVIII 61	II 659
—— A diſcourſe of coffee -	*Houghton*	XXI 311	— 660
COHESION. Some experiments concerning the coheſion of lead -	*Deſaguliers*	XXXIII 345	VI 325
—— Queries concerning the cauſe of coheſion of the parts of matter -	*Triewald*	XXXVI 39	— 2 5
—— A remarkable caſe of coheſion of all the inteſtines in a man about 34 years of age	*Jenty*	L 550	
—— New experiments and obſervations concerning electricity - -	*Symmer*	LI 340	
—— Experiments on electricity; with a letter concerning the force of electrical coheſion	*Mitchell*	— 393	
COINS. A letter giving a further account of ſome coins found at Honedon in Suffolk	*Dale*	XVII 874	III 441
—— Letter concerning pewter money coined in Ireland by the late king James	*Thoreſby*	XXIV 1875	V 2 31
—— An eaſy method of procuring the true impreſſion or figure of medals, coins, &c.	*Baker*	XLIII 77	XI 1339
—— Explication of an inedited coin with two legends, in different languages, on the reverſe	*Swinton*	LXI 78	
COINS (ETRUSCAN). Explication of a moſt remarkable monagram on the reverſe of a very antient quinarius, never before publiſhed or explained - - -	*Swinton*	LXIV 318	
—— —— Obſervations upon two antient Etruſcan coins never before illuſtrated or explained - - -	*Swinton*	LIV 99	
—— Elucidation of an Etruſcan coin of Pæſtum in Lucania, emitted from the mint there about the time of the ſocial war	*Swinton*	LVIII 246	
—— Remarks upon two Etruſcan weights or coins never before publiſhed -	*Swinton*	LXI 82	
COINS (NORMAN). Letter concerning ſome Norman coins found at York -	*Thoreſby*	XXIV 2127	V 2 30

	Transf.	Abridg.
COINS (PARTHIAN). A differtation upon a Parthian coin, with characters on the reverfe refembling thofe of the Palmyrenes *Swinton*	XLIX 593	
—— —— Remarks on a Parthian coin with a Greek and Parthian legend - *Swinton*	L 175	
—— —— Conjectures upon an inedited Parthian coin - - *Swinton*	LI 680	
—— —— Defcription of two Parthian coins never hitherto publifhed - *Swinton*	LVI 296	
COIN (PERSIAN). Obfervations upon five antient Perfian coins ftruck in Paleftine, or Phœnicia, before the diffolution of the Perfian empire - - - *Swinton*	LXI 345	
COIN (PHOENICIAN). An attempt to interpret the legend and infcription of a very curious Phœnician medal never hitherto explained *Swinton*	LVII 266	
COIN (PUNIC). Interpretation of the infcription of a Punic coin ftruck in the Ifle of Gozo *Swinton*	LVIII 235	
—— —— Defcription of a Punic coin appertaining to the Ifle of Gozo, hitherto attributed to that of Malta by the learned - *Swinton*	— 261	
—— —— Obfervations on an inedited coin, adorned with two Punic characters on the reverfe - - - *Swinton*	— 265	
—— —— Interpretation of two Punic infcriptions on the reverfes of two Siculo-Punic coins, publifhed by the prince de Torremuzza, and never hitherto explained *Swinton*	LXI 91	
COINS (ROMAN). Letter concerning fome Roman coins, and other matters lately obferved in Lincolnfhire - *Anon.*	XXIII 1156	IV 2 246
Further account - *Thorefby*	— 1158	
—— —— An account of fome Roman coins found at Clifton, near Edlington, Yorkfhire *Thorefby*	XXIV 2149	V - 34
—— —— Part of a letter concerning fome Roman coins found in Yorkfhire - *Thorefby*	XXVI 134	— - 32
—— —— A defcription of fome clay-mould, or concaves of antient Roman coins found in Shropfhire - - *Baker*	XLIV 557	XI 1320
—— —— An abftract of a difcourfe intituled, Reflections on the medals of Pefcennius Niger, and fome circumftances in the hiftory of his life, written in French by - - *M. Claude Gros de Bofe*	XLVI 452	— 1314
—— —— An account of an inedited coin of the emprefs Crifpina - *Swinton*	LVI 27	
—— —— Remarks upon a Denarius of the Veturian		

	Tranſ.	Abridg.
rian family, with an Etruſcan inſcription on the reverſe - *Swinton*	LVIII 253	
—— —— An account of a ſubærated Denarius of the Plætorian family; adorned with an Etruſcan inſcription on the reverſe, never before publiſhed or explained - *Swinton*	LXII 60	
—— —— Further remarks upon a Denarius of the Veturian family; with an Etruſcan inſcription on the reverſe, formerly conſidered *Swinton*	LXIII 22	
COIN (SAMNITE). Some obſervations upon a Samnite Etruſcan coin, never before fully explained - - - *Swinton*	LI 853	
—— —— A diſſertation upon a Samnite Denarius - - - *Swinton*	LII 28	
—— —— An attempt to elucidate two Samnite coins, never before fully explained *Swinton*	LIX 432	
COINS (SAXON). An account of ſome Saxon coins lately found in Suffolk; communicated by - - - *Sir P. S.*	XVI 356	III 436
Remarks by - *W. W.*	— 361	— 438
COINS (SWEDISH). Letter concerning ſome Swediſh coins - - *Thoreſby*	XXIV 1901	V 2 30
COINS (SYRACUSAN). Some obſervations on an inedited Greek coin of Philiſtis queen of Syracuſe, Malta, and Gozo, who had been paſſed over in ſilence by all the antient writers *Swinton*	LX 80	
COLD ANIMAL. See *Animal.*		
COLD (CHEMISTRY). A new frigorific experiment, ſhewing how a conſiderable degree of cold may be produced without the help of ſnow, ice, hail, wind, or nitre, and that at any time of the year - - *Boyle*	I 255	II 161
—— An account of ſome experiments relating to the production of fire and flame; together with an exploſion made by a mixture of two liquors actually cold - - *Slare*	XVIII 201	III 359
—— Obſervations upon the diſſolutions and fermentations, which we may call cold, becauſe they are accompanied with a coolneſs of the liquors into which they paſs - *Geoffroy*	XXII 951	V 421
COLD (DISEASE). Some ſuggeſtions for remedies againſt cold - *Oldenburgh*	I 379	II 639
—— Hiſtorical account of the late general coughs and colds, with ſome obſervations on other epidemical diſtempers - *Molyneux*	XVIII 105	III 271
—— Extract of a letter concerning the bark preventing catching cold - *Salter*	XLIV 1	X 762

—— Re-

[illegible] Gout.

+ Cold (Chemistry) Account of artificial cold produced at Petersburg.	Himsel.	51: 670.
Experiments relating to the cold produced by the evaporation of various fluids.	Cavallo	71: 511.
Account of experiments made by Mr McNab at Henley-house, Hudson's Bay, relating to freezing mixtures	Cavendish	76: 241.
	Beddoes	77: 282
New experiments on the production of artificial Cold. — — —	Walker 79:208	78: 395.
Experiments on the cooling of water below its freezing point. —	Blagden	78: 125.
Account of experiments made by Mr. McNab at Albany Fort, Hudsons Bay, relative to the freezing of Nitrous and Vitriolic Acids — —	Cavendish	— 166.
Experiments on the effect of various substances in lowering the point of congelation in water — — — — — — — — —	Blagden	— 277.
Observations on the best methods of producing artificial cold. — — —	Walker	1795: 270.
On the production of artificial cold by means of Muriate of Lime. — —	———	1801: 120.
On a method of freezing at a distance. —	Wollaston.	1813: 71.
Experiment on the production of cold by the evaporation of the Sulphuret of Carbon. — — — — —	Marcet.	— 252.

	Trans.	Abridg.
—— Remarks upon its effects upon the blood *Hewson*	LX 398	
COLD (Natural philosophy). Account of the experimental history of cold - *Boyle*	I 8	
—— A further account of Mr. Boyle's experimental history of cold - *Oldenburg*	— 46	
—— Promiscuous inquiries chiefly about cold; with answers to some of them by *Hevelius*	— 344	III 631
—— Tables of the barometrical altitudes at Zurich in Switzerland, in the year 1708, by Scheuchzer; and at Upminster in England, by Derham; as also the rain at Pisa in Italy, in 1707 and 1708, by Tilli; and at Zurich in 1708; and at Upminster in all that time; with remarks on the same tables; as also on the winds, heats and colds, and divers other matters occurring in those three different parts of Europe - - *Derham*	XXVI 342	
—— A contrivance to avoid the irregularities in a clock's motion, occasioned by the action of heat and cold upon the rod of a pendulum - - - *Graham*	XXXIV 40	VI 297
—— An observation of the magnetic needle being so affected by great cold, that it could not traverse - - *Middleton*	XL 310	VIII 741
—— The effects of cold; together with observations of the longitude, latitude, and declination of the magnetic needle at Prince of Wales's Fort, upon Churchill River in Hudson's Bay, North America - *Middleton*	XLII 157	— 469
—— A letter concerning a very cold day, and another concerning a very hot day, in June and July 1749 - *Miles*	XLVI 208	X 471
—— A letter concerning the difference of the degrees of cold, marked by a thermometer kept within doors, or without in the open air *Miles*	XLIV 613	— 433
—— ~~Two methods by which the irregularity of the motion of a clock, arising from the influence of heat and cold upon the rod of the pendulum, may be prevented~~ (Clock) ~~*Ellicott*~~	~~XLVII~~ 479	
—— ~~Letter concerning the inventor of the contrivance in the pendulum of a clock, to prevent the irregularities of its motion by heat and cold~~ (Clock) - - ~~*Short*~~	~~— 517~~	
—— Observations on the late severe and cold weather - - - *Arderon*	XLVIII 507	
~~—— An account of artificial cold produced at Petersburg~~ (to Cold (Chemistry) above) ~~*Himsel*~~	~~LI 670~~	

—— State

		Transf.	Abridg.
—— State of the cold at Berlin in the winter of 1762-3 - -	*Pallas*	LIII 62	
—— Account of the degree of cold obferved in Bedfordfhire, Nov. 22, 1763	*Howard*	LIV 118	
—— Some account of the late cold weather, Jan. and Feb. 1767, at London	*W. Watfon*	LVII 443	
At Plymouth -	*Anon.*	— 446	
—— A note concerning the cold of 1740 and 1768 - - -	*Bevis*	LVIII 54	
Obfervations on the fame fubject	*Short*	— 55	
—— Some remarks on the effects of cold in February 1771 -	*Richard Watfon*	LXI 213	
—— An account of the remarkable cold obferved at Glafgow in January 1768	*Wilfon*	— 326	
—— Obfervations on the intenfe cold in the months of Jan. 1767 and 1768, and Nov. 1770, at Franeker -	*Van Swinden*	LXIII 89	
—— An account of a moft extraordinary degree of cold at Glafgow in January 1780; together with fome new experiments and obfervations on the comparative temperature of hoar-froft and the air near to it, made at Glafgow	*Wilfon*	LXX 451	
—— See *Heat* and *Thermometer*.			
Colic. Letter concerning an unufual colic	*Davies*	XXII 965	V 268
—— An account of an extraordinary effect of the colic - -	*St. André*	XXX 580	— 270
—— An account of an extraordinary colic	*Huxham*	XXXVII 236	VII 517
Collision. A remark upon the new opinion relating to the forces of moving bodies, in the cafe of the collifion of non-elaftic bodies	*Eames*	XXXIV 183	VI 287
Cologne. Remarks on the ftones in the county of Naffau, and the territories of Treves and Cologne, refembling thofe of the Giant's Caufway in Ireland - -	*Trembley*	XLIX 581	
Colon. An account of part of the colon hanging out of a wound for 14 years	*Vater*	XXXI 89	VII 513
Colonies. Obfervations on the Roman colonies and ftations in Chefhire and Lancafhire	*Percival*	XLVII 216	
Colour. An effay upon the caufes of the different colours of people in different climates	*Mitchell*	XLIII 102	XI 926
Colours (Chemistry). An experiment of a way of preparing a liquor that fhall fink into and colour the whole body of marble, caufing a picture drawn on a furface to appear alfo in the inmoft parts of the ftone	*Kircher and Bird*	I 125	I 603
—— An account of the ufe of the grain kermes for colouration - -	*Verny*	— 362	II 765

+ Cold. Farther experiments on Cold, made at Glasgow. Wilson. 71: 386.
Frigorific experiments on the mechanical expansion of Air. Darwin. 78: 43.
Experiments on the cooling of Water below its freezing point. Blagden. 78: 125.
Of the influence of Cold upon the health of the Inhabitants of London. Heberden 1796: 279.

Collision. New fundamental experiments upon the collision of bodies. Smeaton. 72: 337.

	Transf.	Abridg.
—— A way of colouring fruit - *Tonge*	V 2074	II 752
—— A way of colouring leaves - *Tonge*	——	——
—— Some obſervations touching colours, in order to the increaſe of dies, and the fixation of colours - - *Liſter*	VI 2132	III 658
—— An account of an inſect feeding upon henbane; the horrid ſmell of which is in that creature ſo qualified, as to become in ſome meaſure aromatical; together with the colour yeilded by the eggs of the ſame - *Liſter*	— 2176	II 783
—— An account of an extraordinary tincture given to a ſtone - - *Reiſel*	XVI 22	I 604
—— A Latin and Engliſh catalogue of ſimple and mixed colours, with a ſpecimen of each colour fixed to its proper name - *Waller*	— 24	— 601,605
—— An experiment in which a ſurpriſing change of colour, from a pale tranſparent or clear liquor, to a very blue ceruleous one, and that in an inſtant, by the admiſſion of air only: was applied to illuſtrate ſome changes of colour, and other effects on the blood of reſpiring animals - - *Slare*	XVII 898	
—— Two letters giving an account of a red colour produced by the mixture of a ſulphureous ſpirit with a volatile alcali - *Gibbons*	XIX 542	— 214
—— To give iron the colour and tincture of copper - - - *Southwell*	XX 296	III 657
—— A way to make two clear ſpirituous inflammable liquors, which differ very little in taſte and ſmell; and being mixed together, do give a fine carnation colour, without either ſenſible fermentation or alteration *Geoffroy*	XXI 43	— 367
—— Method of colouring marbles *Anon.*	XXII 727	IV 2 205
—— An account of two obſervations in gardening, upon the change of colour in grapes and jeſſamine - - *Cane*	XXXI 102	VI 2 340
—— An account of the bones of animals being changed to a red colour by aliment only - - - *Belchier*	XXXIX 287	IX 102
—— Obſervations and experiments with madder root, which has the faculty of tinging the bones of living animals of a red colour - - - *Du-Monceau*	XLI 390	— 103
—— Obſervations of the effects which the farina of peas of different colours have on each other - - - *Henchman*	XLIII 477	

—— An

	Tranſ.	Abridg.
—— An account of a new die from the berries of a weed in South Carolina - *Lindo*	LIII 238	
—— Experiments and obſervations on the agreement between the ſpecific gravities of the ſeveral metals and their colours, when united to glaſs, as well as thoſe of their other proportions - - - *Delaval*	LV 10	
—— An account of rings conſiſting of all the priſmatic colours made by electrical exploſions on the ſurfaces of pieces of metal *Prieſtley*	LVIII 68	
—— A letter on his new phoſphorus receiving ſeveral colours, and only emitting the ſame *Beccaria*	LXI 212	
—— A letter giving ſome account of the roots uſed by the Indians in the neighbourhood of Hudſon's Bay, to dye porcupine quills *Foſter*	LXII 54	
—— Experiments on dying black - *Clegg*	LXIV 48	
—— Experiments on a new colouring ſubſtance from the iſland of Amſterdam, in the South Seas - - - *Woulfe*	LXV 91	
COLOUR (Natural philoſophy). Letter containing his new theory of light and colours *Newton*	VI 3075	I 128
—— Extracts of ſeveral letters concerning the appearance of ſeveral arches of colours contiguous to the inner edge of the common rainbow at Petworth - *Langwith*	XXXII 241	VI 122
Another letter, with ſome reflections on the ſame ſubject - *Pemberton*	— 245	— 123
—— An account of perſons who could not diſtinguiſh colours - *Huddart*	LXVII p. 1, ſ. 260	
—— See *Light*.		
COLT. Obſervations upon a monſtrous head of a colt - - - *Boyle*	I 85	
COBRA DE CABELAS PIETRA DE. See *Serpent-ſtone*.		
COLUBER CERASTES. A letter on the coluber ceraſtes, or horned viper of Egypt *Ellis*	LVI 287	
COLUMNS. An account of two giants cauſways, or groups of priſmatic baſaltine columns, and other curious volcanic concretions, in the Venetian ſtate in Italy; with ſome remarks on the characters of thoſe and other ſimilar bodies, and of the phyſical geography of the countries in which they are found *Strange*	LXV 5	
—— An account of a curious Giants Cauſway, or group of angular columns, newly diſcovered in the Euganean Hills, near Padua in Italy - - - *Strange*	— 418	
COMBINATIONS. The doctrine of combinations and		

...r (Chemistry) Some experiments and observations on the colours used in painting by the ancients. — — — Davy. 1815: 97.

A few facts relative to the colouring matters of some vegetables. Smithson. 1818: 110.

...our (Natural philosophy) on some phenomena of colours exhibited by thin plates. — — Knox. 1815: 161.

On the multiplication of images, and the colours which accompany them in some specimens of calcareous spar. Brewster. → 270.

Coloured rings. Experiments for investigating the cause of the coloured concentric rings, discovered by Sir Isaac Newton, between two objectglasses laid upon one another. Herschel. 1807: 180.
1809: 259.
1810: 149.

Combustion. Some experiments on the combustion of the Diamond and other carbonaceous substances. Davy. 1814:557

		Tranf.	Abridg.
alternations improved and compleated — — — *Thornycroft*		XXIV 1961	IV 60
COMET. The motion of the late comet predicted — — — *Auzout*		I 3	I 436
—— Letter from Rome touching the late comet, and a new one — — *Anon.*		— 17	
Letter from Paris, containing reflections on part of the letter from Rome — *Anon.*		— 18	— 346
—— The motion of the second comet predicted, by the same gentleman who predicted the former — — — *Auzout*		— 36	— 438
—— An account of Hevelius's prodromus cometicus, together with some observations upon it, by a French philosopher — *Oldenburg*		— 104	— 437
—— Of the judgment of some of the English astronomers touching the difference between two learned men, about an observation made of the first of the late two comets *English Astronomers*		— 150	——
—— Observations concerning the comet of 1668, which lately appeared in foreign parts, from Italy — — *Cassini*		III 683	— 438
From Portugal — — *Anon.*		— 684	— 439
—— An account of a new comet seen at Dantzick, March 1672 — *Hevelius*		VII 4017	——
—— Observations of a new comet made at Paris — — — *Cassini*		— 4042	— 440
Reflections on the foregoing observations *Cassini*		— 4048	
—— Observations concerning the comet that was seen in Brasil, 1668 — *Estancel*		IX 91	— 370
—— Observations of the comet of April and May 1677, made at Paris — *Cassini*		XII 868	— 443
At Dantzick — *Hevelius*		— 869	— 444
At Greenwich — *Flamstead*		— 873	— 445
—— An account of the comet of Aug. 1682, at Dantzick — — *Hevelius*		XIII 16	— 446
—— Short history of the comet of 1683, at Dantzick — — *Hevelius*		— 416	— 448
—— An extract of a letter concerning a late comet seen at Rome, June 30, 1684 *Ciampini*		XV 920	— 451
—— An account of a comet seen at Leipsick in Sept. 1686 — *Acta Eruditorum*		XVI 256	— 452
—— Observations of the situation of the new comet of Feb. 1699, at Paris *Anon.*		XXI 79	——
—— A synopsis of cometic astronomy *Halley*		XXIV 1882	IV 345
—— Observations made at Rome of the comet which appeared anno 1664 — *Ray*		XXV 2350	— 339
—— Accurate observations of the remarkable comet			

	Tranſ.	Abridg.
ſeen at the end of the year 1680, at Coburg in Saxony, 13 days before any where elſe *Kirch*	XXIX 170	IV 340
—— An account of a ſmall teleſcopical comet ſeen at London on the 10th of June 1717 *Halley*	XXX 721	— 344
—— Account of the comet ſeen at Berlin in Jan. 1718 - - *Kirch*	— 820	— 342
—— Obſervations on the comet ſeen at Berlin Jan. 18, 1718 - - *Kirch*	XXXII 238	VI 258
—— Obſervations upon the comet that appeared in the months of October, November, and December 1723 - *Bradley*	XXXIII 41	— 259
With ſome curious figures *Lord Paiſley*	— 50	— 265
Obſerved at Albano - *Bianchini*	— 51	— 266
At Liſbon - - *Carboni*	— —	— —
—— Obſervations upon the comet that appeared in October 1723, made at Bombay *Saunderſon*	XXXIV 213	— 267
—— A letter containing an account of a comet ſeen on February 29, 1731-2, from on board the Monmouth, in Table Bay - *Dove*	XXXVII 393	— —
—— A collection of obſervations relating to the comet that appeared in January, February, and March 1736-7, at Oxford *Bradley*	XL 111	VIII 210
At Rome - - *Revillas*	— 118	— 213
At Philadelphia - *Kearſley*	— 119	— 214
At Jamaica - - *Fuller*	— 122	— 215
At Madras - - *Sartorius*	— —	— —
At Liſbon - - *Vanbrugh*	— 123	
—— The parabolic orbit for the comet of 1739, obſerved at Bologna - *Zanotti*	XLI 809	— —
—— Obſervations on the comet of 1743, made at Vienna (Lat.) - *Carnabè*	XLII 457	— 216
—— Obſervations on the late comet made at Sherborn and Oxford; with the elements for computing its motions - *Betts*	XLIII 91	X 111
—— Obſervations on the comet of March 1742, by the Jeſuits at Pekin - *Hodgſon*	XLIV 264	— 116
—— Paths of 19, according to the hypotheſis which makes them, deſcribe a parabola about the ſun - - - *Struyck*	XLVI 89	— 117
—— Obſervations on the comet ſeen at Pekin, 1748 - - - *Hallerſtein*	— 305	— 124
—— Thoughts on comets - *Dunthorne*	XLVII 281	
—— Extract of a letter concerning the return of the comet expected 1757 or 1758 *Barker*	XLIX 347	
—— Obſervations on the comet of September and October 1757, at Greenwich *Bradley*	L 408	

5

—— Ob-

+ Comets. Discovery of a Comet — Pigott 74: 20.
Observations of the same Comet — — — — — ——— — 460.
Advertisement of the expected return of the Comet of 1532 and
1661 in the year 1788 — — — — — — — Maskelyne 76: 426.
An account of a new Comet — — — — — — Miss Herschel 77: 1.
Remarks on the same Comet — — — — — Dr Herschel — 4.
Observations of the same Comet — — — — — Wollaston — 55
Observations on a Comet — — — — — — — Dr Herschel 79: 151
Account of a Comet — — — — — — ———— 1792: 23.
Account of the discovery of a Comet, with observations thereon Gregory 1793: 50.
Observations of the Comet of 1793. — — — Maskelyne — 55.
Account of the discovery of a Comet — — — Miss Herschel 1794: 1.
1796: 131.
Observations of the Comet which was expected to appear last January
in its return from the Sun. Dr Herschel. 1807: 264.
Observations of a Comet, made with a view to investigate its
magnitude, and the nature of its illumination. ———— 1808: 145.
Observations of a Comet, with remarks on the construction
of its different parts. — — — Herschel. 1812. 115.
Observations of a second Comet, with remarks on its
construction — — — Herschel, 1812: 229
A new method of deducing a first approximation to the orbit
of a Comet from three geocentric observations — Ivory 1814: 121.

COMets

		Transf.	Abridg.
—— Observations on the comet of Sept. and Oct. 1757, at the Hague — *Klinkenberg*		L 483	
—— An account of the comet of May 1759 *Bevis*		LI 93	
Another account — *Munckley*		— 94	
—— Observations on the comet of Jan. 1760, at London — — *Short*		— 465	
At Cambridge — *Michell*		— 466	
At London — — *Munckley*		— 467	
At Lowick, near Thropston, Northamptonshire — — *Day*		— 469	
—— Observations of the comet seen at Paris, Feb. 1760 — — *De la Caille*		— 635	
—— An account of the comet seen at Paris in June 1762 — — *De la Lande*		LII 581	
—— Observations of the comet of May 1759, made at the Hague — — *Gabry*		LIII 3	
—— A table of the places of the comet discovered at the Observatory of the Marine at Paris, Jan. 3, 1764, about 8 o'clock in the evening, in the constellation of the Dragon, concluded from its situation with regard to the stars — — *Messier*		LIV 151	
—— A memoir, containing the history of the return of the famous comet of 1682; with observations of the same made at Paris from January to June 1759 — *Messier*		LV 294	
—— A discovery; with observations of two new comets in the Marine Observatory at Paris, March 1766 — *Messier*		LVI 57	
—— A letter giving an account of a comet seen April 9. 1766 — — *Brice*		— 66	
—— Thoughts concerning comets *Winthorp*		LVII 132	
—— Extract of two letters on a new comet observed Jan. 10, 1771, at Paris *Messier*		LXI 104	
—— A disquisition of the periodical time of the comet of 1770 — — *Lexell*		LXX 68	
COMPASS. Undertakings concerning the variation of the magnetical compass, and the inclination of the inclinatory needle, as the result and conclusion of 38 years magnetical study — — *Bond*		VIII 6065	I 587
—— A theory of the variation of the magnetical compass — — *Halley*		XIII 208	II 610
—— Letter concerning a new sort of a magnetical compass; with several curious magnetical experiments — *De la Hire*		XVI 344	— 620
—— The variation of the compass, or magnetical needle,

	Tranſ.	Abridg.
needle, in the Atlantick and Ethiopick Oceans, 1706 - - *Maxwell*	~~XXV 2433~~	
—— Some remarks on the variations of the magnetical compaſs, publiſhed in the Memoirs of the Academy of Sciences, with regard to the general chart of thoſe variations made by E. Halley; as alſo concerning the longitude of the Magellan Streights - *Halley*	~~XXIX 165~~	~~IV 453~~
—— The variation of the magnetical compaſs obſerved in a paſſage from Cape St. Lucar, in California, to the Iſle of Guan, or Guana, one of the Ladrones; with ſome remarks thereon - - - *Rogers*	~~XXXI 173~~	~~VI 2 286~~
—— A new and exact table, collected from ſeveral obſervations taken in four voyages to Hudſon's Bay from London: ſhewing the variation of the magnetical needle, or ſea compaſs, in the pathway to the ſaid bay, according to the ſeveral longitudes and latitudes, from 1721 to 1725 - - *Middleton*	~~XXXIV 73~~	~~— 297~~
—— A new and exact table collected from ſeveral obſervations taken from the year 1721 to 1729, in nine voyages to Hudſon's Bay, in North America: ſhewing the variation of the compaſs, according to the latitudes and longitudes, accounting the longitude from the meridian of London - - *Middleton*	~~XXXVII 71~~	~~— 300~~
—— The uſe of a new azimuth-compaſs for finding the variation of the compaſs, or magnetic needle, at ſea, with greater eaſe and exactneſs than by any yet contrived for that purpoſe - - *Middleton*	XL 395	VIII 374
—— A letter ſhewing, that the electricity of glaſs diſturbs the mariner's compaſs, and alſo nice balances - - *Robins*	XLIV 242	X 328
—— On the effects of lightening in deſtroying the polarity of the mariner's compaſs; to which are ſubjoined, ſome remarks by Gowin Knight - - - *Waddell*	XLVI 111	X 695
—— A deſcription of a mariner's compaſs contrived by Gowin Knight -	— 505	— 689
—— An account of ſome improvements of the mariner's compaſs, in order to render the card and needle propoſed by Dr. Knight of general uſe - - *Smeaton*	— 513	— 693
—— The variation of the compaſs; containing 1719 obſervations to, in, and from, the Eaſt Indies,		

Condensor. On a new construction of a condensor and Air-pump.

Austin. 1803 : 158.

	Transf.	Abridg.
Guinea, West Indies, and Mediterranean, with the latitudes and longitudes at the time of observations - *Douglas*	LXVI 18	
—— Tract of his majesty's armed brig Lion, from England to Davis's Streights and Labrador; with observations for determining the longitudes by sun and moon, and errors of common reckoning; also the variation of the compass and dip of the needle, as observed during the said voyage in 1776 *Pickersgill*	LXVIII 1057	
—— See Needle. Magnet		
CONCEPTION. An account of the dissection of a bitch whose cornua uteri being filled with the bones and flesh of a former conception, had, after a second conception, the ova affixed to several parts of the abdomen - *Anon.*	XIII 183	II 904
—— A letter on a false conception *Cole*	XV 1045	III 220
—— Account of the bones of a fœtus voided per anum, some years after conception *Morley*	XIX 486	
—— An account of an extra-uterine conception - - - *Myddelton*	XLIII 336	XI 1010
CONCOCTION. A short discourse concerning concoction - - *Havers*	XXI 233	III 95
CONCRETIONS (Anatomy). The figures of some very extraordinary calculous concretions found in the kidney of a woman - *Lucas*	XLIV 465	XI 1001
CONCRETIONS (Natural history). A letter concerning certain chalky tubulous concretions, called malm - - *Needham*	XLII 634	VIII 732
—— An account of two giants causways, or groups of prismatic basaltine columns, and other volcanic concretions, in the Venetian state in Italy; with some remarks on the characters of these and other similar bodies, and on the physical geography of the countries in which they are found - *Strange*	LXV 5	
CONDUCTOR. An account of the appearance of lightening on a conductor, fixed from the summit of the main-mast of a ship down to the water - - *Winn*	LX 188	
—— An account of the effects of lightening on a house which was furnished with a pointed conductor, at Tenterden in Kent; to which are added, some remarks by Mr. Henley *Haffenden*	LXV 336	
—— New experiments and observations on the nature and use of conductors *Wilson*	LXVIII 245	

—— Ex-

	Transf.	Abridg.
—— Experiments in electricity; being an attempt to shew the advantage of elevated conductors - - - *Nairne*	LXVIII 823	
—— New experiments upon the Leyden phial, respecting the termination of conductors *Wilson*	— 999	
—— See *Lightening.*		
CONES. An investigation of a general theorem for finding the length of any arc of any conic hyperbola by means of two elliptic arcs, with some other new and useful theorems deduced therefrom - - *Landen*	LXV 283	
CONFORMATION. A remarkable conformation or lusus naturæ in a child *Warwick*	XLII 152	XI 316
—— Two observations of a diseased conformation in bodies - - *Haller*	XLIV 527	— 1062
—— Diseased conformations found in bodies *Haller*	XLVI 172	
CONGELATION. Account of a sudden congelation - - - *Hollman*	XLIII 239	X 450
CONGELATION. See *Frost.*		
CONGLACIATION. See *Frost.*		
CONIC SECTIONS. Some simple properties of conic sections, deduced from the nature of focus's, &c. - - *De Moivre*	XXX 622	IV 3
—— —— The motion of projectiles near the earth's surface, considered independent of the properties of the conic sections *Simpson*	XLV 137	X 196
—— —— Some new properties in conic sections, discovered by - *Edward Waring*	LIV 193	
—— —— A disquisition concerning certain fluents which are assignable to the arc of conic sections; wherein are investigated some new and useful theorems for computing such fluents - - - *Landen*	LXI 298	
—— —— Properties of the conic sections; deduced by a compendious method *Jones*	LXIII 340	
CONJUNCTION. A short account of the three great conjunctions of Saturn, Jupiter, and Mars, at Dantzick, in 1682 and 1683 *Hevelius*	XIII 325	I 395,425
—— An astronomical dissertation on the visible conjunction of the inferior planets with the sun - - - *Halley*	XVII 511	— 427
CONNOUGH WORM. See *Worm.*		
CONSERVATORIES. Instances, hints, and applications, relating to a main point, solicited in the preface to this fourth volume; concerning the use may be made of vaults, deep wells, and cold conservatories, to find out the cause, or to		

promote

4 Conic sections. Of the rectifications of the conic sections. — — — — Kallins. 1802 : 448.

	Transf.	Abridg.
promote the generation of salt, minerals, metals, crystal; gems, stones of divers kinds; and helps to conserve long, or to hasten putrefaction, fertility of any kind of land, &c. *Beale*	IV 1135	II 363
CONSTANTINOPLE. Historical observations relating to Constantinople - *Smith*	XIII 335	III 465
—— A continuation of the historical observations relating to Constantinople - *Smith*	XIV 431	— 473
—— Journal of a voyage from London to Constantinople - - *Smith*	XIX 597	
—— See *Population.*		
CONTAGION. A discourse of the usefulness of inoculation of the horned cattle, to prevent the contagious distemper among them *Layard*	L 528	
CONSTITUTIONS. Some observations of odd constitutions of bodies - *Oldenburg*	I 138	— 10
CONTRACTION. A cure of muscular contraction by electricity - *Partington*	LXVIII 97	
CONTRAYERVA. An account of the contrayerva - - - - *Houston*	XXXVII 195	VI 2 331
CONTUSION. Account of a rupture of the ilium from an internal contusion, unattended with any external wound - *Wolfius*	XL 61	IX 160
CONVULSIONS. The history of periodical convulsions - - - *Cole*	XV 1113	III 35
—— The history of a convulsive disease returning every eight years - *Cole*	— 1115	— 36
—— An account of an unusual medicinal case of an hæmorrhage of bloody tears in convulsion fits - - - *Monginot*	XXII 756	V 355
—— Of the extraordinary effects of musk in convulsive disorders - *Wall*	XLIII 212	XI 1044
—— Case of a boy troubled with convulsive fits cured by the discharge of worms *Oram*	L 518	
———————— - *Gaze*	— 521	
———————— - *Wall*	— 836	
—— An account of some extraordinary effects arising from convulsions - *W. Watson*	— 743	
COOKERY. An account of the Moorish way of dressing their meat (with some remarks) in West Barbary, from Cape Spartel to Cape de Geer - - - - *Jones*	XXI 248	III 626
COPERNICUS. An account of a portrait of Copernicus, presented to the Royal Society by Dr. Wolf of Dantziek - *Wolf*	LXVIIp.1 f33	
COPPER. Account of the copper-mine at Herrn Ground in Hungary - *Brown*	V 1042	II 562

—— The

	Transf.	Abridg.
—— The method, manner, and order of the tranfmutation of copper into brafs, &c. *Povey*	XVII 735	II 565
—— Letters concerning feveral copper-mines, in anfwer to fome queries of Dr. Lifter *Davies*	— 737	— 563
—— The method, manner, and order of tranfmuting of copper into brafs, &c. - *Povey*	XXII 474	— 565
—— An account of an human body found in a copper-mine - - *Leyel*	XXXIII 136	VI 2 204
—— Letter concerning the copper-fprings in the county of Wicklow, in Ireland *Henry*	XLVII 500	
—— Second letter concerning the copper-fprings in the county of Wicklow, in Ireland *Henry*	XLVIII 94	
—— A letter containing experiments on the copper-fprings in Wicklow, in Ireland, and obfervations thereon - - *Bond*	— 181	
—— An account of the copper-fprings lately difcovered in Pennfylvania - *Rutty*	XLIX 648	
—— Actual fire in detonation, produced by the contact of tinfoil, with the falt compofed of copper and the nitrous acid - *Higgins*	LXIII 137	
—— A new method of affaying copper-ore *Fordyce*	LXX 30	
COPPERAS. An account of the way of making Englifh green copperas - *Colwall*	XII 1058	
CORAL. Some obfervations, on coral, large oyfters, rubies, the growing of a fort of Ficus Indica, the gods of the Ceylanefe, &c. made in Ceilan - - - *Strachan*	XXIII 1248	V 2 181
—— A defcription of fome corals, and other curious fubmarines, lately fent from the Philippine Ifles by G. J. Cameli - *Petiver*	— 1419	IV 2 286
—— Microfcopical obfervations on the pumice ftone, coral, fpunges, &c. - *Leewenhoek*	XXIV 2158	VI 2 267
—— Microfcopical obfervations on red coral - - - *Leewenhoek*	XXVI 126	V - —
—— New difcoveries relating to the hiftory of coral - - - *Donati*	XLVII 95	
—— An account of a MS treatife fent to the Royal Society, intituled, " A treatife upon coral, and feveral other productions of the fea, in order to illuftrate the natural hiftory thereof," by the Sieur de Peyffonel *W. Watfon*	— 445	
—— Letter concerning the formation of corals and corallines - - *Parfons*	— 505	
—— An account of a curious flefhy coral-like fubftance, with fome obfervations on it by Mr. John Ellis - - *Schloffer*	XLIX 449	

—— Ex-

4 Copper. Analysis of the red octaedral Copper Ore of Cornwall. Chenevix. 1801:

Analysis of a new species of Copper Ore. Thomson. 1814: 45.

	Transf.	Abridg.
—— Extract of a letter giving an account of coral, and that it is a mass of animals of the polype-kind - - *Trembley*	L 59	
—— An account of a red coral from the East Indies of a very singular kind - *Ellis*	— 188	
—— See *Polypus.*		
CORALLINE. Observations on a remarkable coralline - - - *Ellis*	XLVIII 115	
—— A letter concerning the animal life of those corallines that look like minute trees, and grow upon oysters and fucus's all around the sea-coast of this kingdom - *Ellis*	— 627	
—— Letter concerning a species of corallines *Ellis*	— 504	
—— An account of some fungitæ, and other curious coralloid fossil bodies - *Pennant*	XLIX 513	
—— Observations on corallines, and the polypus's and other sea animals living on them *Baster*	L 258	
Remarks on the above observations *Ellis*	— 280	
—— An historical memoir concerning a genus of plants, called Lichen by Micheli, Haller, and Linnæus, and comprehended by Dillenius under the terms, usnea, coralloides, and lichnoides; tending principally to illustrate their several uses - - *W. Watson*	— 652	
—— Letter on the animal nature of the genus of zoophytes called corallina - *Ellis*	LVII 404	
—— An account of the actinia sociata, or clustered animal-flower, lately found on the sea-coasts of the new-ceded islands - *Ellis*	— 428	
CORBRIDGE. See *Antiquities.*		
CORD. Part of a letter concerning the improvement of the weather-cord - *Arderon*	XLIV 169	X 453
CORK. A course of experiments to ascertain the specific buoyancy of cork in different waters; the respective weights and buoyancy of salt water and fresh water; and for determining the exact weight of human and other bodies in fluids - - - *Wilkinson*	LV 95	
COR LEONIS. An observation on an occultation of cor leonis by the moon, on Thursday, March 12, 1747, in Surrey Street in the Street, London, with a reflecting telescope, made by Mr. Short, which magnified about 100 times *Bevis*	XLIV 455	— 110
CORN. Letter concerning the smut of corn; translated from the French by T. S. *Pluche*	XLI 357	VIII 817
—— A letter with some microscopical observations on		

	Transf.	Abridg.
the farina of the red lily, and of worms discovered in smutty corn — *Needham*	XLII 634	VIII 817
—— An account of the maize, or Indian corn *Cooke*	XLVI 205	
CORNEA. Observations upon incisions of the cornea - - - *Gandolphe*	XXVI 387	V 286
—— The case of a wound in the cornea of the eye, cured by - *Thomas Baker*	XLI 135	IX 121
—— Extract of a letter concerning the particulars of the cure of a wound in the cornea, and of a laceration of the uvea in the eye of a woman - - - *Aery*	XLV 411	XI 954
—— A description of a new method of opening the cornea, in order to extract the crystalline humour - - *Sharp*	XLVIII 161	
—— A second account of a new method of opening the cornea for taking away the cataract *Sharp*	— 322	
—— See *Cataract, Couching, Eye*.		
CORNUA UTERI. An account of the dissection of a bitch, whose cornua uteri being filled with the bones and flesh of a former conception, had, after a second conception, the ova affixed to several parts of the abdomen *Anon.*	XIII 183	II 904
CORNEL. An account of the cornel caterpillar *Skelton*	XLV 281	
CORNISH DIAMONDS. An enquiry into the original state and properties of spar and sparry productions, particularly the spars or crystals found in the Cornish mines, called the Cornish diamonds - - *Borlace*	XLVI 250	X 642
CORNUA AMMONIS. A letter concerning some vertebræ of ammonitæ, or cornua ammonis *Miles*	— 37	— 641
CORNWALL. An account of some mineral observations touching the mines of Cornwall and Devon; wherein is described the art of training a load; the art and manner of digging the ore, and the way of dressing and blowing tin *Anon.*	VI 2096	II 365
—— The improvement of Cornwall by sea sand *Anon.*	X 293	— 729
—— See *Antiquities, Barrows*.		
CORONA SOLIS MARINA AMERICANA. Observations upon the corona solis marina Americana; the American sea sun-crown *Peyssonel*	L 843	
CORONOPUS. Letter concerning the use of the star of the earth, coronopus, or buck's-horn plantain in the cure of the bite of a mad dog *Steward*	XL 449	VIII 83
CORRUPTION. Divers means for preserving from corruption dead birds, intended to be sent to remote countries, so that they may arrive there in good condition. Some of the same means

A description of a process, by which corn tainted with must
y be completely purified.' – – – Hatchett. 1817.36

Corundum. On the Corundum stone from Asia. . — — — - Greville. 1798: 403.

Description of the Corundum stone, and its varieties, commonly known by the names of Oriental Ruby, Sapphire &c. Bournon. 1802: 233.

Analysis of Corundum, and of some of the substances which accompany it. Chenevix. — 327.

+ Cotes's theorem. On a remarkable application of Cotes's theorem. — — — — Herschel. 1813. 8.

		Tranf.	Abridg.
may be employed for preserving quadrupeds, reptiles, fishes, and insects *Reaumur*		XLV 309	
CORTEX ELEUTHERIÆ. An account of the quantity of resin in the cortex eleutheriæ *Brown*		XXXII 81	VII 738
CORTEX PERUVIANUS. See *Bark*.			
CORTEX WINTERANUS. An account of the true cortex winteranus, and the tree that bears it *Sloane*		XVII 922	II 666
—— —— See *Cinnamon Tree*.			
COSTERUS. See *Printing*.			
COSTIVE. An extraordinary case of a costive person, with a note, by W. Cowper *Sherman*		XXIV 2111	V 273
COTTON. Microscopical observations on the corneous fibres of a muscle, and the cortical and medullar part of the brain; as also of moxa and cotton *Leewenhoek*		XII 899	III 684
—— An extract of a letter containing microscopical observations on the seeds of cotton *Leewenhoek*		XVII 949	— 685
COUCHING. An account of some observations made by a young gentleman who was born blind, or lost his sight so early, that he had no remembrance that he had ever seen, and was couched between 13 and 14 years of age *Cheselden*		XXXV 447	VI 2 251
—— See *Cataract, Cornea, Eye*.			
COUGHS. Historical account of the late general coughs and colds, with some observations on other epidemical distempers *Molyneux*		XVIII 105	III 271
—— Letter concerning a substance coughed up resembling the vessels of the lungs *Bussiere*		XXII 545	— 68
—— An account of a polypus coughed up by the wind-pipe *Samber*		XXXIV 262	VII 503
—— A case wherein part of the lungs were coughed up *W. Watson*		XLI 623	IX 137
—— Cases of the remarkable effects of blisters in lessening the quickness of the pulse in coughs, attended with infarction of the lungs and fever *Whytt*		L 569	
COW. Letter concerning the bones of a dead fœtus taken out of the uterus of a cow *Sherman*		XXVI 450	V 54
—— An account of some trials to cure the ill taste of milk, which is occasioned by the food of cows, either from turnips, cabbages, or autumnal leaves, &c; also to sweeten stinking water *Hales*		XLIV 339	
—— See *Cattle, Distemper*.			

	Tranſ.	Abridg.
Cow (Sea). Account of the ſea cow, and the uſe made of it - *Shuldham*	XLV 249	
Crab. Some obſervations on the cancer major - - - - *Collinſon*	XLIV 70	X 864
Further obſervations - *Collinſon*	XLVII 40	
—— Letter concerning the ſhells of crabs *Parſons*	— 439	
Crabs Eyes. Letter concerning crabs eyes *King*	XXII 672	II 831
—— —— A letter concerning an extraordinary fiſh, called in Ruſſia quab, and concerning the ſtones called crabs eyes - *Baker*	XLV 174	XI 876
Crab Stones. An obſervation of the immoderate and fatal uſe of crab ſtones, and ſuch like abſorbent earths; and from whence have proceeded ſtones in the ſtomach and reins *Breynius*	XLI 557	IX 171
Crab Trees. How to multiply crab-ſtocks, and propagate trees by layers - *Tonge*	V 2074	II 752
Cramp. An account of an extraordinary cramp - - - - *Freind*	XXII 799	V 208
Crane. Some obſervations on the crane, with improvements on that machine *Deſaguliers*	XXXVI 194	
—— The deſcription of a new and ſafe crane which has four different powers, invented by *Ferguſon*	LIV 24	
Credibility, A calculation upon the credibility of human teſtimony - *Anon.*	XXI 359	III 662
Crispina. See *Coin.*		
Crocus Autumnalis Sativus. See *Saffron.*		
Crocodiles. An account of lacerta (crocodilus) ventre marſupio donato, faucibus merganſeris roſtrum æmulantibus - *Edwards*	XLIX 639	
Croton Spicatum. A deſcription and figure of the croton ſpicatum, a new ſpecies of plant from America - - *Bergius*	LVIII 132	
Crounian Lectures. See *Muſcles.*		
Croyland. See *Shrine.*		
Crural Artery. See *Artery.*		
Crust. Of hydatides incloſed with a ſtony cruſt in the kidney of a ſheep - *Cowper*	XXV 2304	V 54
Crystal. An obſervation of optick glaſſes made of rock-cryſtal - - *Divini*	I 362	I 195
—— Account of ſundry experiments made upon a cryſtal-like body ſent from Iſland *Bartholin*	V 2039	
—— Reflections concerning the formation of cryſtals - - - *Lane*	VII 4068	II 465
—— Of the origin of white vitriol, and the figure of its cryſtals, not yet accounted for *Liſter*	XXI 331	— 537
— A letter containing ſome microſcopical obſerva-		

tions

Cretinism. Some account of Cretinism. – – – – – – – – – – 1808: 111.

4 Crystal. On the oblique refraction of Iceland Crystal. — — — Wollaston. 1802: 381.

On the primitive crystals of Carbonate of Lime, Bitter spar, and Iron-spar. — — — — — — Wollaston. 1812: [illegible]

On the elementary particles of certain Crystals. Wollaston 1813: 51[illegible]

On the effects of simple pressure in producing that species of Crystallization which forms two oppositely polarised images and exhibits the complementary colours by polarised light. — — Brewster. 1815 [illegible]

On the communication of the structure of doubly refracting crystals to glass, Muriate of Soda, Fluor spar, and other substances, by mechanical compression and dilatation — — 1816.

	Tranſ.	Abridg.
tions upon the cryſtallized particles of ſilver diſſolved in aquafortis - *Leewenhoek*	XXVII 20	V 2 267
—— A deſcription of ſome rare cryſtals lately diſcovered - - *Scheuczer*	XXXIV 260	VI 2 226
—— An account of perfect minute cryſtal ſtones - - - *Parſons*	XLIII 468	X 612
—— An enquiry into the original ſtate and properties of ſpar and ſparry productions, particularly the ſpars or cryſtals found in the Corniſh mines, called the Corniſh diamonds - - - *Borlace*	XLVI 250	— 642
—— An account of the double refractions in cryſtals - - - *Beccaria*	LII 486	
—— An attempt to account for the formation of ſpars and cryſtals - *King*	LVII 58	
—— On the cryſtallizations obſerved on glaſs *Keir*	LXVI 530	
CRYSTALLINE. Letter concerning the icy and cryſtalline mountain of Helvetia, called the Gletſcher - - *Muraltus*	IV 982	II 465
—— A farther deſcription and repreſentation of the icy mountain called the Gletſcher, in the canton of Berne, in Helvetia - *Juſtel*	VIII 6191	— —
CRYSTALLINE HUMOURS. An extract of a letter containing microſcopical obſervations on cryſtalline humours - *Leewenhoek*	XVII 949	III 685
—— A deſcription of a new method of opening the cornea, in order to extract the cryſtalline humour - - *Sharp*	XLVIII 161	
CUBE. Of the weight of a cubic foot of divers grain - *Phil. Soc. at Oxford*	XV 926	I 522
Further liſt of ſpecific gravities of bodies *ibid.*	— 927	— 523
—— Cubic and biquadratic equation conſtructed by a parabola and circle - *Halley*	XVI 335	— 63
—— The ſpecific gravity of ſeveral metalline cubes, in compariſon with their like bulks of water - - *Hauksbee*	XXVII 521	
—— A method of extending Cardan's rule for reſolving one caſe of a cubick equation $x^3 - qx = r$ to the other caſe of the ſame equation, which it is not naturally fitted to ſolve, and which is therefore called the irreducible caſe - - - *Maſeres*	LXVIII 902	
- - - *Maſeres*	LXX 85	
—— Of cubic equations and infinite ſeries *Hutton*	— 387	
CUCKOW. A deſcription of a new ſpecies of cuckow - - - *Sparrman*	LXVII p. 1. fol. 38.	

	Tranf.	Abridg.
—— A defcription of the cuculus lævis ceruleo flavefcens cui in fupremo Branchiarum opercula; or the yellow gurnard - *Tyfon*	XXIV 1749	IV 2 181
CUNTUR. An account of a prodigious large feather of the bird cuntur, brought from Chili, and fuppofed to be a kind of vultur *Sloane*	XVIII 61	II 860
CUP. An attempt to explain an antient Greek infcription engraven upon a curious bronze cup with two handles, and publifhed with a draught of the cup by Dr. Pocock, in his defcription of the Eaft, vol. II. part II. page 207 *Ward*	XLVI 488	XI 1278
CUPPING. A farther account of fome experiments of injecting claret, &c. into the abdomen after cupping - - *Warrick*	XLIX 485	
CUPPING-GLASSES. On the application of an air-pump to cupping-glaffes - *Luffkin*	XXI 287	III 265
—— —— Letter concerning the application of the pneumatick engine to cupping-glaffes *Luffkin*	— 408	— —
CURE. An extraordinary cure of a horfe that was ftaked into his ftomach - *Wallis*	XIX 118	
—— An abftract of a remarkable cafe and cure of a woman from whom a fœtus was extracted, which had been lodged in one of the fallopian tubes thirteen years - *Mounfey*	XLV 131	XI 1202
CURIOSITIES. Account of fome natural ones from New England - *Winthrop*	V 1151	II 832–3 III 564
—— Extract of two letters from Rome, concerning fome ftatues, pictures, and other curiofities, found in a fubterraneous town lately difcovered near Naples - - *Paderni*	XLI 484	IX 440
Extract of another letter on the fame fubject - - - *Knapton*	— 489	— 442
Extract of another letter on the fame fubject - - - *Crifpe*	— 493	— 444
CURRANTS. An extract of a letter containing microfcopical obfervations on currants *Leewenhoek*	XVII 949	— 685
—— Some obfervations concerning the virtue of the jelly of black currants in curing inflammations in the throat - - *Baker*	XLI 655	VIII 838
CURRENT. An account of the current of the tides about the Orcades - *Anon.*	VIII 6139	II 290
—— A conjecture about an under-current at the Streights mouth - *Thomas Smith*	XIV 564	— 288
—— Of the currents at the Streights mouth *Anon.*	XXXIII 191	VI 2 171
—— Obfervations upon the currents of the fea at the Antilles of America - *Peyffonel*	XLIX 624	
Mediterranean - *Peyffonel*	— 634	

+ ~~Cuckoo. Observations on the natural history of the Cuckoo.~~ ~~Jenner~~ ~~77:~~ ~~216~~

+ Cuckoo. Observations on the natural history of the Cuckoo. Jenner. 78: 219

Current. Observations on ~~the~~ a Current, that often prevails to the Westward of Scilly, endangering the safety of Ships that approach the British Channel. Rennell. 1793:182.

Some further observations on the current that often prevails to the westward of the Scilly islands. ——— 1815:182.

		Transf.	Abridg.
Bizerty in Barbary, 1724 -	*Peyssonel*	XLIX 635	
Marseilles - -	*Peyssonel*	— 637	
Bonne (called also Hipone) in Barbary	*Peyssonel*	— 638	
CURVE. Short and easy method of drawing tangents to all geometrical curves, without any labour of calculation - -	*Slusius*	VII 5143	I 18
—— Easy way of demonstrating his method of drawing tangents to all sorts of curves, without any labour of calculation -	*Slusius*	VIII 6059	— 21
—— Analytic investigation of the curve of quickest descent - -	*Sault*	XX 425	— 463
—— Some easy methods for the measuring of curve-lined figures, plain and solid	*Wallis*	XXII 547	— 58
—— The method of squaring any kind of curves, or reducing them to more simple curves	*De Moivre*	XXIII 1113	IV 15
—— Of the tangents of curves deduced immediately from the theory of Maxima and Minima - - -	*Ditton*	— 1333	— 7
—— The curve assigned by Cassini to the planets as their orbit, considered and rejected	*Gregory*	XXIV 1704	— 206
—— On the length of curve lines -	*Craig*	XXVI 64	— 43
—— A ready description and quadrature of a curve of the third order, resembling that commonly called the foliate -	*De Moivre*	XXIX 329	— 24
—— Treatise on the construction and measure of curves - -	*Maclaurin*	XXX 803	— 51
—— A new universal method of describing all curves of every order, by the help only of given angles and right lines -	*Maclaurin*	— 939	— 57
—— The general quadrature of trinomial hyperbolic curves contained in two theorems	*Klingerstein*	XXXVII 45	VI 82
—— A general method of describing curves by the intersection of right lines; moving about points in a given plane -	*Brakenridge*	XXXIX 25	VIII 58
—— A letter concerning the description of curve lines - -	*Maclaurin*	— 143	
—— An abstract of what has been printed since the year 1721, as a supplement to a treatise concerning the description of curve lines published in 1719, and of what the author proposes to add to that supplement -	*Maclaurin*	— 148	
—— Of the cardoide curve, so called from its figure - - -	*Castilioneus*	XLI 778	— 108
—— A general investigation of the nature of the curve, formed by the shadow of a prolate spheroid, upon a plane standing at right angles to the axis of the shadow -	*Witchell*	LVII 28	

Solutio problematis de curvis inveniendis quæ quadam ratione in situ inverso disposita se intersecare possunt in angulo dato. XXXII. 106 VI. 85.

		Tranſ.	Abridg.
—— A ſpecimen of a new method of comparing curvilineal areas; by which many ſuch areas may be compared, as have not yet appeared to be comparable by any other method	*Landen*	LVIII 174	
—— Some new theorems for computing the areas of certain curved lines -	*Landen*	LX 441	
—— Directions for making the beſt compoſition for the metals of reflecting teleſcopes; together with a deſcription of the proceſs for grinding, poliſhing, and giving the great ſpeculum the true parabolic curve -	*Mudge*	LXVII 296	
CUSANUS. See *Cycloid.*			
CUSTOMS. Extracts of ſome letters on the cuſtoms, manners and language of the northern Indians of America - -	*Johnſon*	LXIII 142	
CUTICULA. Microſcopical obſervations concerning the cuticula -	*Leewenhoek*	IX 121	III 683
—— Microſcopical obſervations about the cuticula - - -	*Leewenhoek*	XIV 568	— 684
CUTICULAR GLOVE. See *Skin.*			
CUTTING, MARGARET. See *Speech, Tongue.*			
CYANUS. Account of the Cyanus foliis radicalibus partim integris, partim pinnatis, bractea calycis ovali, flore ſulphureo -	*Haller*	XLIII 94	X 702
CYCLE. A method for finding the number of the Julian period for any year aſſigned; the number of the cycle of the ſun; the cycle of the moon, and of the indictions for the ſame year being given; together with a demonſtration of that method - -	*Collins*	II 568	III 399
CYCLOID. A demonſtration of the ſynchroniſm of the vibrations made in a cycloid	*Anon.*	VIII 6032	I 462
—— Letter aſſerting the firſt invention and demonſtration of the equality of the curve line of a paraboloid to a ſtrait line to Mr. Wm. Neile; and next the finding a ſtrait line equal to that of a cycloid, and of the parts thereof to Sir Chriſtopher Wren -	*Wallis*	— 6146	— 116
Another letter to the ſame purpoſe	*Lord Brounker*	— 6149	— —
Another - -	*Wren*	— 6150	— —
—— Letter concerning the ſpaces in the cycloid, which are perfectly quadrable	*Wallis*	XVIII 111	— —
—— Letter concerning the cycloid known to cardinal Cuſanus about the year 1450, and to Carolus Bovillus about 1500 -	*Wallis*	XIX 561	— —
CYDER. Of an excellent liquor made with cyder-apples and mulberries -	*Colepreſs*	II 502	

—— Some

+ Curves. Methodus inveniendi lineas Curvas ex proprietatibus variationis Curvaturæ,
Landerbeck 73:456. 74:477.

	Transf.	Abridg.
—— Some communications concerning cyder *Reed*	VI 2128	II 656
—— Some considerations of what choice of apples for the delicacy of the liquor in peculiar seasons; and for easy and speedy propagation: pears for some lands proper; their choice for manifold uses, especially for pleasant, or for lasting liquor; and how to be planted or ordered to the best advantage - *Beal*	— 2144	— 653
—— An account of some improvements which may be made in cyder and perry - *Miles*	XLIII 516	
CYGNUS. A figure of the stars in the constellation of Cygnus; together with the new star in it, discovered some years since, and very lately seen by M. Hevelius again - *Hevelius*	I 372	I 453
—— See *Swan*.		
CYLINDERS. The best proportions for steam-engine cylinders of a given content considered *Blake*	XLVII 197	
CYLINDROID. The generation of an hyperbolical cylindroid demonstrated, and the application thereof for grinding hyperbolical glasses, hinted at - - *Wren*	IV 961	— 188
CYPRUS. A letter concerning the Cyprus of the antients - - *Garcin*	XLV 564	X 741
CYSTIS. Case of a large quantity of matter or water contained in cystis's or bags adhering to the peritonæum, and not communicating with the cavity of the abdomen - *Graham*	XLI 708	IX 187
—— An account of an extraordinary cystis in the liver, full of water - *Jernegan*	XLIII 305	XI 971

D.

	Transf.	Abridg.
DALMATIA. Observations on travels from Venice, through Istria, Dalmatia, Greece, and the Archipelago to Smyrna - *Vernon*	XI 573	
DAMPIER'S POWDER. The effects of Dampier's powder in curing the bite of a mad dog *Fuller*	XL 272	IX 224
Another case drawn up by - - - *Hartley and Sandys*	— 274	— 224
DAMPS (In mines, pits, &c.) A relation of persons killed with subterraneous damps *Moray*	I 44	II 373
—— Letter concerning the damps in the mines of Hungary, and their effects *Browne*	IV 965	— —
—— Extract of a letter containing some observations about damps - - *Lister*	X 391	— 375

	Tranſ.	Abridg.
—— A letter containing a farther account of damps in mines - - *Jeſſop*	X 450	II 376
—— Obſervations on a ſubterranean fire in a coal mine near Newcaſtle - *Hodgſon*	XI 762	— 383
—— A relation of ſome ſtrange phænomena, accompanied with miſchievous effects in a cole-work in Flintſhire - *Moſtyn*	XII 895	— 378
—— An account of the burning of ſeveral hay-ricks by a fiery exhalation or damp: and of the infectious quality of the graſs of ſeveral grounds - - - *Floyd*	XVIII 49	— 181
—— Farther account of the fiery exhalation in Merionydhſhire - - *Lhwyd*	— 223	— 180
—— An attempt made to ſhew how damps or foul air may be drawn out of any ſort of mines, &c. by an engine - *Deſaguliers*	XXXV 353	VI 2 193
—— A brief account of ſome of the effects and properties of damps, from obſervations of the effects of opening an old well at Boſton in New England, July 19, 1729 *Greenwood*	XXXVI 184	— - 195
—— An account of the damp air in a coal-pit of Sir James Lowther, Bart. ſunk within 20 yards of the ſea - - *Lowther*	XXXVIII 109	VIII 656
—— An experiment to ſhew that ſome damps in mines may be occaſioned only by the burning of candles under ground, without the addition of any noxious vapour, even when the bottom of the pit has a communication with the outward air, unleſs the outward air be forcibly driven in at the ſaid communication or pipe - - *Deſaguliers*	XXXIX 281	
—— An obſervation of an extraordinary damp in a well in the Iſle of Wight - *Cooke*	XL 379	— 658
—— See *Flame.*		
DANTZICK. A relation of an inland ſea near Dantzick, yeilding at a certain ſeaſon of the year a green ſubſtance, which cauſeth certain death - - - *Kirkby*	VII 4069	II 491
DARIEN. Part of a journal kept from Scotland to New Caledonia in Darien, with a ſhort account of that country - *Wallace*	XXII 536	III 561
DARKNESS. An account of a remarkable darkneſs at Detroit in America, Oct. 19, 1762 *Stirling*	LIII 63	
DATE. An account of an antient mantle-tree in Northamptonſhire, on which the date of it (for the year 1133) is expreſſed by the nume-		

On the means of procuring a steady light in coal-mines without the danger of explosion — — Clanny. 1813: 200.

On the fire-damp of coal mines, and on methods of lighting the mines so as to prevent explosion. — — Davy. 1816: 1

An account of an invention for giving light in explosive mixtures of fire-damp in coal mines, by consuming the fire-damp. ——— ——— 23.

Further experiments on the combustion of explosive mixtures confined by wire-gauze, with some observations on flame. ——— ——— 115.

Some new experiments and observations on the combustion of gaseous mixtures, with an account of a method of preserving a continued light in mixtures of inflammable gases and air without flame. ——— 1817: 77.

		Transf.	Abridg.
ral figures, which shews the great antiquity of those figures in England - *Wallis*		XIII 399	I 107
—— Extract of a letter concerning an antient date found at Widge Hall in Hertfordshire *Cope*		XXXIX 119	IX 420
Remarks on the above date *Ward*		— 120	— 421
Further account of it - *Gulston*		— 122	
—— Remarks upon an antient date, over a gateway, near the cathedral at Worcester *Ward*		— 136	
—— An account of an antient date in Arabian figures, upon the north front of the parish church of Rumsey in Hampshire *Barlow*		XLI 652	— 432
—— A brief inquiry into the reading of two dates in Arabian figures cut upon stones, which were found in Ireland - *Ward*		XLIII 283	XI 1260
—— A description of an antient date in Arabian figures at Walling, near Aldermanston, Berkshire - - *Ward*		XLV 603	— 1267
DATE-STONES. An extract of a letter containing microscopical observations on date stones - - - *Leewenhoek*		XLII 949	III 685
DAVENPORT (ANN). The case of Ann Davenport - - - *Fynney*		LXVII 458	
DAVIS's QUADRANT. A description of a water-level to be fixed to Davis's quadrant, whereby an observation may be taken at sea in thick and hazy weather without seeing the horizon - - - *Leigh*		XL 413	VIII 360
DAVIS's STREIGHTS. Track of his majesty's armed brig Lion, from England to Davis's Straights and Labrador; with observations for determining the longitude by sun and moon, and error of common reckoning: also the variation of the compass and dip of the needle, as observed during the said voyage in 1776 - - - *Pickersgill*		LXVIII 1057	
DAY. Letter proposing a new place for the first meridian, and pretending to evince the equality of all natural days; as also to shew a way of knowing the true place of the moon *Anon.*		X 425	I 270
Answered by - *Flamstead*		— 429	— —
—— A letter concerning a very cold day, and another a very hot day, in June and July 1749 - - - *Miles*		XLVI 208	X 471
DEAD BODIES. A letter concerning the body of a woman found in a morass in the Isle of Axholm in Lincolnshire - *Stovin*		XLIV 571	XI 1326

	Transf.	Abridg.
—— —— An account of the dead bodies of a man and woman who were preſerved 49 years in the Moors in Derbyſhire - *Balguy*	XXXVIII 413	VIII 706
—— —— Extract of ſeveral letters concerning a body found in a vault in the church of Staverton in Devonſhire, intire, after being buried upwards of 80 years *Huxham and Tripe*	XLVII 253	
—— —— Some account of a body lately found in uncommon preſervation under the ruins of the abbey at St. Edmundſbury, Suffolk; with ſome reflections upon the ſubject *Collignon*	LXII 465	
Dead Sea. Experiments by way of analyſis upon the water of the dead ſea, upon the hot ſprings near Tiberiades, and upon Hammon Pharoan water - - *Perry*	XLII 48	— 645
Deafness. An account of an experiment concerning deafneſs - - *Holder*	III 665	III 42
—— Method of inſtructing perſons deaf and dumb - - - *Wallis*	XX 353	— 393
—— An account of a young lady born deaf and dumb taught to ſpeak - *Ellis*	XXIII 1416	V 2 134
—— An account of two deaf perſons who can ſpeak and underſtand one another by the motion of the lips - - *Waller*	XXV 2468	— 219
—— A relation of a deaf and dumb perſon who recovered his hearing and ſpeech after a violent fever: with ſome other medical and chirurgical obſervations - *Martin*	— 2469	— 357
—— A method propoſed to reſtore the hearing, when injured from an obſtruction of the tuba euſtachiana - - *Wathen*	XLIV 213	
—— Upon the ſound and hearing of fiſhes by Jac. Theod. Klein; or ſome account of a treatiſe intitled, An enquiry into the reaſons why the author of an epiſtle concerning the hearing of fiſhes, endeavours to prove they are all mute and deaf - - *Brockleſby*	XLV 233	XI 883
—— See *Speech*.		
Deal Rod. The deſcription of an hygrometer made of a deal rod - *Arderon*	XLIV 184	X 757
Dean. An account of the iron works in the foreſt of Dean - - *Powle*	XII 931	II 558
Deaths. Some obſervations on the motion of diſeaſes, and on the births and deaths of men, and other animals, in different times of the Νυχθήμερον - - *Paſchall*	XVII 815	III 311
—— An account of the opening of the body of a		

boy

Dead Sea. An analysis of the waters of the Dead Sea and the River Jordan.
Marcet. 1807: 296.

*Deafness. Account of an operation for the removal of a particular species of Deafness.
Cooper. 1801: 435.

		Tranſ.	Abridg.
boy who died ſuddenly, and what obſervable was found therein - *Preſton*		XIX 362	III 32
—— Obſervations on the death of a dog, on firing a volley of ſmall ſhot - *Clarke*		— 779	— 650
—— Obſervations on a caſe publiſhed in the laſt volume of the Medical Eſſays, &c. of recovering a man dead in appearance, by diſtending the lungs with air - *Fothergill*		XLIII 275	XI 969
—— An extract of an Italian treatiſe written by Joſ. Bianchini, upon the death of the counteſs Cornelia Zangari and Bandi of Ceſena. To which are ſubjoined, an account of the death of Io Hitchell, who was burned to death by lightening; and of Grace Pett at Ipſwich, whoſe body was conſumed to a coal *Rolli*		— 447	— 1068
—— On the digeſtion of the ſtomach after death - - - *John Hunter*		LXII 447	
—— See *Diſſection*.			
DEATH WATCH. An account of the death-watch - - - *Allen*		XX 376	II 785
—— —— Letter concerning the inſect which is commonly called the death-watch *Derham*		XXII 832	V 27
—— —— A ſupplement to the account of the pediculus pulſatorius, or death-watch; ſerving to the more perfect natural hiſtory of that inſect - - - *Derham*		XXIV 1586	— 8
—— —— An account of the ſcarabæus galeatus pulſator, or the death-watch *Stackhouſe*		XXXIII 159	VII 407
DECIMAL. See *Fractions*.			
DECLINATION. Some remarks upon the method of obſerving the differences of right aſcenſion and declination by croſs hairs in a teleſcope *Halley*		XXXI 113	VI 165
—— Deſcription of a method of meaſuring differences of right aſcenſion and declination with Dollond's micrometer; together with other new applications of the ſame *Maſkelyne*		LXI 536	
DEER. A diſcourſe concerning the large horns frequently found under ground in Ireland; concluding from them, that the great American deer, called a mooſe, was formerly common in that iſland - *Molyneux*		XIX 489	II 432
—— Method of catching fowl and deer in the iſland of Ceilan - - *Strachan*		XXIII 1094	V 2 179
—— A deſcription of the mooſe deer of New England - - *Dudley*		XXXI 65	
- - - *Dale*		XXXIX 384	IX 84
—— Ac-			

	Transf.	Abridg.
—— Account of the horn of a large deer found in the heart of an oak - *Clark*	XLI 235	VIII 847
—— An account of two extraordinary deers horns, found under ground in different parts of Yorkshire - - *Knowlton*	XLIV 124	X 601
DEGREE. Letter concerning a place in New York for measuring a degree of latitude *Alexander*	XLI 383	
—— Proposal of a method for measuring degrees of longitude upon parallels of the æquator *Mitchell*	LVI 119	
—— Letter containing a short account of the measurement of three degrees of latitude under the meridian of Vienna - *Liesganig*	LVIII 15	
—— Introduction to the following observations made by Ch. Mason and Jer. Dixon, for determining the length of a degree of latitude in the provinces of Maryland and Pennsylvania, in North America - *Maskelyne*	— 270	-
Observations, &c. *Mason and Dixon*	— 274	
Length of a degree of latitude in the provinces of Maryland and Pennsylvania, deduced from the observations of Mess. Mason and Dixon - - - *Maskelyne*	— 323	
—— Kepler's method of computing the moon's parallaxes in solar eclipses, demonstrated and extended to all degrees of the moon's latitude; as also to the assigning the moon's correspondent apparent diameter: together with a concise application of this form of calculation to those eclipses - - *Pemberton*	LXI 437	
DELGOVICIA. Extract of a letter concerning the situation of the antient town Delgovitia - - - *Knowlton*	XLIV 100	XI 1245
—— A dissertation on the situation of the antient Roman station of Delgovitia in Yorkshire - - - *Burton*	— 541	— 1246
DELIRIUM. Account of one who had no ear to music naturally, singing several tunes when in a delirium - - *Doddridge*	— 596	X 1084
—— Case of the efficacy of bark in the delirium of a fever - - *Munckley*	L 609	
DELUGE. Some considerations about the cause of the universal deluge - *Halley*	XXXIII 118	VI 2 1
Some further thoughts on the same *Halley*	— 123	— - 4
—— An extract of a philosophical account of a new opinion concerning the origin of petrefactions found in the earth, which has hitherto been		

ascribed

Delphinus gangeticus. & description of its teeth. Home. 1818: 417.

Denmark. The latitudes and longitudes of several places in Denmark, calculated from the trigonometrical operations. Bugge 1794: 43.

+ Density. Experiments to determine the density of the earth. Cavendish 1798: 469.

+ Derbyshire denudation. An account of the great Derbyshire denudation. — — — — — — — — Farey. 1811.

On a new detonating compound. Davy. 1813.

Detonating substance. Some further observations on a detonating substance. — .... — Davy. 1813.

	Tranf.	Abridg.
ascribed to the universal deluge, by Lazzaro Moro Antonio - *Ehrhart*	XLIV 163	X 615
—— An attempt to account for the universal deluge - - - *King*	LVII 44	

DENARIUS. See *Coin*.

DENMARK. Remarks in a late journey into Denmark and Holland - *Oliver*	XXIII 1400	V 2 128
DENSITY. An account of an experiment touching the different densities of common water from the greatest degrees of heat in our climate, to the freezing point observed by a thermometer - - - *Haukſbee*	XXVI 267	VI 2 181
—— An enquiry concerning the figure of such planets as revolve about an axis, supposing the density continually to vary from the center to the surface - *Clairaut*	XL 277	VIII 90
—— An essay on the connection between the parallaxes of the sun and moon; their densities, and their disturbing motions on the ocean - - - *Murdock*	LVIII 24	
—— An account of the calculations made from the survey and measures taken at Schehallien, in order to ascertain the mean density of the earth - - - *Hutton*	LXVIII 689	

—— See *Air*.

DENTARIA HEPTAPHYLOS. An account of aphyllon and dentaria heptaphylos of Clusius, omitted by Mr. Ray - *W. Watson*	XLVII 428	

DESCARTES. See *Equations*.

DETONATION. Actual fire and detonation produced by the contact of tin-foil with the salt composed of copper and the nitrous acid *Higgins*	LXIII 137	
DETROIT. An account of a remarkable darkness at Detroit in America, Oct. 19, 1762 *Stirling*	LIII 63	

DEVIZES. See *Antiquities*.

DEVON. An account of some mineral observations touching the mines of Cornwall and Devon; whereby is described the art of training a load, the art and manner of digging the ore, and the way of dressing and blowing the tin *Anon.*	VI 2096	II 565
DEW. Account of an extraordinary meteor, or kind of dew like butter, that fell in Ireland *Van Bp. of Cloyne*	XIX 224	—
—— A relation of observations concerning the falling dew, made at Medioburg in Zeland by Leonard Stocke, upon an open lead plain of the astronomical turrit of John Munk, in the		

night

	Transf.	Abridg.
night between the 25th and 26th of July 1741; with figures of the flocks of snow observed at the same place, Jan. 1742 (Lat.) *Stocke*	XLII 112	VIII 502
DIAGONALS. A letter gratulatory to M. Hevelius for his organographia, and particularly concerning divisions by diagonals - *Wallis*	IX 243	
DIAMETERS. A way for taking the diameters of planets - - *Auzout*	I 373	I 194
—— A way for knowing the parallax of the moon; as also why, in the solar eclipse of July 2. 1666, the diameter of the moon did increase about the end - *Auzout*	— —	— 217
—— A letter touching the invention of dividing a foot into many thousand parts, for mathematical purposes - - *Townley*	II 457	— 218
More ways for the same purpose *Hook*	— 459	— 220
A description of the instrument for dividing a foot into many thousand parts, and thereby measuring the diameters of planets to great exactness - - *Townley*	— 541	— 219
—— Kepler's method of computing the moon's parallaxes in solar eclipses, demonstrated and extended to all degrees of the moon's latitude, as also to the assigning the moon's correspondent diameter; together with a concise application of this form of calculation to those eclipses - - - *Pemberton*	LXI 437	
—— A new and general method of finding simple and quickly-converging series; by which the proportion of the diameter of a circle to its circumference may easily be computed to a great number of places of figures *Hutton*	LXVI 476	
DIAMONDS. A note about some unusual diamonds *Anon.*	IX 26	II 187
—— A description of the diamond mines - - *Earl Marshal of England*	XII 907	— 467
—— Experiments of the luminous qualities of amber, diamonds, and gum-lac *Wall*	XXVI 69	IV 2 275
—— Microscopical observations on the configuration of diamonds - *Leewenhoek*	— 479	V 2 267
—— A letter concerning diamonds lately found in Brazil - - *Sarmento*	XXXVII 199	IV 2 182
—— A letter concerning the specific gravity of diamonds - - *Ellicott*	XLIII 468	X 612
—— An enquiry into the original state and properties of spar and sparry productions, particularly the spars or crystals found in the Cornish mines, called the Cornish diamonds *Borlace*	XLVI 250	— 642
— On the particles and structure of adamant Leeuwenhoeck	XXXII 199	VI 2 226
— On the nature of the Diamond. Tennant. 1797: 123.		
— On the cutting Diamond. Allen & Pepys. 1807: 267. Wollaston. 1816: 265.		

DIAbetes mellitus. On the non-existence of sugar in the blood of persons labouring under Diabetes mellitus. — Wollaston. 1811: 96.

[illegible] See Ships.

4 Differential. On the integration of certain differential expressions, with which problems in physical astronomy are connected. Woodhouse. 1804: 219.

Two general propositions [illegible] method of differences. Knight. 1817: 234.

[illegible]

Dip. A method of measuring the Dip at sea. - - - - - - Wollaston. 1803: 9.

		Tranſ.	Abridg.
DIAPHRAGM. Of the ſtructure of the midriff - - -	*Leewenhoek*	XXXII 400	VII 687
—— A letter concerning two poſthumous letters of Ant. à Leewenhoek, relating to the diaphragm - - -	*Hoogvlietius*	— 435	
—— On the palpitation of the diaphragm - - -	*Leewenhoek*	— 436	— 562
—— Hiſtory of a ſplit one in a child of ten months old, accompanied with part of the inteſtines being thrown into the thorax	*Fothergill*	XLIV 11	XI 1078
DIARIES. See *Meteorological.*			
DIFFERENTIAL. A letter concerning the diſpute about the invention of the method of fluxions, or differential method; with M. Leibnitz, his anſwer - -	*Conti*	XXX 923	IV 162
—— The Newtonian differential method illuſtrated 4 - - -	*Stirling*	— 1050	— 141
DIGESTION. Obſervations on theſe three chemical operations, digeſtion, fermentation, and triture or grinding (hitherto in the author's opinion not ſufficiently regarded) by which many things of admirable uſe may be performed - - -	*Langelot*	VII 5052	III 315
—— Obſervations about digeſtion, and the motion of the blood in a fever -	*Leewenhoek*	XIII 347	— 684
—— A diſcourſe concerning digeſtion	*Leigh*	XIV 694	— 94
—— Experiments relating to digeſtion	*Muſgrave*	— 699	— 93
—— On the digeſtion of the ſtomach after death - - -	*John Hunter*	LXII 447	
DIOPTRICK PROBLEM. Why four convex glaſſes in a teleſcope ſhew objects erect	*Molyneux*	XVI 169	I 189
DIPPING NEEDLE. See ~~Needle.~~ Magnet (Inclination) pag. 293.			
DISEASES. Obſervation on a human body dead of odd diſeaſes - -	*Fairfax*	II 546	III 76
—— An account of the diſeaſes of dogs, and ſeveral receipts for the cure of their madneſs, and of thoſe bitten by them: extracted from the papers of Sir T. Mayerne, by - -	*Sir Theodore de Vaux*	XVI 408	II 870 III 283
—— Some obſervations on the motion of diſeaſes, and on the births and deaths of men and other animals, in the different times of the Νυχθήμερον - - -	*Paſchall*	XVII 815	— 311
—— An account of a very large diſeaſed kidney found on the diſſection of a body; with the ſymptoms of the diſeaſe before death, and an explanation of the phænomena	*Cooper*	XIX 301	— 143

	Transf.	Abridg.
—— Part of a letter giving an account of several magnetical experiments; and of one who pretended to cure or cause diseases, by applying a sympathetick powder to the urine - - - *Leeuwenhoek*	XIX 512	III 685
—— Particular observations upon different maladies - - - *Gailhard*	— 717	— 288
—— Of the diseases and remedies incident to northern countries - *Lloyd*	XXI 311	— 606
—— An attempt to prove the antiquity of the venereal disease long before the discovery of the West Indies - - *Beckett*	XXX 839	IV 329
—— A letter concerning the antiquity of the venereal disease - - *Beckett*	XXXI 47	VII 652
—— A letter to Dr. Halley in answer to some objections made to the history and antiquity of the venereal disease - *Beckett*	— 108	— 663
—— An extract from the books of the town council of Edinburgh, relating to a disease there, supposed to be venereal, in the year 1497 *Macky*	XLII 420	IX 213
—— A short account of the disease of which Joseph Bolognini died (Lat.) - *De Camillis*	XLIII 40	XI 1059
—— Two observations of a diseased conformation in bodies - - *Haller*	XLIV 527	— 1062
—— Diseased conformation found in dead bodies - - - *Haller*	XLVI 172	
—— Two singular cases of diseased knee-joints successfully treated; the first by topical applications, the second by operation *Warner*	XLIX 452	
—— A further account of the effects of electricity in the cure of some diseases - *Brydone*	L 695	
—— An account of a cure of a diseased eye *Layard*	— 747	
—— Extract of a letter relating to an extraordinary agitation of the sea at Barbadoes, Mar. 31, 1761, and an epidemical disorder in that island - - - *Mason*	LII 477	
—— An account of an extraordinary disease among the Indians in the island of Nantucket, and Martha's vineyard in New England *Oliver*	LIV 386	
—— An account of the disease called Ergot in French, from its supposed cause, viz. vitiated rye - - - *Tissot*	LV 106	
—— Observations on the population and diseases of Chester, in the year 1774 - *Haygarth*	LXVIII 131	

—— See *Distemper* and *Epidemy.*

DISEASED CATTLE. See *Cattle, Distemper.*

DISSECTION OF ANIMALS. An account of the dis-

		Tranf.	Abridg.
——— section of a porpus; with some observations omitted by Rondeletius - *Ray*		VI 2274	II 839
——— Observations on the dissection of a rat *R. W.*		XVII 594	
——— Observations on the dissection of a paroquet - - - *Waller*		XVIII 153	— 855
——— An account of the dissection of a dog who had mercury injected into one of the jugulars *Pitt*		XX 184	III 234
——— Some observations made on an ostrich dissected by order of Sir Hans Sloane - *Ranby*		XXXIII 223	VII 435
——— Observations upon the dissection of an ostrich - - - *Warren*		XXXIV 113	— 437
——— Some material observations upon dissecting an ostrich - - *Ranby*		XXXVI 275	— —
——— A letter concerning a cluster of small teeth observed at the root of each fang, or great tooth in the head of a rattle-snake, upon dissecting it - - *Bartram*		XLI 358	IX 60
DISSECTION (Of human bodies). An account of an egg found in the tuba fallopiana of a woman lately dissected; with several remarks touching generation - - *Buissiere*		XVIII 11	III 211
——— Relation of an extraordinary child of six years old, who in face, &c. was as large as a full-grown woman; and of what appeared on the dissection of the body - *Sampson*		XIX 80	— 20
——— An account of a very large diseased kidney found on the dissection of a lady; with the symptoms of the disease before her death, and an explanation of their phænomena *Cowper*		— 301	— 143
——— An anatomical account of some remarkable things found on the dissection of a woman who died of a dropsy, after the paracentesis was performed; with a small reflection on the causes of dropsies - - *Preston*		— 330	— 141
——— A relation of a strange symptom attending a hydrops pectoris, and the reason of it, as it appeared on the dissection of the body *Doudy*		— 390	— 77
——— Dissection of a woman who died in child-bed - - - *Silvestre*		XXII 787	V 303
——— Some uncommon observations on the dissection of morbid bodies - *Vaughan*		XXIII 1244	— 261
——— An account of a dropsical body dissected by - - - *Lafage*		XXIV 1977	— 291
——— A letter giving an account of some anatomical observations made on a body dissected at Padua, by Mr. John Ray - *Dale*		XXV 2282	— 184

	Trans.	Abridg.
—— An account of the diſſection of a perſon who died of an ulcer in the right kidney *Douglas*	XXVII 32	V 257
—— An account of what appeared on the diſſection of Mr. Dove - *Cowper*	— 512	— 325
—— An account of the diſſection of a child *Blair*	XXX 631	— 275
—— Some obſervations made in the diſſection of three ſubjects - - *Ranby*	XXXV 413	VII 560
Dissolution. Obſervations upon the diſſolutions and fermentations which we may call cold, becauſe they are accompanied with a coolneſs of the liquors into which they paſs *Geoffroy*	XXII 951	V 421
Distances. Inſtance to Mr. Hook, for communicating a contrivance of making, with a glaſs of a ſphere of 20 or 40 foot diameter, a teleſcope drawing ſeveral hundred feet: and his offer of recompenſing that ſecret with another, teaching to meaſure with a teleſcope the diſtances of objects upon the earth *Auzout*	I 123	
—— Of the correſpondence to be procured for the finding out the true diſtance of the ſun and moon from the earth by the parallax, obſerved under or near the ſame meridian *Oldenburg*	— 151	I 300
—— A true copy of a paper found in the hand-writing of Sir Iſaac Newton among the papers of Dr. Halley, deſcribing an inſtrument for obſerving the moon's diſtance from the fixed ſtars at ſea - -	XLII 155	VIII 129
—— Some experiments in order to diſcover the height to which rockets may be made to aſcend, and to what diſtance their light may be ſeen *Ellicott*	XLVI 578	X 202
—— A letter containing the reſults of obſervations of the diſtance of the moon from the ſun and fixed ſtars, made in a voyage from England to the iſland of St. Helena, in order to determine the longitude of the ſhip from time to time; together with the whole proceſs of computation uſed on this occaſion *Maſkelyne*	LII 558	
—— Of the moon's diſtance and parallax *Murdock*	LIV 29	
—— Conciſe rules for computing the effects of refraction and parallax, in varying the apparent diſtance of the moon from the ſun or a ſtar: alſo an eaſy rule of approximation for computing the diſtance of the moon from a ſtar; the longitudes and latitudes of both being given, with demonſtrations of the ſame *Maſkelyne*	— 263	
—— A method by which a glaſs of a ſmall plano-convex ſphere, may be made to refract the rays		

Distances. A catalogue of north polar distances of some of the principal fixed stars. — — — — — — — Pond. 1813:75

Catalogue of north polar distances of 84 principal fixed stars, deduced from observations made with the mural circle at the Royal Observatory. — — — — — — 280

Determination of the north polar distances and proper motion of 30 fixed stars. — — — — 1815:33

Distilling. On the means of producing a double distillation by the same heat. Tennant. 1814:587

	Tranf.	Abridg.
of light to a focus of a far greater diftance than is ufual - - *Hook*	I 202	I 193
DISTEMPERS. Hiftorical account of the late general coughs and colds; with fome obfervations on other epidemic diftempers - *Molyneux*	XVIII 105	III 271
DISTEMPERS (Amongft cattle). An account of a murraine in Switzerland, and the method of its cure - - *Wincler*	XIII 93	II 869
Further confirmation - *Slare*	— 94	— 870
—— A differtation concerning the dreadful contagious diftempers feizing the black cattle in the Venetian territories, and efpecially about Padua - - *Ramazzini*	XXIX 46	V 183
A receipt for the above diftemper	— 50	
—— A brief account of the contagious difeafe which raged among the milch cows near London, 1714, and of the methods that were taken for fuppreffing it - - *Bates*	XXX 872	— 48
—— An account of the diftemper raging among the cow-kind in the neighbourhood of London; together with fome remarks propofed for their recovery - - *Mortimer*	XLIII 532	XI 916
Further obfervations - *Mortimer*	— 549	— 917
—— A third account of the diftemper among the cows - - *Mortimer*	XLIV 4	— 921
—— Concerning the burying of cows, dead of the diftemper, in lime or not - *Milner*	— 224	— 925
—— A difcourfe of the ufefulnefs of inoculation of the horned-cattle to prevent the contagious diftemper among them - *Layard*	L 528	
—— Letters relative to the diftemper among the horned-cattle - *Layard*	LXX 536	
DISTILLING. A letter concerning a new contrivance of applying receivers to retorts in diftillation - - - *Langrifh*	XLIII 254	XI 1225
—— An account of the great benefit of blowing fhowers of frefh air up through diftilling liquors - - *Hales*	XLIX 312	
—— Experiments on applying the Rev. Dr. Hales' method of diftilling falt-water to the fteam-engine - - *Fitzgerald*	L 53	
—— Experiments on the diftillation of acids, volatile alkalies, &c. fhewing how they may be condenfed without lofs, and how thereby we may avoid noxious and difagreeable fumes *Woulfe*	LVII 517	
—— See *Water*.		
DIVIDING. A letter touching the invention of divid-		

ing

	Transf.	Abridg.
ing a foot into many thoufand parts, for mathematical purpofes - *Townley*	II 457	I 218
More ways for the fame purpofe *Hook*	— 459	— 220
† A defcription of an inftrument for dividing a foot into many thoufand parts, and thereby meafuring the diameters of planets to great exactnefs - - *Anon.* (see Division, below)	— 541	— 219
DIVING. A table fhewing to what degree air is compreffible in fea-water from the depth of one foot to 1947 feet; ufeful to divers *Anon.*	VI 2192	II 201
A fupplement - - *Anon.*	— 2239	— 202
—— The art of living under water: or, a difcourfe concerning the means of furnifhing air at the bottom of the fea, in any ordinary depths - - - *Halley*	XXIX 492	IV 2 188
—— A letter concerning an improvement of the diving-bell - - *Triewald*	XXXIX 377	VIII 634
DIVISIBILITY. Some theorems refpecting the infinite divifibility of matter - *Keill*	XXIX 82	IV 423
DIVISION. A letter gratulatory to M. Hevelius for his organographia, and particularly concerning divifions by diagonals - *Wallis* (See Dividing, above. See Astronomical Instruments)	IX 243	
—— Propofitions felected from a paper on the divifion of right lines, furfaces and folids *Glenie*	LXVI 73	
DOG IN GENERAL. An account of an eafier and fafer way of transfufing blood, viz. by the veins only - - *King*	II 441	
—— An experiment of bleeding a mangy into a found dog - - *Coxe*	— 451	III 229
—— Letter touching the transfufion of blood *Denis*	— 453	— —
—— Of making a dog draw his breath like a broken-winded horfe; with obfervations *Lower*	— 544	— 65
—— Obfervations on the death of a dog on firing a volley of fmall fhot - *Clarke*	XIX 779	— 650
—— An account of what happened on fyringing warm water into the thorax of a bitch - - - *Mufgrave*	XX 181	— 78
—— An account of the diffection of a dog who had mercury injected into one of the jugulars *Pitt*	— 184	— 234
—— Letter concerning a polypus found in a dog - - - *Mufgrave*	XXII 690	— 85
—— Obfervations on part of the inteftine of a dog fuccefsfully cut away - *Shipton*	XXIII 1299	V 275
—— A letter giving an account of two women being poifoned by the fimple-diftilled water of laurel-leaves, and of feveral experiments upon dogs;		

Dividing. An account of a method of dividing Astronomical and other Instruments by ocular inspection.

Troughton. 1809: 105.

On an improvement in the manner of dividing Astronomical instruments. Cavendish. — 221.

On a method of examining the divisions of Astronomical instruments. Lax. — 232.

Dog. (Natural history) Observations tending to shew that the Wolf, Jackal and Dog, are all of the same species. Hunter 77: 253. 79: 160.

	Tranſ.	Abridg.
by which it appears that this laurel-water is the moſt dangerous poiſon hitherto known - - - *Madden*	XXXVII 85	VI 2 374
—— Some experiments concerning the poiſonous quality of the ſimple-diſtilled water from the Lauro-ceraſus, or common laurel, made upon dogs at Topping Hall, Eſſex, 1731; and others made before the Royal Society in their repoſitory - - *Mortimer*	— 163	— — —
Dog (Mad). Relation of a man bitten with a mad dog, and dying of the diſeaſe called hydrophobia - - *Liſter*	XIII 162	II 276
—— —— A receipt to cure mad dogs, or men or beaſts, bitten by mad dogs *Gourdon*	XVI 298	III 283
—— —— An account of the diſeaſes of dogs, and ſeveral receipts for the cure of their madneſs, and of thoſe bitten by them; extracted from the papers of Sir T. Mayerne, by - - *Sir Theodore de Vaux*	— 408	III 283
—— —— On the venomous bite of a mad dog - - - *Anon.*	XVIII 24	— 281
—— —— Letter concerning the cure of the bitings of mad creatures; with a remark on the ſame by Hans Sloane - *Dampier*	XX 49	— 284
—— —— An obſervation of two boys bit by a mad dog - - *Liſter*	— 247	
—— —— Letter concerning the bitings of mad dogs, &c. - - *De la Pryme*	XXIII 1073	IV 2 218
—— —— A letter containing ſome experiments made upon mad dogs with mercury *James*	XXXIX 244	IX 218
—— —— Remarks on the cure of the bite of a mad dog - - *Mortimer*	— 313	— 221
—— —— The caſe of a lad bitten by a mad dog - - - *Nourſe*	XL 5	— 222
—— —— The effects of Dampier's powder in curing the bite of a mad dog - *Fuller*	— 272	— 224
Another caſe drawn up by *Hartley and Sandys*	— 274	— —
—— —— Letter concerning the virtues of the ſtar of the earth, coronopus, or buck's-horn plantain, in the cure of the bite of a mad dog - - - *Steward*	— 449	VIII 83
—— —— Caſe of a perſon bit by a mad dog *Peters*	XLIII 257	
—— —— An account of a horſe bit by a mad dog - - - *Starr*	XLVI 474	XI 913
—— —— An account of an hydrophobia *Wilbraham*	XLVII 412	
Dog Mercury. Part of a letter concerning the		

ſtrange

	Transf.	Abridg.
ftrange effects from the eating dog-mercury; with remarks thereon by Hans Sloane *Baxter*	XVII 875	II 640
DOVE (MR.) An account of what appeared on the diffection of the body of Mr. Dove *Cowper*	XXVII 512	V 325
DOVER. Letter relating to that ifthmus, or neck of land, which is fuppofed to have joined England and France in former times, where now is the paffage between Dover and Calais *Wallis*	XXII 967	IV 2 227
DRAGON-FLY. Some obfervations on the dragon-fly, or libella of Pennfylvania *Bartram*	XLVI 323	XI 845
DRAWING. A new way of orthographically delineating by parallel vifual rays the poftures and actions of an human body, exactly obferving the fymmetry and proportion of the parts - - - *Saint-Clare*	VIII 6079	I 599
—— The principal properties of the engine for turning ovals in wood or metal, and of the inftrument for drawing ovals upon paper demonftrated - - *Ludlam*	LXX 378	
DREAM. The cafe of Henry Axford, who recovered the ufe of his tongue, after having been four years dumb, by means of a frightful dream - - - *Squire*	XLV 148	XI 958
DRILLS. Concerning the magnetifm of drills *Ballard*	XX 417	
DRINK. An account of a woman in the fhire of Rofs, living without food or drink *Mackenfie*	LXVII 1	
DROPSY. An account of a notable cafe of a dropfy, miftaken for gravidation in a young woman; enlarging the obfervations of the fame cafe by Dr. Tulpius - - *Anon.*	IX 131	III 139
—— Anatomical obfervations in the body of a woman about 50 years of age, who died hydropical in her left tefticle - *Sampfon*	XII 1000	— 206
—— An account of an uncommon cafe of a dropfy between the coats of the womb *Anon.*	XVIII 20	— 205
—— An anatomical account of fome remarkable things found on the diffection of a woman, who died of a dropfy, after the paracentefis was performed; with a fmall reflection on the caufes of the dropfy - *Prefton*	XIX 330	— 141
—— A relation of a ftrange fymptom attending a hydrops pectoris, and the reafon of it, as it appeared on the diffection of the body *Doudy*	— 390	— 77
—— An obfervation concerning a very odd kind of dropfy, or fwelling in one of the ovaries of a woman - - *Sloane*	XXI 150	— 207

—— An

+Drawing. Sketches and descriptions of three instruments for drawing Architecture and Machinery in Perspective. Peacock. 75:366.

+ Dropsy. An extraordinary case of a Dropsy of the Ovarium. Martineau. 74:471.

	Trans.	Abridg.
—— An account of a dropsical body dissected by - - - *Lafage*	XXIV 1977	V 291
—— An account of an hydrops ovarii, with a new and exact figure of the glandulæ renales, and of the uterus in a puerpera *Douglas*	XXV 2317	— 294
—— A relation of an hydropical case, in which the gall-bladder was distended to an unusual bigness - - *Yonge*	XXVII 426	— 292
—— An account of a dropsy in the left ovary of a woman, aged 58, cured by a large incision made in the side of the abdomen *Houstoun*	XXXIII 8	VII 541
—— A remarkable case of a gentlewoman who died of an hydrops ovarii in the 33d year of her age, after having been tapped 57 times *Belchier*	XXXVII 279	— 544
—— The case of Mr. Cox, surgeon, of Peterborough, who fell into a pestilential fever, upon tapping a corpse lately dead of an hydropsy - - - *Cox*	XLI 168	IX 212
—— The case of an extraordinary dropsy *Short*	XLII 223	— 150
—— An improvement on the practice of tapping, whereby that operation, instead of a relief for symptoms, becomes an absolute cure for an ascites; exemplified in the case of Jane Roman - - *Warrick*	XLIII 12	XI 1030
—— A method of conveying liquors into the abdomen during the operation of tapping *Hales*	— 20	
—— Further accounts of the success of injecting medicated liquors into the abdomen, in the case of an ascites - *Warren*	— 47	
—— Account of an uncommon dropsy from the want of a kidney; and a large saccus that contained the water - - *Glass*	XLIV 337	— 1027
—— An account of some cases of dropsies cured by sweet oil - - *Oliver*	XLIX 46	
—— An account of a successful operation for the hydrops pectoris - *Moreland*	LVI 302	
—— An account of an extraordinary dropsical case - - - *Latham*	LXIX 54	
DROPSY. See *Hydrocephalus.* See *Injections.*		
DROWNING. A comparison of the times wherein animals may be killed by drowning, or with drawing the air - - *Boyle*	V 2028	II 490
—— Relation of a girl three years old, who remained a quarter of an hour under water without drowning - - *Green*	XLI 166	IX 241
—— Proposals for the recovery of people apparently drowned - *John Hunter*	LXVI 412	

	Tranf.	Abridg.
Drugs. An account of part of a collection of curious plants and drugs lately given to the Royal Society by the East India Company; with their names, virtues, and descriptions *Sloane*	XXII 759	II 752
First book of East India plants by S. Brown; with some remarks by - *J. Petiver*	— 581	
Second book, with remarks, by *J. Petiver*	— 699	— —
Third book, with remarks, by *J. Petiver*	— 843	V 2 325
Fourth book, with remarks, by *J. Petiver*	— 9, 2	V 183
Fifth book, with remarks, by *J. Petiver*	— 1007	V 2 325
Sixth book, with remarks, by *J. Petiver*	XXIII 1055	— — —
Seventh book, with remarks, by *J. Petiver*	— 1251	— — —
Eighth book, with remarks, by *J. Petiver*	— 1450	
—— Observations on the class of sweet tastes, made by comparing the tastes of sweet plants with Mr. L'Emery's chymical analysis of them in his treatise of drugs - *Floyer*	— 1160	V 406
Dryness. Observations on the annual evaporation at Liverpool, in Lancashire, and on evaporation, considered as a test of the moisture or dryness of the atmosphere - *Dobson*	LXVII 244	
Dublin. An account of the houses and hearths in Dublin, in 1695 and 1696 - *Anon.*	XXII 518	III 665
Ducks. Observations made about the lasting of ducks, included in the exhausted receiver - - - *Boyle*	V 2011	II 215
Duckweed. A letter concerning animalcula on the roots of duckweed, &c. - *Leewenhoek*	XXIV 1784	V 2 267
—— A letter concerning some further microscopical observations on the animalcula found upon duckweed - *Leewenhoek*	XXVIII 160	— — —
Ducts. A new discovery of the communication of the ductus thoracicus with the emulgent vein - - - *Pecquet*	II 461	III 258
—— A letter concerning the jaundice; occasioned by a stone obstructing the ductus communis bilarius, which was afterwards voided by stool - - - *Musgrave*	XXV 2233	V 279
—— Annotations upon a discovery pretended to have been made by M. Pecquet, of a communication between the ductus thoracicus and the inferior vena cava - *Needham*	VII 5007	III 259
—— Observations on the salival duct *Bartholini*	XIV 749	— 58
—— An account of two glands, and their excretory ducts, lately discovered in human bodies - - - *Cowper*	XXI 364	— 194

	Tran.	Abridg.
—— An account of an excretory duct from the glandula renalis - - *Valſa'va*	XXXIII 190	VII 540
—— An enquiry into a diſcovery ſaid to have been made by Signor Valſalva, of an excretory duct from the glandula renalis to the epididymis - - *Ranby*	— 270	— 541
—— Account of an oſſification of the thoracic duct - - - *Cheſton*	LXX 323	
Continuation of the caſe of James Jones *Cheſton*	— 578	
DUDLEY FOSSIL. Letter concerning a non-deſcript petrified inſect - *Lyttleton*	XLVI 598	X 656
Further account of the before-mentioned Dudley foſſil - - *Pococke*	— 600	— —
A letter concerning the foſſil found at Dudley, in Staffordſhire - - *Da Coſta*	XLVIII 286	
DULWICH. An account of a new purging ſpring diſcovered at Dulwich in Surrey *Martyn*	XLI 835	VIII 653
DUMB. See *Deaf.*		
DUNBAR. An account of a production of nature at Dunbar in Scotland, like that of the Giants Cauſeway in Ireland *Biſhop of Oſſory*	LII 98	
DUNMORE PARK. A letter containing an account of the cavern in Dunmore Park, near Kilkenny in Ireland - - *Walker*	LXIII 16	
DURA MATER. An anatomical experiment made to diſcover the true cauſe of the motion of the dura mater - - *Ridley*	XXIII 1480	V 201
DURHAM. See *Antiquities, Inſcription.*		
DUST. An account of an earthquake felt at Glaſgow and Dumbarton Dec. 30, 1755; alſo of a ſhower of duſt falling on a ſhip between Shetland and Iceland - *Whytt*	XLIX 509	
DWARF. An account of a dwarf; together with a compariſon of its dimenſions with thoſe of a child under four years of age *Baker*	XLVI 467	XI 1207
—— Letter concerning a dwarf *Browning*	XLVII 278	
DYAL. Account of F. Lynus's dyals at Liege *Ellis*	XXIII 1416	V 2 134
—— An inſtrument for ſeeing the ſun, moon, and ſtars, paſs the meridian of any place: uſeful for ſetting watches in all parts of the world with the greateſt exactneſs; to correct ſun-dyals, and to aſſiſt in the diſcovery of the longitude of places - *Derham*	XXIV 1578	IV 464
—— A new method of conſtructing ſun-dyals for any given latitude, without the aſſiſtance of dialing-ſcales or logarithmic calculations *Ferguſon*	LVII 389	
DYING. See *Colours.*		

	Tranf.	Abridg.
DYNAMICS. Principia dynamica five principia mechanices metaphysica - *Jurin*	XLIV 103	X 183
DYSENTERY. Extract of a letter containing some remarks upon the dysentery in 1762 *W. Watson*	LII 646	

E.

	Tranf.	Abridg.
EAGLES. Letter on the Roman eagles *Musgrave*	XX 145	
EAR. Letter concerning the organ of hearing *Vieussens*	XXI 370	III 43
——— Part of a letter concerning some things observable in the anatomy of a human ear *Adams*	XXV 2414	V 206
——— A description of the organ of hearing in the elephant, with the figures and situation of the ossicles, labyrinth, and cochlea, in the ear of that animal - - *Blair*	XXX 885	— 82
——— A description of some instruments for the ears *Cleland*	XLI 847	IX 124
——— Account of one who had no ear to music naturally, singing several tunes when in a delirium - - - *Doddridge*	XLIV 596	XI 1084
——— An account of the case of a boy who had the malleus of each ear, and one of the incus's, dropt out - - *Morant*	LII 264	
EARTH (AGRICULTURE). Advertisements occasioned by the remarks printed in No. XIV. upon frosts in some parts of Scotland, differing in their anniversary seasons and force from our ordinary frosts in England: of black winds and tempests, of the warm and fertilizing temperature and steams of the earth, stones, rocks, springs, waters (some in some places more than others in other places), of petrifying and metallizing waters; with some hints for the horticulture of Scotland - *Beal*	X 337	
EARTH. Speculations of the changes likely to be discovered in the earth and moon by their respective inhabitants - *Auzout*	I 120	I 198
——— Instance to Mr. Hook for communicating a contrivance of making, with a glass of a sphere of 20 or 40 feet diameter, a telescope drawing several hundred feet; and his offer of recompensing that secret with another, teaching to measure with a telescope the distances of objects from the earth - *Auzout*	— 122	
——— Of the correspondency to be procured for the finding out the true distance of the sun and moon from the earth, by the parallax observed under or near the same meridian *Oldenburg*	— 151	— 300

Ear. On the structure and uses of the membrana tympani of the Ear. Home. 1800 : 1.

Observations on the effects which take place from the destruction of the membrana tympani of the Ear. Cooper. —— 151.

1801 : 435.

Earth.

Astronomical observations on the rotation of the Planets round their Axes, made with a view to determine whether the Earth's diurnal motion is perfectly equable.

Herschel 71:115.

		Transf.	Abridg.
—— An account of a controverfy between Stephano de Angelis of Padua and J. B. Riccioli, concerning the motion of the earth	*Gregory*	III 693	
—— Extract of a letter touching Hugens' thoughts of Mr. Hooke's obfervations for proving the motion of the earth -	*Hugens*	IX 90	
Extract of a letter on the faid fubject	*Caffini*	— —	
—— A breviate of Mr. Picart's account of the meafure of the earth -	*Oldenburg*	X 261	— 587
—— An account of the caufe of the change of the variation of the magnetical needle; with an hypothefis of the ftructure of the internal parts of the earth - -	*Halley*	XVII 563	II 615
—— A differtation concerning the figure of the earth - -	*Defaguliers*	XXXIII 201	VI 2 250
—— The differtation concerning the figure of the earth continued -	*Defaguliers*	— 239	
—— A differtation concerning the figure of the earth, part II. -	*Defaguliers*	— 277	VI 384
—— An experiment to illuftrate what has been faid concerning the figure of the earth	*Defaguliers*	— 344	— 400
—— A phyfical hiftory of the earth and air for the year 1732 - -	*Cyrillus*	XXXVIII 184	VIII 625
—— Of the figure of the earth, and the variation of gravity on the furface -	*Stirling*	XXXIX 98	— 324
—— Obfervations on an eclipfe of the earth, May 3, 1734 - -	*De Revillas*	— 294	— 138
—— Inveftigations to prove, that the figure of the earth nearly approaches to an ellipfe, according to the laws of attraction in an inverfe ratio of the fquare of the diftances	*Clairauet*	XL 19	— 329
—— A propofal for the meafurement of the earth in Ruffia; read at a meeting of the Academy of Sciences of St. Peterfbourg, Jan. 21, 1737, by -	*Mr. Jof. Nic. de l'Ifle*	— 27	— 339
—— Letter containing the actual menfuration of the bafis - -	*De l'Ifle*	— 50	— 351
—— An account of a machine to reprefent eclipfes of the earth - -	*Segner*	XLI 781	X 157
—— A new and particular method of calculating eclipfes of the earth; and of any appulfes of the moon to planets and fixed ftars	*Gerften*	XLIII 22	
—— The motion of projectiles near the earth's furface, confidered independent of the properties of the conic fections -	*Simpfon*	XLV 137	— 196
—— Some obfervations on Norwood's meafure of the figure of the earth -	*De la Lande*	LII 369	

—— An

		Tranf.	Abridg.
—— An account of the calculations made from the furvey and meafures taken at Schehallien, in order to afcertain the mean denfity of the earth - - -	*Hutton*	LXVIII 689	
EARTH (Natural philofophy). The defcription of a well and earth in Lancafhire taking fire by a candle approached to it -	*Shirley*	II 482	III 149
—— An account of a ftrange kind of earth taken up near Smyrna, of which is made foap; together with the way of making it	*Smith*	XIX 228	II 457
—— An account of a very odd eruption of fire out of a fpot of earth near Fierenzola in Italy	*St. Clair*	XX 378	— 385
—— A defcription of the feveral ftrata of earths, ftone, coals, &c. found in a coal-pit at the weft end of Dudley, Staffordfhire: to which is added, a table of the fpecifick gravity of each ftratum -	*Fettiplace and Haukfbee*	XXVII 541	IV 2 182
—— A letter giving an account of a very uncommon finking of the earth, near Folkeftone in Kent - - - See Grounds	*Sachetti*	XXIX 469	— 2 248
—— An account of the feveral ftrata of earths and foffils found in finking the mineral wells at Holt - -	*Lewis*	XXXV 489	VI 2 225
—— An extract of a philofophical account of a new opinion concerning the origin of petrifactions found in the earth, which has hitherto been afcribed to the univerfal deluge	*Ehrhart*	XLIV 163	X 615
—— An account of an uncommon phænomenon in Dorfetfhire, of flame arifing out of the earth - - -	*Stephens*	LII 119	
EARTH (MEDICINE). An obfervation of the immoderate and fatal ufe of crab-ftones, and fuch like abforbent earths, from whence have proceeded ftones in the ftomach and kidnies	*Breynius*	XLI 557	IX 171
EARTHEN-WARE. A method of making a gold-coloured glazing for earthen-ware	*Heinfius*	XLII 188	IX 499
EARTHQUAKES (Nature and caufes). Of the nature of earthquakes; more particularly of the origin of the matter of them, from the pyrites alone - - -	*Lifter*	XIV 512	II 420
—— On the caufes of earthquakes	*Stukeley*	XLVI 641	
Continued - -	*Stukeley*	— 657	X 529
—— Some confiderations on the caufes of earthquakes - - -	*Hales*	— 669	— 535
—— Conjectures concerning the caufe and obfervations upon the phænomena of earthquakes	*Michell*	LI 566	

—— The

Earths (Chemistry) Observations on the affinities which the earths have been supposed to have for each other, in the humid way. Chenevix. 1802:327.

Electro-chemical researches on the decomposition of the Earths; with observations on the metals obtained from the alkaline Earths. Davy. 1808:333

	Transf.	Abridg.
—— The philosophy of earthquakes *Stukeley*	XLVI 731	X 541
EARTHQUAKE (Particular). A relation concerning the earthquake near Oxford, Jan, 19, 1665 *Wallis*	I 166	II 395
A confirmation of the former account, and the concomitants thereof - *Boyle*	— 179	— —
—— An account of the earthquake at Oxford, and the parts adjacent, Sept. 17, 1683 *Pigot*	XIII 311	- 396,400
—— A letter with an account of the late earthquake in Sicily - - *Hartop*	XVII 827	— —
Another account from an Italian paper of - - - *P. Ales Burgos*	— 830	— 401
—— An account of the earthquakes in Sicilia on Jan. 9 and 11, 1692-3 - *Bonajutus*	XVIII 2	— 406
—— A letter with an account of the earthquakes in Peru, Oct. 20, 1687; and at Jamaica, Feb. 19, 1687-8, and June 7, 1692 *Sloane*	— 78	
—— An account of the earthquake at Lima, Oct. 20, 1687 - *Alvarez de Toledo*	— 81	— 410
—— A relation of the bad condition of the mountains about the Tungarouse, and Batavian Rivers having their source from thence, occasioned by the earthquake between the 4th and 5th of Jan. 1699: drawn up from the account given by Tommagon Porbo Nata (who hath been there). - - - - *Tommagon*	XXII 595	— 419
—— Part of two letters concerning an earthquake, which happened in some places of the north of England Dec. 28, 1703 - - *Thoresby*	XXIV 1555	IV 2 210
—— A letter concerning a shock of an earthquake felt in the neighbourhood of Sutton, near Dartford in Kent, August 1727 *Barrel*	XXXV 305	VI 2 200
—— Part of a letter giving an account of the late earthquake at Boston in New England, Oct. 29, 1727 - - *Colman*	XXXVI 124	— - 201
—— The history of the earthquake felt at Apulia, and almost all the kingdom of Naples, 1731 - - - *Cyrillus*	XXXVIII 79	VIII 682
—— A letter containing an account of an earthquake at Annapolis in Maryland, Sept. 5, 1725 *Lewis*	— 119	— 685
—— An account of the several earthquakes which have happened in New England since the first settlement of the English in that country, especially of the last, which happened in Oct. 29, 1727 - - *Dudley*	XXXIX 63	— —
—— An account of a shock of an earthquake felt in Sussex Oct. 25, 1734 *Duke of Richmond*	— 361	— 690
Another account at Havant *Bayley*	— 362	— —

		Transf.	Abridg.
—— Account of an earthquake in Northamptonshire, October 1731 - -	*Wasse*	XXXIX 361, 367	VIII 692
—— Account of an earthquake at Naples	*Temple*	XLI 340	— 684
—— An account of an earthquake at Scarborough - - -	*Johnson*	— 804	IX 502
—— A journal of the shocks of earthquakes felt in New England, from the year 1727 to the year 1741 - -	*Plant*	XLII 33	VIII 693
—— Account of the earthquakes felt at Leghorn Jan. 1742; with some observations	*Pedini*	— 77	— 697
—— A letter concerning the earthquake at Taunton - - -	*Foster*	XLV 398	X 488
—— Account of an earthquake Feb. 8, 1749-50, felt at London - -	*Baker*	XLVI 601	— 489
- - -	*Knight*	— 603	— 490
At Eltham -	*Freeman*	— 605	— 491
Tooting - -	*Miles*	— 607	— 492
Chelsea - -	*Martyn*	— 609	— 493
Harwich - -	*Trembley*	— 610	— 493
Danbury in Essex -	*Lethieullier*	— 611	— 478
Plymouth -	*Barlow*	— 692	
- - -	*Vanbrugh*	— 693	
- - -	*Slade*	— 694	
—— An account of an earthquake March 8, 1749-50, at London - -	*Folkes*	— 613	— 494, 495
- - -	*Birch*	— 615	— 496
- - -	*Baker*	— 617	— —
Tooting - -	*Miles*	— 619	
Kensington Gravel Pitts -	*Clare*	— 620	— 497
London - -	*Layard*	— 621	— —
London - -	*Pickering*	— 622	— 498
As seen in the Inner Temple garden by Robert Shaw - -	*Burrow*	— 626	— 499
A more full account from Tooting	*Miles*	— 628	— 500
Chelsea - -	*Martyn*	— 630	— 501
London - -	*Russel*	— 631	— —
London - -	*Parsons*	— 633	— 502
Southwark - -	*Burrow*	— 637	— 503
London - -	*Mortimer*	— 638	— 504
Addition to his former accounts from Tooting - - -	*Miles*	— 639	— —
London - -	*Cooper*	— 647	— 505
Kensington; given by Tho. Burrat	*Folkes*	— 681	
Account of the roof of a pot-house at Lambeth being thrown down by the earthquake - - -	*Jackson*	— 700	— 507

—— Ac-

		Tranf.	Abridg.
—— Account of an earthquake March 18 and 19, 1749-50, at Portfmouth -	*Oakes*	XLVI 646	X 507
Another account from Portfmouth	*Anon.*	— 647	— 505
Portfmouth - -	*Taylor*	— 649	— 507
Ifle of Wight - -	*Cooke*	— 651	— 508
Southampton - -	*Anon.*	— 652	— 508
Hackney - -	*Newcome*	— 653	— —
Eaft Sheen - -	*Burrow*	— 655	— 509
Bridgeport - -	*Downe*	— 688	
—— Account of an earthquake felt at Chefter Apr. 2, 1750 - -	*Anon.*	— 683	— 510
Flintfhire - -	*Pennant*	— 687	— 511
Warrington, Lancafhire -	*Seddon*	— 695	— —
—— Account of an earthquake felt Mar. 14, 1749-50, at Eaft Molefey -	*Bowman*	— 684	— 509
—— An account of an earthquake felt May 4, 1749, at Wenbourn in Dorfetfhire -	*Baker*	— 689	— 512
—— An account of an earthquake felt July 1, 1747, at Taunton in Somerfetfhire -	*Baker*	— —	— —
—— An account of an earthquake felt Oct. 11, 1749, in France - -	*Reaumur*	— 691	— 526
—— Letter concerning earthquakes at Smyrna - - -	*Mackenzie*	— 700	— —
—— Letter concerning the fhock of an earthquake felt at Newton in Northamptonfhire Sept. 30, 1750 - -	*Folkes*	— 701	— 514
St. Edmund's Bury, Suffolk -	*Burrow*	— 702	— —
Narborough, Leicefterfhire -	*Burrow*	— —	— —
Northamptonfhire -	*Nixon and Cave*	— 705	— 515
Further particulars -	*Nixon*	— 710	— 516
- - -	*Dodderidge*	— 712	— 517
Dean - -	*Anon.*	— 723	— 523
Tooting - -	*Miles*	— 726	— —
Peterborough - -	*Smith*	— 727	— 524
—— An account of an earthquake felt Aug. 23, 1750, at Spalding in Lincolnfhire	*Johnfon*	— 725	
Ditto - -	*Green*	— —	
—— An account of an earthquake felt at York Apr. 19, 1754 - -	*Baker*	XLVIII 564	
—— Account of an earthquake at Conftantinople Sept. 16, 1754 -	*Mackenzie*	— 819	
—— An account of feveral earthquakes lately felt at Conftantinople May 15, 1755	*Porter*	XLIX 115	
—— An account of an earthquake Nov. 1, 1755, as felt in the lead-mines in Derbyfhire - - -	*Bullock*	— 398	

		Transf.	Abridg.
An account of the earthquake at Lisbon Nov. 1, 1755	*Wolfal*	XLIX 402	
- - -	*Saccheti*	— 409	
Zsusqueira - -	*Latham*	— 411	
Colares (20 miles from Lisbon)	*Stoqueler*	— 413	
Oporto - -	*Henkel*	— 418	
Ditto - -	*Plummer*	— 419	
Ditto - -	*Knowler*	— 421	
Ditto - -	*Muysson*	— 422	
Madrid - -	*Anon.*	— 423	
Cadiz - -	*Bewick*	— 424	
Ditto - -	*Ulloa*	— 427	
Barbary - -	*Fowke*	— 428	
Madeira - -	*Heberden*	— 432	
Ditto - -	*Chambers*	— 435	
Neufchâtel in Swisserland	*De Valtravers*	— 436	
Geneva, Nov. 9 -	*Trembley*	— 438	
Boston in New England, Nov. 18	*Anon.*	— 439	
New York, Nov. 18 -	*Colden*	— 433	
Pennsylvania, Nov. 18 -	*Anon.*	— 444	
—— An extraordinary and surprising agitation of the waters, though without any perceptible motion of the earth, having been observed in various parts of this island, both maritime and inland, on the same day, and chiefly about the time that the more violent commotions of both earth and waters so very extensively affected many very distant parts of the globe, the following accounts relating to the former have been transmitted to the Society; in which are specified the times and places when and where they happened - -		— 351	
Portsmouth - -	*Robertson*	— —	
Sussex and Surrey -	*Webb*	— 353	
Guildford - -	*Adee*	— 357	
Petworth - -	*Hodgson*	— 358	
Cranbrook - -	*Tempest*	— 360	
Chevening - -	*Pringle*	— —	
Rotherhith - -	*Mills*	— 361	
Peerless Pool, London -	*Birch*	— 362	
Rochford in Essex -	*Thomlinson*	— 364	
Reading - -	*Philips*	— 365	
Ditto - -	*Blair*	— 367	
Shirburn Castle, Oxfordshire	*Lord Parker*	— 368	
Devonshire, Cornwall, Plymouth, Mountsbay, Penzance, &c. -	*Huxham*	— 371	
Mountsbay - -	*Borlace*	— 373	

		Transf.	Abridg.
Swanzey - -	*Blair*	— 379	
Norwich - -	*Arderon*	— 380	
Yarmouth - -	*Barber*	— —	
Hawkeshead in Cumberland	*Harrison*	— 381	
Durham - -	*Cowper*	— 385	
Edinburgh - -	*Stevenson*	— 387	
Luss in Scotland -	*Colquhoun*	— 389	
Kinsale - -	*Nicola*	— 393	
Toplitz in Bohemia -	*Steplin*	— 395	
Hague - -	*De Hondt*	— 396	
Leyden - -	*Allamand*	— 397	
—— Extract of a letter concerning the earthquakes at Manilla, 1750 -	*Pye*	— 459	
—— An account of the earthquake felt at Glasgow Dec. 30, 1755, and Dumbarton; also of a shower of dust falling on a ship between Shetland and Iceland -	*Whytt*	— 509	
—— Extract of a letter concerning the earthquake on the 14th of November 1755, in Valais in Swisserland - -	*Trembley*	— 511	
—— Extract of a letter concerning the earthquake felt at Leyden, Leige, Maestricht, Nimeguen, Arnheim, &c. Dec. 26, 1755	*Allamand*	— 512	
—— An extract of a letter concerning an earthquake at the Hague, on Wednesday the 18th of February 1756 -	*Grovestins*	— 544	
—— An account of an earthquake felt in Holland Feb. 18, 1756 -	*Allamand*	— 545	
—— An account of the earthquakes felt at Brussels Dec. 26, 27, and Feb. 18, 1756	*Pringle*	— 546	
—— An account of the agitation of the waters on the 1st of November 1756, in Scotland and Hamburgh - -	*Pringle*	— 550	
—— Account of the earthquake felt Feb. 18, along the coast of England, between Margate and Dover - -	*Warren*	— 579	
—— Extract of a letter concerning the earthquakes felt at Turin Dec. 9, 1755, and March 8, 1756 - -	*Donati*	— 612	
—— An account of a continued succession of earthquakes at Brigue in Valais - -	*Rector of the College of Jesuits*	— 616	
—— Extract of a letter relating to the agitation of the waters observed at Dartmouth Nov. 1, 1755 - -	*Holdsworth*	— 643	
—— An account of the late earthquakes felt at Maes-			

	Tranſ.	Abridg.
tricht, from Feb. 18, to the beginning of April 1756 - - *Vernede*	XLIX 663	
—— An account of the agitation of the ſea at Antigua Nov. 1, 1755 - *Affleck*	— 668	
—— An account of the extraordinary agitation of the waters in ſeveral ponds in Hertfordſhire Nov. 1. 1755 - *Rutherforth*	— 684	
—— An account of an earthquake felt at Colen, Leige, Maeſtricht, &c. on the 19th of Nov. 1756 - - *Trembley*	— 893	
—— An account of the earthquake felt in New England, and the neighbouring parts of America, Nov. 18, 1755 - *Winthrop*	L 1	
—— Extract of a letter mentioning a ſlight ſhock of an earthquake Aug. 13, 1756, at Turin, and another Nov. 9, 1756, at Genoa *Trembley*	— 58	
—— An account of an earthquake in Cornwall July 15, 1757 - - *Huxham*	— 429	
—— An account of an earthquake felt in the iſland of Sumatra in the Eaſt Indies, in Nov. and Dec. 1756 - - *Perry*	— 491	
—— An account of the earthquake in the weſt parts of Cornwall July 15, 1757 - *Borlace*	— 499	
—— An account of an earthquake felt at Lingfield in Surrey, and Eden Bridge in Kent, Jan. 24, 1758 - - *Burrow*	— 614	
—— Obſervations upon a ſlight earthquake, though very particular, which may lead to the knowledge of the cauſe of great and violent ones - - - *Peyſſonel*	— 645	
—— An account of the late earthquakes in Syria - - - *Ruſſell*	LI 529	
—— Conjectures concerning the cauſe, and obſervations upon the phænomena of earthquakes, particularly that of Nov. 1, 1755 *Michell*	— 566	
—— An account of an earthquake at Liſbon May 31, 1761 - - *Anon.*	LII 141	
—— Another account of the earthquake at Liſbon May 31, 1761 - *Molloy*	— 142	
—— An account of the earthquake felt in the iſland of Madeira Mar. 31, 1761 *Thomas Heberden*	— 155	
—— An account of an earthquake in Siberia Nov. 28, 1761 - - *Weymarn*	LIII 201	
—— An account of an earthquake Apr. 2, 1762, at Chaltigaon: tranſlated from the Perſian *Gulſton*	— 252	
Another account from Calcutta *Hirſt*	— 256	
Another account from Chattigong *Gulſton*	— 263	

—— Another

+Earthquakes, several felt in Wales.		Pennant	71: 193.
at Hafodunos near Denbigh, Aug. 29. 1780.	—	Lloyd	331.
in Northwales, Oct. 5. 1782.	— — — — —	———	73: 104.
in Italy, from February to May 1783.	— —	Sir Wm Hamilton	169.
in Calabria, March 28. 1783.	— — — — — —	Ippolito	209. & app. 1.
in the Northern part of England, Aug. 11. 1786.	— —	More	— — 77: 35.
in Scotland, Aug. 11. 1786	— — — — —	Brydone	— — 69.
in Lincolnshire, Febr. 25. 1786.	— — — — —	Turnor	1792: 283.
in Various parts of England, Nov. 18. 1795.	— — —	Gray	1796: 353.

	Tranf.	Abridg.
—— Another account of feveral from Apr. 2 to 19, 1762, in the province of Iflamabad, with the damages attending them: tranflated from the Perfian - - *Verelft*	LIII 265	
—— An account of an earthquake felt at Lifbon Dec. 26, 1764 - - *Anon.*	LV 43	
—— Abftract of a letter containing an account of an earthquake at Macao Nov. 23, 1767 *De Vifme*	LIX 71	
—— An account of the earthquake which was felt at Manchefter and other places, on Sept. 14, 1777 - - *Henry*	LXVIII 221	
East Burne. See *Antiquities.*		
Easter. Letter concerning the obfervation of Eafter on April 24, 1698 - *Wallis*	XX 185	III 402
—— A calculation for finding Eafter *Thorefby*	XXIV 1901	V 2 27
—— An explanation of the rule for finding Eafter - - - *Jackman*	— 2123	— - —
East Indies. A narrative of fome obfervations made upon feveral voyages, to find a way for failing about the North to the Eaft Indies, and for returning the fame way from hence hither; together with inftructions given by the Dutch Eaft India Company for the difcovery of Jeffo, near Japan: to which is added, a relation of failing through the Northern America to the Eaft Indies - *Van Nierop*	IX 197	
—— —— Part of a letter from Fort St. George in the Eaft Indies, giving an account of the long worm, which is troublefome to the inhabitants of thofe parts - - *Lifter*	XIX 417	III 138
—— —— Account of fome animals fent from the Eaft Indies, with remarks by J. Petiver *Brown*	XXII 859	
—— —— A defcription of a bird from the Eaft Indies - - *Edwards*	LXI 55	
—— —— The procefs of making ice in the Eaft Indies - *Sir Robert Barker*	LXV 252	
—— —— Journal of a voyage to the Eaft Indies, in the fhip Grenville, in the year 1775, captain Burnet Abercrombie - *Dalrymple*	LXVIII 389	
Eaton. See *Stiptick.*		
Ecchoes. A letter concerning fome extraordinary ecchoes - - *Southwell*	XLIV 219	X 246
Echinites. A defcription of a curious echinites - - - *Baker*	— 432	— 634
—— A letter concerning two beautiful echinites - - - *Da Cofta*	XLVI 143	— 635
Echinus. Remarks upon a petrified echinus of a		

	Tranſ.	Abridg.
ſingular kind, found on Bunnan's Land, in the pariſh of Bovingdon in Hertfordſhire, which is a clay, and ſuppoſed to have been brought with the chalk dug out of a pit in the field - - *Parſons*	XLIX 155	
—— An account of a remarkable echinus *Brander*	— 295	
ECLIPSES. A method for obſerving the eclipſes of the moon free from the common inconveniencies - - - *Rook*	I 388	I 300
—— Obſervations on an eclipſe of the earth May 3, 1734 - - *De Revillas*	XXXIX 294	VIII 138
—— An account of a machine to repreſent eclipſes of the earth (Lat.) - *Segner*	XLI 781	— 157
—— A new and particular method of calculating eclipſes of the earth; and of any appulſes of the moon to planets and fixed ſtars *Gerſten*	XLIII 22	
—— Letter concerning the year of the eclipſe foretold by Thales - *Coſtard*	XLVIII 17	
—— Letter concerning the eclipſe mentioned by Xenophon - - *Coſtard*	— 155	
—— An account of the eclipſe predicted by Thales - - - *Stukeley*	— 221	
—— Kepler's method of computing the moon's parallaxes in ſolar eclipſes, demonſtrated and extended to all degrees of the moon's latitude; as alſo to the aſſigning the moon's correſpondent apparent diameter; together with a conciſe application of this form of calculation to thoſe eclipſes - *Pemberton*	LXI 437	
ECLIPSES OF THE SUN AND MOON. See *Sun*, *Moon*.		
ECLIPTIC. Some more accurate obſervations about Jupiter's tranſits near fixed ſtars; uſeful for determining the inclination of that planet to the ecliptique - - *Flamſtead*	VIII 6033	I 401
—— An account ſhewing, that the latitude of Nurenburg has continued without ſenſible alteration for 200 years laſt paſt; as likewiſe the obliquity of the ecliptick, by comparing them with what was obſerved by B. Walther in 1487 - - *Wurtzelbaur*	XVI 403	— 262
—— A propoſal to make the poles of a globe of the heavens move in a circle round the poles of the ecliptic - - *Latham*	XL 201	VIII 217
—— A contrivance to make the poles of the diurnal motion, in a cœleſtial globe, paſs round the poles of the ecliptic - *Senex*	— 203	— —

	Transf.	Abridg.
—— A treatiſe on the preceſſion of the equinoxes, and in general on the motion of the nodes, and the alteration of the inclination of the orbit of a planet to the ecliptick *Silvabelle*	XLVIII 385	
—— An enquiry into the quantity and direction of the proper motion of Arcturus; with ſome remarks on the diminution of the obliquity of the ecliptic - - *Hornſby*	LXIII 93	
EDEN. An account of a remarkable decreaſe of the river Eden in Cumberland Dec. 28, 1762 - - - - *Milbourne*	LIII 7	
EDINBURGH. A compariſon of the heat of London and Edinburgh - *Roebuck*	LXV 459	
EDWARDS. An account of what appeared moſt remarkable on opening the body of Anne Edwards, who died Jan. 5, 1729-30, having a large umbilical rupture - *Ranby*	XXXVII 221	VII 516
EELS. Method of taking eels in froſty weather *Anon.*	I 323	II 837
—— An abſtract of a letter concerning the ſcales of eels - - *Leewenhoek*	XV 883	III 684
—— Microſcopical obſervations on eels, mites, the ſeeds of figs, ſtrawberries, &c. *Leewenhoek*	XIX 269	— 685
—— Of the manner of generation of eels *Allen*	— 664	II 837
—— An account of a very large eel lately caught at Malden in Eſſex; with ſome conſiderations about the generation of eels - *Dale*	XX 90	— —
—— Manner of obſerving the circulation of blood in an eel - - *Leewenhoek*	XXVI 444	V 2 388
—— Obſervations on the mouths of the eels in vinegar, and alſo a ſtrange aquatic animal *Baker*	XLII 416	IX 38
—— A letter concerning the minute eels in paſte being viviparous - *Sherwood*	XLIV 67	XI 799
—— Abſtract of a letter concerning the peculiar aſcent of eels - - *Arderon*	— 395	— 874
EFFERVESCENCE. A memoir on the lacrymæ batavicæ, or glaſs drops, the tempering of ſteel, and effervelcence, accounted for by the ſame principle - - *Le Cat*	XLVI 175	X 560
—— The ſtrange effects of ſome effervefcent mixtures - - *Mounſay*	L 19	
EFFLUVIA. Several experiments ſhewing the ſtrange effects of the effluvia of glaſs, produceable on the motion and attrition of it *Haukſbee*	XXV 2372	IV 2 180
—— An account of the repetition of an experiment touching motion given bodies, included in a glaſs by the approach of a finger		

	Transf.	Abridg.
near its outfide; with other experiments on the effluvia of glafs - *Haukfbee*	XXVI 82	IV 2 181
—— A letter of weighing the ftrength of electrical effluvia - - *Ellicott*	XLIV 96	X 324
—— Experiments upon air, and the effects of different kinds of effluvia upon it *White*	LXVIII 194	
—— Account of the manner in which the Ruffians treat perfons affected with the fumes of burning charcoal, and other effluvia of the fame nature - - *Guthrie*	LXIX 325	
EFT. Some remarks concerning the circulation of the blood, as feen in the tail of a water-eft through a folar microfcope - *Miles*	XLI 725	IX 69
—— A letter concerning the property of water-efts, in flipping off their fkins as ferpents do *Baker*	XLIV 529	XI 857
EGGS. An account of an infect feeding upon herbane, the horrid fmell of which is in that creature fo qualified thereby as to become in fome meafure aromatical; together with the colour yeilded by the eggs of the fame *Lifter*	VI 2176	II 783
—— An account of what hath been of late obferved of eggs to be found in all forts of females - - - *Kirkringius*	VII 4018	I 251,440
—— Account of a fmall egg found within an ordinary one - *De Vallemont*	XIX 632	II 904
EGYPT. Inquiries to be made in Egypt *Henfhaw*	II 470	III 632
—— A narrative of fome obfervations lately made by certain miffionaries in the Upper Egypt *Anon.*	VI 2151	— 527
—— An explanation of the cuts of two porphyry pillars in Egypt - *Huntington*	XV 1252	— 530
—— Extract of a letter concerning a fuppofed connection between the hieroglyphical writing of antient Egypt, and the characteriftic writing which is in ufe at this day among the Chinefe - - - *Morton*	LIX 489	
ELASTICITY. A remark upon the new opinion relating to the forces of moving bodies, in the cafe of the collifion of non-elaftic bodies - - - *Eames*	XXXIV 183	VI 287
—— An experiment to prove that water, when agitated by fire, is infinitely more elaftic than air in the fame circumftances - *Clayton*	XLI 162	VIII 466
—— A narrative of a new invention of expanding fluids, by their being conveyed into certain ignited veffels, where they are immediately rarified into an elaftic impelling force, fufficient to give motion to hydraulopneumatical and		

other

	Tranſ.	Abridg.
other engines, for raiſing water, and other uſes, &c. - - *Payne*	XLI 821	VIII 638
—— An attempt to explain ſome of the principal phænomena of electricity by means of an elaſtic fluid - - *Cavendiſh*	LXI 584	
—— Continuation of an experimental enquiry concerning the nature of the mineral elaſtic ſpirit or air contained in the Pouhon water, and other acidulæ - - *Brownrigg*	LXIV 357	
—— Experiments for diſcovering the various elaſticity of the air in different parts of Switzerland - - *Scheuchzer*	XXIX 266	IV 2 16
—— Some thoughts and conjectures concerning the cauſe of elaſticity - *Deſaguliers*	XLI 175	VIII 439
—— See *Air.*		
ELDEN HOLE. An account of Elden Hole in Derbyſhire, with ſome obſervations upon it - - *King and Lloyd*	LXI 250	
ELDER. A letter on the effects of elder, in preſerving growing plants from inſects and flies *Gullet*	LXII 348	
ELECTRICITY. A catalogue of electrical bodies *Plot*	XX 384	III 491
—— An account of an experiment touching the extraordinary electricity of glaſs, produceable on a ſmart attrition of it; with a continuation of experiments on the ſame ſubject, and other phænomena - - *Haukſbee*	XXV 2327	IV 2 180
A continuation - *Haukſbee*	— 2332	— — —
—— An account of ſome experiments touching the electricity and light produceable on the attrition of ſeveral bodies - - *Haukſbee*	XXVI 87	
—— An account of ſome new electrical experiments - - - *Gray*	XXXI 104	VI 2 7
—— A letter containing ſeveral experiments concerning electricity - - *Gray*	XXXVII 18	— - 9
—— A letter concerning the electricity of water *Gray*	— 227	— - 22
—— A letter containing a further account of his experiments concerning electricity *Gray*	— 285	— - 139
—— Two letters containing farther accounts of his experiments concerning electricity *Gray*	— 397	VII 4 96
—— A letter concerning electricity *Du Fay*	XXXVIII 258	VIII 393
—— Experiments and obſervations upon the light that is produced by communicating electrical attraction to animal or inanimate bodies; together with ſome of its moſt ſurpriſing effects - - - *Gray*	XXXIX 16	— 397
—— A letter containing ſome experiments relating to electricity - - *Gray*	— 166	— 401

	Tranſ.	Abridg.
—— A letter concerning the revolutions which ſmall pendulous bodies will, by electricity, make round larger ones, from eaſt to weſt, as the planets do round the ſun - *Gray*	XXXIX 220	
—— An account of ſome electrical experiments intended to be communicated to the Royal Society - - *Gray*	— 400	VIII 404
—— Some electrical experiments chiefly regarding the repulſive force of electrical bodies *Wheler*	XLI 98	— 406
—— Account of ſome of the electrical experiments made by Granville Wheeler at the Royal Society's houſe May 11, 1731 *Mortimer*	— 112	— 412
—— Letter of remarks on the late Stephen Gray; his electrical circular experiment *Wheler*	— 118	— 415
—— Some thoughts and experiments concerning electricity - - *Deſaguliers*	— 186	— 419
—— Experiments made before the Royal Society Feb. 2, 9, and 16, 1737-8 *Deſaguliers*	— 193	— 422
—— Some electrical experiments made at the prince of Wales's at Cliefden Apr. 15, 1738, where the electricity was conveyed 420 feet in a direct line - - *Deſaguliers*	— 209	— 429
—— Something concerning electricity *Deſaguliers*	— 634	— 430
—— An account of ſome electrical experiments made before the Royal Society Jan. 22 and Mar. 15, 1741 - - *Deſaguliers*	— 637	— 432
—— Several electrical experiments made at various times before the Royal Society *Deſaguliers*	— 661	— 433
—— Further obſervations concerning electricity - - - *Deſaguliers*	XLII 14	— 435
—— Some conjectures concerning electricity, and the riſe of vapours - *Deſaguliers*	— 140	— 437
—— An account of the electrical fire *Hollman*	XLIII 239	X 271
—— Letter on firing phoſphorus by electricity *Miles*	— 290	— 272
—— Some new obſervations in electricity *Winkler*	— 307	
—— Obſervations of luminous emanations from human bodies and from brutes: with ſome remarks on electricity - *Miles*	— 441	— 278
—— Abſtract of a letter on electricity *De Bozes*	— 419	— 277
—— Experiments and obſervations tending to illuſtrate the nature and properties of electricity - - - *W. Watſon*	— 481	— 280
—— Extracts of two letters concerning the effects of a cane of black ſealing-wax, and a cane of brimſtone, in electrical experiments *Miles*	XLIV 27	— 317
—— Further experiments and obſervations tending to		

	Transf.	Abridg.
illustrate the nature and properties of electricity - - *W. Watson*	XLIV 41	X 290
—— Extracts of two letters containing several electrical experiments - *Miles*	— 53	— 319
—— Part of a letter concerning the light caused by quickfilver shaken in a glass tube proceeding from electricity - - *Trembley*	— 58	— 321
—— Part of a letter concerning electrical fire *Miles*	— 78	— 322
—— A letter on weighing the strength of electrical effluvia - - *Ellicott*	— 96	— 324
—— Part of two letters containing some electrical observations - - *Miles*	— 158	— 325
—— An extract of a letter concerning the effects of electricity upon himself and his wife *Winkler*	— 211	— 327
—— A letter shewing, that the electricity of glass disturbs the mariner's compass, and also nice balances - - *Robins*	— 242	— 328
—— Extract of a letter concerning some new electrical experiments lately made at Paris - - - *Needham*	— 247	— 329
—— Extract of a memoir concerning the communication of electricity; read at the meeting of the Royal Academy of Sciences at Paris Nov. 12, 1746 - *Le Monnier*	— 290	— 336
—— Part of a letter concerning the effect of electricity on vegetables - *Browning*	— 373	— 342
—— Observations upon so much of M. le Monnier, jun. memoir, lately presented to the Royal Society, as relates to the communicating the electric virtue to non-electrics - *W. Watson*	— 388	— 339
—— A letter which gives a description and the figures of his electrical pyrorganum *Winkler*	— 497	— 345
—— A continuation of a paper concerning electricity, from vol. XLIII. pag. 501 *W. Watson*	— 695	
—— A sequel to the experiments and observations tending to illustrate the nature and properties of electricity - - *W. Watson*	— 704	— 290
—— A collection of electrical experiments *W. Watson*	XLV 49	— 347
—— Some further inquiries into the nature and properties of electricity - *W. Watson*	— 93	— 368
—— Part of a letter concerning electricity *Nollet*	— 187	— 3[illegible]2
—— Several essays towards discovering the laws of electricity - - *Ellicott*	— 195	— 386
- - -	— 203, 213	— 389, 394
—— A letter concerning a fustian-frock being set on fire by electricity - *Roche*	— 323	— 406

—— Ex-

		Tranſ.	Abridg.
—— Extract of a letter concerning ſome electrical experiments	*Hales*	XLIV 409	X 406
—— An account of the experiments made by ſome gentlemen of the Royal Society, in order to meaſure the abſolute velocity of electricity - - -	*W. Watſon*	XLV 491	— 407
—— Extract of a letter on the electricity of glaſs that has been expoſed to ſtrong fires	*Boſe*	XLVI 189	— 329
—— Letter declaring that he, as well as many others, have not been able to make odours paſs through glaſs by means of electricity; and giving a particular account of profeſſor Boſe at Wittemberg, his experiment of beatification, or cauſing a glory to appear round a man's head by electricity - -	*W. Watſon*	— 348	— 410
—— Extract of a letter accompanying an examination of certain phænomena in electricity - - -	*Nollet*	— 368	— 414
—— An account of B. Franklin's treatiſe of experiments and obſervations on electricity, made at Philadelphia - -	*W. Watſon*	XLVII 202	
—— An account of experiments relating to odours paſſing through electrified globes and tubes - - -	*Winkler*	— 231	
An account of the reſult of ſome experiments made here with globes and tubes, tranſmitted by Mr. Winkler, in order to verify the facts above-mentioned - - -	*W. Watſon*	— 236	
—— An account of the phænomena of electricity in vacuo - -	*W. Watſon*	— 362	
—— Letter concerning the ſucceſs of the late experiments in France -	*Mazeas*	— 534	
—— Extracts of two letters relating to the extracting electricity from the clouds	*Nollet*	— 553	
Another letter on the ſame -	*Moliere*	— 559	
—— Letter concerning an electrical kite	*Franklin*	— 565	
—— Letter concerning the electrical experiments in England upon thunder-clouds	*W. Watſon*	— 567	
—— Letter concerning ſome electrical experiments made at Paris - -	*Wilſon*	XLVIII 347	
—— Electrical experiments, with an attempt to account for their ſeveral phænomena; together with ſome obſervations on thunder-clouds - - -	*Canton*	— 350	
—— Obſervations upon the electricity of the air made			

at

		Tranſ.	Abridg.
at the Chateau de Maintenon in June, July, and October 1753 -	*Mazeas*	XLVIII 377	
—— An additional remark to one of W. Watſon, in his account of the Abbé Nollet's letter concerning electricity -	*Birch*	— 484	
—— Anſwer to ſeveral queries concerning his experiment of electricity with a kite	*Lining*	— 757	
—— Anſwer to Dr. Lining's query relating to the death of profeſſor Richman	*W. Watſon*	— 765	
—— Account of two electrical experiments	*Winkler*	— 772	
—— Letter concerning ſome new electrical experiments -	*Canton*	— 780	
—— An account of the death of Mr. George-William Richman, occaſioned by an electrical ſhock collected from thunder; tranſlated from the High Dutch -	*Anon.*	XLIX 61	
—— Electrical experiments made in purſuance of thoſe of Mr. Canton, dated Dec. 3, 1753; with an explanation by -	*Franklin*	XLIX 300	
—— Extract of a letter concerning electricity - - -	*Franklin*	— 305	
—— A retractation of his former opinion concerning the explication of the Leyden experiment - - -	*Wilſon*	— 682	
—— An account of ſome electrical experiments - - -	*Wilſon*	LI 83	
- - -	*Delaval*	— —	
—— Experiments on the tourmalin	*Wilſon*	— 308	
—— New experiments and obſervations concerning electricity - -	*Symmer*	— 340	
—— A letter concerning the force of electrical coheſion - -	*Mitchell*	— 390	
—— Experiments in electricity -	*Beccaria*	— 514	
With remarks -	*Franklin*	— 525	
—— Further experiments in electricity	*Wilſon*	— 896	
—— A letter to Mr. B. Wilſon concerning electricity - -	*Bergman*	— 907	
—— An account of ſeveral experiments in electricity - -	*Delaval*	LII 353	
—— A letter concerning Mr. Canton's experiment - - -	*Franklin*	— 456	
—— A letter containing ſome remarks on Mr. Delaval's electrical experiments -	*Canton*	— 457	
—— New experiments in electricity	*Kinnerſley*	LIII 84	
—— Obſervations in electricity, and on a thunderſtorm - -	*Bergman*	— 97	

—— Ex-

		Tranſ.	Abridg.
—— Experiments on the tourmalin -	*Wilſon*	LIII 436	
—— A letter containing ſome experiments in electricity - -	*Bergman*	LIV 84	
—— New experiments in electricity	*Beccaria*	LVI 105	
—— On the nature of the tourmalin	*Bergman*	— 236	
—— A deſcription of an approved apparatus for performing electrical experiments, in which the lectrical power is increaſed, the operation entirely ſecured from receiving any accidental ſhocks, and the whole rendered more convenient - -	*L'Epinaſſe*	LVII 186	
—— A ſpecimen of ſome new experiments in electricity - -	*Beccaria*	— 297	
—— An account of rings conſiſting of all the priſmatic colours, made by electrical exploſions on the ſurface of pieces of metal	*Prieſtley*	LVIII 68	
—— Experiments on the lateral force of electrical exploſions - -	*Prieſtley*	LIX 57	
—— Various experiments on the force of electrical exploſions - -	*Prieſtley*	— 63	
—— An inveſtigation of the lateral exploſion, and of the electricity communicated to the electrical circuit, in a diſcharge	*Prieſtley*	LX 192	
—— Theorems concerning the electrical atmoſphere - - -	*Beccaria*	— 277	
—— An attempt to explain ſome of the principal phænomena of electricity by means of an elaſtic fluid - -	*Cavendiſh*	LXI 584	
—— A letter incloſing an account of ſome obſervations on atmoſpherical electricity, in regard of frogs, mites, &c. with ſome remarks - - -	*Ronayne*	LXII 137	
—— An account of ſeveral electrical experiments made by Mr. W. Henley -	*Prieſtley*	— 359	
—— Extract of a letter on ſome electrical experiments made with charcoal -	*Kinnerſley*	LXIII 38	
—— A letter containing ſome new electrical experiments, July 7, 1772 -	*Brydone*	— 163	
—— An extract of a letter on ſome improvements in the electrical machine -	*North*	— 333	
—— Of the electric property of the torpedo	*Walſh*	— 461	
—— Electrical experiments made with a machine of his own workmanſhip; a deſcription of which is prefixed - -	*Nairne*	LXIV 79	
—— An account of ſome new experiments in electricity, containing, 1. An enquiry whether vapour be a conductor of electricity. 2. Some			

+ Electricity

On the method of rendering very sensible the weakest electricity. Volta. 72:237. app. VII.

Electrical experiments made in order to ascertain the non-conducting power of a perfect vacuum &c. — Morgan 75:272.

An account of a doubler of electricity — — — — — Bennet 77:288.

Observations on the manner in which glass is charged with the electric fluid, and discharged — — — — — — — Gray 78:121.

Description of a new electrical instrument capable of collecting together a diffused or little condensed quantity of Electricity. — — Cavallo. 78:255.

Description of an instrument which, by the turning of a winch, produces the two states of electricity, without friction or communication with the earth. — — — — — Nicholson — 403.

Experiments and observations on electricity — — — — ———— 79:265.

A meteorological Journal, principally relating to atmospheric electricity, kept at Knightsbridge, from May 9. 1789 to May 8. 1790. — Read 81:185.
May 9. 1790 to May 8. 1791. ———— 1792:225.

Account of some discoveries lately made by Mr. Galvani, of Bologna, with experiments and observations on them. — Volta 1793:10.

Experiments and observations made with the Doubler of Electricity, with a view to determine its real utility, in the investigation of the Electricity of atmospheric air, in different degrees of purity — — Read 1794:266.

Observations on the influence which incites the muscles of Animals to contract in Mr Galvani's experiments — — — Wells 1795:246.

On the electricity excited by the mere contact of conducting substances of different kinds — — — — — — — Volta 1800:403

Experiments on the chemical production and agency of electricity. Wollaston. 1801:427

On some chemical agencies of electricity. — — — — — Davy. 1807:1.

On some new electrochemical researches on various objects, particularly the metallic bodies from the Alkalies and Earths, and on some combinations of Hydrogene. ———— 1810:16.

On some new electro-chemical phenomena — Brande 1814:51.

	Tranſ.	Abridg.
experiments to aſcertain the direction of the electric matter in the diſcharge of the Leyden bottle. 3. Experiments on the lateral exploſion in the diſcharge of the Leyden bottle. 4. The deſcription and uſe of a new prime conductor. 5. Miſcellaneous experiments made principally in 1771 and 1772. 6. Experiments and obſervations on the electricity of frogs, in purſuance of thoſe made by Thomas Ronayne, Eſq; with a plan of an electrical journal - - *Henly*	LXIV 389	
—— An account of ſome attempts to imitate the effects of the torpedo by electricity *Cavendiſh*	LXVI 196	
—— Extraordinary electricity of the atmoſphere, obſerved at Iſlington in the month of October 1775 - - *Cavallo*	— 407	
—— Experiments and obſervations on a new apparatus, called, a machine for exhibiting perpetual electricity - - *Henly*	— 513	
—— An account of ſome new experiments in electricity - - *Cavallo*	LXVII 1 48	
—— Experiments and obſervations in electricity - - - *Henly*	— 1 85	
—— New electrical experiments and obſervations - - - *Cavallo*	— 388	
—— An account of ſome electrical experiments *Swift*	LXVIII 155	
—— Reaſons for diſſenting from the report of the committee appointed to conſider of Mr. Wilſon's experiments; including remarks on ſome experiments exhibited by Mr. Nairne - - - *Muſgrave*	— 801	
—— Experiments on electricity; being an attempt to ſhew the advantage of elevated pointed conductors - - *Nairne*	— 823	
—— On the uſe of an amalgam of zinc for the purpoſe of electrical excitation - *Higgins*	— 861	
—— New experiments upon the Leyden phial, reſpecting the termination of conductors *Wilſon*	— 999	
—— A ready way of lighting a candle by a very moderate electrical ſpark - *Ingenhouſz*	— 1022	
—— Obſervations and experiments tending to confirm Dr. Ingenhouſz's theory of the electrophorus; and to ſhew the impermeability of glaſs to the electric fluid - *Henly*	— 1049	
—— Account of ſome experiments in electricity - - - *Swift*	LXIX 454	
—— Improvements in electricity by *Ingenhouſz*	— 661	

—— An

		Transf.	Abridg.
—— An account of some new experiments in electricity, with the description and use of two new electrical instruments -	*Cavallo*	LXX 15	
—— An account of the effect of electricity in shortening of wires -	*Nairne*	— 334	
ELECTRICITY (Medicine). A discovery in electricity useful to medicine (Lat.)	*Winkler*	XLV 262	X 399
—— A letter concerning several medical experiments of electricity - -	*Baker*	— 270	— 404
—— Accounts of the effects of electricity in the county hospital at Shrewsbury	*Hart*	XLVIII 786	
—— An account of a cure of a paralytic arm by electricity - -	*Hart*	XLIX 558	
—— An instance of the electrical virtue in the cure of a palsy - -	*Brydone*	L 392	
—— An account of the effects of electricity in paralytic cases - -	*Franklin*	— 481	
—— A further account of the effects of electricity in the cure of some diseases -	*Brydone*	— 695	
—— Case of a paralytic patient cured by an electrical application -	*Himsel*	LI 179	
—— Observations upon the effects of electricity applied to a tetanus, or muscular rigidity of four months continuance -	*W. Watson*	LIII 10	
—— Account of a locked jaw and paralysis cured by electricity - -	*Spry*	LVII 88	
—— A cure of a muscular contraction by electricity - - -	*Partington*	LXVIII 97	
—— An account of the cure of St. Vitus's Dance by electricity -	*A. Fothergill*	LXIX 1	
ELECTRICAL [redacted] See *Gymnotus Electricus.* Torpedo.			
ELECTROMETER. Description of an electrometer invented by Mr. Lane; with an account of some experiments made by him with it	*Lane*	LVII 451	
—— An account of a new electrometer contrived by Mr. William Henly, and of several electrical experiments made by him -	*Priestley*	LXII 359	
—— New electrical experiments and observations, with an improvement of Mr. Canton's electrometer - -	*Cavallo*	LXVII 388	
ELECTROPHORUS. Electrical experiments to explain how far the phænomena of the electrophorus may be accounted for by Dr. Franklin's theory of positive and negative electricity	*Ingenhousz*	LXVIII 1027	
—— Observations and experiments tending to confirm Dr. Ingenhousz's theory of electropho-			

+Electrical Fishes. Account of a new electrical fish. - - - Paterson 76:382.

+Electrometer. Account of a new — Brook. 72:384.
Description of a new Electrometer - - - Bennet 77: 26, 32.
Of the methods of manifesting the presence, and ascertaining the quality, of small quantities of natural or artificial electricity. Cavallo. 78: 1.

4 Elephant. Observations on the manners, habits, and natural history of the Elephant. Corse 1799: 31.

Observations on the different species of Asiatic Elephants, and their modes of dentition. —— —— 205.

	Trans.	Abridg.
rus; and to ſhew the impermeability of glaſs to electric fluid - - *Henly*	LXVIII 1049	
Elephant. An account of the ſkeleton of an elephant lately dug up at Tonna *Tentzelius*	XIX 757	II 438
—— An account of the taking and training of elephants in Zeylan - *Strachan*	XXIII 1051	V 2 176
—— A full and exact deſcription of all the bones of an elephant, with their ſeveral dimenſions. To which are premiſed, an hiſtorical account of the natural endowments and ſeveral wonderful performances of elephants, with the manner of taking and training them; an anatomical account of its parts, &c. - *Blair*	XXVII 53	
A continuation - - *Blair*	— 117	V 82
—— Some remarks upon the diſpoſition of the parts; and microſcopical obſervations upon the contexture of the ſkin of elephants *Leewenhoek*	— 518	
—— A deſcription of the organ of hearing in the elephant, with the figures and ſituation of the oſſicles, labyrinth and cochlea, in the ear of that animal - - *Blair*	XXX 885	— 82
—— An account of elephants teeth and bones found under ground, Part I. - *Sloane*	XXXV 457	VI 2 205
Part II. - - *Sloane*	— 497	— - 211
—— Obſervations, and a deſcription of ſome mammoth's bones dug up in Siberia, proving them to have belonged to elephants - *Breyne*	XL 124	IX 87
—— Letter concerning an extraordinary large foſſil-tooth of an elephant - *Baker*	XLIII 331	X 599
—— An account of ſeveral bones of an elephant found at Leyſdown in the Iſle of Sheppey - - - *Jacob*	XLVIII 626	
—— Obſervations on the bones commonly ſuppoſed to be elephants bones, which have been found near the river Ohio in America *William Hunter*	LVIII 34	
—— A diſſertation on the bones and teeth of elephants, and other beaſts, found in North America, and other northern regions, by which it appears they are the bones of indigenous beaſts - - - *Raſpe*	LIX 126	
Ellicott. Obſervations for proving the going of Mr. Ellicott's clock at St. Helena *Maſon*	LII 534	
—— See *Clock*.		
Ellipse. A direct and geometrical method by which the aphelia, excentricities, and proportions of the orbs of the primary planets may be determined, without ſuppoſing the equality of the angle of		

	Tranf.	Abridg.
motion at the other focus of the planet's ellipfis - - - *Halley*	XI 683	I 258
—— Inveftigation to prove, that the figure of the earth approaches nearly to an ellipfis, according to the laws of attraction in an inverfe ratio of the fquare of the diftances *Clairault*	XL 19	VIII 329
ELLIPTIC. An inveftigation of a general theorem for finding the length of any arc of any conic hyperbola by means of two elliptic arcs; with fome other new and ufeful theorems deduced therefrom - - *Landen*	LXV 283	
ELMS. An extract of a letter concerning the propagation of elms by feed - *Buckley*	XVII 971	II 667
EMBALMING. An abftract of Νεκροκηδεια; or the art of embalming - - *Greenhill*	XXIV 1101	
EMBRYO. Hiftoria et explicatio figurarum embryon feptimanarum & placentam cotiledoformen exhibentium - - *Hartmann*	XX 66	III 208
—— A letter concerning a child born with an extraordinary tumour near the anus, containing fome rudiments of an embryo in it *Huxham*	XLV 325	XI 1020
EMERY. Some obfervations on the formation of emery-ftone - - *Brice*	LVI 229	
EMETICK. A folution of the problem for determining the dofes of purging and emetick medicines, to be given according to the different ages and conftitutions of the patient *Cockburn*	XXIV 2119	V 273
EMPIRICISM. Poftfcript againft empiricifm *Banyer*	XLII 633	
EMPYEMA. Cafe of the operation of the empyema - - - *Warner*	XLVII 407	
—— The cafe of the operation for the empyema fuccefsfully performed - *Warner*	XLVIII 270	
—— A remarkable cafe of an empyema *Warner*	LI 194	
EMULGENT VEIN. A new difcovery of the communication of the ductus thoracicus with the emulgent vein - - *Pecquet*	II 461	III 258
EMULGENTS. Anatomical obfervations of an abcefs in the liver; a great number of ftones in the gall-bag and bilious veffels; an unufual conformation of the emulgents and pelvis; a ftrange conjunction of both kidnies, and a great dilatation of the vena cava - *Tyfon*	XII 1035	— 81
ENCAUSTIC. Experiments concerning the encauftic painting of the ancients - *Colebrooke*	LI 40	
—— A letter concerning the fuccefs of the former experiments - *Colebrooke*	— 53	
—— See *Painting*.		

ENCRINUS.

Emery. On the composition of Emery. — — — — - - - Tennant, 1802: 398.

	Tranſ.	Abridg.
Encrinus. See *Star Fiſh.*		
Engine. A deſcription of Dr. Charles Wren's engine deſigned for grinding hyperbolical glaſſes, as it was in a manner promiſed, vol. III. p. 962 - - *Wren*	IV 1059	I 189
—— A new engine to make linen cloth without the help of an artificer - *De Gennes*	XII 1007	— 501
—— Letter concerning Dr. Papin's way of raiſing water - - *Vincent*	XV 1238	— 539
—— Letter concerning Dr. Papin's new water engine - - *Tenon*	— 1254	— —
—— A full deſcription, with the uſe, of the new contrivance for raiſing water - *Papin*	— 1274	— 540
—— An account of an engine that conſumes ſmoak, ſhewn lately at St. German's fair in Paris *Juſtell*	XVI 78	III 638
—— Anſwer to ſeveral objections made by Mr. Nuis againſt his engine for raiſing water by the rarefaction of the air - *Papin*	— 263	I 542
—— A deſcription of an engine to raiſe water by the help of quickſilver, invented by *J. Haſkins* And improved by - *Deſaguliers*	XXXII 5	VI 352
—— An account of ſeveral experiments concerning the running of water in pipes, as it is retarded by friction and intermediate air; with a deſcription of a new machine, whereby pipes may be cleared of air as the water runs along without ſtand pipes, or the help of any hand *Deſaguliers*	XXXIV 77	— 347
—— An account of a new engine for raiſing water by horſes, or other animals drawing, without any loſs of power; with the ſtrokes of the piſton made of any length, to prevent the loſs of water by the too frequent opening of valves *Churchman*	XXXVIII 402	VIII 322
—— A narrative of a new invention of expanding fluids, by their being conveyed into certain ignified veſſels, where they are immediately rarified into an elaſtic impelling force ſufficient to give motion to hydraulopneumatical and other engines, for raiſing water, and other uſes, &c. - - *Payne*	XLI 821	— 638
—— The greateſt effect of engines with uniformly accelerated motions conſidered *Blake*	LI 1	
—— A method of leſſening the quantity of friction in engines - - *Fitzgerald*	LIII 139	
—— Short and eaſy methods for finding the quantity and weight of water contained in a full pipe of any given height and diameter of bore; and, conſequently, to find what degree of power		

	Transf.	Abridg.
would be required to work a common pump, or any other hydraulic engine, when the diameter of the pump bore, and the height to which the water is to be raifed therein are given *Ferguson*	LV 61	
—— An account of a machine for raifing water, executed at Oulton in Chefhire in 1772 *Whitehurft*	LXV 277	
—— A new theory of the engine for driving piles *Bugge*	LXIX 120	
—— The principal properties of the engine for turning ovals in wood or metal, and of the inftrument for drawing ovals upon paper, demonftrated - - *Ludlam*	LXX 378	
—— See *Cloth*, *Fire*, *Hydraulic*, *Machine*.		
England. A difcourfe tending to prove at what time and place Julius Cæfar made his firft defcent upon Britain - *Halley*	XVII 495	III 412
—— An advertifement neceffary for all navigators bound up the Channel of England *Anon.*	XXII 725	I 585
—— Letter relating to that ifthmus, or neck of land, which is fuppofed to have joined England and France in former times, where now is the paffage between Dover and Calais *Wallis*	— 967	IV 2 227
—— A demonftration of the numbers of acres contained in England, or South Britain, and the ufe which may be made of it *Grew*	XXVII 266	— 449
Engrafting. Some Hortulan communications about the curious engrafting of oranges and lemons, or citrons, upon one another's trees; and of one individual fruit, half orange and half lemon, growing on fuch trees, &c.	II 553	II 658
Engraving. Some obfervations upon gems, or precious ftones; more particularly fuch as the ancients ufed to engrave upon *Dingley*	XLIV 502	X 610
Entrails. An obfervation about the epiploon, or the double membrane, which covers the entrails of animals, and is filled with fat - - *Malpighi and Fracaffati*	II 553	II 658
Ephemeron. Some obfervations on a fort of libella, or ephemeron - - *Collinfon*	XLIV 329	XI 844
Epicycloid. The quadrature of a portion of the epicycloid - - *Cafwel*	XIX 113	I 31
Epidemical Diary. A meteorological, barometrical, thermometrical, epidemical and magnetical diary kept at Utrecht 1729 *Van Mufchenbroek*	XXXVII 357	VII 2 71
1730 and 1731 - -	— 408	— 4 86,90
Epidemick Diseases. Hiftorical account of the late general coughs and colds; with fome obfervations on other epidemick diftempers *Anon.*	XVIII 105	III 271

	Transf.	Abridg.
—— —— Extract of a letter relating to an extraordinary agitation of the sea at Barbadoes Mar. 31, 1761, and an epidemical disorder in that island - - *Mason*	LII 477	
Epileptic Fits. An account of a polypus found in the heart of a person who died epileptical *Gould*	XIV 537	III 70
—— —— An account of strange epileptick fits *Leigh*	XXIII 1174	V 211
—— —— Observation of remarkable appearances in the brain of three persons who died of epilepsies - - *Rhætus*	XXXV 315	VII 486
Epiploon. An observation about the epiploon, or the double membrane, which covers the entrails of animals, and is filled with fat - - *Malpighi and Fracassati*	I 553	II 658
Epsom Salt. Observations and experiments on the sal catharticum amarum, commonly called the Epsom salt - - *Brown*	XXXII 348	VII 729
Further observations - *Brown*	— 372	— 732
Equations. An account concerning the resolution of equations in numbers - *Collins*	IV 929	I 60
—— Cubic and biquadratic equations constructed by a parabola and circle - *Halley*	XVI 335	— 63
—— Of the number of roots in cubic and biquadratic equations, and their limits *Halley*	— 387	— 68
—— A new, accurate and easy method of finding the roots of equations of every kind, without previous reduction - - *Halley*	XVIII 136	— 81
—— A method of extracting the root of an infinite equation - - *De Moivre*	XX 190	— 95
—— Universal solution of cubic and biquadratic equations, viz. analytical, geometrical, and mechanical - - *Colson*	XXV 2353	IV 66
—— Analytical solution of certain equations of the third, fifth, seventh, ninth, and higher dimensions to infinity in finite terms, like that by Cardan's rules for cubics - *De Moivre*	— 2368	— 77
—— An attempt towards the improvement of the method of approximating, in the extraction of the roots of equations in numbers *Taylor*	XXX 610	— 80
—— A letter concerning equations with impossible roots - - *Maclaurin*	XXXIV 104	VI 19
—— A method of determining the number of impossible roots in adfected equations *Campbell*	XXXV 515	— 9
—— A second letter concerning the roots of equations, with the demonstration of other rules in algebra - - *Maclaurin*	XXXVI 59	— 25

		Tranf.	Abridg.
—— Of the reduction of radical expreſſions (or of the extraction of any root of a poſſible or impoſſible binomial) to more ſimple terms (Lat.) *De Moivre*		XL 463	VIII 1
—— Extract of a letter containing a commodious diſpoſition of equations for exhibiting the relations of goniometrical lines - *Jones*		XLIV 560	X 14
—— The application of Dr. Saunderſon's theorem for ſolving unlimited equations to a curious queſtion in chronology - *Horsfall*		LVIII 100	
—— Directions for making a machine for finding the roots of equations univerſally; with the manner of uſing it - *Rowning*		LX 240	
—— A method of extending Cardan's rule for reſolving one caſe of a cubic equation $x^3 - qx = r$ to the other caſe of the ſame equation, which it is not naturally fitted to ſolve, and which is therefore called the irreducible caſe *Maſeres*		LXVIII 902	
Appendix - - *Maſeres*		LXX 85	
—— A conjecture concerning the method by which Cardan's rules for reſolving the cubic equation $x^3 + qx = r$ in all caſes (or in all magnitudes of the known quantities q and r) and the cubic equation $x^3 - qx = r$ in the firſt caſe of it (or when r is greater than $\frac{2q\sqrt{q}}{3\sqrt{3}}$, or $\frac{rr}{4}$ is greater than $\frac{q^3}{27}$) were probably diſcovered by Scipio Ferreus of Bononia, or whoever elſe was the firſt inventor of them - *Maſeres*		LXX 221	
+ —— Of cubic equations and infinite ſeries *Hutton*		— 387	
EQUATION OF TIME. Some remarks upon the equation of time, and the true manner of computing it - - *Maſkelyne*		LIV 336	
EQUATOR. A reſolution of a general propoſition for determining the horary alteration of the poſition of the terreſtrial equator from the attraction of the ſun and moon; with ſome remarks on the ſolutions given by other authors to that difficult and important problem - *Simpſon*		L 416	
—— Propoſal of a method for meaſuring degrees of longitude upon parallels of the equator *Michell*		LVI 119	
EQUATORIAL TELESCOPE. The deſcription and uſes of an equatorial teleſcope - *Short*		XLVI 241	— 154
—— —— Deſcription and uſe of a new-conſtructed equatorial teleſcope, or portable obſervatory - - - *Nairne*		LXI 107	
			—— An

+ Equations. Extract of a letter from the Earl of Stanhope. 71:195.

Hints relating to the use which may be made of the tables of natural and logarithmic sines &c in the numerical resolution of affected equations. Wales 71:45.

On the roots of equations. Wood. 1798:369

Essay on the resolution of Algebraic equations: attempting to distinguish particularly, the real principle of every method, and the true causes of the limitations to which it is subject. Wilson. 1799:26

Methods of clearing equations of quadratic, cubic, quadratocubic, and higher surds. Allman. 1814:23.

On circulating functions, and on the integration of a class of equations of finite differences into which they enter as coefficients. Herschel. 1818:14

+Equatorial. An account of the Equatorial instrument. Shuckburgh. 1793: 67.

+Equinoxes. On the precession of the Equinoxes. - - - - Vince. 77: 363.
Robertson. 1807: 57.

[illegible]

Ether. Method of purifying it. Cavallo 71: 519.

	Transf.	Abridg.
—— An account of an apparatus applied to the equatorial inftrument for correcting the errors arifing from the refraction in altitude *Dollond*	LXIX 332	
EQUILIBRIUM. An account of an experiment explaining a mechanical paradox, viz. that two bodies of equal weight, fufpended on a certain fort of balances, do not lofe their equilibrium by being removed one farther from, the other nearer to, the center - *Defaguliers*	XXXVII 125	VI 310
EQUINOXES. A treatife on the preceffion of the equinoxes, and in general on the motion of the nodes, and the alteration of the inclination of the orbit of a planet to the ecliptic *Silvabelle*	XLVIII 385	
—— Effay on the preceffion of the equinoxes, and the nutation of the earth's axis *Walmefley*	XLIX 704	
—— A theory of the irregularities that may be occafioned in the annual motion of the earth by the actions of Jupiter and Saturn *Walmefley*	— 737	
—— On the preceffion of the equinoxes produced by the fun's attraction - *Milner*	LXIX 505	
EQUULEUS. An account of the equuleus *Ward*	XXXVI 231	VII 4 31
ERATOSTHENES. Κοσκινον Ερατοσθενους, or the fieve of Eratofthenes; being an account of his method of finding out the prime numbers *Horfley*	LXII 327	
ERGOT. An account of the difeafe called Ergot in French, from its fuppofed caufe, viz. vitiated rye - - *Tiffot*	LV 106	
ERIOCAULON. A letter on a rare plant found in the Ifle of Skye, fuppofed to be the eriocaulon decangulare - - *Hope*	LIX 241	
ESSAY INSTRUMENT. A new-invented effay-inftrument defcribed, with its ufes - *Boyle*	X 329	I 516
Extract of a letter relating to the effay-inftrument - -	— 353	— 520
ETRUSCAN. See *Coin*, *Infcription*.		
EVACUATION. A new trocart for the puncture in the hydrocephalus, and for other evacuations which are neceffary to be made at different times - - - *Le Cat*	XLVII 267	
EVAPORATION. A differtation on the nature of evaporation, and feveral phænomena of air, water, and boiling liquors - *Hamilton*	LV 146	
—— Obfervations on the annual evaporation at Liverpool in Lancafhire; and on evaporation confidered as a teft of the moifture or drynefs of the atmofphere - *Dobfon*	LXVII 1 244	
On Evaporation — — — — De Luc	1792: 400	

EUCLID.

	Trans.	Abridg.
EUCLID. A new and easy way of demonstrating some propositions in Euclid - *Ash*	XIV 672	I 7
—— Pappus of Alexandria's two general propositions taking in a great part of Euclid's porisms, restored by - - *Simpson*	XXXII 330	VI 76
EUGANEAN HILLS. An account of a curious giants causeway, or group of angular columns, newly discovered in the Euganean Hills, near Padua in Italy - - *Strange*	LXV 418	
EUPHORBIUM. An account of a lady who swallowed euphorbium - - *Willis*	LI 662	
EURE. An account of an aqueduct designed for carrying the River Eure to Versailles - - - *Anon.*	XV 1016	I 594
EURIPUS. A letter concerning the flux of the Euripus - - *Babin*	VI 2153	II 289
EXCENTRICITIES. Considerations concerning M. Cassini's geometrical and direct method for finding the apogees, excentricities and anomalies of the planets - *Mercator*	V 1168	I 253
—— A direct and geometrical method by which the aphelia, excentricities, and proportions of the orbs of the primary planets may be determined, without supposing the equality of the angle of motion at the other focus of the planets ellipsis - - *Halley*	XI 683	— 258
EXCENTRICITY. See *Planet.*		
EXCREMENTS. Letter on animalcula in the excrements of frogs - *Leewenhoek*	XXII 509	III 688
EXCRESCENCES. A considerable account touching vegetable excrescences - *Lister*	VI 2254	II 768
Another letter enlarging his communication on vegetable excrescences - *Lister*	— 2284	- 768,770
With some additions - *Lister*	— 3002	— 768
—— An account of one who had horny excrescences, or extraordinary large nails on his fingers and toes - - *Locke*	XIX 694	
—— Two letters concerning horn-like excrescences growing on the fingers, &c. - *Wroe*	XXIV 1899	V 387
—— Letter concerning the extirpation of an excrescence from the womb - *Burton*	XLVI 520	X 1022
—— Observations on fungous excrescences of the bladder; a cutting forceps for extirpating those excrescencies; and canulas for treating these diseases - - *Le Cat*	XLVII 292	
EXCRETORY DUCTS. An account of two glands,		

Eudiometer. An account of a new — Cavendish 73: 106.
A new Eudiometer, accompanied with experiments, elucidating its application. Pepys. 1807: 247.

	Tranf.	Abridg.
and their excretory ducts, lately difcovered in human bodies - *Cowper*	XXI 364	III 194
—— —— An account of an excretory duct from the glandula renalis - *Valfalva*	XXXIII 190	VII 540
—— —— An enquiry into a difcovery, faid to have been made by Sig. Valfalva, of an excretory duct, from the glandula renalis to the epididymis - - *Ranby*	— 270	— 541
EXHALATION. Letters concerning the caufes of the afcent of vapour and exhalation, and thofe of winds; and of the general phænomena of the weather and barometer - *Eeles*	XLIX 124	
—— An extract of an effay entituled, On the ufes of a knowledge of mineral exhalations, when applied to difcover the principles and properties of mineral waters, and the nature of burning fountains, and of thofe poifonous lakes which the antients called averni - *Brownrigg*	LV 236	
EXOCÆTUS VOLITANS. A defcription of the exocætus volitans, or flying fifh - *Brown*	LXVIII 791	
EXOSTOSES. A cafe of extraordinary exoftofes on the back of a boy - - *Freke*	XLI 369	IX 253
—— See *Bone*.		
EXOTIC. An account of the bifhop of London's garden at Fulham, with a catalogue of the exotic trees remaining in it June 25, 1751 *W. Watfon*	XLVII 241	
EXPANSION. Experiments concerning the expanfion of animal juices - *Boyle*	V 2043	
—— An account of an experiment made to afcertain the proportion of the expanfion of the liquor in the thermometer, with regard to the degrees of heat - - *Taylor*	XXXII 291	VI 2 49
EXPERIMENTS. Some obfervations and experiments made, and in a letter communicated to the publifher for the Royal Society, by the learned and inquifitive - *Martin Lifter*	IX 221	II 431, 466, 491, 505, 548, 555, 624
—— An account of fome experiments made before the Royal Society by F. Slare, with fhort applications of them to phyfical matters. 1. A parallel between lightening and a phofphorus. 2. By mixing two liquors actually cold, to produce fuch fparkling and fiery bodies as are not only vifible in the dark, but at noon day in the enlightened air. 3. By the addition of an oil to the foregoing mixture to produce a flame. 4. A refutation of Borrichius's experiment that pretends to accenfion.	XIII 289	III 350, 352

	Tranſ.	Abridg.
5. A new experiment with ebullition and incaleſcence. 6. Of cold produced without ebullition; giving ſome account of hyſterical paroxyſms. 7. Of cold produced by a very great ebullition, wherein the cold and hot fits of an ague are reſembled by a mixture of liquors		
—— A miſcellaneous catalogue of mean, vulgar, cheap and ſimple experiments - *Petty*	XV 849	III 683
EXPLOSION. An account of ſome experiments relating to the production of fire and flame, together with an exploſion, made by the mixture of two liquors actually cold - *Slare*	XVIII 201	— 359
—— An account of a fire-ball ſeen in the air, and of an exploſion heard Dec. 11, 1741, near London - - *Lord Beauchamp*	XLI 870	VIII 523
In Suſſex - - *Fuller*	— 871	— —
In Kent - - *Goſtlin*	— 872	— 524
—— Letter concerning an exploſion in the air, heard at Norwich June 7, 1750 - *Arderon*	XLVI 698	X 513
—— An account of rings, conſiſting of all the priſmatic colours made by electrical exploſions on the ſurface of pieces of metal *Prieſtley*	LVIII 68	
—— Experiments on the lateral force of electrical exploſions - - *Prieſtley*	LIX 57	
Various experiments on the force of electrical exploſions - - *Prieſtley*	— 63	
—— An inveſtigation of the lateral exploſion, and of the electricity communicated to the electrical circuit in a diſcharge - *Prieſtley*	LX 192	
—— A letter containing a ſhort account of an exploſion of air in a coal-pit at Middleton, near Leeds in Yorkſhire - *Bernard*	LXIII 217	
EYE. An obſervation containing a blemiſh in a horſe's eye, not hitherto diſcovered by any author - - - *Lower*	II 613	II 864
—— Several caſes relating chiefly to the eyes - - - *Turbervile*	XIV 737	III 34
—— Obſervations about the chryſtalline humour of the eye - - *Leewenhoek*	— 790	
—— An account of an extraordinary hæmorrhage at the glandula lacrimalis - *Havers*	XVIII 51	II 252
—— Letter concerning the eyes of beetles *Leewenhoek*	XXII 69	III 685
—— Letter concerning crabs eyes - *King*	— 672	II 831
—— An account of the Frieſland boy with letters in his eye - - *Ellis*	XXIII 1416	V 2 235
—— Letter concerning the chryſtalline humour in the		

+ Eye. Observations on the structure of the Eyes of Birds. – – – – 1795: 263.
The Croonian lecture, in which some of the morbid actions of the straight muscles and cornea of the Eye are explained, and their treatment considered. Home. 1797: 1.
An account of the orifice in the retina of the human eye, discovered by Professor Soemmering; to which are added proofs of this appearance being extended to the eyes of other animals. —— 1798: 332
The Bakerian Lecture. On the mechanism of the Eye. Young. 1801. 23.
The Croonian Lecture. On the power of the Eye to adjust itself to different distances, when deprived of the crystalline lens. Home. 1802: 1.

Eye-glasses. A new construction of Eye-glasses for such telescopes as may be applied to mathematical instruments. Ramsden 73: 94.

	Transf.	Abridg.
eye of whales, fish, and other creatures, and of the use of the eye-lids - *Leewenhoek*	XXIV 1723	V 2 267
~~—— An extraordinary case of a partial sight of objects - - - *Vater*~~	~~XXXIII 147~~	~~VII 490~~
—— An explication of the instruments used in a new operation of the eyes - *Cheselden*	XXXV 451	— 493
—— A letter concerning a very large tumour of the eye - - *Klein*	XXXVII 427	
—— The case of a wound in the cornea of the eye cured by - *Thomas Baker*	XLI 135	IX 121
—— A description of needles made for operations on the eyes - - *Cleland*	— 847	— 124
—— A remarkable cure performed on the eye of a young woman in Scotland - *Hope*	XLIII 194	XI 951
—— A letter concerning the stones called crabs eyes - - *Baker*	XLV 174	— 876
—— Extract of a letter containing the particulars of the cure of a wound in the cornea, and of a laceration of the uvea in the eye of a woman - - - *Aery*	— 411	— 954
—— A letter concerning a large piece of lath being thrust into a man's eye, who recovered of it - - - *Hassel*	— 520	— 955
—— A description of a new method of opening the cornea, in order to extract the crystalline humour - - *Sharp*	LXVIII 161	
—— A second account of a new method of opening the cornea for taking away the cataract *Sharp*	— 322	
—— A remarkable case of a morbid eye *Spry*	XLIX 18	
—— An account of a case of a diseased eye *Layard*	L 747	
—— Case of a man wounded in the left eye by a small sword - - *Geach*	LIII 234	
see Sight + EYE LIDS. Letter concerning the chrystalline humour in the eye of whales, fish, and other creatures, and of the use of the eye-lids - - - *Leewenhoek*	XXIV 1723	V 2 267
—— Letter concerning an uncommon palsey in the eye-lids - - *Cantwell*	XL 311	IX 121

F.

FABA S. IGNATII. An account of the virtues of Faba S. Ignatii - *Anon.*	XXI 87	II 648
Further account of the same - *Camelli*	— 88	— 649
Letter on Swammerdam's treatise, *De Faba S. Ignatii* - - *Hutton*	— 365	— —

	Trans.	Abridg.
FACE. A relation of two monſtrous pigs with the reſemblance of human faces - *Floyer*	XXI 431	II 900
—— An account of an unuſual blackneſs of the face - - - *Yonge*	XXVI 424	V 199
Further account - *Yonge*	— 432	— —
FAIRBURN. An account of the ſulphureous mineral waters of Caſtle Leod and Fairburn in the county of Roſs, and of the ſalt purging water of Pitkeathly in the county of Perth, Scotland - - *Monro*	LXII 15	
FALKLAND ISLANDS. An account of Falkland Iſlands - - - *Clayton*	LXVI 99	
FALL OF WATER. Part of a letter giving a relation of a wonderful fall of water from a ſpout upon the Moors in Lancaſhire *Richardſon*	XXX 1097	IV 2 108
FALLS. An account of the falls of the river Niagara, taken at Albany Oct. 10, 1721 *Boraſſaw*	XXXII 69	VI 2 173
FALLOPIAN TUBE. An account of an egg found in the tuba fallopiana of a woman lately diſſected; with ſeveral remarks touching generation - - - *Buiſſiere*	XVIII 11	III 211
FALLOPIAN TUBES. An abſtract of a remarkable caſe and cure of a woman, from whom a fœtus was extracted that had been lodged in one of the fallopian tubes thirteen years *Mounſey*	XLV 131	XI 1012
FARINA. Some experiments concerning the impregnation of the ſeeds of plants - *Logan*	XXXIX 192	VIII 804
—— A letter with ſome microſcopical obſervations on the farina of the red lily, and of worms diſcovered in ſmutty corn - *Needham*	XLII 634	— 816
—— Obſervations of the effects which the farina of peas of different colours have on each other - - - *Henchman*	XLIII 477	
—— The effects which the farina of bloſſoms of different ſorts of apple-trees had on the fruit of a neighbouring tree - *Cook*	— 525	X 751
—— A letter containing ſome microſcopical obſervations on the farina fœcundans of the holyoak and the paſſion flower - *Badcock*	XLIV 150	— 753
Further obſervations and experiments on the paſſion flower and its farina *Badcock*	— 166	— 756
—— A letter concerning the farina fœcundans of the yew-tree - - *Badcock*	— 189	— 757
—— A letter concerning a mixed breed of apples from the mixture of farina - *Cooke*	XLV 602	— 752
—— Part of a letter concerning the effects of the mixture of the farina of apple-trees *Cooke*	XLVI 205	— —

Fairy-rings. On Fairy-rings. - - - - - - - - Wollaston. 1807 : 133.

+ Fat. On the conversion of the substance of a Bird into a hard fatty matter. Smith^d. 1792: 197.

On the conversion of animal muscle into a substance much resembling Spermaceti. Gibbes. 1794: 169.

On the formation of Fat in the intestines of living animals 1795: 239.

Home. 1813: 146.

Fecundation of vegetables. An account of some experiments on the — Knight 1799. 195.

	Transf.	Abridg.
FARTHINGS. An account of what happened to a child who swallowed two copper farthings *Baynard*	XX 424	III 92
FASCINATION. Conjectures on the charming or fascinating power attributed to the rattle-snake; grounded on credible accounts, experiments, and observations - *Sloane*	XXXVIII 321	IX 55
FAT. An observation about the epiploon, or the double membrane, which covers the entrails of animals, and is filled with fat - - *Malpighi and Fracassati*	II 553	II 658
—— Microscopical observations concerning fat - - - *Leewenhoek*	IX 128	
—— A letter concerning the particles of fat - - - *Leewenhoek*	XXXII 93	VII 469
—— Extract of a letter concerning two men of an extraordinary bulk and weight *Knowlton*	XLIV 100	XI 1245
—— Letter concerning Mr. Bright, the fat man, at Malden in Essex - *Coe*	XLVII 188	
FECUNDITY. Remarks on the very different accounts that have been given of the fecundity of fish, with fresh observations on that subject *Harmer*	LVII 280	
FEET. The description and use of the pores in the skin of the hands and feet - *Grew*	XIV 566	III 9
—— Case of Nicholas Reeks, who was born with his feet turned inwards, which came to rights after being some time used to sit cross-legged - - - *Milner*	XLVI 239	XI 1113
FEMALES. An account of what has been of late observed of eggs to be found in all sorts of females - - *Kerkringius*	VII 4018	
FERMAT (M. DE). Character of M. de Fermat - - - *Oldenbourg*	I 15	
FERMENTATION. Observations on these three chymical operations, digestion, fermentation, and triture, or grinding (hitherto, in the author's opinion, not sufficiently regarded), by which many things of admirable use may be performed - - - *Langelot*	VII 5052	III 315
—— A way to make two clear spirituous inflammable liquors, which differ very little in taste and smell; and being mixed together, do give a fine carnation colour, without either sensible fermentation or alteration - *Geoffroy*	XXI 43	— 367
—— Observations upon the dissolutions and fermentations which we may call cold, because they are accompanied with a coolness of the liquors into which they pass - *Geoffroy*	XXII 951	V 421

Subject	Author	Transf.	Abridg.
Fern. A letter concerning the feed of fern	*Miles*	XLI 770	VIII 809
Ferreus Scipio. See *Equation.*			
Fertility. Inftances, hints, and regulations relating to a main point, folicited in the preface to this fourth volume, concerning the ufe to be made of vaults, deep wells, and cold confervatories, to find out the caufe or to promote the generation of falt, minerals, metals, cryftals, gems, ftones of divers kinds; and helps to conferve long or to haften putrefaction, fertility of any kind of land, &c.	*Beale*	IV 1135	II 728
Fever. Obfervations on diffection, and the motion of the blood in a fever -	*Leewenhoek*	XIII 347	III 384
—— A difcourfe of the operation of a blifter when it cures a fever -	*Cockburn*	XXI 161	— 260
—— A letter concerning the whitenefs on the tongue in fevers - -	*Leewenhoek*	XXV 2456	V 2 267
—— A relation of a deaf and dumb perfon who recovered his hearing and fpeech after a violent fever; with fome other medical and chirurgical obfervations -	*Martin*	— 2469	V [357]
—— A letter containing his obfervations upon the white matter on the tongues of feverifh perfons - - -	*Leewenhoek*	XXVI 210	V 2 267
—— Of the ufe of cold water in fevers	*Cyrillus*	XXXVI 142	VII 635
—— A letter relating to the cure of intermitting fevers at Tunis - -	*Shaw*	— 177	— 640
—— The cafe of Mr. Cox, furgeon, of Peterborough, who fell into a peftilential fever upon tapping a corpfe late dead of an hydropfy - - -		XLI 168	IX 212
—— An account of feveral perfons feized with the gaol fever working in Newgate, and of the manner in which the infection was communicated to one intire family -	*Pringle*	XLVIII 42	
—— An account of thofe malignant fevers that raged at Rouen at the end of the year 1753, and the beginning of 1754 -	*Le Cat*	XLIX 49	
—— Cafe of the efficacy of bark in the delirium of a fever - -	*Munckley*	L 609	
—— Letter on the good effects of the quaffi roots in fevers at Antigua -	*Farley*	LVIII 80	
—— Obfervations of a fick man furprizingly recovered from a fever -	*Benvenuti*	— 189	
—— Cafe of a man feized with a fever from the effects of meal-duft -	*Latham*	LX 451	
Fibres. A difcourfe concerning the fpiral, inftead of			

the

	Transf.	Abridg.
the supposed annular structure of the fibres of the intestines - - *Cole*	XI 603	III 88
—— Extract of a letter concerning the fibres of the muscles - - *Leewenhoek*	XXIX 55	V 390
—— Observations upon the membranes enclosing the fasciculi of fibres, into which a muscle is divided - - *Leewenhoek*	XXXI 129	VII 464
Observations on the muscular fibres of different animals - *Leewenhoek*	— 134	
- - - *Leewenhoek*	XXXII 72	— 468
—— An observation on the double fibres observable in the skeletons prepared from green leaves *Hollman*	XLI 789	VIII 818
Conjectures on the use of double fibres in some leaves, &c. - - *Hollman*	— 796	— 820
FIELDING. A brief narrative of the shot of Dr. Robert Fielding with a musket bullet, and its strange manner of coming out of his head, where it had laid near 30 years: written by himself - - *Fielding*	XXVI 317	V 205
FIGURES. An account of an antient mantle-tree in Northamptonshire, on which the date of it (for the year 1133) is expressed by the numeral figures, which shews the great antiquity of those figures in England -	XIII 399	I 107
—— On the use of numeral figures in England, as old as 1090 - - *Luffkin*	XXI 287	— 108
—— Letter concerning the use of the numeral figures in England in 1090 - *Wallis*	XXII 677	— —
—— Extract of a letter concerning an antient date found at Widgel Hall in Hertfordshire *Cope*	XXXIX 119	IX 420
Remarks on the above date - *Ward*	— 120	— 421
Further accounts of it - *Gulston*	— 122	
—— Some considerations on the antiquity and use of the Indian characters or figures *Cope*	— 131	— 426
—— Remarks upon an antient date over a gateway, near the cathedral at Worcester *Ward*	— 136	
—— An account of an antient date in Arabian figures, upon the north front of the parish church of Rumsey in Hampshire. *Barlow*	XLI 652	— 254
—— A brief inquiry into the reading of two dates in Arabian figures cut upon stones, which were found in Ireland - *Ward*	XLIII 283	XI 1260
—— A description of an antient date in Arabian figures at Walling, near Aldermarston, Berkshire - - *Ward*	XLV 603	— 1267
—— Concerning the various figures of the salts contained in several substances *Leewenhoek*	XV 1073	III 685

	Tranf.	Abridg.
—— Some eafy methods for the meafuring of curve-lined figures, plain and folid *Wallis*	XXII 547	I 58
—— A fpecimen of the general method of determining the quadratures of figures *Craig*	XXIII 1346	IV 26
—— An inquiry concerning the figure of fuch planets as revolve about an axis, fuppofing the denfity continually to vary from the center to the furface - - *Clairault*	XL 277	VIII 90
FILE. Account of a file rendered magnetical by lightening - - *Bremond*	XLI 614	— 506
FILTRING STONE. An account of the filtring ftone of Mexico, and compared with other ftones; by which it is fhewn, that it is of little or no ufe in purifying the waters which have paffed through it - - *Vaterus*	XXXIX 106	— 728
FINGER. An account of a periodical evacuation of blood at the end of one of the fingers - - - *Dublin Society*	XV 989	III 252
—— An account of one who had horny excrefcences or extraordinary large nails on his fingers and toes - - *Locke*	XIX 694	— 13
—— Two letters on horn-like excrefcences growing on the fingers, &c. - *Wroe*	XXIV 1899	V 378
FINLANDERS. A letter giving an account of the Norwegian Fins, or Finlanders - *Kinck*	XXXV 357	VII 4 44
FIRE. An experiment to prove that water, when agitated by fire, is infinitely more elaftic than air in the fame circumftance - *Clayton*	XLI 162	VIII 466
—— A propofal for checking in fome degree the progrefs of fires - - *Hales*	XLV 277	XI 1391
Additions - - *Mortimer*	— 382	— 1392
—— Extract of a letter concerning the everlafting fire in Perfia - *Mounfey*	— 296	X 267
—— An account of the cafe of a man who died of the effects of the fire at Eddyfton Lighthoufe, by melted lead running down his throat *Spry*	XLIX 477	
Another account - *Huxham*	— 483	
—— An account of a woman accidentally burnt to death at Coventry - *Wilmer*	LXIV 340	
—— Defcription of a moft effectual method of fecuring buildings againft fire *Lord Mahon*	LXVIII 884	
FIRE BALL. A letter giving an account of a fiery meteor feen in Jamaica to ftrike into the earth, with remarks on the weather, earthquakes, &c. of that ifland - - *Barham*	XXX 837	IV 2 31
—— —— An account of a fire-ball feen in the air,		

and

		Tranſ.	Abridg.
and of the exploſion heard Dec. 11, 1741, near London	*Lord Beauchamp*	XLI 870	VIII 523
In Suſſex	*Fuller*	— 871	— —
In Kent	*Goſtlin*	— 872	— 524
—— —— Account of a fire-ball ſeen in the air Dec. 11, 1741	*Maſon*	XLII 1	— —
—— —— An account of a fire-ball ſeen Dec. 11, 1741	*Cooke*	— 25	— 525
—— —— An account of the fire-ball ſeen Dec. 11, 1741	*Gordon*	— 58	— —
	Collinſon	— 60	
The appearance of a fiery meteor as ſeen by	*Cradock*	XLIII 78	
Account of a fiery meteor ſeen in the air July 14, 1745	*Coſtard*	— 522	
Account of a fiery meteor ſeen Dec. 16, 1742	*Mortimer*	— 524	
—— —— An account of an extraordinary fire-ball burſting at ſea	*Chalmers*	XLVI 366	X 480
—— —— An account of a fire-ball ſeen in the air July 22, 1750	*Smith*	XLVII 1	
Another account of the ſame	*Baker*	— 3	
—— —— Account of a fire-ball ſeen at Hornſey	*Hirſt*	XLVIII 773	
—— —— Several accounts of a fiery meteor which appeared Nov. 26, 1758; collected by	*Pringle*	LI 218	
Remarks on the ſeveral accounts of the fiery meteor which appeared Nov. 26, 1758, and on other ſuch bodies	*Pringle*	— 259	
—— —— Account of a fiery meteor ſeen at the Hague	*Gabry*	LIII 5	
—— —— An account of ſeveral fiery meteors ſeen in North America	*Winthorp*	LIV 185	
Account of a fiery meteor ſeen on the 10th of February in the ſhire of Berwick	*Brydone*	LXIII 163	
FIRE (Chemiſtry). An account of ſome experiments relating to the production of fire and flame; together with an exploſion made by the mixture of two liquors actually cold	*Slare*	XVIII 201	III 359
—— Thoughts on Dr. Hales new method of diſtillation by the united force of air and fire	*Brownrigg*	XLIX 534	
—— Actual fire in detonation, produced by the contact of tinfoil, with the ſalt compoſed of copper and the nitrous acid	*Higgins*	LXIII 137	
—— Experiments on ignited bodies	*Roebuck*	LXVI 509	
FIRE (Electricity). Two letters concerning the ro-			

	Tranſ.	Abridg.
tatory motion of glaſs tubes about their axes, when placed in a certain manner before the fire - - - *Wheler*	XLIII 341	X 551
—— Letter concerning electrical fire *Miles*	XLIV 78	— 322
—— A letter concerning a fuſtian-frock being ſet on fire by electricity - *Rocke*	XLV 323	— 406
—— Extract of a letter concerning the electricity of glaſs that has been expoſed to ſtrong fires *Boſe*	XLVI 189	— 329
FIRE ENGINE. An account of Mr. T. Savery's engine for raiſing water by the help of fire *Savery*	XXI 228	I 544
—— —— The beſt proportions for ſteam-engine cylinders of a given content conſidered *Blake*	XLVII 197	
—— —— An engine for raiſing water by fire: being an improvement of Savery's conſtruction to render it capable of working itſelf; invented by M. de Moura of Portugal; deſcribed by - - - *J. Smeaton*	— 436	
—— —— Experiments on applying the Rev. Dr. Hales method of diſtilling ſalt water to the ſteam-engine - *Fitzgerald*	L 53	
—— —— Farther experiments for increaſing the quantity of ſteam in a fire engine *Fitzgerald*	— 370	
—— —— An attempt to improve the manner of working the ventilators by the help of fire-engines - - *Fitzgerald*	— 727	
FIRE (Natural hiſtory). A letter rectifying the relation of ſalamanders living in fire *Steno*	I 377	II 816
—— The deſcription of a well and earth in Lancaſhire taking fire by a candle approached to it - - - *Shirley*	II 482	III 149
—— Obſervations on a ſubterranean fire in a coal mine near Newcaſtle - *Hodgſon*	XI 762	II 383
—— An account of a very odd erruption of fire out of a ſpot of earth near Fierenzola in Italy - - - *St. Clair*	XX 378	— 385
—— See *Diſtillation.*		
FISH. Account of a ſtrange and curiouſly-contrived fiſh from New England - *Winthrop*	V 1151	— 832
—— Thoughts about the ſtellar fiſh deſcribed vol. V. p. 1151 - *Willoughby*	— 1201	
—— Phænomena afforded by ſhell-fiſhes in an exhauſted receiver - - *Boyle*	— 2023	I 304
—— Of the phænomena of a ſcale-fiſh in an exhauſted receiver - *Boyle*	— 2024	
—— A conjecture concerning the bladders of air that are found in fiſhes by A. I. and illuſtrated by		

an

		Tranſ.	Abridg.
an experiment ſuggeſted by the Hon. Robert Boyle - -	*A. I.*	X 310	II 846
— Account of a poiſonous fiſh in one of the Bahama Iſlands - -	*Locke*	X 312	— 824
— Conſiderations on the ſwimming-bladders in fiſhes - -	*Ray*	— 349	I 846
— Obſervations on the purple-fiſh -	*Cole*	XV 1278	II 823, 832
— A general idea of the ſtructure of the internal parts of fiſh - -	*Preſton*	XIX 419	— 847
— Letter concerning a ſhower of fiſhes	*Conny*	XX 289	— 144
— Letter concerning the chryſtalline humour in the eye of whales, fiſh, and other creatures, and of the uſe of the eye-lids	*Leewenhoek*	XXIV 1723	V 2 267
— A letter concerning the circulation of the blood in fiſhes - -	*Leewenhoek*	XXVI 250	— — —
— An account of ſome experiments touching the keeping of fiſhes in water under different circumſtances - -	*Haukſbee*	XXVII 431	IV 2 182
— Obſervations on the muſcular fibres of fiſh - - -	*Leewenhoek*	XXXI 190	VII 431
— An account of a narhual, or unicorn fiſh, lately taken in the river Oſt, in the Dutchy of Bremen, 1736 - -	*Steigerthal*	XL 147	IX 71
A deſcription of the ſame fiſh	*Hampe*	— 149	— 72
— A method of preparing ſpecimens of fiſh by drying their ſkins -	*Gronovius*	XLII 52	
— A letter on keeping of ſmall fiſh in glaſs jars; and of an eaſy way of catching fiſh	*Arderon*	XLIV 23	XI 869
— Abſtract of a letter concerning ſome obſervations made on the banſticle, or prickleback, and alſo on fiſh in general -	*Arderon*	— 424	— 872
— Extract of a letter concerning the hearing of fiſh - -	*Arderon*	XLV 149	— 880
— A letter concerning an extraordinary fiſh, called in Ruſſia, Quab; and concerning the ſtones called crabs-eyes - -	*Baker*	— 174	— 876
— Upon the ſounds and hearing of fiſhes by Jac. Theod. Klein; or ſome account of a treatiſe intituled, " An enquiry into the reaſons why the author of an epiſtle concerning the hearing of fiſhes endeavours to prove they are all mute and deaf - -	*Brockleſby*	— 233	— 883
— Divers means for preſerving from corruption dead birds intended to be ſent to remote countries, ſo that they may arrive there in good condition. Some of the ſame means may be			

employed

	Transf.	Abridg.
employed for preserving quadrupeds, reptiles, fishes, and insects - *Reaumur*	XLV 309	
—— Observations on keeping fish in glasses *Arderon*	— 321	XI 871
—— The description of a fish shewed to the Royal Society by Ralph Bigland *Mortimer*	XLVI 518	— 879
Experiments of fish and flesh preserved in lime-water - - *Hume*	XLVIII 163	
—— An account of some trials to keep water and fish sweet with lime-water - *Hales*	— 826	
—— An account of Mr. Tull's method of castrating fish - - *W. Watson*	— 870	
—— An account of four undescribed fishes of Aleppo - - - *Russel*	XLIX 445	
—— An account of a remarkable fish taken in the King's Road near Bristol - *Ferguson*	LIII 170	
—— Account of a fish from Batavia, called Jaculator - - - *Schlosser*	LIV 89	
Some farther account of the Jaculator fish, from Mr. Hommel of Batavia; together with the description of another species by Dr. Pallas - - - *Hommel and Pallas*	LVI 186	
—— A letter on some particular fish found in Wales - - - *Barrington*	LVII 204	
—— Remarks on the very different accounts that have been given of the fecundity of fish, with fresh observations on that subject *Harmer*	— 280	
—— An account of the lymphatic system in fish - - - *Hewson*	LIX 204	
—— A letter containing an account of a singular fish from the South Seas - *Tyson*	LXI 247	
—— An account of some curious fishes sent from Hudson's Bay - - *Forster*	LXIII 149	
—— An account of some poisonous fish in the South Seas - - *Anderson*	LXVI 544	
—— A description of the exocætus volitans, or flying-fish - - *Brown*	LXVIII 791	
FISHERY. A letter concerning pearl-fishing in the north of Ireland - *Redding*	XVII 659	II 828
—— An account of a voyage to Chusan in China; with a description of the island, of the several sorts of teas, of the fishing and agriculture of the Chinese, &c. with several observations not hitherto taken notice of - *Cunningham*	XXIII 1201	V 2 171
—— An account of the discovery of the manner of making isinglass in Russia; with a particular description of its manufacture in England, from the produce of British fisheries *Jackson*	LXIII 1	

FISTULA

+ Fish. Great quantity thrown ashore in the island of Sumatra. Marsden. 71: 383.
On the arrangement and mechanical action of the muscles of fishes. Carlisle. 1806: 1.
Experiments to ascertain the influence of the spinal marrow
on the action of the heart in fishes. —— Clift. 1815: 91.

Flame. Some observations on flame. — — Davy. 1816: 115.

Some researches on flame. Davy. 1817: 45.

Floating bodies. The construction and analysis of geometrical propositions, determining the positions assumed by homogeneal bodies which float freely, and at rest, on a fluid's surface; also determining the stability of ships, and of other floating bodies. Atwood. 1796: 46.

		Tranf.	Abridg.
Fistula Lacrymalis. Some thoughts on the operation of the fistula lachrymalis	*Hunauld*	XXXIX 54	IX 122
——— A new method of treating the fistula lachrymalis	*Blizard*	LXX 239	
Fits. An account of strange epileptick fits	*Leigh*	XXIII 1174	V 366
——— Case of a boy troubled with convulsive fits cured by a discharge of worms	*Oram*	L 518	
Another account	*Gaze*	— 521	
More observations	*Wall*	— 836	
Fixed Air. See *Air*.			
Flame. An account of some observations relating to the production of fire and flame; together with an explosion made by a mixture of two liquors actually cold	*Slare*	XVIII 201	III 259
——— An account of an uncommon phænomenon in Dorsetshire, of flame arising out of the earth	*Stephens*	LII 119	
Flamingo. The natural history and description of the phænicopterus, or flamingo; with two views of the head and three of the tongue	*Douglass*	XXIX 523	V 63
Flanel. Extract of a letter concerning the property of new flanel sparkling in the dark	*Cooke*	XLIV 457	X 343
Fleas. Letter concerning the generation of fleas	*Cestone*	XXI 42	II 789
——— Microscopical observations on the proboscis of fleas	*Leeuwenhoek*	XXV 2305	V 2 267
Flesh. Experiments on fish and flesh preserved in lime water	*Hume*	XLVIII 163	
——— An account of a curious fleshy coral-like substance, with some observations on it by Mr. John Ellis	*Schlosser*	XLIX 449	
Flies. A letter on the effects of elder, in preserving growing plants from insects and flies	*Gullet*	LXII 348	
Flood. Letter giving an account of a viscous slime left after a flood in the territory of the Landgrave of Thuringue; with observations	*Böse*	XLVIII 358	
Florentine Philosophers. See *Frost*.			
Flowers. Several experiments concerning the preserving of flowers, fruit, &c.	*Southwell*	XX 42	II 623, 750
——— A letter giving an account of tulips, and of such bulbous plants, flowering much sooner when their bulbs are placed upon bottles filled with water, than when planted in the ground	*Triewald*	XXXVII 79	VI 2 54
An account of the same experiments tried the next year by	*Miller*	— 81	— 355

FLU

	Transf.	Abridg.
—— Experiments and observations on bulbous roots, plants, and seeds, growing in water *Curteis*	XXXVIII 267	VIII 825
—— A letter concerning a zoophyton somewhat resembling the flower of marygold *Hughes*	XLII 590	IX 111
—— Observations upon the sex of flowers, occasioned by a letter upon the same subject by Mr. Mylius of Berlin - - *W. Watson*	XLVII 169	
FLUENTS. Of the fluents of multinomials and series affected by radical signs, which do not begin to converge till after the second term - - - *Simpson*	XLV 328	X 1
—— A disquisition concerning certain fluents which are assignable by the arcs of the conic sections; wherein are investigated some new and useful theorems for computing such fluents *Landen*	LXI 298	
FLUIDS (ANIMAL). Experiments to prove the existence of a fluid in the nerves - *Stuart*	XXXVII 327	VI 2 22
—— Experiments on animal fluids in the exhausted receiver - *Darwin*	LXIV 344	
FLUIDS (Natural philosophy). New experiments made about the superficial figures of fluids, especially of liquors contiguous to other liquors - - - *Boyle*	XI 775	I 526
- - - - *Boyle*	— 799	— 531
—— A description of the apparatus for making experiments on the refractions of fluids; with a table of the specifick gravities, angles of observations, and ratio of refractions of several fluids - - *Hauksbee*	XXVII 204	IV 2 182
—— Experiments relating to the resistance of fluids made before the Royal Society *Desaguliers*	XXXI 142	VI 299
—— A narrative of a new invention of expanding fluids, by their being conveyed into certain ignited vessels, where they are immediately rarified into an elastic impelling force sufficient to give motion to hydraulopneumatical, and other engines, for raising water, and other uses, &c. - - - *Payne*	XLI 821	VIII 638
—— Experiments and observations on the compressibility of water, and some other fluids *Canton*	LIV 261	
—— A course of experiments to ascertain the specific buoyancy of cork in different waters; the respective weights and buoyancy of salt water and fresh water; and for determining the exact weight of human and other bodies in fluids - - - *Wilkinson*	LV 95	
—— An attempt to explain some of the principal phæ-		

nomena

+ Fluents. A new method of finding fluents by continuation. Vince. 76: 432.

+ Fluids (Animal). Observations on Albumen, and some other Animal Fluids; with remarks on their analysis by electro-chemical decomposition. Brande. 1809: 373.

Experiments to prove that fluids pass directly from the stomach to the circulation of the blood, and from thence into the cells of the spleen, the gall bladder and urinary bladder, without going through the thoracic duct. Home. 1811: 163.

Chemical researches on the blood, and some other animal Fluids. Brande. 1812: 90.

4 Fluids. An essay on the cohesion of fluids. - - - - - - - - - - -Young. 1805: 65.

[illegible] Acid.

Fluor Spar. Some experiments and observations on the substances produced in different chemical processes on Fluor Spar. Davy. 1813:

	Tranf.	Abridg.
nomena of electricity by means of an elaftic fluid - - *Cavendifh*	LXI 584	
—— Obfervations and experiments tending to confirm Dr. Ingenhoufz's theory of the electrophorus, and to fhew the impermeability of glafs to electric fluid - - *Henly*	LXVIII 1049	
—— See *Water*.		
FLUX. An account of an extraordinary flux of the blood by the penis - *Howman*	XXXII 418	VII 539
—— A difcourfe concerning the difficulty of curing fluxes - - *Cockburn*	XXXVII 385	— 641
FLUXIONS. Some remarkable fpecimens of the doctrine of fluxions, or examples wherein the ufe and excellence of that method in folving geometrical problems is fhewn *De Moivre*	XIX 52	I 34
—— A letter concerning the difpute about the invention of the method of fluxions, or differential method; with M. Leibnitz's anfwer *Conti*	XXX 923	IV 162
FLY. An account of a kind of fly that is viviparous - - - *Lifter*	VI 2170	II 787
—— Account of a viviparous fly - *Lifter*	XIV 592	— —
—— An account of the infect called the vegetable fly - - *W. Watfon*	LIII 271	
FOCUS. A method by which a glafs of a fmall plano-convex fphere may be made to refract the rays of light to a focus of a far greater diftance than is ufual - - *Hook*	I 202	I 193
—— A direct and geometrical method by which the aphelia, excentricities, and proportion of the orbs of the primary planets may be determined, without fuppofing the equality of the angle of motion at the other focus of the planet's ellipfis - - *Halley*	XI 683	— 258
—— An inftance of the excellence of the modern algebra, in the refolution of the problem of finding the foci of optick glaffes univerfally *Halley*	XVII 960	— 183
—— Some fimple properties of conic fections, deduced from the nature of focus's *De Moivre*	XXX 622	IV 3
FOETUS. A way of preferving birds taken out of the fhells, and other fmall fœtus's *Boyle*	I 199	III 650
—— Extract out of the third and feventh Venetian Giornale de Letterati, concerning the formation of fœtus's -	VI 2224	
—— An account of an odd fœtus lately born at Paris - - - - *Denys*	VIII 6157	— 23
—— An account concerning the formation of a fœtus in the tefticle - *St. Maurice*	XIII 285	— 212

	Transf.	Abridg.
—— An account of a fœtus lying without the uterus in the belly - - *Savard*	XIX 314	III 214
—— A letter giving an account of the bones of a fœtus voided per anum, some years after conception - - *Morley*	— 486	
—— An account of a fœtus voided by the ulcerated navel of a negro - - *Brodie*	— 580	— 219
—— Account of a woman who voided the bones of a fœtus above the os pubis, and by other extraordinary ways *Philosophical Society at Oxford*	XX 292	— —
—— An extract of a relation containing a remarkable history of a fœtus without the womb *Fern*	XXI 121	- 214,216
—— An account of a woman who voided the greatest part of a fœtus by the navel *Birbeck*	XXII 1000	V 305
—— Letter concerning the bones of a human fœtus voided through an impostume in the groin - - - *Skippon*	XXIV 2077	— 306
—— An account of a puppy in the womb, that received no nourishment by the mouth *Brady*	— 2176	- 34[353]
—— An account of several extra-uterine fœtus's *Yonge*	XXVI 424	— 306
Further account - *Yonge*	— 432	
—— Letter concerning the bones of a dead fœtus taken out of the uterus of a cow *Sherman*	— 450	— 54
—— Account of a child's crying in the womb - - - *Derham*	— 485	— 310
A short dissertation on the child's crying in the womb - *Derham*	— 487	— —
—— An account of a fœtus that continued 46 years in the mother's body *Steigertahl*	XXXI 126	VII 554
—— An account of an extra-uterine fœtus taken out of a woman after death, that had continued five years and a half in the body *Houston*	XXXII 387	— 555
—— Case of the head and ribs of a fœtus brought forth by the anus - *Lindestolpe*	XXXIII 171	— 557
—— An account of the præternatural delivery of a fœtus at the anus - *Nourse*	XXXVI 435	— 559
—— Case of a woman who had a fœtus in her abdomen for nine years - *Bromfeild*	XLI 697	IX 191
—— An account of a monstrous fœtus resembling a hooded monkey - *Gregory*	— 764	— 315
—— Case of the bones of a fœtus coming away by the anus - - *Winthrop*	XLIII 304	XI 1015
—— A letter concerning the bones of a fœtus voided per anum - - *Simon*	— 529	— 1016
—— An account of a child being taken out of the abdomen, after having lain there upwards of 16 years - - *Myddleton*	XLIV 617	— 1017

—— A let-

+ Foetus. On the aeration of the foetal blood in different classes of animals. Home. 1810: 205.

	Transf.	Abridg.
——— A letter concerning the bones of a fœtus being discharged through an ulcer near the navel - - - *Drake*	XLV 121	XI 1019
——— An abstract of the remarkable case and cure of a woman, from whom a fœtus was extracted that had been lodged in one of the fallopian tubes thirteen years - *Mounsey*	— 131	— 1012
——— An account of double fœtus's of calves *Le Cat*	— 497	— 1216
——— Some accounts of the fœtus in utero, being differently affected by the small-pox *W. Watson*	XLVI 235	— 1042
——— An account of a monstrous fœtus without any mark of sex - - *Baster*	— 479	— 1208
——— Case of a woman from whom the bones of a fœtus were extracted - *Debenham*	XLVII 92	
——— Some observations proving, that the fœtus is in part nourished by the liquor amnii *Fleming*	XLIX 254	
——— An account of a monstrous human fœtus having neither head, heart, lungs, stomach, spleen, pancreas, liver nor kidnies - *Le Cat*	LVII 1	
——— History of a fœtus born with a very imperfect brain; to which is subjoined, a supplement of the essay on the use of ganglions *Johnston*	— 118	
——— An account of a very small fœtus brought into the world, at the same time with a child at its full growth - - *Warner*	LX 453	
Fogs. A letter inclosing an account of some observations on atmospherical electricity, in regard of fogs, mists, &c. with some remarks *Ronayne*	LXII 137	
——— An account of some new experiments in electricity, containing, 1. An enquiry whether vapour be a conductor of electricity. 2. Some experiments to ascertain the direction of the electric matter in the discharge of the Leyden bottle. 3. Experiments on the lateral explosion in the discharge of the Leyden bottle. 4. The description and use of a new prime conductor. 5. Miscellaneous experiments made principally in 1771 and 1772. 6. Experiments and observations on the electricity of fogs, in pursuance of those made by Thomas Ronayne, Esq. with a plan of an electrical journal, &c. - - *Henley*	LXIV 389	
Foliate. A ready description and quadrature of a curve of the third order, resembling that commonly called foliate - *De Moivre*	XXIX 329	IV 24
Folkestone. Account of a very uncommon sinking of the earth near Folkestone in Kent *Sachetti*	— 469	IV 2 248

	Tranſ.	Abridg.
Food. An abſtract concerning a ſtrange preſervation of four men in a mine 24 days without food - - - *Anon.*	XIV 577	
—— A query concerning the food of the humming bird - - *Grew*	XVII 815	II 854
—— Letter concerning men's feeding on fleſh *Wallis*	XXII 769	V 1
Anſwer - - *Tyſon*	— 774	
Second letter - - *Wallis*	— 783	
—— Copy of an affidavit made in Scotland of a boy's living a conſiderable time without food *Blair*	XXXI 28	VII 668
—— An account of ſome trials to cure the ill taſte of milk, which is occaſioned by the food of cows, either from turnips, cabbages, or autumnal leaves, &c: alſo to ſweeten ſtinking water - - - *Hales*	XLIV 339	
—— An account of a woman in the ſhire of Roſs living without food or drink *Mackenzie*	LXVII 1	
—— See *Boulimia.*		
Foot (Mathematics). A letter touching the invention of dividing a foot into many thouſand parts for mathematical purpoſes - *Townley*	II 457	I 218
More ways for the ſame purpoſes	— 459	— 220
A deſcription of the inſtrument for dividing a foot into many thouſand parts, and thereby meaſuring the diameters of planets to great exactneſs - -	— 541	— 219
—— An enquiry into the meaſure of the Roman foot - - - *Raper*	LI 774	
Foot (Phyſic). Account of a briſtle that was lodged in a gentleman's foot, and cauſed a violent inflammation - - *Arderon*	XLIV 192	XI 1114
Foramen Ovale. An extraordinary caſe of the foramen ovale of the heart being open in an adult - - *Amyand*	XXXIX 172	IX 134
A letter concerning the foramen ovale being found open in the hearts of adults, and of the figure of the canal of the urethra *Le Cat*	XLI 681	— —
Force. An account of ſome experiments for trying the force of great guns - *Greaves*	XV 1090	I 495
—— Some experiments and obſervations on the force of the preſſure of the water at great depths	XVII 504	— 521
—— On the laws of centripetal force - *Keill*	XXVI 174	IV 359
—— A letter concerning an experiment, whereby it has been attempted to ſhew the falſity of the common opinion in relation to the force of bodies in motion - *Pemberton*	XXXII 57	VI 276

	Trans.	Abridg.
—— An account of ſome experiments made to prove, that the force of moving bodies is proportionable to their velocities *Deſaguliers*	XXXII 269	VI 281
—— Animadverſions upon ſome experiments relating to the force of moving bodies; with two new experiments on the ſame ſubject - - - *Deſaguliers*	— 285	— 221
—— A remark upon the new opinion relating to the forces of moving bodies, in the caſe of the colliſion of non-elaſtic bodies *Eames*	XXXIV 183	— 287
—— Remarks upon a ſuppoſed demonſtration, that the moving forces of the ſame body are not as the velocities, but as the ſquares of the velocities - - *Eames*	— 188	— 289
—— Remarks upon ſome experiments in hydraulics, which ſeem to prove, that the forces of equal moving bodies are as the ſquares of their velocities - - *Eames*	XXXV 343	— 292
—— A letter occaſioned by the preſent controverſy among mathematicians, concerning the proportion of velocity and force in bodies in motion - - - *Samuel Clarke*	— 381	— 294
—— An account of an experiment contrived by G. J. s'Graveſande, relating to the force of moving bodies; ſhewn to the Royal Society by - - - *Deſaguliers*	XXXVIII 143	VIII 235
—— Some electrical experiments chiefly regarding the repulſive force of electrical bodies *Wheeler*	XLI 98	— 406
—— A narrative of a new invention of expanding fluids, by their being conveyed into certain ignified veſſels, where they are immediately rarified into an elaſtic impelling force ſufficient to give motion to hydraulopneumatical and other engines, for raiſing water and other uſes, &c. - - - *Payne*	— 821	— 638
—— Some new thoughts for diſcovering whether pendulums are obſtructed by any centrifugal force - - *Polenus*	XLII 299	— 250
—— An inquiry into the meaſure of the force of bodies in motion; with a propoſal of an experimentum crucis, to decide the controverſy about it - - *Jurin*	XLIII 423	X 174
—— An eſſay on the force of percuſſion - - - *Richardſon*	LVIII 17	
—— A letter containing a demonſtration of a law of motion, in the caſe of a body deflected by two		

		Tranſ.	Abridg.
forces tending conſtantly to two fixed points	*Robertſon*	LIX 74	
Forceps. Obſervations on fungous excreſcences of the bladder, a cutting forceps for extirpating theſe excreſcences, and canulas for treating theſe diſeaſes	*Le Cat*	XLVII 292	
Forehead. Part of two letters concerning a prodigious os frontis in the medicine ſchool at Leyden	*Molyneux*	XV 880	III 2
Fossil. Of the abundance of foſſil wood found under ground in Lincolnſhire	*Anon.*	V 2050	II 423
—— Letter concerning Broughton in Lincolnſhire; with obſervations on the ſhell-fiſh obſerved in the quarries about that place	*De la Pryme*	XXII 677	— 428
—— Obſervations on the foſſils of Reculver Cliffe; with a note by the publiſher, H. Sloane	*Gray*	— 762	IV 461
—— Part of two letters concerning foſſils	*Lhwyd*	XXIV 1566	IV 2 264
—— A letter concerning Harwich Cliffe, and the foſſil ſhells found there	*Dale*	— 1568	— — —
—— A letter concerning ſome foſſils of Swiſſerland	*Leewenhoek*	— 1774	V 2 267
—— A catalogue of foſſils, ſhells, metals, minerals, &c. which J. J. Scheuchzer of Zurich ſent to J. Petiver	*Petiver*	— 2042	IV 2 286
—— A catalogue of the minerals, petrified ſhells, and other foſſils, ſent from C. M. Spener, of Berlin, to J. Petiver	*Petiver*	— 2082	— — —
—— Advertiſement of a collection of ſpecimens of foſſils to be had of Alb. Thomas, for one guinea a ſet	*Thomas*	XXVI 77	— — —
—— An account of the impreſſion of the almoſt entire ſkeleton of a large animal in a very hard ſtone found at Elſton, near Newark, Nottinghamſhire	*Stukeley*	XXX 963	— - 272
—— An account of elephants teeth and bones found under ground	*Sloane*	XXXV 457	
—— Of foſſil teeth and bones of elephants, part II.	*Sloane*	— 497	VI 2 211
—— An account of the ſeveral ſtrata of earth and foſſils found in ſinking the mineral well at Holt	*Lewis*	— 489	— - 225
—— A letter ſerving to accompany the pictures of an extraordinary foſſil ſkull of an ox with the cores of the horns	*Klein*	XXXVII 427	VII 4 01
—— A letter concerning the manuring of land with foſſil ſhells	*Pickering*	XLIII 191	X 796

—— Let-

Forest, submarine, on the east coast of England. Correa. 1799. 145.

+ Fossils. Account of a Stag's head and horns found at Alport in Derbyshire. Barker. 75:353.
Account of a substance found in a clay-pit. Wiseman. 1798: 567.

An account of some organic remains found near Brent-
ford, Middlesex. — — — — — Trimmer. 1813: 131.

On a fossil human skeleton from Guadeloupe. — — Konig. 1814:107.

Some account of the fossil remains of an animal more nearly
allied to Fishes than any of the other classes of animals. —
Some further account of the fossil remains of an animal, Home. — 571.
of which a description was given to the Society in 1814. — 1816:318.

An account of some fossil remains of the Rhinoceros,
discovered by Mr. Whitby, in a cavern inclosed in the lime-
stone rock, from which he is forming the Breakwater at
Plymouth. — — — 1817:176.

Additional facts respecting the fossil remains of an animal,
on the subject of which two papers have been printed in the
On a submarine forest, on the coast of England. Correa. 1799. 145.
Philos. Transact., showing that the bones of the sternum resemble those of the Ornithorhynchus paradoxus. — 1818. 24.

		Tranſ.	Abridg.
—— Letter concerning an extraordinary large foſſil tooth of an elephant	*Baker*	XLIII 331	X 599
—— An account of ſome foſſils found in Ireland	*Simon*	— 529	— 670
—— Letter concerning a non-deſcript petrified inſect	*Lyttleton*	XLVI 598	— 656
Further account of the before-mentioned Dudley foſſil	*Anon.*	— 600	— —
—— An account of ſome uncommon foſſil bodies	*Baker*	XLVIII 117	
—— A letter concerning the foſſil found at Dudley in Staffordſhire, and deſcribed, N° 496	*Da Coſta*	— 286	
—— An account of ſome fungitæ, and other curious coralloid foſſil bodies	*Pennant*	XLIX 513	
—— Account of a remarkable foſſil orthoceratites	*Wright*	— 670, 672	
—— An account of ſome foſſile fruits, and other bodies, found in the iſland of Shepey	*Parſons*	L 396	
—— A ſhort deſcription of ſome high mountains, in which there is a great quantity of foſſile wood	*Hollman*	LI 506	
—— An account of ſome very large foſſil teeth found in North America	*Collinſon*	LVII 464	
Sequel to the account	*Collinſon*	— 468	
—— Some account of a foſſil lately found near Chriſt Church in Hampſhire	*Barrington*	LXIII 171	
FOUNTAINS. A particular account of the origin of fountains; and to ſhew that the rain and ſnow waters are ſufficient to make fountains and rivers run perpetually	*Anon.*	X 447	II 329
—— An account of boiling and other fountains	*Robinſon*	XV 1036	— 349
—— An extract of an eſſay entituled, On the uſes of a knowledge of mineral exhalations when applied to diſcover the principles and properties of mineral waters, and the nature of burning fountains, and of thoſe poiſonous lakes which the antients called Averni	*Brownrigg*	LV 236	
FOWL. Anatomical obſervations in the heads of fowl made at ſeveral times	*Moulen*	XVII 711	— 860
—— Method of catching fowl and deer in the iſland of Ceilan	*Strachan*	XXIII 1094	V 2 179
—— Letter concerning a pin found in the gizard of a fowl	*Regnart*	XXIV 2055	V 53
FRACASSATI. A confirmation of the experiments			

	Tranf.	Abridg.
made by Sign. Fracaffati in Italy, by injecting acid liquors into the blood - *Boyle*	II 551	III 232
FRACTIONS. The reduction of rational fractions into more fimple ones - *De Moivre*	XXXII 162	VI 51
—— An inveftigation of fome theorems which fuggeft fome remarkable properties of the circle, and are of ufe in refolving fractions whofe denominations are certain multinomials into more fimple ones - - *Landen*	XLVIII 566	
—— Of the theory of circulating decimal fractions - - - *Robertfon*	LVIII 207	
FRACTURE. Obfervations on a fracture in the upper part of the thigh bone - *Douglas*	XXIX 499	V 388
—— Part of a letter concerning a cafe of chirurgery, which is commmonly miftaken for a fracture of the patella - - *Deverel*	XXXI 44	VII 678
—— The defcription and draught of a machine for reducing fractures of the thigh *Ettrick*	XLI 562	IX 254
—— Obfervations of a fracture of the os humeri by the power of the mufcles only *Amyand*	XLIII 293	XI 1103
An account of the fracture of the os ilium, and its cure - - *Layard*	— 537	— 1110
—— An account of the extraction of three inches and ten lines of the bone of the upper arm, which was followed by a regeneration of the bony matter; with a defcription of a machine made ufe of to keep the upper and lower pieces of the bone at their proper diftances, during the time that the regeneration was taking place, and which may alfo be of fervice in fractures happening near the head of that bone *Le Cat*	LVI 270	
—— An account of a new-invented inftrument for fractured legs - - *Sharp*	LVII 80	
FRAGILITY. An account of fome experiments lately made in Holland upon the fragility of unannealed glafs veffels - *Anon.*	XLIII 505	— 1343
FRANCE. Obfervations made in the fouthern parts of France - - - *De Martel*	V 1179	II 425, 657, 309
—— Letter relating to that ifthmus, or neck of land, which is fuppofed to have joined England and France in former times, where now is the paffage between Dover and Calais *Wallis*	XXII 967	IV 2 227
FRANCFORT. Letter concerning ofteocolla, and other obfervables near Francfort on the Oder - - - *Beckman*	III 771	II 148, 461 III 603
FRICTION. Some obfervables on the effects of touch and friction - *Oldenburg*	I 206	— 10

—— An

Freezing Mixtures. see Cold (Chemistry).

+ Friction. On the motion of Bodies affected by friction. Vince. 75:165.

FRIction FRO

	Transf.	Abridg.
—— An account of several experiments concerning the running of water in pipes, as it is retarded by friction and intermixed air; with a description of a new machine, whereby pipes may be cleared of air as the water runs along without stand-pipes, or the help of any hand - - - *Desaguliers*	XXXIV 77	VI 347
—— An examination of M. Perault's new-invented axis in peritrochio, said to be void of friction: with an experiment to confirm the reasoning made upon an axis in peritrochio, first used in M. Perault's manner, then in the common way - - - *Desaguliers*	XXXVI 222	— 317
A farther examination of the above	— 228	— 20
—— An account of two experiments of the friction of pullies - *Desaguliers*	XXXVII 394	— 322
—— A method of lessening the quantity of friction in engines - - *Fitzgerald*	LIII 139	
—— See *Engine*.		
FRIGHT. The case of Henry Axford, who recovered the use of his tongue after having been four years dumb, by means of a frightful dream - - - *Squire*	XLV 148	XI 958
FRIULI. Letter concerning the mines of mercury in Friuli - - *Pope*	I 21	II 577
—— A letter concerning the mines of Friuli; confirming as well the account given on that subject, vol. I. p. 21, as enlarging the same with some additions - *Brown*	IV 1080	— 579
FROGS. The phænomena afforded by them in an exhausted receiver - *Boyle*	V 2015	— 523
—— Anatomical observations on the structure of the lungs of frogs, tortoises, &c. and perfecter animals - - *Malpighi*	VI 2149	— 817
—— Observations about generation by an animalcula of the male seed: animals in the seed of a frog: and some other observables in the parts of a frog. - - *Leewenhoek*	XIII 347	III 684
—— Some observations made on the spawn of frogs, and the production of tadpoles therein. *Waller*	XVII 523	II 818
—— Letter on animalcula in the excrements of frogs - - - *Leewenhoek*	XXII 509	III 688
FROG FISH. Some account of the rana piscatrix - - - *Parsons*	XLVI 126	XI 866
—— —— An account of the frog-fish of Surinam - - - *Edwards*	LI 653

		Transf.	Abridg.
FROST. Method of taking eeles in frosty weather - - -	*Anon.*	I 323	II 837
—— An experiment concerning the progress of artificial conglaciation, and the remarkable accidents therein, observed by the Florentine philosophers - -	*Anon.*	V 2020	— 252
—— An account of a strange frost which hath done much hurt about Bristol; together with some useful hints suggested upon that occasion	*Beale*	VII 5138	— 150
A confirmation of the account	*Wallis*	VIII 5196	— 152
—— Advertisements occasioned by the remarks printed in N° 14, upon frosts in some parts of Scotland, differing in their anniversary seasons and force from our ordinary frosts in England	*Beale*	X 337	
—— A discourse concerning the effects of the great frost on trees and other plants in 1683; drawn from the answers to some queries sent into divers countries by R. Plott, and from several observations made at Oxford by J. Bobart - - - -	*Anon.*	XIV 766	— 155, 751
—— A discourse concerning the rising and falling of the quicksilver in the barometer, and what may be gathered from its great rise in frosty weather, as to a healthy or sickly season	*Lister*	— 790	— 18
—— Some experiments about freezing, and the difference between common fresh water ice, and that of the sea water: also a probable conjecture about the original of the nitre of Egypt - - -	*Lister*	XV 836	— 164
—— Some experiments about freezing	*Desmasters*	XX 384	— 165
Further experiments about freezing	*Desmasters*	— 439	— —
—— An account of an experiment touching the different densities of common water from the greatest degrees of heat in our climate, to the freezing point observed by a thermometer - - -	*Hauksbee*	XXVI 267	IV 2 182
—— An experiment touching the freezing of common water, and water purged of air	*Hauksbee*	— 302	— — —
—— An account of an experiment touching the freezing of common water tinged with a liquid, said to be extracted from shell-lac	*Hauksbee*	— 304	— — —
—— The history of the great frost in the winters 1708 and 1709 - -	*Derham*	— 454	— — 113
—— A letter concerning the frost in January 1730-1 - - -	*Derham*	XXXVII 16	IV 275
—— Experiments and observations of the freezing of water in vacuo -	*Fahrenheit*	XXXIII 78	VI 2 51

—— A le-

+ Frost. Account of a remarkable frost June 23. 1783. Cullum. 74: 416.

	Tranf.	Abridg.
— A letter concerning an extraordinary inftance of the almoft inftantaneous freezing of water; and giving an account of tulips, and fuch bulbous plants, flowering much fooner when their bulbs are placed upon bottles filled with water, than when planted in the ground - - - - *Triewald*	XXXVII 79	VI 2 54
— An examination of fea water frozen, and melted again, to try what quantity of falt is contained in fuch ice: made in Hudfon's Straights by captain Chriftopher Middleton, at the requeft of C. Mortimer - *Middleton*	XLI 806	VIII 643
— The fuppofed effect of boiling upon water, in difpofing it to freeze more readily, afcertained by experiments - *Black*	LXV 124	
— An account of the fuccefs of fome attempts to freeze quickfilver, at Albany Fort in Hudfon's Bay, in the year 1775; with obfervations on the dipping needle - *Hutchins*	LXVI 174	
— Obfervations made during the late froft, at Northampton Jan. 1776 - *A. Fothergill*	— 587	
— An account of a moft extraordinary degree of cold at Glafgow in January 1780; together with fome new experiments and obfervations on the comparative temperature of hoar-froft and the air near to it; made at Glafgow - - - *Patrick Wilfon*	LXX 451	
FRUIT. An experiment of making cherry-trees that have withered fruit to bear full and good fruit, and of recovering the almoft-withered fruit - - - *Merret*	II 455	II 652
— Inftances fhewing the correfpondence of the pith and timber with the feed of the plant; as alfo of the bark, or fap in the bark, with the pulp of the fruit, or fome encompaffing coat or cod containing the feed - *Beal*	IV 919	— 710
— A way of colouring leaves, fruit, &c. *Tonge*	V 2074	--681,752
— An eafy way of raifing Fruit Trees *Lewis*	VIII 6067	— 654
— A way of making all forts of plants, trees, fruits, and legums, grow to an extraordinary bignefs - - *Anon.*	X 356	III 749
— Several experiments concerning the preferving of flowers, fruits, &c. - *Southwell*	XX 42	II623,750
— Letter concerning fome infects obferved on fruit trees - - *Leewenhoek*	XXII 659	III 686
— The effects which the farina of the bloffoms of		

	Trans.	Abridg.
different sorts of apple-trees had on the fruit of a neighbouring tree - *Cook*	XLIII 525	I 602
—— An account of some fossile fruits, and other bodies, found in the island of Shepey - - - *Parsons*	L 396	
—— Experiments on checking the too luxuriant growth of fruit trees, tending to dispose them to produce fruit - *Fitzgerald*	LII 71	
Fucus. A letter concerning the animal life of those corallines that look like minute trees and grow upon oysters and fucus's all around the sea-coast of this kingdom - *Ellis*	XLVIII 627	
Fuller's Earth. An account of the pits for Fuller's earth in Bedfordshire *Holloway*	XXXII 419	VI 2 220
Fungous. Observations on fungous excrescences of the bladder; a cutting forceps for extirpating those excrescences; and a canula for treating these diseases - - *Le Cat*	XLVII 292	
Fungus. Observations on the poisonous qualities of some sorts of fungi - *W. Watson*	XLIII 51	X 790
—— An account of a new species of fungus - - - *Martyn*	— 263	X 705
—— Account of a new plant of the order of Fungi - - - - Woodward	74:423	
G.		
GALL BEE. An account of a gall bee *Allen*	XX 376	II 785
Gall (Bladder.) An extract of a letter containing microscopical observations on the gall and scales of fish - *Leewenhock*	XVII 949	III 685
—— —— An essay upon the use of the bile in the animal œconomy, founded on an observation of a wound in the gall-bladder - *Stuart*	XXXVI 341	VII 572
—— —— A relation of an hydropical case, in which the gall-bladder was distended to an unusual bigness - - *Yonge*	XXVII 426	V 292
—— —— Epistola de cadavere aperto, in quo non exstitit vesica fellea; et de streno gibboso - - - *Huber*	XLVI 92	XI 972
Gall Stones. An account of two extraordinary cases of gall-stones - *Johnstone*	L 543	
Ganglions. History of a fœtus born with a very imperfect brain: to which is subjoined, a supplement of the essay on the use of ganglions - - - *Johnston*	LVII 118	
—— Experiments in support of the uses ascribed to		

Functions. An essay towards the calculus of functions. Part 1. — Babbage. 1815: 389.
On the development of exponential functions; together with several new theorems relating to finite differences. — Herschel. 1816: 25.
An essay towards the calculus of functions. Part 2. — Babbage. 1816: 179.
On the fluents of irrational functions. — Bromhead. — 335.
On circulating functions and on the integration of a class of equations of finite differences into which they enter as co-efficients. Herschel. 1818: 144.

Galls. Observations on an astringent vegetable substance from China. Brande. 1817: 39.

Galvanism. An account of some Galvanic combinations, formed by the arrangement of single metallic plates and fluids, analogous to the new Galvanic apparatus of Mr. Volta. Davy. 1801: 397.
An account of some experiments, performed with a view to ascertain the most advantageous method of constructing a Voltaic Apparatus, for the purposes of chemical research. Children. 1809: 32.
An account of some experiments with a large Voltaic battery — 1815: 363.

Ganges (River) Account of — Rennell 71: 87.

Gaz. see Air.

Experiments and observations made with the view of ascertaining the nature of the Gaz produced by passing electric discharges through water. Pearson. 1797:142.

Experiments on carbonated hydrogenous Gas, with a view to determine whether Carbon be a simple or compound substance. Henry. —— 401.

Experiments on the quantity of Gases absorbed by water, at different temperatures, and under different pressures. —— 1803. 29.

An account of the application of the Gas from Coal to economical purposes. Murdoch. 1808. 124.

Description of an apparatus for the analysis of the compound inflammable Gases by slow combustion; with experiments on the Gas from Coal, explaining its application. Henry. —— 282.

	Transf.	Abridg.
the glanglions of the nerves in Philofophical Tranfactions, vol. LIV and vol. LVII. - - - *Johnftone*	LX 30	
GANGRENE. A letter concerning a woman of 62 years of age, that loft her leg and greateft part of her thigh by a gangrene - *Calep*	XXVI 41	V 389
—— A letter concerning the cure of dry gangrenes, together with a new-invented inftrument for the extirpation of tumours out of the reach of the furgeon's fingers - *Le Cat*	XLVI 72	XI 1084
GARDEN. Account of damage done to Mr. Evelyn's garden by the preceding winter *Evelyn*	XIV 559	II 153
—— Some account of the remains of John Tradefcant's garden at Lambeth *William Watfon*	XLVI 160	X 740
GARDENIA. An account of the plants Halefia and Gardenia - - *Ellis*	LI 929	
—— An account of the Gardenia *Solander*	LII 654	
GARDENING. How to multiply crab-ftocks, and propagate trees by layers - *Tonge*	V 2074	II 752
—— Some communications on the feafon for tranfplanting vegetables - *Reed*	VI 2128	— 655
—— Some confiderations on the beft feafon for tranfplantation - - *Beal*	— 2144	— —
—— Advertifements occafioned by the remarks printed in N° XIV. upon frofts in fome parts of Scotland, differing in their anniverfary feafons and force from our ordinary frofts in England: of black winds and tempefts: of the warm and fertilizing temperature and fteams of the earth, ftones, rocks, fprings, waters (fome in fome places more than others in other places) of petrifying and metallizing waters: with fome hints for the horticulture of Scotland - - - *Beal*	X 337	
—— An account of two obfervations in gardening, upon the change of colour in grapes and jeffamine - - *Cane*	XXXI 102	VI 2 340
GASCOIGNE. See *Micrometer*.		
GEASTER. An account of a plant called the geafter volvæ radiis et operculo elevatis, little known or hitherto undefcribed (Lat.) - - - *W. Watfon*	XLIII 234	X 703
GENERATION. Some anatomical obfervations on the parts of generation - *Clarck*	III 672	III 290
—— Inftances, hints, and applications, relating to a main point, folicited in the preface to this		

	Trans.	Abridg.
fourth volume, concerning the use made of vaults, deep wells, and cold conservatories, to find out the cause, or to promote the generation of, salts, minerals, metals, crystals, gems, and stones of divers kinds - *Beale*	IV 1135	
—— Some observations concerning the organs of generation - *King and De Graeff*	— 1403	III 192
—— A letter concerning spontaneous generation - - - - *Ray*	VI 2219	II 765
—— An account of what hath been of late observed of eggs to be found in all sorts of females - - - *Kerkringius*	VII 4018	
—— Letter on the parts of generation *Leewenhoek*	XIII 74	III 684
—— Observations about generation, by an animalcula of the male seed; of animals in the seed of a frog: and of some other observables in the parts of a frog - *Leewenhoek*	— 347	— —
—— An abstract of a letter concerning generation by an insect - - *Leewenhoek*	XV 1120	II 911
—— A discourse concerning the modern theory of generation - - *Garden*	XVII 474	— 907
—— Examination of the testicles of a rat, and the seed of muscles, oysters, &c. *Leewenhoek*	— 593	III 685
—— An account of an egg found in the tuba fallopiana of a woman lately dissected; with several remarks touching generation *Buissiere*	XVII 1I1	— 211
—— Letter on the generation of animals - - - *Josephus de Aromatariis*	— 150	
—— The history of the generation of an insect, called the wolf; with observations on insects bred in rain water, cheese, &c. - - - - *Leewenhoek*	— 194	III 685
—— Of the manner of generation of eels *Allen*	XIX 664	II 837
—— An account of a very large eel lately caught at Malden in Essex, with some considerations about the generation of eels - *Dale*	XX 90	— —
—— An objection to the new hypothesis of the generation of animalcula in semine masculino - - - *Lister*	— 337	III 685
—— An extract of a letter concerning the generation of fleas - - *Cestone*	XXI 42	II 789
—— Answer to the objections made to his opinions concerning the animalcula in semine masculino - - *Leewenhoek*	XXI 270	III 686
—— Several microscopical observations and experiments concerning the animalcula in se-		

mine

+ Generation. On the comparative influence of male and female parents on their offspring. Knight. 1809 : 392.

On the mode of generation of the Lamprey and Myxine. Home. 1815 : 265.

	Tranſ.	Abridg.
mine maſculino of cocks and ſpiders breath, &c. - *Leewenhoek*	XXIII 1137	V 2 264
—— Part of a letter containing ſome microſcopical obſervations upon the animalcula in ſemine maſculino of young rams *Leewenhoek*	XXVII 316	— - 267
—— Obſervations upon the generation of plants *Blair*	XXXI 216	VI 2 345
—— On the præternatural ſtructure of the genital parts of a woman - *Huxham*	XXXII 408	VII 546
Hiſtory of the ſame woman *Oliver*	— 413	— 548
—— Letter on the generation of animals - - - *Leewenhoek*	— 438	— 473
—— A letter containing the account of a remarkable generation of inſects at Annapolis in Maryland - - *Lewis*	XXXVIII 119	IX 1
—— Some reflections on generation and monſters, with a deſcription of ſome particular monſters - - - *De Superville*	XLI 294	— 304
—— See *Conception, Eels, Fleas.*		
GENERATION (Natural Philoſophy). Letter concerning the generation of hail, thunder and lightening, and the effects thereof *Wallis*	XIX 653	II 183
GENEVA. An accurate deſcription of the lake of Geneva - -	VII 5043	— 317
GENTIAN. An account of the poiſonous root lately found among the Gentian *Brocklesby*	XLV 240	X 772
GEOCENTRIC. Account of the eclipſes of Jupiter's ſatellites for 1686, and a table of the parallaxes of Jupiter's orb; and an ephemeris of Jupiter's geocentric places for the ſame year - - - *Flamſtead*	XV 1215	I 453
GEOGRAPHY. A method for determining the geographical longitude of places, from the appearance of the common meteor, called falling ſtars - - *Lynn*	XXXV 351	VI 400
—— A letter containing a geographical deſcription and map of the kingdom of Tunis; with a poſtſcript relating to the cure of intermittent fevers in thoſe parts - *Shaw*	XXXVI 177	— 423
—— Some account of the knowledge of geography amongſt the Chineſe - *Gaubil*	XLVI 327	X 255
—— Of the beſt form of geographical maps - - - - *Murdock*	L 553	
—— An account of two giants cauſeways, or groups of priſmatic baſaltine columns, and other curious volcanic concretions, in the Venetian ſtate in Italy; with ſome remarks on the characters		

of

	Tranſ.	Abridg.
of theſe and other ſimilar bodies, and on the phyſical geography of the countries in which they are found - *Strange*	LXV 5	
—— See *Maps*.		
GEOMETRY. Animadverſions of Dr. Wallis upon Mr. Hobbes's book, De Principiis & Ratiocinatione Geometrarum - - *Wallis*	I 289	
—— An anſwer to Mr. Hobbes's Roſetum Geometricum - - *Wallis*	VI 2202	I 247
—— Conſiderations concerning the geometric and direct method of Signor Caſſini, for finding the apogees, excentricities, and anomalies of the planets - - *Mercator*	V 1168	— 253
—— A direct and geometrical method by which the aphelia excentricities and proportions of the orbs of the primary planets are diſcovered, without ſuppoſing the equality of the angle of motion at the other focus of the planet's ellipſis - - - - *Halley*	XI 683	— 258
—— Some remarkable ſpecimens of the doctrine of fluxions, or examples wherein the uſe and excellence of that method in ſolving geometrical problems is ſhewn - *De Moivre*	XIX 52	— 34
—— Univerſal ſolution of cubic and biquadratic equations, viz. analytical, geometrical, and mechanical - - *Colſon*	XXV 2353	IV 66
—— A handful of geometrical flowers exhibited to the Royal Society by - *Guido Grandi*	XXXII 355	VI 67
—— A diſcourſe on the locus for three and four lines celebrated among the ancient geometers - - - *Pemberton*	LIII 496	
—— Geometrical ſolutions of three celebrated aſtronomical problems - *Pemberton*	LXII 434	
—— Propoſitions ſelected from a paper on the diviſion of right lines, ſurfaces, and ſolids *Glenie*	LXVI 73	
GEORGE II. Obſervations concerning the body of his late majeſty, Oct. 26, 1760 *Nicholls*	LII 265	
GERMANY. Some obſervations on the country of Germany - - *Brice*	LVI 229	
GIANT. Account of one Edward Melloon, born at Port Leiceſter in Ireland, who was of an extraordinary ſize - *Muſgrave*	XX 184	III 1
—— An eſſay concerning giants; occaſioned by ſome further remarks on the large human os frontis, or forehead bone, mentioned in the Ph. Tranſ. vol. XV. page 880 - *Molyneux*	XXII 487	— 2
—— A picture of the ſize of a gigantic bone; with a		

4 Geometry. General theorems, chiefly porisms, in the higher geometry. Brougham. 1798: 378.

Georgian Planet. Account of a Comet. Herschel. 71: 492.

A Letter to Sir Jos. Banks (on the name to be given to it) —— 73: 1.

On the diameter and magnitude of the Georgium Sidus. —— 4.

Account of the discovery of two Satellites revolving round it —— 77: 125.

On the Georgian Planet and its Satellites - - - - —— **78: 364.**

On the discovery of four additional Satellites of the Georgium Sidus. The retrograde motion of its old Satellites announced; and the cause of their disappearance at certain distance from the planet explained. —— 1798: 47.

A series of observations of the satellites of the Georgian planet, including a passage through the node of their orbits, with an introductory account of the telescopic apparatus that has been used on this occasion; and a final exposition of some calculated particulars deduced from the observations. - - - —— 1815: 293.

	Tranf.	Abridg.
problem for determining the fize of the giant according to the rules of the art of drawing - - - *Klein*	XLI 308	IX 311
—— See *Skeleton.*		
GIANTS CAUSEWAY. Letter concerning the Giants Caufeway in Ireland - *Sir R. B.*	XVII 708	II 511
—— —— An account of the Giants Caufeway in Ireland - - *Foley*	XVIII 170	— 512
—— Anfwers to Sir Richard Buckeley's queries relating to the Giants Caufeway; wrote down when we were upon the caufeway *Anon*	— 173	— 513
Some notes upon the foregoing account, ferving to further illuftrate the fame *Molyneux*	— 175	— —
—— —— Some additional obfervations on the Giants Caufeway in Ireland - *Molyneux*	XX 209	— 514
—— —— An account of the Giants Caufeway in Ireland - - *Pococke*	XLV 124	X 594
—— —— Further account of the Giants Caufeway in the county of Antrim in Ireland *Pococke*	XLVIII 226	
Letter on the fame fubject - *Pococke*	— 238	
—— —— Remarks on the ftones in the county of Naffau, and the territories of Treves and Colen, refembling thofe of the Giants Caufeway in Ireland *Trembly*	XLIX 581	
—— —— An account of a production of nature at Dunbar in Scotland, like that of the Giants Caufeway in Ireland - *Bp. Offory*	LII 98	
—— —— An account of fome productions of nature in Scotland refembling the Giants Caufeway in Ireland - *Mendez da Cofta*	— 103	
—— —— An account of two giants caufeways, or groups of prifmatic bafaltine columns, and other volcanic concretions, in the Venetian ftate in Italy; with fome remarks on the characters of thofe and other fimilar bodies, and on the phyfical geography of the countries in which they are found - *Strange*	LXV 5	
—— —— An account of a curious giants caufeway, or group of angular columns, newly difcovered in the Euganean Hills, near Padua in Italy - - - *Strange*	— 418	
GIBRALTAR. See *Bones.*		
GILLAROO TROUT. Of the gillaroo trout *Barrington*	LXIV 116	
Account of the ftomach of the gillaroo trout - - - *Henry Watfon*	— 121	
—— —— Obfervations on the gillaroo trout, com-		

monly

	Tranſ.	Abridg.
monly called in Ireland the gizzard trout - - - *John Hunter*	LXIV 310	
GIN-SENG. The deſcription of a Tartarian plant, called gin-ſeng; with an account of its virtues - - - *Jartoux*	XXVIII 237	IV 2 314
—— A new genus of plants called araliaſtrum, of which the famous zin-zin, or gin-ſeng of the Chineſe, is a ſpecies - *Vaillant*	XXX 705	— - 319
GIRARD (ALBERT). An explication of an obſcure paſſage in Albert Girard's commentary upon S. Stevins's works - *Simpſon*	XLVIII 368	
GIRL. An account of a girl in Ireland who had ſeveral horns growing on her body *Aſh*	XV 1202	III 12
—— An extraordinary caſe of three pins ſwallowed by a girl, and diſcharged at her ſhoulder - - - *Lyſons*	LIX 9	
GIZARD. Letter concerning a pin found in the gizard of a fowl - *Regnart*	XXIV 2055	V 53
GIZARD TROUT. See *Gillaroo Trout.*	LXIV 310	
GLANDS. Remarks on the glandulæ renales *Tyſon*	XII 1039	III 146
—— Letter concerning a horn hanging to the neck of an ox; with obſervations on horns and glandules in general - *Malpighius*	XIV 601	II 865
—— Obſervations of a large bed of glands obſerved in the ſtomach of a pike - *Muſgrave*	— 699	III 93
—— An extract giving an account of a large præternatural glanduloſe ſubſtance found between the heart and pericardium of an ox - - *Philoſophical Society at Oxford*	XV 860	— 69
—— A remarkable account of a liver appearing glandulous to the eye - *Brown*	— 1266	— 83
—— A relation of a petrified glandula pinealis, lately found in the diſſection of a brain *King*	XVI 228	— 157
—— An account of an extraordinary hæmorrhage at the glandula lacrimalis - *Anon.*	XVIII 51	— 152
—— An account of two glands, and their excretory ducts, lately diſcovered in human bodies *Cowper*	XXI 364	— 194
—— An account of an hydrops ovarii, with a new and exact figure of the glandulæ renales, and of the uterus in a puerpera *Douglas*	XXV 2317	V 274
—— An account of an excretory duct from the glandula renalis - - *Valſalva*	XXXIII 190	VII 540
—— An enquiry into a diſcovery ſaid to have been made by Signor Valſalva of an excretory duct, from the glandula renalis to the epididymis - - - *Ranby*	— 270	— 541

+ Gizard. On the Gizzards of grazing Birds. — — — — Home. 1810:18

A description of the solvent Glands and Gizzards of the Ardea argala, the Casuarius Emu, and the long-legged Casowary
from New South Wales. — — — — — — Home. 1813:77

Glands. Experiments to ascertain the coagulating power of the secretion of the gastric Glands. Home. 1813:96

On the colouring matter of the black Bronchial Glands and of the black spots of the Lungs. — Pearson. — 159.

Observations on the gastric glands of the human stomach, and the contraction which takes place in that viscus. Home. 1817:347.

A description of the Solvent Glands and Gizzards of the Ardea argala, the Casuarius Emu, and the long-legged Casowary from New South Wales. Home. 1812:77.

	Trans.	Abridg.
—— An account of a large glandular tumor in the pelvis; and of the pernicious effects of crude mercury given inwardly to the patient *Cantwell*	XL 139	IX 184
GLASS. The recovery of the art of making red glass - - *Colepresse*	III 743	III 685
—— A method of making a gold-coloured glazing for earthen ware - - *Heinsius*	XLII 188	IX 499
—— A dissertation on the antiquity of glass in windows - - *Nixon*	L 601	
—— Additional observations upon some plates of white glass found at Herculaneum *Nixon*	LII 123	
GLASS. (Electricity). An account of an experiment touching the extraordinary electricity of glass, produceable on a smart attrition of it; with a continuation of experiments on the same subject, and other phænomena - - *Hauksbee*	XXV 2327	IVp.2.180
- - - - *Hauksbee*	— 2332	— — —
—— Several experiments shewing the strange effects of the effluvia of glass, produceable on the motion and attrition of it - - *Hauksbee*	— 2372	— — —
—— An account of the repetition of an experiment touching motion in given bodies included in a glass by the approach of a finger near its outside: with other experiments on the effluvia of glass - - *Hauksbee*	XXVI 82	— - 181
—— Part of a letter concerning the light caused by quicksilver shaken in a glass tube, proceeding from electricity - *Trembley*	XLIV 58	X 321
—— A letter shewing, that the electricity of glass disturbs the mariner's compass, and also nice balances - - - *Robins*	— 242	— 328
—— Extract of a letter on the electricity of glass that has been exposed to strong fires *Bose*	XLVI 189	— 329
—— Letter declaring that he, as well as many others, have not been able to make odours pass through glass by means of electricity; and giving a particular account of professor Bose at Witemberg, his experiment of beatification, or causing a glory to appear round a man's head by electricity - *William Watson*	— 348	— 410
—— Observations and experiments tending to confirm Dr. Ingenhousz's theory of the electrophorus; and to shew the impermeability of glass to the electric fluid - *Henly*	LXVIII 1049	
GLASSES. (Natural History). Observations concerning keeping fish in glasses - *Arderon*	XLV 231	
—— An account of glasses of a new contrivance for		

preserving

		Transf.	Abridg.
─── preserving pieces of anatomy, or natural history, in spirituous liquors — Le Cat		XLVI 6	─ 1349
Continued — Le Cat		─ 88	───
─── On the crystallizations observed on glass Keir		LXVI 530	
GLASS (OPTICS). An account of the improvement of optic glasses — Campani		I 2	I 193
─────── Mr. Hook's treatise entituled, An account of micrographia, or the physiological description of minute bodies made by magnifying glasses — Oldenburg		I 27	
─── Judgment touching the apertures of object glasses and their proportions, in respect of the several lengths of telescopes, together with a table thereof — Auzout		─ 55	I 191
─── Considerations upon Mr. Hook's new instrument for grinding of optic glasses — Auzout		─ 56	─ 215
Mr. Hook's answer — Hook		─ 63	─ 192
─── A farther account touching Signor Campani's book and performances about optic glasses — Auzout		─ 69	
Sig. Campani's answer, and M. Auzout's animadversions thereon Campani and Auzout		─ 74	
─── Of M. Hevelius's promise of imparting to the world his invention of making optic glasses, and of the hopes given by M. Hugens of Zulichem, to perform something of the like nature; as also of the expectations conceived of some ingenious persons in England to improve telescopes Hevelius, Hugens, and Du-Sons		─ 98	─ 193
─── Of M. de Sons progress in working parabolar glasses — Oldenburg		─ 119	───
─── Instance to Mr. Hook for communicating a contrivance of making, with a glass of a sphere of 20 or 40 foot diameter, a telescope drawing several hundred feet; and his offer of recompensing that secret with another, teaching to measure with a telescope the distances of objects from the earth — Auzout		─ 122	
─── An account of the trials made in Italy of Campani's new optic glasses — Anon.		─ 131	I 485
─── A method by which a glass of a small planoconvex sphere may be made to refract the rays of light to a focus of a far greater distance than is usual — Hook		─ 202	I 193
─── A contest between two artists about optic glasses — Ciampani and Divini		─ 239	───
			─── An

	Tranſ.	Abridg.
—— An obſervation of optic glaſſes made of rock cryſtal - - *Divini*	— 362	— 195
—— An account of the invention of grinding optic and burning glaſſes of a figure not ſpherical - - - *Smethwick*	III 631	— 194
—— Method of poliſhing teleſcopical glaſſes by a turn-lathe; as alſo the making of an extraordinary burning glaſs at Milan - *Anon.*	— 795	— —
—— The deſcription of a way ſaid to be new and univerſal, for working convex ſpherical glaſſes upon a plane for all practicable lengths, without other diſhes or concave moulds *Mancini*	III 837	
—— The generation of an hyperbolical cylindroid demonſtrated, and the application thereof for grinding hyperbolical glaſſes hinted at *Wren*	IV 961	I 188
—— A deſcription of Dr. Chr. Wren's engine deſigned for grinding hyperbolical glaſſes, as it was in a manner promiſed, vol. III. p. 962 - - - *Wren*	— 1059	— 189
—— The effects of the different refractions of the rays in teleſcopical glaſſes - *Anon.*	VIII 6086	— 156
—— A ſure and eaſy way to make all ſorts of great teleſcopical glaſſes, with a generous offer of furniſhing induſtrious aſtronomers with them - - - *Borelli*	XI 691	— 195
—— Letter about the making of microſcopes with very ſmall and ſingle glaſſes, and of ſome other inſtruments - *Butterfield*	XII 1026	— 208
—— A dioptrick problem why four convex glaſſes in a teleſcope ſhew objects erect *Molyneux*	XVI 169	— 189
—— A way for myopes to uſe teleſcopes without eye-glaſſes; an object becoming as uſeful to them, and ſometimes more, than a combination of glaſſes - - *Deſaguliers*	XXX 1017	IV 188
—— A new method of improving and perfecting catadioptrical teleſcopes, by forming the ſpeculums of glaſs inſtead of metal *Smith*	XLI 326	VIII 113
—— Letters relating to a theorem of Mr. Euler, for correcting the aberrations in the object-glaſſes of refracting teleſcopes; by - - *Short, Euler, and Dollond*	XLVIII 287	
—— A report concerning the microſcope glaſſes ſent as a preſent to the Royal Society by father Torre of Naples - *Baker*	LVI 67	
—— A method of working the object glaſſes of refracting teleſcopes truly ſpherical *Short*	LIX 507	
GLASS. (Natural Philoſophy). An account of an experiment		

	Transf.	Abridg.
riment touching the direction of a drop of oil of oranges, between two glafs planes, towards any fide of them that is neareft preffed together - - - *Haukfbee*	XXVII 395	IV 2 182
—— An account of an experiment concerning the angle required to fufpend a drop of oil of oranges at certain ftations, between two glafs planes, placed in the form of a wedge - - - *Haukfbee*	— 473	— - —
—— Part of a letter concerning the afcent of water between two glafs planes - *Taylor*	— 538	— 423
- - - *Haukfbee*	— 539	IV 2 182
—— An account of an experiment touching the proportions of the afcent of fpirit of wine between two glafs planes, whofe furfaces were placed at certain different diftances from each other - - *Haukfbee*	XXVIII 151	— - 183
Account of fome further experiments *Haukfbee*	— 153	— - —
Further account - *Haukfbee*	— 155	— - —
—— An account of fome new experiments relating to the action of glafs tubes upon water and quickfilver - - *Jurin*	XXX 1083	IV 428
—— Two letters concerning the rotatory motion of glafs tubes about their axis, when placed in a certain manner before the fire *Wheler*	XLIII 341	X 551
—— An account of fome experiments lately made in Holland, upon the fragility of unannealed glafs veffels - - *Anon.*	— 505	XI 1343
—— A memoir on the Lacrymæ Batavicæ, or glafs drops; the tempering of fteel and effervefcence, accounted for by the fame principle - - - *Le Cat*	— 175	X 560
—— Experiments and obfervations on the agreement between the fpecific gravities of the feveral metals and their colours, when united to glafs, as well as thofe of their other proportions - - - *Delaval*	LV 10	
GLETCHER. Letter concerning the icy and cryftalline mountains of Helvetia, called the Gletfcher - - *Muraltus*	IV 982	II 465
—— A further defcription and reprefentation of the icy mountain, called the Gletfcher, in the canton of Berne in Helvetia - *Juftel*	VIII 6191	— —
GLOBE. The defcription of a cœleftial globe made by M. Didier - *L'Alleman*	XII 905	— 378
—— A propofal to make the poles of a globe of the		

heavens

Globes. Description of an improvement in the application of the Quadrant of Altitude to a Celestial Globe, for the Resolution of Problems dependant on Azimuth and Altitude. — — — — — — — — — Smeaton 79: 1.

Glossopora. Observations on the Hirudo complanata, and H. stagnalis, now formed into a distinct genus under the name, Glossopora. Johnson. 1817: 339.

+ Gold. Experiments on mixing Gold with Tin. — — — Alchorne 74. 463.
An account of the late discovery of native Gold in Ireland. Lloyd. 1796: 34.
A mineralogical account of the native Gold lately discovered in Ireland. Mills — 38.
The action of Nitre on Gold — — — — — — — — Tennant 1797: 219.
Experiments and observations on the various alloys, on the specific gravity, and on the comparative wear of Gold. — — — — Hatchett. 1803: 43.

Goniometer. Description of a reflective Goniometer. — Wollaston. 1809: 253.

	Transf.	Abridg.
heavens move in a circle round the poles of the ecliptic - - *Latham*	XL 201	VIII 217
—— A contrivance to make the poles of the diurnal motion in a cœlestial globe pass round the poles of the ecliptic - - *Senex*	— 203	— 217
—— An account of an improvement in the terrestrial globe - *Harris*	XLI 321	VIII 352
—— An improvement of the cœlestial globe *Ferguson*	XLIV 535	X 156
—— Letter concerning the large globes prepared by her late husband, and now sold by herself - - - *Mrs. Senex*	XLVI 290	— 158
GLOBES (Natural philosophy). An account of experiments relating to odours passing through electrified globes and tubes *Winkler*	XLVII 231	
An account of the result of some experiments made here with globes or tubes, transmitted by M. Winkler, in order to verify the facts above-mentioned - *W. Watson*	— 236	
GLOW-WORMS. Some observations concerning glow-worms - - *Templer*	VI 2177	II 760
Further observations - *Templer*	— 3035	— —
—— —— Observations on the cicindela volans, or flying glow-worm; with the figure *Waller*	XV 841	— 761
GNATS. Letter concerning gnats *Leewenhoek*	XXII 509	III 688
—— Some observations on swarms of gnats, particularly on one seen at Oxford Aug. 20, 1766 - - - - *Swinton*	LVII 111	
GODFREY. See *Quadrant*.		
GOLD. Of the incalescence of quicksilver with gold - - - - *B. R.*	X 515	II 580
—— Experiments of refining gold with antimony - - - *Goddard*	XII 953	— 595
—— A way of gilding gold upon silver *Southwell*	XX 296	III 657
—— A method of making a gold-coloured glazing for earthen-ware - *Heinsius*	XLII 188	IX 499
—— Sequel to the case of Mr. Butler of Moscow, who was strangely affected by mixing verdigris and false leaf-gold with aquafortis *Baker*	LIV 15	
GONIOMETRY. Extract of a letter containing a commodious disposition of equations for exhibiting the relations of goniometrical lines *Jones*	XLIV 560	X 14
GOOD HOPE. See *Cape*.		
GOOSEBERRIES. An extract of a letter containing microscopical observations on the seeds of gooseberries - - *Leewenhoek*	XVII 949	III 685
GORGONIA. On the nature of the gorgonia; that it		

	Transf.	Abridg.
is a real marine animal, and not of a mixed nature, between animal and vegetable - Ellis	LXVI 1	
GOUT. An abstract of a letter concerning the parts of the brain of several animals, the chalk-stones of the gout, the leprosy, and the scales of eels - - Leewenhoek	XV 883	III 684
—— An extract of a letter concerning the causes of the gout - - Pinelli	XXXV 491	VII 623
GOZO. See *Coin*.		
GRAFT. Some communications on the descent of sap - - - - Reed	VI 2128	II 690,775
Some considerations on Mr. Reed's letter, shewing in what sense the sap may be said to descend, and to circulate in plants, and the graft to communicate with the stock - Beal	— 2144	— 690
GRAIN. Of the weight of a cubic foot of divers grain - - Phil. Soc. at Oxford	XV 926	I 522
Further list of the specific gravities of bodies - - - - Anon.	— 927	— 523
—— Letter about the grains resembling wheat which fell lately in Wiltshire - Cole	XVI 281	
GRANARIES. A description of several kinds of granaries, as those of London, of Dantzick, and in Muscovy - Merret and others	II 464	II 628
GRANGE (LE). Observations on the case of Mr. Le Grange - - Stuart	XL 325	IX 146
GRANTHAM. See *Pavement*.		
GRAPES. An account of two observations in gardening, upon the change of colour in grapes and jessamine - - Cane	XXXI 102	VI 2 340
GRASS. An account of grass found in the wind-pipes of some animals - - Anon.	I 100	II 869
—— An account of the burning of several hay-ricks by a fiery exhalation or damp; and of the infectious quality of the grass of several grounds - - - Floyd	XVIII 49	— 181
—— Part of two letters concerning several plants which may be usefully cultivated for producing grass or hay - - Lister	XIX 412	I 748
—— A letter concerning the grubbs destroying the grass in Norfolk - Baker	XLIV 576	XI 821
—— An account of an inverted iris observed on the grass in September, and another in October 1751 - - Webb	XLVII 248	
GRASSHOPPERS. An account of an extraordinary swarm of grasshoppers in Languedoc Justell	XVI 147	II 788
GRAVIDATION. An account of a notable case of a		

+ Gout. On gouty concretions. Wollaston. 1797: 386.

Experiments and observations to prove that the beneficial effects of many medicines are produced through the medium of the circulating blood, more particularly that of the colchicum autumnale upon the Gout. — Home. 1816: 257.

An appendix to a paper on the effects of the colchicum autumnale in Gout. — — — — 262.

Some further observations on the use of colchicum autumnale in Gout. — — — — 1817: 262.

Granite. Observations on the affinity between Basaltes and Granite. Beddoes. 81: 48.

	Transf.	Abridg.
dropsy, mistaken for gravidation in a young woman; enlarging the observation of the same case, made by Dr. Tulpius - *Anon.*	IX 131	III 139
GRAVITY (in general). On the center of gravity of hyperbola's - - *Wallis*	VII 5074	
— A discourse concerning gravity and its properties, wherein the descent of heavy bodies and the motion of projects is briefly but fully handled: together with the solution of a problem of great use in gunnery - *Halley*	XVI 3	— 472
— Experiments concerning the time required in the descent of different bodies, of different magnitudes and weights, in common air, from a certain height - - *Hauksbee*	XXVII 196	— - 182
— Of the figure of the earth, and the variation of gravity on the surface - *Stirling*	XXXIX 98	VIII 324
— Astronomical observations made in the forks of the river Brandivine in Pennsylvania, for determining the going of a clock sent thither by the Royal Society, in order to find the difference of gravity between the Royal Observatory at Greenwich and the place where the clock was set up in Pennsylvania *Mason and Dixon*	LVIII 329	
— On the computation of the sun's distance from the earth by the theory of gravity *Horsley*	LIX 153	
— Reflections on the communication of motion by impact and gravity - *Milner*	LXVIII 344	
GRAVITY. (Specific). An invention for estimating the weight of water in water with ordinary balances and weights - *Boyle*	IV 1001	I 520
— Of the weight of a cubic foot of divers grains - - - *Phil. Soc. at Oxford*	XV 926	— 522
— A further list of specific gravities of bodies - - - - *Anon.*	— 927	— 523
— A discourse on this problem; why bodies, dissolved in menstrua specifically lighter than themselves, swim therein *W. Molyneux*	— 88	— 355
Some reflections on the foregoing paper - - - *T. Molyneux*	— 93	— 537
— Observations on the comparative, intensive or specific gravities of various bodies *J. C.*	XVII 694	— 524
— An account of an experiment touching the proportion of the weight of air to the weight of a like bulk of water, without knowing the quantity of either - *Hauksbee*	XXV 2221	IV 2 180
— An experiment touching the weighing of bodies of the same species, but of very unequal sur-		

faces

	Transf.	Abridg.
faces in common water, being of an equal weight in common air - *Hauksbee*	XXVI 306	— - 181
—— Of several metalline cubes, in comparison with their like bulks of water - *Hauksbee*	XXVII 521	
—— A description of the several strata of earth, stone, coal, &c. found in a coal-pit at the west end of Dudley, Staffordshire. To which is added, a table of the specific gravity of each stratum - - *Fettiplace and Hauksbee*	— 541	— - 182
—— A caution to be used in examining the specific gravity of solids by weighing them in water - - - *Jurin*	XXXI 223	VI 327
—— The specific gravities of certain matters observed at different times for various purposes - - - *Fahrenheit*	XXXIII 114	VI 329
—— A letter concerning the specific gravity of diamonds - - *Ellicott*	XLIII 468	X 612
—— Tables of specific gravities; extracted from various authors; with some observations upon the same - - *Davies*	XLV 416	— 206
—— An essay towards ascertaining the specific gravity of living men - *Robertson*	L 30	
—— Experiments and observations on the agreement between the specific gravities of the several metals and their colours when united to glass, as well as those of their other proportions - - *Delaval*	LV 10	
—— A course of experiments to ascertain the respective weights and buoyancy of salt water and fresh water, and for determining the exact weight of human and other bodies in fluids - - - *Wilkinson*	— 95	
GREATRIX. A letter concerning the cures done by Mr. Greatrix the stroker - *Thoresby*	XXI 332	II 11
GREECE. Observations in travels from Venice through Istria, Dalmatia, Greece, and the Archipelago to Smyrna - *Vernon*	XI 573	
GREEK. An attempt to explain an antient Greek inscription engraven upon a curious bronze cup with two handles, and published with a draught of the cup by Dr. Pococke, in his description of the East, vol. II. part II. pag 207 - - *Ward*	XLVI 488	X 1278
—— Remarks on a Parthian coin with a Greek and Parthian legend - *Swinton*	L 175	
—— Some observations on an inedited Greek coin of Philistis queen of Syracuse, Malta and		

Gravity (Specific)

Of various saline substances. R. Kirwan. 71: 7. 72: 179.

Remarks on specific gravities taken at different degrees of heat, and an easy method of reducing them to a common standard. Kirwan 75: 267.

Description of an instrument for ascertaining the specific gravities of fluids. Schmeisser. 1793: 164.

Greenwich (Royal Observatory at) Concerning its latitude and longitude, with remarks on a memorial of the late M. Cassini de Thury. Maskelyne 77: 151.

Account of the mode proposed to be followed in determining the relative situation of the Royal Observatories of Greenwich and Paris. Roy — 188.

Account of the trigonometrical operation, whereby the distance between the meridians of the Royal Observatories of Greenwich an Paris has been determined. — — — — — — — — — — 80: 111.

Remarks on M. G. Roy's account of the trigonometrical operation - Dalby — 593.

+ Ground. Account of a subsidence of the ground near Folkstone in Kent. Lyon. King. 76: 220.

Account of a sinking in of the ground (near Ketton in Rutland) Barker. 79: 164.

	Trans.	Abridg.
Gozo, who had been passed over in silence by all the antient writers - *Swinton*	LX 80	
—— —— An enquiry into the value of Greek and Roman money - *Raper*	LXI 462	
GREEK. See *Coin.*		
GREEN HOUSE. An account of the lately-invented stove for preserving plants in the green-house in winter - - *Cullum*	XVIII 191	II 750
GREENE. An account of the death of Dr. Greene, by a hurt in riding out - *Cameron*	XLIV 609	XI 1112
GREENLAND. Inquiries to be made in Greenland - - - *Royal Society*	II 554	III 631
GREEN WEEDS GROWING IN WATER. Letter concerning green weeds growing in water, and animalculæ found about them *Leewenhoek*	XXIII 1304	
Two letters from a gentleman in the country relating to the same - *Anon.*	—. 1494	V 2 225
GREENWICH. A letter concerning observations to be made on the parallax of the moon at St. Helena, and recommending the same to be made at Paris and Greenwich, to settle the difference of longitude between Paris and St. Helena - - - *De La Caille*	LII 21	
- - - *Maskelyne*	— 26	
GREYHOUND. An account of an animal resembling a whelp voided per anum, by a male greyhound - - *Halley*	XIX 316	II 904
GRINDING. An account of the invention of grinding optick and burning glasses of a figure not spherical - - *Smethwick*	III 631	I 194
GROIN. Letter concerning the bones of a human fœtus voided through an imposthume in the groin - - *Skippon*	XXIV 2077	
—— Of a bubonocele, or rupture in the groin, and the operation made on it - - *Amyand*	XL 361	IX 161
GROTTA DE' CANI. Extract of the observations made in Italy on the Grotta de' Cani *Nollet*	XLVII 48	
GROUND. An uncommon sinking of the ground at Lymne in Kent - - *Anon.*	XXXV 551	VI 2 203
—— A narrative of an extraordinary sinking down and sliding away of some ground at Pardines, near Auvergne - - *Anon.* (See Earth)	XLI 272	VIII 704
—— An account of the sinking down of a piece of ground at Horseford in Norfolk *Arderon*	XLIII 527	X 587
+ —— Observations on the heat of the ground on mount Vesuvius - - *Howard*	LXI 53	
GRUBBS. A letter concerning the grubbs which destroy the grass in Norfolk - *Baker*	XLIV 576	XI 821

Guaiacum. Chemical experiments on. Brande. 1806. 89.

	Transf.	Abridg.
GUAIANA. Inquiries for Guaiana and Brasil - - - *Royal Society*	II 422	III 632
GUILDING. A way of gilding gold upon silver - - - *Southwell*	XX 296	— 657
GUINEA. Inquiries to be made in Guinea *Hill*	II 472	— 632
—— A catalogue of some Guinea plants sent to James Petiver, with their native names and virtues, and remarks on them by *Petiver*	XIX 677	II 752
GULLET. An account of a wound which the late lord Carpenter received at Brihuega, where a bullet remained near his gullet for a year, wanting a few days - *Carpenter*	XL 316	
GUM LAC. Experiments of the luminous qualities of amber, diamonds, and gum lac *Wall*	XXVI 69	IV 2 275
GUNNERY. Experiments for improvement in the art of gunnery, viz. the point-blank distance, the quantity of powder for the just charge of any piece, and what gun shoots farthest *Moray*	II 473	I 493
—— A description of the uses of a certain powder for yeilding very close and smooth metal, and of easy carriage, &c. (for casting of guns) *Anon.*	VIII 6040	II 557
—— An account of some experiments for trying the force of great guns - *Greaves*	XV 1090	I 495
—— A discourse concerning gravity and its properties, wherein the descent of heavy bodies, and the motion of projects, is briefly but fully handled; together with the solution of a problem of great use in gunnery *Halley*	XVI 3	— 472,473
—— An account of an experiment of shooting by the rarefaction of the air - *Papin*	— 21	— 496
—— A proposition of general use in the art of gunnery; shewing the rule of laying a mortar to pass, in order to strike any object above or below the horizon - *Halley*	XIX 68	— 481,483
—— The report of the committee of the Royal Society appointed to examine some questions in gunnery *Committee of the Royal Society*	XLII 172	VIII 253
GUN POWDER. Experiments for improvement in the art of gunnery, viz. the point-blank distance, the quantity of powder for the just charge of any piece, and what gun shoots farthest *Moray*	II 473	I 493
—— —— An extract of a letter containing several observations on gun-powder *Leewenhoek*	XVII 754	III 685
—— —— An experiment of firing gun-powder on a red-hot iron in vacuo Boyliano *Hauksbee*	XXIV 1806	IV 2 171
—— —— An account of an experiment touching the quantity of air produced from a certain		

Gulf-stream. On the heat of the water in the Gulf-stream. Blagden. 71: 334.

+ Gun-powder. New experiments on — Thompson 71:229.
Experiments to determine the force of fired Gunpowder ——— 1797: 222.

		Transf.	Abridg.
quantity of gun-powder fired in common air	*Haukſbee*	XXV 2409	IV 2 181
—— —— The force of fired gun-powder, and the initial velocities of cannon balls determined by experiments; from which is alſo deduced the relation of the initial velocity to the weight of the ſhot and the quantity of powder	*Hutton*	LXVIII 50	
—— —— A new theory of gun-powder	*Ingenhouſz*	LXIX 376	
GUN-SHOT WOUND. Caſe of a boy who died of a gun-ſhot wound	*Woolcomb*	LX 94	
GUNTER'S SCALE. The conſtruction of the logarithmic lines on Gunter's ſcale	*Robertſon*	XLVIII 96	
GURNARD (YELLOW). A deſcription of the *cuculus lævis cœrulæo-flaveſcens, cui in ſupremo capite branchiarum opercula*, or the yellow gurnard	*Tyſon*	XXIV 1749	V 36
GUTS. Some anatomical obſervations and experiments concerning the unalterable characters of the whiteneſs of the chyle within the lacteous veins; together with divers particulars obſerved in the guts, eſpecially ſeveral ſorts of worms found in them	*Liſter*	VIII 6060	II 696
—— The anatomy of the ſlime within the guts, and the uſe thereof	*Leewenhoek*	XIV 586	III 684
—— Some obſervations on wounds in the guts	*Amyand*	XXXIX 329	IX 153
—— An inſtance of the gut ilium cut through by a knife, and cured	*Travers*	L 35	
GYMNOTUS ELECTRICUS. Experiments and obſervations on the gymnotus electricus, or electrical eel	*Williamſon*	LXV 94	
—— —— An account of the electrical eel	*Garden*	— 102	
—— —— An account of the gymnotus electricus	*J. Hunter*	— 395	
Haddocks, Observations on the remarkable failure of Haddocks, on the coasts of Northumberland, Durham and Yorkshire	Abbs	1792: 367.	

H.

HADLEY. A letter concerning obſervations with Mr. Hadley's reflecting teleſcopes	*Pound*	XXXII 382	VI 221
HÆMATITES. Extract of ſome letters concerning iron ore, and more particularly of the hæmatites wrought into iron at Melthorp forge in Lancaſhire	*Sturdie*	XVII 695	II 551
HÆMOPTYSIS. An uncommon caſe of an hæmoptyſis	*Darwen*	LI 526	

	Transf.	Abridg.
HÆMORRHAGE. An account of an extraordinary hæmorrhage at the glandula lacrimalis - *Anon*	XVIII 51	III 252
—— Letter concerning a very extraordinary periodical hæmorrhage - *Mufgrave*	XXII 864	V 239
—— Two remarkable medical cafes; one of an extraordinary hæmorrhage, the other of an afcites, cured by tapping - *Banyer*	XLII 628	IX 151, 193
—— Experiments concerning the ufe of the agaric of oak in ftopping hæmorrhages *Sharp and Warner*	XLVIII 588	
HAIL. An account of hail-ftones of an unufual bignefs; with reflections on them *Fairfax*	II 481	
—— The relation of a ftorm of thunder, lightening, and hail, at Oundle in Northamptonfhire - - - *W. R.*	XVII 710	
—— Extract of a letter giving an account of an unufual ftorm of hail, which fell at Lifle in Flanders May 25, 1686 - *Anon.*	— 858	II 145
—— Account of an extraordinary hail in Chefhire April 29, 1697 - *Halley*	XIX 570	— —
A larger account of the fame ftorm *Anon.*	— 572	— 146
—— An account of a great hail-ftorm at Hitchin in Hertfordfhire May 4, 1697 - *Tailor*	— 577	— 147
—— Relation of a great hail-ftorm in Herefordfhire in June 6, 1697 - *Anon.*	— 579	— —
Another account of the fame ftorm in Monmouthfhire - - *Lhwyd*	— —	— 148
—— Letter concerning the generation of hail, thunder and lightning, and the effect thereof *Wallis*	— 653	— 183
—— A letter giving an account of the damage done by a ftorm of hail, which happened near Rotherham in Yorkfhire - *Thorefby*	XXVII 514	IV 2 109
—— An account of an extraordinary ftorm of hail in Virginia July 9, 1758 *Fauquier*	L 746	
HAIR. Microfcopical obfervations on the ftructure of the hair - - *Leewenhoek*	XII 1003	
—— An account of balls of hair taken from the uterus and ovaria of feveral women *Yonge*	XXV 2387	
—— Account of a bunch of hair voided by urine - - *Yonge*	XXVI 414	V 284
—— Obfervations on the cafe related by Mr. Yonge - - - *Leewenhoek*	— 416	— —
—— Cafe of a gentlewoman who voided with her urine hairy cruftaceous fubftances; with Sir H. Sloane's anfwer, containing feveral obfervations of extraordinary fubftances voided by the urinary paffages *Powell and Sloane*	XLI 699	IX 180
—— Cafe of hair voided by urine - *Knight*	— 705	— 182

	Transf.	Abridg.
—— Observatio de ovarii steatomate & de pilis ibidem inventis - - *Haller*	XLIII 71	XI 1009
—— Part of two letters concerning the sparkling of flannel and the hair of animals in the dark - - - *Cooke*	XLV 394	X 343
HAIR (Astronomy). Some remarks upon the method of observing the differences of right ascension and declination by cross hairs in a telescope - - *Halley*	XXXI 113	VI 165
HALES. The conclusion of Dr. Desaguliers' account of Mr. Hales's vegetable staticks *Desaguliers*	XXXV 323	VI 2 158
—— Thoughts on Dr. Hales's new method of distillation by the united force of air and fire - - - *Brownrigg*	XLIX 534	
HALESIA. An account of the plants halesia and gardenia - - *Ellis*	LI 929	
HALLEY. Some remarks on the variation of the magnetical compass, published in the memoirs of the Academy of Sciences, with regard to the general chart of those variations made by Halley; as also concerning the longitude of Magellan Straights - *Anon.*	XXIX 165	IV 453
—— A true copy of a paper found in the hand-writing of Sir Isaac Newton, among the papers of the late Dr. Halley; describing an instrument for observing the moon's distances from the fixed stars at sea - - *Newton*	XLII 155	
—— A view of the relation between Dr. Halley's tables and the notions of Mr. de Buffon, for establing a rule for the probable duration of the life of a man - *Kerseboom*	XLVIII 239	
HALO. Observation of one May 12, 1667 - - *Philosophical Academy at Paris*	V 1065	
Discourse concerning the cause of halo's and parelia's - - *Huygens*	— —	
—— An account of an unusual parhelion and halo Apr. 7, 1699 - - *Gray*	XXII 535	II 188
—— An account of two mock sun's, and an arc of a rain-bow inverted, with an halo, and its brightest arc seen on Sunday and Monday, Oct. 22 and 23, 1721, at Lyndon in Rutland *Whiston*	XXXI 212	VI 2 76
—— An account of an halo observed at Rome Aug. 11, 1732 - *De Revillas*	XXXIX 118	VIII 108
—— A letter giving a representation of an halo, or mock sun, observed July 11, 1749 *Arderon*	XLVI 196	XI 1295

—— An

	Transf.	Abridg.
—— An account of a remarkable halo May 20, 1737 - - - *Barker*	LII 3	
HAMMAM PHAROAN WATER. Experiments, by way of analysis, upon the water of the dead sea, upon hot springs near Tiberiades, and upon Hamman Pharoan water - *Perry*	XLII 48	VIII 643
HAMPSHIRE. See *Camps.*		
HANDS. The description and use of the pores in the skin of the hands and feet - *Grew*	XIV 566	III 9
HARBOURS. A recommendation of Hadley's quadrant for surveying, especially the surveying of harbours; together with a particular application of it to some cases of pilotage *Michell*	LV 70	
HARDOUIN. A remark on F. Hardouin's amendment of a passage in Pliny's natural history, lib. II. p. 74, by - - *Folkes*	XLIV 365	XI 1378
HARES. Observations on various sorts of worms, as well human as from hares - *Limbourg*	LVI 126	
—— Investigation of the specific character which distinguish the rabbit from the hare *Barrington*	LXII 4	
HARROWING. See *Sembradore.*		
HARTSELL SPAW WATER. Occasional remarks on the Hartsell Spaw, and their comparison with other waters of the same class - *Rutty*	LI 470	
HARTZ MINES. Barometrical observations on the depth of the mines in the Hartz - *De Luc*	LXVII 401	
—— —— A second paper concerning some barometrical measures in the mines of the Hartz *De Luc*	LXIX 485	
HARWICH. A letter concerning Harwich Cliff, and the fossil shells there - *Dale*	XXIV 1568	IV 2 264
HATCHET. Part of a letter concerning the remains of an ancient temple in Ireland, and of a stone hatchet of the antient Irish *Bp. of Cork*	XLII 581	IX 457
HAY. An account of the burning of several hayricks by a fiery exhalation or damp; and of the infectious quality of the grass of several grounds - *Floyd*	XVIII 49	II 181
—— Part of two letters concerning several plants which may be usefully cultivated for producing grass or hay - *Lister*	XIX 412	I 748
HEAD. Observations upon a monstrous head of a colt - - *Boyle*	I 85	
—— Anatomical observations in the heads of fowl, made at several times - *Moulen*	XVII 711	II 860
—— An abstract of an account of five pair of muscles, which serve for different motions of the head - - *Dupre*	XXI 13	
With remarks by - *Wm. Cowper*	— —	

Harmattan, a singular African Wind, Account of — M. Dobson. 71:46.

Harrogate. Observations on the sulphur wells at Harrogate. Watson. 76:171.

+ Hearing. Account of the organ of hearing in Fish. J. Hunter. 72:379.
The physiology of the Stapes, one of the bones of the organ of hearing, deduced from a comparative view of its structure and uses in different animals. Carlisle. 1805:198.
An account of some peculiarities in the structure of the organ of hearing in the Balaena mysticetus of Linnaeus. Home. 1812:83.

	Transf.	Abridg.
—— A letter concerning worms in the heads of sheep - - - *Thorpe*	XXIV 1806	V 16
—— A remarkable cure of a wound of the head, complicated with a large fracture and depression of the skull, the dura mater and brain wounded and lacerated. - *Cagna*	XLI 495	IX 118
—— An account of some extraordinary tumours upon the head of a labouring man *Parsons*	L 350	
—— An account of a monstrous human foetus, having neither head, heart, lungs, stomach, spleen, pancreas, liver, nor kidnies - *Le Cat*	LVII 1	
—— Account of an extraordinary large head *Benvenuti*	LVIII 190	
HEALTH. A discourse concerning the rising and falling of the quicksilver in the barometer, and what may be gathered from its great rise in frosty weather, as to a healthy or sickly season - - - *Lister*	XIV 790	II. 18, 274
—— Observations on the expectations of lives, the increase of mankind, the influence of great towns on population, and particularly the state of London with respect to healthfulness and number of inhabitants - *Price*	LIX 89	
—— The method taken for preserving the health of the crew of his majesty's ship the Resolution, during their late voyage round the world *Cook*	LXVI 402	
HEARING. A description of the organ of hearing in the elephant; with the figures and situation of the ossicles, labyrinth and cochlea in the ear of that animal - - *Blair*	XXX 885	V 82
—— Extract of a letter concerning the hearing of fish - - - *Ardenon*	XLV 149	XI 880
—— Upon the sounds and hearing of fish by Jac. Theod. Klein, or some account of a treatise entituled, An enquiry into the reasons why the author of an epistle concerning the hearing of fishes, endeavours to prove they are all mute and deaf - - *Brocklesby*	—— 233	—— 883
—— See *Deafness*.		
HEART. Of the motion of the separated heart of a cold animal in the exhausted receiver *Boyle*	V 2027	
—— Observations upon the motion of the hearts of two urchins, after their being cut out *Templer*	VIII 6016	III 69
—— An account of a polypus found in the heart of a person who died epileptical - *Gould*	XIV 537	I 279
—— An extract giving an account of a large præternatural glandulose substance found between the heart and pericardium of an ox	XV 860	III 69

	Transf.	Abridg.
—— An account of an extraordinary aneuriſma of the arteria aorta near the baſis of the heart, with the ſymptoms thereof - *La Fage*	XXII 666	
—— A diſcourſe concerning ſome influence of reſpiration on the motion of the heart, hitherto unobſerved - - *Drake*	XXIII 1217	V 253
—— An account of the left ventricle of the heart of an amazing magnitude - *Douglaſs*	XXIX 326	— 231
—— A diſcourſe of the power of the heart *Jurin*	XXX 863	
Concluſion of the diſcourſe - *Jurin*	— 929	
—— Letter on the ſtrength of the heart *Keill*	— 995	— 244
—— Letter in defence of his doctrine of the power of the heart againſt the objections of Dr. Keill - - - *Jurin*	— 1039	— 247
—— An extraordinary caſe of the foramen ovale of the heart, being found open in an adult - - - *Amyand*	XXXIX 172	IX 134
—— Short account of Dr. A. Stuart's paper concerning the muſcular ſtructure of the heart - - - *Mortimer*	XLI 675	— 131
—— A letter concerning the foramen ovale being found open in the hearts of adults, ~~and of the figure of the canal of the urethra~~ - - - *Le Cat*	— 681	— 134
—— Caſe of the heart of a child turned upſide down - - - *Torres*	— 776.	— 135
—— A letter concerning a polypus at the heart - - - *Templeman*	XLIV 285	XI 1021
—— The caſe of a man whoſe heart was found enlarged to a very uncommon ſize *Pulteney*	LII 344	
—— An account of a blow upon the heart, and of its effects - - *Akenſide*	LIII 353	
—— An account of a monſtrous human fœtus, having neither head, heart, lungs, ſtomach, ſpleen, pancreas, liver, nor kidnies - *Le Cat*	LVII 1	
—— See *Polypus*.		
HEARTHS. An account of the houſes and hearths in Dublin in 1695 and 1696	XXII 518	III 665
—— A ſcale of the gradation of heat	XXII 824	IV 2 1
—— An account of an experiment touching the different denſities of common water from the greateſt degrees of heat in our climate, to the freezing point, obſerved by a thermometer - - - *Haukſbee*	XXVI 267	— 181
HEAT (Philoſophy). An account of an experiment made to aſcertain the proportion of the expan-		

ſion

4 Heart. Observations on the foramina Thebesii of the heart. Abernethy. 1798: 103.
A description of a very unusual formation of the human heart. Wilson. — 346.
A description of malformation in the heart of an Infant. Standert. 1805: 228.
On the functions of the Heart. Young. 1809: 1.

On some physiological researches, respecting the influence of the brain on the action of the heart, and on the generation of animal heat. Brodie. 1811: 36

Experiments made with a view to ascertain the principle on which the action of the heart depends, and the relation which subsists between that organ and the nervous system. Philip. 1815: 65.
Experiments to ascertain the influence of the spinal marrow on the action of the heart in fishes. Clift. — 91.
Some additional experiments and observations on the relation which subsists between the nervous and sanguiferous systems. Philip. — 424.

Heart wood. On its office. Knight. 1818: 137.

+Heat. New experiments upon heat — — — — — — Thompson 76: 273. 1792: 48.

An experiment on heat — — — — — — — — Fordyce 77: 310.

An inquiry concerning the source of the heat which is excited by friction. Rumford. 1798: 80.

An inquiry concerning the weight ascribed to heat. —— 1799: 179.

Investigation of the powers of the prismatic colours to heat and illuminate objects, with remarks, that prove the different refrangibility of radiant heat. Herschel. 1800: 255.

Experiments on the refrangibility of the invisible rays of the sun. —— —— 284.

solar, and on the terrestrial rays that occasion heat; with a comparative view of the laws to which light and heat, or rather the rays which occasion them, are subject, in order to determine wether they are the same or different. —— —— 293, 437.

Quelques remarques sur la chaleur, et sur l'action des corps qui l'interceptent. Prevost. 1802. 403.

An account of a curious phenomenon observed on the Glaciers of Chamouny, together with some occasional observations concerning the propagation of heat in fluids. Rumford. 1804: 23.

An enquiry concerning the nature of heat, and the mode of its communication. —— —— 77.

On new properties of heat as exhibited in its propagation along plates of glass. — Brewster. 1816: 46.

New experimental researches on some of the leading doctrines of caloric; particularly on the relation between the elasticity, temperature, and latent heat of different vapours; and on thermometric measurement and capacity. — — Ure. 1818: 3[illegible]

[illegible] (Experimentat[illegible])

	Trans.	Abridg.
sion of the liquor in the thermometer, with regard to the degrees of heat - *Taylor*	XXXII 291	VI 2 49
—— Experiments about the degrees of the heat of some boiling liquors - - *Fahrenheit*	XXXIII 1	— —
—— A contrivance to avoid the irregularities in a clock's motion, occasioned by the action of heat and cold upon the rod of the pendulum - - - - *Graham*	XXXIV 40	VI 297
—— The description and manner of using an instrument for measuring the degrees of the expansion of metal by heat - - *Ellicot*	XXXIX 297	VIII 464
—— ~~Two methods by which the irregularity of the motion of a clock arising from the influence of the heat and cold upon the rod of the pendulum may be prevented~~ (Cold) - ~~*Ellicot*~~	~~XLVII 479~~	
—— ~~Letter concerning the inventor of the contrivance in the pendulum of a clock to prevent the irregularities of its motion by heat and cold~~ - - - (Clock) - ~~*Short*~~	~~XLVII 517~~	
—— Observations for settling the proportion which the decrease of heat bears to the height of situation - - *Thomas Heberden*	LV 126	
—— Experiments on animals and vegetables, with respect to the power of producing heat - - - *John Hunter*	LXV 446	
—— Experiments on ignited bodies - *Roebuck*	LXVI 509	
—— Experiments on ignited substances *Whitehurst*	— 575	
—— Of the heat of animals and vegetables - - - - *John Hunter*	LXVIII 7	
+ —— On the variation of the temperature of boiling water - - - *Shuckburgh*	LXIX 362	
HEAT (Meteorology). Tables of the barometrical altitudes, at Zurich in Switzerland, in the year 1708, by Scheuchzer; and at Upminster in England, by Derham. As also the rain at Pisa, in Italy, in 1707 and 1708, by Tilli; and at Zurich in 1708, and at Upminster in all that time: with remarks on the same tables; as also on the winds, heats, and colds; and divers other matters occurring in these three different parts of Europe - *Derham*	XXVI 342	
—— A letter concerning a very cold day, and another a very hot day, in June and July 1749 - - - - - - *Miles*	XLVI 208	X 471
—— Two letters concerning the heat of the weather in July and September 1750 - - *Miles*	XLVI 571	X 474

	Transf.	Abridg.
—— Letter concerning the hot weather July 1750 - - - - - *Arderon*	XLVI 573	X 474
—— An account of extraordinary heat in February 1749-50 - - - *Miles*	— 619	
—— Remarks on the heat of the air in July 1759 - - - - - *Huxham*	L 428	
—— —— —— —— *W. Watson*	— 429	
—— An account of the heat of the weather in Georgia - - - - *Ellis*	— 754	
—— Account of the heat of the climate at Bengal - - - - *Martin*	LVII 217	
—— Account of the extraordinary heat observed at Rome in the summer 1768 - - *Byres*	LVIII 337	
—— Observation on the heat of the ground on Mount Vesuvius. - - - *Howard*	LXI 53	
—— A comparison of the heat at London and Edinburgh - - - - *Roebuck*	LXV 459	
HEATED ROOM, Experiments and observations in an heated room - - - *Blagden*	— 111	
—— —— Experiments in an heated room *Dobson*	— 463	
—— —— Further experiments and observations in an heated room - - *Blagden*	— 484	
HEAVENS, An account of a pyramidal appearance in the heavens, observed near Upminster in Essex - - - - - *Derham*	XXV 2411	IV 2 133
HEEL. An account of stitching the great tendon between the calf of the leg and the heel, with its union, and cure after an entire division of it, with remarks - - - *Cowper*	XXI 153	III 298
HEIGHT. (in general) Experiments touching the time required in the descent of different bodies of different magnitudes and weights, in common air, from a certain height - *Hauksbee*	XXVII 196	IV 2 182
—— An account of an extraordinary meteor, seen all over England, on the 19th of March 1712-3, with demonstration of the uncommon height thereof - - - *Halley*	XXX 978	IV 2 156
—— Observation on the height to which rockets will ascend - - - *Robins*	XLVI 131	X 201
—— Some experiments in order to discover the height to which rockets may be made to ascend, and to what distance their light may be seen - - - - *Ellicot*	— 578	X 202
—— Observations for settling the proportion which the decrease of heat beareth to the height of situation - - *Thomas Heberden*	LV 126	

—— Of

+ Heat (Meteorology)

Experiments to investigate the variation of local Heat - - - Six { 78: 103. 74: 428.

Table of the mean heat of every month for ten years in London. Heberden 78: 66.

Heavens. Account of some observations tending to investigate the construction of the Heavens Herschel 74: 437. 75: 213. (79: 212.)

Astronomical observations relating to the construction of the Heavens, arranged for the purpose of critical examination, the result of which seems to throw some new light upon the organization of the celestial bodies. 1802: 477. 1811: 269.

Astronomical observations relating to the sidereal parts of

Hejera. On the Eva of the Mahometans, called Hejera. - - Marsden. 78: 414.

the heavens and its connection with the nebulous parts; arranged for the purpose of critical examination 1814: 248.

	Tranſ.	Abridg.
—— Of the different quantities of rain which appear to fall, at different heights, over the ſame ſpot of ground - - *W. Heberden*	LIX 359	
—— A letter giving an account of ſome experiments made in North Wales, to aſcertain the different quantities of rain, which fell at the ſame time, at different heights - *Barrington*	LXI 294	
HEIGHTS (meaſured by the barometer). A diſcourſe of the rule of the decreaſe of the height of the mercury in the barometer, according as places are elevated above the ſurface of the earth, with an attempt to diſcover the true reaſon of the riſing and falling of the mercury upon change of weather - *Halley*	XVI 104	II 14
—— A proſpect of the weather, winds, and height of the mercury in the barometer, on the firſt day of the month, and of the whole rain in every month, in 1703 and beginning of 1704, at Townley, in Lancaſhire, by *R. Townley*; and at Upminſter by - - *W. Derham*	XXIV 1877	
—— A propoſal for meaſuring heights of places by help of the barometer of Mr. Patrick, in which the ſcale is greatly enlarged - - *Halley*	XXXI 116	VI 2 28
—— Obſervations concerning the height of the barometer, at different elevations above the ſurface of the earth - - - *Nettleton*	XXXIII 308	VI 2 44
—— Experiments and obſervations made in Britain, in order to obtain a rule for meaſuring heights with the barometer - - *Roy*	LXVII 653	
HELENA (ST.) A letter recommending to make at St. Helena a ſeries of obſervations for diſcovering the parallax of the moon *De la Caille*	LII 21	
—— —— A letter concerning obſervations to be made on the parallax of the moon at St. Helena, and recommending the ſame to be made at Paris and Greenwich, to ſettle the longitude between Paris and St. Helena - - *Maſkelyne*	— 26	
HELSINGLAND. An explanation of the Runic characters of - - - *Celſius*	XL 7	IX 438
HELMONT. See *Laudanum*.		
HELVETIA. Letter concerning the icy and cryſtalline mountain of Helvetia, called the Gletſcher - - - - *Muraltus*	IV 982	II 465
—— A farther deſcription and repreſentation of the icy mountain called the Gletſcher, in the canton of Berne, in Helvetia - - *Juſtel*	VIII 6191	— —

	Transf.	Abridg.
HEMLOCK. Two obfervations, the one concerning the effects of a poifonous one; the other concerning the virtues of the leaves of hemlock - - - - *Ray*	XIX 634	II 641
—— An account of the poifonous qualities of hemlock-water-drop-wort - - *Ray*	XX 84	— —
—— An account of fome perfons poifoned by eating boiled hemlock - *W. Watfon*	XLIII 18	
—— A farther account of the poifonous effects of the oenanthe aquatica fucco virofo crocante, of Lobel, or hemlock-drop-wort *W. Watfon*	L 856	
—— An account of the cicuta, recommended by Dr. Storke - - - *W. Watfon*	LII 89	
—— Cafe of a cancer in which green hemlock was applied - - - *Colebrook*	LIII 346	
—— Obfervations and experiments on different extracts of hemlock - - *Morris*	LIV 172	
—— Sequel to the cafe of Anne James, who had taken the green hemlock - *Colebrooke*	LV 271	
HEMP-SEED. A difcovery of an indiffoluble falt arifing from Hemp-feed put into water till it becomes putrid - - - *Ellis*	LIX 138	
HENBANE. An account of a colour yielded by the eggs of an infect feeding on henbane	VI 2176	II 783
—— An account of fymptoms arifing from eating the feeds of henbane, with their cure, &c. and fome occafional remarks - *Sloane*	XXXVIII 99	VIII 841
—— Letter concerning the poifon of henbane roots - - - *Patouillet*	XL 446	— —
—— The effects of the hyofcyamus albus, or white henbane - - *Stedman*	XLVII 194	
HEPHATITIS. A hephatitis, with unfavourable fymptoms, fuccefsfully treated - *Smith*	LVI 92	
HERB. Some attempts made to prove that herbs of the fame make or clafs, for the generality, have the like effect and tendency to work the fame effects - - - *Petiver*	XXI 289	II 704
HERCULANEUM. An account of the difcovery of the remains of a city under-ground, near Naples - - - - - *Sloane*	XLI 345	IX 440
—— Extracts of two letters from Rome, concerning fome antient ftatues, pictures, and other curiofities, found in a fubterraneous town lately difcovered near Naples - *Paderni*	XLI 484	— —
Extract of another letter on the fame fubject - - - - *Knapton*	— 489	IX 442

Hemisphere. Of the penetration of a hemisphere by an indefinite number of equal and similar Cylinders. — — — Knight. 1812 : 310.

+ Hemp-seed. Experiments with Chinese Hemp-seed. Fitzgerald. 72:46.

	Transf.	Abridg.
Extract of another on the same subject *Crispe*	XLI 493	IX 444
— Extract of a letter, giving a short account of some of the principal antique pictures found in the ruins of Herculaneum at Portici, Naples - - - *Hoare*	XLIV 567	XI 1305
— Account of the method of opening the manuscripts found at Herculaneum *Condamine*	— 622	
— Remarks on the principal paintings found in the subterraneous city of Herculaneum *Blondeau*	XLVI 14	— 1307
— Letter concerning the ruins of Herculaneum - - - *Freeman*	XLVII 131	
— Extract of a letter from Naples concerning Herculaneum, containing an account and description of the place, and what has been found in it - -	— 150	
— Letter concerning the antiquities dug up from the antient Herculaneum, Nov. 18, 1752 - - - *Paderni*	XLVIII 71	
— Letter relating to some antiquities at Herculaneum - - *Spence*	— 486	
— Extract of a letter from the keeper of the Museum Herculaneum at Naples *Paderni*	— 634	
— Letter relating to the late discoveries at Herculaneum - - *Paderni*	— 821	
Another letter - - *Gray*	— 825	
— Extracts of two letters concerning the late discoveries at Herculaneum - *Paderni*	XLIX 109	
— Copy of a letter concerning the books and antient writings dug out of the ruins of an edifice near the site of the old city of Herculaneum, to Monsignor Cerati of Pisa; with a translation by Mr. Locke - *Anon.*	— 112	
— An account of the late discoveries of antiquities at Herculaneum, &c. - *Paderni*	— 490	
— An account of the late discoveries of antiquities at Herculaneum, &c. - *Paderni*	L 49	
— An account of some of the antiquities discovered at Herculaneum, &c. - *Nixon*	— 88	
— An account of the late discoveries of antiquities at Herculaneum, and of an earthquake there, and eruption of mount Vesuvius Mar. 24, 1758 - - *Paderni*	— 619	
— Additional observations upon some plates of white glass found at Herculaneum *Nixon*	LII 123	
HERMAPHRODITE. An exact narrative of an hermaphrodite in London - *Allen*	II 624	III 305

— Letter

	Transf.	Abridg.
—— Letter concerning a very extraordinary hermaphrodite at Thoulouſe - *Veay*	XVI 282	II 606
—— An account of an hermaphrodite lobſter examined and diſſected purſuant to an order of the Society - - *Nicholls*	XXXVI 290	VII 421
—— Letter concerning the hermaphrodite ſhewn in London - - *Parſons*	XLVII 142	
HERNIA. An account of an extraordinary Hernia Inguinalis - - *Huxham*	XLI 640	IX 164
—— Two medico-chirurgical obſervations on the hydatides, and conſequences of an incompleat hernia, and on the function of the inteſtines expoſed to ſight - *Le Cat*	— 712	— 189
—— An account of ſeveral caſes of hernias, and diſorders of the urethra - *Le Cat*	XLVII 324	
—— An account of a hernia of the urinary bladder including a ſtone - - *Pott*	LIV 61	
—— An account of an uncommon large hernia *Carliſle*	LVI 133	
—— An account of an hydro-enterocele appearing like a hydro-ſarcocele, and ending in the death of the patient, in which the inteſtine had paſſed from the hernial ſac into that of the hydrocele, by which the ſtrangulation was formed - - - *Le Cat*	LVII 293	
—— See *Rupture.*		
HERRN GROUND. Account of the copper ground in Hungary - - *Brow*	V 1042	II 562
HERTFORDSHIRE. See *Antiquities.*		
HESIOD. A letter concerning the ages of Homer and Heſiod - - *Coſtard*	XLVIII 441	
HESSIA. A letter containing a ſhort account of ſome baſalt hills in Heſſia - *Raſpe*	LXI 580	
HESSIAN BELLOWS. See *Bellows.*		
HEVELIUS. Obſervations on a treatiſe of Mr. Hevelius, deſigned to prove, that the lungs do not divide and expand the blood, but on the contrary cool and condenſe it - *Nicholls*	XXXVI 163	VII 500
HIERO. Deſcriptio Fontis Hieronis in Metallifodinis Chemnicenſibus in Hungaria, anno 1756 extructi, with a theory of congelation, drawn from ſome appearances of ice and ſnow there - - - *Wolfe*	LII 542	
HIEROGLYPHICS. Extract of a letter concerning a ſuppoſed connection between the hieroglyphical writing of antient Egypt, and the characteriſtic writing which is in uſe at this day among the Chineſe - - *Morton*	LIX 489	

4. Hermaphrodites. An account of the dissection of an hermaphrodite Dog, to which are prefixed some observations on hermaphrodites in general. Home. 1799. 157.

Hirudines. Observations on the Hirudo vulgaris. Johnson. 1817: 13.
Observations on the H. complanata, and H. stagnalis, now formed
into a distinct genus under the name Glossopora. —— —— 339.

	Tranf.	Abridg.
HILL. An account of the subsiding or sinking down of a hill near Clogher in Ireland - - - *Bishop of Clogher*	XXVIII 267	IV 2 250
—— A proposal for measuring the attraction of some hills in this kingdom by astronomical observations - - *Maskelyne*	LXV 495	
—— An account of a volcanic hill near Inverness - - - *West*	LXVII 385	
—— Calculations to determine at what point in the side of a hill its attraction will be the greatest, &c. - - *Hutton*	LXX 1	
—— See *Mountains*.		
HIPPOCRATES. Letter concerning the quadrature of the parts of the lunula of Hippocrates Chius, performed by Mr. John Perks; with the further improvement of the same by Dr. David Gregory and John Caswell - *Wallis*	XXI 411	I 27
—— The dimension of the solids generated by the conversion of Hippocrates lunula, and of its parts about several axes, with the surfaces generated by that conversion *De Moivre*	XXII 624	— 29
HIRTA. A description of the island Hirta *Moray*	XII 927	III 541
HIRUDINELLA MARINA. A description of the hirudinella marina, or sea leach - *Garcin*	XXXVI 377	VII 418
HISTORY. A description of a mathematical historical table - - *Mangold*	XI 667	
HITCHCOCK. Case of Hannah Hitchcock; one of whose ureters was grown up *Huxham*	XLIII 207	XI 1007
HITCHELL (JOHN). An account of the death of John Hitchell, who was burnt to death by lightning - - - *Roin*	— 447	— 1068
HOG. The anatomy of the Mexico musk-hog *Tyson*	XIII 359	II 873
HOLLAND. Remarks in a late journey into Denmark and Holland - - *Oliver*	XXIII 1400	V 2 128
HOLLANDIA (NOVA). Some late observations in Nova Hollandia - *Witsen*	XX 361	III 620
HOLLY. A remark concerning the sex of Holly - - - *Martyn*	XLVIII 613	
HOLT WATERS. An account of the several strata of earth found in sinking the mineral wells at Holt - - *Lewis*	XXXV 489	VI 2 225
—— —— A letter giving a farther account of the nature and virtues of the Holt waters *Lewis*	XXXVI 43	— 176
HOLY-OAK. A letter containing some microscopical observations on the fari a foecundans of the holy-oak and the passion flower *Badcock*	XLIV 150	X 753

Further

	Tranſ.	Abridg.
Further obſervations and experiments on the paſſion flower and its farina *Badcock*	XLIV 166	X 756
Homer. A letter concerning the ages of Homer and Heſiod - - *Coſtard*	XLVIII 441	
Horace. Some thoughts concerning the antient Greek and Roman lyre; and an explanation of an obſcure paſſage in one of Horace's Odes *Molyneux*	XXIII 1267	IV 474
Horizon. A propoſition of general uſe in the art of gunnery; ſhewing the rule of laying a mortar to paſs, in order to ſtrike any object above or below the horizon - *Halley*	XIX 68	I 481,483
— The deſcription of a new quadrant for taking an altitude without an horizon, either at ſea or land - - *Elton*	XXXVII 273	
— A ſpirit-level to be fixed to a quadrant for taking a meridional altitude at ſea when the horizon is not viſible - *Halley*	XXXVIII 167	VIII 357
— An attempt to explain the phænomenon of the horizontal moon, appearing bigger than when elevated many degrees about the horizon; ſupported by an experiment - *Deſaguliers*	XXXIX 390	— 130
An explication of the experiment *Deſaguliers*	— 390	— 131
Some thoughts on the ſun and moon when near the horizon, appearing larger than when in the zenith - - *Logan*	— 404	VII 377
— A deſcription of a water-level to be fixed to Davis's quadrant, whereby an obſervation may be taken at ſea in thick and hazy weather, without ſeeing the horizon - - *Leigh*	XL 413	VIII 360
— The deſcription and uſe of an apparatus added as an improvement to Davis's quadrant, conſiſting of a mercurial level for taking the coaltitude of ſun or ſtar at ſea, without the uſual aſſiſtance of the ſenſible horizon which frequently is obſcured - *Leigh*	— 417	— 362
— See *Moon and Sun.*		
Horns. Account of a kidney of an unuſual ſhape and texture taken out of the body of a man; with obſervations on horns and glandules in general - - *Malpighius*	XIV 601	II 865
— An account of a girl in Ireland who had ſeveral horns growing on her body - *Aſh*	XV 1202	III 12
— An account of one who had horny excreſcences, or extraordinary large nails on his fingers and toes - - *Locke*	XIX 594	
— Two letters on horn-like excreſcences growing on the fingers, &c. - - *Wroe*	XXIV 1899	V 387
— An account of a pair of very large horns found in Lapping - - - - Sloane	XXXII 222	VII 441

— A

† Horizon. Observations on horizontal refractions which affect the appearance of terrestrial objects, and the dip, or depression of the horizon of the sea. Huddart 1797: 29.

+ Horns. Observations on certain horny excrescences of the human body. Home. 81: 95.

		Trans.	Abridg.
—— Of the horn of a large deer found in the heart of an oak - - - - -	Clark	XLI 235	VIII 847
~~—— A letter containing an account of a rhinoceros with a double horn with a figure~~ see rhino.	~~Sloane~~	~~XLVI 118~~	~~XI 910~~
—— Some account of a sheep having a monstrous horn growing from his throat	*Parsons*	XLIX 183	
+ ~~—— A letter concerning the double horns of the~~ see rhinoceros - -	~~*Parsons*~~	~~LVI 32~~	
HORNS (Fossil). A discourse concerning the large horns frequently found under ground in Ireland; concluding from them, that the great American deer, called a moose, was formerly common in that island -	*Molyneux*	XIX 489	II 432 III 544
—— An account of horns found under ground in Ireland - -	*Kelly*	XXXIV 122	VI 2 224
~~—— An account of a pair of very extraordinary large horns found in Wapping some years since; with a probable account whence they came, and to what animal they belonged~~ see above	~~*Sloane*~~	~~— 222~~	~~VII 441~~
—— A letter serving to accompany the pictures of an extraordinary fossil skull of an ox with the cores of the horns - -	*Klein*	XXXVII 427	— 495, IV 4–101
~~—— Of the horn of a large deer found in the heart of an oak~~ see above - -	~~*Clark*~~	~~XLI 235~~	~~VIII 847~~
—— An account of two extraordinary deers horns found under ground in different parts of Yorkshire - -	*Knowlton*	XLIV 124	X 601
HORROX. A letter concerning Mr. Horrox's lunar system - -	*Flamstead*	X 368	I 453
HORSES. An observation concerning a blemish in a eye; not hitherto discovered by any author - - -	*Lower*	II 613	II 684
—— An account of a stone fastened to the back-bone of a horse -	~~*Giornale de Letterati*~~	VII 4094	III 164
—— An extraordinary cure of a horse that was staked into his stomach -	*Wallis*	XIX 118	
—— An account of a new engine for raising water by horses - -	*Churchman*	XXXVIII 402	VIII 322
—— Account of a horse bit by a mad dog	*Starr*	XLVI 474	XI 913
—— Extract of a letter concerning some remarkable experiments made upon the arteries of horses with the powder of lycopherdon, or lupi crepitus: by Monsieur La Fosse	*Latterman*	XLIX 37	
HORSEFORD. An account of the sinking down of a piece of ground at Horseford in Norfolk - - -	*Arderon*	XLIII 527	X 587
HOT HOUSES. An account of the Indian hot houses - - -	*Dudley*	XXXIII 129	VII 669

	Tranf.	Abridg.
HOUSES. An account of the houses and hearths in Dublin in 1695 and 1696	XXII 518	III 665
HOUR. Letter concerning the drawing the meridian line by the pole star, and finding the hour by the same — Gray	— 815	IV 462
HOWELL (MARY). The case of Mary Howell, who had a needle run into her arm and came out at her breast	XLI 767	IX 238
HUDSON's BAY. Observations on the state of the air, winds, weather, &c. at the Prince of Wales's Fort on the north-west coast of Hudson's Bay, in 1768 and 1769 — Dymond and Wales	LX 137	
—— —— An account of birds sent from Hudson's Bay; with observations relative to their natural history; and Latin descriptions of some of the most uncommon — Forster	LXII 382	
HUMBER. An account of the sunk island in Humber, some years since recovered from the sea — — — Chamberlayne	XXX 1014	IV 2 251
HUMMING BIRD. The description of the American tomineius, or humming bird — Grew	XVII 760	II 854
—— —— A query concerning the food of the humming bird — — Grew	— 815	— —
HUMOUR. Observations about the chrystalline humour of the eye — Leewenhoek	XIV 790	
HUNGARIAN BOLUS. Of the Hungarian bolus of the same effects with the bolus armenus Anon.	I 11	— 457
HUNGARY. Inquiries to be made in Hungary and Transylvania — Royal Society	II 467	III 631
—— Letter concerning the damps in the mines of Hungary, and their effects — Browne	IV 965	II 373
—— Directions and enquiries, with their answers, concerning the mines, minerals, baths, &c. of Hungary, &c. Oldenburg and Brown	V 1189	— 523, 585
Account of stone quarries and talcum rocks in Hungary — — Anon.	— 1044	— 339
—— An account of the tokay wines in Hungary — — — Douglass	LXIII 292	
HURRICANES. Relation of two hurricanes in Northamptonshire Oct. 30, 1669, and Oct. 13, 1670 — — Templer	VI 2156	— 102, 103
—— Observations of his own experiences upon hurricanes, and their prognostics — Langford	XX 407	— 105
—— An account of a violent hurricane in Huntingdonshire Sept. 8, 1741 — Fuller	XLI 851	VIII 491
HUSBANDRY. Divers rural and œconomical enquiries recommended to observation and trial Anon.	IX 240	III 683
		—— Some

4 Hydraulics. Hydraulic investigations, subservient to an intended Croonian lecture on the motion of the blood. Young. 1808 : 164.

	Trans.	Abridg.
—— Some agrestic observations and advertisements - - - *Beale*	XII 816	II 744
Continuation of the hortulan and rural advertisements - - *Beale*	— 846	— 745
HYADES. An advertisement to astronomers, of the advantage that may accrue from the observation of the moon's frequent appulses to the hyades, during the three next ensuing years *Anon.*	XXX 692	IV 298
HYDATIDES. Lumbricus hydropicus, or an essay to prove, that hydatides, often met with in morbid animal bodies, are a species of worms, or imperfect animals - *Tyson*	XVII 506	III 133
—— A relation of a person who voided many hydatides in her urine - *Davies*	XXII 897	V 2 283
—— A letter concerning hydatides voided by stool - - - *Musgrave*	XXIV 1797	V 281
—— Of hydatides inclosed with a stony crust in the kidney of a sheep - *Cowper*	XXV 2304	— 54
—— An observation of a tumour on the neck full of hydatides, cured by - *Hewnden*	— 2344	— 216
—— An account of a great quantity of hydatides found in the abdomen - *Thorpe*	XXXI 17	
—— An observation of hydatides voided per vaginam - - - *W. Watson*	XLI 711	IX 188
—— Two medico-chirurgical observations on the hydatides, and consequences of an incomplete hernia, and on the functions of the intestines exposed to sight - *Le Cat*	— 712	— 189
HYDRAULICS. Remarks upon some experiments in hydraulics, which seem to prove, that the forces of equal moving bodies are as the squares of their velocities - *Eames*	XXXV 343	VI 292
—— Short and easy methods for finding the quantity and weight of water contained in a full pipe of any given height and diameter of bore; and, consequently, to find what degree of power would be required to work a common pump, or any other hydraulic engine, when the diameter of the pump-bore, and the height to which the water is to be raised therein, are given *Ferguson*	LV 61	
HYDRAULIC ENGINE. A description of an hydraulic engine - *Journal des Scavans*	XI 679	I 557
HYDRAULOPNEUMATICS. A narrative of a new invention of expanding fluids by their being conveyed into certain ignified vessels, where they are immediately rarified into an elastic impelling force sufficient to give motion to hydrau-		

Subject	Author	Trans.	Abridg.
lopneumatical and other engines for raising water, and other uses, &c. -	*Payne*	XLI 821	VIII 638
Hydrocephalus. A new trocart for the puncture in the hydrocephalus and for other evacuations, which are necessary to be made at different times - -	*Le Cat*	XLVII 267	
Hydro-enterocele. An account of an hydro-enterocele, appearing like a hydro-sarcocele, and ending in the death of the patient, in which the intestines had passed from the hernial sac into that of the hydrocele, by which the strangulation was formed -	*Le Cat*	LVII 293	
Hydrologia. Some reflections made on the enlarged account of Dr. Witties answer to hydrologia chymica, chiefly concerning the cause of the sudden loss of the virtues of mineral waters - - -	*Foot*	IV 1050	II 365
Hydrometer. Account of a new kind of hydrometer - -	*Clarke*	XXXVI 277	VI 326
Hydrophobia. Relation of a man bitten with a mad dog, and dying of the disease called hydrophobia - -	*Lister*	XIII 162	II 276
—— A remarkable account of an hydrophobia - - -	*Howman*	XV 916	III 280
—— An account of three cases of the hydrophobia - - -	*Mead*	XXVI 433	V 367
—— An account of the case of a supposed hydrophobia - -	*Earl of Morton*	LV 139	
Hydro-sarcocele. An account of an hydro-enterocele appearing like a hydro-sarcocele, and ending in the death of the patient; in which the intestine had passed from the hernial sac into that of the hydrocele, by which the strangulation was formed -	*Le Cat*	LVII 293	
Hydrops Ovarii. An account of an hydrops ovarii, with a new and exact figure of the glandulæ renales, and of the uterus in a puerpera - - -	*Douglas*	XXV 317	— 294
—— —— A remarkable case of a gentlewoman who died of a hydrops ovarii in the 33d year of her age, after having been tapped fifty-seven times - - -	*Belchier*	XXXVII 279	VII 544
Hydrostatic. A description of a new essay-instrument, together with the hydrostatical principle it is founded on - -	*Boyle*	X 329	I 516
Extract of a letter relating to the essay-instrument - -	*Anon.*	— 353	— 520

HYGRO-

+Hygrometer. A second paper on Hygrometry. - - - - - De Luc. 81: 1; 389.

	Trans.	Abridg.
HYGROMETER. Letter of a contrivance of an uncommon hygroscope - *Anon.*	XI 647	II 36
—— A description of his hygroscope in two several contrivances; together with some observations made thereon - - *Conyers*	— 715	— 37
—— A letter concerning a new hygroscope invented by - - *Molyneux*	XV 1032	— 40
—— Description of the hygrometer *Pickering*	XLIII 6	
—— Extract of a letter describing an improved hygroscope - - *Arderon*	XLIV 95	X 453
—— Part of a letter concerning an improvement of the weather cord - *Arderon*	— 169	— —
—— The description of an hygrometer made of a deal rod - - *Arderon*	— 184	— 454
—— The description of a new hygrometer invented by - - *James Ferguson*	LIV 259	
—— Description of a new hygrometer *Smeaton*	LXI 198	
—— Account of a new hygrometer *De Luc*	LXIII 404	
HYGROSCOPE. See *Hygrometer*.		
HYOSCYAMUS ALBUS. The effects of the hyoscyamus albus - - *Stedman*	XLVII 194	
HYPERBOLA. The squaring of the hyperbola by an infinite series of rational numbers; together with its demonstration - *Brouncker*	III 645	I 10
—— Answer to the animadversions of Mr. Hugenius upon Dr. Gregory's book, De vera circuli & hyperbolæ quadratura, as published in the journal Des Scavans - *Gregory*	— 732	
—— Some considerations upon M. Hugens's letter, printed in vindication of his examen of the book entituled, Vera circuli & hyperbolæ quadratura - - *Gregory*	— 882	— 407
—— The generation of an hyperbolical cylindroid demonstrated, and the application thereof, for grinding hyperbolical glasses, hinted at *Wren*	IV 961	— 188
—— A description of Dr. Chr. Wren's engine, designed for grinding hyperbolical glasses, as it was in a manner promised, vol. III. p. 962 - - - *Wren*	— 1059	— 189
—— On the center of gravity of hyperbolas *Wallis*	VII 5074	
—— A compendious and facile method for constructing the logarithms, exemplified and demonstrated from the nature of numbers, without any regard to the hyperbola; with a speedy method for finding the number from the logarithm given - - *Halley*	XIX 58	— 108

		Tranf.	Abridg.
—— The construction and properties of a new quadratrix to the hyperbola — *Perks*		XXV 2253	IV 37
—— The general quadrature of trinomial hyperbolic curves; delivered in two theorems *Klingerstein*		XXXVII 45	VI 82
—— An investigation of a general theorem for finding the length of any arc of any conic hyperbola by means of two elliptic arcs; with some other new and useful theorems deduced therefrom — *Landen*		LXV 283	
HYPNUM TERRESTRE. A letter concerning the seeding of mosses; and in particular of the hypnum terrestre trichoides, luteovirenus, vulgare, majus capitulis erectis. Raii Synopf. Edit. III. p. 84 — *Hill*		XLIV 60	X 758
HYPOCAUSTUM. A description of a Roman sudatory, or hypocaustum, found at Wroxeter in Shropshire, 1701 — *Lister*		XXV 2225	
— — *Harwood*		— 2228	
Two letters relating to Wroxeter, and the hypocausta of the antients — *Baxter*		— —	
—— An account of the remains of a Roman hypocaustum, or sweating room, discovered under ground at Lincoln in 1739 — *Sympson*		XLI 855	IX 455

Jackal. Observation, J. tending to show that the Wolf, Jackal and Dog, are all of the same species. Hunter. 77: 253. 79: 160.

JACULATOR. An account of a fish from Batavia called jaculator — *Schlosser*		LIV 89	
—— Some further intelligence relating to the jaculator fish, from Mr. Homnel at Batavia; together with the description of another species by Dr. Pallas — *Schlosser*		LVI 186	
JAMAICA. Observations made at Jamaica *Stubbes*		II 495	
An enlargement of the observations *Stubbes*		III 699	
—— Some particulars referring to the observations made at Jamaica — *Norwood*		— 824	III 559
—— Observations on the eclipse of the moon June 18, 1722, and the longitude of Port Royal in Jamaica determined thereby — *Halley*		XXXII 235	VI 190 / VII 617
JAMES (ANNE). See *Hemlock*.			
JAPAN. Some observations concerning Japan, in answer to queries sent by Mr. Oldenburg *M. I.*		IV 983	III 620
—— A summary relation of what hath been hitherto discovered in the matter of the North East passage — *Anon.*		X 417	— 610

—— Ex-

+ On the rectification of the hyperbola. Hellins. 1811: 110

Hyperoxymuriate. On the action of acids on the salts usually called hyperoxymuriates, and on the gases produced from them. Davy. 1815: 214.

James's Powder. Experiments and observations to investigate its composition. Pearson. 81: 317.
Observations and experiments upon Dr. James's powder, with a method of preparing, in the humid way, a similar substance. Chenevix. 1801: 375.

Ice. Account of the method of making Ice at Benares. 1793 : 56 & 129.

On ice found in the bottom of rivers. Knight. 1816 : 286.

	Tranf.	Abridg.
—— Extract from a journal kept by C. P. Thunberg, M. D. during his voyage to, and residence in, the empire of Japan - *Thunberg*	LXX 1	
JAVA-MAJOR. Answer to some of the queries which were recommended by Sir R. Moray to Sir P. Vernatti, president at Java Major *Vernatti*	III 863	— 617
JAUNDICE. Letter concerning a contumacious jaundice, accompanied with a very odd case in vision - - *Dale*	XVIII 158	— 286
—— A letter concerning the jaundice, occasioned by a stone obstructing the ductus communis bilarius, which was afterwards voided by stool - - - *Musgrave*	XXV 2233	V 279
—— Part of a letter concerning a child born with the jaundice upon it, received from its father; and of the mother taking the same distemper from her husband the next time of being with child - - - *Cooke*	XLVI 205	XI 1063
JAW. Observations upon the effects of electricity applied to a tetanus, or muscular rigidity of four months continuance - *W. Watson*	LIII 10	
—— Case of a locked jaw - *Woolcombe*	LV 85	
—— Account of a locked jaw and paralysis, cured by electricity - - *Spry*	LVII 88	
ICE. A way of preserving ice and snow by chaff *Ball*	I 139	III 240
—— Some experiments shewing the difference of ice made without air, from that which is produced with air - - *Rinaldini*	VI 2169	II 164
—— Some experiments about freezing, and the difference between common fresh water ice and that of the sea water: also a probable conjecture about the original of the nitre of Egypt *Lister*	XV 836	— —
—— New experiments upon ice - *Nollet*	XL 307	VIII 503
—— An examination of sea water frozen and melted again, to try what quantity of salt is contained in such ice; made in Hudson's Straights by Capt. Christopher Middleton, at the request of C. Mortimer - *Middleton*	XLI 806	— 643
—— The process of making ice in the East Indies - - *Sir Robert Barker*	LXV 252	
—— Experiments on water obtained from the melted ice of sea water, to ascertain whether it be fresh or not, &c. - *Nairne*	LXVI 249	
—— See *Frost*.		
ICELAND. Account of sundry experiments made upon a crystal-like body sent from Iceland - - - *Bartholin*	V 2039

		Transf.	Abridg.
——— An answer to some philosophical inquiries concerning that country — *Biornonius*		IX 238	III 609
ICHNEUMON WORMS. Some considerable observations upon that kind of wasps called Vespæ Ichneumones, especially their several ways of breeding: and among them that odd way of laying their eggs in the bodies of caterpillars, &c. — *Willoughby*		VI 2279	II 769
A letter enlarging his observations about Ichneumon worms — *Lister*		— 2284	— 770
——— — *Lister*		— 3002	— 912
ICONANTIDIPTIC TELESCOPE. An account of an Iconantidiptic telescope — *Jeaurat*		LXIX 130	
ICY MOUNTAIN. Letter concerning the icy or crystalline mountains of Helvetia, called the Gletscher — *Muraltus*		IV 982	— 465
——— ——— A further description and representation of the icy mountain, called the Gletscher, in the canton of Berne in Helvetia — *Justel*		VIII 6191	— —
——— ——— Part of a letter concerning the icy mountains in Switzerland — *Burnet*		XXVI 316	
IDIOT. An account of an idiot at Ostend — *Amyand*		— 170	V 278
JELLY. Some observations concerning the virtue of the jelly of black currants in curing inflammations in the throat — *Baker*		XLI 655	VIII 838
JENKINS (HENRY). Account of one Henry Jenkins who attained the age of 169 years; with remarks — *Robinson*		XIX 266	III 307
——— — *Hill*		— 543	
JESSAMINE. An account of two observations in gardening, upon the change of colour in grapes and jessamine — *Cane*		XXXI 102	VI 2 340
JESSO. A narrative of some observations made upon several voyages, to find a way for sailing about the North to the East Indies, and for returning the same way from thence hither; together with instructions given by the Dutch East India Company for the discovery of Jesso near Japan. To which is added, a relation of sailing through the Northern America to the East Indies — *Van Nierop*		IX 197	
JESSOP'S WELL. An examination of the strength of several of the purging waters, especially that of Jessop's Well — *Hales*		XLVI 446	X 574
Letter on the virtues of Jessop's Well — *Adee*		— 451	— —

IGNIS

Images. On the multiplication of images, and the colours which accompany them in some specimens of calcareous Spar.
Brewster. 1815. 270.

Impregnation. An experimental inquiry concerning animal impregnation.
Haighton 1797:159.
Experiments in which, on the third day after impregnation, the ova of Rabbits were found in the fallopian tubes; and on the fourth day after impregnation in the uterus itself; with the first appearance of the foetus.
Cruikshank. ——197.

	Tranſ.	Abridg.
IGNIS FATUUS. Of the meteor called an ignis fatuus, from obſervations made in England, and others in Italy - *Derham and Dereham*	XXXVI 204	VI 2 147
ILIAC PASSION. Of an iliac paſſion; occaſioned by an appendix in the Ilium - *Amyand*	XLIII 369	XI 1066
—— An account of an Iliac paſſion, from a palſy in the large inteſtines - *De Caſtro*	XLVII 123	
ILIUM. Account of a rupture of the Ilium, from an external contuſion, without any external wound - - - *Wolfius*	XL 61	IX 160
—— An inſtance of the gut ilium, cut through by a knife, and cured - *Travers*	L 35	
ILLNESS. A ſhort account of Dr. Maty's illneſs, and of the appearances in the dead body - - *Hunter and W. Watſon*	LXVII 608	
IMAGINATION. A relation of an extraordinary effect of the power of imagination - *Aſh*	XVI 334	
—— An account of a child born with a large wound in the breaſt, ſuppoſed to proceed from the force of imagination - *Cyprianus*	XIX 291	III 222
—— Letter concerning the effects of imagination, &c. - - *Aſh*	XX 293	——
IMITATION. An account of a man of a ſtrange imitating nature - - *Garden*	XII 842	— 8
IMPACT. Reflections on the communication of motion by impact and gravity - *Milner*	LXVIII 344	——
IMPOSTUME. Letter concerning the bones of a human fœtus voided through an impoſtume in the groin - - *Skippon*	XXIV 2077	V 306
—— Account of an extraordinary impoſtumation of the liver - - *Short*	XXXVII 184	VII 506
—— Account of a young lady who had an extraordinary impoſtume formed in her ſtomach *Layard*	XLVI 406	XI 1023
IMPREGNATION. Some experiments concerning the impregnation of the ſeeds of plants *Logan*	XXXIX 192	VIII 804
—— Thoughts on the different impregnations of mineral waters; more particularly concerning the exiſtence of ſulphur in ſome of them *Rutty*	LI 275	
—— A letter on the ſexes of plants, and impregnation of vegetables - *Styles*	LV 258	
INCALESCENCE. Of the incaleſcence of quickſilver with gold - - *B. R.*	X 515	II 580
INCISION. An account of a dropſy in the left ovary of a woman aged 58, cured by a large inciſion made in the ſide of the abdomen *Houſtoun*	XXXIII 8	VII 541
INCRUSTATION. See *Bones*.		
INCUS. An account of the caſe of a boy who had the		

	Transf.	Abridg.
malleus of each ear, and one of the incus's, drop out - - *Morant*	LII 264	
Index Glass. Remarks on Hadley's quadrant, tending principally to remove the difficulties which have hitherto attended the use of the back observation, and to obviate the errors that might arise from a want of parallelism in the two surfaces of the index glass - *Maskelyne*	LXII 99	
Indictions. A method for finding the numbers of the Julian period for any year assigned, the number of the cycle of the sun, the cycle of the moon, and of the indictions for the same year being given; together with a demonstration of that method - *Collins*	II 568	III 399
Indies. Some observations concerning a possible passage to the East Indies, by the Northern America, westward - - *Anon.*	IX 207	
—— Some observations sent from the East Indies, in answer to some queries sent thither *Waller*	XX 273	— 618
—— An account of some Indian plants, &c. with their names, descriptions, and virtues *Petiver*	— 313	II 725
—— Letter concerning some Indian manuscripts lately sent to the university of Oxford *Lewis*	— 421	— 397
—— A letter containing some observations on the mechanic arts of the Indians - *Papin*	XXVIII 225	— — 182
—— A letter containing some observations on the physick of the Indians - *Papin*	— —	— — —
—— An account of the Indian hot-houses *Dudley*	XXXIII 129	VII 669
—— An abstract of a letter concerning experiments made on the Indian magnetick sand - - - *Muschenbroek*	XXXVIII 297	IV 2 253
—— Some considerations on the antiquity and use of the Indian characters or figures - *Cope*	XXXIX 131	IX 426
—— Account of an antidote to the Indian poison in the West Indies - *Milward*	XLII 2	— 335
—— An account of the male and female cochineal insect that breed on the cactus opuntia, or Indian fig, in South Carolina or Georgia *Ellis*	LII 661	
—— An account of an extraordinary disease among the Indians in the islands of Nantuket and Martha's Vineyard in New England *Oliver*	LIV 386	
—— Some attempts to ascertain the utmost extent of the knowledge of the antients in the East Indies - - *Caverhill*	LVII 155	
—— A description and figure of the nyctanthes elongata, a new Indian plant - *Bergius*	LXI 289	

+ Indians. Particulars relative to the nature and customs of the Indians of North America. McCausland 76:229.

	Trans.	Abridg.
—— A letter giving some account of the roots used by the Indians in the neighbourhood of Hudson's Bay, to dye porcupine quills - - - *Forster*	LXII 54	
—— Extracts of some letters on the customs, manners and language of the northern Indians of America - - *Johnson*	LXIII 142	
INDIAN CORN. See *Maize*.		
INDIGO PLANT. The effects of the opuntia, or prickly pear; and of the Indigo plant in colouring the juices of living animals *Baker*	L 296	
INDUSTRIA (CITY). Some account of a curious tripos and inscription found near Turin, serving to discover the true situation of the antient city of Industria - - *Baker*	XLIII 540	XI 1240
INFANT. An anatomical observation of four ureters in an infant - - *Tyson*	XII 1939	III 146
—— Account of an infant musician - *Burney*	LXIX 183	
INFECTION. An account of several persons seized with the gaol fever working in Newgate, and of the manner in which the infection was communicated to one intire family *Pringle*	XLVIII 42	
INFINITE. The squaring of the hyperbola by an infinite series of rational numbers; together with its demonstration - *Brouncker*	III 645	I 10
—— An account of the several species of infinite quantity, and of the proportion they bear one to the other - - *Halley*	XVII 556	—— 102
—— A method of raising an infinite multinomial to any given power, or extracting any given root of the same - *De Moivre*	XIX 619	—— 90
—— A method of extracting the root of an infinite equation - - *De Moivre*	XX 190	I 95
—— Analytical solution of certain infinitesimal equations - - *De Moivre*	XXV 2368	IV 77
—— Some theorems respecting the infinite divisibility of matter - - *Keill*	XXIX 82	IV 423
—— A solution of the 15th general problem proposed by D. De Moivre, in his treatise De Mensura Sortis - - *Bernouilli*	—— 133	V. 2. 255
Another general solution of the preceding problem, with the assistance of combinations or infinite series - *De Moivre*	—— 145	—— 266
—— Of cubic equations and infinite series *Hutton*	LXX 387	
INFLAMMABLE LIQUORS. A way to make two clear spirituous inflammable liquors, which differ		

	Transf.	Abridg.
very little in taste and smell; and being mixed together, do give a fine carnation colour, without either sensible fermentation or alteration - - - *Geoffroy*	XXI 43	III 367
INFLAMMATIONS. Some observations concerning the virtue of the jelly of black currants in curing inflammations in the throat - - *Baker*	XLI 655	VIII 838
—— An account of a bristle that was lodged in a gentleman's foot, and caused a violent inflammation - - *Arderon*	XLIV 192	XI 1114
—— Case of a young lady who drank sea water for an inflammation and tumour in the upper lip - - - *Lewington*	LV 6	
INFUSION INTO VEINS. Account of the success of some experiments of infusing medicines into human veins - - *Anon.*	III 766	III 234
INGUINAL RUPTURE. Of an inguinal rupture, with a pin in the appendix cœci, incrusted with stone See *blood* - - *Amyand*	XXXIX 329	IX 153
INJECTION. A confirmation of the experiments made by Sig. Fracassati in Italy, by injecting acid liquors into the blood - *Boyle*	II 551	III 233
—— Anatomical inventions and observations, particularly the origin of the injection into veins - - - - *Clarck*	III 672	— 290
—— An account of the dissection of a dog who had mercury injected into one of the jugulars *Pitt*	XX 184	— 234
—— Further accounts of the success of injecting medicated liquors into the abdomen, in the case of an ascites - - *Warren*	XLIII 47	X 1009
INOCULATION. An account, or history, of the procuring the small-pox by incision or inoculation, as it has for some years been practised at Constantinople, 1713 - *Timonius*	XXIX 72	V 370
—— A new and safe method of procuring the small-pox by transplantation, lately invented and drawn into use - *Pylarinus*	— 393	— 377
—— The way of proceeding in the small-pox inoculated in New England - *Newman*	XXXII 33	VII 601
—— A letter concerning the inoculation of the small-pox - - *Nettleton*	— 35	— 602
Further account - *Nettleton*	— 49	— 608
—— Part of a letter concerning the inoculation of the small-pox, and the mortality of that distemper in the natural way - *Nettleton*	— 209	— 609
A further account, containing a comparison of		

Inflammation, spontaneous. Account of one. Humfries. 1794: 426.

Inks. Observations on ancient Inks, with the proposal of a new method of recovering the legibility of decayed writings. Blagden. 77: 451.

	Transf.	Abridg.
the danger in the natural way, and by inoculation - - - *Jurin*	XXXII 213	VII 611
——— Success of inoculation at Boston in New England - - - *Osborne*	— 225	— 617
——— A method of procuring the small-pox, used in South Wales - *Williams*	— 262	— 618
——— Another letter on the same subject *Williams*	— 264	— 619
——— Another account from Haverford-West *Wright*	— 267	— 620
——— Part of a letter concerning the effects of inoculation in New England - *Robie*	XXXIII 67	— 621
——— A letter concerning some children inoculated with the small-pox, at Haverford-West in Pembrokeshire - - *Davis*	XXXVIII 121	
——— An abstract from Timoni's history of the inoculated small-pox - *Horseman*	— 296	IX 210
——— A letter concerning inoculation *Brooke*	XLVII 470	
——— Letter from Geneva concerning the success of inoculation there - *Anon.*	— 503	
——— Letter from Salisbury concerning the success of inoculation - *Brown*	— 570	
——— Letter on the success of inoculation at Geneva - - - *Bonnet*	XLVIII 818	
——— Account of the practice of inoculation at Constantinople, - - *Porter*	XLIX 104	
——— An account of inoculation in the year 1736 - - - *Sloane*	— 516	
——— Historical memoirs relating to the practice of inoculation for the small-pox in the British American provinces, particularly in New England - - - *Gale*	LV 193	
——— A short account of the manner of inoculating the small-pox on the coast of Barbary, and at Bengal in the East Indies - *Chais*	LVIII 128	
——— An account of inoculation in Arabia *Russell*	— 140	
——— See *Small Pox.*		
INOCULATION OF CATTLE. A discourse on the usefulness of inoculation of the horned cattle, to prevent the contagious distemper among them - - - *Layard*	L 528	
INSCRIPTION. Letter concerning a Runic inscription at Beau-Castle - *Nicolson*	XV 1287	III 433
——— Letter on a Runic inscription at Bridekirk - - - *Nicolson*	— 1291	— 435
——— An uncommon inscription lately found on a very great basis of a pillar dug up at Rome; with an interpretation of the same - *Vossius*	XVI 172	— 446
——— Some account of the antient state of the city of		

Palmyra,

	Tranſ.	Abridg.
Palmyra, with ſhort remarks upon the inſcriptions found there - *Halley*	XIX 160	III 518
—— An account of an Etruſcan inſcription found on an old urn at Rome - *Pulleyn*	— 537	— 448
—— An account of an inſcription found at Rome in the language of the Palmereni *Pulleyn*	— —	— 526
—— Letter concerning ſome Roman inſcriptions found near Durham *Chriſtopher Hunter*	XXII 657	— 426
—— Letter on the various readings of an inſcription which is written upon the ſtatue of Tages by four Etruſcan alphabets - *Hickes*	XXIV 2076	V 306
—— Letter concerning a Roman inſcription lately found at York - *Thoreſby*	— 2145	V 2 35
—— A letter concerning ſome Roman inſcriptions found at York; proving, that the ninth legion ſome time reſided there - *Thoreſby*	XXV 2194	— - 41
—— Inſcriptio Tarraconenſis, with a comment - - - *Muſgrave*	XXVIII 157	— - 110
—— Extract of a letter giving an account of a Roman inſcription lately dug up in the north of England; with ſome hiſtorical and chronological remarks thereon - *Chr. Hunter*	XXX 701	— - 49
—— Remarks on a fragment of an old Roman inſcription lately found in the north of England - - - *Jurin*	— 813	— - 43
—— A diſcourſe occaſioned by an inſcription found at Langcheſter, in the Biſhoprick of Durham - - - *Gale*	— 823	— - 50
—— Extract of a letter giving an account of an ancient Roman inſcription found at Caerleon upon Uſk; with ſome conjectures thereon *Rice*	— 945	
—— An account of a Roman inſcription found at Chicheſter - *Gale*	XXXII 391	VII 4 23
—— Account of two pigs of lead found near Ripley with this inſcription on them, Imp. Caes. Domitiano, Aug. Coſ. VII. - *Kirſhaw*	XLI 560	IX 420
—— Remarks upon an inſcription cut formerly in a window belonging to the pariſh church of Rumſey in Hampſhire - *Ward*	XLIII 79	
—— A letter ſerving to accompany a copy of an antient Roman inſcription at Rocheſter in Northumberland, and two others at Riſingham - - - *Chr. Hunter*	— 159	X 1271
—— An explanation of a Roman inſcription found not long ſince at Silcheſter in Hampſhire *Ward*	— 200	XI 1264
—— Some account of a curious tripos and inſcription		

4

found

	Trans.	Abridg.
found near Turin, serving to discover the true situation of the antient city Industria *Baker*	XLIII 540	X 1240
— An explanation of an antient inscription discovered at Rutchester, the last station in England, upon the Roman wall, 1744 - *Taylor*	XLIV 344	XI 1284
— Copy of a Roman inscription found at Bath - - - *Stukeley*	XLV 409	— 1272
— Remarks upon an antient Roman inscription found in that part of Italy which formerly belonged to the Sabines - *Ward*	XLVI 293	— 1273
— An attempt to explain an antient Greek inscription engraven upon a curious bronze cup with two handles, and published with a draught of the cup by Dr. Pocock, in his description of the East, vol. II. part II. pag. 207 *Ward*	— 488	— 1278
— An attempt to explain an antient Roman inscription cut upon a stone lately found at Bath *Ward*	XLVIII 332	
— An account of a Roman inscription found at Malton in Yorkshire, in the year 1753 *Ward*	XLIX 69	
— An account of four Roman inscriptions cut upon three large stones found in a ploughed field near Wroxeter in Shropshire, in the year 1752; with some observations upon them *Ward*	— 196	
— Some considerations on two large pieces of lead with Roman inscriptions upon them, found several years since in Yorkshire *Ward*	— 686	
— An account of some subterraneous apartments with Etruscan inscriptions and paintings, discovered at Civita Turchino in Italy *Wilcox*	LIII 127	
— Observations on two antient Roman inscriptions discovered at Netherby in Cumberland *Taylor*	— 133	
— Copies of some Roman inscriptions at Tunis in Africa - - *Carlos*	— 211	
— An attempt to explain a Punic inscription lately discovered in the island of Malta *Swinton*	— 274	
— Some remarks upon the first part of Mr. L'Abbé Barthelemi's memoirs on the Phœnician letters, relative to the inscription in the island of Malta - - - *Swinton*	LIV 119	
— Remarks on the Palmyrene inscription at Teive - - - - *Swinton*	LVI 4	
— An attempt to explain the legend and inscription of a very curious Phœnician medal never hitherto explained - *Swinton*	LVII 266	
— Interpretation of the inscription of a Punic coin struck in the isle of Gozo - *Swinton*	LVIII 235	
— Description of a Punic coin appertaining to the		

isle

		Tranſ.	Abridg.
iſle of Gozo, hitherto attributed to that of Malta by the learned	*Swinton*	LVIII 261	
—— Interpretation of two Punic inſcriptions on the reverſes of two Siculo-Punic coins, publiſhed by the prince of Torremuzza, and never hitherto explained	*Swinton*	LXI 91	
—— An account of a ſubærated Denarius of the Prætorian family; adorned with an Etruſcan inſcription on the reverſe; never before publiſhed or explained	*Swinton*	LXII 60	
INSECTS. Some obſervations of ſwarms of ſtrange inſects in New England, and the miſchiefs done by them	*Anon.*	I 137	II 762
—— Obſervations on ſome inſects and their innoxiouſneſs	*Fairfax*	— 392	
—— Experiments on what happened to ſome creeping inſects in vacuo Boileano	*Boyle*	V 2051	— 463
—— Phænomena ſuggeſted by winged inſects in vacuo Boileano	*Boyle*	— 2053	
—— Account of an inſect likely to yield an acid liquor	*Liſter*	— 2067	— 792
—— Obſervations on inſects lodging themſelves in old willows	*King*	— 2098	— 772
- - - -	*Willoughby*	— 2100	— 773
—— An obſervation concerning certain inſect-huſks of the kermes kind	*Liſter*	VI 2165	— 776
—— An account of an inſect feeding upon henbain; the horrid ſmell of which is, in that creature, ſo qualified thereby, as to become in ſome meaſure aromatical, together with the colour yielded by the eggs of the ſame	*Liſter*	— 2176	— 783
—— Account of the kind of inſect hatched of the Engliſh kermes, alſo the uſe of theſe purple inſect-huſks for tinging; together with a compariſon of this Engliſh kermes with the ſcarlet kermes of the ſhops	*Liſter*	— 2196	— 766
—— An account of the inſects ſmelling of muſk	*Ray*	— 2219	— 765
—— Confirmation of the obſervation about muſk-ſcented inſects; adding ſome notes upon Dr. Swammerdam's book of inſects, and on that of Steno concerning petrified ſhells	*Liſter*	— 2281	— 783
—— Diſcovery of another muſk-ſcented inſect	*Liſter*	— 3002	—784,792
—— A letter concerning animated horſe hairs; rectifying a vulgar error	*Liſter*	VII 4064	— 771
—— An abſtract of a letter concerning generation by an inſect	*Leeuwenhoek*	XV 1120	— 911
—— The hiſtory of the generation of an inſect by			

him

Account of insects in the barks of decaying elms and ashes. Dudley. XXIV: 1859. V: 13.

	Tranf.	Abridg.
him called the wolf; with obfervations on infects bred in rain water, in apples, cheefe, &c. - - - *Leewenhoek*	XVIII 194	III 685
—— Letter concerning fwarms of infects that of late years have much infefted fome parts of the province of Connought in Ireland *Molyneux*	XIX 741	II 778
—— Part of a letter concerning feveral infects *Dale*	XXI 50	— 912
—— Letter concerning fome infects obferved upon fruit trees - - *Leewenhoek*	XXII 659	III 686
—— Letter concerning the infect called libella *Poupart*	— 673	II 762
—— Some obfervations concerning infects in Virginia; with remarks by J. Petiver *Banifter*	— 807	V 183
—— Letter concerning fome remarkable plants and infects obferved in Spain - *Breynius*	XXIV 2045	— 10
—— Two cafes of infects voided by the urinary paffage - - *Turner*	XXXIII 410	VII 539
—— Some corrections and amendments concerning the generation of the infect called coccus radicum, in his natural hiftory thereof *Breynius*	XXXVII 444	— 476
—— A letter containing the account of a remarkable generation of infects at Annapolis in Maryland - - *Lewis*	XXXVIII 119	IX 1
—— A picture and defcription of a water-infect not before defcribed (Lat.) - *Klein*	XL 150	— 6
A defcription of the fame fort of infect found in Kent; with an addition by - - - *Mortimer and Brown*	— 153	— 7
—— An abftract of fome new obfervations upon infects - - *Bonnet*	XLII 458	— 39
—— Obfervations upon feveral fpecies of fmall water-infects of the polypus kind *Trembley*	XLIV 627	XI 807
—— Divers means for preferving from corruption dead birds intended to be fent to remote countries, fo that they may arrive there in good condition. Some of the fame means may be employed for preferving quadrupeds, reptiles, fifhes, and infects - *Reaumur*	XLV 309	
—— Letter concerning a non-defcript petrified infect - - - *Lyttelton*	XLVI 598	X 656
Further account of the before-mentioned Dudley foffil - - - *Mortimer*	— 600	——
—— An account of fome remarkable infects of the polype kind, found in the waters near Bruffels in Flanders - - *Brady*	XLIX 248	
—— Account of a remarkable marine infect *Dupont*	LIII 57	
—— Obfervations on fome bivalve infects found in common water - *Muller*	LXI 230	

	Tranf.	Abridg.

—— A letter on the effects of elder, in preserving growing plants from insects and flies. *Gullet* LXII 348

INSTRUMENTS (for anatomical uses). An explication of the instruments used in a new operation of the eyes. - - *Cheselden* XXXV 451 — VII 493

—— A description of some instruments for the ears - - - *Cleland* XLI 847 — IX 124

—— A letter concerning the cure of a dry gangrene; together with a new-invented instrument for the extirpation of tumours out of the reach of the surgeon's fingers - XLVI 72 — XI 1084

—— An account of a new-invented instrument for fractured legs - - *Sharp* LVII 80

See Machines (Chirurgical)

INSTRUMENTS (Mathematical). Considerations upon Mr. Hook's new instrument for grinding of optick glasses - - *Auzout* I 56 — I 215

Answer - - - *Hook* — 63 — 192

—— A letter touching the invention of dividing a foot into many thousand parts for mathematical purposes - - *Townley* II 457 — 218

More ways for the same purpose *Hook* — 459 — 220

A description of the instrument for dividing a foot into many thousand parts, and thereby measuring the diameters of planets to great exactness - - *Hook* — 541 — 219

—— The description of an instrument invented divers years ago for drawing the out-lines of any object in perspective - *Wren* IV 898 — 598

—— Extract of two letters concerning an instrument to shew the moon's true place to a minute or two - - *Flamstead* IX 219 — 453

—— Account of a new essay-instrument *Boyle* X 329 — 516

Extract of a letter relating to the essay-instrument - - — 353 — 520

—— Letter about the making of microscopes with very small and single glasses, and of some other instruments - - *Butterfield* XII 1026 — 127, 208

—— Further remarks on the instrument, proposed by an anonymous French author, for effecting a perpetual motion - *Anon.* XVI 138

—— An instrument for seeing the sun, moon, or stars, pass the meridian of any place: useful for setting watches in all parts of the world with the greatest exactness, to correct sun-dials, to assist in the discovery of the longitude of places - - - - *Derham* XXIV 1578 — IV 464

—— Ex-

Instruments (Mathematical)

A description of a Transit Circle for determining the place of Celestial objects as they pass the Meridian. Wollaston. 1793: 133.

An improved method of dividing astronomical circles, and other instruments. Kater. 1814: 419.

Description of a new instrument for performing mechanically the involution and evolution of numbers. Roget. 1815: 9.

	Transf.	Abridg.
—— Extracts from Mr. Gascoigne's and Mr. Crabtree's letters, proving Mr. Gascoigne to have been the inventor of the telescopick sights of mathematical instruments, and not the French - - - *Derham*	XXX 603	— 345
—— A description of a new instrument for taking angles - - *Hadley*	XXXVII 147	VI 139
—— An account of observations made on board the the Chatham Yatch Aug. 30-31, and Sept. 1, 1732, for the trial of an instrument for taking angles - - *Hadley*	— 341	— 428
—— The description and use of an instrument for taking the latitude of a place at any given time of the day - - *Graham*	XXXVIII 450	VIII 371
—— A true copy of a paper found in the hand-writing of Sir Isaac Newton, among the papers of Dr. Halley, describing an instrument for observing the moon's distance from the fixed stars at sea - - *Newton*	XLII 155	— 129
—— An explanation of a new instrument made for measuring small angles - *Dollond*	XLVIII 551	
—— An account of the meteorological instruments used at the Royal Society's house *Henry Cavendish*	LXVI 375	
—— Account of a new instrument for measuring small angles, called the prismatic micrometer - - - *Maskelyne*	LXVII 799	
—— An account of the apparatus applied to the equatorial instrument, for correcting the errors arising from the refraction in altitude *Dollond*	LXIX 332	
—— An account of some new experiments in electricity, with the description and use of two new electrical instruments - *Cavallo*	LXX 15	
INSTRUMENTS (Musical) Account of a musical instrument brought from the isle of Amsterdam in the South Seas 1774, by captain Furneaux *Steele*	LXV 67	
—— See *Telescope*, *Microscope*, *Micrometer*, &c. in their places Equatorial		
INTEREST. Rules for correcting the usual methods of computing amounts and present values by compound as well as simple interest, and of stating interest accounts - *Watkins*	XXIX 111	V 2 243
—— Investigations of twenty cases of compound interest - - *Robertson*	LX 508	
INTERPOLATIONS. Problems concerning interpolations - - - *Waring*	LXIX 59	
INTESTINES. A discourse concerning the spiral, in-		

		Trans.	Abridg.
stead of the supposed annular structure of the fibres of the intestines -	*Cole*	XI 603	III 88
—— Letter concerning a child who had its intestines, mesentery, &c. in the cavity of the thorax	*Holt*	XXII 992	V 260
—— Observations on part of the intestines of a dog successfully cut away -	*Shipton*	XXIII 1299	— 275
—— Account of a pain in the belly arising from the intestines being concreted into a cartilaginous substance - -	*Mesaporitus*	XXIV 2114	V 2 35
—— Microscopical observations on the blood vessels, and membranes of the intestines - - -	*Leewenhoek*	XXVI 53	V 2 267
—— Account of a rupture of the ilium from an external contusion, attended with no external wound - -	*Wolfius*	XL 61	IX 160
—— Two medico-chirurgical observations on the hydatides, and consequences of an incompleat hernia, and on the functions of the intestines exposed to sight -	*Le Cat*	XLI 712	— 189
—— An account of an iliac passion from a palsy in the large intestines -	*De Castro*	XLVII 123	
—— An account of a very remarkable case of a boy who, notwithstanding that a considerable part of his intestines were forced out by the fall of a cart upon him, and afterwards cut off, recovered, and continues well	*Needham*	XLIX 238	
—— A remarkable case of cohesions of all the intestines in a man of about 34 years of age	*Jenty*	L 550	
—— An extraordinary cure of wounded intestines - - -	*Nourse*	LXVI 426	
—— See *Particular intestines in their places.*			
Inventions. A paper asserting some mathematical inventions to their true authors	*Gregory*	XVIII 233	I 116
Inundation. An account of an extraordinary inundation in the island of Mauricius	*Diodati*	XX 268	II 329
—— A letter giving an account of some inundations in Ireland, 1708 -	*Derham*	XXVI 308	IV 2 193
—— An account of a surprizing inundation in the valley of St. John's, near Keswick in Cumberland, Aug. 22, 1749 -	*Anon.*	XLVI 362	X 584
Jointed Worm. Lumbricus latus, or a discourse of the jointed worm -	*Tyson*	XIII 113	III 121
Joints. Two singular cures of diseased knee-joints successfully treated; the first by topical applications, the second by operation	*Warner*	XLIX 452	
—— Account of the case of the first joint of the			

Introsusception. History and dissection of an extraordinary — Lettsom, Whately. 76: 305.

Investigation. On the independence of the analytical and geometrical methods of investigation, and on the advantages to be derived from their separation. Woodhouse. 1802: 85.

Iodine. Some experiments and observations on a new substance which becomes a violet gas by heat. Davy. 1814 174.
Further experiments and observations on Iodine. — — 487.
Some experiments on a solid compound of iodine and oxygene, and on its chemical agencies. — 1815: 203.

Jordan. Analysis of the water of the River Jordan. Marcet. 1807: 296.

	Transf.	Abridg.
thumb torn off, with the flexor tendon in its whole extent torn out - *Home*	L 617	
IPECACUANHA. Of the use of the root ipecacuanha for loosenesses; translated from a French paper, with notes, by - *H. Sloane*	XX 69	III 114
—— A short account of the different kinds of ipecacuanha - - *Douglas*	XXXVI 152	VI 2 327
—— Medico-physical observations on ipecacuanha (Lat.) - - *Gmelin*	XLIII 382	X 761
IRELAND. Of the bogs and loughs of Ireland *King*	XV 948	II 732
—— A discourse concerning the large horns frequently found under ground in Ireland; concluding from them, that the great American deer, called a moose, was formerly common in that island - - *Molyneux*	XIX 489	— 432 III 544
—— Several observations relating to the antiquities and natural history of Ireland, in travels through that kingdom - - *Lhwyd*	XXVII 503	V 2 125
—— Some further observations relating to the antiquities and natural history of Ireland *Lhwyd*	— 524	— — 126
—— An account of horns found under ground in Ireland - - *King*	XXXIV 122	VI 2 224
—— Part of a letter concerning the remains of an antient temple in Ireland, and of a stone hatchet of the antient Irish - *Bp. of Cork*	XLII 581	IX 457
—— See *Figures, Population.*		
IRIS. Observations on an evening, or rather nocturnal solar iris, June 5, 1757 *Edwards*	L 293	
—— See *Rainbow.*		
IRON. An account of two mineral substances found in some coal and iron mines in England *Jessop*	VIII 6179	II 458
—— An account of the iron works in the forest of Dean - - *Powle*	XII 931	— 558
—— Several observations of the respect of the needle to a piece of iron held perpendicular; made by a master of a ship crossing the equinoctial line, 1684 - - *Anon.*	XV 1213	
—— Extracts of some letters concerning iron ore; and more particularly of the hæmatites wrought into iron at Milthorpe forge in Lancashire - - - *Sturmie*	XVII 695	— 551
—— To give iron the colour and tincture of copper - - - *Southwell*	XX 296	III 157
—— A letter concerning the magnetic quality acquired by iron upon standing for a long time in the same posture - *Leewenhoek*	XXXII 72	VI 2 277 VII 468

	Tranſ.	Abridg.
—— An hiſtorico-phyſical obſervation on the waters of Neuſohl, which are impregnated with braſs, and change iron into braſs - *Belius*	XL 351	VIII 645
—— A letter concerning melting iron with pit-coal - - - *Maſon*	XLIV 370	X 671
—— An account of a mountain of iron ore at Taberg in Sweden - *Aſcanius*	XLIX 30	
—— Obſervations on ſand iron - *Ellicot*	LIII 48	
—— A letter on the ſolubility of iron in ſimple water, by the intervention of fixed air *Lane*	LIX 216	
—— Account of a ſpecimen of native iron *Steblin*	LXIV 461	
—— Account of the iron ore lately found in Siberia - - - *Pallas*	LXVI 523	
—— Experiments on ignited ſubſtances *Whitehurſt*	— 575	
IRREDUCIBLE CASE. A method of extending Cardan's rule for reſolving one caſe of a cubic equation $x^3 - qx = r$ to the other caſe of the ſame equation, which it is not naturally fitted to ſolve, and which is therefore called the irreducible caſe - - *Maſeres*	LXX 85	
IRREGULARITIES. Of the irregularities in the planetary motions cauſed by the mutual attraction of the planets - *Walmeſly*	LII 275	
ISINGLASS. An account of the diſcovery of the manner of making iſinglaſs in Ruſſia; with a particular deſcription of its manufacture in England, from the produce of Britiſh fiſheries - - - *Jackſon*	LXIII 1	
ISLAND. An account of the ſunk iſland in the Humber, lately recovered from the ſea *Chamberlane*	XXX 1014	IV 2 251
—— Part of a letter concerning a new iſland lately raiſed out of the ſea near Tercera *Forſter*	XXXII 100	VI 2 203
—— On the formation of iſlands - *Dalrymple*	LVII 394	
—— See *Santerini*.		
ISOPERIMETRICAL PROBLEMS. An inveſtigation of a general rule for the reſolution of iſoperimetrical problems of all orders - *Simpſon*	XLIX 4	
—— —— A further attempt to facilitate the reſolution of iſoperimetrical problems *Simpſon*	L 623	
ISTHMUS. Letter relating to that iſthmus, or neck of land, which is ſuppoſed to have joined England and France in former times, where now is the paſſage between Dover and Calais *Wallis*	XXII 967	IV 2 227
ISTRIA. Obſervations in travels from Venice through		

+ Iron. An account of a mass of native Iron, found in South America. De Celis. 78:37. 183.

An account of some appearances attending the conversion of cast into malleable Iron. Beddoes. 81:173.

1792: 257.

~~Experim~~ Remarks on the properties and composition of the different states of Iron. Pearson. 1795: 322.

Experiments and observations on various kinds of native Iron. Howard. 1802: 168.

Observations and experiments on the mass of native Iron found in Brazil. — — — — — — Wollaston. 1816: 270.

	Transf.	Abridg.
Iſtria, Dalmatia, Greece, and the Archipelago, to Smyrna - - *Vernon*	XI 573	
Italy. Letter concerning the ſtate of learning, and ſeveral particulars obſerved by him lately in Italy - - *Silveſtre*	XXII 627	III 603
—— Some curious remarks in his travels through Italy - - *More*	XLVI 464	XI 1331
—— An inveſtigation of the difference between the preſent temperature of the air in Italy, and ſome other countries, to what it was ſeventeen centuries ago - *Barrington*	LVIII 58	
—— See *Antiquities*.		
Judda. A letter accompanying a new chart of the Red Sea, with two draughts of the roads of Mocha and Judda, and ſeveral obſervations made during a voyage to that ſea *Newland*	LXII 77	
—— Remarks and obſervations made on board the ſhip Kelſall, on a voyage to Judda and Mocha in 1769 - - *Newland*	— 79	
Jugular. An account of the diſſection of a dog who had mercury injected into one of the jugulars - - - - *Pitt*	XX 184	III 234
Juices. Queries concerning vegetation, eſpecially the motion of the juices of vegetables *Anon.*	III 797	II 752
—— Experiment concerning the expanſion of blood, and other animal juices - *Boyle*	V 2043	
—— Extracts of divers letters touching ſome inquiries and experiments of the motion of ſap in trees, and relating to the queſtion of the circulation of the ſame - *Liſter*	VI 2119	— 686
A letter relating to ſome particulars in Mr. Liſter's communications - *Willoughby*	— 2125	— 685
Extract of a letter both in relation to the farther diſcovery of the motion of juices in vegetables, and removing the difference noted in Mr. Willoughby's letter - *Anon.*	— 2126	— 686
—— A deſcription of an odd kind of muſhroom yeilding a milky juice much hotter upon the tongue than pepper - *Liſter*	VII 5116	— 623
—— An account of the nature and differences of the juices, more particularly, of our Engliſh vegetables - - *Liſter*	XIX 365	— 696
—— The effects of the opuntia, or prickly pear, and of the Indigo plant in colouring the juices of living animals - - *Baker*	L 296	
Julian Period. A problem for finding the year of		

	Tranf.	Abridg.
the Julian Period by a new and very eafy method - - *De Billy*	I 324	III 398
—— —— A method for finding the number of the Julian Period for any year affigned; the number of the cycle of the fun; the cycle of the moon; and of the indictions for the fame year being given; together with a demonftration of that method - - *Collins*	II 568	— 399
—— —— See *Style.*		
Ivory. Microfcopical obfervations of ivory - - - *Leewenhoek*	XII 1003	
Jupiter. A fpot in one of the belts of Jupiter *Hook*	I 3	I 382,400
—— Some obfervations concerning Jupiter: of the fhadow of his fatellites, feen by a telefcope, paffing over the body of Jupiter *Oldenburg*	— 143	— 383
—— Of a permanent fpot in Jupiter; by which is manifefted the converfion of Jupiter about his own axis *Hook, Caffini, and Oldenburg*	——	— 400
—— A more particular account of thofe obfervations about Jupiter, than were mentioned in N° VIII. - - - - - *Boyle*	— 171	——
—— Some particulars from foreign parts concerning the permanent fpot in Jupiter - *Anon.*	— 209	— 382
—— Obfervations lately made at London concerning the planet Jupiter - - *Hook*	— 245	——
—— Obfervations of a tranfit of the moon by Jupiter Sept. 30, 1671 - *Hevelius*	VI 3031	— 347
—— Obfervations of Jupiter's tranfit near two fixed ftars, in Derby, Feb. and March 1671 *Flamftead*	VII 4036	
—— An account of the return of a great permanent fpot in the planet Jupiter - *Caffini*	VII 4039	- 382,400
—— Some more accurate obfervations about Jupiter's tranfits near fixed ftars; ufeful for determining the inclination of that planet to the ecliptic - - - *Flamftead*	VIII 6033	— 401
—— A fhort account of the three great conjunctions of Saturn, Jupiter, and Mars, at Dantzick, in 1682 and 1683 - *Hevelius*	XIII 325	- 357,395
—— Two aftronomical obfervations of the eclipfes of the planet Jupiter by the moon, in March and April 1686, at London *Hook and Halley*	XVI 85	— 364
—— Several obfervations of the eclipfe of Jupiter by the moon Mar. 31, 1686, at Paris *Caffini*	XVI 175	-- 363
At Avignon - - *Bonfa*	— 176	——
At Nurenberg - - *Zimmerman*	— 177	— 360
- - - - *Wurtzelbaver*	——	— 364

Dantzick

	Transf.	Abridg.
Dantzick - - - *Hevelius*	XVI 178	I 361
—— An account of an occultation of Jupiter by the moon June 6, 1744, at London *Bevis*	XLIII 65	I 95
—— A theory of the irregularities that may be occasioned in the annual motion of the earth by the actions of Jupiter and Saturn *Walmesley*	XLIX 737	
—— An account of an appulse of the moon to Jupiter; observed at Chelsea - *Dunn*	LIII 31	
JUPITER'S SATELLITES. Prediction of the eclipses of Jupiter's satellites 1671; calculated for Uraniburg - - - *Cassini*	VI 2238	
—— —— An account of an occultation of the first of the satellites of Jupiter by the shadow of this planet - - - *Hevelius*	— 3029	I 557
—— —— Some advertisements to astronomers about the configurations by him given of the satellites of Jupiter for 1676 and 1677, for the verification of their hypothesis - *Cassini*	XI 681	— 409
—— —— An account of the eclipses or ingresses of Jupiter's satellites into his shadow, and such emersions of them as will be visible at Greenwich in the last three months of 1683 - - - - - *Flamstead*	XII 322	
—— —— A letter from Flamstead concerning the eclipses of Jupiter's satellites for 1684, with the catalogue of them, and informations concerning its use - - -	XIII 404	
—— —— Concerning the eclipses of Jupiter's satellites for 1685; with a catalogue of them, and information concerning its use *Flamstead*	XIV 760	— 557
—— —— Account of the eclipses of Jupiter's satellites for 1686, and a table of the parallaxes of Jupiter's orb; and an ephemeris of Jupiter's geocentric places for the same year *Flamstead*	XV 1215	— 563
—— —— Description and uses of an instrument for finding the distances of Jupiter's satellites from his axis, with the help of the table of parallaxes and catalogue of eclipses: printed in the preceding Transactions - *Flamstead*	— 1262	— 404
—— —— Calculation of the eclipses of Jupiter's satellites for 1687, &c. - *Flamstead*	XVI 199	
—— —— A catalogue of all the eclipses of Jupiter's satellites visible in 1688 - *Flamstead*	— 435	— 559
—— —— New and exact tables for the eclipses of the first satellite of Jupiter, reduced to the Julian style, and meridian of London - - - *Cassini and Halley*	XVIII 237	— 409

	Transf.	Abridg.
—— —— Curious obfervations of the tranfit of the body and fhade of Jupiter's fourth fatellite over the difc of the planet - *Pound*	XXX 900	IV 07
—— —— New and accurate tables for the ready computing of the eclipfes of the firft fatellite of Jupiter by addition only - *Pound*	— 1021	IV 308
—— —— Obfervations on the fatellites of Jupiter and Saturn made with his reflecting telefcope - - - *Hadley*	XXXII 385	VI 221
—— —— Obfervations of the eclipfes of the firft fatellite of Jupiter in 1723 and 1724, at New York - - - *Burnet*	XXXIII 162	— 409
—— —— Obfervations on the immerfions and emerfions of the innermoft fatellite of Jupiter 1723 and 1724, at Lifbon *Carbone and Capaffo*	— 185	
—— —— The longitude of Lifbon, and the fort of New York, from Wanfted and London; determined by eclipfes of the firft fatellite of Jupiter - - *Bradley*	XXXIV 85	— 412
—— —— Obfervationes aliquot circum-Jovialium habitæ anno 1724 - *Bianchini*	— 176	— 238
—— —— Obfervations of the eclipfes of Jupiter's fatellites from 1700 to the year 1727; with remarks - - *Derham*	XXXV 415	— 225
—— —— The difference in time of the meridians of divers places, computed from obfervations of the eclipfes of Jupiter's fatellites *Derham*	XXXVI 33	— 414
—— —— Obfervations of the eclipfes of Jupiter's fatellites made at Rome and other places *Bianchini*	— 35	
—— —— Extract of a letter containing obfervations of the eclipfes of Jupiter's fatellites, from July 10, 1726, to April 12, 1728; taken at Peterfburgh - - *De Lifle*	— 37	— 243
—— —— A catalogue of the eclipfes of the four fatellites of Jupiter for the year 1732 *Hodgfon*	XXXVII 109	— 270
—— —— Obfervations of the immerfions and emerfions of Jupiter's fatellites, made at Pekin in 1730 and 1731 - *Kegler and Pereira*	— 316	— 249
—— —— A catalogue of eclipfes of Jupiter's fatellites for 1733 - - *Hodgfon*	— 321	
—— —— A catalogue of the eclipfes of Jupiter's fatellites for 1734 - *Hodgfon*	XXXVIII 26	VIII 227
—— —— Obfervations on the eclipfes of Jupiter's fatellites - - *Manfredus*	— 117	— 179
—— —— A catalogue of eclipfes of Jupiter's fatellites for 1735 - *Hodgfon*	— 279	— 227

A

	Trans.	Abridg.
—— —— A catalogue of the eclipses of Jupiter's satellites for 1736, computed to the meridian of the Royal Observatory at Greenwich *Hodgson*	XXXIX 5	—— ——
—— —— The apparent times of such of the immersions and emersions of Jupiter's satellites as are visible at London in 1736; together with their configurations at those times - *Hodgson*	— 13	— 227
—— —— An account of some observations of the eclipses of the first satellite of Jupiter compared with the tables - *Hodgson*	XXXIX 15	VIII 227
—— —— The apparent times of the immersions and emersions of Jupiter's satellites which will happen in the year 1737: computed to the meridian of Greenwich - *Hodgson*	— 177	—— ——
—— —— Some observations of eclipses of Jupiter's satellites, made at Southwick 1730, near Oundle in Northamptonshire - *Lynn*	— 196	— 180
—— —— Extract of a letter concerning the eclipses of Jupiter's satellites Annis 1731 and 1732 - - - - *De l'Isle*	— 221	—— ——
—— —— The immersions and emersions of the four satellites of Jupiter for the year 1738: computed to the meridian of Greenwich *Hodgson*	— 301	— 228
—— —— The apparent times of such of the immersions and emersions of Jupiter's satellites as are visible at London in 1738 *Hodgson*	— 309	—— ——
—— —— The apparent times of the immersions and emersions of Jupiter's satellites for the year 1739: computed to the meridian of the Royal Observatory at Greenwich - *Hodgson*	XL 69	—— ——
—— —— The apparent times of such of the immersions and emersions of Jupiter's satellites as are visible in London in the year 1739 *Hodgson*	— 76	
—— —— The apparent times of the immersions and emersions of the four satellites of Jupiter, 1740, at Greenwich - *Hodgson*	— 332	—— ——
At London - - *Hodgson*	— 340	
—— —— An occultation of Jupiter and his satellites by the moon Oct. 28, 1740 *Bevis and Short*	XLI 647	— 184
—— —— A catalogue of the immersions and emersions of the satellites of Jupiter that will happen in the year 1750; of which there are 173 of the first, 85 of the second, 94 of the third, and none of the fourth, by reason of its great latitude; in all 322: computed by the Flamsteadian tables, corrected - *Hodgson*	XLV 373	X 159

	Tranſ.	Abridg.
—— —— A catalogue of the immerſions and emerſions of the ſatellites of Jupiter for 1751 - - *Hodgſon*	XLVI 282	— —
—— —— Obſervations on the eclipſes of Jupiter's ſatellites made at Liſbon in 1753 *Chevalier*	XLVIII 546	
—— —— Obſervations on the eclipſes of Jupiter's ſatellites at Liſbon in 1754 - - *Chevalier*	XLIX 48	
—— —— Obſervations on the eclipſes of Jupiter's ſatellites made at Liſbon in 1757 *Chevalier*	L 378	
—— —— Elements of new tables of the motions of Jupiter's ſatellites - *Dunthorne*	LII 105	
—— —— A letter containing an eſſay of a new method for determining the longitude of places, from obſervations of the eclipſes of Jupiter's ſatellites - - *Wargentin*	LVI 278	
—— —— Obſervations of ſome immerſions of Jupiter's firſt ſatellite, obſerved in Pennſylvania - - - *Maſon and Dixon*	LVIII 329	
—— —— Eclipſes of Jupiter's firſt ſatellite obſerved at Greenwich in the year 1769 *Maſkelyne*	LIX 399	
—— —— Eclipſes of Jupiter's firſt ſatellite; obſerved at Glaſgow with an eighteen-inch reflector of Mr. Short's - *Wilſon*	— 402	
—— —— A ſeries of aſtronomical obſervations at the Obſervatory of the Marine at Paris: to wit, 1. Of Jupiter's ſatellites in the years 1767 and 1768. 2. On the ſhadows of Jupiter's ſatellites. 3. On the variation of the belts on the diſc of that planet. 4. Of a ſpot on the diſc of the third ſatellite - *M. Meſſier*	— 454	
—— —— Obſervations of the immerſions and emerſions of Jupiter's firſt ſatellite, made at Funchal in Madeira, from 1763 to 1768, with a reflecting teleſcope of eighteen inches focus - - - *Heberden*	LX 502	
—— —— A letter containing a propoſal of ſome new methods of improving the theory of Jupiter's ſatellites - *Bailly*	LXIII 185	
—— —— Account of ſome eclipſes of Jupiter's ſatellites obſerved near Quebec - *Holland*	LXIV 171	
—— —— Obſervations of the immerſions and emerſions of the ſatellites of Jupiter, taken at Gaſpee in 1768 - - *Sproule*	— 177	
—— —— Obſervations of eclipſes of Jupiter's ſatellites at ſeveral places of North America *Holland*	— 182	
—— —— Obſervations of eclipſes of Jupiter's firſt		

Jupiter's Satellites. Observations of the changeable brightness of the Satellites of Jupiter, and of the variation in their apparent magnitudes; with a determination of the time of their rotatory motions on their axes. To which is added, a measure of the diameter of the second Satellite, and an estimate of the comparative size of all the four. Herschel. 1797:332.

Eclipses of the Satellites of Jupiter observed at Madras. Goldingham. 1808:322.

Kanguroo. Some observations on the mode of generation of the Kanguroo, with a particular description of the organs themselves. Home. 1795:221.

	Transf.	Abridg.
satellite at Greenwich, compared with observations of the same made by Samuel Holland, Esq. in North America, and the longitudes of the places thence deduced - *Maskelyne*	— 184	
—— Immersions and emersions of Jupiter's first satellite observed at Jupiter's inlet, on the island of Anticosta, North America, and the longitude of the place deduced from comparison with observations made at the Royal Observatory at Greenwich by the Astronome Royal - *Wright and Maskelyne*	— 190	
—— The difference of Longitude of Greenwich and Paris deduced from the eclipses of Jupiter's first satelllite observed during the last ten years, together with a comparative table of the corresponding observations of the first Satellite made in the principal observatories from 1765 to 1776 - - *Wargentin*	LXVII 162	

K.

	Transf.	Abridg.
KAMTCHATKA. An account of that part of America which is nearest to the coast of Kamtchatka, extracted from the description of Kamtchatka, by Professor Krashennicoff *Dumaresque*	LI 477	
KAPANIHANE. An account of a moving bog in Ireland - - - - *Anon.*	XIX 714	II 737
——A true description of the bog of Kapanihane in the county of Limerick, with an account of the motion thereof, June 7, 1697 *Molyneux.*	XIX 714	II 737
KEPLER's Manuscripts. Account of *Hevelius.*	XI 27	
—— Solution of his problem - *Machin*	XL 205	VIII 73
—— His method of computing the moon's parallaxes in solar eclipses, demonstrated and extended to all degrees of the moon's latitude, as also to the assigning the moon's correspondent apparent diameter, together with a concise application of this form of calculation to those eclipses *Pemberton.*	LXI 437	
KERMES. An account of the use of the grain Kermes for colouration - - *Verny.*	I 362	II 765
—— An observation concerning certain insect husks of the Kermes kind - *Lister.*	VI 2165	II 766
—— Account		

	Trans.	Abridg.
——Account of the kind of insect hatched of the English Kermes above described. also the use of these purple insect husks for tinging, together with a comparison of this English purple Kermes, with the scarlet Kermes of the shops *Lister.*	VI 2196	
——Letter enlarging and correcting his former notes upon Kermes; and withal insinuating his conjectures of cochineal's being a sort of kermes - - *Lister.*	VII 5059	
KIDNEY. Anatomical observations of an abscess in the liver; a great number of stones in the gall-bag and bilious vessels; an unusual conformation of the emulgents and pelvis; a strange conjunction of both kidneys, and a great dilation of the vena cava - *Tyson.*	XII 1035	III 81
——Account of a kidney of an unusual shape and texture, taken out of the body of a man, with observations on horns and glandules in general *Malpighius.*	XIV 601	III 682
——An account of a very large diseased kidney, found on the dissection of a lady, with the symptoms of the disease before her death, and an explanation of their phænomena *Cowper*	XIX 301	III 143
——Of hydatides inclosed with a stony crust in the kidney of a sheep - - *Cowper*	XXV 2304	V 54
——An account of the dissection of a person who died of an ulcer in the right kidney *Douglas*	XXVII 32	V 257
——An anatomical description of worms, found in the kidnies of wolves - *Klein.*	XXXVI 269	VII 456
——An uncommon dropsy, from the want of a kidney; and a large saccus that contained the water - - - *Glass*	XLIV 337	IX 1027
——The figures of some very extraordinary calculous concretions formed in the kidney of a woman - - - *Lucas*	— 465	XI 1001
——An account of a monstrous human fœtus, having neither head, heart, lungs, stomach, spleen, pancreas, liver, nor kidnies - *Le Cat.*	LVII 1	
——See *Stone*		
KILCORNY CAVE OF. A description of the Cave of Kilcorny in the Barony of Burren in Ireland *Lucas*	XLI 36	VIII 668
KIRBYTHORE. See ANTIQUITIES.		
KIRCHER. Observations upon father Kircher's opinion concerning the burning of the fleet of		

Kilburn Wells. Description of, and analysis of their water - - - Schmeisser 1792: 115.

Lacca (Gum) Natural history of the insect which produces it. Kerr. 71:374.

Roxburgh 81:228.

Analytical experiments and observations on Lac. — — — Hatchett 1804:191.

Lac, white. Observations and experiments on a waxlike substance, resembling the Pe-la of the Chinese, collected at Madras by Dr. Anderson, and called by him White Lac. Pearson 1794:383.

		Tranf.	Abridg.
Marcellus by Archimedes - *Parsons*	XLVIII 621		
KITE. Letter concerning an electrical kite *Franklin*	XLVII 565		
—— Answer to several queries concerning his experiment of electricity with a kite *Lining*	XLVIII 757		
KITTLING. The phænomena afforded by a newly kittened kitling in the exhausted Receiver *Boyle*	V 2017		
KNEE. An account of an extraordinary tumour in the knee of a person whose leg was taken off *Pierce*	XLI 56	IX 271	
—— Two singular cases of diseases at the knee joints successfully treated, the first by topical applications, the second by *Warner*	XLIX 452		
KNIFE. Case of one who swallowed a knife, which lay in his stomach a year and seven months, and then worked out at an aposthem on his breast - - - *Sloane*	XIX 180		
KNIGHT. An account of the magnetical machine contrived by Dr. Knight - *Fothergill*	LXVI 591		

L.

		Tranf.	Abridg.
LABOURER. Account of some extraordinary tumours upon the head of a labouring man *Parsons*	IV 350		
LABRADORE. Particulars of the country of Labradore, extracted from the papers of lieutenant Roger Curtis, of his majesty's sloop the Otter, with a plane-chart of the Coast - *Curtis*	LXIV 372		
—— Tract of his majesty's armed brig Lion from England to Davis's Straights and Labrador, with observations for determining the longitude by sun and moon, and error of common reckoning; also the variation of the compass and dip of the needle, as observed during the said voyage in 1776 - *Pickersgill*	LXVIII 1057		
—— Two meteorological journals kept at Nain in 57 degrees north latitude, and Okak, in 57 degrees 30 minutes north latitude, both on the coast of Labradore - *De la Trobe*	LXX 657		
LABYRINTH. A description of the organ of hearing in the elephant, with the figure and situation of the ossicles labyrinth and cochlea in the ear of that animal - - *Blair*	XXX 885	V 82	
LACERATION. Extract of a letter, containing the

	Transf.	Abridg.
particulars of the case of a wound in the cornea, and of a laceration of the uvea in the eye of a woman - - *Aery*	XLV 411	XI 954
LACERTA. Letter concerning the circulation of the blood, as seen by the help of a microscope, in lacerta aquatica - *Molyneux*	XV 1236	II 133 III 225
——An account of lacerta (crocodillus) ventre marsupio donato faucibus merganseris rostrum æmulantibus - - *Edwards*	XLIX 639	
LACRYMÆ BATAVICÆ. A memoir on the Lacrymæ Batavicæ; or glass drops, the tempering of steel and effervescence accounted for by the same principle - - - *Le Cat.*	XLVI 175	X 560
LACTEALS. Some anatomical observations and experiments concerning the unalterable character of the whiteness of the chyle within the lacteous veins; together with divers particulars observed in the guts, especially several sorts of worms found in them - *Lister*	VIII 6060	III 101
——An account of an experiment made for altering the colour of the chyle in the lacteal veins *Lister*	XIII 6	III 102
——Endeavours to prove that the lacteals frequently convey liquors that are not white *Musgrave*	XIV 812	— —
——Letter concerning powdered blues passing in the lacteal veins - *Lister*	XXII 819	V 259
——An experiment made for the transmitting of a blue coloured liquor into the lacteals *Musgrave*	XXII 996	V 259
——Account of an experiment, by which it appears that salt of steel does not enter into the lacteal vessels; with remarks - *Wright*	L 594	
LAGOPUS. Observations on the lagopus, or ptarmigan - - - *Barrington*	LXIII 224	
LAKES. Extracts of several letters from Edinburgh, giving an account of an obelisk thrown down by a violent wind, of an extraordinary lake in lord Lovat's lands in Scotland, of Lake Ness, and of a petryfiing rivulet - *Mackenzy*	X 307	III 603
——Observations concerning the lake of Mexico *Journal des Sçavans*	XI 758	II 320
——Letter concerning the lake Ness, &c. *Fraser*	XXI 230	— 322
——Observations on the lake Vetter *Hearne*	XXIV 1938	
——A description of a large lake called Malholm tarn, near Shipton in Craven, Yorkshire *Fuller*	XLI 612	VIII 641
——Account of vegetable balls which grow in a lake near the Humber in Yorkshire, with re-		

marks

Lamprey. On the mode of generation of the Lamprey and Myxine. — Home. 1815: 265.

Subject	Author	Trans.	Abridg.
marks by W. Watson	*Dixon*	XLVII 498	
LAMA. Experiments made on a great number of animals, with the poison of Lama's and of Ticunas	*Herissant*	— 75	
LAMB. Account of a monstrous lamb	*Doddridge*	XLV 502	XI 1218
LAMPAS. Declaration of the Council of the Royal Society passed Nov. 20, 1676. relating to some passages in a late book of Mr. Hook, entituled, Lampas, &c.	*Council of the Royal Society*	XI 749	I 586
LAMPS. A discourse concerning the sepulchral lamps of the ancients, shewing the possibility of their being made divers ways	*Plot*	XIV 806	III 636
——An easy contrivance of a lamp to be always kept full whilst it burns	*St. Clair*	XX 378	II 385
LANCASHIRE. Observations on the Roman colonies and stations in Cheshire and Lancashire	*Percival*	XLVII 216	
LAND. Instances, hints, and applications relating to a main point solicited in the preface to the fourth volume; concerning the use may be made of vaults, deep wells, and cold conservatories, to find out the cause, or to promote the generation, of salt, minerals, metals, cristals, gems, stones of divers kinds, and helps to conserve long, or to hasten putrefaction, fertility of any land, &c.	*Beale*	IV 1135	II 728
——Part of a letter concerning the manuring of land in Devonshire with sea sand	*Bury*	XXVI 142	IV 2 301
——A letter concerning the manuring of land with fossil shells	*Pickering*	XLIII 191	X 796
LANGCHESTER. V. *Inscription*			
LANGUAGE. An explication of all the inscriptions in the Palmyrene language and character hitherto published	*Swinton*	XLVIII 690	
——Extracts of some letters on the customs, manners, and language of the Northern Indians of America	*Johnson*	LXIII 142	
——An account of the Romansh language	*Planta*	LXVI 129	
——See *Deafness*, *Speech*			
LANGUEDOC. See *Ocean*			
LAPIS CALAMINARIS. An account of digging and preparing the Lapis Calaminaris	*Pooley*	XVII 672	II 554
LAPLAND. A relation of the small creature called sable mice, which have lately come in troops into Lapland, about Thorne, and other places adjacent to the mountains, in innumerable multitudes	*Rycaut*	XXI 110	II 871

	Transf.	Abridg.
Larum. Account of the weavers alarm, vulgo larum - - - - *Arderson*	XLIII 555	XI 1392
Laryngotomy. An argument for the more frequent use of laryngotomy, urged from a remarkable cure in chirurgery - *Musgrave*	XXI 398	III 61
Lath. A letter concerning a large piece of lath being thrust into the eye of a man who recovered of it - - - *Kepel*	XLV 520	XI 955
Latitude. The description and use of an instrument for taking the latitude of a place at any time of the day - - *Graham*	XXXVIII 450	III 371
—— Some considerations on a late treatise intituled A new Set of logarithmic solar Tables, &c. intended for a more commodious method of finding the latitude at sea by two observations of the sun - - - *Pemberton*	LI 910	
—— A new method of constructing sun-dials for any given latitude, without the assistance of dialling scales or logarithmic calculations *Ferguson* (see Sun-Dial)	~~LVII 389~~	
Latitude of Places. An account of the latitude of Constantinople and Rhodes - *Greaves*	XV 1295	I 564
—— An account shewing that the latitude of Nurenburg has continued without sensible alteration for 200 years last past, as likewise the obliquity of the ecliptick, by comparing them with what was observed by B. Walther in 1487 *Wurtzelbaur*	XVI 43	I 262
—— An account of the eclipse of the moon observed at Moscua in Russia, April 5, 1688, compared with the same observed at Leipsick, whereby the longitude of the former is ascertained, together with the latitude of several principal places in the empire of Russia *Timmerman*	XVII 453	I 564
—— A new and exact table, collected from several observations taken in four voyages to Hudson's Bay from London, shewing the variation of the magnetical needle, or sea compass, in the path-way to the said bay, according to the several longitudes and latitudes from 1721 to 1725 - - *Middleton*	~~XXXIV 73~~	~~VI 2 297~~
—— A new and exact table, collected from several observations taken from the year 1721 to 1729, in nine voyages to Hudson's Bay, in North America, shewing the variation of the		

compass,

+ Latitude. A method of finding the latitude of a place, by means of two altitudes of the sun and the time elapsed betwixt the observations. Lax. 1799: 74.

	Trans.	Abridg.
compass, according to the latitudes and longitudes, accounting the longitude from the meridian of London - *Middleton*	XXXVII [illegible]	[illegible] 330
—Observations of latitude and variation taken on board the Hartford, in her passage from Java Head to St. Helena, 1731-2 - *Halley*	— 331	— 421
—Observations made of the latitude, variation of the magnetic needle, and weather, in a voyage from London to Hudson's Bay, 1735 *Middleton*	XXXIX 270	VIII 376
—Letter concerning a place in New York for measuring a degree of latitude - *Alexander*	XLI 383	
—The effects of cold, together with observations of the longitude, latitude, and declination of the magnetic needle at Prince of Wales's Fort upon Churchill River in Hudson's Bay, North America - *Middleton*	XLII 157	VIII 469
—A letter concerning the variation of the magnetic needle, with a sett of tables annexed, which exhibit the result of upwards of fifty thousand observations in six periodic reviews from 1700 to 1756, and are adapted to every five degrees of latitude and longitude in the more frequented oceans *Mountain and Dodson*	L 349	
—Letter containing a short account of the measurement of three degrees of latitude under the meridian of Vienna - *Liesganig*	LVIII 15	
—Observations made on the islands of St. John and Cape Breton, to ascertain the longitude and latitude of those places, agreeable to the orders and instructions of the commissioners for trade and plantations - *Holland*	— 46	
—Introduction to the following observations made by Ch. Mason and Jer. Dixon, for determining the length of a degree of latitude in the provinces of Maryland and Pennsylvania in North America - *Maskelyne*	— 270	
Observations, &c. - *Mason and Dixon*	— 274	
—Length of a degree of latitude in the province of Maryland and Pennsylvania, deduced from the observations of Messieurs Mason and Dixon *Maskelyne*	— 323	
—A determination of the latitude of Stamford in Lincolnshire - *Barker*	LXI 227	
—Astronomical observations made at Leicester for determining the latitude of that place *Ludlow*	LXV 366	

—The

	Trans.	Abridg.
—— The variation of the compass, containing 17[illegible]0 observations to, in, and from, the East-Indies, Guinea, West Indies, and Mediterranean, with the latitudes and longitudes at the time of observation - - *Douglas*	LXVI 18	
—— The latitude of Madrass in the East-Indies, deduced from observations - *Stephens*	LXIX 182	
—— Two meteorological journals kept at Nain in 5[illegible] degree north latitude, and at Okak in 57 degrees 30 minutes north latitude, both on the coast of Labradore - *De la Trobe*	—— 657	
LAUDANUM. An account of two sorts of Helmontian laudanum, together with the way of F. M Van Helmont preparing his laudanum *Boyle*	IX 147	II 642
LAUREL WATER. A letter giving an account of two women being poisoned by the simple distilled water of laurel leaves; and of several experiments upon dogs, by which it appears that this laurel water is the most dangerous poison hitherto known - - *Madden*	XXXVII 85	VI 2 374
—— Some experiments concerning the poisonous quality of the simple distilled water from the lauro-cerasus or common laurel, made upon dogs at Toppingo Hall, Essex; and others made before the Royal Society in their repository *Mortimer*	—— 163	—— ——
—— Letter on the poison of laurel water *Rutty*	XLI 63	VIII 844
LAY-WELL. An extract of a letter, giving an account of an experiment made in the Bay of Biscay of sinking a bottle, close corked, under various depths of water, and of Lay-well, which ebbs and flows - - *Oliver*	XVII 908	II 305
—— Answer to several queries relating to Lay-Well *Oliver*	—— 910	—— ——
LAYERS. How to multiply crab-stocks, and propagate trees by layers - - *Tonge*	V 2074	—— 752
LEACH. A description of the hirudinella marina, or Sea Leach - - - *Garcin*	XXXVI 377	VII 418
LEAD. Of a peculiar lead ore in Germany, and the use thereof - - *Anon*	I 10	II 576
—— A further account of some rock plants growing in the lead mines of Mendip Hills *Beaumont*	XIII 276	—— 503
—— Some experiments concerning the cohesion of Lead - - - *Desaguliers*	XXXIII 345	VI 325

†Latitudes of Places. Of York - - - - - - - - - - Pigott 76: 409.
Of some remarkable places near the Severn - - - - - - - ——— 80: 385.

		Tranf.	Abridg.
——An account of the case of a man who died of the effects of the fire at Eddystone light-house by melted lead running down his throat	*Spry*	XLIX 477	
	Huxham	— 483	
——A short account of some specimens of native lead found in a mine of Monmouthshire	*Morris*	LXIII 20	
——Chemical experiments and observations on lead-ore -	*Richard Watson*	LXVIII 863	
LEADEN COFFIN. Vide *Antiquities*			
LEARNING. Letter concerning the state of learning, and several particulars observed by him lately in Italy - -	*Silvestre*	XXII 627	III 603
LEATHER. Brief directions how to tan leather according to the new invention of the honourable Charles Howard of Norfolk, experimented and approved of by divers of the principal tanners using Leadenhall-Market -	*Howard*	IX 93	II 668
——An improved method of tanning leather	*Macbride*	LXVIII 111	
LEAVES. A way of colouring leaves, fruit, &c.	*Tonge*	V 2074	— 752
——Two observations, the one concerning the effects of a poisonous root, the other concerning the virtues of the leaves of hemlock	*Ray*	XIX 634	— 640
——An account of the veins and arteries of leaves	*Nicholls*	XXXVI 371	VI 2 340
——An observation on the double fibres observable in the skeletons prepared from green leaves	*Hollman*	XLI 789	VIII 818
——Conjectures on the use of double fibres in some leaves, &c. - -	*Hollman*	— 796	— 820
LEECH. Of the long continuance of one alive in the vacuum made in the pneumatical engine	*Boyle*	V 2049	III 147
——The anatomical history of the Leech	*Poupart*	XIX 722	II 819
LEG. An account of stitching the great tendon between the calf of the leg and heel, with its union and cure, after an entire division of it; with remarks - -	*Cowper*	XXI 153	III 298
——A letter concerning a woman of 62 years of age, that lost her leg and greatest part of her thigh, by a gangrene - -	*Calep*	XXVI 41	V 389
——An account of an extraordinary tumour in the knee of a person whose leg was taken off	*Peirce*	XLI 56	IX 271

	Trans.	Abridg.
——An account of a new-invented instrument for fractured legs - *Sharp*	LVII 80	
LEGION. Letter concerning the Roman legion *Musgrave*	XXVIII 80	V 2 110
LEGUMS. A way of making all sorts of plants, trees, fruits, and legums, grow to an extraordinary bigness - - *Anon*	X 356	II 749
LEIBNITZ. Letter of Dr. Wallis giving an account of some late passages between him and Mynheer Leibnitz of Hanover - *Wallis*	XXI 273	II 2
——Letter of Dr. Wallis to G. G. Leibnitz *Wallis*	— 280	— —
——A solution of the problem of G. G. Leibnitz, proposed to the English - *Taylor*	XXX 695	IV 46
LEICESTER. Astronomical observations made at Leicester for determining the latitude of that place - *Ludlam*	LXV 366	
L'EMERY. Observations on the class of sweet tastes, made by comparing the taste of sweet plants, with Mr. L'Emery's chymical analysis of them in his treatise of drugs *Floyer*	XXIII 1160	V 406
LEMON. Some hortular communications about the curious engrafting of oranges and lemons or citrons, upon one anothers trees, and of one individual fruit half orange and half lemon growing on such trees, &c. - *Anon*	II 553	II 658
LENS. A proposition relating to the combination of transparent lenses with reflecting planes *Hadley*	XXXIX 185	VIII 111
—— The figure of a machine for grinding lenses spherically, invented by Samuel Jenkins *Jenkins*	XLI 555	VIII 281
LEPROSY. An abstract of a letter concerning the parts of brain of several animals, the chalk stones of the gout, the leprosy, and the scales of eels - - *Leewenhoeck*	XV 883	III 684
—— An account of a visitation of the leprous persons in the isle of Gaudeloupe - *Peyssonell*	L 38	
LETTERS (Antiquities). Some remarks on the first part of Mr. L'Abbé Barthelemy's memoir on the Phœnician letters relative to a Phœnician inscription in the island of Malta *Swinton*	LIV 119	
——Farther remarks upon Mr. l'Abbé Barthelemy's memoir on the Phœnician letters, containing his reflections on certain Phœnician monuments, and the alphabet resulting from them - - - *Swinton*	— 393	
LETTERS (Natural History) An account of the Friesland		

Lever. Observations on the fundamental property of the Lever, with a proof of the principle assumed by Archimedes, in his demonstration. Vince. 1794.

		Tranf.	Abridg.
boy with letters in his eye — *Ellis*	XXIII 1416	V 2 134	
——— Account of letters found in the middle of a beech tree — — *Klein*	XLI 231	VIII 845	
LEVELS. A new contrivance for taking levels — — — — *Desaguliers*	XXXIII 165	VI 271	
——— A description of a water-level to be fixed to Davis's quadrant, whereby an observation may be taken at sea in thick and hazy weather without seeing the horizon — *Leigh*	XL 413	VIII 360	
——— The description and use of an apparatus added as an improvement to Davis's quadrant, consisting of a mercurial level for taking the co-altitude of sun or star at sea without the usual assistance of the sensible horizon which frequently is obscured — *Leigh*	XL 417	— 362	
LEVERS. An account of the advantages of a newly invented machine much varied in its effects, and very useful for determining the perfect proportion between different moveables acting by levers and wheel and pinion — *Le Cerf*	LXVIII 950		
LEYDEN BOTTLE. An account of some new experiments in electricity, containing, 1. An enquiry whether vapour be a conductor of electricity. 2. Some experiments to ascertain the direction of the electric matter in the discharge of the Leyden bottle. 3. Experiments on the lateral explosion in the discharge of the Leyden bottle. 4. The description and use of a new prime conductor, 5. Miscellaneous experiments made principally in 1771 and 1772. 6. Experiments and observations on the electricity of fogs in pursuance of those made by Thomas Ronayne, Esq. with a plan of an electrical Journal, &c. — *Henley*	LXIV 389		
LIBELLA. Letter concerning the insect called libella — — *Poupart*	XXII 673	II 762	
——— Some observations on a sort of libella or ephemeron — — — *Collinson*	XLIV 329	XI 844	
——— Some observation on the dragon-fly, or libella of Pensylvania — — *Bartram*	XLVI 323	— 845	
——— A further account of the libella or May-fly — — — — *Bartram*	— 400	— 846	
LICHEN. An historical memoir concerning a genus of plants called Lichen by Micheli, Haller, and Linnæus, and comprehended by Dillenius under the terms usnea, coralloides, and lichenoides, tending principally to illustrate their several uses. — *W. Watson*	L 652

	Tranſ.	Abridg.
Life. An experiment of preſerving animals alive by blowing through their lungs with bellows - - - *Hook*	II 539	III 66
—— An eſtimate of the degrees of the mortality of nations, drawn from curious tables of the births and funerals of the city of Breſlaw, with an attempt to aſcertain the price of annuities upon lives - - *Halley*	XVII 596	
—— A view of the relation between Dr. Halley's tables, and the notions of Mr. de Buffon for eſtabliſhing a rule for the probable duration of the life of man *Kerſeboom*	XLVIII 239	
—— A letter concerning the value of an annuity for life, &c. the probability of ſurvivorſhips *Dodſon*	— 487	
—— A letter concerning the animal life of thoſe Corallines that look like minute trees, and grow upon oyſters, and fucus's, all around the ſea-coaſt of this kingdom - *Ellis*	XLVIII 627	
—— Obſervations on the expectations of lives, the increaſe of mankind, the influence of great towns on population, and particularly the ſtate of London with reſpect to health, fulneſs, and number of inhabitants *Price*	LIX 89	
—— See *Annuities, Mortality, Population*		
Light (in general) An experiment to examine what figure and celerity of motion begetteth or encreaſeth light and flame - *Beale*	I 226	III 639
—— Of the light produced by inflammation *Fordyce*	LXVI 504	
New experiments concerning the relation between light and air in ſhining wood and fiſh *Boyle*	II 581	II 206
—— Experiments of the luminous qualities of amber, diamonds, and gum-lac - *Wall*	XXVI 69	IV 2 275
—— Obſervations of luminous emanations from human bodies and from brutes; with ſome remarks on electricity - - *Miles*	XLIII 441	X 278
Light, Meteors in the Air. Part of a letter concerning a glade of light obſerved in the heavens March 28, 1706 *Derham*	XXV 2220	IV 2 133
—— Account of ſeveral meteors or lights in the ſky *Halley*	XXIX 159	IV 2 135
—— An account of the late ſurprizing appearance of lights ſeen in the air on the 6th of March 1715-6, with an attempt to explain the principal phænomena thereof - *Halley*	— 406	— — 138

Light. Observations and experiments on the light of bodies in a state of combustion. Morgan 75: 190.

Experiments and observations on the production of light from different bodies, by heat and by attrition. T. Wedgwood 1792: 28, 270

An account of a method of measuring the comparative intensities of the light emitted by luminous bodies. Thompson 1794: 67.

Experiments and observations on the Inflection, Reflection and Colours of light. Optics Brougham. 1796: 227.

Farther experiments and observations on the affections and properties of light. ——— 1797: 352.

Quelques remarques d' Optique, principalement relatives à la Reflexibilité des rayons de la lumiere. Prevost 1798: 311.

An enquiry concerning the chemical properties that have been attributed to Light. Rumford ——— 449.

Experiments and observations on the Light which is spontaneously emitted, with some degree of permanency, from various bodies. Hulme. 1800: 161.

with some experiments and observations on solar light, when imbibed by Canton's phosphorus. ——— 1801: 403.

+ Light. Meteors in the air.

Account of a luminous appearance in the heavens. Cavallo. 71: 329.

Account of some luminous Arches - - - - - - - - Hey. 80: 32.

Wollaston — 43.

Hutchinson — 45.

Franklin — 46.

Pigott — 47.

On the height of the luminous arch which was seen on Feb. 23. 1784.

Cavendish — 101.

	Trans.	Abridg.
Of the same seen on the ocean, near the coast of Spain, with an account of the return of the same sort of appearance on March 31, and April 1, and 2 - - *Halley*	— 430	— - 151
—— An account of a luminous appearance in the air at Dublin, Jan. 12, 1719-20 - *Percival*	XXXI 21	VI 2 81
—— An account of a luminous appearance in the sky seen at London, March 13, 1734-5 *Bevis*	XLI 347	VIII 517
—— An account of a luminous arch Feb. 16, 1749 *Cooper*	XLVI 647	X 507
LIGHT (Electrical) An account of an experiment touching the production of a considerable light upon a slight attrition of the hands on a glass globe exhausted of its air; with other remarkable occurrences - *Hauksbee*	XXV 2277	IV 2 180
—— An account of an experiment touching the production of light by the effluvia of one glass falling on another in motion *Hauksbee*	XXV 2413	— - —
—— An account of some experiments touching the electricity and light producible on the attrition of several bodies - - *Hauksbee*	XXVI 87	
—— An account of an experiment touching the production of light within a globe glass, whose inward surface is lined with sealing wax, upon an attrition of its outside - *Hauksbee*	— 219	— 181
—— An account of an experiment touching an attempt to produce light on the inside of a glass globe lined with melted flowers of sulphur, as in the experiments of sealing-wax and pitch *Hauksbee*	— 439	— - 182
—— An account of an experiment concerning an endeavour to produce light through a metallick body, under the circumstances of a vacuum and attrition - - *Hauksbee*	XXVII 328	— - —
—— Experiments and observations upon the light that is produced by communicating electrical attraction to animals or inanimate bodies, together with some of its most surprizing effects *Gray*	XXXIX 16	VIII 397
—— Observations of luminous emanations from human bodies and from brutes, with some remarks on electricity - *Miles*	XLIII 441	X 278
—— Part of a letter concerning the light caused by quicksilver shaken in a glass tube, proceeding from electricity - - *Trembley*	XLIV 58	X 321
LIGHT (Optics) Of the means to illuminate an ob-		

	Transf.	Abridg.
ject in what proportion one pleaseth, and of the distances requisite to burn bodies by the sun - - - *Auzout*	I 68	I 280
—— A method by which a glass of a small plano-convex sphere may be made to refract the rays of light to a focus of a far greater distance than is usual - - - *Hook*	I 202	I 193
—— —— Letter containing his new theory of light and colours - - *Newton*	VI 3075	— 128
Some experiments proposed in relation to Mr. Newton's theory of light, with observations thereon by - *Newton*	VII 4059	— 135
Letter of animadversions upon I. Newton's theory of light - - *Pardies*	— 4087	— 137
Answer - - *Newton*	— 4091	— 139
A series of queries to be determined by experiments, positively and directly concluding his new theory of light and colours. *Newton*	VII 5004	— 197
Second letter to Mr. Newton's answer to his first letter - - *Pardies*	— 5012	— 141
Answer - - *Newton*	— 5014	— 142
Answer to some considerations on his doctrine of light and colours - *Newton*	— 5084	— 144 — 202
Considerations upon Mr. Newton's doctrine of colours, as also upon the effects of the different refractions of the rays in telescopical glasses in a letter from Paris - *Anon*	VIII 6086	— 156
Answer further explaining his theory of light and colours, and particularly that of whiteness, together with his continued hopes of perfecting telescopes by reflection rather than refraction - - - *Newton*	— 6087	— 158
Letter concerning the number of colours, and the necessity of mixing them for the production of white, as also touching the cause why a picture cast by glasses into a darkened room appears so distinct notwithstanding its irregular refraction, being an immediate answer to that from Paris - *Newton*	— 6108	— 157
An answer by the same Parisian philosopher	— 6112	— 158
A letter animadverting upon Sir Isaac Newton's theory of light and colours *Linus*	X 217	I 161
Answer - - *Newton*	— 218	
A letter, being a reply to the letter printed vol. X. 219. by way of answer to the former letter of Mr. Linus concerning Newton's theory		

of

		Tranſ.	Abridg.
of light and colours -	*Linus*	— 499	— 162
Conſiderations on the reply, together with further directions how to make the experiments controverted aright -	*Newton*	— 500	
Another letter relating to the ſame argument	*Newton*	— 503	— 164
—— A particular anſwer to Mr. Linus's letter about an experiment relating to the new doctrine of light and colours -	*Newton*	XI 556	— 163
—— Letter concerning Mr. Newton's experiments of the coloured ſpectrum, together with ſome exceptions againſt his theory of light and colours - - -	*Lucas*	— 692	— 165
Anſwer - -	*Newton*	— 698	— 168
—— A demonſtration concerning the motion of light - - -	*Romer*	XII 893	— 409
—— Some queries concerning the nature of light and diaphanous bodies - -	*Halley*	XVII 998	II 252
—— —— An account of ſome experiment of light and colours formerly made by Sir Iſaac Newton, and mentioned in his opticks, lately repeated before the Royal Society	*Deſaguliers*	XXIX 433	IV 173
A plain and eaſy experiment to confirm Sir Iſaac Newton's doctrine of the different refrangibility of the rays of light -	*Deſaguliers*	— 448	— 481
—— Some experiments made in order to diſcover the height to which rockets may be made to aſcend, and to what diſtance their light may be ſeen - - - -	*Ellicott*	XLVI 578	X 202
—— Diſcourſe concerning the cauſe of the different refrangibility of the rays of light	*Melvil*	XLVIII 261	
—— A compariſon between the notions of M. de Courtivron and Mr. Melvil concerning the difference of refrangibility of the rays of light - - - -	*Clairaut*	— 776	
—— An account of ſome experiments concerning the different refrangibility of light -	*Dollond*	L 733	
—— Diſſertation on the aberration of light refracted at ſpherical ſuperficies and lenſes	*Klingenſtierna*	LI 944	
—— A letter containing a theorem of the aberration of the rays of light refracted through a lens, on account of the imperfection of the ſpherical figure - -	*Maſkelyne*	LII 17	
—— Rules and examples for limiting the caſes in which the rays of refracted light may be re united into a colourleſs pencil -	*Murdoch*	LIII 173	

See Spectra (Ocular)
Vision
~~Heat~~ +

	Transf.	Abridg.
—— Difficulties in the Newtonian theory of light considered and removed - *Horsley*	LX 417	
—— A supplement concerning difficulties in the Newtonian theory of light - *Horsley*	LXI 547	
—— Phases of the transit of Venus supposed to be retarded by the aberration of light *Winthorp*	LX 358	
—— On the effect of the aberration of light on the time of a transit of Venus over the sun *Price*	— 536	
LIGHT (Phosphorus) Experiments on the production and propagation of the light from the phosphorus in vacuo - *Hauksbee*	XXIV 1865	IV 2 181
—— An easy method of making phosphorus that will imbibe and emit light like the Bolognian stone, with experiments and observations - - - - - *Canton*	LVIII 337	
LIGHTNING. An account of a young man slain with thunder and lightning, Dec. 22, 1698 *Thoresby*	XXI 51	II 179
—— Two letters of the effects of lightning in Northamptonshire, July 3, 1725 - *Wasse*	XXXIII 366	VI 2 70
—— An account of persons killed by lightning at Worcester - - - *Beard*	XXXIV 118	— - 72
—— An account of an extraordinary effect of lightning in communicating magnetism at Wakefield in Yorkshire - - *Dod*	XXXIX 74	VIII 504
A farther account of the above lightning - - - *Cookson*	— 75	— 505
—— An extract of a letter concerning the crooked and angular parts of lightnings in thunder storms - - *Logan*	XXXIX 240	— 507
—— An account of a file rendered magnetical by lightning - - *Bremond*	XLI 614	— 506
—— Part of a letter concerning some extraordinary effects of lightning - - *Lord Petre*	XLII 136	— 507
—— An extract of an Italian treatise, written by Jos. Bianchini, upon the death of the Countess Cornelia Zangari and Bandi of Cesena; to which are subjoined accounts of the death of Jos. Hitchell, who was burned to death by lightning, and of Grace Pett at Ipswich, whose body was consumed to a coal - - *Rolli*	XLIII 447	XI 1068
—— A letter concerning the effects of lightning in destroying the polarity of a mariner's compass; to which are subjoined some remarks thereon by Gowin Knight - *Waddell*	XLVI 111	X 695
—— An account of the burning of the steeple of Danbury in Essex, Feb. 5, 1749-50 *Lethieullier*	XLVI 611	X 478

—— Letter

+Light (Optics)

Experiment proposed for determining, by the aberration of the fixed Stars, whether the Rays of light, in pervading different media, change their velocity according to the law which results from Sr. I. Newton's Ideas concerning the cause of refraction; and for ascertaining their velocity in every medium whose refractive density is known. Wilson. 72: 58.

Investigation of the powers of the prismatic colours to heat and illuminate Objects. Herschel. 1800: 255.

A comparative view of the laws to which Light and Heat, or rather the rays which occasion them, are subject. —— — 293.

Outlines of experiments and inquiries respecting Sound and Light. —— Young —106.

The Bakerian Lecture. On the theory of Light and Colours. — — — —— 1802. 12.

A method of examining refractive and dispersive powers, by prismatic reflection. Wollaston. —365.

An account of some cases of the production of colours, not hitherto described. Young. —387.

On some properties of light. — — — — Brewster. 1813: 101.

On the affections of Light transmitted through crystallized bodies. — — 1814: 187.

On the polarisation of light by oblique transmission through all bodies, whether crystallized or uncrystallized. — — — —— —219.

On new properties of Light exhibited in the optical phenomena of Mother of Pearl, and other bodies to which the superficial structure of that substance can be communicated. —397.

Results of some recent experiments on the properties impressed upon light by the action of Glass raised to different temperatures, and cooled under different circumstances. — — —436.

Additional observations on the optical properties and structure of heated glass and unannealed glass drops. — — —— 1815. 1.

Experiments on the depolarisation of Light as exhibited by various mineral, animal, and vegetable bodies, with a reference of the phenomena to the general principles of polarisation. — — —— —29.

On the laws which regulate the polarisation of light by reflection from transparent bodies. — — —— —125.

On some phenomena of colours, exhibited by thin plates — Knox. — 161.

On the multiplication of images, and the colours which accompany them in some specimens of calcareous spar. — Brewster —270.

On the dispersive power of the Atmosphere, and its effect on astronomical observations. — — — Lee —375.

On the laws of polarisation and double refraction in regularly crystallized bodies. — — — Brewster. 1818: 199.

LIG

		Tranf.	Abridg.
—— Letter concerning the effects of lightning - - - - - Franklin	XLVII 289		
—— An account of the effects of lightning at South Molton in Devonshire - Palmer	— 330		
—— Part of a letter in relation to the effects of lightning at Plymouth - Huxham	XLIX 16		
—— An account of the effects of lightning in the Danish church in Wellclose-Square Brander	— 298		
—— A letter concerning the effects of lightning at Darking in Surry - Child	— 309		
—— An account of the effects of lightning upon the steeple and church of Lestwithiel in Cornwall, Jan. 25, 1757 - Smeaton	L 198		
—— An account of some extraordinary effects of lightning, July 16, 1759 - Mountaine	LI 286		
With remarks - - Knight	— 294		
—— Extract of a letter concerning a person struck by lightning at Duloe, June 26, 1756 - - - - Huxham	LII 517		
—— Some suggestions concerning the preventing the mischiefs which happen to ships and their masts by lightning - W. Watson	— 629		
—— An account of the effects of lightning at South Weald, in Essex, June 18, 1764 Heberden	LIII 198		
—— Observation upon the effects of lightning, with an account of the apparatus proposed to prevent its mischiefs to buildings, more particular to powder magazines, being answers to questions proposed by M. Calandrini of Geneva - - - - W. Watson	LIV 201		
—— An account of the effects of lightning on St. Bride's Church, Fleet-Street, June 18, 1764 - - - - Delaval	— 227		
in Essex-Street - - Lawrence	— 235		
—— Considerations to prevent lightning from doing mischief to great works, high buildings, and large magazines - Wilson	— 247		
—— An account of the effects of lightning on three ships in the East Indies, Aug. 1, 1750 Veicht	— 284		
—— Proposal of a method for securing the cathedral of St. Paul's from damage by lightning; in consequence of a letter from the dean and chapter of St. Paul's to James West, Esq. Committee of the Royal Society	LIX 160		
—— An account of the appearance of lightning on a conductor fixed from the lee-mast of the main-

		Transf.	Abridg.
mast of a ship down to the water -	*Winn*	LX 188	
— An account of the death of a person destroyed by lightning in the chapel in Tottenham-Court-Road, and its effects on the building, as observed by Messrs. Henley, Nairne, and Jones - -	*Henley*	LXII 131	
— A report of the committee appointed by the Royal Society to consider of a method for securing the powder magazine at Purfleet from lightning -	*Committe of the Royal Society*	LXIII 42	
Mr. Wilson's dissent to part of the above report - -	*Wilson*	— 48	
Answer of the committee to the objections	*Committee of the Royal Society*	— 66	
— Observations upon lightning, and the method of securing buildings from its effects	*Wilson*	— 49	
— A letter to Sir John Pringle on pointed conductors	*Cavendish, Watson, Franklin, Robertson*	— 66	
— An account of the effects of lightning at Steeple Aston and Holt, in the county of Wilts on the 20th of June, 1772.	*Eliot, Wainhouse, Pitcairn, Paradise*	— 231	
— Experiments concerning the different efficacy of pointed and blunted rods, in securing buildings against the stroke of lightning -	*Henley*	LXIV 133	
— An account of a storm of lightning observed on the 1st of March, 1774, near Wakefield in Yorkshire - -	*Nicholson*	— 350	
— An account of the effects of lightning on a house, which was furnished with a pointed conductor, at Tenterden in Kent; to which are added some remarks by Mr. Henley -	*Haffenden*	LXV 336	
— An account of a very extraordinary effect of lightning on a bullock, at Swanborow, in the parish of Ilford, near Lewes in Sussex, in sundry letters from -	*Lambert and Green*	LXVI 463	
— Sundry papers relative to an accident from lightning at Purfleet, May 15, 1777	*Nickson*	LXVIII 232	
Report of the committee appointed by the Royal Society for examining the above	*Committee of the Royal Society*	— 236	
Mr. Wilson's dissent from the above report	*Wilson*	— 239	
Mr. Wilson's letter to the king Nov. 12, 1777	*Wilson*	— 243	

— New

Lightning.

Account of the Storm & lightning at East-bourn Sept. 17, 1780. O. S. Brereton. 71: 42.
Proceedings relative to the accident by lightning at Heckingham. 72: 355.
Account of a Thunder-storm in Scotland - - - - - - Brydone 77: 61.
Remarks on Mr Brydone's account of a Thunder-storm in Scotland. Earl Stanhope — 130.
Account of some extraordinary effects of Lightning - - - - - - Withering 80: 293.

+ Lime. On different sorts of Lime used in agriculture. Tennant. 1799: 305.

	Trans.	Abridg.
—— New experiments and observations on the nature and use of conductors - *Wilson*	LXIX 160	
—— Account of the effects of lightning on board the Atlas - - *Cooper*	— 245	
LILY. A letter with some microscopical observations on the Farina of the red lily - *Needham*	XLII 634	VIII 816
LIMAX. Observations on the limax non cochleata purpur ferens, the naked snail producing purple - - *Peyssonel*	L 585	
LIMBS. Extract of a letter relating to the case of mortification of limbs in a family at Wattisham in Suffolk - - *Wollaston*	LII 523	
Another account - - *Bones*	— 526	
Second account - - *Bones*	— 529	
Further account - - *Wollaston*	— 584	
LIME. A letter concerning the relief he found in the stone in the use of Alicant soap and lime-water - *Lucas*	XLIV 463	XI 1000
—— Two letters on the property of quick lime - - - - *Alston*	XLVII 265	
—— Experiments of fish and flesh preserved in lime water - - *Hume*	XLVIII 163	
—— An account of some trials to keep water and fish sweet with lime-water - *Hales*	— 826	
—— Observations on the lithontriptic virtue of lime-water - - - - *Whytt*	L 386	
LIME-TREES. An extract of a letter containing microscopical observations on lime-trees *Leewenhoek*	XVII 949	III 685
LIMPET FISH. An account of the patella, or limpet fish of Bermuda - - *Forbes*	L 859	
LINCOLNSHIRE. An account of some observables in Lincolnshire, not taken notice of in Camden or any other author - *Merret*	XIX 343	III 333
—— —— A table of the washes in Lincolnshire - - - *Merret*	— 392	II 267
LINE. Three letters asserting the first invention and demonstration of the equality of the curve line of a paraboloid to a straight line, and next the finding a straight line, equal to that of the cycloid, and of the parts thereof *Wallis, Brouncker, and Wren*	VII 6146	I 116
—— A new universal method of describing all curves of every order by the assistance only of angles and right lines - *Maclaurin*	XXX 939	IV 57
—— A general method of describing curves, by the intersection of right lines, moving about		

	Transf.	Abridg.
points in a given plane - - *Braikenridge*	XXXIX 25	VIII 58
—— Letter concerning two species of lines of the third order not mentioned by Sir Isaac Newton nor Mr. Sterling - *Stone*	XLI 318	— 72
—— Extract of a letter containing a commodious disposition of equations for exhibiting the relations of goniometrical lines - *Jones*	XLIV 560	X 14
—— A discourse on the locus for three and four lines celebrated among the ancient geometers - - - - *Pemberton*	LIII 496	
Linen Cloth. A new engine to make linen cloth without the help of an artificer - *De Gennes*	XII 1007	I 501
Lips. Part of a letter concerning two deaf persons who can speak and understand one another by the motion of their lips - *Waller*	XXV 2468	V 2 219
—— Case of a young lady who drank sea-water for an inflammation and tumour in the upper lip - - - *Lavington*	LV 6	
Liquor. An experiment of a way of preparing a liquor that shall sink into and colour the whole body of marble, causing a picture drawn on a surface to appear also in the inmost parts of the stone - - *Kircher and Bird*	I 125	I 603
—— Of an excellent liquor made with cyder, apples, and mulberries - - *Colepress*	II 502	
Liquors (Chemistry) The strange and secret changes of liquors examined - - *Beale*	V 1131	II 712
—— Observations on several passages in the two last months Transactions relating to mixing and fermenting liquors in vacuo - *Anon.*	X 533	
—— An historical account of a strangely self-moving liquor - - *Boyle*	XV 1188	III 367
—— An account of some experiments relating to the production of fire and flame, together with an account of an explosion made by the mixture of two liquors actually cold - - *Slare*	XVIII 201	III 359
—— A way to make two clear spirituous inflammable liquors, which differ very little in taste and smell and being mixed together do give a fine carnation colour, without either sensible fermentation or alteration - *Geoffroy*	XXI 43	III 367
—— Observations upon the dissolutions and fermentation which we may call cold, because they are accompanied with a coolness of the liquors into which they pass - *Geoffroy*	XXII 951	V 421
—— An account of the great benefit of blowing		

showers

	Tranf.	Abridg.
ſhowers of freſh air up through diſtilling liquors - - *Hales*	XLIX 312	
—— A diſſertation of the evaporation and ſeveral phænomena of air, water, and boiling liquors *Hamilton*	LV 146	
LIQUORS (Medical) Account of the riſe and attempts of a way to convey liquors immediately into the maſs of blood - *Oldenburg*	I 128	II 364
—— Some experiments of injecting liquors into the veins of animals - - *Fracaſſati*	II 490	III 232
—— A confirmation of the experiments made by Sign. Fracaſſati in Italy, by injecting acid liquors into the blood - *Boyle*	II 551	— 233
—— Endeavours to prove that the lactea's frequently convey liquors that are not white *Muſgrave*	XIV 812	III 102
—— An experiment made for the tranſmitting of a blue coloured liquor into the lacteals *Muſgrave*	XXII 996	V 259
—— An account of a perſon vomitting blood by drinking exceſſive cold liquors in winter *Michelotti*	XXXVII 129	
—— An obſervation of a white liquor reſembling milk, which appeared inſtead of ſerum, ſeparated from the blood after it had ſtood ſome time - - - - *Stuart*	XXXIX 289	VII 508
—— An improvement on the practice of tapping, whereby that operation, inſtead of a relief for ſymptoms, becomes an abſolute cure for an aſcites, exemplified in the caſe of Jane Roman - - - - *Warrick*	XLIII 12	IX 193
A method of conveying liquors into the abdomen during the operation of tapping *Hales*	— 20	XI 1030
—— Some obſervations proving that the fœtus is in part nouriſhed by the liquor amnii *Fleming*	LXIX 254	
LIQUORS (Natural Hiſtory) The cauſes of mineral ſprings further enquired; and the ſtrange and ſecret changes of liquors examined *Beale*	IV 1131	II 712
—— Account of an inſect likely to yield an acid liquor - - *Liſter*	V 2067	— 792
LIQUOR (Natural Philoſophy) Experiments about the degree of the heat of ſome boiling liquors. *Fahrenheit*	XXXIII 1	VI 2 49
LISBON. The longitude of Liſbon, and the Fort of New York, from Wanſtead and London, determined by eclipſes of the firſt ſatellite of Jupiter - - *Bradley*	XXXIV 85	VI 412
LIVER. Anatomical obſervation of an abſceſs in the liver; a great number of ſtones in the gall bag and bilious veſſels; an unuſual conformation		

	Tranſ.	Abridg.
of the emulgents and pelvis; a ſtrange conjunction of both kidnies, and a great dilatation of the vena cava - *Tyſon*	XII 1035	II 81
—— A remarkable account of a liver appearing glandulous to the eye - - *Brown*	XV 1266	— 83
—— Letter concerning the worms in ſheeps livers - - - *Leeuwenhoek*	XXII 509	— 688
—— Part of a letter concerning worms obſerved in ſheeps livers and paſture grounds *Leeuwenhoek*	XXIV 1522	V 2 266
—— Account of an extraordinary impoſtumation of the liver - - *Short*	XXXVII 184	VII 506
—— An account of an extraordinary cyſtis, in the liver, full of water - *Jernegan*	XLIII 305	XI 971
—— An account of a monſtrous human fœtus, having neither head, heart, lungs, ſtomach, ſpleen, pancreas, liver, nor kidnies *Le Cat*	LVII 1	
Lizard. An advertiſement neceſſary for all navigators bound up the channel of England on account of the Lizard and Scilly being laid down too far northerly, and the change of the variation of the compaſs - - *Anon*	XXII 725	I 585
Lizard Scaly. An account of a new ſpecies of the manis or ſcaly lizard, extracted from the German relations of the Daniſh Royal Miſſionaries in the Eaſt Indies of the year 1765, publiſhed at Hall, in Saxony - *Hampe*	LX 36	
Load-Stone. Of a conſiderable load-ſtone digged out of the ground in Devonſhire *Cotton*	II 423	
Obſervations concerning load-ſtones and ſea compaſſes - - *Oldenburg*	— 423	— 601
—— —— A letter concerning the load-ſtone; where chiefly the ſuggeſtion of Gilbert, touching the circumvolution of a globous magnet, called Terrella; and the variation of the variation is examined - - - *Petit*	— 27	— 607
—— —— An account of experiments concerning the proportional power of the load-ſtone at different diſtances - - *Haukſbee*	XXVII 506	IV 2 295
—— —— An account of a treatiſe entituled calculations and tables relating to the attractive virtue of load-ſtones by lord Paiſley *Anon.*	XXXVI 245	VI 2 304
—— —— An abſtract of a letter concerning the making of magnets without a load-ſtone - - - *Marcel*	XXXVII 294	— - 270
—— —— Account of Dr. Knight's method of making artificial load-ſtones - *Wilſon*	LXIX 51	
—— —— See *Magnet*		

		Tranſ.	Abridg.
LOAM. A letter concerning Windſor loam	*Hill*	XLIV 458	X 605
LOBE. An uncommon obſervation of a defect in the right lobe of the lungs -	*Paiton*	LV 79	
LOBLOLLY BAY. The figure and characters of that elegant American evergreen called by the gardiners Loblolly Bay, taken from bloſſoms blown near London -	*Ellis*	LX 518	
LOBSTER. An account of an hermaphrodite lobſter examined and diſſected purſuant to an order of the ſociety - -	*Nicholls*	XXXVI 290	VII 421
LOCUS. A diſcourſe on the locus for three and four lines celebrated among the ancient geometers - - -	*Pemberton*	LIII 496	
LOCUSTS. An account of locuſts lately obſerved in Wales - -	*Floyd*	XVIII 45	II 777
Another account - -	*Anon*	— 48	
—— A narrative of the deſtruction of the canker-worms and locuſts which deſtroyed the fields near Wirtemberg for ſeveral years	*Wardle*	XXXVIII 294	
—— An account of the locuſts which did vaſt damage in Walachia, Moldavia, and Tranſylvania, in the year 1747 and 1748; and of ſome ſwarms of them, which in the months of July and Auguſt 1748 came into Hungary and Poland - - -		XLVI 30	XI 840
—— An account of a ſingular ſpecies of locuſt	*Felton*	LIV 53	
—— Obſervations on the cicada or locuſt of North America - -	*Collinſon*	— 65	
LOG. An account of a new machine, called the marine ſurveyor, contrived for the menſuration of the way of a ſhip at ſea, more correctly than by the log, or any other method hitherto uſed for that purpoſe, together with ſeveral teſtimonials ſetting forth the uſefulneſs of this invention - -	*Saumarez*	XXXIII 411	VII 444
—— A further account of a new machine called the marine ſurveyor, deſigned for the menſuration of the way of a ſhip at ſea, more certainly, than by the log at preſent in uſe, or any other method hitherto invented for that purpoſe - - -	*Saumarez*	XXXVI 45	VI 456
LOGARITHM. Account of the logarithmotechnia of Mercator - -	*Wallis*	III 759	
Illuſtration of the ſame -	*Mercator*	— 759	— —
—— —— A compendious and facile method for conſtructing the logarithms, exemplified and demonſtrated from the nature of numbers,			

without

	Tranſ.	Abridg.
without any regard to the hyperbola, with a ſpeedy method for finding the number from the logarithm given - *Halley*	XIX 58	I 108
—— —— An eaſy demonſtration of the analogy of the logarithmic tangents to the meridian line, or ſum of the ſecants, with various methods for computing the ſame to the utmoſt exactneſs - - *Halley*	— 202	— 577
—— —— The quadrature of the logarithmic curve - - - *J. Craig*	XX 373	— 56
—— —— Logarithmotechnia generalis *J. Craig.*	XXVII 191	IV 156
—— —— Logometria - - *Cotes*	XXIX 5	IV 171
—— —— A new method for making logarithms, and finding the number correſponding to a logarithm given, with tables - *Long*	— 52	— 160
—— —— Letter containing an explanation of the late Dr. Halley's demonſtration of the analogy of the logarithmic tangents to the meridian line or ſum of the ſecants - *Robertſon*	XLVI 559	X 256
—— —— The conſtruction of the logarithmic lines on the Gunter's ſcale - *Robertſon*	XLVIII 96	
—— —— Letter about logarithms - *Dodſon*	— 273	
—— —— Some conſiderations on a late treatiſe, intituled, A new ſet of Logarithmic Solar Tables, &c. intended for a more commodious method of finding the latitude at ſea by two obſervations of the ſun - *Pemberton*	LI 910	
—— —— Obſervations on an infinite ſeries ſaid to expreſs the value of the ſum of the logarithms of the natural numbers from unity to any number *Bayes*	LIII 269	
—— —— A new method of conſtructing ſun-dials for any given latitude, without the aſſiſtance of dialling ſcales or logarithmic calculations - - - *Ferguſon*	LVII 389	
—— —— On the nature and conſtruction of logarithms - - *Jones*	LXI 455	
—— —— Theorems for computing logarithms *Hellins*	LXX 307	
Loins. An account of a præternatural tumour on the loins of an infant, attended with a cloven ſpine - - - *Rutty*	XXXI 98	VII 676
London. An extract of two eſſays in political arithmetic, concerning the comparative magnitude of London and Paris - - *Petty*	XVI 152	
A further aſſertion of the propoſition, and vindication from the objection of ſome learned perſons of the French Nation - *Petty*	— 237	

—— Some

+Logarithms. The principles and illustration of an advantageous method of arranging the differences of Logarithms, on lines graduated for the purpose of computation. Nicholson 77:246.

Mr Jones's computation of the hyperbolic logarithm of 10 improved: being a transformation of the series which converge by the powers of 80. Hellins 1796:135.

New method of computing Logarithms. — — — — Manning. 1806:327.

On the construction of Logarithmic tables. — Knight. 1817:217.

	Trans.	Abridg.
—— Some reflections on Mr. de Lisle's comparison of the magnitude of Paris with London, and several cities, printed in the memoirs of the academy of sciences at Paris in 1725 *Davall*	XXXV 432	VI 426
—— A letter concerning the number of inhabitants within the London bills of mortality - - - *Brakenridge*	XLVIII 788	
—— Observations on the expectations of lives, the increase of mankind, the influence of great cities on population, and particularly the state of London with the respect to healthfulness and the number of its inhabitants - *Price*	LIX 89	
—— A comparison of the heat of London and Edinburgh - - *Roebuck*	LXV 459	
LONDON BRIDGE. Problems concerning the fall of water under Bridges, applied to the falls under London and Westminster Bridges *Robertson*	L 492	
LONGEVITY. An account of the longevity of the inhabitants of the Bermudas - *Stafford*	III 792	III 561
—— An anatomical account concerning Thomas Parre, who died in London aged 152 years and nine months - - *Harvey*	— 886	— 306
—— A letter concerning a way for the prolongation of human life - - *De Martel*	V 1179	— 309
—— Account of some very aged persons in the North of England - *Lister*	XIV 597	— 304
—— Account of Henry Jenkins, a Yorkshire man, who attained the age of 169 years, with remarks - - *Robinson*	XIX 266	— 307
—— Note confirming the great age of Henry Jenkins - - - *Hill*	— 543	— 367
—— An account of examples of long life *Degg*	XXXV 363	VI 429
LONGITUDE (ATTEMPTS FOR THE DISCOVERY OF) A narrative concerning the success of pendulum-watches at sea for discovering the longitude *Holmes*	I 13	I 555
—— —— Instructions concerning the use of pendulum-watches for finding the longitude at sea, together with a method of a journal for such watches - - *Huygens*	IV 937	— 547 — 555
—— —— An instrument for seeing the sun, moon, or stars pass the meridian of any place. Useful for setting watches in all parts of the world with the greatest exactness, to correct sun-dials, and to assist in the discovery of the longitudes of places - - *Derham*	XXIV 1578	IV 464
—— —— A new and exact table collected from seve-		

	Trans.	Abridg.
ral observations taken in four voyages to Hudson's Bay from London; shewing the variation of the magnetical needle or sea-compass, in the path way to the said Bay, according to the several latitudes and longitudes from 1721 to 1725 - - *Middleton*	XXXIV 73	VI - 297
—— —— A method for determining the geographical longitude of places, from the appearance of the common meteors, called falling stars *Lynn*	XXXV 351	— 400
—— —— A proposal of a method for finding the longitude at sea, within a degree or twenty leagues; with an account of the progress made therein, by a continued series of accurate observations of the moon *Halley*	XXXVII 185	— 401
—— —— A letter concerning the variation of the magnetic needle, with a set of tables annexed, which exhibit the result of upwards of fifty thousand observations, in six periodic reviews from 1700 to 1756, and are adapted to every five degrees of latitude and longitude in the more frequented oceans *Mountain and Dodson*	L 329	
—— —— Letter giving an account of observations at sea for finding out the longitude by the moon - - *Horsley*	LIV 329	
—— —— Proposal of a method for measuring degrees of longitude upon parallels of the equator - - *Mitchell*	LVI 119	
—— —— A letter containing an essay of a new method of determining the longitude of places from observations of the eclipses of Jupiter's satellites - - *Wargentin*	— 278	
LONGITUDE OF PLACES. An account of an eclipse of the moon observed at Moscua in Russia, April 5, 1688, compared with the same observed at Lipsick, whereby the longitude of the former is ascertained, together with the latitude of several principal places in the empire of Russia - *Timmerman*	XVI 53	I 564
—— —— An account of some eclipses of the sun and moon observed by Thomas Brattle at Cambridge, four miles from Boston in New England, whence the difference of the longitude between Cambridge and London is determined from the observation of one of them made at London - - *Hodgson*	XXIV 1630	IV 451
—— —— Concerning the true longitude of the Magellan Streights - *Halley*	XXIX 165	IV 453

—— An

+ Longitude. Recommendation of the method of determining the longitude of Places by observations of the Moon's transit over the Meridian — — Pigott 76:409.

	Transf.	Abridg.
—— —— An obfervation of the end of the total lunar eclipfe, March 5, 1718, obferved near the Cape of Good Hope, ferving to determine the longitude thereof, with remarks thereon *Halley*	XXX 992	IV 451
—— —— The longitude of Buenos Ayres, determined from an obfervation made there by Pere Feuillée - - *Feuillée*	XXXII 2	
—— —— The longitude of Fort-Royal in Jamaica, determined by the eclipfe of the moon, June 18, 1722 - - *Halley*	— 235	
And of Carthagena in America - *Halley*	— 237	VI 408
—— —— The difference of the meridians of Lifbon, Paris, and London - *Carbo*	XXXII 1186	— 410
—— —— The longitude of Lifbon, and the fort of New-York, from Wanfted and London, determined by eclipfes of the firft fatellite of Jupiter - - *Bradley*	XXXIV 85	— 412
~~—— —— A new and exact table, collected from feveral obfervations taken from the year 1721 to 1729, in nine voyages to Hudfon's Bay, in North-America, fhewing the variation of the compafs according to latitudes and longitudes, accounting the longitude from the meridian of London - - *Middleton*~~	~~XXXVII 71~~	~~VI 2 300~~
—— —— Obfervations on the longitude, ~~latitude, and declination of the magnetic needle, and the effects of cold at~~ of Prince of Wales's Fort, upon Churchill-River in Hudfon's Bay, North-America - - *Middleton*	XLII ~~157~~ 169	VIII 469
—— —— A letter containing the refults of obfervations of the diftance of the moon from the fun and fixed ftars, made in a voyage from England to the ifland of St. Helena, in order to determine the longitude of the fhip from time to time; together with the whole procefs of computation ufed on this occafion *Mafkelyne*	LII 558	
—— —— Propofals to determine the exact difference of longitude betwixt London, Paris, and Greenwich by occultations of fixed ftars by the moon *Mafkelyne*	— 607	
—— —— The difference of longitude between the royal obfervatories of Greenwich and Paris, determined by the obfervations of the tranfits of Mercury over the fun in 1723, 1736, 1743, and 1753 - *Short*	LIII 158	
—— —— Obfervations made on the iflands of St.		

John

	Trans.	Abridg.
John and Cape-Breton, to ascertain the longitude and latitude of those places - *Holland*	LVIII 46	
—— —— Astronomical observations for ascertaining the longitude of several places in North-America - - *Holland*	LXIV 182	
—— —— Observations of eclipses of Jupiter's first satellite at Greenwich, compared with the observations of the same made by Samuel Holland, Esq. in North-America, and the longitudes of the places thence deduced *Maskelyne*	— 184	
Immersions and emersions of Jupiter's first satellite, observed at Jupiter's inlet in the island of Anticosti in North-America, and the longitude of the place deduced from comparison, with observations made at the royal observatory at Greenwich by the Astronomer Royal *Wright and Maskelyne*	— 190	
—— —— The variation of the compass, containing 1710 observations to, in, and from, the East-Indies, Guinea, West-Indies, and Mediterranean, with the latitudes and longitudes at the time of observation - - *Douglas*	~~LXVI 18~~	
—— —— A letter concerning the difference of longitude of the royal observatories at Paris and Greenwich, resulting from the eclipses of Jupiter's first satellite, observed during the last ten years: to which is added a comparative table of the corresponding observations of the first satellite made in the principal observatories - - - *Wargentin*	LXVII 162	
—— —— Track of his majesty's armed brig Lion from England to Davis's Streights and Labrador, with observations for determining the longitude by sun and moon and error of common reckoning; also the variation of the compass and dip of the needle, as observed during the said voyage in 1776 - *Pickersgill*	LXVIII 1057	
—— —— of Cork, deduced from astronomical observations - - *Longfield*	LXIX 163	
—— —— See *Compass*		
LOOSENESS. Of the use of the root ipecacuanha for loosenesses, translated from a French paper with notes by - - *H. Sloane*	XX 69	III 114
LOTTERIES. An arithmetical paradox concerning the chances of lotteries - - *Roberts*	XVII 677	— 679
LOUGHS. Of the bogs and loughs of Ireland *King*	XV 948	II 732
LOUGH NEAGH. A letter concerning the petrefac-		

tions

+ Longitude (of Places) of Cambridge in New England. Willard 71: 502.

York — — — — — — — E. Pigott 76: 409.

Result of Calculations of the observations made at various places of the Eclipse of the Sun, which happened on June 3, 1788. Piazzi 79: 55.

Of some remarkable places near the Severn . . . — — — — — E. Pigott 80: 385.

of Dunkirk and Paris from Greenwich, deduced from the triangular measurement in 1787, 1788, supposing the earth to be an ellipsoid. Dalby. 81: 236.

Luminous Animals. Observations upon — - - - Macartney. 1810: 258.

	Transf.	Abridg.
tions of Lough Neagh in Ireland: to which is annexed a lettter from the right reverend doctor George Berkley, lord bishop of Cloyne, to Thomas Prior, Esq. - *Simon*	XLIV 305	X 616
LOWDELL. The case of Grace Lowdell, aged about sixty, who had an extraordinary tumour on her thigh - - *Chandler*	XLI 365	IX 236
LUMBAGO. The history of a convulsive rheumatic lumbago - - *Pitt*	XVIII 58	III 263
LUMBRICUS HYDROPICUS, or an essay to prove that the hydatides, often met with in morbid animal bodies, are a species of worms or imperfect animals - - *Tyson*	XVII 506	— 133
—— —— LATUS, or a discourse on the jointed worm *Tyson*	XIII 113	— 121
—— —— TERES, or some anatomical observations on the round worm bred in human bodies *Tyson*	— 154	— 130
LUMINOUS APPEARANCES IN THE AIR. Vide *Lights* (Astronomical)		
LUMINOUS EMANATIONS. Vide *Lights* (Natural History)		
LUNATIONS. Short and easy methods for finding the quantity of time contained in any given number of mean lunations, and the number of mean lunations in any given quantity of time *Ferguson*	LV 61	
LUNGS. An experiment of preserving animals alive by blowing through their lungs with bellows *Hook*	I 539	III 66
Some anatomical observations about the structure of the lungs of frogs, tortoises, &c. and perfecter animals, as also on the texture of the spleen, &c. - - *Malpigh.*	VI 2149	II 817
—— Letter concerning the structure of the lungs *Templer*	VII 5031	III 64
—— An account of some animals, that having lungs are yet without the arterious vein; together with some other curious particulars *Swammerdam*	VIII 6040	— 256
—— An account of an experiment of the injection of Mercury into the blood, and its ill effects on the lungs - - *Moulin*	XVII 486	— 233
—— Observations about the polypus of the lungs, with Dr. Lister's opinion - *Clark*	XIX 779	— 68
—— Letter concerning a substance coughed up re-		

		Transf.	Abridg.
sembling the vessels of the lungs	*Bussiere*	XXII 545	III 68
—— A letter concerning the cure of an apostemation of the lungs - -	*Wright*	XXIII 1379	V 223
An answer - -	*Cowper*	— 1386	— 227
—— Observations on a treatise of M. Hevelius, designed to prove that the lungs do not divide and expand the blood, but on the contrary cool and condense it - -	*Nicholls*	XXXVI 163	VII 500
—— A case wherein part of the lungs were coughed up - - -	*W. Watson*	XLI 623	IX 137
—— Case of a lad shot through the lungs drawn up by N. Peters - -	*Hallett*	XLIII 151	XI 966
—— Observations on a case published in the last volume of the Medical Essays, &c. of recovering a man dead in appearance by distending the lungs with air -	*Fothergill*	— 275	— 969
—— Cases of the remarkable effects of blisters in lessening the quickness of the pulse in coughs attended with an infarction of the lungs and a fever - - -	*Whytt*	L 569	
—— Case of an extraneous body forced into the lungs - - -	*Martin*	LV 39	
—— An uncommon anatomical observation of a defect in the right lobe of the lungs	*Paitoni*	— 79	
—— An account of a monstrous human fœtus, having neither head, heart, lungs, stomach, spleen pancreas, liver, nor kidney -	*Le Cat*	LVII 1	
LUNI-SOLAR TABLES. Emendations and notes upon the antient astronomical observations of Albatenius, with the restoration of his luni-solar tables - -	*Halley*	XVII 913	III 522
LUNULA. Letter concerning the quadrature of the parts of the lunula of Hippocrates Chius, performed by Mr. John Perks; with the further improvements of the same by Dr. David Gregory and John Caswell -	*Wallis*	XXI 411	I 27
—— The dimensions of the solids generated by the conversion of Hippocrates's lunula, and of its parts about several axes, with the surfaces generated by that conversion	*De Moivre*	XXII 624	I 29
LUPI-CREPITUS. Extract of a letter concerning some remarkable experiments made upon the arteries of horses, with the powder of lycoperdon, or lupi-crepitus, by Monsieur La Fosse	*Latterman*	XLIX 37	
LUSUS NATURAE. A remarkable conformation, or			

+ Lungs. On the colouring matter of the black Bronchian glands and of the black spots of the Lungs. — — — Pearson. 1813:159
On the effects of galvanism in restoring the due action of the lungs.
Philip. 1817:22.

Lusus naturae. An account of a family having hands and feet with supernumerary fingers and toes. Carlisle. 1814: 9.

		Transf.	Abridg.
lusus naturae in a child -	*Warwick*	XLII 152	IX 316
LUXATION. An account of a complete luxation of a thigh-bone, in an adult person, by external violence - -	*White*	LI 676	
—— An account of a case of a luxated thigh-bone reduced - -	*Young*	— 846	
LYCOPERDON. Extract of a letter concerning some remarkable experiments made upon the arteries of horses, with the powder of lycoperdon, or lupi-crepitus, by Monsieur La Fosse	*Latterman*	XLIX 37	
—— A letter concerning the use of lycoperdon, in stopping blood after amputation	*Parsons*	— 38	
LYMNE. An uncommon sinking of the ground at Lymne in Kent - -	*Anon.*	XXXV 551	VI 2 203
LYMPHATICK VESSELS. Letters touching the true use of the lymphatick vessels, &c.	*De Bills*	III 791	III 262
—— Observations on the origin and use of the lymphatick vessels of animals, being an extract from the Gulstonian lecture	*Akenside*	L 322	
—— An account of the lymphatick system in birds - -	*Hewson*	LVIII 217	
—— An account of the lymphatick system in amphibious animals -	*Hewson*	LIX 198	
—— An account of the lymphatick system in fish - - -	*Hewson*	— 204	
—— A description of the lymphaticks of the urethra and neck of the bladder	*Henry Watson*	— 392	
—— On the degrees of heat which coagulates the limph and serum of the blood, with an enquiry into the causes of the inflammating crust, or size as it is called	*Hewson*	~~LX 384~~	
LYNCURIUM. Some observations concerning the lyncurium of the ancients -	*W. Watson*	LI 394	
LYNUS. Account of Fr. Lynus's dials at Liege	*Ellis*	XXIII 1416	V 2 134
LYRE. Some thoughts concerning the ancient Greek and Roman lyre, and an explanation of an obscure passage in one of Horace's odes	*Molyneux*	— 1267	IV 474

M.

	Tranf.	Abridg.
MACHINES (Chirurgical). The description and draught of a machine for reducing fractures of the thigh - *Ettrick*	XLI 562	IX 254
—— Description of a machine for dressing and curing unwieldy patients - *Le Cat*	XLII 364	— 272
—— An account of the extraction of three inches and ten lines of the bone of the upper arm, which was followed by a regeneration of the bony matter; with a description of a machine made use of to keep the upper and the lower pieces of the bone at their proper distances during the time that the regeneration was taking place; and which may also be of service in fractures happening near the head of that bone *Le Cat*	LVI 270	
MACHINES (Mechanical) An account of a catadioptrick telescope, made by John Hadley, Esq. with the description of a machine contrived for applying it to use - *Hadley*	XXXII 303	
—— An account of a new machine called the marine surveyor, intended for the mensuration of the way of a ship in the sea, more correctly than by the log, or any other method hitherto used for that purpose, together with several testimonials setting forth the usefulness of this invention - - - *Saumarez*	XXXVI 45	VI 456
—— Account of a machine to represent eclipses of the earth - - *Segner*	XLI 781	VIII 157
—— A scheme of a diary of the weather, together with draughts and descriptions of machines subservient thereto - - *Pickering*	XLIII 1	XI 1226
—— A description of a machine to blow fire by the fall of water - - *Stirling*	— 315	X 205
—— A machine for sounding the sea at any depth, or in any part, invented by Mr. William Cock in the year 1738, in a voyage to Georgia *Anon.*	XLIV 146	— 261
—— Account of a machine to write down extempore voluntaries, or other pieces of music *Creed*	— 445	— 265
—— An account of a machine for killing whales *Bond*	XLVII 429	

Instruments (anatomical)

	Transf.	Abridg.
—— Some experiments upon a machine for measuring the way of a ſhip at ſea - *Smeaton*	XLVIII 532	
—— An experimental enquiry concerning the natural powers of water and wind to turn mills and other machines depending on a circular motion *Smeaton*	LI 100	
—— Directions for making a machine for finding the roots of equations univerſally, and the means of uſing it - - *Rowning*	LX 240	
—— An account of the magnetical machine contrived by Dr. Knight - *Fothergill*	LXVI 591	
—— Of the degrees and quantities of winds neceſſary to move the heavier kinds of wind-machines *Stedman*	LXVII 493	
—— Account of advantages of a newly-invented machine much varied in its effects, and very uſeful for determining the perfect proportion between different moveables acting by levers and wheel and pinion - *Le Cerf*	LXVIII 950	
MACKENBOY. Letter concerning the effects of Mackenboy, or Tithimalus Hibernicus *Aſhe*	XX 293	
MACREUSE. Some obſervations on the French Macreuſe - - *Robinſon*	XV 1036	II 850
A letter concerning the French macreuſe *Ray*	— 1041	— —
MADDER ROOTS. Obſervations and experiments with madder root, which has the faculty of tinging the bones of living animals of a red colour - - *Du Monceau*	XLI 390	IX 103
See *Bones*		
MADEIRA. Of the increaſe and mortality of the inhabitants of the iſland of Madeira -	LXII 461	
MADNESS. An account of the diſeaſes of dogs, and ſeveral receipts for the cure of their madneſs, and of thoſe bitten by them, extracted from the papers of Sir T. Mayerne by Sir Theodore de Vaux - - - *Mayerne*	XVI 408	II 870 III 282
—— A letter touching the efficacy of camphire in maniacal diſorders - *Kinneir*	XXXV 347	VII 632
—— See *Dog*, *Hydrophobia* - -		
MADRASS. The method of making the beſt mortar at Madraſs in the Eaſt-Indies - *Pyke*	XXXVII 231	VI 465
MAGELLAN. Some remarks on the variation of the magnetical compaſs publiſhed in the memoirs of the academy of ſciences, with regard to the general chart of thoſe variations made by E. Halley, as alſo concerning of longitude of Magellan Straights - *Halley*	XXIX 165	IV 453

MAGNET.

	Tranf.	Abridg.
MAGNET. Accounts of a confiderable load-ftone digged out of the ground in Devonfhire *Cotton*	II 413	
—— Obfervations about load-ftones and fea-compaffes - - - *Oldenburg*	— 423	II 601
—— Anfwer to fome magnetical enquiries *Sellers*	— 478	— —
—— A letter about the load-ftone; where chiefly the fuggeftion of Gilbert touching the circumvolution of a globous magnet, called terrella, and the variation of the variation is examined - - *Petit*	II 527	— 607
—— A retraction of the feventh and laft paragraph of Mr. W. Molyneux's letter, v. XIV. p. 552, concerning lough-neagh ftone, and its non-application to the magnet upon calcination *Molyneux*	XIV 820	— 323
—— A paper about magnetifm, or concerning the changing and fixing the polarity of a piece of iron - - *J. C.*	XVIII 257	— 603
—— An account of experiments concerning the proportion of the power of the load-ftone at different diftances - - *Haukfbee*	XXVII 506	IV 2 295
—— An account of fome magnetical obfervations made in the months of May, June, and July, 1732, in the Atlantic and weftern ocean; ~~alfo the defcription of a water fpout~~ *Harris*	XXXVIII 75	VIII 742
—— An account of an experiment in order to difcover the law of magnetical attraction *Taylor, Haukfbee*	XXIX 294	— - 297
—— A meteorological, barometrical, thermometrical, epidemical, and magnetical diary kept at Utrecht, 1729 - *Van Mufchenbrock*	XXXVII 357	VII 471
1730 and 1731 - *Van Mufchenbrock*	— 408	— - 86 — - 90
—— An obfervation of the magnetic-needle being fo affected by great cold that it could not traverfe - - *Midaleton*	XL 310	VIII 741
—— Abftract of a letter on giving magnetifm and polarity to brafs - - *Arderon*	L 774	
MAGNET (Artificial) A letter concerning the magnetick quality acquired by iron, upon ftanding for a long time in the fame pofture *Leeuenhoeck*	XXXII 72	VI 2 277
—— An abftract of a letter concerning the making of magnets without a load-ftone - *Marcel*	XXXVII 294	— - 270
—— Account of a file rendered magnetical by lightning - - *Bremond*	XLI 614	— 506
—— A method of making artificial magnets without		

Undertakings concerning the inclination of the inclinatory needle Bond 8:6065. I 587

	Tranſ.	Abridg.
the uſe of natural ones - *Canton*	XLVII 31	
—— An account of the magnetical machine, contrived by the late Dr. Gowin, Knight *Fothergill*		
—— Account of Dr. Knight's method of making artificial load-ſtones - *Wilſon*	LXVI 591	
MAGNET. (Declination of the) A letter concerning the preſent declination of the magnetic needle and the tides - - *D: B.*	LXIX 51	
—— An obſervation concerning the declination of the needle made at Rome about the beginning of 1670 - - *Auzout*	~~III 726~~	~~II 607~~
—— Letter concerning ſome ſuppoſed alteration of the meridian line, which may affect the declination of the magnetic needle and the pole's elevation - *Wallis*	~~V 1184~~	~~— 608~~
—— —— Obſervations on the dipping needle made at London 1723 - - *Graham*	~~XXI 285~~	~~I 265~~
—— —— Obſervations of the declination of the magnetic needle, the effects of cold, longitude and latitude made at prince of Wales's Fort, upon Churchill-River in Hudſon's Bay, North-America - - *Middleton*	XXXIII 332	VI 2 28
—— Experiments on two dipping needles which were made agreeable to a plan of the reverend Mr. Michell - - *Nairne*	~~XLII 157~~	~~VIII 469~~
—— —— Deſcription of a new dipping needle *Lorimer*	LXII 476	
—— —— Experiments made on the dipping needle by deſire of the Royal Society 1775 *Hutchins*	LXV 79 — 129	
—— —— An account of obſervations on the dipping needle, made at Albany Fort, in Hudſon's Bay - - - *Hutchins*	LXVI 174	
MAGNETS (Experiments with) An account of ſome magnetical experiments - *Colepreſs*	II 502	
—— A narrative of the ſtrange effects of thunder upon a magnetic card - - *Anon.*	XI 647	II 180
—— Several obſervations of the reſpect of the needle to a piece of iron held perpendicular, made by the maſter of a ſhip croſſing the equinoctial line 1684 - - *Anon.*	XV 1213	
—— Letter concerning a new ſort of a magnetical compaſs, with ſeveral curious magnetical experiments - - *De la Hire*	XVI 344	II 620
—— Part of a letter giving an account of ſeveral mag-		

Inclination

netical

MAGnets (Experiments with)

	Trans.	Abridg.
netical experiments, and of one who pretended to cure or cause diseases at a distance, by applying a sympathetick powder to the urine *Leeuenhoek*	XIX 512	III 685
Concerning the magnetism of drills *Ballard*	XX 417	
—— An account of some magnetical experiments and observations - *Derham*	XXIV 2136	IV 2290
Farther observations and remarks - *Anon.*	— 2138	— - 291
—— An extract of a letter giving an account of some experiments relating to magnetism *Taylor*	XXXI 204	VI - 253
—— A letter on the strength of magnets. *Muschenbroek*	XXXIII 370	— - 255
—— An account of a treatise entitled "Calculations and tables relating to the attractive virtue of load-stones" - - *Anon.*	XXXVI 245	— - 304
—— Magnetical observations and experiments *Savery*	XXXVI 295	— - 260
—— An abstract of a letter concerning experiments made on the Indian magnetick sand *Muschenbroeck*	XXXVIII 297	VIII 737
—— An account of an extraordinary effect of lightning in communicating magnetism, at Wakefield in Yorkshire - - *Dod*	XXXIX 74	— 504
A farther account of the above lightning *Cookson*	— 75	— 505
—— Extract from the journal books of the Royal Society concerning magnets having more poles than two - - - *Eames*	XL 383	— 740
—— An account of some magnetical experiments made before the Royal Society, June 24, 1736 and April 24, 1737 - *Desaguliers*	— 385	— —
—— An account of some magnetical experiments shewed before the Royal Society Nov. 15, 1744 - - - *Knight*	XLIII 161	X 678
—— A letter concerning the poles of Magnets being variously placed - *Knight*	— 361	— 688
—— A collection of magnetical experiments in the years 1746 and 1747 - *Knight*	XLIV 656	— 681
—— Some new method of suspending magnetical needles - - - *Ingen-Housz*	LXIX 537	
MAGNETS. (Variation) The variation of the magnetic needle predicted for many years following *Oldenburg*	III 789	II 610
—— —— Observation on the variation of the magnet at Dantzick in 1670 - *Hevelius*	V 2059	— 609
—— Undertakings concerning the variation of the

+ Magnetical Experiments and Observations   Cavallo   76:62. 77:6

A new suspension of the magnetic Needle, intended for the discovery of minute quantities of magnetic attraction, with new experiments on the magnetism of Iron filings and Brass.   Bennet 1792:81.

On the magnetic attraction of oxides of Iron.   Lane. 1805: 281.

Declination of the magnetic Needle at Bristol in 1668, observed by S. Sturmy. 3:726. II 607.
Rome in 1670   by A. Auzout. 5:1184. — 608.

Variation of the compass in the Atlantick and Ethiopick Oceans 1706. Maxwell 25 n. 310: 2433. IV 455.
Remarks on the Variation of the compass published in the memoirs of the Roy. Acad. of Sciences, with regard to the general chart of those variations made by E. Halley 29: 165. — 453.

Table of the variation of the magnetical needle in the pathway to Hudson's bay, from observations in 4 voyages, from 1721 to 1725 Middleton 34: 73. VI: 2: 297.
—— —— from observations in 9 voyages from 1721 to 1729. —— 37: 71. —— 300.

	Tranſ.	Abridg.
variation of the magnetical compaſs, and the inclination of the inclinatory needle; as the reſult and concluſion of 38 years magnetical ſtudy - - - - *Bond*	VIII 6065	I 587
—— A theory of the variation of the magnetical compaſs - - - *Halley*	XIII 208	II 610
—— Account of the variation of the needle at Cabo Cors Caſtle, on the coaſt of Guiney *Heathcott*	XIV 578	
—— Repetition of the obſervations on the variation of the magnetic needle made at Norimberg ſome years paſt, in the preſent year 1685 *Volckamer, Wurtelbaur, and Eimmart*	XV 1253	— 609
—— An account of the cauſe of the change of the variation of the magnetical needle, with an hypotheſis of the ſtructure of the internal parts of the earth - - *Halley*	XVII 563	— 615
—— A demonſtration of an error committed by common ſurveyors in comparing of ſurveys taken at long intervals of time, ariſing from the variation of the magnetic needle *Molyneux*	XIX 625	I 125
—— Obſervations on the thermometer and magnetic needle in his voyage to the Cape of Good Hope 1700 - - *Cuningham*	XXII 577	
—— Letter concerning captain Edmund Halley's map of magnetic variations, and ſome other things things relating to the magnet - *Wallis*	XXIII 1106	IV 2 286
—— Obſervations upon the variation of the needle made in the Baltick in 1720. - *Sanderſon*	XXXI 120	
—— The variation of the magnetical compaſs obſerved in a paſſage from Cape St. Lucar in Calefornia to the iſle of Guam or Guana, one of the Ladrones, with ſome remarks thereon *Rogers*	— 173	VI 2 286
—— Obſervation of the variation on board the Royal African Pacquet in 1721 in the Ethiopic Ocean - - - *Cornwall*	XXXII 55	— - 289
—— An account of obſervations made of the variation of the horizontal needle at London, in the latter part of the year 1722, and beginning of the year 1723 - *Graham*	XXXIII 96	— - 290
—— An account of an unuſual agitation in the magnetical needle, obſerved to laſt ſome time in a voyage from Maryland - *Hoxton*	XXXVII 53	— - 304
—— Obſervations of the variations of the needle and weather, made in a voyage to Hudſon's Bay in 1731 - *Middleton*	XXXVIII 127	VIII 468

	Tranf.	Abridg.
—— Obfervations of the latitude, variation of the magnetic needle, and weather, made in a voyage from London to Hudfon's Bay, 1735 *Middleton*	XXXIX 270	VIII 376
—— The variation of the magnetic needle as obferved in three voyages from London to Maryland - - *Hoxton*	XLI 171	— 744
—— Some obfervations made during the laft three years of the quantity of the variation of the magnetic horizontal needle to the weftward *Graham*	XLV 279	X 698
—— Letter concerning the variation of the magnetic needle - - *Wargentin*	XLVII 126	
—— An attempt to point out, in a concife manner, the advantages which will accrue from a periodic review of the variation of the magnetic needle throughout the known world, addreffed to the Royal Society by William Mountaine and James Dodfon, and requefting their contribution thereto, by communicating fuch obfervations concerning it as they have lately made and can procure from their correfpondents in foreign parts *Mountaine and Dodfon*	XLVIII 875	
—— A letter concerning the variation of the magnetic needle, with a fet of tables annexed, which exhibit the refult of upwards of fifty thoufand obfervations in fix periodic reviews from 1700 to 1756; and are adapted to every five degrees of latitude and longitude in the more frequented oceans *Mountaine and Dodfon*	L 329	
—— An attempt to account for the regular diurnal variation of the horizontal magnetic needle; and alfo for its irregular variation at the time of an aurora borealis - *Canton*	LI 398	
—— A letter containing fome obfervations on the variation of the magnetic needle, made on board the Montagu man of war in 1760, 1761, 1762 - - - *Rofs*	LVI 216	
—— The variation of the compafs; containing 1719 obfervations to, in, and from, the Eaft-Indies, Guinea, Weft-Indies, and Mediterranean, with the latitudes and longitudes at the time of obfervation - *Dougla*	LXVI 18	
—— Track of his majefty's armed brig Lion from England to Davis's Straights and La-		

brador,

Variation of the magnetic needle at Prince of Wales's fort, Churchill river, Hudson's bay
by C. Middleton 42:181. VIII 469.

+ Observations of the diurnal variation of the Magnetic Needle at Fort Marlborough in the Island of Sumatra. Macdonald. 1796: 340.

, and in the Island of St. Helena ——— 1798: 397.

Concerning the differences in the magnetic needle, on board the Investigator, arising from an alteration in the direction of the ship's head. Flinders. 1805: 186.

Observations on the permanency of the variation of the compass at Jamaica. Robertson. 1806: 348.

Observations on the Variation, and on the Dip of the magnetic Needle, made at the apartments of the Royal Society, between the years 1786 and 1805 incl. Gilpin. ——— 385.

	Transf.	Abridg.
brador, with observations for determining the longitude by sun and moon, and error of common reckoning; also the variation of the compass and dip of the needle as observed during the said voyage in 1776 - *Pickersgill*	LXVIII 1057	
—— See *Compass, Loadstone* - -		
MAGNETICAL SAND. Letter concerning magnetical sand - - *Butterfield*	XX 336	II 577
MAGNITUDE. Experiments concerning the time required in the descent of different bodies of different magnitudes and weights in common air from a certain height - *Hauksbee*	XXVII 196	IV 2 182
—— The general mathematical laws which regulate and extend proportion universally, or a method of comparing magnitudes of any kind together, in all the possible degrees of increase and decrease - - *Glenie*	LXVII 450	
MAIZE. The description, culture, and use of maize *Winthorp*	XII 1065	II 630
—— The extract of a letter concerning the improvements to be made by maize; with a note on the same by John Ray - *Bulkley*	XVII 938	— 634
—— An account of the maize or Indian corn *Cooke*	LXI 205	X 752
MALACCA. A letter containing a technical description of an uncommon bird from Malacca - - - *Badenach*	LXII 1	
MALHOLM TARN. A description of a large lake called Malholm Tarn, near Skipton, in Craven, Yorkshire - - *Fuller*	XLI 612	VIII 641
MALLEUS. An account of the case of a boy who had the Malleus of each ear, and one of the incus drop out - - *Morant*	LII 264	
MALLOW. A letter concerning the wonderful increase of the seed of plants, *e. g.* of the upright mallow - - *Hobson*	XLII 32 o	VIII 824
MALM. A letter concerning certain chalky tubulous concretions, called malm - *Needham*	— 634	— 732
MALPIGHI. Extract of a letter giving an account of Mr. Malpighi, the circumstances of his death, and what was found remarkable at the opening of his body - - - *Lancisi*	XIX 467	III 31
MALT. An account of the manner of making malt in Scotland - - *Moray*	XII 1069	II 627
MALTA. Some remarks on the first part of Mr. L'Abbé Barthelemi's memoirs on the Phoenician letters relative to the inscription in the island of Malta - - *Swinton*	LIV 119

	Trans.	Abridg.
MALTA. See *inscription* - - -		
MALTON. See *inscription* - - -		
MALVERN HOLY WELL. An essay on the waters of the Holy Well at Malvern, Worcestershire *Wall*	XLIX 459	
—— —— A letter concerning the good effects of Malvern Waters in Worcestershire *Wall*	L 23	
MAMMOTH. Observations, and a description of some Mammoth bones dug up in Siberia, proving them to have belonged to elephants *Breyne*	XL 124	IX 87
MAN. An account of a man of a strange imitating nature - - - *Gasaen*	XII 842	III 8
—— The anatomy of a decrepid old man of 109 years - - - *Scheuchzer*	XXXII 313	VII 689
—— Letter concerning a man who lived eighteen years on water - - *Campbell*	XLII 240	IX 238
—— Extract of a letter concerning two men of an extraordinary bulk and weight - *Knowlton*	XLIV 100	XI 1245
—— An essay towards ascertaining the specific gravity of living men - - *Robertson*	L 30	
—— See *Annuities*, *Mortality*, *Population*		
MANCHENILLE APPLE. Singular observations upon the Manchenille apple - *Peyssonel*	L 772	
MANCHESTER. See *Population*		
MANDEVILLE, Sir JOHN. Account of Sir John Mandeville's tomb at Leige - - *Ellis*	XXIII 1416	V 2 134
MANGE. An experiment of bleeding a mangy into a sound dog - - - *Coxe*	II 451	III 229
MANGOSTANS. The settling of a new genus of plants called after the Malayans Mangostans *Garcin*	XXXVIII 232	VIII 755
MANILLA. Extract of a letter describing the island of Manilla - - - *Pye*	XLIX 458	
MANIS. See *Lizard*		
MANNA. Observations on the manna Persicum *Fothergill*	XLIII 86	IX 1299
With additions in the Abridgment -		IX 1299
—— Letter concerning the method of gathering of manna near Naples - - *More*	XLVI 470	
—— Some account of the manna tree - *Cirillo*	LX 233	X 776
MANNERS. Extracts of some letters on the customs, manners, and language of the Northern Indians of America - - - *Johnson*	LXIII 142	
MANTLE TREE. An account of an antient mantle tree in Northamptonshire, on which the date of it (for the year 1133) is expressed by the		

	Author	Trans.	Abridg.
numeral figures, which shews the great antiquity of those figures in England		XIII 399	I 107
MANUFACTURE. An account of a balance of a new construction, supposed to be of use in the woollen manufacture	*Ludlam*	LV 205	
—— An account of the discovery of the manner of making isinglass in Russia, with a particular description of its manufacture in England, from the produce of British fisheries	*Jackson*	LXIII 1	
MANURE. Part of a letter concerning the manuring of land in Devonshire with sea sand	*Bury*	XXVI 142	IV 2 301
—— A letter concerning the manuring of land with fossil shells	*Pickering*	XLIII 191	X 796
MANUSCRIPTS. An account of Kepler's manuscripts	*Hevelius*	IX 27	
—— A letter concerning some Indian manuscripts, lately sent to the university of Oxford	*Lewis*	XX 421	II 397
—— Extract of a letter concerning seignior Redi's manuscripts	*Anon.*	XXI 42	— 789
—— Letter judging of the age of MSS. the style of learned authors, painters, musicians, &c.	*Wanley*	XXIV 1993	V 2 1
—— A letter giving an account of what manuscripts were left by Mr. John Ray	*Dale*	XXV 2282	V 184
—— Remarks on a vellum manuscript	*Schelhammer*	XXVII 459	
—— Account of the method of preserving the manuscripts found at Herculaneum	*Condamine*	XLIV 622	
MAPS. An advertisement of a way of making more lively counterfeits of nature in wax, than are extant in painting; and of a new kind of maps in low relief; both practised in France	*Anon*	I 99	I 193
—— An ingenious proposal for a new sort of maps of countries, together with tables of sands and clays, such chiefly as are found in the north parts of England	*Lister*	XIV 739	II 450
—— An account of a large and curious map of the great Tartary	*Witsen*	XVII 499	
—— A letter containing a geographical description and map of the kingdom of Tunis, with a postscript relating to the cure of intermittent fevers, in those parts	*Shaw*	XXXVI 177	VI 423
—— The construction and use of spherical maps, or such as are delineated upon portions of a spherical surface.	*Colson*	XXXIX 204	VIII 354
—— Of the best form of geographical maps	*Murdock*	L 553	

	Transf.	Abridg.
—— A short dissertation on maps and charts *Mountaine*	L 563	
—— Some account of a new map of the river Volga *Forster*	LVIII 214	
MARBLES. An experiment of a way of preparing a liquor that shall sink into and colour the whole body of marble, causing a picture, drawn on a surface, to appear also in the inmost parts of the stone - *Kercher and Bird*	I 125	I 603
—— A suggestion for retrieving the art of hardening and tempering steel for cutting porphyre and other hard marbles - *Anon.*	VIII 6010	II 599
—— Method of colouring marbles - *Anon.*	XXII 727	IV 2 205
—— An extract of a letter concerning a quarry of marble in the county of Farnanagh in Ireland *Nevill*	XXVIII 278	—— 206
—— Experiments on several pieces of marble stained by Robert Chambers - *Da Costa*	LI 30	
—— A dissertation on the manner of producing white marble - *Raspe*	LX 47	
MARINE INSECT. An account of a remarkable marine insect - *Dupont*	LIII 57	
MARINE PRODUCTION. An account of a remarkable marine production - *Russell*	LII 554	
MARINERS BOW. An account of Thomas Godfrey's improvement of Davis's quadrant transferred to the mariners bow - *Logan*	XXXVIII 441	VIII 366
MARLE. Experiments upon the different kinds of Marle found in Staffordshire - *Withering*	LXIII 161	
MARS. Observations of the planet Mars made at London in February and March, 1665-6 *Hook*	I 239	I 423
Observations made in Italy, confirming the former and withal fixing the period of the revolution of Mars - *Cassini*	I 242	
—— An observation of the planet Mars *Flamstead*	VII 5118	—— 424
—— Observations on Mars in the autumn of 1736 made at Berlin - *Kirch*	XLI 573	
—— (Occultations of) An occultation of Mars, and certain fixt stars, observed at Dantzig, September 1, 1676 - *Hevelius*	XI 721	—— 350
—— An observation of Mars covered by the Moon, Aug. 21, at Greenwich - *Flamstead*	—— 723	
Oxford - *Halley*	—— 724	—— ——
—— Observations of the occultation of Mars by the the moon, October 7, 1736, Fleet-street *Graham*	XL 100	VIII 186

Covent-

+Mars. On the remarkable appearances at the Polar Regions of the Planet Mars, the inclination of its Axis, the position of its Poles, and its spheroidical figure, with hints relating to its real diameter and Atmosphere. Herschel. 74: 233.

Astronomical observations made with a view to determine the heliocentric longitude and motion of its nodes, and the inclination of its orbit. Bugge. 80: 29.

		Tranſ.	Abridg.
Covent-garden - -	Bevis	XL 101	
—— (Conjunctions of) A ſhort account of three great conjunctions of Saturn, Jupiter, and Mars, at Dantzick, in 1682 and 1683	Hevelius	XIII 325	I 357
—— (Parallax of) Compariſon of obſervations made relating to the parallax of Mars at the Cape of Good Hope, by Mr. De La Caillè, and at Greenwich by Dr. Bradley	De L'Iſle	XLVIII 512	
MARSHES. On the noxious quality of putrid marſhes	Prieſtley	LXIV 90	
Farther Proofs of the inſalubrity of marſhy ſituations - -	Price	LXIV 96	
MARSUPIALE AMERICANUM ſeu CARIGUEYX, the anatomy of an Opoſſum -	Tyſon	XX 105	II 881
MARTIN. Account of the houſe martin, or Martlet	White		
—— Of the houſe and Sand-Martin -	White	LXIV 196	
—— Of the torpidity of ſwallows and martins	Corniſh	LXV 258	
—— Account of the free martin -	Hunter	— 343	
MARYGOLD. A letter concerning a zoophyton ſomewhat reſembling the flower of the marygold	Hughes	LXIX 279	
MARYLAND. Remarks on ſome animals, plants, &c. ſent from Maryland - -	Petiver	XLII 590	IX 111
—— Letter concerning ſeveral obſervables in Maryland - - - -	Jones	XX 393	II 253
MATHEMATICS. A letter concerning ſome miſtakes, to be found in a book intituled, "Specimina Mathematica F. du Laurens," eſpecially touching a certain problem affirmed to have been propoſed by Dr. Wallis, to the mathematicians of all Europe, to ſolve it	Wallis	XXI 436	III 600
Animadverſions on a printed paper intituled, reſponſio F. du Laurens ad epiſt. D. Walliſii ad Oldenburgium - -	Wallis	III 654	
Second letter on the ſame paper -	Wallis	— 744	
Continuation of the ſecond letter -	Wallis	— 775	
—— An anſwer to four papers of Mr. Hobb's, lately publiſhed - -	Wallis	— 825	
—— Anſwer to the book intituled Lux Mathematica	Wallis	VI 2241	
—— A deſcription of a mathematic hiſtorical table	Mangola	VII 5067	
		XI 667	

	Tranf.	Abridg.
MATHEMATICS A paper afferting fome mathematical inventions to their true authors *Gregory*	XVIII 233	I 116
—— A folution of two mathematical problems propofed by John Bernouilli - *Anon.*	XIX 384	— 463
—— Letter of Dr. Wallis, giving an account of fome late paffages between him and Myn Heer Leibnitz of Hanover - - *Wallis*	XXI 273	II 2
—— Some eafy methods for the meafuring of curvelined figures, plain and folid - *Wallis*	XXII 547	I 58
—— A folution of the problem propofed in the French Diary, Feb. 1403, by John Bernoulli *Craig*	XXIV 1527	IV 35
—— A general folution of a mathematical problem formerly propofed to the Englifh in the Acta Lipfienfia - - *Anon.*	XXIX 399	IV 45
—— Extracts from Mr. Gafcoigne's and Mr. Crabrie's letters, proving Mr. Gafcoigne to have been the inventor of the telefcopick fights of mathematical inftruments, and not the French *Derham*	XXX 603	— 345
—— A folution of the problem of G. G. Leibnitz, lately propofed to the Englifh *Taylor*	XXX 695	— 46
—— Problem folved by - - *Waring*	LIII 294	
—— Two theorems - - *Waring*	LV 143	
—— A demonftration of two theorems mentioned in Article XXV. of the Philofophical Tranfactions for the year 1775 - *Hutton*	LXVI 600	
—— The general mathematical laws which regulate and extend proportion univerfally; or a method of comparing magnitudes of any kind together, in all the poffible degrees of increafe and decreafe - - - - *Glenie*	LXVII 450	
MATLOCK. Account of the petrefactions near Matlock Baths in Derbyfhire, with conjectures concerning petrefactions in general *Gilks*		
—— Experiments and obfervations on the waters of Buxton and Matlock in Derbyfhire *Percival*	XLI 352	VIII 707
—— A defcription of a petrified ftratum formed from the waters of Matlock in Derbyfhire *Dobfon*	LXII 455	
	LXIV 124	
MATTER. Some theorems refpecting the infinite divifibility of matter - - *Keill*	XXIX 82	IV 423
—— An account of an experiment to fhew by a new proof, that bodies of the fame bulk do not contain equal quantities of matter, and, that therefore there is an interfperfed vacuum *Defaguliers*	XXXI 81	VI 2 157

†Matter (Physic.) On expectorated Matter. Pearson. 1809:313.

Measurement. Account of the measurement of a base on Hounslow heath. Roy. 75:385.

Considerations on the convenience of measuring an arch of the meridian, and of the parallel of longitude, having the observatory of Geneva for their common intersection. Pictet. 81:106

An account of the measurement of a base line upon the sea beach near Porto novo, on the coast of Coromandel Topping 1792:99.

An abstract of the results deduced from the measurement of an arc on the meridian, extending from Latitude 8° 9' 38",4, to Lat. 18° 3' 23",6 N. being an amplitude of 9° 53' 45" 2. Lambton. 1818:486.

On the length of the French Metre estimated in parts of the English standard. Kater. 1818:103.

	Transf.	Abridg.
—— Queries concerning the cause of cohesion of the parts of matter - - *Triewald*	XXXVI 39	— - 5
—— (Physic) Case of a large quantity of matter or water contained in cystes or bags adhering to the peritonaeum, and not communicating with the cavity of the abdomen - *Graham*	XLI 708	IX 187
MATRIX. An account of a woman who had a double matrix - - - *Vassal*	IV 969	III 205
MATY. A short account of Dr. Maty's illness, and of the appearance in the dead body, which was examined on the 3d of August 1776, the day after his decease *Hunter and Watson*	LXVII 608	
MAXIMA. Of the tangents of curves deduced immediately from the theory of maxima and minima *Ditton*	XXIII 1333	IV 7
MAY-DEW. Some observations and experiments upon May-Dew - - - *Henshaw*	I 33	II 141
MAY-FLIES. A further account of the libellæ or May-flies - - *Bartram*	XLVI 400	XI 846
MEAD. An abstract of Dr. Mead's mechanical account of poisons - - *Marlana*	XXIII 1320	
MEAL DUST. Case of a man seized with a fever from the effects of meal dust - *Latham*	LX 451	
MEASURES. An account of the standard measures preserved in the capitol at Rome - *Folkes*	XXXIX 262	IX 486
—— Of the measure and motion of running water *Jurin*	XLI 5	VIII 282
—— An account of the analogy betwixt English weights and measures of capacity *Barlow*	XLI 457	IX 488
—— An account of the proportions of the English and French measures and weights from the standard of the same kept at the Royal Society	XLII 185	IX 489
—— A new experiment of the proportion of the English and French measures *Maskelyne and Bird*	LVIII 326	
MECHANICS. Universal solution of cubic and biquadratic equations, viz. analytical, geometrical, and mechanical - - *Colson*	XXV 2353	IV 66
MECHANICS. An account of an experiment explaining a mechanical paradox, viz. that two bodies of equal weight, suspended on a certain sort of balance, do not lose their equilibrium, by being removed one farther from, the other nearer to the center - *Desaguliers*	XXXVII 125	VI 310
—— A letter containing some observations upon the		

See Weights

MED

		Tranf.	Abridg.
mechanic arts of the Indians — *Papin*		XXVIII 225	V 2 182
—— Dynamic principles, or metaphysical principles of mechanics — — *Jurin*		XLIV 103	X 183
—— The properties of the mechanic powers demonstrated, with some observations on the methods that have been commonly used for that purpose — — *Hamilton*		LIII 103	
—— A memoir concerning the most advantageous construction of water-wheels, &c. *Mallet*		LVII 372	
—— An experimental examination of the quantity and proportion of mechanic power, necessary to be employed in giving different degrees of velocity to heavy bodies, from a state of rest *Smeaton*		LXVI 450	
MEDALS. An easy method of procuring the true impression or figure of medals, coins, &c. *Baker*		XLIII 77	
—— See *Coins*			
MEDICAL. Some new experiments of injecting medicated liquor into the veins, together with the considerable cures performed thereby *Fabritius*		II 564	III 234
—— An account of some chymical, medicinal, and anatomical particulars — *Behm*		III 650	III 84 — 351
—— Relation of an uncommon case in physic at Dantzick — — — *Kirkby*		VIII 6093	— 110
—— A letter containing some considerable observations in the practise of physic — *Turbervill*		XV 839	— 33
—— A relation of four extraordinary medico-chirurgical cases — — *Greenhill*		XXII 617	— 93 — 113
—— An account of an unusual medicinal case *Monginot*		— 756	IV 355
—— A relation of a deaf and dumb person who recovered his hearing and speech after a violent fever: with some other medical and chirurgical observations — — *Martin*		XXV 2469	V [357] V 2 127
—— Two medico-chirurgical observations on the hydatides and consequences of an incompleat hernia, and on the functions of the intestines exposed to sight — — *Le Cat*		XLI 712	IX 189
—— Various medico-chirurgical observations *Schlichting*		XLII 270	— 232
—— Observations on a case published in the last volume of the medical essays, &c. of recovering a man dead in appearance, by distending the lungs with air — — *Fothergill*		XLIII 275	XI 969

Medulla spinalis. A letter on a canal in the medulla spinalis of some Quadrupeds. Sewall. 1809: 146.

	Transf.	Abrid.
MEDICINAL SPRING. An account of a medical spring in Dorsetshire - *Highmore*	IV 1128	II 333
—— —— Letter concerning a medicated spring in Glamorganshire - - *Aubry*	XIX 727	— —
—— —— An account of a new medicinal well lately discovered near Moffat in Annandale, in the county of Dumfries - - *Walker*	L 117	
MEDICINES. A problem proposed to the practisers of physic, by - - - *Cockburn*	XXIV 1753	
—— A solution of the problem for determining the doses of purging and emetic medicines *Cockburn*	— 2119	V 273
—— A letter containing some observations upon the physic of the Indians - *Papin*	XXVIII 225	— 2 182
—— A letter concerning the operation of medicines *Quincy*	XXXI 71	VII 586
—— The effects of the Tonquinese medicine *Reid*	XLIII 212	XI 1044
—— Mead's physical observations on ipecacuanha *Gmelin*	— 382	X 761
—— A brief botanical and medical history of the solanum lethale, bella donna, or deadly night-shade - - - - *W. Watson*	L 62	
—— A letter concerning the medicinal effects of a poisonous plant exhibited instead of the water parsnip - - *Pulteney*	XLII 469	
—— A description of three substances mentioned by the Arabian physicians, in a paper sent from Aleppo, and translated from the Arabic by *Channing*	LVII 21	
MEDITERRANEAN. Advice touching the conjunction of the Ocean with the Mediterranean *Petit*	I 41	III 683
—— A narrative of the conjunction of the Ocean and the Mediterranean by a canal cut through Languedoc in France - - *Anon.*	IV 1123	— —
—— Some additions to the narrative about the conjunction of the Ocean and Mediterranean by a canal in France - - *Froidour*	VII 4080	— —
MEGAMETER. Account of a new megameter *Boscovich*	LXVII 789	
MELLOON. Account of one Edward Melloon, born at Port Leicester in Ireland, who was of an extraordinary size - - *Musgrave*	XX 184	— 1
MELONS. Way of ordering melons *De la Quintenie*	IV 901	II 638
Further directions - - *De la Quintinie*	— 923	— 639
—— Some microscopical observations and curious re-		

	Tranſ.	Abridg.
marks on the vegetation and exceeding quick propagation of moldineſs, on the ſubſtance of a melon - - - *Bradley*	XXIX 490	IV 2 308
—— A letter concerning the vegetation of melon-ſeed forty-two years old - *Triewald*	XLII 115	VIII 824
—— Letter concerning the vegetation of melon-ſeed thirty-three years old - - *Gale*	XLIII 265	X 761
MEMBRANES. A further account concerning the exiſtence of veins in all kinds of plants; together with a diſcovery of the membranous ſubſtance of thoſe veins, and ſome acts in plants reſembling thoſe of ſenſe; and alſo the agreement of the venal juice in vegetables with the blood of animals, &c. - *Liſter*	VII 5131	II 693
—— Microſcopical obſervations on the blood-veſſels and membranes of the inteſtines *Leeuenhoek*	XXVI 53	V 2 267
—— Obſervations upon the membranes encloſing the faſciculi of fibres, into which a muſcle is divided - - *Leeuenhoek*	XXXI 129	VII 464
MEMORY. Account of the ſtrength of memory when applied with due attention - *Wallis*	XV 1269	III 661
MENDIP. A curious deſcription of the ſtrata obſerved in the coal-mines of Mendip in Somerſetſhire - - *Strachey*	XXX 968	IV 2 260
MENE. Letter concerning the ſtocking the river Mene with oyſters - - *Rowlands*	XXXI 250	VII 420
MENSES. A letter containing the caſe of a woman who had her menſes regularly to 70 years of age - - - - *Yonge*	XXVIII 236	V 360
MENSTRUA. A diſcourſe on this problem; why bodies diſſolved in menſtrua ſpecifically lighter than themſelves ſwim therein *W. Molyneux*	XVI 88	I 535
With ſome reflections - *T. Molyneux*	— 93	— 537
MERCATOR. An eaſy mechanical way to divide the nautical meridian line in Mercator's projection, with an account of the relation of the ſame meridian line to the curva catenaria *Perks*	XXIX 331	IV 456
—— Remarks on the cenſure of Mercator's chart, in a poſthumous work of Mr. Weſt of Exeter *Dunn*	LIII 66	
A defence of Mercator's chart againſt the cenſure of Mr. Weſt - *Mountaine*	— 69	
MERCURIAL LEVEL. The deſcription and uſe of an apparatus added as an improvement to Davis's quadrant, conſiſting of a mercurial level, for taking the altitude of ſun or ſtar, at ſea, with-		

+ Membrane. Observations on the component parts of Membrane. Hatchett. 1800: 327.

	Transf.	Abridg.
out the usual assistance of the sensible horizon, which frequently is obscured - *Leigh*	LX 417	VIII 362
MERCURY. Part of a letter concerning the strange effects from the eating Dog Mercury, with remarks thereon by Hans Sloane *Baxter*	XVII 875	II 640
—— (Mineral) Letter concerning the mines of Mercury in Friuli - *Pope*	I 21	II 577
—— (Medicine) An account of an experiment of the injection of Mercury into the blood, and its ill effects on the lungs - *Moulin*	XVII 486	III 233
—— An account of the dissection of a dog who had Mercury injected into one of the jugulars *Pitt*	XX 184	— 234
—— A Letter containing some experiments made upon mad dogs with Mercury - *James*	XXXIX 244	IX 218
—— An account of what was observed upon opening the corpse of a person who had taken several ounces of crude Mercury internally; and of a plum-stone lodged in the coats of the rectum *Madden*	— 291	— 152
—— An account of a large glandular tumor in the pelvis; and of the pernicious effects of crude Mercury given inwardly to the patient *Cantwell*	XL 139	— 184
MERCURY (Barometer) A relation of some mercurial observations, and their result - *Oldenburg*	I 153	II 2
—— A prospect of the weather, winds, and height of the Mercury in the barometer, on the first day of the month, and of the whole rain in every month in 1703, and beginning of 1704 at Townley in Lancashire, by R. Townley, and at Upminster, by W. Derham *Townley and Derham*	XXIV 1877	
—— Several experiments on the mercurial phosphorous - - - - *Hauksbee*	— 2129	IV 2 180
MERCURY (the planet) An observation of a transit of Mercury under the sun, Oct. 31, 1690, at Nuremberg - - *Wurtzelbaur*	XVII 483	I 426
—— An account of the appearance of Mercury, passing over the sun's disk, on the 29th of October, 1723, determining the mean motion, and fixing the nodes of that planet's orb *Halley*	XXXIII 228	VI 253
—— Observations of the transit of Mercury over the sun, Oct. 31, 1736, Fleet-Street *Graham*	XL 102	VIII 194
Manfredi	— 103	
Weidler	— 110	— 198

—— An

	Trans.	Abridg.
—— An account of Mercury eclipsed by Venus, observed at Greenwich, May 17, 1737 *Bevis*	XL 394	VIII 207
—— An account of a transit of Mercury over Venus, May 17, 1737, at Greenwich - *Bevis*	XLI 630	
—— A synopsis of the calculation of the transit of Mercury over the disk of the sun, 25th of October, 1743 - - *Catlyn*	XLII 235	— 204
—— A letter concerning the transit of Mercury over the sun, April 21, 1740, at Cambridge in New *Winthrop*	— 572	— 199
—— An account of the transit of Mercury over the sun, Oct. 25, 1743, in the morning *Graham*	— 578	— 202
—— A letter of the transits of Mercury over the sun, Oct. 31, 1736, and Oct. 25, 1743 *Bevis*	— 622	— 198
—— Some observations concerning Mercury *Bevis*	XLIII 48	X 104
—— Observations of Mercury seen over the sun, Nov. 5, 1743, at Giesa - *Gersten*	XLIV 376	— —
—— Observations on the transit of Mercury over the sun, May 6, 1753 - - *Short*	XLVIII 192	
—— Letter concerning the transit of Mercury over the sun, May 6, 1753, as observed at the island of Antigua - *Tyrrel and Shervington*	— 318	
—— An account of a memoir read at the academy of sciences at Paris by M. de Barros, concerning certain phænomena, observed by him at Paris in the last transit of Mercury over the sun *Short*	— 361	
—— ~~The difference of longitude between the Royal Observatories of Greenwich and Paris, determined by the observations of the transits of Mercury over the Sun in 1723, 1736, 1743, 1753 - - - Short~~	~~LIII 158~~ See Longitude	
—— Observation of the transit of Mercury over the sun, Oct. 25, 1743 - - *Winthrop*	LIX 505	
—— An account of the transit of Mercury at Noriton in Pennsylvania, Nov. 9, 1769 *Smith*	LX 504	
—— Account of an observation of the transit of Mercury over the sun, Nov. 9, 1769, at Cambridge in New England - - *Winthrop*	LXI 51	
+ MERIDIAN. Of a correspondency to be procured for the finding out the true distance of the sun and moon, from the earth by the parallax, observed under, or near, the same meridian *Oldenburg*	I 151	I 300
—— Letter proposing a new place for the first meridian		

Observation of the passage of Mercury over the sun, Oct. 31. 1738. Huxham 41: 645. IX 164

+ Mercury. Transitus Mercurii in ejus exitu a disco Solis 10 Nov. 1769 observatus. Mohr 61:433.

Observation of the transit of Mercury over the Sun Nov. 12. 1782, observed at Cook's town near Dungannon in Ireland Hamilton 73:483.

Observation du Passage de Mercure sur le disque du Soleil le 12 Nov. 1782, faites à l'Observatoire Royal de Paris, avec des reflexions sur un effet qui se fait sentir dans ces mêmes observations semblable à celui d'un refraction dans l'Atmosphere de Mercure. Wallot 74:312.

Observation of the Transit of Mercury over the Sun, made at Louvain May 3. 1786.
N. Pigott 76:384.
E. Pigott — 389.
at Dresden Köhler 77:47.
at St. Petersburg. Rumovski — 48.

Observation of the Right Ascension and Declination of Mercury out of the meridian, near his greatest elongation, Sept. 1786. Smeaton — 318

Observations of the Transit of Mercury over the Disk of the Sun. Herschel. 1803:214.

Mere of Diss. Account of the effect of the Mere of Diss, upon various substances immersed in it. Wiseman. 1798:568.
Analysis of the water of the Mere of Diss. - - - - - - Hatchett. — 572.

4 Meridian. An account of the measurement of an arc of the Meridian, extending from Dunnose, in the Isle of Wight, Lat. 50°37'8", to Clifton, in Yorkshire, Lat. 53°27'31", in course of the operations carried on for the Trigonometrical survey of England, in 1800–1802. Mudge. 1803:383.

Observations on the measurement of three degrees of the Meridian conducted by Lieut. Col. William Mudge. ——— Rodriguez. 1812:321

An abstract of the results deduced from the measurement of an arc of the meridian, extending from latitude 8°9'38",4. to latitude 18°3'23",6, N. being an amplitude of 9°53'45",2. Lambton 1818:486.

	Tranf.	Abridg.
dian, and pretending to evince the equality of all natural days, as alfo to fhew a way of knowing the true place of the moon *Profeffor of Seville*	X 425	I 270
Anfwer to the above letter - *Flamftead*	— 429	— 556
—— An inftrument for feeing the fun, moon, or ftars pafs the meridian of any place, ufeful for fetting watches in all parts of the world with the greateft exactnefs, to correct fun-dials, to affift in the difcovery of the longitudes of places - - - *Derham*	XXIV 1578	IV 464
—— Obfervations on the meridian heighth of the fun, to inveftigate the elevation of the pole at Lifbon - - *Carbone*	XXXIV 95	
—— The difference in time of the meridians of diverfe places, computed from obfervations of the eclipfes of Jupiter's fatellites - *Derham*	XXXVI 33	VI 414
—— See *Longitude*		
MERIDIAN LINE. An eafy demonftration of the analogy of the logarithmic tangents to the meridian line, or fum of the fecants, with various methods for computing the fame to the utmoft exactnefs - - *Halley*	XIX 202	I 577
—— —— Letter concerning fome fuppofed alteraration of the meridian line; which may affect the declination of the magnetic needle, and the poles elevation - - *Wallis*	XXI 285	— 265
—— —— New way of drawing the meridian line *Gray*	XXII 762	IV 461
—— —— Letter concerning drawing the meridian line by the pole ftar, and finding the hour by the fame - - *Gray*	— 815	— 462
—— —— An eafy mechanical way to divide the nautical meridian line in Mercator's projection, with an account of the relation of the fame meridian line to the curva catenaria *Perks*	XXIX 331	— 456
—— Letter containing an explanation of the late Dr. Halley's demonftration of the analogy of the logarithmic tangents to the meridian line, or the fum of the fecants - *Robertfon*	XLVI 559	X 256
MESENTERY. Account of an unufual rupture of the mefentery - - *Swammerdam*	X 273	III 118
—— Letter concerning a child who had its inteftines, mefentery, &c. in the cavity of the thorax - - - *Holt*	XXII 992	V 260
METAL (In general) A defcription of the ufes of a		

certain

		Tranf.	Abridg.
——— certain powder for yielding very close and smooth metal, and of easy carriage, &c. for casting of guns - - - *Anon.*		VIII 6040	II 557
——— A catalogue of fossils, shells, metals, minerals, &c. which J. J. Scheuzhzer of Zurich sent to J. Petiver - - *Petiver*		XXIV 2042	IV 2 286
——— Experiments concerning the effects of air passed through red-hot metals - *Hauksbee*		XXVII 199	—— - 182
——— The specific gravity of metalline cubes, in comparison of their like bulks of water *Hauksbee*		—— 521	
——— Some observations towards composing a natural history of mines and metals - *Nicholls*		XXXV 401	VII 4 102
——— A second letter containing farther observations towards composing a natural history of mines and metals - - *Nicholls*		—— 480	II 187
——— The description and manner of using an instrument for measuring the degrees of the expansion of metals by heat - *Ellicott*		XXXIX 297	VIII 464
METAL. (Use of, in making instruments) A new method of improving and perfecting catadioptrical telescopes, by forming the speculums of glass instead of metal - - *Smith*		XLI 326	—— 113
——— A discourse concerning the usefulness of thermometers in chemical experiments, and concerning the principles on which the thermometers now in use have been constructed; together with the description and uses of a metalline thermometer newly invented by *Mortimer*		XLIV 672	X 435
——— A letter concerning a metalline thermometer in the museum of the Society at Spalding *Johnson*		XLV 128	—— 446
——— A description of a metalline thermometer *Fitzgerald*		LI 823	
——— Directions for making the best composition for the metals of reflecting telescopes; together with a description of the process for grinding, polishing, and giving the great speculum the true parabolic curve - *Mudge*		LXVII 296	
——— The principal properties of the engine for turning ovals in wood or metal, and of the instrument for drawing ovals upon paper demonstrated - - *Ludlam*		LXX 378	
METAL. (Chemistry) How terrestrial streams may be the generative cause both of minerals and metals, and of all the peculiarities of springs *Beale*		V 1154	
——— A continuation of the discourse concerning			

vitriol

Metals. On the cause of the additional weight which metals acquire by being calcined. — Fordyce. 1792: 374.

Observations on some ancient metallic arms and utensils, with experiments to determine their composition. — Pearson. 1796: 395.

An analysis of a mineral substance from North America, containing a metal hitherto unknown. — Hatchett. 1802: 49.

On the identity of Columbium and Tantalum. — Wollaston. 1809: 246.

On two metals, found in the black powder remaining after the solution of Platina. — Tennant. 1804: 411.

On a new metal found in crude Platina. — — — — — — Wollaston. — 419.

On the discovery of Palladium, with observations on other substances found with Platina. — —— 1805. 316.

	Transf.	Abridg.
vitriol, fhewing, that vitriol is ufually produced by fulphur, acting on and coagulating with a metal, and then making out, that alum is likewife the refult of the faid fulphur; as alfo evincing, that vitriol, fulphur, and alum do agree in the faline principle; and laftly, declaring the nature of the falt in brimftone, and whence it is derived - *Anon.*	IX 66	II 544
—— Experiments and obfervations on the agreement between the fpecific gravities of the feveral metals and their colours when united to glafs, as well as thofe of their other proportions - - - *Delaval*	LV 10	
—— An account of rings confifting of all the prifmatic colours, made by explofions on the furface of pieces of metal - *Prieftley* (See Acids)	LVIII 68	
METAPHYSICS. Principia dynamica five principia mechanices - - - *Jurin*	XLIV 103	X 183
METEORS. An account of a confiderable meteor feen in many diftant places in England, Sept. 20, 1676 - - - *Wallis*	XII 863	II 200
—— An account of an extraordinary meteor, or kind of dew refembling butter, that fell laft winter and fpring in Ireland - - *Van*	XIX 224	
Bifhop of Cloyne - -	— —	
—— A letter giving an account of fome appearances in the heavens in Ireland, 1708		IV 2 134
Derham	XXVI 308	— - 193
—— A letter giving an account of a meteor which was feen in Yorkfhire, and other neighbouring counties, upon May 18, 1710 *Thorefby*	XXVII 322	— - 134
—— Account of feveral meteors or lights in the fky *Halley*	XXIX 159	IV - 135
—— A letter giving a relation of a fiery meteor feen in Jamaica, to ftrike into the earth; with remarks on the weather, earthquakes, &c. of that ifland - - *Barham*	XXX 837	— - 131
—— An account of the extraordinary meteor feen all over England, on the 19th of March, 1718-9, with a demonftration of the uncommon heighth thereof - - *Hadley*	— 978	— - 156
—— A defcription of the great meteor feen on the 6th of March, 1715-6 - - *Cotes*	XXXI 66	— - 82
—— A method for determining the geographical longitude of places from the appearance of the		

		Trans.	Abridg.
common meteors called falling stars	*Lynn*	XXXV 351	VI 400
—— A new method for composing a natural history of meteors	*Greenwood*	— 390	VI 2 390
—— Of the meteor called an Ignis Fatuus, from observations made in England and others in Italy	*Derham and Dereham*	XXXVI 204	— 147
—— An account of a meteor seen in the air in the day-time on Dec. 8, 1733	*Crocker*	XLI 346	VIII 517
—— Notices of some meteors observed at Philadelphia	*Breintnall*	— 359	— 518
—— An account of several	*Short*	— 625	— —
—— An account of a meteor seen at Peckham Dec. 11, 1741	*Milne*	XLII 138	— 521
—— An account of a meteor seen near Holkam in Norfolk, Aug. 1741	*Lord Lovell*	— 183	— —
—— Appearance of a fiery meteor seen, by Craddock		XLIII 78	X 478
—— Account of a fiery meteor seen in the air July 14, 1745	*Costard*	XLIII 522	
December 16, 1742	*Mortimer*	— 524	
—— An extraordinary meteor seen in the county of Rutland, which resembled a water-spout	*Barker*	XLVI 248	— 479
—— Several accounts of a fiery meteor which appeared Nov. 26, 1758, collected by J. Pringle,		LI 218	
Remarks on the several accounts of the fiery meteor which appeared Nov. 26, 1718, and other such bodies	*Pringle*	— 259	
—— An account of a meteor seen at Shefford in Berkshire, Oct. 20, 1759; with some observations of the weather of the preceding winter	*Forster*	— 299	
Another account of the same meteor at Bath	*Colebrooke*	— 301	
Another account at Chigwell-Row, Essex	*Dutton*	— 302	
—— An account of a meteor seen in New England, May 10, 1760, and of a whirlwind felt in that country July 10, 1760	*Winthorp*	LII 6	
—— An account of a remarkable meteor seen at Oxford, Sept 21, 1760	*Swinton*	— 99	
—— An observation of a fiery meteor seen at the Hague, Dec. 21, 1758	*Gabry*	LIII 5	
—— An account of a remarkable meteor October 6, 1763	*Dunn*	— 351	
—— An account of several fiery meteors seen in North-America	*Winthorp*	LIV 185	

—— An

+ Meteor. Description of a Meteor, observed Aug. 18. 1783.	Cavallo.	74: 108.
Account of the Meteors of Aug. 18. and Oct. 4. 1783. —	Aubert	— 112.
Observations on a Meteor seen Aug. 18. 1783. — — —	Cooper	— 116.
	Edgeworth	— 118.
Account of some late fiery meteors, with observations.	Blagden	— 201.
Account of an observation of the Meteor of Aug. 18. 1783.	N. Pigott	— 457.

Conf Fireball

	Trans.	Abridg.
—— An account of a remarkable meteor seen at Oxford, March 5, 1764 - - *Swinton*	LIV 326	
—— An account of a remarkable meteor seen at Oxford, April 23, 1764 - - *Swinton*	— 332	
—— Description of a meteor seen at Oxford, Oct. 12, 1766 - - - *Swinton*	LVII 108	
—— An account of an extraordinary meteor seen at Oxford, Oct. 24, 1769 - - *Swinton*	LX 532	
—— A letter containing an account of a fiery meteor seen on the 10th of February 1772, in the shire of Berwick - *Brydone*	LXIII 163	
—— See *Aurora Borealis, Lights in the Air*		
METEOROLOGICAL OBSERVATIONS. A letter concerning the use which may be made of the following history of the weather - *Plot*	XV 930	II 46
Observations of the wind, weather, and height of Mercury in the barometer at Oxford *Plot*	— 932	
—— —— A discourse concerning weather *Garden*	— 991	— 118
—— —— A discourse of the rule of the decrease of the height of the Mercury in the barometer, according as places are elevated above the surface of the earth, with an attempt to discover the true reason of the rising and falling of the Mercury upon change of weather - - - *Hall*	XIV 104	— 14
—— —— An account of the quantity of rain falling monthly for several years successively at Townley in Lancashire - *Townley*	XVIII 51	— 43
—— —— A letter about a contrivance to measure the height of the Mercury in the barometer by a circle on one of the weather plates, with a register of the weather, &c. for 1679 - - - *Derham*	XX 45	— 12
—— —— Part of a letter accompanying his observations of the Mercury in the barometer, rains, winds, &c. for the year 1698 *Derham*	XXI —	— 73
—— —— Observations on what rain fell at Townley in Lancashire in 1697 and 1698, with some other observations on the weather *Townley*	— 47	— 86
—— —— Some observations on the sun's altitude, with the changes of the weather at Emay, in China - - *Cunningham*	— 323	— —
—— —— Observations on the weather 1699, made at Upminster in Essex - *Derham*	XXII 527	— 90

	Trans.	Abridg.
—— —— Some observations on the weather, &c. for some years past - - *Derham*	XXIII 1443	IV 2 62
—— —— Observations of the weather made in a voyage to China, 1700 - *Cunningham*	XXIV 1639	
A register of the wind and weather in China, with the observations of the mercurial barometer at Chusan, from Nov. 1700 to Jan. 1702 *Cunningham*	— 1648	— - 26
—— —— A prospect of the weather, winds, and height of the Mercury in the barometer on the first day of the month, and of the whole rain in every month in 1703 and beginning of 1704, at Townley in Lancashire, and at Upminster, - *Townley and Derham*	— 1877	
—— —— A register of the weather kept at Oates in Essex, 1692 - - *Locke*	— 1917	— - 48
—— —— An account of a storm of rain that fell at Denbigh in Wales - - *Anon.*	XXV 2342	
—— Meteorological tables kept at Upminster, 1705 *Derham*	— 2378	— - 70
—— —— Part of a letter concerning a storm of thunder, lightning, and rain at Leeds in Yorkshire, Aug. 5, 1708 - *Thoresby*	XXVI 289	V 2 40
—— —— Tables of the barometical altitudes at Zurich in Switzerland, in the year 1708, by Scheuchzer, at Upminster, in England, by Derham; as also, of the rain at Pisa, in Italy, in 1707 and 1708, by Tilli; and at Zurich, in 1708; and at Upminster in all that time: with remarks on the same tables, as also on the winds, heats, and colds, and divers other matters occurring in those three different parts of Europe - - - - *Derham*	XXVI 342	
—— —— A meteorological, barometical, thermometrical, epidemical, and magnetical diary kept at Utrecht, 1729 - *Van Muschenbroek*	XXXVII 357	VII 4 71
1730, 1731 - - -	— 408	— - 86
		— - 90
—— —— An account of the rain which fell every year at Upminster, in Essex, during the last eighteen years, with remarks upon that of the year 1714; also a comparison of what has been observed of that kind at Paris, by M. De la Hire - - *Derham*	XXIX 130	IV 2 100
—— —— An account of an Aurora Borealis seen at Cruwys Moreland, in Devonshire, February		

	Tranf.	Abridg.
bruary 6, 1720-1, with an account of the weather before and after it - *Cruwys*	XXXI 186	VI 2 89
—— —— A letter concerning the effects of a violent fhower of rain in Yorkfhire, May 18, 1722 - - *Thorefby*	XXXII 101	— - 58
—— —— An account of the depth of rain fallen from April 1, 1722 to April 1, 1723, at Waddrington, in Northumberland *Horfley*	— 328	
—— —— An invitation to an affociation for forming meteorological diaries, with a fpecimen *Jurin*	— 422	— - 122
—— —— Obfervations on the weather in a voyage to Hudfon's Bay, 1730 - *Middleton*	XXXVII 76	— - 55
—— —— Obfervations made at Padua in fix years *Polenus*	— 201	— - 131
—— —— An abftract of meteorological diaries communicated to the Royal Society, with remarks, Part I. - - *Derham*	— 261	— - 139
—— —— An abftract of the meteorological diaries, made at Peterfburg, and at Lunden in Sweden, 1724 and 1725, Part II. with remarks upon them - - *Confett and Derham*	XXXVIII 101	VIII 555
—— —— Obfervations on the variations of the needle and weather, made in a voyage to Hudfon's Bay in 1731 - *Middleton*	— 127	— 268
—— —— An abftract of the meteorological diaries communicated to the Royal Society for 1726, with remarks upon them, Part III. *Derham*	— 334	IX 339
—— —— An abftract of meteorological diaries, communicated to the Royal Society in 1727, with remarks, Part IV. - *Derham*	— 405	
—— —— Aftronomical, phyfical, and meteorological obfervations in 1733, at Wirtemberg *Weidler*	XXXIX 238	VIII 178 — 550
—— —— Obfervations made of the latitude, variation of the magnetic needle and weather, made in a voyage from London to Hudfon's Bay, 1735 - - *Middleton*	— 270	— 376
—— —— An account and abftract of the meteorological diaries, communicated to the Royal Society for 1729, 1730 - *Hadley*	XL 154	— 578
—— —— A fummary of fix years meteorological obfervations made at Padua - *Polenus*	— 39	

—— Collec-

	Tranf.	Abridg.
—— —— Collections from the diary of the weather and barometer, in order to fettle rules for foretelling the weather by the barometer *Beighton*	XL 259	
—— —— A defcription of a water-level to be fixed to Davis's quadrant, whereby an obfervation may be taken at fea, in thick and hazy weather, without feeing the horizon *Leigh*	XL 413	VIII 360
—— —— Extract from the diaries of the weather, kept at Rome - - *Revillas*	XLI 193	— 422
—— —— An inquiry into the caufes of a dry and wet fummer - - *Anon.*	— 519	— 482
—— —— A letter containing remarks on the weather, and accompanying three fynoptical tables of meteorological obfervations for fourteen years from 1726 to 1739 *Lynn*	— 686	— 604
—— —— An account and abftract of the meorological obfervations for the years 1731-32-33-34-35 - - *Hadley*	XLII 243	— 589
—— —— Meteorological obfervations made at Charles-Town, in South-Carolina *Jurin*	— 491	IX 276
—— —— A fcheme of a diary of the weather, together with draughts and defcriptions of machines fubfervient thereto - *Pickering*	XLIII 1	XI 1226
—— —— A letter concerning the weather in South-Carolina, with abftracts of the tables of his meteorological obfervations in Charles-Town *Lining*	XLV 336	X 456
—— —— On the correfpondence of the barometer with the air and weather - *Holman*	XLVI 101	— 428
—— —— Two letters concerning the heat of the weather in July and September, 1750 *Miles*	— 571	— 474
Letter concerning the hot weather July, 1750 *Arderon*	— 573	— —
—— —— Obfervations of the weather in Madeira *Heberden*	XLVII 357	
—— —— Letter concerning the quantity of rain which fell at Leyden in 1731 *Van Hazen*	— 360	
—— —— Extract of a regifter of the barometer, thermometer, and rain, at Lyndon in Rutland, 1772 - - *Barker*	XLVIII 221	
—— —— A letter concerning the quantity of rain fallen at Charles-Town in South-Carolina from Jan. 1738 to Dec. 1752 *Lining*	— 284	
—— —— State of the weather at Dublin from March 7, 1752 to Feb. 28, 1753 - *Simon*	— 30	

	Transf.	Abridg.
—— —— Letter concerning the late hard weather *Miles*	— 525	
—— —— A continuation of an account of the weather in Madeira - - *Heberden*	— 617	
—— —— Letters concerning the cause of the ascent of vapour and exhalation, and those of winds; and the general phænomena of the weather and barometer - - *Eeles*	XLIX 124	
—— —— An account of the quantity of rain fallen in Antigua for four years 1750 to 1754. *Byam*	— 295	
—— —— Journal of the weather in Dublin for the year 1753, 1754, 1755 - *Simon*	— 759	
—— —— An account of the heat of the weather in Georgia - - *Ellis*	L 754	
—— —— A thermometrical account of the weather in Maryland, for one year from Sept. 1753 *Brooke*	LI 58	
Ditto from three years from Sept. 1754 *Brooke*	— 70	
—— —— An account of a meteor at Shefford in Berkshire, Oct. 20, 1759, with some observations of the weather of the preceding winter *Forster*	— 299	
—— —— State of the weather at Turin, 1759 *Bruni*	— 839	
—— —— An account of the rain fallen in a foot square at Norwich from 1750 to 1762 *Anderson*	LIII 9	
—— —— An account of the quantity of rain fallen Cornwall in 1762 - - *Borlase*	— 27	
—— —— An account of the late mild weather in Cornwall, winter of, 1762 - *Borlase*	— —	
—— —— An account of the quantity of rain fallen at Mount's Bay in Cornwall, and of the weather at that place in June and July 1763 *Borlase*	LIV 59	
—— —— Physical observations, conjectures, and suppositions - - *Franklin*	LV 182	
—— —— abstract of a journal of the weather in Quebec, between the first of April 1765 to the 30th of April 1766 - - *Murdock*	LVI 291	
—— —— Observations for 1767 made at Carlysle *Carlyle*	LVIII 83	
Bridgewater - - - - -	— 87	
Ludgvan in Cornwall - - *Borlase*	— 89	

—— Obser-

	Transf.	Abridg.
——— Observations on the barometer, thermometer, and rain at Plymouth 1767 - *Farr*	— 136	
——— Observations in Poland on the winter of 1768 *Wolfe*	— 151	
——— Observations made at Stockholm in the winter of 1767-8 - - - *Wargentin*	LVIII 152	
——— Abstract from a meteorological register kept at Plymouth during the year 1768 - *Farr*	LIX 81	
——— Meteorological Observations for 1768, made at Bridgewater in Somersetshire, and at Ludgvan in Mount's Bay, Cornwall *Mille*	— 155	
——— Of the different quantities of rain which appear to fall, at different heights, over the same spot of ground - - - *Heberden*	— 359	
——— Observations on the state of the air, winds weather, &c. at Prince of Wales's Fort, on the north-west coast of Hudson's Bay in 1768 and 1769 - - *Dymond and Wales*	LX 137	
——— Meteorological observations for 1769 made at Bridgewater in Somersetshire - *Milles*	— 228	
At Ludgvan in Cornwall - *Borlase*	— 230	
——— Meteorological observations at Ludgvan in Mount's Bay, Cornwall, 1770 - *Borlase*	LXI 195	
——— A letter concerning observations of the quantities of rain fallen at Lyndon, in Rutlandshire, for several years - - *Barker*	— 221	
A second letter on the same subject, and determining the latitude of Stamford in Lincolnshire - - - *Barker*	— 227	
——— Meteorological observation at Caen in Normandy, for 1765, 66, 67, 68, and 1769 *Pigot*	— 274	
——— A letter giving an account of some experiment made in North Wales, to ascertain the different quantities of rain, which fell at the same time at different heights - *Barrington*	— 294	
——— Extract of a meteorological register at Lyndon in Rutlandshire - - *Barker*	LXII 42	
——— Meteorological observations at Ludgvan in Mount's Bay, Cornwall - *Borlase*	— 365	
——— Extract of a register of the barometer, thermometer, and rain at Lyndon in Rutland, 1773 *Barker*	LXIV 202	
——— A meteorological journal for the year 1774, kept at the Royal Society's house by order of the President and Council - -	LXV 139

Meteorological Observations

Observations on the Dryness of the year 1788. Hutchinson. 79: 37.

METeorological Observations

	Transf.	Abridg.
An abridged state of the weather at London in the year 1774, collected from the meteorological journal of the Royal Society *Horsley*	LXV 167	
—— Extract of a register of the barometer, thermometer, and rain, at Lyndon in Rutland, 1773 *Barker*	LXV 199	
—— Meteorological observations made at Chislehurst in Kent in 1774 - *Wollaston*	— 290	
—— Meteorological journal kept at the house of the Royal Society by order of the President and Council for 1775 and 1776	LXVI 319	
An abridged state of the weather at London for one year, commencing with the month of March, 1775, collected from the meteorological journal of the Royal Society *Horsley*	— 354	
—— Extract of a meteorological journal for the year 1775 kept at Bristol - *Farr*	— 367	
—— Extract of a register of the barometer, thermometer, and rain at Lyndon, in Rutland, 1775 *Barker*	— 370	
—— An account of the meteorological instruments used at the Royal Society's House *Henry Cavendish*	— 375	
—— Extract of a meteorological journal for the year 1776, kept at Bristol - *Farr*	LXVII 353	
—— —— Extract of a register of barometer, thermometer, and rain, at Lyndon in Rutland, 1776 *Barker*	— 350	
—— Meteorological journal kept at the house of the Royal Society by order of the President and Council in 1776	— 357	
—— A meteorological diary kept at Fort St. George in the East Indies - *Roxburgh*	LXVIII 180	
—— Abstract of a register of the barometer, thermometer, and rain, at Lyndon, in Rutland 1777 - - - *Barker*	— 554	
—— Journal of weather at Montreal - *Barr*	— 559	
—— Extract of meteorological observations kept at Hawkhill near Edinburgh 1773 to 1776 *M'Govan*	— 564	
—— Extract of a meteorological journal kept at Bristol, 1777 - - - *Farr*	— 567	
—— Journal of the quantity of rain that fell at Holme, near Manchester from 1765 to 1769, and at Barrowby, near Leeds, from 1772 to 1777 - - - *Lloyd*	— 571	
at Barrowby near Leeds from 1778 to 1781 *Lloyd*	72: 71	
		—— Meteo-

Meteorological Observations

	Transf.	Abridg.
—— Meteorological journal kept at the houſe of the Royal Society, by order of the Preſident and Council 1777 - - -	LXVIII 573	
—— Meteorological journal kept by order of the Royal Society 1778 - -	LXIX 295	
—— Regiſter of the barometer, thermomerer, and rain, at Lyndon, in Rutland - *Barker*	— 547	
—— Meteorological journal kept at Briſtol, 1778 *Farr*	— 551	
—— Two meterological journals kept at Nain in 57 degrees north latitude, and Okak in 57 degrees 30 minutes north latitude, both on the coaſt of Labradore - - *Anon.*	— 657 71: 197	
—— A continuation of a meteorological diary, kept at St. George's Fort, on the coaſt of Coromandel, from March 1777 to May 1778 *Roxburgh*	LXX 246	
—— A journal of the weather at Montreal from Dec. 1778 to April 1779 - - *Barr*	— 272	
—— Meteorological journal kept at the Houſe of the Royal Society from Jan. 1778 to Jan. 1779	— 279 1780: 71: [illegible]	
—— Regiſter of the barometer, thermometer, and rain, at Lyndon, in Rutland, 1779 *Barker*	— 47 1781: 72: 285	
—— Journal of the weather at Senegambia, during the prevalence of a very fatal putrid diſorder, with remarks on that country - *Schotte*	— 478	
Mexico. Narrative of a voyage from Spain to Mexico, and of the minerals of that kingdom *Anon.*	III 81	II 588
—— Obſervations concerning the lake of Mexico *Journal des Scavans*	IX 758	— 320 III 564
—— An account of the filtering ſtone of Mexico, compared with other ſtones, by which it is ſhewn that it is of little or no uſe in purifying the waters which have paſſed through it *Vaterus*	XXXIX 106	VIII 728
Mice. A relation of the ſmall creatures called ſable-mice, which have lately come in troops into Lapland, about Thorne, and other places adjacent to the mountains, in innumerable multitudes - - - *Rycaut*	XXI 110	II 871
Micrometer. On the application of the micrometer to the microſcope - - *Hollman*	XLIII 239	X 29
—— Letter concerning a paper of Servington Savery, relating to his invention of a new micrometer *Short*	XLVIII 165	
—— A letter concerning Mr. Gaſcoigne's invention		

1787. 78: 191. 1788. 79: 113
1789. 80. append. 1790 81. append.
1780: 71: 351 | 1781: 72: 281
~~1782. 73: [illegible]~~
See Heat

+ Meteorological Observations. at Minehead in Somersetshire 1782. Atkins. 74: 58.

Register of the Barometer Thermometer and Rain at Lyndon in Rutland; also of the Rain at South Lambeth and at Selbourn, Hampshire. Barker, White

1782. 73: 242.

also at Fyfield, Hampshire – – – – – – – – 1783. 74: 283.

1784. 75: 481.

1785. 76: 236.

1786. 77: 368.

1787. 78: 408.

1788. 79: 162.

1789. 81: 89.

1790. — 278.

1791. 1792: 362.

In this all the places 1792. 1793: 220.

at Rutland 1793. 1794: 174.

1797. 1799: 24. 1794. 1795: 410.

1798. 1800: 46. 1795. 1796: 483.

1796. 1798: 130.

Meteorological journal kept at Knightsbridge from May 9. 1789 to May 8. 1790. Read. 81: 185.

May 9. 1790 to May 8. 1791. — 1792: 225.

+ Micrometer. Description of a Lamp-Micrometer. Herschel 72: 163.
Description of a simple Micrometer for measuring small angles with the Telescope. Cavallo. 81: 283.
Description of a single-lens Micrometer — — - Wollaston. 1813: 119.

		Transf.	Abridg.
of the micrometer - -	*Bevis*	XLVIII 190	
—— Defcription of a method of meafuring differences of right afcenfion and declination, with Dollond's micrometer, together with other new applications of the fame -	*Mafkelyne*	LXI 536	
—— Directions for ufing the common micrometer, taken from a paper in the late Dr. Bradley's hand-writing - -	*Bradley*	LXII 46	
—— Account of a new micrometer -	*Bofcovich*	LXVII 789	
—— Account of a new inftrument for meafuring fmall angles, called the prifmatic micrometer	*Mafkelyne*	— 799	
—— A defcription of two new micrometers	*Ramfden*	LXIX 419	
MICROSCOPE. A defcription of a microfcope of a new fafhion, by the means whereof there has been feen an animal leffer than any of thofe hitherto feen - -	*Anon.*	III 842	I 207
—— Letter about the making of microfcopes with very fmall and fingle glaffes, and of fome other inftruments - -	*Butterfield*	XII 1026	— 208
—— A letter giving a further account of his water-microfcope - - -	*Gray*	XIX 353	— 209
—— Letter concerning making water fubfervient to the viewing both near and diftant objects, with the defcription of a natural reflecting microfcope - -	*Gray*	— 539	— 195
—— The defcription and manner of ufing a late invented fet of fmall pocket microfcopes made by James Wilfon, which with great eafe are applied in viewing opake, tranfparent, and liquid objects, &c. - -	*Wilfon*	XXIII 1241	IV 199
—— A letter concerning the making of microfcropes	*Adams*	XXVII 24	— 203
—— Some account of Mr. Leeuwenhoek's curious microfcopes - -	*Folkes*	XXXII 446	VI 129
—— Account of a catoptric microfcope	*Barker*	XXXIX 259	VIII 120
—— An account of Mr. Leeuwenhoek's microfcopes	*Baker*	XLI 503	— 121
—— On the application of the micrometer to the microfcope - -	*Hollman*	XLIII 239	X 29
—— Obfervations on fallacies in vifion through compound microfcopes -	*Gmelin*	XLIII 382	— 761
—— An account of fome new microfcopes made at Naples, and their ufe in viewing the fmalleft objects - - -	*Stiles*	LV 246	

	Tranf.	Abridg.
—— A report concerning the microscope glasses, sent as a present to the Royal Society by Father di Torre of Naples - - *Baker*	LVI 67	
MICROSCOPIC OBSERVATIONS. An account of micrographia, or the physiological descriptions of minute bodies, made by magnifying glasses *Oldenburg*	I 27	
—— —— Some observations made with a microscope contrived by M. Leeuwenhoek *Leeuwenhoek*	VIII 6037	III 683
—— Figures of some of Mr. Leeuwenhoek's microscopical observations with their explication *Leeuwenhoek*	— 6116	— —
More microscopical observations *Leeuwenhoek*	IX 23	— —
—— Microscopical observations concerning blood, milk, bones, the brain, spittle, cuticula, &c. *Leeuwenhoek*	— 121	— —
Observations about sweat, fat, tears *Leeuwenhoek*	— 128	
More observations from Mr. Leeuwenhoek, Sept. 7, 1674 - - *Leeuwenhoek*	— 178	
—— Microscopical observations concerning the optic nerve - - *Leeuwenhoek*	X 378	— —
Microscopical observations about the texture of the blood, the sap of plants, the figure of sugar and salt, and the probable cause of the difference of their tastes - *Leeuwenhoek*	— 380	— —
—— Concerning the texture of trees, and a remarkable discovery in wine, with notes thereon *Leeuwenhoek*	XI 653	II 873
—— Observations concerning some little animals observed in rain, well, sea, and snow-water; as also in water wherein pepper had lain infused *Leeuwenhoek*	XII 821	I 368
With the manner of observing them *Leeuwenhoek*	— 844	III 683
—— Observations of the carneous fibres of a muscle, and the cortical and medullar part of the brain; as also of moxa and cotton *Leeuwenhoek*	— 899	— 684
—— Microscopical observations of the structure of teeth and other bones - *Leeuwenhoek*	— 1002	— —
—— Observations of ivory - *Leeuwenhoek*	— 1003	
—— Microscopical observations of the structure of the hair - - *Leeuwenhoek*	— —	
—— Animalculæ observed in semine humano *Leeuwenhoek*	— 1040	
Answered by - - *Oldenburg*	— 1043	

Microscope. On a periscopic Camera obscura and Microscope.

Wollaston. 1812:370.

	Tranſ.	Abridg.
Anſwered by - - *Leeuwenhoek*	— 1044	
With extracts of ſeveral other letters *Leeuwenhoek*	— 1045	
—— Obſervations about generation by an animalcule of the male ſeed; animals in the ſeed of a frog; ſome other obſervables in the parts of a frog - - - - - *Leeuwenhoek*	XIII 347	III 684
—— Microſcopical obſervations about animals in the ſcurf of the teeth, the ſubſtance called worms in the noſe, the cuticula conſiſting of ſcales *Leeuwenhoek*	XIV 568	— —
—— An abſtract of a letter concerning the parts of the brain of ſeveral animals, the chalk-ſtones of the gout, the leproſy, and the ſcales of eels *Leeuwenhoek*	XV 883	— —
—— An abſtract of a letter concerning generation by an inſect - - *Leeuwenhoek*	— 1120	
—— Letter concerning the circulation of the blood, as ſeen by the help of a microſcope, in the lacerta aquatica - - - *Molyneux*	— 1236	— 225
—— Microſcopical examination of the teſticles of a rat, and the ſeed of muſcles, oyſters, &c. *Leeuwenhoek*	XVII 593	— 685
—— concerning animalcules found in teeth, of the ſcalineſs of the ſkin, &c. *Leeuwenhoek*	— 646	— 684
—— An extract of a letter containing ſeveral obſervations on the texture of the bones of animals compared with that of wood, on the bark of trees, on the little ſcales found on the cuticula, &c. - - *Leeuwenhoek*	— 838	— 685
—— An extract of a letter containing obſervations on the ſeeds of cotton, palm, or date-ſtones, cloves, nutmegs, gooſeberries, currants, tulips, caſſia, lime-tree; on the ſkin of the hand, and pores, of ſweat, the cryſtalline humour, optic nerves, gall, and ſcales of fiſh; and the figures of ſeveral ſalt particles, &c. *Leeuwenhoek*	— 949	— —
—— Some microſcopical obſervations of vaſt numbers of animalcula ſeen in water - *Harris*	XIX 254	— 652
—— Microſcopical obſervations on eels, mites, the ſeeds of figs, ſtrawberries, &c. *Leeuwenhoek*	— 269	— 685
—— Microſcopical obſervations and experiments *Gray*	— 280	I 209 III 653
—— Letter concerning the eyes of beetles *Leeuwenhoek*	XX 169	— 685

—— Letter

	Tranſ.	Abridg.
—— Letter concerning the circulation and ſtagnation of blood in tadpoles - *Leeuwenhoek*	XXII 447	III 685
—— Letter concerning the worms in ſheeps livers, gnats and animalcula in the excrement of frogs, &c. - - *Leeuwenhoek*	— 509	— 688
—— Obſervations on the circulation and globules in the blood of fiſh - - *Leeuwenhoek*	— 552	— 686
—— Letter concerning worms pretended to be taken from the teeth - - *Leeuwenhoek*	— 635	— 686
—— Letter concerning excreſcences growing on willow leaves - - *Leeuwenhoek*	— 786	V 2 266
—— Letter concerning the ſpawn of codfiſh, &c. *Leeuwenhoek*	— 821	— - —
—— Letter concerning ſeveral microſcopical obſervations - - - *Leeuwenhoek*	— 903	— - 238
—— Several microſcopical obſervations and experiments concerning the animalculæ in ſemine maſculino of cocks and ſpiders, *Leeuwenhoek*	XXIII 1137	— - 264
—— Microſcopical obſervations ſent to Sir C. H. *Anon.*	— 1357	— - 229
—— Letter concerning the ſeeds of oranges *Leeuwenhoek*	— 1461	— - 266
—— A letter concerning the fleſh of whales, cryſtaline humour of the eyes of whales, fiſh, and other creatures, and the uſe of the eye-lids *Leeuwenhoek*	XXIV 1723	— - 267
—— A letter concerning animalculæ on the roots of duck-weed - - - *Leeuwenhoek*	— 1784	— - 267
—— Several microſcopical obſervations on the pumice-ſtone, coral, ſpunges, &c. *Leeuwenhoek*	— 2158	— - —
—— Microſcopical obſervations on the ſeeds of ſeveral Eaſt-India plants - - *Leeuwenhoek*	XXV 2205	— - —
—— Microſcopical obſervations on the blood veſſels, and membranes of the inteſtines *Leeuwenhoek*	XXVI 53	— - —
—— Microſcopical obſervations upon the tongue *Leeuwenhoek*	— 111	— - —
—— Microſcopical obſervations on red coral *Leeuwenhoek*	— 126	— - —
—— Microſcopical obſervations on the palates of oxen - - - *Leeuwenhoek*	— 294	— - —
—— A letter containing ſome microſcopical obſervations upon the chryſtalized particles of ſilver diſſolved in aqua-fortis - *Leeuwenhoek*	XXVII 20	— - —
—— Part of a letter containing ſome microſcopical obſervations upon the animalculæ in ſemine of young rams - - - *Leeuwenhoek*	— 316	— - —
—— A letter containing the obſervations upon the ſeminal veſſels, muſcular fibres, and blood of whales - - *Leeuwenhoek*	— 438	— - —

—— Some

Milky Way. Astronomical observations and experiments tending to investigate the local arrangement of the celestial bodies in space, and to determine the extent and condition of the Milky Way. Herschel. 1817:302

		Transf.	Abridg.
—— Some remarks upon the disposition of the parts and microscopical observations upon the contexture of the skin of elephants *Leeuwenhoek*	XXVII 518	
—— Some microscopical observations upon muscles, and the manner of their production *Leeuwenhoek*	— 529	
—— A letter containing some further microscopical observations on the animalculæ found upon duck-weed, &c. - - *Leeuwenhoek*	XXVIII 160	V 2 267
—— Some microscopical observations and curious remarks on the vegetation and exceeding quick propagation of mouldiness on the substance of a melon - - *Bradley*	XXIX 490	IV 2 308
—— Observations upon the vessels in several sorts of wood, and upon the muscular fibres of different animals - - *Leeuwenhoek*	XXXI 134	VI 2 336
—— Observations upon a fœtus, and the parts of generation of a sheep - *Leeuwenhoek*	XXXII 151	VII 445
—— Some remarks concerning the circulation of the blood, as seen in the tail of a water eft, through a solar microscope - - *Miles*	XLI 725	IX 69 VIII 816
—— A letter with some microscopical observations concerning certain chalky tubulous concretions called malm, on the farina of the red lily, and on worms in smutty corn - *Needham*	XLII 634	— 817
—— Microscopical observations, Dec. 26, 1755 *Wright*	XLIX 553	
—— Microscopic observations on the human blood *Styles and Torre*	LV 252	
MIGUEL, SAINT. An account of the island of St. Miguel - - - *Masson*	LXVIII 601	
MILK. Anatomical observatios of milk found in the veins instead of blood - - *Boyle*	I 100	II 869
A further account of an observation about white blood - - *Boyle*	— 117	III 239
—— Microscopical observations concerning blood, milk, bones, the brain, spittle, and cuticula *Leeuwenhoek*	IX 121	— 683
—— An observation of a white liquor resembling milk, which appeared instead of serum separated from the blood after it had stood some time - - - *Stuart*	XXXIX 289	IX 193
—— An account of some trials to cure the ill taste of milk, which is occasioned by the food of cows either from turnips, cabbages, or autumnal leaves, &c. also to sweeten stinking water *Hales*	XLIX 339	
MILLS. Part of a letter containing a description of a		

water

	Transf.	Abridg.
water wheel for mills invented by Mr. Philip Williams - - *Arderon*	XLIX 1	X 247
MILTHORPE FORGE. Extracts of some letters concerning iron ore, more particularly of the hæmatites wrought into iron at Milthorpe forge in Lancashire - - *Stuechi*	XVII 695	II 551
MINES AND MINERALS.		I 498
Letter concerning the mines of Mercury in Friuli - *Pope*	I 21	II 577
—— Of the mineral of Liege yielding both brimstone and vitriol, and the way of extracting them out of it, used at Liege - *Anon.*	I 45	II 530
—— An account how adits and mines are wrought at Liege without air-shafts - *Moray*	— 79	— 372
—— Articles of enquiries concerning mines *Boyle*	— 342	
—— Observations made in mines and at sea, occasioning a conjecture about the origin of wind *Colepresse*	II 481	— 105
—— An answer to some enquires formerly published concerning mines - *Glanvill*	— 525	— 573
Additional answers to the queries on mines *Glanvill*	III 767	— 574
—— Narrative of the minerals of Mexico *Anon.*	— 817	III 588
—— A particular account of divers minerals sent from the lately burning Mount Ætna *Anon.*	IV 1041	II 390
—— Account of the copper mine in Hern Ground in Hungary - - *Brown*	V 1042	— 562
—— A relation concerning the quicksilver mines of Friuli; confirming as well the account given on that subject, vol. I. p. 21. as enlarging the same, with some additions - *Brown*	IV 1080	— 579
—— Instances, hints, and applications relating to a main point solicited in the preface to this fourth volume; concerning the use may be made of vaults, deep wells, and cold conservatories, to find out the cause or to promote the generation of salt, minerals, metals, crystal, gems, stones of divers kinds, and helps to conserve long, or to hasten putrefaction, fertility of any kind of ground, &c. - - *Beale*	— 1135	
—— A relation concerning the sal-gemmæ mines in Poland - - - *Anon.*	V 1099	II 524
—— How terrestrial streams may be the generative cause both of minerals and metals, and of all the peculiarities of springs - *Beale*	V 1154	
—— Directions and enquiries, with their answers, concerning the mines, &c. of Hungary,		

Tran-

	Tranf.	Abridg.
Tranfylvania, Auftria, and other countries neighbouring to thofe *Oldenburgh and Brown.*	— 1189	II 523 — 585
—— An account of fome mineral obfervations touching the mines of Cornwall and Devon; wherein is defcribed the art of training a load; the art and manner of digging the ore, and the way of dreffing and blowing tin *Anon.*	VI 2096	— 565
—— An account of two uncommon mineral fubftances found in fome coal and iron mines in England - - *Jeffop*	VIII 6179	— 458
—— Some obfervations and experiments about vitriol, tending to prove the nature of that fubftance, and to give further light in the enquiry after the principles and properties of other minerals - - - *Anon.*	IX 41	— 451
—— Two letters concerning rock plants, and their growth - - *Beaumont*	XII 724	II 503
—— A defcription of the diamond mines *Earl Marfhal of England.*	— 907	— 467
—— A relation of the tin-mines, and working of tin in the county of Cornwall - *Merret*	— 949	— 572
—— A further account of fome rock plants growing in the lead mines of Mendip Hills	XIII 276	— 503
—— An account of a ftrange prefervation of four men in a mine 24 days without any food *Anon.*	XIV 577	
—— A catalogue of foffils, fhells, metals, minerals, &c. which J. J. Scheuchzer of Zurich fent to Mr. Petiver - - *Anon.*	XXIV 2042	IV 2 286
—— A curious defcription of the ftrata obferved in the coal mines of Mendip in Somerfetfhire *Strachey*	XXX 968	— - 260
—— Some obfervations towards compofing a natural hiftory of mines and metals - *Nicholls*	XXXV 402	VI 2 185
—— A fecond letter to Dr. Rutty, containing farther obfervations towards compofing a natural hiftory of mines and metals - *Nicholls*	— 480	— - 187
—— An account of the feveral ftrata of earths and foffils found in finking the mineral well at Holt - - *Lewis*	XXXV 489	VI 2 225
—— Some obfervations on the mines of Spain and Germany - - *Bowles*	LVI 229	
—— A fhort account of fome fpecimens of native lead found in a mine in Monmouthfhire *Morris*	LXIII 20	
—— Barometrical obfervations on the depth of the mines in the Hartz - - *De Luc*	LXVII 401	
A fecond paper concerning fome barometrical		

	Transf.	Abridg.
measures in the mines of the Hartz *De Luc*	LXIX 485	
—— Experiments on some mineral substances *Woulfe*	LXIX 11	
—— (Damps in) A relation of persons killed with subterraneous damp - - - *Murray*	I 44	II 373
—— Letter concerning the damps in the mines of Hungary, and their effects - *Browne*	IV 965	— —
—— Some observations about damps *Lister*	X 391	— 375
—— A letter containing a farther account of damps in mines - - *Jessop*	— 450	— 376
—— Observations on a subterranean fire in a coal mine near Newcastle - *Hodgson*	XI 762	— 383
—— A relation of some strange phænomena accompanied with mischievous effects in a coal-work in Flintshire - - *Mostyn*	XII 895	— 378
—— An account of the burning of several hay-ricks by a fiery exhalation or damp; and of the infectious quality of the grass of several grounds *Floyd*	XVIII 49	— 181
Farther account of the fiery exhalation in Merionethshire - - *Lhwyd*	— 223	— 180
—— An attempt made to shew how damps or foul air may be drawn out of any sorts of mines, &c. by an engine - - *Desaguliers*	XXXV 353	VI 2 193
—— A brief account of the effects and properties of damps from observations of the effects on opening an old well at Boston in New England, July 19, 1729 - *Greenwood*	XXXVI 184	— 195
—— An account of the damp air in a coal-pit of Sir James Lowther, sunk within 20 yards of the sea - - *Lowther*	XXXVIII 109	VIII 656
—— An experiment to shew that some damps in mines may be occasioned only by the burning of candles under ground, without the addition of any noxious vapour, even when the bottom of the pit has a communication with the outward air, unless the outward air be forceably driven in, out of the said communication or pipe *Desaguliers*	XXXIX 281	
—— An observation of an extraordinary damp in a well in the Isle of Wight - *Cooke*	XL 379	— 658
MINERAL WATERS. See *Water*		
MINIMA. Of the tangents of curves deduced immediately from the theory of maxima and minima - - - *Ditto*	XXIII 1333	IV 7
MINIUM. A description of a Swedish stone, which		

Minerals. Analysis of a mineral substance from New South Wales. Wedgwood. 80:306.

Analysis of the earthy substance from New South Wales, called Sydneja, or Terra australis. Hatchett. 1798:110.

Observations on a new species of hard carbonate of Lime, also on a new species of Oxide of Iron. Bournon. 1808:325.

An account of some analytical experiments on a mineral production from Devonshire, consisting principally of Alumine and Water. Davy. 1805:155.

Experiments on a mineral substance formerly supposed to be Zeolite; with some remarks on two species of Uran-glimmar. Gregor. —— 331.

Description of the mineral bason in the counties of Monmouth, Glamorgan, Brecon, Carmarthen and Pembroke. Martin. 1806:342

4 Minium. Account of a discovery of native minium. — — — — — Smithson. 1806: 267.

4 Mirrors. Observations and experiments relating to the causes, which often affect mirrors, so as to prevent their shewing objects distinctly. Herschel. 1803: 217.

	Tranf.	Abridg.
affords fulphur, vitriol, allum, and minium *Talbot*	I 375	III 364
MINORCA. Extract of a letter from Minorca, being an addition to Dr. Cleghorn's account of Minorca, 1775 - - - *Small*	LXVI 439	
MIRROR. Part of a letter giving an account of a new mirror, which burns at sixty-six feet distance, invented by M. de Buffon *Needham*	XLIV 493	X 195
Concerning the same mirror burning at 150 feet distance - - *Nicolini*	— 495	— 194
See *Burning-glass*		
MISLETO. A letter concerning the propagation of misleto - - *Barrel*	XXXIV 215	VI 2 348
—— Observations of a difference of sex in misleto *Barrel*	XXXV 547	— 251
MISTS. A letter inclosing some observations on atmospherical electricity; in regard to fogs, mists, &c. with some remarks - *Ronayne*	LXII 137	
—— Account of an extraordinary appearance in a mist - - - - *Cockin*	LXX 157	
MITES. Experiment on the necessity of air to the motion of mites - - *Boyle*	V 2054	
—— Microscopical observations on mites, *Leeuwenhoek*	XIX 269	III 685
—— Additional observations upon the production of mites - - *Leeuwenhoek*	XXVII 398	V 2 267
MITHRAS. Account of a bas-relief of Mithras found at York, explained by - *Stukeley*	XLVI 214	XI 1311
MIXTURE. Two letters, giving an account of a red colour produced by mixture of a sulphureous spirit with a volatile Alcali - *Gibbons*	XIX 542	I 214
—— The strange effects of some effervescent mixtures - - *Mounsey*	L 19	
MOCHA. A letter accompanying a new chart of the Red Sea, with two draughts of the Roads of Mocha and Judda, and several observations made during a voyage on that sea *Newland*	LXI. 77	
—— Remarks and observations made on board the ship Kelsall, on a voyage to Judda and Mocha in 1769 - - *Newland*	— 79	
MODES. An explanation of the Modes or tones in the ancient Grecian music - *Styles*	LI 695	
MOFFATT. An account of a new medicinal well lately discovered near Moffatt, in Annandale, in the county of Dumfries - *Walker*	L 117	
MOISTURE. Observations on the annual evaporation at Liverpool, in Lancashire, and evaporation

	Transf.	Abridg.
considered as a test of the moisture or dryness of the atmosphere - - *Dobson*	LXVII 244	
Mole. Several letters concerning a particular nævus maternus, or mole - *Steigertahl*	XXXIII 347	VII 485
—— Account of a mole from North America *Barrington*	LXI 292	
Molosses. An account of a new sort of molosses made of apples - - *Dudley*	XXXII 231	VI 2 379
Molucco Islands. A farther relation of the horrible burning of some mountains of the Molucco islands - - *Witsen*	XIX 529	II 394
See *Volcanoes*		
Mombazza Pietra Di. A letter concerning the pietra di mombazza, or the rhinoceros stone *Sloane*	XLVI 118	XI 910
Monagram. Explication of a most remarkable monagram, on the reverse of a very ancient quinarius, never before published or explained *Swinton*	LXIV 318	
Money. An enquiry into the value of Greek and Roman Money - - *Raper*	LXI 462	
Monkey. Account of a monstrous fœtus, resembling a hooded monkey - *Gregory*	XLI 764	IX 315
—— An account of a very small Monkey *Parsons*	XLVII 146	
—— Abstract of a letter containing a short description of a singular species of monkies without tails, found in the interior part of Bengall *De Visme*	LIX 71	
Monks-hood. The case of a man who was poisoned by eating monks-hood, or napellus *Bacon*	XXXVIII 287	VIII 842
Monochord. A question in musick lately proposed to Dr. Wallis concerning the division of the monochord or section of the musical canon, with his answer to it - - *Wallis*	XX 80	I 610
Monsoons. An historical account of the trade-winds, and monsoons, observable in the seas between and near the tropicks, with an attempt to assign the physical cause of the said winds *Halley*	XVI 153	II 153
See *Winds*		
Monsters. Observations upon a monstrous head of a colt - - - *Boyle*	I 85	
—— An account of two monstrous births at Paris *Anon.*	II 479	
—— An account of two monstrous births in Devonshire - - - *Colepress*	— 480	— 900
—— Account of two odd monsters - *Grandi*	V 1188	III 301

—— Anato-

+ Moisture. Experiments made to determine the positive and relative quantities of moisture absorbed from the Atmosphere by various substances, under similar circumstances Thompson 77:240.

Molybdate. An analysis of the Carinthian Molybdate of Lead, with experiments on the Molybdic Acid. Hatchett. 1796:285.

Monoculus Polyphemus Linn. Microscopic description of its eyes. André. 72:440.

		Transf.	Abridg.
—— Anatomical obfervations on a monftrous birth at Plymouth	*Durfton*	V 2096	III 301
—— A relation of a monftrous birth	*Morris*	XII 961	— 302
—— The anatomy of a monftrous pig	*Anon.*	XIII 188	II 904
—— The defcription of a monftrous child born in South Jutland	*Krabe*	XIV 599	III 304
—— A difcourfe on the diffection of a monftrous double cat	*Mullen*	XV 1135	II 901
—— An account of a child born with a large wound in its breaft, fuppofed to proceed from the force of imagination	*Cyprianus*	XIX 291	III 222
—— A relation of two monftrous pigs, with the refemblance of human faces	*Floyer*	XXI 431	II 900
—— Letter concerning a child who had its inteftines, mefentery, &c. in the cavity of the thorax	*Holt*	XXII 992	V 269
—— Account of monfters, and monftrous productions	*Camelli*	XXV 2266	— 183
—— Part of a letter concerning a monftrous birth	*Taylor*	— 2345	— 309
—— A letter giving an account of fome monftrous births in Ireland, 1708	*Derham*	XXVI 308	— 309
—— An account of a monftrous birth in Lorrain	*Mac Laurin*	XXXII 346	VII 688
—— Cafe of a child born with the bowels hanging out of its belly	*Amyand*	XXXVII 258	— 516
—— Account of a monftrous boy	*Cantwell*	XLI 137	IX 314
—— Some obfervations on generation, and on monfters, with a defcription of fome particular monfters	*De Superville*	— 294	— 304
—— Account of a monftrous child born of a woman under fentence of tranfportation	*Sheldrake*	— 341	— 313
—— An account of a monftrous fœtus refembling a hooded monkey	*Gregory*	— 764	— 315
—— A cafe of the heart of a child turned upfide down	*Torres*	— 776	— 315
—— A remarkable conformation, or lufus naturæ in a child	*Warwick*	XLII 152	— 316
—— Account of a monftrous lamb	*Doddridge*	XLV 502	XI 1281
—— An account of a preternatural conjuction of two female children	*Parfons*	— 526	XI 1209
—— An account of a monftrous fœtus without any mark of fex	*Bafter*	XLVI 479	— 1208
—— An account of a double child born at Hebus, near Middleton, in Lancafhire	*Percival*	XLVII 360	
—— Anatomico-medical obfervations of a monftrous double-bodied child, born Oct. 16, 1701, in			

Pannonia,

		Trans.	Abridg.
Pannonia, and who died Feb. 23, 1723	*Torkes*	L 311	
Another account	*Burnet*	— 315	
Another account	*Du Plessis*	— 317	
Another account	*Driesschius*	— 318	
—— An account of a monstrous human fœtus, having neither head, heart, lungs, stomach, spleen, pancreas, liver, nor kidnies.	*Le Cat.*	LVII 1	
—— An account of an extraordinary acephalous birth	*Cooper*	LXV 311	
—— See *Calf*, *Child*, *Fœtus*			
MONUMENT. An account of some experiments about the height of the Mercury in the barometer at the top and bottom of the Monument, and also about portable barometers	*Derham*	XX 2	II 14
—— An account of a remarkable monument found near Ashford, in Derbyshire	*Evatt*	LII 544	
MOON. Speculations of the changes likely to be discovered in the earth and moon by their respective inhabitants	*Auzout*	I 120	I 198
—— Of the correspondency, to be procured, for the finding out the true distance of the sun and moon from the earth, by the parallax observed under (or near) the same meridian	*Oldenburg*	I 151	I 300
—— A method for finding the number of the Julian period for any year assigned, the number of the cycle of the sun, the cycle of the moon, and of the indictions, for the same year, being given, together with a demonstration of that method	*Collins*	II 568	III 399
—— Its appulses to Saturn, and the fixed stars observable in the year 1671 foretold and reduced to the meridian and latitude of London	*Flamstead*	V 2029	I 453
—— Letter concerning the appulses of the moon for 1673, and the other planets to the fixed stars, together with an observation of the planet Mars	*Flamstead*	VII 5118	I 424
—— The appulses of the moon and other planets to the fixed stars predicted for 1674	*Flamstead*	VIII 6155	III 149
—— Letter on Mr. Horrox's instrument to shew the moon's true place to a minute or two	*Flamstead*	IX 219	I 453
—— A letter concerning Mr. Horrox's lunar system,	*Flamstead*	X 368	— —

—— Letter

+ Monsters. Account of a monstrous birth. Torlese. 72: 44.
monster of the human species. Reichel, Anderson. 79: 157.
Account of a Child with a double head — — — — — — — Home. 80: 296.
Description of an extraordinary production of human generation, 1799: 28.
with observations. — — — — — — Clarke 1793: 154.
Account of a monstrous Lamb. — — — — Carlisle. 1801: 139.
Description of an extraordinary human foetus. — — — Gibson 1810: 123.

	Trans.	Abridg.
Letter proposing a new place for the first meridian, and pretending to evince the equality of all natural days, as also to shew a way of knowing the true place of the moon — *Anon.*	X 425	I 556
Answered — *Flamstead*	— 429	— —
Observations of the spot Plato in the moon the 16th of August, 1725, with a telescope of his own 150 palms long — *Compani*	XXIV 181	VI 220
A letter giving an account of a lunar rainbow observed in Derbyshire, 1710-11 — *Thoresby*	XXVII 320	IV 2 131
An advertisement to astronomers of the advantages that may accrue from the observations of the moon's frequent appulses to the hyades, during the three next ensuing years — *Halley*	XXX 692	IV 298
An attempt to explain the phænomenon of the horizontal moon appearing bigger than when elevated many degrees above the horizon, supported by an experiment — *Desaguliers*	XXXIX 390	VIII 130
An explication of the above — *Desaguliers*	— 392	— 131
Some thoughts concerning the sun and moon, when near the horizon, appearing larger than when in the zenith — *Logan*	— 404	— 377
An astronomical dissertation on the lunar atmosphere — *De Fouchy*	XLI 261	— 172
A true copy of a paper found in the hand-writing of Sir Isaac Newton, among the papers of the late Dr. Halley, containing a description of an instrument for observing the moon's distance from the fixed stars at sea — *Newton*	XLII 155	VIII 129
A new method of calculating eclipses, particularly of the earth, and of any appulses of the moon to planets and fixed stars — *Gersten*	XLIII 22	X 55
A letter concerning the moon's motion — *Dunthorne*	XLIV 412	— 78
An observation of an extraordinary lunar circle, and of two paraselenes made at Paris, Oct. 20, 1747 — *Grischow*	XLV 524	— 483
A letter concerning the acceleration of the moon — *Dunthorne*	XLVI 162	— 84
A letter concerning the mean motion of the moon's apogee — *Murdocke*	XLVII 62	
An account of a remarkable appearance in the moon, April 22, 1751 — *Short*	XLVII 164	
An account of a prize of 100 ducats, offered by		

the

	Trans.	Abridg.
the Academy of Sciences at Peterſburg, for the beſt anſwer to the queſtion, " Whether the " theory of Sir Iſaac Newton is ſufficient to " explain all the irregularities which are found " in the motion of the moon?" *Euler*	XLVII 263	
—— A reſolution of a general Propoſition for determining the horary alteration of the poſition of the terreſtrial equator, from the attraction of the ſun and moon; with ſome remarks on the ſolutions given by other authors to that difficult and important problem - *Simpſon*	L 416	
—— A letter concerning obſervations to be made on the parallax of the moon at St. Helena, and recommending the ſame to be made at Paris and Greenwich *Le Caille and Maſkelyne*	LII 21 & 26	
—— Certain reaſons for a lunar atmoſphere *Dunn*	— 578	
—— An account of an appulſe of the moon to the planet Jupiter obſerved at Chelſea *Dunn*	LIII 31	
—— Of the moon's diſtance and parallax *Murdock*	LIV 29	
—— Conciſe rules for computing the effects of refraction and parallax in varying the apparent diſtance of the moon from the ſun or a ſtar; alſo an eaſy rule of approximation for computing the diſtance of the moon from a ſtar, the longitudes and latitudes of both being given with demonſtrations of the ſame *Maſkelyne*	— 263	
—— Short and eaſy methods for finding the quantity of time contained in any given number of mean lunations, and the number of mean lunations in any given quantity of time *Ferguſon*	LV 61	
—— An eſſay on the connection between the parallaxes of the ſun and moon; their denſities; and their diſturbing forces on the ocean *Murdock*	LVIII 24	
—— Kepler's method of computing the moon's parallaxes in ſolar ecliplſes, demonſtrated and extended to all degrees of the moon's latitude, as alſo to the aſſigning the moon's correſpondent apparent diameter, together with a conciſe application of this form of calculation to thoſe eclipſes - *Pemberton*	LXI 437	
—— Aſtronomical obſervations relating to the mountains of the moon - *Herſchel*	LXX 507	

Moon. (Occultations, tranſits, and conjunctions) Conjunction of the moon and Venus on the

Moon. Remarkable phænomena in an Eclipse of the Moon. — —Herschel. 1792:27.
Observations on the atmospheres of Venus and the Moon, their respective densities, perpendicular heights, and the twilights occasioned by them. - - - Schroeter —309.
An account of an appearance of light, like a Star, seen in the dark part of the Moon, March 7. 1794, at Norwich. Wilkins 1794:429.
An account of an appearance of light, like a Star, seen lately in the dark part of the Moon by Th. Stretton, in St. John's Square, Clerkenwell, London. Maskelyne —435.

	Tranſ.	Abridg.
11th of October, 1670 - *Hevelius*	V 2023	I 304
—— Obſervations of a tranſit of Jupiter near the moon, Sept. 20, 1671 - *Hevelius*	VI 3031	— 347
—— An obſervation of Mars covered by the moon. Aug. 21, 1676, at Dantzig - *Hevelius*	XI 721	
At Greenwich - - *Flamſtead*	— 723	
—— At Oxford - - - *Halley*	— 724	— 350
—— An account of an occultation of Venus by the moon, Sept. 19, 1729, at Berlin *Kirchius*	XXXVI 256	VI 352
—— An obſervation of the moon's tranſit by Aldebaran, April 3, 1736, London - *Bevis*	XL 90	VIII 133
—— Obſervations of the occultation of Mars by the moon, October 7, 1716, Fleet-ſtreet *Graham*	— 100	— 186
Covent-garden - - - *Bevis*	— 101	
—— An occultation of Aldebaran by the moon, Dec. 12, 1738 - - *Graham*	XLI 632	— 135
—— An occultation of Jupiter and his ſatellites by the moon, Oct. 28, 1748 - *Graham*	— 647	— 184
An account of an occultation of Jupiter by the moon, June 6, 1744 - *Bevis*	XLIII 65	
—— An obſervation on an occultation of Cor Leonis by the moon, on Thurſday March 12, 1747, in Surry-ſtreet, in the Strand, London, with a reflecting teleſcope made by Mr. Short, which magnified about 100 times *Bevis*	XLIV 455	X 1 0
—— An occultation of the planet Venus by the moon in the day-time obſerved at London, April 16, 1751 - - *Bevis*	XLVII 159	
—— The ſame obſerved at Greenwich *Bradley*	— 201	
—— Account of occultations of Anta es, Mars, and Mercury by the moon, that will happen in the year 1763, proper to determine the exact difference of longitude betwixt London, Paris, and Greenwich - - *La Lande*	LII 607	
—— Occultation of fixed ſtars by the moon, obſerved at Greenwich, 1769 - *Maſkelyne*	LIX 399	
—— Obſervation of the moon's paſſage over the Pleiades in 1767. - *M. Meſſier*	LIX 454	
—— An account of an occultation of the ſtar ζ Tauri by the moon, obſerved at Leiceſter *Ludlam*	LX 355	
—— Occultation of the ſtars α and γ Tauri, and other ſtars, by the moon *Wargentin and Lexel*	LXV 280	
—— Occultation of α and γ Tauri obſerved at Leiceſter - - *Ludlam*	— 370	

	Trans.	Abridg.
MOON. (Eclipſe of the) Obſervation of an eclipſe of, Sept. 29, 1670 - - *Hevelius*	V 2023	I 304
—— Obſervations on the eclipſe of the moon, Sept. 8, 1671 London - - *Street*	VI 2272	— 306
Ecton, in Northamptonſhire, - *Palmer*	— —	— 307
Paris - - - *Bullialdus*	— —	~~VI 2272~~
—— Obſervations upon the eclipſe of the moon, Sept. 8, 1671 - - *Hook*	VI 2296	I 227
—— Obſervations on a lunar eclipſe, Sept. 18, 1671 *Hevelius*	— 3028	— 307
—— Obſervations on the eclipſe of the moon, Sept. 8, 1671 - - *Fogelius*	— 3033	— 308
—— An account of what hath been obſerved concerning the late eclipſe of the moon, Jan. 1 1674-5, London - - *Hook*	IX 237	— —
Derby - - - *Flamſtead*	— —	— —
Paris - - *Bullialdus*	— 238	— —
—— A more particular account of the laſt eclipſe of the moon, Jan. 11, 1675, as it was obſerved at Paris - *Caſſini, Picard, and Roens*	X 257	— —
—— Obſervation on an eclipſe of the moon, Jan. 11, 1675, with the occultation of certain fixed ſtars at Dantzig - *Hevelius*	— 289	— 310
—— Account of the total eclipſe of the moon, June 26, 1675, obſerved at London - *Flamſtead*	— 371	— 314
At Paris - - *Bullialdus*	— 372	— 315
—— Obſervations on the ſame made at Paris, proper to compare with thoſe made in London -	— 383	— —
A letter relating to the foregoing obſervations *Caſſini*	— 390	— 560
—— A letter containing obſervations of the late lunar eclipſe, Dec. 21, 1675 *Flamſtead*	— 495	— 316
—— Conſiderations on Mr. Flamſtead's account of the ſame, and obſervations on the ſame *Caſſini*	XI 561	— 317
Anſwer - - *Flamſtead*	— 565	— 562
—— Obſervation of the lunar eclipſe of Oct. 29, 1678, at Paris - - *Caſſini*	XII 1015	— 320
—— An obſervation of the lunar eclipſe Aug. 19, 1681, made at St. Lawrence or Madagaſcar *Heathcot*	XIII 15	— 568
—— Obſervations on the eclipſe of the moon, Feb. 11, 1682, - - *Flamſtead*	— 89	— 326
—— Obſervations on the ſame 11, 1682, at Paris *Anon.*	— 145	— 330
At Dantzick - - *Hevelius*	— 146	— 331
—— An account of a ſmall lunar eclipſe of June 16,		

1684

	Transf.	Abridg.
1684, observed at Greenwich - *Flamstead*	XIV 689	I 334
—— Eclipses totalis lunæ cum mora, Dec. 10, 1685, observata Gedani - - *Hevelius*	XV 1256	— 335
—— Two observations on the eclipse of the moon, Nov. 30, 1685, at Nuremberg *Eimmart and Wurtzelbaur*	XVI 146	— 338
—— Observations on the eclipse of the moon, Nov. 30, 1685, at Paris - *Jacobs*	— 199	— 338
—— Observations on an eclipse of the moon, Nov. 19, 1686, Dublin - - *Molyneux*	— 236	
—— An account of an eclipse of the moon, observed at Moscua in Russia, April 5, 1688, compared with the same, observed at Leipsick, whereby the longitude of the former is ascertained: together with the latitude of several principal places in the empire of Russia *Tinnermann*	XVII 453	— 139
—— Eclipse of the moon, observed Oct. 19, 1697, at Chester - *Halley*	XIX 784	— 340
		— 301
—— At Rotterdam - - - *Cassini*	XX 15	— 340
—— Eclipse of the moon, April 17, 1707, observed at Zurich - *Jacobs and Scheuchzer*	XXV 2394	IV 272
—— The same observedat Boston, in New-England *Brattle*	— 2471	— 271
—— A letter giving an account of the eclipse of the moon, Sept. 18, 1708, at Upminster *Derham*	XXVI 308	— 275
—— An account of the moon's eclipse, Feb. 2, 1709-10, observed at Streatham, near London, and compared with the calculation *Cressener*	XXVII 16	— 275
—— Observation of the eclipse of the moon on Jan. 12, 1711-2 - - *Derham*	— 522	— 277
—— An observation of the end of the total lunar eclipse on the 5th of March, 1718, observed near the Cape of Good Hope, serving to determine the longitude thereof. With remarks thereon - - - *Halley*	XXX 992	— 451
—— Observations on the eclipse of the moon, June 18, 1722, and the longitude of Port Royal in Jamaica, determined thereby *Halley*	XXXII 235	VI 190
—— Observations made in Italy of an eclipse of the moon, Sept. 8, 1718 *Poleni and Margagni*	XXXIII 71	— 185
Bologna - *Rondelli, Nadio, & Parisi,*	— 72	— 186
- - *Eustachius & Monfredi*	— 75	— 187
- - - *Ghisilieri*	— 77	— 189
—— An observation of the eclipse of the moon,		

	Trans.	Abridg.
Nov. 1, 1724, at Lisbon *Carbone and Capasso*	XXXIII 180	VI 191
A comparison of the observations made at Lisbon and Paris - - *Carbone*	— 187	VII 680
—— Observations of the eclipse of the moon, October 10, 1725, made at Bristol *Burroughs*	XXXIV 37	VI 196
Eclipse of the moon at Padua, October 2, 1726 - - *Polenu*	— 158	
—— Observations on the eclipse of the Moon, Oct. 21, 1725, at Albano - *Bianchini*	— 179	— 194
—— Observations upon an eclipse of the moon, Oct. 21, 1724, at Gomroon, in Persia *Saunderson*	— 213	— 267
—— An account of an eclipse of the moon, Oct. 10 1726, Lisbon - - *Carbone*	XXXV 338	— 196
—— An observation of the eclipse of the moon at Castle Dobbs, near Carrickfergus, in Ireland, Feb. 2, 1728-9 - - *Dobs*	XXXVI 140	— 201
—— Observations of an eclipse of the moon, Feb. 2, 1729, at Rome and Paris - *Carbone*	— 170	— 202
Padua - - *Polenus*	— 173	— 203
—— Observations on an eclipse of the moon, Oct. 31, 1724, at Rome - *Blanchini*	— 174	— 205
—— Observations of an eclipse of the moon, July 29, 1729, Wirtemberg - *Weidler*	— —	— —
Padua - - *Polenus*	— 176	— 206
—— Two observations of the total eclipse of the moon, July 28, 1729, Bologna *Manfredi*	— 215	— 207
—— Observations on an eclipse of the moon, Feb. 2, 1730, at Lisbon - - - *Carbone*	— 363	— 213
—— Extract of a letter containing an account of an observation of an eclipse of the moon, July 29 1729, made in Barbadoes - *Stevenson*	— 440	
—— Observations of the eclipse of the moon, June 28, 1721, at Cambridge, in New England *Robie*	XXXVII 272	— 215
—— An observation of the eclipse of the moon, Dec. 1, 1732, made at Rome *Bottarius and Manfredi*	XXXVIII 85	VIII 161
—— An observation on the eclipse of the moon, Nov. 20, 1732, London - *Graham*	— 88	
—— Observations on the eclipse of the moon, Oct. 2, 1735, at Wirtemberg - - *Weidler*	XXXIX 359	— 164
—— A collection of the observations made on the eclipse of the moon on March 15, 1735-6, which were communicated to the Royal Society		
—— In Fleet-street - - *Graham*	XL 14	— 164
—— At Greenwich - - *Halley*	— —	
Fleet-street, London - *Celsius*	— 15	— 165

		Transf.	Abridg.
Covent-Garden - -	*Bevis*	XL 16	
Yeovil in Somersetshire -	*Milner*	— 18	
— A collection of the observations of the lunar eclipse, Sept. 8, 1736			
— In Fleet-street, - -	*Graham*	— 92	
Covent-garden - -	*Bevis*	— 93	
Wirtemberg - -	*Weidler*	— 94	
Hudson's Bay - -	*Middleton*	— 96	
— Observation of an eclipse of the moon, Jan. 2, 1740 - -	*Graham*	XLI 633	VIII 172
— Observation of the eclipse of the moon, Dec. 21, 1740, at the island of St. Catherine, on the coast of Brasil - -	*Legge*	XLII 18	— 170
— A letter concerning the same eclipse, New England - - -	*Winthrop*	— 572	— 170
— Eclipse of the moon, Oct. 22, 1743, in the morning - -	*Graham*	— 580	— 172
— Eclipse of the moon, Dec. 12, 1749, observed at Earith, near St. Ives, Huntingdonshire	*Elstobb*	XLVI 280	X 91
— The same observed at Rome, -	*Maire*	— 321	— —
— Eclipse of the moon observed in London, June 8, 1750 - -	*Catlin and Short*	— 323	— 92
— The same observed at Wirtemberg, June 19, 1750 - - -	*Bose*	— 570	— —
— Eclipse of the moon observed at London, Dec. 2, 1750 - -	*Bevis and Short*	— 575	— 94
— An account of the eclipse of the moon, Nov. 21, 1751 - - - -	*Short*	XLVII 317	
— Lunæ defectus elbis observatus, 27 Martii, 1755	*Barbosa*	XLIX 265	
— The same made at Lisbon -	*Chevalier*	L 374	
— Observations on the eclipse of the moon, Feb. 4, 1757, made at Lisbon -	*Chevalier*	— 376	
— Observations on the eclipse of the moon, July 30, 1757, at Madrid, and Jan. 24, 1758	*Wendlingen*		
— Observations on the eclipse of the moon, July 30, 1757, made at Lisbon		— 640	
	Chevalier	— 769	
— An account of the eclipse of the moon, Nov. 22, 1760, London - - -	*Short*	LI 936	
— Observations on an eclipse of the moon, May 18, 1761, in Sweden - -	*Wargentin*	LII 208	
— An account of the eclipse of the moon, May 8, 1762, in the morning observed in London	*Short*	LII 542	

— An

		Tranſ.	Abridg.
	Bevis	— 543	
—— An account of the ſame at Leyden	*Luloſs*	LII 650	
—— Obſervations of an eclipſe of the moon, Nov. 28 1762, at Calcutta - -	*Hirſt*	LIII 262	
—— Obſervation of the eclipſe of the moon, March 17, 1764, London -	*Bevis*	LIV 107	
—— Obſervations on the ſame at Schwezinga	*Mayer*	— 165	
—— Obſervation of the end of the ſame eclipſe obſerved in Pennſylvania	*Maſon and Dixon*	LVIII 329	
—— An account of the eclipſe of the moon, November 12, 1769, made at Hawkhill, near Edinburgh - -	*Lind*	LIX 363	
—— Obſervations on the eclipſe of the Moon, Dec. 12, 1769, Greenwich -	*Maſkelyne*	— 399	
—— Obſervation of a partial eclipſe of the moon, Jan. 3, and of a total one, Dec. 23, 1768	*M. Meſſier*	— 454	
—— An account of an eclipſe of the moon at Pekin, Oct. 23, 1771 - -	*Cipolla*	LXIV 39	
—— An account of an eclipſe of the moon at Pekin, Nov. 12, 1761 - -	*Cipolla*	— 43	
—— An account of the lunar eclipſe, Oct. 11, 1772, obſerved at Canton -	*Blake*	— 46	
Moon. (Applied to finding the longitude) An inſtrument for ſeeing the ſun, moon, or ſtars paſs the meridian of any place; uſeful for ſetting watches in all parts of the world with the greateſt exactneſs, to correct ſun-dials, to aſſiſt in the diſcovery of the longitude of places	*Derham*	XXIV 1578	IV 464
—— A letter containing the reſults of obſervations of the diſtance of the moon from the ſun and fixed ſtars, made in a voyage from England to the iſland of St. Helena, in order to determine the longitude of the ſhip from time to time; together with the whole proceſs of computation uſed on this occaſion -	*Maſkelyne*	LII 558	
—— Letter giving an account of obſervations at ſea for finding out the longitude by the moon	*Horſley*	LIV 329	
—— Tract of his majeſty's armed brig Leon from England to Davis's Streights and Labrador, with obſervations for determining the longitude by ſun and moon, and error of common			

Morne Garou, a mountain in the Island of St. Vincent.
Account of it, with a description of the Volcano on its summit. Anderson. 75:16.

		Transf.	Abridg.
reckoning; also the variation of the compass and dip of the needle as observed during the said voyage in 1776 — *Pickersgill*		LXVIII 1057	
MOORS. An account of the Moorish way of dressing their meat (with some remarks) in West Barbary, from Cape Spartel to Cape de Geer *Jones*		XXI 248	III 626
MOOSE DEER. A discourse concerning the large horns frequently found under-ground in Ireland, concluding from them that the great American deer, called a Moose, was formerly common in that island — *Molyneux*		XIX 489	II 432 III 544
——— A description of the moose deer in America *Dudley*		XXXI 165	VII 447
——— A letter containing the description of the moose deer of New England — *Dale*		XXXIX 384	IX 84
MORASS. A letter concerning the body of a woman found in a morass, in the Isle of Axholm, in Lincolnshire — — *Stovin*		XLIV 571	VIII 187
MORBID. Some uncommon observation on the dissection of morbid bodies — *Vaughan*		XXIII 1244	V 261
—— A remarkable case of a morbid eye *Spry*		LXIX 18	
MORBUS STRANGULATORIUS. An account of the morbus strangulatorius — — *Starr*		XLVI 435	XI 959
MORTALITY. An estimate of the degrees of the mortality of mankind, drawn from various tables of the births and funerals at the city of Breslaw, with an attempt to ascertain the price of annuities upon lives *Halley*		XVII 596	
—— A view of the relation between Dr. Halley's tables, and the notions of M. de Buffon, for establing a rule for the probable duration of the life of man — — *Kerseeboom*		XLVIII 239	
—— A letter concerning the value of an annuity for life, and the probability of survivorship *Dodson*		— 487	
—— Observations on the expectations of lives, the increase of mankind, the influence of great towns on population, and particularly the state of London with respect to healthfulness, and the number of inhabitants *Price*		LXX 89	
MORTALITY (Bills of) The general bill of christenings and burials in London, 1685. —		XV 1245	III 665
—— Bill of mortality of London, 1616, and 1687		XVI 445	— —
—— Some further considerations on the Breslaw bills of mortality, by the same as the former		XVII 655	— 677

	Tranſ.	Abridg.
—— An extract of all perſons that died in 1695, in Frankfort on the Maine, conſummate matrimony, receive baptiſm, and where buried	XIX 559	III 667
—— The number of perſons who have been chriſtened, married, and buried in the Old, Middle, and Lower Marck, 1698 -	XXII 471	
—— An account of the perſons married, chriſtened, and deceaſed in all the dominions of the Elector of Brandenburg in 1698 -	— 508	
—— Of ſeveral conſiderable towns in Europe, from Chriſtmas 1716 to Chriſtmas 1717, extracted from the Acta Breſlavienſia - *Sprengell*	XXXII 454	VII 446
—— The remainder of the bills of mortality, &c. of the ſeveral towns of Europe, extracted from the Breſlaw Acts - - *Sprengell*	XXXIII 24	
—— An farther account of the bills of mortality, &c. of ſeveral conſiderable towns in Europe, for the years 1722 and 1723, extracted from the Acta Breſlavienſia - *Sprengell*	XXXV 365	— - 60
—— Bills of mortality in ſeveral parts of Europe, for the years 1724 and 1725, extracted from the Acta Breſlavienſia - *Scheuchzer*	XXXVI 110	— - 64
—— For the town of Dreſden, from the year 1617, to 1717, containing the numbers of marriages, births, burials, and communicants - - *Sprengell*	XXXVIII 89	IX 318
—— For the imperial city of Augſburg, from the year 1501 to 1720 incluſive, containing the number of births, marriages, and burials *Sprengell*	— 94	— 322
Remarks upon the aforeſaid bills of mortality for the cities of Dreſden and Augſburgh *Maitland*	— 98	— 325
—— An account of births and burials, with the number of inhabitants at Stoke Damerell, in the county of Devon - *Barrow*	XXXIX 171	— —
—— An abſtract of the bills of mortality in Bridge-Town, in Barbadoes, for the years 1737—1744 - - - *Clark*	XLV 345	XI 1219
—— A letter concerning an improvement of the bill of mortality - - - *Dodſon*	LXVII 333	
—— An extract of the regiſter of the pariſh of Holy-Croſs, in Salop, from Michaelmas, 1750, to Michaelmas, 1760 - *More*	LII 140	
—— An extract from the regiſter of Holy-Croſs, in Salop, from Michaelmas, 1760, to Michaelmas, 1770 - - *Gorſuch*	LXI 57	
—— from Michaelmas 1770, to Michaelmas 1780.	72: 53.	

—— Ob-

+ Mortality.

Calculations of the number of deaths which happen in consequence of parturition, with an attempt to ascertain the chance of life at different periods. Bland. 71: 355.

Observations on the Bills of Mortality at York - - - White 72:35.

Observations on some causes of the excess of mortality of males above the females Clarke 76:349.

	Transf.	Abridg.
—— Observations on the bill of mortality in Chester for the year 1772 - *Haygarth*	LXIV 67	
—— Bill of mortality of the town of Warrington, for 1773 - - - *Aikin*	— 438	
—— Bill of mortality for Chester, for the year 1773 *Haygarth*	LXV 85	
—— Observations on the difference between the duration of human life in towns and in country parishes and villages - - *Price*	— 424	
—— An account of baptisms, marriages, and burials during forty years, in the parish of Blandford Forum, Dorset - *Pulteney*	LXVIII 615	
MORTAR. A proposition of general use in the art of gunnery, shewing the rule of laying a mortar to pass, in order to strike any object above or below the horizon - - *Halley*	XIX 68	I 81
—— The method of making the best mortar at Madrass in East-India - - *Pyke*	XXXVII 231	VI 465
—— See *Gunnery* - - -		
MORTIFICATION. Part of a letter concerning the coming off of the scapula and head of the os humeri, upon a mortification *Derante*	XXXII 15	VII 676
—— An abstract of a book, entituled, A short account of mortifications, and of the surprizing effects of the bark, in putting a stop to their progress - - *Douglas*	XXXVII 429	— 645
—— A remarkable case of the efficacy of bark in a mortification - - - *Grindall*	L 379	
—— Extract of a letter relating to the case of mortification of limbs in a family at Wattisham, in Suffolk - - *Wollaston*	LII 523	
Another account - - *Bones*	— 526	
Second account - - - *Bones*	— 529	
Further account - - *Wollaston*	— 584	
MOSAIC WORK. Part of a letter concerning an antient tessellated, or Mosaick, work at Leicester *Carte*	XXVII 324	
MOSSES. An account of mosses in Scotland *Earl of Cromertie*	— 296	IV 2 253
An answer to the above - *Sloane*	— 302	— 256
—— An account of a moving moss in the neighbourhood of Church-Town in Lancashire *Richmond*	XLIII 282	X 596
—— A letter concerning the manner of feeding mosses; and in particular of the hypnum terrestre trichoides lute-ovirens vulgare ma-

	Tranſ.	Abridg.
jus, capitulis erectis; Raii Synopſ. Ed. III. p. 84 - - - - *Hill*	XLIV 60	X 758
—— The ſubſtance of ſome experiments of planting of ſeeds in moſs - - *Bennet*	XLV 156	— 795
—— Experiments and obſervations on a blue ſubſtance found in the peat-moſs in Scotland *Douglas*	LVIII 181	
MOTION. A ſummary of the general laws of motion *Wallis*	III 864	III 457
—— Theory of motion - - - - *Wren*	— 867	I 459
—— A ſummary account of the laws of motion *Hugens*	IV 925	— 460
—— Some propoſitions on the parabolic motion of projectiles, written in 1710 - *Taylor*	XXXI 151	VI 299
—— (Aſtronomy) A letter concerning the moon's motion - - *Dunthorne*	XLIV 412	X 78
—— —— A letter concerning the mean motion of the moon's apogee - *Murdocke*	XLVII 62	
—— —— An account of a prize of 100 ducats offered by the Academy of Sciences at Peterſburg, for the beſt anſwer to the queſtion, "Whether the theory of Sir Iſaac Newton is "ſufficient to explain all the irregularities "which are found in the motion of the "moon?" - - - - *Euler*	— 263	
—— —— Of the irregularities in the planetary motions cauſed by the mutual attraction of the planets - - *Walmeſley*	LII 275	
—— —— An eſſay on the connection between the parallaxes of the ſun and moon; their denſities; and their diſturbing forces on the ocean - - - *Murdock*	LVIII 24	
—— (Mechanics) Letter concerning a movement that meaſures time after a peculiar manner, with an account of the reaſon of the ſaid motion - - - *Wheeler*	XIV 647	I 468
—— A diſcourſe proving from experiments, that the larger the wheels of a coach, &c. are, the more eaſily they may be drawn over a ſtone, or ſuch like obſtacle that lies in the way *Anon.*	XV 856	I 503
—— —— Obſervations on a French paper concerning perpetual motion - *Papin*	XV 1240	— 504
—— A diſcourſe concerning gravity, and its properties, wherein the deſcent of heavy bodies, and the motion of projects, is briefly, but fully handled; together with the ſolution of a problem of great uſe in gunnery - *Halley*	XVI 3	— 472

Motacilla. Account of a (new) English Bird of the genus Motacilla. Lightfoot. 75: 8.

+Motion (Astronomy) On the proper motion of the Sun and Solar System. Herschel. 73: 247.

+ Motion (Mechanics) Of the rotatory motion of a Body of any form whatever, revolving, without restraint, about any Axis passing through its center of gravity. Landen 75:311.

On spherical motion - - - - - - - - - - - Wildbore 80:496.

Observations on the theory of the motion and resistance of fluids, with a description of the construction of experiments, in order to obtain some fundamental principle - - - - Vince 1795:24.

Experiments upon the resistance of bodies moving in fluids. —— 1798:1.

	Tranf.	Abridg.
—— —— Further remarks on the inftrument propofed by an anonymous French author for effecting a perpetual motion - - *Papin*	XVI 138	
—— —— An anfwer to the author of the perpetual motion - - *Papin*	— 267	
—— Experiments about the motion of pendulums in vacuo - - *Derham*	XXIV 1785	IV 2 168
—— —— Remarks of fome attempts made towards a perpetual motion - - *Defaguliers*	XXXI 234	VI 323
—— The greateft effect of engines, with uniformly accelerated motions confidered - *Blake*	LI 1	
—— An experimental enquiry concerning the natural powers of water and wind to turn mills and other machines depending on a circular motion - - *Smeaton*	— 100	
—— A letter containing a demonftration of a law of motion, in the cafe of a body deflected by two forces, tending conftantly to two fixed points *Robertfon*	LIX 74	
—— A new theory of the rotatory motion of bodies affected by forces difturbing fuch motion *Landen*	LXVII 266	
—— An inveftigation of the principles of progreffive and rotatory motion - *Vince*	LXX 546	
—— (Force of moving bodies) A letter concerning an experiment, whereby it has been attempted to fhew the falfity of the common opinion, in relation to the force of bodies in motion *Pemberton*	XXXII 57	— 276
—— An account of fome experiments made to prove that the force of moving bodies is proportionable to their velocities - *Defaguliers*	— 269	— 281
—— Animadverfions upon fome experiments relating to the force of moving bodies; with two new experiments on the fame fubject *Defaguliers*	— 285	— 285
—— A remark upon the new opinion relating to the forces of moving bodies, in the cafe of the collifion of non-elaftic bodies - *Eames*	XXXIV 183	— 287
—— Remarks upon a fuppofed demonftration, that the moving forces of the fame body are not as the velocities, but as the fquares of the velocities - - - *Eames*	— 188	— 289
—— A letter occafioned by the prefent controverfy among mathematicians, concerning the proportion of velocity and force in bodies in motion - - *Samuel Clarke*	XXXV 381	— 294
—— An account of an experiment contrived by G.		

	Tranf.	Abridg.
J. Gravefande, relating to the force of moving bodies, fhewn to the Royal Society by *Defaguliers*	XXXVIII 143	VIII 235
—— An enquiry into the meafure of the force of bodies in motion; with a propofal of an experimentum crucis to decide the controverfy about it - - - *Jurin*	XLIII 423	VIII 174
—— An experimental examination of the quantity and proportion of mechanic power, neceffary to be employed in giving different degrees of velocity to heavy bodies from a ftate of reft *Smeaton*	LXVI 450	
—— Reflections on the communication of motion by impact and gravity - - *Milner*	LXVIII 344	
—— (Motion of fluids) An account of the motion of running water - - *Jurin*	XXX 748	IV 435
—— A defence of the differtation of the motion of running water, againft the animadverfions of P. A. Michelotti - - *Jurin*	XXXII 179	VI 431
—— Remarks upon fome experiments in hydraulics, which feem to prove that the forces of equal moving bodies are as the fquares of their velocities - - - *Eames*	XXXV 343	— 292
—— Of the meafure and motion of running water *Jurin*	XLI 5	VIII 282
With the conclufion - *Jurin*	— 65	
—— (Motion of the earth) An account of a controverfy between Stephano de Angelis of Padua, and J. B. Riccioli, concerning the motion of the earth - - - *Gregory*	III 693	
—— Extract of a letter touching his thoughts of Mr. Hooke's obfervations for proving the motion of the earth - - *Hugens*	IX 90	
—— Extract of another letter relating to the fame fubject - - - *Caffini*		
—— (Electricity) An account of the repetition of an experiment touching motion, given bodies included in a glafs, by the approach of a finger near its outfide; with other experiments on the effluvia of glafs - *Haukfbee*	XXVI 82	VI 2 81
—— (Heat) An experiment to examine what figure and celerity of motion begetteth or increafeth light and flame - - - *Beale*	I 226	
—— Two letters concerning the rotatory motion of glafs tubes about their axes when placed in a certain manner before the fire *Wheeler*	XLIII 341	X 551 III 639

Motion (Anatomy) Some account of the feet of those animals whose progressive motion can be carried on in opposition to gravity. Home. 1816: 149.
Further observations on the feet of animals whose progressive motion can be carried on against gravity. — — —— —— 322.

Motion (Natural history of vegetables) On the motions of the Tendrils of plants. — — — — — — — Knight. 1812: 314.

Observations intended to show that the progressive motion of Snakes is partly performed by means of the ribs Home. 1812 : 163

	Tranſ.	Abridg.
Motion. (Anatomy) An abſtract of an account of five pair of muſcles, which ſerve for different motions of the head - *Dupre*	XXI 13	
With remarks by - *W. Cowper*	— —	— —
—— —— An obſervation upon the motion of the hearts of two urchins, after being cut out *Templer*	VIII 6016	III 69
—— (Natural hiſtory of vegetables) Queries concerning vegetation, eſpecially the motion of the juices of vegetables - *Anon.*	III 797	II 752
—— Experiments concerning the motion of the ſap in trees - *Willoughby and Wray*	IV 963	— 682
—— Extracts of divers letters touching ſome enquiries and experiments, touching the motion of ſap in trees, and relating to the queſtion of the circulation of the ſame - *Liſter*	VI 2119	— 686
A letter relating to ſome particulars in Mr. Liſter's communications - *Willoughby*	— 2125	— 685
Extract of a letter both in relation to the further diſcovery of the motion of juices in vegetables, and removing the difference noted in Mr. Willoughby's letter - *Anon.*	— 2126	— 686
—— Some conſiderations on the deſcent of ſap *Reed*	— 2128	— 687 — 690
Some conſiderations on Mr. Reed's letter, ſhewing in what ſenſe the ſap may be ſaid to deſcend, and to circulate in plants, and the graft to communicate with the ſtock *Beal*	— 2144	— —
—— Obſervations and experiments relating to the motion of ſap in vegetables *Bradley*	XXIX 486	IV 2 302
Mouldiness. Some microſcopical obſervations and curious remarks on the vegetation and exceeding quick propagation of mouldineſs on the ſubſtance of a melon - *Bradley*	XXIX 490	IV 2 308
—— Letter concerning the green mould on firewood - - - *Miles*	XLVI 334	X 748
Mountains. Letter concerning the icy and cryſtalline mountain of Helvetia, called the Gletſcher - - *Muraltus*	IV 982	II 465
—— Experiment concerning reſpiration upon very high mountains - - *Boyle*	V 2038	
—— A farther deſcription and repreſentation of the icy mountain called the Gletſcher in the canton of Bern, in Helvetia - - *Juſtel*	VIII 6191	— —
—— A diſcourſe of the rule of the decreaſe of the height of the Mercury in the barometer, ac-		

for Sap

cording

	Trans.	Abridg.
cording as places are elevated above the surface of the earth, with an attempt to discover the true reason of the rising and falling of the Mercury upon change of weather *Halley*	XVI 104	II 14
—— A relation of the small creatures called sable mice, which have lately come in troops into Lapland, about Thorne, and other places adjacent to the mountains, in innumerable multitudes - - - *Rycaut*	XXI 110	— 871
—— A relation of the bad condition of the mountains about the Tungarouse and Batavian rivers, having their source from thence, occasioned by the earthquake between the 4th and 5th of January, 1699, drawn up from the account given by Tommagon Porbo Nata who had been there - -	XXII 595	— 419
—— The barometrical method of measuring the height of mountains, with two new tables, shewing the height of the atmosphere at given altitudes of Mercury - - *Scheuchzer*	XXXV 537	VI 2 30
—— Remarks on the height of mountains in general, and of those of Swisserland in particular, with an account of the rise of some of the most considerable rivers of Europe - *Scheuchzer*	— 577	— - 35
—— An account of a mountain of iron-ore at Taberg in Sweden - - *Ascanius*	XLIX 30	
—— A short description of some high mountains on which are a great quantity of fossil wood *Hollman*	LI 506	
—— Observations made in Savoy, in order to ascertain the height of mountains by means of the barometer; being an examination of Mr. de Luc's rules delivered in his "Recherches sur les Modifications de l'Atmosphere" *Schuckburg*	LXVII 513	
—— Astronomical observations relating to the mountains of the moon - - *Herschel*	LXX 507	
MOUTH. Letter concerning scales within the mouth *Leeuwenhoek*	XIV 586	III 684
MOXA. Observations on moxa and cotton *Leeuwenhoek*	XII 899	— —
MULBERRY-TREES. A letter concerning an unusual way of propagating mulberry-trees in Virginia, for the better improvement of the silk-work; together with some particulars, tending to the good of that plantation *Moray*	I 201	II 653
—— Of an excellent liquor made with cyder, apples, and mulberries - - *Colepress*	II 502	

Mountains. Observations on the heights of mountains in the north of England. — — Greatorex. 1818: 398.

+ Multinomials (Functions of) on the expansion of any functions of multinomials. Knight: 1811: 49

+ Mummies. Observations on some Egyptian Mummies opened in London. Blumenbach. 1794: 177
Some account of two Mummies of the Egyptian Ibis. - - - - Pearson. 1805: 264

		Tranf.	Abridg.
—— Note of Pliny about the bleeding of the	*Lifter*	III 2069	
MULTINOMIAL. A method of raifing an infinite multinomial to any given power, or extracting any given root of the fame	*De Moivre*	XIX 619	I 90
—— Of the fluents of multinomials, and feries affected by radical figns, which do not begin to converge till after the fecond term	*Simpfon*	XLV 328	X 1
—— An inveftigation of fome theorems, which fuggeft fome remarkable properties of the circle, and are of ufe in refolving fractions, whofe denominators are certain multinomials into more fimple ones	*Landen*	XLVIII 566	
MUMMY. An account of a mummy infpected at London, 1763	*Hadley*	LIV 1	
MURAL QUADRANT. A defcription of an aftronomical mural quadrant, freed from many of the inconveniencies it has hitherto laboured under	*Gerften*	XLIV 507	— 143
MURRAIN IN CATTLE. Vide *Cattle, Diftempers, Inoculation*			
MUSA. Some remarks on the family of plants called mufa	*Garcin*	XXVI 377	VI 2 361
MUSEUM. Letter concerning feveral obfervables in Mr. Thorefby's mufeum	*Thorefby*	XXIII 1070	— - 274 V - 220
—— A catalogue of foffils, fhells, metals, minerals, &c. which J. J. Scheuchzer, of Zurich, fent to J. Petiver	-	XXIV 2042	IV 2286
MUSCLE (fifh). Examination of the tefticles of a rat, and the feed of mufcles, oyfters, &c.	*Leeuwenhoek*	XVII 593	III 685
MUSCLE (Anatomy). Microfcopical obfervations of the carneous fibres of a mufcle	*Leeuwenhoek*	XII 899	III 684
—— A letter containing obfervations upon the feminal veffels, mufcular fibres, and blood of whales	*Leeuwenhoek*	XXVII 438	V 2 267
—— An extract of a letter concerning the fibres of the mufcles	*Leeuwenhoek*	XXIX 55	V 390
—— Concerning the frame and texture of the mufcles	*Muys*	— 59	— 393
—— Obfervations upon the membranes enclofing the fafciculi of fibres, into which a mufcle is divided	*Leeuwenhoek*	XXXI 12	VII 464
—— Obfervations on the mufcular fibres of different animals	*Leeuwenhoek*	— 134	— 468
—— Obfervations on the mufcular fibres of fifh	*Leeuwenhoek*	— 190	— 431

—The

	Trans.	Abridg.
—— A letter concerning the muscular fibres in several animals - - *Leeuwenhoek*	XXXII 72	— 468
—— Crounian lecture on muscular motion -	XL *Supplem.*	
—— The Crounian lectures on muscular motion, read before the Royal Society in 1744 and 1745 - - - *Parsons*	XLIII *Supp.*	XI 1226
—— Observations concerning the salt marsh muscle, the oyster-banks, and the fresh-water muscle of Pennsylvania - - *Bartram*	— 157	XI 860
—— Observations of a fracture of the os humeri, by the power of the muscles only - *Amyand*	— 293	— 1103
—— Observations and experiments upon animal bodies, digested in a philosophical analysis, or enquiry into the cause of voluntary muscular motion - - *Morton*	XLVII 305	
—— The case of William Carey, whose muscles began to be ossified - *Henry*	LI 89	
A further account - - *Henry*	— 91	
A further account - - *Henry*	LII 143	
—— Observations upon the effects of electricity applied to a tetanus, or muscular rigidity of four months continuance - *Watson*	— 10	
—— A cure of a muscular contraction by electricity *Partington*	LXVIII 97	
—— Some microscopical observations upon muscles, and the manner of their production *Leeuwenhoek*	XXVII 529	
MUSHROOM. A description of an odd kind of mushroom yielding a milky juice, much hotter to the tongue than pepper - *Lister*	VII 5116	II 623
—— A letter concerning the seeds of mushrooms *Pickering*	XLII 593	VIII 812
Some remarks of the above *W. Watson*	— 599	— 815
—— Further remarks concerning mushrooms, occasioned by the Rev. Mr. Pickering's paper, with observations on the poisonous faculty of some sort of fungi - *W. Watson*	XLIII 51	X 790
—— On the propagation and culture of mushrooms *Pickering*	— 96	X 788
—— See *Fungus*		
MUSIC. Letter concerning a new musical discovery *Wallis*	XII 839	I 606
—— A discourse concerning the musical notes of the trumpets and trumpet-marine, and of the defects of the same - *Roberts*	XVII 559	— 607
—— A question in music lately proposed to Dr. Wallis, concerning the division of the mono-		

1746. Parsons. XLIV after 333.
1747. Langrish —— after 749.
1787. Fordyce. 78:23.
1790. Home, 1795: 202.
1793. Some facts relative to the late Mr. J. Hunters preparation for the Croonian lecture. Home. 1794:21.
1794. Home. 1795:1.
1795. Home 1796:1.
1796. —— 1797:1.
1798. —— 1799:1.
1799. —— 1800:1.
1800. —— 1801:1.
1801. —— 1802:1.
1804. Carlisle. 1805:1.
1805. —— 1806:1.
1808. Young 1809:1.
1809. Wollaston 1810:1.

chord

+ Music. Of the temperament of those musical Instruments, in which the Tones, Keys, or Frets, are fixed, as in the Harpsichord, Organ, Guitar &c. Cavallo. 78: 238.

	Transf.	Abridg.
chord, or section of the musical canon; with his answer to it - - *Wallis*	XX 80	I 610
—— Letter concerning the strange effects reported of musick in former times beyond what is reported of later ages - - *Wallis*	— 297	— 618
—— The theory of musick reduced to arithmetical and geometrical proportions - *Salmon*	XXIV 2069	
—— A letter of the various genera and species of music among the ancients, with some observations concerning their scale - *Pepusch*	XLIV 266	X 261
—— A letter, inclosing a paper of the late Rev. Mr. Creed, concerning a machine to write down extempore voluntaries, or other pieces of music *Freke*	— 445	— 265
—— Account of one, who had no ear to music naturally, singing several tunes when in a delirium *Doddridge*	— 596	XI 1084
—— An explanation of the modes or tones in the ancient Græcian music - *Stiles*	LI 695	
MUSICIAN. Account of a very remarkable young musician - *Barrington*	LX 54	
—— Account of an infant musician - *Burney*	LXIX 183	
MUSK. The extraordinary effect of musk in convulsive disorders - - *Wall*	XLIII 212	— 1044
—— A remarkable instance of the happy effects of musk, in a very dangerous case *Parsons*	XLIV 75	— 1055
MUSK SMELLING ANIMALS. An account of some insects smelling of musk - *Ray*	VI 2219	II 783
Confirmation of the observation about musk-scented insects, adding some notes upon Dr. Swammerdam's book of insects, and on that of Steno, concerning petrified shells *Lister*	— 2281	II 783
Discovery of another musk-scented insect *Lister*	— 3002	— 792
MUSK HOG. Tajacu seu aper Mexicanus moschiferus, or the anatomy of the Mexico musk-hog *Tyson*	XIII 359	— 873
MUSTELA. The figure of the mustela fossilis *Gronovius*	XLIV 451	XI 874
MYOPES. A way for Myopes to use telescopes without eye-glasses, an object glass becoming as useful to them, and sometimes more so than a combination of glasses *Desaguliers*	XXX 1017	IV 188

	Transf.	Abridg.
MYRRH. Some obfervations upon myrrh, made in Abyffinia in the year 1771, fent to Dr. Hunter, with fpecimens, in February, 1775 *Bruce*	LXV 408	

N.

	Transf.	Abridg.
NÆVUS MATERNUS. Several letters concerning a particular nævus maternus, or mole *Steigertahl*	XXXIII 347	VII 485
NAIL. An account of one who had horny excrefcencies, or extraordinary large nails on his fingers and toes - - - *Locke*	XIX 694	
NAIN. Two meteorological journals kept at Nain, in 57 degrees north latitude, and at Okak, in 57 degrees 30 minutes north latitude, both on the coaft of Labradore - *De la Trobe*	LXIX 657	
NAMUR. Account of the cachot, or rooms cut in the rock of the caftle in Namur - *Ellis*	XXIII 1416	V 2 134
NAPELLUS. See *Monk's Hood*		
NAPLES. Remarks upon the nature of the foil of Naples, and its neighbourhood *Hamilton*	LXI 1	
Extract of another letter on the fame fubject *Hamilton*	— 48	
—— See *Catacombs*		
NARHUAL, OR UNICORN FISH. An account of a Narhual, or Unicorn Fifh, lately taken in the river Oft, in the Dutchy of Bremen, 1739 *Steigertahl*	XL 147	IX 71
A defcription of the fame fifh *Hampe*	— 149	— 72
NASSAU. Remarks on the ftones in the Country of Naffau, and the territories of Cleves and Colen, refembling thofe of the Giants Caufeway in Ireland - - *Trembly*	XLIX 581	
NATRON. Experiments and obfervations about the natron of Egypt, and the Nitrian water *Leigh*	XIV 609	II 525
NATURAL HISTORY (Mifcellaneous). General heads for a natural hiftory of a country, great or fmall - - *Boyl*	I 186	III 361
—— —— Divers inftances of peculiarities of nature,		

both

Myxine. On the mode of generation of the Lamprey and Myxine. — Home. 1815: 265.

Nardus indica. Account of — — — — — — — — Blane. 80: 284.

Narhual. On the tusks of the Narwhale. — — Home. 1813: 126.

	Transf.	Abridg.
both in men and brutes - *Fairfax*	II 549	III 191 — 287
—— —— An account of some of the natural things, with which Sig. P. Boccone of Sicily hath lately presented the Royal Society *Anon.*	VIII 6158	II 492 — 493 — 821
—— —— Observations in natural history made in Scotland - - - *Mackenzie*	X 396	III 539
—— —— Extracts of four letters relating to the natural productions of Virginia - *Banister*	XVII 667	II 822 III 631
With an additional note - *Hooke*	— 691	II 786
—— —— Some observations concerning some wonderful contrivances of nature in a family of plants in Jamaica, to perfect the individuum, and propagate the species, with several instances analogous to them in European vegetables - - - *Sloane*	XXI 113	— 669
—— —— Some natural observations made in the parishes of Kinardsey and Donington, in Shropshire - - *Plaxton*	XXV 2418	V 2 112
—— —— A letter containing several observations in natural history, made in travels through Wales *Lhwyd*	XXVII 462	V 34 V 2 117
With further account of the birds mentioned in it - - - *Lhwyd*	— 466	V 34
And farther observations - *Lhwyd*	— 467	V 2 118
—— —— Letter giving a further account of what he met with remarkable in natural history and antiquities in his travels through Wales *Lhwyd*	— 500	— - 120
—— —— Several observations relating to the antiquities and natural history of Ireland, in his travels through that kingdom - *Lhwyd*	— 503	— - 125
Some farther observations - *Lhwyd*	— 524	— - 126
—— —— Extracts of letters containing observations in natural history and antiquities in his travels through Wales and Scotland - *Lhwyd*	XXVIII 93	— - 120 — - 123
—— —— Several observations in natural history, made at North Bierley, in Yorkshire *Richardson*	XXVIII 167	— - 115
—— —— An account of some observations relating to natural history, made in a Journey to the Peak in Derbyshire - - *Martyn*	XXXVI 22	VI - 190 — - 333
—— —— A remark on T. Hardouin's amendment of a passage in Pliny's natural history, lib. II. 74 - - - *Folkes*	XLIV 365	XI 1378
—— —— An account of glasses of a new contrivance		

for

		Tranf.	Abridg.
for preserving pieces of anatomy or natural history in spirituous liquors — *Le Cat*		XLVI 6	XI 1349
Addition — — *Le Cat*		— 88	— —
—— A specimen of the natural history of the Volga — *Forster*		LVII 312	
—— An account of birds sent from Hudson's Bay, with observations relative to their natural history; and Latin descriptions of some of the most uncommon — — *Forster*		LXII 382	
NAVEL. Account of a fœtus voided by the ulcered navel of a negro in Nevis — *Brodie*		XIX 580	III 219
—— Account of a woman who voided the greatest part of a fœtus by the navel — *Birbeck*		XXII 1000	
—— Account of a rupture of the — *Taube*		XLIII 50	XI 1027
—— A letter concerning the bones of a fœtus being discharged through an ulcer near the navel *Drake*		XLV 121	— 1019
NAVIGATION. Certain problems touching some points of navigation — — *Mercator*		I 215	I 576
—— A summary relation of what hath hitherto been discovered in the matter of the North-East Passage — — *Anon.*		X 417	III 610
—— What a compleat treatise of navigation should contain — — *Petty*		XVII 657	I 571
—— A method for rowing men of war in a calm *Du Quet*		XXXI 239	VI 439
—— An account of a new machine, called the marine surveyor, contrived for the mensuration of the way of a ship in the sea, more correctly than by the log, or any other method hitherto used for that purpose, together with several testimonials setting forth the usefulness of this invention, — — *Saumarez*		XXXIII 411	— 444
NAVIGATORS. An advertisement necessary for all Lizard and Scilly navigators bound up the channel of England laid down too far northerly *Anon.*		XXII 725	— 585
NAUTILITES. A beautiful Nautilite shewn to the Royal Society by the Rev. Charles Lyttleton		XLV 320	X 639
NEAGH. A letter concerning Lough-Neagh in Ireland, and its petrifying qualities *Molyneux*		XIV 552	II 322
—— A retraction of the 7th and last paragraph of Mr. W. Molyneux's letter, vol. XIV. p. 552, concerning Lough-Neagh Stone, and its non-application to the magnet upon calcination *Molyneux*		— 820	— 323

+ Nebulæ. Account of one in Coma Berenices. E. Pigott. 71: 82.
Catalogue of one thousand new Nebulæ and clusters of Stars. Herschel. 76: 457.
Cat. of a second thousand of new Nebulæ and clusters of Stars. —— 79: 212
On nebulous stars, properly so called. - - - - - - - —— 81: 71.
Catalogue of 500 new nebulæ, nebulous stars, planetary nebulæ, and clusters of stars. - - - - - - - - - —— 1802: 477.

+ Nerves. Experiments on the Nerves, particularly on their reproduction. Cruikshank. 1795: 177.
An experimental inquiry concerning the reproduction of Nerves. Haighton. —— 190.
Experiments and observations upon the structure of nerves. Home. 1799: 1.
On the irritability of Nerves. —— 1801: 1.
Experiments and observations on the influence of the Nerves of the 8th pair on the secretions of the Stomach. Brodie. 1814: 102
On the influence of the Nerves upon the action of the Arteries. — — — Home. —— 583.
Experiments made with a view to ascertain the principle on which the action of the Heart depends and the relation which subsists between that organ and the Nervous system. — — Philip. 1815: 65.

	Tranf.	Abridg.
—— An anfwer to fome queries concerning Lough-Neagh - - - - *Smyth*	XV 1168	II 324
—— Some obfervations of Lough-Neagh in Ireland *Nevill*	XXVIII 260	V 2 193
—— A letter concerning the petrifaction of Lough Neagh, with a letter from the bifhop of Cloyne on the fame fubject - *Simon and Berkley*	XLIV 305	X 616
NEBULÆ. An account of feveral nebulæ, or lucid fpots like clouds, lately difcovered among the fixed ftars by help of the telefcope - *Halley*	XXIX 390	IV 225
NECK. Letter concerning a horn hanging to the neck of an ox, with obfervations on horns and glandules in general - - *Malpighius*	XIV 601	II 865
—— An obfervation of an infant, where the brain was depreffed into the hollow of the vertebræ of the neck - - - *Tyfon*	XIX 533	III 26
—— An account of a very large tumour in the fore part of the neck - - - *Douglas*	XXV 2214	V 213
—— An obfervation of a tumour on the neck full of hydatides cured by - *Hewnden*	—— 2344	—— 216
NEEDLE. See *Magnet*		
NEGRO. An account of a negro boy that is dappelled in feveral parts of his body with white fpots - - - - *Byrd*	XIX 781	II 8
—— An account of the remarkable alteration on the colour of a negro woman - *Bate*	LI 759	
—— An account of a white negro fhewn before the Royal Society - - *Parfons*	LV 45	
NERVES. Obfervations concerning the optic-nerve *Leeuwenhoek*	X 378	III 683
—— Obfervations on the optic-nerve *Leenwenhoek*	XVII 949	—— 685
—— Experiments to prove the exiftence of a fluid in the nerves - - *Stuart*	XXXVII 327	VII 585
—— Effay on the ufe of the ganglions of the nerves *Johnftone*	LIV 177	
NESS. Letter concerning the Lake Nefs, &c. *Frafer*	XXI 230	II 322 III 538
NESTS. An account of fome very curious wafps nefts made of clay in Pennfylvania - *Bartram*	XLIII 363	
—— Some obfervations upon an American wafps neft *Mauduit*	XLIX 205	XI 847
See Java Swallows		
NEW CALEDONIA. See *Darien*		
NEW ENGLAND. Account of fome natural curiofities, and a very ftrange and curioufly contrived fifh from New England - *Winthrop*	V 1151	III 564

—— Natural

	Tranſ.	Abridg.
—— —— Natural obſervations made at Boſton in New England - - *Bullivant*	XX 167	III 565
—— —— An extract of ſeveral letters from Cotton Mather from New England - *Mather*	XXIX 62	V 159
—— —— Obſervations of remarkable inſtances of the nature and power of vegetation in New England - - - *Dudley*	XXXIII 194	VI 2 342
—— —— An account of an extraordinary diſeaſe among the Indians in the iſlands of Nantucket and Martha's Vineyard in New England - - - *Oliver*	XLIV 386	
NEWGATE. An account of ſeveral perſons ſeized with the gaol fever, working in Newgate, and of the manner in which the infection was communicated to one intire family *Pringle*	XLVIII 42	
NEWTON. A demonſtration of the 11th propoſition of Sir Iſaac Newton's treatiſe of quadratures *Robins*	XXXIV 230	VI 60
—— A demonſtration of Sir Iſaac Newton's formula for raiſing a multinomial to any power *Caſtilloneus*	XLII 91	VIII 10
—— A true copy of a paper found in the hand-writing of Sir Iſaac Newton, among the papers of the late Dr. Halley, deſcribing an inſtrument for obſerving the moon's diſtance from the fixed ſtars at ſea - - *Anon.*	— 155	— 129
—— An account of a prize of 100 ducats offered by the Academy of Sciences at Peterſburg, for the beſt anſwer to the queſtion, "Whether the "theory of Sir Iſaac Newton is ſufficient to "explain all the irregularities which are "found in the motion of the moon?" *Euler*	XLVII 263	
—— Remarks upon a paſſage in Caſtillione's life of Sir Iſaac Newton - - *Winthrop*	LXIV 153	
—— See *Chronology, Equation, Light*		
NEW YORK. The longitude of Liſbon, and the Fort of New York, from Wanſtead and London, determined by eclipſes of the firſt ſatellite of Jupiter - - - *Bradley*	XXXIV 85	VI 412
NIAGARA RIVER. An account of the Falls of the river Niagara taken at Albany, Oct. 10, 1741 *Boraſſaw*	XXXII 69	VI 2 173
NIGHTSHADE. A brief botanical and medical hiſtory of the ſolanum lethale, bella-donna, or deadly nightſhade - *W. Watſon*	L 62	
NIN-ZIN or GINSENG. A new genus of plants, called Araliaſtrum, of which the famous nin-zin or		

Nerves. Some additional experiments and observations on the relation which subsists between the nervous and sanguiferous systems. — — Phil. Tr. 1815: 424.

+ Nitre. The action of it on Gold and Platina. - - - - Tennant. 1797: 219.

+ Nitrous Acid. Experiments on the phlogistication of Spirit of Nitre. Priestley. 79: 139.
On the production of nitrous Acid and nitrous Air - - - - Milner — 300.

		Transf.	Abridg.
ginfeng of the Chinefe is a fpecies	*Vaillant*	XXX 705	IV 2 219
NISOL. An hiftorico-phyfical obfervation on the brafs-waters of Nifol, commonly called Cement-Wafzfer, changing iron to brafs	*Belius*	XL 351	VIII 645
NITRE. A probable conjecture about the original of the nitre of Ægypt	*Lifter*	XV 836	II 529
—— A catalogue of thofe oils that will take fire with a great noife, when the compound fpirit of nitre is poured upon any of them; and of thofe oils which do only make a great noife and explofion, but will not take fire, and alfo of them that do not make effervefcence or explofion	*Anon.*	XVIII 200	III 358
—— An experiment concerning the nitrous particles in the air	*Clayton*	XLI 62	VIII 465
—— Manner of preparing nitre in Poland	*Wolf*	LIII 356	
NITRIAN WATER. Experiments and obfervations about the natron of Egypt, and the nitrian water	*Leigh*	XIV 609	III 525
NITROUS ACID. Actual fire in detonation, produced by the contact of tinfoil, with the falt compofed of copper and the nitrous acid	*Higgins*	LXIII 137	
—— —— See *Acid*			
NITROUS AIR. See *Air*			
NODES. An account of the appearance of Mercury paffing over the fun's difk, on the 29th of October, 1723, determining the mean motion, and fixing the nodes of that planet's orb	*Halley*	XXXIII 228	VI 253
—— A treatife on the preceffion of the equinoxes, and in general on the motion of the nodes, and the alteration of the inclination of the orbit of a planet to the ecliptic	*Silvabelle*	XLVIII 385	
NOLI ME TANGERE. See *Cancer*			
NORFOLK. Extract of a letter concerning obfervations on the precipices or cliffs on the north eaft coaft of Norfolk	*Arderon*	XLIV 275	X 589 — 592
—— An account of large fubterraneous caverns in the chalk hills near Norwich	*Arderon*	XLV 244	— 593
NORFOLK BOY. Obfervations on the hiftory of the Norfolk boy	*Wall*	L 836	
NORTH EAST PASSAGE. A fummary relation of what hath been hitherto difcovered in the matter of the North Eaft Paffage	*Anon.*	X 417	III 610

	Transf.	Abridg.
NORTHERN COUNTRIES. Of the diseases incident to, and remedies of northern countries *Lloyd*	XXI 310 311	II 660
NORTHERN REGIONS. A dissertation on the bones and teeth of elephants, and other beasts found in North America, and other northern regions, by which it appears they are the bones of indigenous beasts - - *Raspe*	LIX 126	
NORWOOD. Some observations on Norwood's measure of the figure of the earth *De la Lande*	LII 369	
NOSE. Anatomical observations on the structure of the nose - - *Vernoy*	XII 976	III 56
—— Microscopical observations on the substance called worms in the nose - - *Leeuwenhoek*	XIV 568	— 684
NOTES. A discourse concerning the musical notes of the trumpet, and trumpet marine, and of the defects of the same - *Roberts*	XVII 559	I 607
NOVA-ZEMBLA. A letter containing a true description of Nova-Zembla, together with an intimation of the advantage of its shape and position - - - *Anon.*	IX 3	— 570
NOURISHMENT. An account of a puppy in the womb that received no nourishment by the mouth - - - *Brady*	XXIV 2176	V 34
NUMBERS. The squaring of the hyperbola, by an infinite series of rational numbers, together with its demonstration - *Brouncker*	III 645	I 10
—— An account concerning the resolution of equations in numbers - - *Collins*	IV 929	— 60
—— A compendious method for constructing the logarithms, exemplified and demonstrated from the nature of numbers, without any regard to the hyperbola, with a speedy method for finding the number from the logarithm given *Halley*	XIX 58	— 108
—— On the use of numeral figures in England, as old as 1090 - - *Luffkin*	XXI 287	III 265
—— Letter concerning the use of the numeral figures in England in 1090 *Wallis*	XXII 677	I 108
—— An attempt towards the improvement of the method of approximating in the extraction of the roots of equations in numbers *Taylor*	XXX 610	IV 80
—— Κοσκινον Ερατοσθενους, or, the Sieve of Eratosthenes, being an account of his method of finding all the prime numbers *Horsley*	LXII 327	

ee figures.

Some properties of the Sum of the Divisors of Numbers - - - Waring 78: 388

—— See *Equations*

Numeral figures, see Figures.

	Tranf.	Abridg.
—— See *Equations*		
NUREMBERG. An account shewing that the latitude of Nuremberg has continued without sensible alteration for 200 years last past, as likewise the obliquity of the ecliptic, by comparing them with what was observed by B. Walther, in 1487 - - *Wurtzelbaur*	XVI 403	I 262
NUTMEGS. An extract of a letter containing microscopical observations - *Leeuwenhoek*	XVII 949	III 685
NUX VOMICA. An account of the virtues of Faba S. Ignatii - - *Anon.*	XXI 87	II 648
—— Farther and more exact account of the same Igasur, seu nux vomica legitima serapionis *Camelli*	— 88	— 649
—— Letter on Swammerdam's treatise "de Faba S. Ignatii" - - - *Hotton*	— 365	— 648 — 652
NYCTANTHES ELONGATA. A description and figure of the nyctanthes elongata, a new Indian plant - - - *Bergius*	LXI 289	
NYL-GHAU. An account of the Nyl-ghau, an Indian animal not hitherto described *William Hunter*	— 170	

O.

	Tranf.	Abridg.
OAK-TREES. An account of grass in moors soon parched up in the shape of trees, under which oak trees are found - - *Beale*	I 323	— 423
—— Thoughts about the dwarf-oaks described in vol. V. p. 1151 - - *Willoughby*	V 1200	— 833
—— An account of two oak trees struck by thunder, and of the horn of a large deer found in the heart of an oak - - *Clark*	XLI 235	VIII 847
—— Experiments concerning the use of the agaric of oak in stopping hæmorrhages *Sharp, Warner*	XLVIII 588	
—— A letter giving an account of a new species of oak - - - *Holwell*	LXII 128	
—— See *Agaric*		
OBJECT GLASSES. Judgment touching the apertures of object-glasses, and their proportions in respect of the several lengths of telescopes, together with a table thereof *Auzout*	I 55	I 191
—— Instance

	Trans.	Abridg.
— — Instance to Mr. Hooke for communicating a contrivance of making, with a glass of a sphere of 20 or 40 feet diameter, a telescope, drawing several hundred feet; and his offer of recompensing that secret with another, teaching to measure, with a telescope, the distances of objects upon the earth *Auzout*	I 123	
— — A way for Myopes to use telescopes without eye-glasses, an object-glass alone becoming as useful to them, and sometimes more, than a combination of glasses *Desaguliers*	XXX 1017	IV 188
— — Letters relating to a theorem of Mr. Euler for correcting the aberrations in the object-glasses of refracting telescopes, by *Short, Euler, and Dollond*	XLVIII 287	
— — An account of some new microscopes made at Naples, and their use in viewing the smallest objects - - *Stiles*	LV 246	
— — A method of working the object-glasses of refracting telescopes truly spherical *Short*	LIX 507	
— — See *Telescopes*		
OBSERVATORY. Letter concerning the remains of the observatory of the famous Tycho Brahe *Gourdon*	XXII 691	I 216
— The difference of longitude between the Royal Observatories of Greenwich and Paris, determined by the observations of the transits of Mercury over the sun in 1723, 1736, 1746, 1753 - - - *Short*	LIII 158	
~~— Description and use of a new constructed equatorial or portable observatory *Nairne*~~	~~LXI 107~~	
~~— A comparative table of the corresponding observations of the first satellite, made in the principal observatories - *Wargentin*~~	~~LXVII 162~~	
— An account of the Bramin's observatory at Benares - - *Barker*	— 598	
OBSTRUCTION. A method proposed to restore the hearing, when injured from an obstruction of the tuba eustachiana - *Wathen*	XLIV 213	
OCCULTATION. An occultation of Mars, and certain fixed stars, observed at Dantzig, Sept. 1, 1676, - - *Hevelius*	XI 721	I 350
— An observation of Mars covered by the moon, Aug. 21, 1676, at Greenwich - *Flamstead*	— 723	
Halley	— 724	— —
— An account of an occultation of Venus by the		

[illegible] [illegible]les. See Ships.

+ Observatory. Further particulars respecting the Observatory at Benares. Williams. 1793: 45.

	Transf.	Abridg.
moon, Sept. 19, 1729, at Berlin *Kirchius*	XXXVI 256	VI 352
—— Observations of the occultation of Mars by the moon, Oct. 7, 1736, Fleet-street *Graham*	XL 100	VIII 186
Covent-garden - - *Bevis*	— 101	
—— Observations of an occultation of Palilicius, at Berlin, Dec. 23, 1738 - - *Kirchius*	XLI 223	— 134
Witenberg - - - *Weidler*	— 225	
—— An occultation of Jupiter and his satellites by the moon, Oct. 28, 1740 - *Graham*	XLI 647	— 184
—— An account of an occultation of Jupiter by the moon, June 6, 1744, London - *Bevis*	XLIII 65	X 95
—— An observation on an occultation of Cor Leonis, by the moon, on Thursday, March 12, 1747, in Surry-street, in the Strand, London, with a reflecting telescope, made by Mr. Short, which magnified above 100 times *Bevis*	XLIV 455	— 110
—— An occultation of the planet Venus by the moon in the day-time, observed at London, April 16, 1751 *Bevis*	XLVII 159	
—— Observations of the occultations of Venus by the moon, April 16, 1751 *Bradley*	— 201	
—— Account of occultations of the fixed stars by the moon, that will happen in 1763, proper to determine the exact difference of longitude betwixt London, Paris, and Greenwich *De la Lande*	LII 607	
—— Occultation of fixed stars by the moon, observed at Greenwich, 1769 *Maskelyne*	LIX 399	
—— An account of an occultation of the star ξ Tauri by the moon, observed at Leicester *Ludlam*	LX 355	
—— Occultation of α and γ Tauri by the moon *Lexel*	LXV 280	
—— See *particular Occultations in their Places*		
OCEAN. Advice touching the conjunction of the Ocean with the Mediterranean - *Petit*	I 41	III 683
—— A narrative of the conjunction of the two seas, the Ocean, and the Mediterranean, by a channel cut out through Languedoc in France *Oldenburg*	IV 1123	——
—— Additions to the narrative about the conjunction of the ocean and the Mediterranean, by a channel in France - *Froidour*	VII 4080	III 683
—— An essay on the connection between the parallaxes of the sun and moon, their densities,		

	Transf.	Abridg.
and their disturbing forces on the ocean *Murdock*	LVIII 24	
ODOURS. Letter declaring that he, as well as many others, have not been able to make odours pass through glass by means of electricity, and giving a particular account of Professor Bose, at Wittemberg, his experiments of beatification, or causing a glory to appear round a man's head by electricity - *W. Watson*	XLVI 348	X 410
—— An account of experiments relating to odours passing through electrified globes and tubes *Winkler*	XLVII 231	
With an account of the result of some experiments made here with globes and tubes, transmitted by Mr. Winkler, in order to verify the facts above mentioned *W. Watson*	— 236	
OENANTHE AQUATICA. Critical observations concerning the œnanthe aquatica succo viroso crocante, of Lobel *W. Watson*	XLIV 227 L 856	— 765
OIL. An account of the making pitch, tar, and oil, out of a blackish stone in Shropshire *Ele*	XIX 544	
—— Letter concerning the efficacy of oil of olives in curing the bite of vipers - *Williams*	XL 26	IX 66
—— An account of some cases of dropsies cured by sweet oil - *Oliver*	XLIX 46	
OIL OF ORANGES. An account of an experiment touching the direction of a drop of the oil of oranges, between two glass planes, towards any side of them that is nearest, pressed together - - *Hauksbee*	XXVII 395	IV 2 182
—— —— An account of an experiment, concerning the angle required to suspend a drop of oil of oranges, at certain stations, between two glass planes, placed in the form of a wedge *Hauksbee*	— 473	— —
OKAK. Two meteorological journals kept at Nain, in 57 degrees north latitude, and at Okak, in 57 degrees 38 minutes, north latitude, both on the coast of Labradore *De la Trobe*	LXIX 657	
OMBRIÆ. An account of certain transparent pebbles, mostly of the shape of the ombriæ *Lister*	XVII 778	II 467
OMBROMETER. Description of the ombrometer *Pickering*	XLIII 12	XI 1030

Cythae. Observations on the genus Cythae of Rafinesque; with a description of a new species. — — Acad. 1817: 298.

Ophidium barbatum Linn. Account of — Broussonet 71: 436.

	Trans.	Abridg.
Omentum. Observations on a large omentum *Huxhan.*	XXXIII 60	VII 518
Opal. Letter about the making of counterfeited opal - - *Colepress.*	III 743	III 685
Ophris. An account of a species of ophris, supposed to be the plant mentioned by Gronovius in the Flora Virginica, p. 185 *Ehret*	LIII 81	
Opium. Of the use of opium amongst the Turks *Smyth*	XIX 288	II 643
—— An account of a person who took a great quantity of opium without causing sleep *Anon.*	XXII 999	V 357
Opossum. Carigueya seu Marsupiale Americanum, or the anatomy of an opossum - *Tyson*	XX 105	II 881
—— The anatomy of a male opossum with observations - - *Cowper*	XXIV 1565	
—— The anatomy of a male opossum, with observations on the opossum, and a new division of terrestrial brute animals, particularly those that have feet formed like hands, where an account is given of some animals not yet described - - - *Tyson*	— —	V 177
—— A letter to Dr. Tyson, giving an account of the anatomy of those parts of a male opossum that differ from the female - *Cowper*	— 1576	— 169
Optick Glasses. An account of an improvement of optick glasses - *Ciampani*	I 2	I 193
—— —— Considerations upon Mr. Hooke's new instrument for grinding of optick glasses *Auzout*	— 56	— 215
Answered - - - *Hooke*	— 63	— 192
—— —— A further account touching Signor Campani's book and performances about optick glasses - *Auzout*	— 69	
Sig. Campani's answer, and M. Auzout's animadversions thereon - - -	— 74	
—— —— Of M. Hevelius's promise of imparting to the world his invention of making optick glasses, and of the hopes given by M. Hugens of Zulichem, to perform something of the like nature; as also of the expectations conceived of some ingenious persons in England, to improve telescopes - - *Hevelius Hugens & Du Sons*	— 98	— 193
—— —— An account of the tryals, made in Italy, of Campani's new optick glasses - *Anon.*	I 131	I 193 II 845
—— —— A contest between two artists about optick glasses - *Campani & Divini*	— 209	I 193

—— An

	Tranf.	Abridg.
—— —— An obfervation of optick glaffes made of rock-cryftal - - *Divini*	I 362	I 195
—— —— An account of the invention of grinding optic and burning glaffes of a figure not fpherical - - *Smethwick*	III 631	— 194
—— A letter concerning an optical experiment, conducive to a decayed fight - *Anon.*	— 727	III 41
Another, confirming the former, and adding fome other obfervations about fight *Anon.*	— 729	II 864
A note relating to the above *Anon.*	— 765	
Another note on the fame, about the fmall empty tubes - - *Anon.*	— 802	
—— A contrivance to make the picture of any thing appear on a wall, cup-board, or within a picture-frame, &c. in the midft of a light room *Hooke*	— 741	I 206
—— Letters about an optic problem of Alhazen *Slufius, Hugenius*	VIII 6119	— 172 — 174
Continuation of the letters *Slufius, Hugenius*	— 6140	II 290
Some optical affertions concerning the rainbow - - - *Linus*	X 386	I 315
—— An inftance of the excellence of the modern dern algebra in the refolution of the problem of finding the foci of optic glaffes univerfally *Halley*	XVII 960	— 183
—— An account of an optical experiment made before the Royal Society - *Defaguliers*	XXXII 206	VI 145
—— Experiments made in Auguft, 1728, before the Royal Society upon occafion of Signor Rizzetti's opticks with an account of that book *Defaguliers*	XXXV 607	— 110
—— An obfervation made in opticks *Edwards*	LIII 229	
—— See *Light and Colours.*		
OPTIC NERVE. Microfcopical obfervations concerning the optic nerve - *Leeuwenhoek*	X 378	III 683
—— —— Obfervations on the cryftalline humours, optic nerves, &c. - *Leeuwenhoek*	XVII 949	— 685
OPUNTIA. The effects of the opuntia, or prickly-pear, and of the indigo plant, in colouring the juices of living animals - *Baker*	L 296	
ORANG-OUTANG. Account of the organs of fpeech of the Orang-outang - *Camper*	LXIX 139	
ORANGES. Some hortulan communications about the curious engrafting of oranges and lemons, or citrons, upon one another's trees, and of one individual fruit, half orange and half lemon, growing on fuch trees - *Anon.*	II 553	II 568

4 Optics. Experiments and calculations relative to physical optics. Young. 1804:1.

Organic remains. See Fossils.

Ornithorhynchus paradoxus. Some observations on its head. Home. 1800: 432.

A description of the anatomy of the Ornithorhynchus paradoxus. —— 1802: 67.

Hystrix. —— —— 348.

	Transf.	Abridg.
—— A philological obſervation concerning oranges and lemons, both ſeparately, and in one piece, produced on one and the ſame tree, at Florence *Nate*	X 313	— 658
ORATAVA. An account of a journey from the port of Oratava, in the iſland of Teneriffe, to the top of the pike in that iſland, in Aug. 1715, with obſervations made thereon, by *Edens*	XXIX 317	V 2 148
ORBS. A direct and geometrical method by which the aphelia, excentricities and proportions of the orbs of the principal planets may be determined without ſuppoſing the equality of the angle of motion at the other of focus the planet's ellipſis - - *Halley*	XI 683	I 258
—— An account of the appearance of Mercury paſſing over the ſun's diſk, on the 29th of October, 1723; determining the mean motion, and fixing the nodes of that planet's orb *Halley*	XXXIII 228	VI 253
ORBIT. The curve aſſigned by Caſſini to planets as their orbit, conſidered and refuted *Gregory*	XXIV 1704	IV 206
—— The parabolic orbit for the comet of 1739, obſerved at Bologna - - *Zanotti*	XLI 809	VIII 215
—— A treatiſe on the preceſſion of the equinoxes, and in general on the motion of the nodes, and the alteration of the inclination of the orbit of a planet to the ecliptick *Silvabelle*	LXVIII 385	
ORCADES. An account of the current of the tides about the Orcades - - *Anon.*	VIII 6139	II 290
ORES. An examination of various ores in the muſeum of Dr. W. Hunter *Fordyce and Alchorne*	LXIX 529	
ORGAN. Letter on ſome ſuppoſed imperfections in an organ - - *Wallis*	XX 249	I 612
ORKNEY. An abſtract from an account of the iſlands of Orkney, by *James Wallace*	XXII 543	
ORRERY. The phænomena of Venus repreſented in an orrery made by Mr. James Ferguſon, agreeable to the obſervations of Signior Bianchini - - -	XLIV 127	X 95
ORTHOCERATITES. An account of a remarkable foſſil orthoceratites - *Wright*	XLIX 670	
Another account - *Wright*	— 672	
—— An account of a rare ſpecies of, found in Sweden - - - *Himſel*	L 692	
OSCILLATION. On the finding of the centre of oſcillation - - *Taylor*	XXVIII 11	IV 384

	Tranf.	Abridg.
Os FEMORIS. Account of a callus that supplied the loss of the os femoris — *Sherman*	XXVI 450	V 54
Os FRONTIS. See *Bone*		
Os HUMERI. An account of the cure of two sinuous ulcers possessing the space of the whole arm, with the extraordinary supply of a callus, which fully answers the purposes of the os humeri lost in time of cure — *Fowler*	XXV 2466	V 388
——— Part of a letter concerning the coming off of the scapula and head of the os humeri, upon a mortification — *Derante*	XXXII 15	VII 676
——— Observations of a fracture of the os humeri by the power of the muscles only — *Amyand*	XLIII 293	XI 1103
——— An account of a woman enjoying the use of her right arm after the head of the os humeri was cut away — *Bent*	LXIV 353	
——— A case in which the head of the os humeri was sawn off, and yet the motion of the limb preserved — *Orred*	LXIX 6	
Os ILIUM. An account of a fracture of the os ilium, and its cure — *Layard*	XLIII 537	X 1110
Os PUBIS. Account of a woman who voided the bones of a fœtus above the os pubis, and by other extraordinary ways *Phil. Society at Oxford*	XX 292	III 219
OSSICLES. A description of the organ of hearing in the elephant, with the figures and situation of ossicles, labyrinth, and cochlea, in the ear of that animal — *Blair*	XXX 885	V 82
OSSIFICATION. Account of an ossification of the thoracic duct — *Chefton*	LXX 323	
Continuation of the case of James Jones *Chefton*	— 578	
OSTEOCOLLA. Letter concerning osteocolla, and other observables near Francfort on the Oder *Beckman*	III 771	II 461
——— An enquiry concerning the stone osteocolla *Beurerus*	XLIII 373	X 602
OSTRACITES. Part of a letter concerning the virtues of the ostracites, with a remark of Mr. Lister's on it — *Cay*	XXI 81	II 505
OSTRICH. Some observations made in an ostrich dissected by order of Sir Hans Sloane *Ranby*	XXXIII 223	VII 435
——— Observations upon the dissection of an ostrich *Warren*	XXXIV 113	— 437

——— Some

Ovum. On the passage of the Ovum from the ovarium to the uterus in women. — — — Home. 1817: 252.
The distinguishing character between the Ova of the Sepia, and those of the Vermes testacea that live in water explained — — — 297.

+ Ovarium. An experiment to determine the effect, of extirpating one Ovarium, upon the number of young produced. Hunter. 77: 233.
An account of a particular change of structure in the human ovarium. Baillie 79: 71.
The case of a full grown woman in whom the Ovaria were deficient. Pears. 1805: 225.

Oxalic acid. On Oxalic Acid. – – – – – – – Thompson. 1808: 63.

Oxygene. See [illegible].

Oxymuriatic acid. Researches on the oxymuriatic acid, its nature and combinations. Davy. 1810: 231.
On some of the combinations of oxymuriatic gas and Oxygene, and on the chemical relations of these principles, to inflammable bodies. Davy. 1811: 1.
On a combination of oxymuriatic gas and oxygene gas. Davy. 1811: 155

		Tranf.	Abridg.
——— Some material observations upon dissecting an ostrich - - - *Ranby*		XXXVI 275	VII 437
OTIS MINOR. Letter concerning the pheasant of Pennsylvania - - *Edwards*		XLVIII 499	
OVA. An account of the dissection of a bitch, whose cornua uteri being filled with the bones and flesh of a former conception, had, after a second conception, the ova affixed to several parts of the abdomen - - - *Anon.*		XIII 183	II 964
OVALS. The principal properties of the engine for turning ovals in wood or metals, and of the instrument for drawing ovals upon paper, demonstrated - - *Ludlam*		LXX 378	
OVARIUM. An observation concerning a very odd kind of dropsy or swelling of one of the ovaries of a woman - - *Sloane*		~~XXI 150~~ *(see Dropsy)*	~~III 207~~
——— An account of balls of hair taken from the uterus and ovaria of several women *Yonge*		XXV 2387	
——— An account of a dropsy in the left ovary of a woman aged 58, cured by a large incision made in the side of the abdomen *Houstoun*		~~XXXIII 8~~ *(see Dropsy)*	~~VII 541~~
——— Two newly discovered arteries, in women, going to the ovaria - - *Ranby*		XXXIV 159	— 541
OX. Letter concerning a horn hanging to the neck of an ox, with observations on horns and glandules in general - - *Malpighius*		XIV 601	II 865
——— An extract giving an account of a large præter-natural glandulose substance, found between the heart and pericardium of an ox *Anon.*		XV 860	III 69
——— Microscopical observations on the palates of oxen *Leeuwenhoek*		XXVI 294	V 2 267
——— A letter serving to accompany the pictures of an extraordinary fossil-skull of an ox, with the cores of the horns - *Klein*		XXXVII 427	VII 4 101
OXYOIDES. Memoirs containing a description of a new family of plants called oxyoides *Garcin*		XXXVI 377	VI 2 357
OYLS. A catalogue of those oyls that will take fire with a great noise and explosion, when the compound spirit of nitre is poured upon any of them, and of those oyls which do only make a great noise and explosion, but will not take fire; and also of those that do not make effervescence or explosion - *Anon.*		XVIII 200	III 358

	Transf.	Abridg.
OYSTERS. Obfervations about fhining worms in oyfters - - *Auzout*	I 203	III 826
—— Microfcopical examination of the tefticles of a rat, and the feed of mufcles and oyfters, &c. *Leeuwenhoek*	XVII 593	— 685
—— Obfervations on young oyfters *Leeuwenhoek*	XIX 790	— 685
—— Account of beds of oyfter-fhells found near Reading, Berkfhire - - *Brewer*	XXII 844	
—— Part of a letter concerning the ftocking the river Mene with oyfters - *Rowlands*	XXXI 250	VII 420
—— Obfervations on the oyfter-banks of Pennfylvania - - *Bartram*	XLIII 157	XI 860
—— A letter concerning the animal-life of thofe corallines, that look like minute trees, and grow upon oyfters and fucus's all around the fea-coaft of this kingdom (see Corallines) *Ellis*	XLVIII 627	

P.

PÆSTUM. Elucidation of an Etrufcan coin of Pæftum, in Lucania, emitted from the mint there, about the time of the focial war *Swinton*	LVIII 246	
PAGAN TEMPLE. An explanation of the figures of a Pagan temple, and unknown characters, at Canara, in Salfet - - *Stuart*	XXVI 372	V 260
PAIN. An account of the probable caufes of the pain in Rheumatifms; as alfo of the cure of a total fuppreffion of urine, not caufed by the ftone, by the ufe of acids - *Baynard*	XIX 19	III 265
PAINTING. A relation of the conferences held at Paris, in the Royal Academy, for the improvement of the arts of painting and fculpture *Journal des Scavans*	IV 953	I 603
—— Letter judging of the age of painters by the ftyle - - *Wanley*	XXIV 1993	V 21
—— An account of the principles of printing, in imitation of painting - *Blon*	XXXVII 101	VI 469
—— Extract of a letter concerning an ancient method of painting, revived by Count Caylus *Mazeas*	XLIX 652	

Painting. Some experiments and observations on the colours
used in painting by the Ancients. — Davy. 1815: 97.

Palladium. Enquiries concerning the nature of a metallic substance
lately sold in London, as a new metal, under the title of Palladium. Chenevix. 1803: 290.
On the Discovery of Palladium Wollaston. 1805: 316.
On native Palladium from Brazil. ——— 1809: 189.

	Trans.	Abridg.
— Observations on the Abbé Mazeas's letter on the count de Caylus's method of imitating the ancient painting in burnt-wax *Parsons*	XLIX 655	
— Experiments concerning the encaustic painting of the ancients *Colebrooke*	LI 40	
A letter concerning the success of the former experiments *Colebrooke*	— 53	
— An account of some subterraneous apartments with Etruscan inscriptions and paintings discovered at Civita Turchino, in Italy *Wilcox*	LIII 127	
PALATE. Microscopical observations on the palates of oxen - *Leeuwenhoek*	XXVI 294	VI 2 267
PALILICIUS. Observation of an occultation of Palilicius, at Berlin, Dec. 23, 1738 *Kirchius*	XLI 223	VIII 134
Wirtenberg *Weidler*	— 225	
PALM-STONES. Microscopical observations on palm and date stones, *Leeuwenhoek*	XVII 949	III 685
PALMYRA. A relation of a voyage from Aleppo to Palmyra, in Syria *Halifax*	XIX 83	— 505
— An extract of the journals of two several voyages of the English merchants of the factory of Aleppo, to Tadmor, anciently called Palmyra - *Anon*	— 129	— 492
— Some account of the ancient state of the city of Palmyra, with short remarks upon the inscriptions found there - *Halley*	— 160	— 518
— A dissertation upon a Parthian coin, with characters on the reverse, resembling those of the Palmyrenes — - - *Swinton*	XLIX 593	
PALPITATION. On the palpitation of the diaphragm *Leeuwenhoek*	XXXII 436	VII 562
PALSY. An abstract of a letter, giving an instance of the bath water curing the palsy, and barrenness - *Pierce*	XV 944	II 339
— Letter concerning a periodical palsy - *Musgrave*	XX 257	III 33
— Letter concerning an uncommon palsy in the eye-lids - - *Cantwell*	XL 311	IX 121
— An account of an Iliac passion from a palsy in the large intestines - *De Castro*	XLVII 123	
— An account of a cure of a paralytic arm by electricity - - *Hart*	XLIX 558	
— An instance of the electrical virtue in the cure of a palsy - - *Brydone*	L 392	

	Trans.	Abridg.
—— An account of the effects of electricity in paralytic cases - - *Franklin*	— 481	
—— The case of a paralytic patient cured by an electrical application - *Himsel*	LI 179	
PANCREAS. An account of a monstrous human fœtus, having neither head, heart, lungs, stomach, spleen, pancreas, liver, nor kidneys *Le Cat*	LVII 1	
PANTHEON. An account of the alterations making in the pantheon at Rome - *Anon.*	L 115	
PAPAVER CORNICULATUM LUTEUM. An account of some effects of the papaver corniculatum luteum - - *Newton*	XX 263	III 297
PAPER. Some account of the paper money current among the Chinese - *Gaubil*	XLVI 327	XI 1364
—— An account of an essay on the origin of a natural paper, found near the city of Cortona, in Tuscany - - *Strange*	LIX 50	
—— Of the culture and use of the son or sun-plant of Hindostan, with an account of the manner of manufacturing the Hindostan paper *Ironside*	LXIV 99	
—— The principal properties of the engine for turning ovals in wood or metal, and of the instrument for drawing ovals upon paper demonstrated - - *Ludlam*	LXX 378	
—— See *Asbestus*		
PAPIN. Letter concerning Dr. Papin's way of raising water - - *Vincent*	XV 1238	I 539
—— Letter concerning Dr. Papin's new water engine - - - *Tenon*	— 1254	— —
PAPPUS OF ALEXANDRIA. Two general propositions of his, taking in a great part of Euclid's porisms restored - - *Simpson*	XXXII 330	VI 76
PARABOLA. Cubic and biquadratic equations constructed by one parabola and circle *Halley*	XVI 335	I 63
—— Some propositions on the parabolic motion of projectiles, written in 1710 - *Taylor*	XXXI 151	VI 299
—— The parabolic orbit for the comet of 1739, observed at Bologna - *Zanotti*	XLI 809	VIII 215
—— A short narrative of the structure and effect of parabolic burning-glasses, made by Mr. Hoesen, of Dresden, and an account of experiments made with them on the fusion of different substances - - *Wolfe*	LIX 4	
—— Directions for making the best composition for		

Parallax. On the annual parallax of α Lyræ. — — — — Brinkley, 1810: 204.

On the parallax of α Aquilæ. — — Pond. 1818: 477.

	Transf.	Abridg.
the metals of reflecting telescopes; together with a description of the process for grinding, polishing, and giving the great speculum the true parabolic curve - *Mudge*	LXVII 296	
PARABOLOEID. Letter asserting the first invention and demonstration of the equality of the curve line of a paraboloeid to a straight line, and next the finding a straight line equal to that of a cycloid, and of the parts thereof *Wallis*	VIII 6146	I 193
Two other letters to the same purpose *Anon.*	— 6149	
PARABOLIC GLASSES OF M. DE SONS. Progress in working parabolar glasses - *Oldenburg*	I 119	
—— A short narrative of the structure and effect of parabolic burning glasses made by Mr. Hoesen, of Dresden, and an account of experiments made with them on the fusion of different substances - - *Wolf.*	LIX 4	— 116 — —
PARALLAX. See *Eclipse, Moon, Planets, Sirius, Sun, Stars*		
PARACENTESIS. An anatomical account of some remarkable things found on the dissection of a woman who died of a dropsy, after the Paracentesis was performed, with a small reflection on the causes of the dropsy - *Preston*	XIX 330	III 141
PARAGUAY. Astronomical observations made at Paraguay, in South America, from 1706 to 1730 - - *De Castro Sarmiento*	XLV 667	X 118
PARASELENES. An observation of an extraordinary lunar circle, and of two paraselenes made at Paris, Oct. 20, 1747 - *Grischow*	— 524	— 483
PARDINES. A narrative of an extraordinary sinking down and sliding away of some ground at Pardines, near Auvergne - *Anon.*	XLI 272	
PAREIRA BRAVA. An extract of a letter concerning pareira brava, a root from Brasil, where it is called the Universal Remedy, with the preparations of it - *Helvetius*	XXIX 365	V 404
PARENCHYMOUS. Some considerations concerning the parenchymous parts of the body *King*	I 316	III 17
PARHELIA. An account of four suns seen in France *Journal des Scavans*	— 219	II 186
—— An account of two parhelias or mock suns lately seen in Hungary, Jan. 30, 1668 *Brown*	IV 953	— 186
—— Discourse concerning the cause of halos and parhelias - - *Hugens*	— 1086	— 185 — 189

	Transf.	Abridg.
PARHELIA. Extract of a letter concerning some parhelia seen at Sudbury, in Suffolk, Dec. 28, 1698 - - - *Petit*	XXI 107	II 187
— An observation of some parhelia seen at Canterbury, Feb. 26, 1692-3. - *Gray*	— 126	— 187
— An account of an unusual parhelion and halo, April 7, 1699 - - *Gray*	XXII 535	— 188
— An account of the appearance of several unusual parhelia, or mock suns, together with several circular arches lately seen in the air *Halley*		
— Observations of a parhelion, Oct. 26, 1721 *Halley*	XXIII 1127	IV 228
— An account of two mock suns, and an arc of a rainbow inverted, with an halo, and its brightest arc seen on Sunday and Monday, Oct. 22 and 23, 1721, at Lyndon, in Rutland - - - *Whiston*	XXXI 211	VI 2 75
— An account of a parhelion, seen in Ireland, March 22, 1721-2. - *Dobbs*	— 212	— 76
— An account of four mock suns, seen at Kensington, March 1, 1726 - *Whiston*	XXXII 89	— 77
— Observations of two, seen December 30, 1735 *Neve*	XXXIV 257	— 79
— An observation of two parhelia, or mock suns, seen at Wirtemberg, in Saxony, Dec. 31, 1735 - - *Weidler*	XL 52	VIII 508
— An observation of three mock suns, seen at London, Sept. 17, 1736 - *Folkes*	— 54	— 509
— A representation of the parhelia seen in Kent, Dec. 19, 1741 - *Miles and Tennison*	— 59	
— Concerning the mock suns seen Dec. 19, 1741 *Collinson*	XLII 46	— 515
— A letter, giving an account of an halo, or mock sun, with a representation, observed July 1749, from Mr. Arderon - *Baker*	— 60	— 525
PARIS. An extract of two essays in political arithmetick, concerning the comparative magnitudes of London and Paris - *Petty*	XLVI 196	XI 1295
A further assertion of the propositions and vindication from the objections of some learned persons of the French nation - *Petty*	XVI 152	
	— 237	
— Some reflections on Mr. de Lisle's comparison of the magnitude of Paris with London and several other cities, printed in the Memoirs of the Academy of Sciences at Paris - - *Davall*	XXXV 432	VI 426
— A letter concerning observations to be made on the parallax of the moon at St. Helena, and re-		

commending

+Parhelia. Description of a set of Halo's and Parhelia seen in 1771 in North-america. Baxter. 77:44.

	Tranf.	Abridg.
commending the corresponding ones to be made at Paris and Greenwich; also observations of Jupiter's satellites, recommended to settle the difference of longitude between Paris, Greenwich, and St. Helena - *Maskelyne*	LII 26	
PAROQUET. Observations in the dissection of a paroquet - - - *Waller*	XVIII 153	II 855
PARR, THOMAS. An anatomical account concerning Thomas Parr, who died in London, aged 152 years and nine months - *Harvey*	III 886	III 306
PARSNIP. A letter concerning the medicinal effects of a poisonous plant exhibited, instead of the water-parsnip - - *Pulteney*	LXII 469	
PARTHIAN COIN. A dissertation upon a Parthian coin, with characters on the reverse, resembling those of the Palmyrene's *Swinton*	XLIX 593	
——— Conjectures upon an in-edited Parthian Coin *Swinton*	LI 680	
——— Description of two Parthian coins, never hitherto published - *Swinton*	LVI 296	
PARTURITION. Dissection of a woman who died in child-bed - - *Silvestre*	XXII 787	V 303
——— An account of an hydrops ovarii, with a new and exact figure of the glandulæ renales, and of the uterus in a puerpera - *Douglas*	XXV 2317	— 294
——— An account of the Cæsarian operation performed by an ignorant butcher - *Copping*	XLI 814	
PASSION FLOWER. A letter containing some microscopical observations on the farina fœcundans of the holyoak and the passion flower *Badcock*	XLIV 150	X 753
Further observations and experiments on the passion flower and its farina - *Badcock*	— 166	— 756
PASTE. A letter concerning the minute eels in paste being viviporous - *Sherwood*	— 67	XI 799
PASTINACA MARINA. An account of the tongue of a pastinaca marina, frequent in the seas about Jamaica, and lately dug up in Maryland and England - - *Sloane*	XIX 674	II 431
PASTURE. Part of a letter concerning worms observed in sheeps livers, and pasture-grounds *Leeuwenhoek*	XXIV 1522	V 2 266
PATAGONIA. An account of the very tall men seen near the Straights of Magellan, in 1764, by the equipage of the Dolphin man of war, under the command of captain Byron *Clarke*	LVII 75	
——— Letter on the inhabitants of the coast of Patagonia - - *Carteret*	LX 20

	Transf.	Abridg.
PATELLA. Part of a letter concerning a case in chirurgery, which is commonly mistaken for a fracture of the patella - - *Deverel*	XXXI 44	VII 678
—— An account of the patella or limpet fish of Bermudas - - - *Forbes*	L 859	
PAVEMENT. An accurate account of a tessellated pavement, bath, and other Roman antiquities lately discovered at East Bourne, in Sussex *Tabor*	XXX 549	V 2 63
—— The rest of the treatise concerning the scite of the ancient city of Anderida, and other remains of antiquity in the County of Sussex *Tabor*	— 783	— 71
—— A description of a Roman pavement found near Grantham, in Lincolnshire, with the oeconomy of the Roman times in this part of England - - *Stukeley*	XXXV 428	VII 4 29
PAUL's, SAINT. Proposal of a method for securing the cathedral of St. Paul's from damage by lightning, in consequence of a letter from the dean and chapter to James West, Esq. *Committee of the Royal Society*	LIX 160	
PEAK. An account of some observations relating to natural history made in a journey to the Peak in Derbyshire - - *Martyn*	XXXVI 22	VI 2 190
PEARS. Some communications concerning cyder *Reed*	VI 2128	II 687
—— The propriety of pears for some lands; their choice for manifold uses, especially for pleasant, or for lasting liquor; and how they are to be planted and ordered to the best advantage *Beal*	— 2144	— 653
—— Account of a double pear - *Anon.*	XXII 470	— —
—— See *Opuntia*		
PEARLS. Extract of two letters concerning the origin of pearls - - *Sandius*	IX 11	— 827
—— A letter concerning pearl-fishing in the North of Ireland - - - *Redding*	XVII 659	I 607
PEAS. Observations of the effects which the farina of peas of different colours have on each other *Henchman*	XLIII 477	
PEAT. An account of the peat-pit near Newbury, in Berkshire - - *Collet*	L 109	
—— Experiments and observations upon a blue substance found in the peat-moss, in Scotland *Douglas*	LVIII 181	

	Trans.	Abridg.
Pebbles. An account of certain transparent pebbles, mostly of the shape of the Ombriæ or Brontiæ *Lister*	XVII 778	II 467
—— Part of a letter concerning the formation of pebbles - *Arderon*	XLIV 467	X 608
Pecquet. Answer to him concerning the opinion that the choroeides is the principal organ of sight - *Marriotte*	V 1023	II 833
Peculiarities. Divers instances of peculiarities of natures, both in men and brutes *Fairfax*	II 549	III 191 — 287
Pediculus Cæti. A description of the pediculus cæti - *Sibbald*	XXV 2314	V 25
Pediculus Pulsatorius. Letter concerning an insect that is commonly called the death-watch - *Derham*	XXII 832	
—— A supplement to the account of the pediculus pulsatorius, or death-watch, serving to the more perfect natural history of that insect *Derham*	XXIV 1586	— 28
Peking. A description of the plan of Peking, the capital of China - *Gaubil*	L 704	
Pelvis. Anatomical observations of an abscess in the liver; a great number of stones in the gall-bag and bilious vessels; an unusual conformation of the emulgents and pelvis; a strange conjunction of both kidnies, and a great dilation of the vena cava - *Tyson*	XII 1035	III 81
—— An account of a large glandular tumour in the pelvis; and of the pernicious effects of crude Mercury, given inwardly to a patient *Cantwell*	XL 139	IX 184
—— An account of a bone found in the pelvis of a man at Brussels - - *Brady*	LI 660	
Pen-Fish. An account of the sea-pen, or Pennatula phosphorea of Linnæus; likewise a description of a new species of sea-pen found on the coast of South-Carolina, with observations on sea-pens in general *Ellis*	LIII 419	
Pendulum. A narrative concerning the success of pendulum-watches at sea for discovering the longitudes - - *Holmes*	I 13	I 555
—— Instructions concerning the use of pendulum-watches, for finding the longitude at sea, together with a method of a journal for such watches - *Hugens*	IV 937	— 547
—— Experiments about the motion of pendulums in vacuo - - *Derham*	XXIV 1785	IV 2 168
—— A contrivance to avoid the irregularities in a		

clock's

	Trans.	Abridg.
clock's motion, occasioned by the action of heat and cold upon the rod of the pendulum *Graham*	XXXIV 40	VI 297
PENDULUM. An account of some observations made in London by Mr. Graham, and at Black River, in Jamaica, by Colin Campbell, concerning the going of a clock, in order to determine the difference between the lengths of isochronal pendulums in those places *Graham, Campbell, and Bradley*	XXXVIII 302	VII 238
—— Experiments concerning the vibrations of pendulums - - *Derham*	XXXIX 201	VIII 245
—— An account of the influence which two pendulum clocks were observed to have upon each other - - - *Ellicott*	XLI 126	— 246
Further observations and experiments *Ellicott*	— 128	
—— A commentary of some new observations to discover whether pendulums are obstructed by any centrifugal force - - *Polenus*	XLII 299	— 250
—— Two methods by which the irregularity of the motion of a clock arising from the influence of heat and cold upon the rod of the pendulum may be prevented - *Ellicot*	XLVII 479	
—— Letter concerning the inventor of the contrivance in the pendulum of a clock to prevent the irregularities of its motion by heat and cold - - - *Short*	— 517	
—— See *Clock*		
PENGUIN. An account of the different species of the birds called penguins - - *Pennant*	LVIII 91	
PENIS. An account of an extraordinary flux of the blood by the penis - *Howman*	XXXII 418	VII 539
PENNATULA PHOSPHOREA. An account of the sea pen, or pennatula phosphorea of Linnæus; likewise a description of a new species of sea pen found on the coast of South Carolina, with observations on sea pens in general *Ellis*	LIII 419	
PEN-PARK-HOLE. A description of Pen-Park-Hole, in Gloucestershire - - *Southwell*	XIII 2	II 370
PENNSYLVANIA. Observations on the oyster banks of Pennsylvania - - *Bartram*	XLIII 157	XI 860
PEPPER. A description of an odd kind of mushroom yielding a milky juice, much hotter upon the tongue than pepper - *Lister*	VII 5116	II 623

+ Pendulum. Account of a new Pendulum. - - - - - - - - - Fordyce. 1794: 2.

An account of experiments for determining the length of the Pendulum vibrating seconds in the latitude of London Kater. 1818: 33.

P Percussion. The Bakerian lecture on the force of percussion. Wollaston. 1806:13.

	Trans.	Abridg.
—— Observations concerning some little animals observed in rain, well, sea, and snow water; as also in water where pepper had laid infused *Leeuwenhoek*	XII 821	III 683
With the manner of observing them *Leeuwenhoek*	— 844	— —
—— A description of the pimienta, or Jamaica pepper tree - - *Sloane*	XVII 462	II 663
—— Several observations and experiments on the animalcula in pepper-water *Sir Edmund King*	— 861	III 654
PERCUSSION. An essay on the force of percussion *Richardson*	LVIII 17	
PERICARDIUM. An extract, giving an account of a large præter-natural substance found between the heart and pericardium of an ox *Anon.*	XV 860	— 69
PERIOSTEUM. Observations upon the bones and the periosteum - - *Leeuwenhoek*	XXXI 91	VII 672
PERITONÆUM. Case of a large quantity of matter or water contained in cystis's or bags adhering to the peritonæum, and not communicating with the cavity of the abdomen *Graham*	XLI 708	IX 187
PERRY. An account of some improvements which may be made in cyder and perry - *Miles*	XLIII 516	
PERSEPOLIS. A letter containing the exact draughts of several unknown characters, taken from the ruins at Persepolis - *Flowers*	XVII 775	III 526
—— A letter, with two draughts of the famous Persepolis - - *Witsen*	XVIII 117	— 527
PERSIA. Inquiries for Persia - *Royal Society*	II 420	— 632
—— Observations upon five antient coins struck in Palestine, or Phœnicia, before the dissolution of the Persian empire - *Swinton*	LXI 345	
PERSON. Part of a letter concerning a person who had a new set of teeth after 80 years of age; with some observations upon the virtues and properties of sugar - - *Slare*	XXVIII 273	V 353
PERSPECTIVE. The description of an instrument, invented divers years ago, for drawing the outlines of any object in perspective *Wren*	IV 898	I 598
PETRIFACTION. Of a place in England, where, without petrifying water, wood is turned into stone - - *Boyle*	I 101	II 325
—— Observables touching petrifaction - *Beale*	— 320	III 149
An addition to the instances of petrifaction *Packer*	— 329	II 325
—— A narrative of two petrifactions in human bodies - - *Kirkby*	VI 2158	III 150 — 158

	Tranſ.	Abridg.
PETRIFACTION. A deſcription of certain ſtones figured like plants, and by obſerving men eſteemed to be plants petrified - *Liſter.*	VIII 6181	II 493
—— Extracts of ſeveral letters from Edinburgh of a petrifying rivulet, &c. - *Mackenzy*	X 307	— 321
Advertiſements of petrifying and metallizing waters in Scotland - *Beal*	— 357	
—— A letter concerning Lough-Neagh, in Ireland, and its petrifying qualities - *Molyneux*	XIV 552	— 322
—— A catalogue of the minerals, petrified ſhells, and other foſſils, ſent from C. M. Spencer of Berlin to J. Petiver - *Anon.*	XXIV 2082	IV 2 286
—— An account of part of two human ſkeletons petrified - - *Scheuczer*	XXXIV 38	VI 2 205
—— Account of the petrifaction near Matlock Baths in Derbyſhire; with conjectures concerning petrifaction in general - - *Gilks*	XLI 352	VIII 707
—— An extract of a philoſophical account of a new opinion concerning the origin of petrifactions found in the earth, which has hitherto been aſcribed to the univerſal deluge, by Sig. Antonio Lazzaro Moro - *Zollman*	XLIV 163	X 615
—— A letter concerning the petrifaction of Lough-Neagh in Ireland, to which is annexed a letter from Dr. Berkley, Biſhop of Cloyne, to Thomas Prior, Eſq. - - *Simon*	— 305	— 616
—— Letter concerning a non-deſcript petrified inſect *Lyttelton*	XLVI 598	— 656
—— A deſcription of a petrified ſtratum, formed from the waters of Matlock in Derbyſhire *Dobſon*	LXIV 124	
—— Account of a petrifaction found on the coaſt of Eaſt Lothian - - *King*	LXIX 35	
PETT. An account of Grace Pett, at Ipſwich, whoſe body was conſumed to a coal - *Rolli*	XLIII 447	XI 1068
PEWTER MONEY. Letter concerning pewter money coined in Ireland, by the late King James *Thoreſby*	XXIV 1875	V 2 31
PHÆNOMENA. Letters concerning the cauſe of the aſcent of vapour and exhalation, and thoſe of winds, and of the general phænomena of the weather and barometer - *Eeles*	XLIX 124	
PHEASANT. Letter concerning the pheaſant of Pennſylvania - - *Edwards*	XLVIII 499	
—— An account of a bird, ſuppoſed to have been bred between a turkey and a pheaſant *Edwards*	LI 833	

+ Petrifactions. Conjectures relative to the Petrifactions found in St. Peter's Mountain near Maestricht — — — — — Camper 76:443.

Phlogiston. Experiments relating to Phlogiston. - - - - Priestley. 73:398. 78:147, 313.
79:7. 289.

	Tranſ.	Abridg.
—— A deſcription of a beautiful Chineſe pheaſant *Edwards*	LV 88	
—— An account of an extraordinary pheaſant *John Hunter*	LXX 527	
PHILIPPINE ISLANDS. An account of the animals in the Philippine Iſlands - *Camelli*	XXIII 1065	V 183
Obſervations on the birds of the Philippine Iſlands - - *Camelli*	— 1394	— —
—— A deſcription of ſome corals, and other curious ſubmarines, lately ſent from the Philippine Iſles, by G. J. Camelli - - *Petiver*	— 1419	IV 2 286
—— An account of the quadrupeds in the Philippine Iſlands - - *Camelli*	XXV 2197	
—— Account of ſome monſters and ſerpents there *Camelli*	— 2266	V 183
—— An account of the ſhells, minerals, and foſſils there - - *Camelli*	— 2397	
—— An extract of two letters concerning the diſcovery of the New Philippine iſlands, with a map of the ſame - *Miſſionary Jeſuits*	XXVI 189	V 2 185 — - 189
PHILISTIS. Some obſervations on an inedited Greek coin of Philiſtis, Queen of Syracuſe, Malta, and Gozo, who had been paſſed over in ſilence by all antient writers - *Swinton*	LX 80	
PHILOSOPHY. Particulars of a philoſophical nature *Hevelius*	V 2023	I 304
—— An intimation of divers philoſophical particulars now undertaken and conſidered by ſeveral ingenious and learned men, here inſerted to excite others to join with them in the ſame or like attempts and obſervations *Anon.*	VI 2216	II 2
—— Some reflections on the Tranſactions of April, 1675, ſent to the publiſher out of the country	X 305	
—— Conſiderations upon N° 133 of theſe tracts *Anon.*	XII 890	
—— Some philoſophical experiments *Southwell*	XX 363	I 214
PHOCA. Some account of the phoca, vitulus marinus, or ſea calf, ſhewed in London, in 1743 *Parſons*	XLII 383	IX 74
—— A diſſertation upon the claſs of phocæ marinæ - - - *Parſons*	XLVII 109	
PHOENICIAN. Some remarks upon the firſt part of M. l'Abbé Barthelemy's memoir on the Phoenician letters, relative to the inſcription in the iſland of Malta - - *Swinton*	LIV 119	
—— Farther remarks upon M. l'Abbé Barthelemy's memoir on the Phœnician letters, containing		

his

	Transf.	Abridg.
his reflections on certain Phœnician monuments, and the alphabets resulting from them - - - *Swinton*	LIV 393	
—— An attempt to interpret the legend and inscription of a very curious Phœnician medal never hitherto explained - - *Swinton*	LVII 266	
PHOENICIA. Observations on five antient Persian coins, struck in Palestine or Phœnicia, before the dissolution of the Persian empire *Swinton*	LXI 345	
PHOENICOPTERUS. The natural history and description of the phœnicopterus or flamingo, with two views of the head, and three of the tongue - - *Douglass*	XXIX 523	V 63
PHOLAS CONOIDES. An account of the pholas conoides - - *Parsons*	LV 1	
PHOSPHORUS. An account of making phosphorus, deposited with the Secretaries of the Royal Society, Oct. 14, 1680, and opened since his death - - *Boyle*	XVII 583	III 346
—— Experiments on the production and propagation of the light from the phosphorus in vacuo *Hauksb*	XXIV 1865	IV 2 181
—— Several experiments on the mercurial phosphorus *Haukfbee*	—— 2129	—— 180
—— A letter concerning firing phosphorus by electricity - - *Miles*	XLIII 290	X 272
—— An easy method of making phosphorus, that will imbibe and emit light, like the Bolognian stone; with experiments and observations *Canton*	LVIII 337	
—— A letter on his new phosphorus receiving several colours, and only emitting the same *Beccaria*	LXI 212	
PHRENSY. An account of the cure of an inveterate phrensy by the transfusion of blood, at Paris *Denis*	II 617	III 291
PHYSIC. See *medicine*		
PHYSICS. (Natural philosophy) Dr. Wallis's opinion concerning the hypothesis physica nova of Dr. Leibnitius - - *Wallis*	VI 2227	
—— A letter in which the laws of attraction and other principles of physics are shewn *Keill*	XXVI 97	VI 353
—— Astronomical, physical and meteorological observations in 1733 at Wirtemberg *Weidler*	XXXIX 238	VIII 178 —— 550
—— A short account of some new astronomical and physical observations made in Asia *Porter*	XLIX 251

Phosphorus. Experiments on Phosphorus. – – – – – Davy. 1810: 231.

New experiments on the combinations of Phosphorus. —— 1818: 316.

	Tranſ.	Abridg.
Physics. Phyſical and meteorological obſervations, conjectures, and ſuppoſitions *Franklin*	LV 182	
—— An eſſay on pyrometry and areometry, and on phyſical meaſures in general - *De Luc*	LXVIII 419	
Physiognomy. Diſcourſe of phyſiognomy *Gwither*	XVIII 118	III 8
Human Physiognomy explained in the Crounian lectures for 1746 Parsons. XLIV after 393.		
Picture. An experiment of a way of preparing a liquor that ſhall ſink into, and colour, the whole body of marble, cauſing a picture drawn on a ſurface, to appear alſo in the inmoſt parts of the ſtone - *Kircher and Bird*	I 125	I 192 — 603
—— A contrivance to make the picture of any thing appear on a wall, cup-board, or within a picture frame, &c. in the midſt of a light room *Hook*	III 741	— 206
—— Extracts of two letters from Rome, concerning ſome antient ſtatues, pictures, and other curioſities found in a ſubterraneous town, lately diſcovered near Naples - *Paderni*	XLI 484	IX 440
Extract of another letter on the ſame ſubject *Knapton*	— 489	— 442
Extract of another letter on the ſame ſubject *Criſp*	— 493	— —
—— Extract of a letter giving a ſhort account of ſome principal antique pictures, found in the ruins of Herculaneum, at Portici, Naples *Hoare*	XLIV 567	XI 1305
—— Remarks on the principal paintings found in the ſubterraneous city of Herculaneum *Blondeau*	XLVI 14	— 1307
—— See *Herculaneum*		
Pig. The anatomy of a monſtrous pig *Anon.*	XIII 188	II 904
—— A relation of two monſtrous pigs, with the reſemblance of human faces - *Floyer*	XXI 431	— 900
Pigeons. Account of a pond in Somerſetſhire, to which pigeons reſort, but cattle will not drink at it - - - *Beale*	I 323	— 332
Further account of the (pond) vitriolate waters, with ſome particulars touching water *Anon.*	— 359	— 332
Pikes. Obſervations of a large bed of glands, obſerved in the ſtomach of a pike - *Muſgrave*	XIV 699	III 93
Pile Engine. A new theory of the pile engine *Bugge*	LXIX 120	
Pilotage. A recommendation of Hadley's quadrant for ſurveying, eſpecially the ſurveying of harbours, together with a particular application of		

it

	Transf.	Abridg.
it to ſome caſes of pilotage - *Michell*	LV 70	
PIMIENTA. A deſcription of the pimienta, or the Jamaica pepper tree - - - *Sloane*	XVII 462	II 663
PIN. Letter concerning a pin, found in the gizard of a fowl - - *Regnart*	XXIV 2055	V 53
—— Of an inguinal rupture, with a pin in the appendix cœci incruſted with ſtone *Amyand*	XXXIX 329	IX 153
—— An extraordinary caſe of three pins ſwallowed by a girl, and diſcharged at her ſhoulder *Lyſons*	LIX 9	
PINE APPLES. On the culture of pine apples *Baſtard*	LXVII 649	
PINIONS. Account of advantages of a newly invented machine much varied in its effects, and very uſeful for determining the perfect proportion between different moveables acting by levers and wheel and pinion - *Le Cerf*	LXVIII 950	
PIPES. An account of ſeveral experiments concerning the running of water in pipes, as it is retarded by friction and intermixed air; with a deſcription of a new machine, whereby pipes may be cleared of air, as the water runs along, without ſtand-pipes, or the help of any hand - - *Deſaguliers*	XXXIV 77	VI 347
—— A propoſal for warming rooms by the ſteam of boiling water conveyed in pipes along the walls - *Cook*	XLIII 370	XI 1391
—— Short and eaſy methods of finding the quantity and weight of water contained in a full pipe of any given height and diameter of bore, and conſequently to find what degree of power would be required to work a common pump, or any other hydraulic engine, when the diameter of the pump-bore, and the height to which the water is to be raiſed, are given *Ferguſon*	LV 61	
PITCH. An account of the making pitch, tar, and oil out of a blackiſh ſtone in Shropſhire *Ele*	XIX 544	
—— The way of making pitch, tar, roſin, and turpentine near Marſeilles - *Bent*	XX 291	
PITH. Inſtances ſhewing the correſpondence of the pith and timber with the ſeed of the plant; as alſo of the bark or ſap in the bark with the pulp of the fruit, or ſome encompaſſing coat or cod containing the ſeed - *Beal*	IV 919	II 710
PITKEATHLY. An account of the ſulphureous mineral waters of Caſtle Lead, and Fairburn, in the		

country

+ Placenta. Account of a tumour found in the substance of the human placenta. Clarke. 1798:361.

	Trans.	Abridg.
county of Ross and of the salt purging water of Pitkeathly, in the county of Perth, in Scotland *Monro*	LXII 15	
Placenta. Account of a placenta cotyledoniformis *Hartmann*	XX 66	III 208
Plætorian. See *coin*		
Plague. An abridgment of a book intitled, A description of the plague, which happened in Dantzick in 1709 - *Gottwald*	XXVIII 101	
—— Remarks upon the plague at Copenhagen in 1711 - - *Chamberlayn*	— 279	V 381
—— An account of the plague at Constantinople *Timon*	XXXI 14	VII 668
—— An account of some experiments made with the bile of persons dead of the plague at Marseilles, with what appeared upon the dissection of the bodies; as likewise some experiments made with the bile of persons dead of other diseases - - *Deidier*	XXXII 20	
—— Part of a letter concerning a new experiment made with the blood of a person dead of the plague - - *Couzier*	— 103	VII 601
—— Extract of a letter concerning an experiment made with the bile of persons dead of the plague - - - *Deidier*	— 105	— 600
—— Extracts of several letters concerning the plague at Constantinople - *Mackensie*	XLVII 384	
—— Farther account of the late plague at Constantinople - - *Mackensie*	— 514	
—— Answer to queries sent to Constantinople concerning the plague - *Porter*	XLIX 96	
—— An account of the plague at Aleppo *Dawes*	LIII 9	
—— An account of the plague at Constantinople *Mackensie*	LIV 69	
Plane. A new invention of a clock ascendant on a plane inclined - *De Gennes*	XII 1006	I 468
—— An account of an experiment touching the direction of a drop of the oil of oranges, between two glass planes, towards any side of them that is nearest pressed together - *Hauksbee*	XXVII 395	IV 2 182
—— An account of an experiment concerning the angle required to suspend a drop of oil of oranges, at certain stations, between two glass planes, placed in the form of a wedge *Hauksbee*	— 473	— - —
—— An account of an experiment touching the proportion of the ascent of spirit of wine between		

		Transf.	Abridg.
two glaſs planes, whoſe ſurfaces are placed at certain different diſtances from each other	*Haukſbee*	XXVIII 151	IV 2 183
An account of ſome further experiments	*Haukſbee*	— 153	— - —
Farther account -	*Haukſbee*	— 155	— - —
PLANE. A general method of deſcribing curves, by the interſection of right lines, moving about points in a given plane	*Braikenridge*	XXXIX 25	VIII 58
—— A propoſition relating to the contraction of tranſparent lenſes with reflecting planes	*Hadley*	— 185	— 111
—— A general inveſtigation of the nature of the curve, formed by the ſhadow of a prolate ſpheroid upon a plane ſtanding at right angles to the axis of the ſhadow -	*Witchell*	LVII 28	
Planets. A way for taking the diameters of planets	*Auzout*	I 373	I 217
—— A letter touching the invention of dividing a foot into many thouſand parts for mathematic purpoſes - -	*Townley*	II 457	— 218
More ways for the ſame purpoſe	*Hook*	— 459	— 220
A deſcription of the inſtrument for dividing a foot into many thouſand parts, and thereby meaſuring the diameter of planets to great exactneſs	*Hook*	— 541	— 219
—— Conſiderations concerning the geometrick and direct method of Signor Caſſini for finding the apogees, excentricities, and anomalies of the planets - -	*Mercator*	V 1168	— 253
—— Letter concerning the appulſes of the moon for 1673, and the other planets to fixed ſtars, together with an obſervation of the planet Mars - -	*Flamſtead*	VII 5118	
—— The appulſes of the moon and other planets to fixed ſtars, predicted for 1674	*Flamſtead*	VIII 6162	III 149
—— A direct and geometrical method by which the aphelia, excentricities, and proportion of the orbs of the primary planets may be found, without ſuppoſing the equality of the angle of motion at the other focus of the planet's ellipſis - -	*Halley*	XI 683	I 258
—— An aſtronomical diſſertation of the viſible conjunction of the inferior planets with the ſun	*Halley*	XVII 511	— 427
—— The curve aſſigned by Caſſini to planets as their orbit, conſidered and rejected	*Gregory*	XXIV 1704	IV 206

Planets. Observations of the rotation of the Planets round their Axes. Herschel. 71: 115.
Observations on the two lately discovered celestial bodies. —— 1802: 213.
Observations on the nature and magnitude of Mr. Harding's lately discovered star. —— 1805: 31.
Observations and measurements of the Planet Vesta Schroeter 1807: 245.
Observations on the nature of the new celestial body discovered by Dr. Olbers. Herschel —— 260.
Direct and expeditious method of calculating the excentric from the mean anomaly of a planet. Robertson 1816: 127

	Transf.	Abridg.
PLANETS. On the method of determining the places of the planets by observing their near appulses to the fixed stars - *Halley*	XXXI 209	VI 170
—— An inquiry concerning the figure of such planets as revolve about an axis, supposing the density continually to vary from the centre towards the surface - *Clairaut*	XL 277	VIII 90
—— A new and peculiar method of calculating eclipses of the earth, and of any appulses of the moon to planets and fixed stars *Gersten*	XLIII 22	X 55
—— Letter concerning the contraction of the orbits of the planets - - *Euler*	XLVI 356	— 142
—— A treatise on the precession of the equinoxes, and, in general, on the motion of the nodes, and the alteration of the inclination of the orbit of a planet to the ecliptic - *Silvabelle*	XLVIII 385	
—— Of the irregularities in the planetary motions, caused by the mutual attraction of the planets *Walmsley*	LII 275	
—— See *particular Planets in their Places*		
PLANTS. An experiment on aloe Americana serratifolia weighed; seeming to import a circulation of the sap in plants - *Merret*	II. 455	II 645
—— Observations concerning quicksilver found at the root of plants - - *Septalius*	II 493	II 425
—— An account of some rare plants in the Bermudas *Stafford*	III 792	III 561
—— Instances shewing the correspondence of the pith and timber, with the seeds of the plant; as also of the bark, with the pulp of the fruit, or some encompassing coat or cod containing the seed - - - *Beal*	IV. 919	— 710 — 655 — 687
—— Some communications on the descent of sap *Reed*	VI. 2128	— 690
Some considerations on Mr. Reed's letter, shewing in what sense the sap may be said to descend and to circulate in plants, and the graft to communicate with the stock *Beal*	—2144	— 653 — 655 — 690
—— An ingenious account of veins by him observed in plants, analogous to human veins *Lister*	—3052	— 691
—— A further account concerning the existence of veins in all kind of plants; together with a discovery of the membranous substance of those veins, and of some acts in plants resembling those of sense; and also of the agreement of

	Tranſ.	Abridg.
the venal juice in vegetables with the blood of animals, &c. - *Liſter*	VII. 5131	II 693
A note upon Mr. Liſter's obſervations concerning the veins of plants - *Wallis*	VIII. 6060	— 696
Letter taking notice of the foregoing intimations - - *Liſter*	——	— —
PLANTS. A way of making all ſorts of plants, trees, fruits, and legums, grow to an extraordinary bigneſs - - *Anon.*	X 356	— 749
—— Microſcopical obſervations about the texture of the blood, ſap of plants, &c. *Leeuwenhoek*	— 380	III 683
—— Two letters concerning the rock plants, and their growth - - *Beaumont*	XI 724	II 497 — 519
—— Obſervations on ſome animals, and of a ſtrange plant made in a voyage into the kingdom of Congo, *M. Ang de Guattini and Dyoniſius of Placenza*	XII 977	
—— A diſcourſe concerning the effects of the great froſt on trees and plants in 1683, drawn from the anſwer to ſome queries ſent into divers countries, by R. Plott, and from ſeveral obſervations made at Oxford - *J. Bobart*	XIV 766	— 155
—— An account of two plants lately brought from the Cape of Good Hope - *Sloane*	XVII 664	— 672
—— Letters concerning the ſeeds of plants, with obſervations on the manner of the propagation of plants and animals. - *Leeuwenhoek*	— 700	III 685
—— Letter concerning the ſeeds of plants *Joſephus de Aromatariis*	XVIII 150	
—— An account of the lately invented ſtove for preſerving plants in the green houſe in winter *Cullum*	— 191	II 750
—— A catalogue of plants growing within the fortifications of Tangier, in 1673 *Spottſwood*	XIX 239	II 752
—— Part of two letters concerning ſeveral plants, that may be uſefully cultivated for producing graſs or hay *Liſter*	— 412	I 748
—— A catalogue of ſome Guinea plants, with their native names and virtues ſent to James Petiver, and remarks on them by *Petiver*	— 677	II 752
—— An account of ſome Indian plants, with their names, deſcriptions, and virtues *Petiver*	XX 313	II 725
—— Remarks on ſome animals, plants, &c. ſent from Maryland *Petiver*	— 393	— 253
—— Some obſervations, concerning ſome wonderful		

		Tranf.	Abridg.
contrivances of nature, in a family of plants in Jamaica, to perfect the individuum, and propagate the fpecies, with feveral inftance analogous to them in European vegetables	*Sloane*	XXI 113	II 669 — 749
Plants. An account of part of a collection of curious plants and drugs, lately given to the Royal Society by the Eaft India Company	*Sloane*	XXII 579	— 762
Firft book of E. India plants, with their names virtues, and defcriptions, by S. Brown, with fome remarks, by	*J. Petiver*	— 581	
Second book, with remarks, by	*J. Petiver*	— 699	— 752
Third book, with remarks, by	*J. Petiver*	— 843	IV 2 323 — — 183
Fourth book, with remarks, by	*J. Petiver*	— 932	
Fifth book, with remarks, by	*J. Petiver*	— 1007	— — 333
Sixth book, with remarks by	*J. Petiver*	XXIII 105	
Seventh book, with remarks, by	*J. Petiver*	— 1251	— — 326
The eighth book, with remarks, by	*J. Petiver*	— 1450	
—— An account of fome ftones and plants lately found in Scotland -	*Sibbald*	XXII 693	
—— An account of fome plants collected at Chufan, in China, by James Cunningham	*Petiver*	XXIII 1419	— — 286
—— New obfervations on the parts and the ufe of the flower in plants - -	*Morland*	— 1474	— — 305
Plantis Philippensibus scandentibus ~~Part 2~~	*Camelli*	XXIV 1707	— — 325
Part ~~1~~ 2	*Camelli*	— 1763	— — —
Part ~~2~~ 3	*Camelli*	— 1809	— — —
—— ~~Account of the plants fent from the Philipines to James Petiver~~ Pars 4	*Camelli*	— 1816	— — —
—— Letter concerning fome remarkable plants and infects obferved in Spain -	*Breynius*	— 2045	V 10
—— Microfcopical obfervations on the feeds of feveral Eaft Indian plants -	*Leeuwenhoek*	XXV 2205	V 2 267
—— An account of divers rare plants, lately obferved in feveral curious gardens about London, and particularly in the Apothecaries Phyfic Garden at Chelfea - -	*Petiver*	XXVII 375	IV 2 325
—— Some farther account of divers rare plants, lately obferved in feveral curious gardens about London and at Chelfea -	*Petiver*	— 416	— — —
—— An extract of a letter giving an account of fome uncommon plants growing about Penfance and St. Ives, in Cornwall -	*Lhwyd*	— 527	
—— An account of divers rare plants, obferved laft fummer in feveral curious gardens, particularly at Chelfea - -	*Petiver*	XXVIII 33	— — —

—— An

	Tranſ.	Abridg.
PLANTS. An account of divers rare plants obſerved 1713, in ſeveral curious gardens about London, and particularly the Society of Apothecaries Phyſic Garden at Chelſea - *Petiver*	XXVIII 177	IV 2 325
—— An extract of a letter containing ſome remarks of an undeſcribed plant, and ſome particulars obſerved in Wales, by - *Lhwyd*	— 275	V 2 122
—— An account of divers rare plants obſerved in 1714, in ſeveral gardens about London, and particularly the Apothecaries Phyſic Garden, at Chelſea - - *Petiver*	XXIX 229 — 269 — 353	IV 2 325 — - —
—— A new genus of plants, called Araliaſtrum, of which the famous nin-zin or gin-ſeng of the Chineſe, is a ſpecies - *Vaillant*	XXX 705	— - 319
—— A diſcourſe concerning a method of diſcovering the virtues of plants by their external ſtructure *Blair*	XXXI 30	VI 2 362
—— Obſervations upon the ſeeds of plants *Leuewenhoek*	— 200	— - 334
—— Obſervations upon the generation of plants *Blair*	— 216	— - 345
—— Obſervations on ſome plants in New England, with remarkable inſtances of the nature and power of vegetation - - *Dudley*	XXXIII 194	— - 342
—— Memoirs containing a deſcription of a new family of plants called Oxyoides - *Garcin*	XXXVI 377	— - 357
—— Some remarks on the family of plants called Muſa - - *Garcin*	— —	— - 360
—— A botanical invitation to forward an hiſtory of the plants in Swiſſerland *Scheuchzer*	XXXVII 219	— - 380
—— The ſettling of a new genus of plants, called after the Maleyans, Mangoſtans *Garcin*	XXXVIII 232	VIII 755
—— Some experiments concerning the impregnation of the ſeeds of plants - *Logan*	XXXIX 192	— 804
—— Botanical obſervations, giving more accurate deſcriptions of certain plants *Moehring*	XLI 211	— 760
—— The diſcovery of a perfect plant in Semine *Baker*	— 448	— 806
—— A catalogue of plants obſerved in a journey over the Tyrol Alps - - *Ehrhart*	— 547	— 768
—— A letter concerning the wonderful encreaſe of the ſeed of plants, *e. g.* of the upright mallow *Hobſon*	XLII 320	— 824
—— The ſubſtance of ſome experiments of planting ſeeds in moſs - - *Bonnet*	XLV 156	X 795
—— An account of the Biſhop of London's Garden		

	Trans.	Abridg.
at Fulham, with a catalogue of the exotic trees remaining in it, June 25, 1751 *W. Watson*	XLVII 241	
Plants. An account of Aphyllon and Dentaria heptaphylos of Clusius, omitted by Mr. Ray *W. Watson*	— 428	
—— An account of some of the more rare English plants observed in Leicestershire *Pultney*	XLIX 803	
—— Some observations upon the sleep of plants; with an account of that faculty, which Linnæus calls Vigilia Florum, with an enumeration of several plants which are subject to that law *Pulteney*	L 506	
—— An account of a species of ophris, supposed to be the plant mentioned by Gronovius, in the Flora Virginia, p. 185 - *Ehret*	LIII 81	
—— An account of a new Peruvian plant, lately introduced into the English gardens; the several characters of which differ from all the genera hitherto described - *Ehret*	— 130	
—— A letter on the sexes of plants, and impregnation of vegetables - - *Styles*	LV 258	
—— A letter on the success of his experiments for preserving acorns for a whole year, without planting them, so as to be in a state fit for vegetation, with a view to bring over some of the most valuable seeds from the East-Indies, to plant for the benefit of our American Colonies - - *Ellis*	LVIII 75	
—— A letter on a rare plant found in the Isle of Skye, supposed to be the Eriocaulon decangulare - - *Hope*	LIX 241	
—— A description and figure of the nyctanthis elongata, a new Indian plant - *Bergius*	LXI 289	
—— A letter on the effects of elder in preserving growing plants from insects and flies *Gullet*	LXII 348	
—— A letter concerning the medicinal effects of a poisonous plant exhibited instead of the water-parsnip - - *Pulteney*	— 469	
—— An account of three journeys from the Cape Town, in the southern parts of Africa, undertaken for the discovery of new plants, towards the improvement of the Royal Botanical Gardens at Kew - *Mason*	LXVI 268	

—— A

	Trans.	Abridg.
—— A catalogue of fifty plants, lately presented to the Royal Society, by the company of Apothecaries of London; pursuant to the direction of Sir Hans Sloane, Bart. President of the College of Physicians, and Vice President of the Royal Society, from 1722 to 1773, XXXII 279, XXXIII 93, 305, XXXIV 125, XXXV 293, XXXVI 1, 219, XXXVII 1, 223, XXXVIII 1, 199, XXXIX 1, 173, XL 1, 143, XLI 1, 291, 406, XLII 620, XLIII 75, 189, 421. XLIV 213, 597, XLVI 43, ~~331~~, 359, 403, XLVII 166, XLVIII 110, 528, XLIX 78, 607, L 236, 648, LI 96, 644, LII 85, 491, LIII 32, LIV 137, LV 91, LVI 250, LVII 470, LVIII 227, LIX 384, LX 541, LXI 390, LXIII 30, LXIV 302		
PLANTS (Chymistry.) A way of extracting volatile salt and spirit out of vegetables - *Coxe*	IX 4	III 333
—— A confirmation of the assertion, that alcalizate or fixed salt, extracted out of the ashes of vegetables, do not differ from each other *Coxe*	— 150	— —
A continuation of the discourse on the identity of all volatile salts and vinous spirits, with two experiments concerning vegetable salts, perfectly resembling the shape of the plants whence they had been obtained *Coxe*	— 169	— —
—— Observations on the class of sweet tastes, made by comparing the tastes of sweet plants with Mr. L'Emery's chymical analysis of them in his treatise of drugs - - *Floyer*	XXIII 1160	V 406
PLANTS. (Fossil) A description of certain stone figured like plants, and by some observing men esteemed to be plants petrified *Lister*	VIII 6181	II 493
—— An account of the impressions of plants on the slates of coals - *Da Costa*	L 228	
PLATINA. Several papers concerning a new semi-metal, called platina - *William Watson*	XLVI 584	X 671
—— Experimental examination of a white metallic substance, said to be found in the gold mines of the Spanish West-Indies, and there known by the appellation of Platina, Platina di Pinto, Juan Blanca. Paper 1, 2, 3, 4 *Lewis*	XLVIII 638	
Paper 5 - - - *Lewis*	L 148	
Paper 6 - - *Lewis*	— 156	
—— Experiments on Platina - *Ingenhousz*	LXV 257	

See Chloranthus.

The action of Nitre on Platina. Tennant. 1797: 219
On the action of Platina and Mercury upon each other. Chenevix. 1805: 104.
On Platina from Brasil. Wollaston. 1809: 189.

PLEIADES.

Platinum. On a new fulminating Platinum. Davy. 1817: 136.

	Transf.	Abridg.
PLEIADES. Obfervations of the moon's paffage over the Pleiades in 1767 - *M. Meffier*	LIX 454	
PLICA POLONICA. An extraordinary cafe *Vater*	XXXVII 50	VII 495
—— A letter concerning a plica Polonica mentioned vol. xxxvii, 50 - - *Klein*	— 427	— —
—— —— A letter concerning a plica Polonica *Ames*	XLIV 556	XI 950
PLINY. Note of Pliny about the bleeding of the mulberry tree - *H. Lifter*	V 2069	
—— Amendments and notes upon three places in the common text of Pliny's Natural Hiftory falfely edited - - *Halley*	XVII 535	
—— A remark on F. Hardouin's amendment of a paffage in Pliny, lib. II. fec. 74 - *Folkes*	XLIV 365	XI 1378
PLUMB-STONE. Account of a ball, extracted from a perfon, who had fuffered by it 30 years, in which was a plumb-ftone - *Young*	XXIII 1279	V 261
Some inftances of other perfons who were hurt by fwallowing plumb-ftones - *Sloane*	— 1283	— 264
—— —— An account of what was obferved upon opening the corpfe of a perfon who had taken feveral ounces of crude mercury internally; and of a plumb-ftone lodged in the coats of the rectum - - *Madden*	XXXIX 291	IX 152
PNEUMATICS. New pneumatical experiments about refpiration - - *Boyle*	V 2011	II 215
—— ENGINE. Vide *air-pump* -		
POESTUM. Vide *Coin*		
POINTS. Concerning the proportion of mathematical points to each other - *Robartes*	XXVII 470	IV 1
POISON. A relation of an inland fea, near Dantzick, yeilding at a certain feafon of the year, a green fubftance, which caufeth certain death *Kirby*	VII 4069	II 491
—— Account of a poifonous fifh in one of the Bahama Iflands - - *J. Locke*	X 312	— 842
—— A difcourfe of the viper, and fome other poifons, wrote by Sir Theodore Mayerne, after difcourfing with Mr. Pontæus - *Mayerne*	XVIII 162	— 645 — 814
—— Two obfervations, the one concerning the effects of a poifonous root, the other concerning the virtues of the leaves of hemlock *Ray*	XIX 634	— 640
—— An account of the poifonous qualities of hemlock-water-drop-wort - *Ray*	XX 84	— 641
—— An abftract of Dr. Mead's mechanical account of poifons - - *Morland*	XXIII 1320	

	Trans.	Abridg.
— Experiments and observations of the effects of several sorts of poisons upon animals, made at Montpellier, in 1678 and 1679 *Courten*	XXVII 485	
— An account of the poison wood tree in New England - - *Dudley*	XXXI 145	VI 2 307
A farther account of the same tree *Sherrard*	— 147	— - 308
— An account of some experiments on the effects of the poison of the rattle-snake *Hall*	XXXV 309	VII 412
— An anatomy of the poisonous apparatus of the rattle snake, with an account of the quick effect of its poison - - *Ranby*	— 377	— 416
— A letter, giving an account of two women being poisoned by the simple distilled water of laurel leaves, and of several experiments upon dogs; by which it appears that this laurel water is the most dangerous poison hitherto known *Madden*	XXXVII 85	VI 2 374
— Some experiments concerning the poisonous quality of the simple distilled water from the lauro-cerasus, or common laurel, made upon dogs at Topping's Hall, Essex, 1731, and others made before the Royal Society in their Repository - - *Mortimer*	— 163	— - —
— The case of a man who was poisoned by eating monk's-hood, or napellus - *Bacon*	XXXVIII 287	VIII 842
— Letter concerning the poison of henbane roots *Patouillat*	XL 446	— 841
— Letter on the poison of laurel water *Rutty*	XLI 63	— 844
— Account of an antidote to the Indian poison in the West-Indies - *Milward*	XLII 2	IX 335
— An account of some persons poisoned by eating boiled hemlock - - *W. Watson*	XLIII 18	X 763
— Farther remarks concerning mushrooms, occasioned by the Rev. Mr. Pickering's paper, with observations on the poisonous quality of some sort of fungi - *W. Watson*	— 51	— 790
— A letter concerning the Indian poison sent over from M. Condamine - *Brocklesby*	XLIV 408	— 1224
— An account of the poisonous root lately found among the Gentian - *Brocklesby*	XLV 240	— 772
— Experiments made on a great number of living animals, with the poison of Lamas, and of Ticunas - - *Herissant*	XLVII 75	
— A farther account of the poisonous effects of the œnanthe aquatica succo viroso crocante of Lobel or hemlock drop-wort - *W. Watson*	L 856	

+ Poison. Experiments and observations on the different modes in which death is produced by certain vegetable poisons. Brodie. 1811. 178

Further experiments and observations on the action of poisons on the animal system. — — — — — — Brodie. 1812. 205

	Transf.	Abridg.
—— An extract of an essay, entitled, On the Uses of a Knowledge of Mineral Exhalations, when applied to discover the principles and properties of mineral waters, the nature of burning fountains, and of those poisonous lakes which the antients called Averni - *Brownrigg*	LV 236	
—— An account of some poisonous fish in the South Seas - - - *Anderson*	LXVI 544	
—— An account of the American poison called Ticunas - - *Fontana*	LXX 163	
POLAND. A relation concerning the sal-gemme-mines in, - - *Anon.*	V 1099	II 524
POLARITY. A paper about magnetism, concerning the changing and fixing the polarity of a piece of iron - - *J. C.*	XVIII 257	— 603
—— Extract of a letter on giving magnetism and polarity to brass - - *Arderon*	L 774	
POLE. Letter concerning some supposed alteration of the meridian line, which may affect the declination of the magnetic needle and the pole's elevation - - *Wallis*	XXI 285	I 265
—— Observations on the elevation of the pole at Lisbon - - *Carbone*	XXXIV 92	
Observations on the meridian height of the sun, to investigate the elevation of the pole at Lisbon - - *Carbone*	— 95	
—— A proposal to make the poles of a globe of the heavens move in a circle round the poles of the ecliptic - - *Latham*	XL 201	VIII 217
—— A contrivance to make the poles of the diurnal motion in a cœlestial globe pass round the poles of the ecliptic - *Senex*	— 203	— —
POLE STAR. Letter concerning the drawing the meridian line by the pole star, and finding the hour by the same - *Gray*	XXII 815	IV 462
POLYGONS. Theorems for making the solution of them as easy as that of triangles by common trigonometry - - *Lexel*	LXV 281	
—— Theorems concerning polygons, inscribing or circumscribing the circle, having the greatest or least area, or greatest or least perimeter *Horsley*	— 301	
POLYNOMIUM. A demonstration of the binomial theorem of Sir Isaac Newton *Castillioneus*	XLII 91	VIII 10
POLYPODIUM. Observations on the seed vessels and seeds of polypodium - *Leeuwenhoek*	XXIV 1868	V 2 267
POLYPUS (Disease) An account of a polypus found in		

 the

		Tranſ.	Abridg.
the heart of a perſon who died epileptical	*Gould*	XIV 537	III 70
—— The original of a polypus -	*Giles*	XIX 472	— 58
—— Obſervation about the polypus of the lungs, with Dr. Liſter's opinion of this obſervation	*Clarke*	— 779	— 68
—— An account of a polypus taken out of the vena pulmonaris, and of the ſtructure of that veſſel	*Cowper*	XXII 797	V 221
—— Letter concerning a polypus found in a dog	*Muſgrave*	— 690	III 85
—— An account of a polypus coughed up by the wind-pipe - -	*Samber*	XXXIV 262	VII 503
—— A letter giving an account of a polypus, reſembling a branch of the pulmonary vein coughed up by an aſtmatic perſon	*Nicholls*	XXXVII 123	— 504
—— A letter concerning polypi taken out of the hearts of ſeveral ſailors, juſt arrived at Plymouth from the Weſt Indies -	*Huxham*	XLII 123	IX 135
POLYPUS. (Animal) Extract of a letter concerning a water inſect, which, being cut into ſeveral pieces, becomes ſo many perfect animals	*Gronovius*	— 218	IX 17
Part of a letter from ——— of Cambridge, occaſioned by what has been reported of the above inſect	*Anon.*	— 227	— 19
—— Several papers relating to the freſh water polypus - -	*Bentick*	XLII ii	— 22
	Trembley	— iii	— 23
	Reaumur	— xii	— 26
These pages come between page 280 *and* 299			
Another account - -	*Folkes*	— 422	VIII 29
—— A further account of the polypus	*Duke of Richmond*	— 510	IX 35
—— Obſervations upon ſeveral ſpecies of ſmall water inſects of the polypus kind -	*Trembley*	XLIV 627	
—— An account of ſome remarkable inſects of the polype kind, found in the waters near Bruſſels in Flanders - -	*Brady*	XLIX 248	
—— Some obſervations on a polype dried	*Baker*	— 616	— 36
—— Obſervation upon ſeveral newly diſcovered ſpecies of freſh water polypes -	*Trembley*	XLIII 169	
—— Extract of a letter giving an account of coral, and that it is a maſs of animals of the polype kind - -	*Trembley*	L 59	
—— Obſervation on corallines, and the polypus, and other ſea animals living on them	*Baſter*	— 258	

Remarks

Ponza (Island) Voyage to the Island of Ponza. Hamilton 70:370.

	Transf.	Abridg.
Remarks on the above obfervations *Ellis*	L 280	
—— See *coral*		
POMERANIA. See *Thunder*		
POMPEY'S PILLAR. New obfervations on what is called Pompey's Pillar, in Egypt *Montagu*	LVII 438	
POND. Account of a pond in Somerfetfhire to which pigeons refort, but cattle will not drink at it *Beale*	I 323	II 332
Further account of the (pond) vitriolate water, with fome particulars touching waters *Beale*	— 359	— —
—— An attempt to account for the rifing and falling of the water of fome ponds near the fea, or ebbing or flowing rivers, where the water is loweft in the pond, at the time of high water in the fea or river, and the water is the higheft in the pond, at the time of low water in the fea or river; as alfo for the increafing or decreafing of the water of fuch poolsor brooks as are higheft in the dry feafons, and loweft in the rainy feafons; with an experiment to illuftrate the folution of the phænomena *Defaguliers*	XXXIII 132	VI 2 165
POPLAR. Obfervations on the black poplar *Willoughby*	V 1201	
POPULATION. An extract of two effays in political arithmetick, concerning the comparative magnitudes of London and Paris *Petty*	XVI 152	
A further affertion of the propofitions and vindication from the objections of fome learned perfons of the French nation - *Petty*	— 237	
—— An account of the number of people in the counties of Ardmagh, Lowth, and Meath, and the city of Dublin; with an eftimate of the number of people in the kingdom of Ireland, 1695-6 - - *South*	XXII 520	
—— An account of the Romifh clergy in Ireland according to the return made 1698 *South*	— 521	III 667
—— The number of people in the city of Briftol calculated from the burials for ten years fucceffively, and alfo from the number of houfes *Browning*	XLVIII 217	
—— A letter concerning the number of inhabitants within the London bills of mortality *Brakenridge*	— 788	
—— Anfwer to fome queries refpecting the population of Conftantinople - *Potter*	XLIX 100	
—— A letter concerning the number of people in England - - *Brakenridge*	— 268	

		Tranſ.	Abridg.
—— A letter concerning the preſent increaſe of the people in Britain and Ireland *Brakenridge*		XLIX 877	
—— An extract of the regiſter of the pariſh of Great Shefford, in Berkſhire, for ten years; with obſervations on the ſame - *Forſter*		L 356	
—— Letter concerning the number of people in England - - - *Forſter*		— 457	
—— An anſwer to the account of the numbers and increaſe of the people of England *Brakenridge*		L 465	
—— Of the increaſe and mortality of the inhabitants in the iſland of Madeira *Thomas Heberden*		LVII 461	
—— Obſervations on the expectations of lives, the increaſe of mankind, the influence of great towns on population, and particularly the ſtate of London with reſpect to healthfulneſs and number of inhabitants - *Price*		LIX 89	
—— Extract of a letter concerning the increaſe of population in Angleſey - *Panton*		LXIII 180	
—— Obſervations on the ſtate of population in Mancheſter, and other adjacent places *Percival*		LXIV 54	
—— Obſervations on the ſtate of population in Mancheſter, and other adjacent places concluded *Percival*		LXV 322	
—— A ſupplement to a paper, entitled, " obſervations on the population of Mancheſter" *Percival*		LXVI 160	
—— Obſervations on the population and diſeaſes of Cheſter, in the year 1774 - *Haygarth*		LXVIII 131	
—— See *Mortality*, *Birth*			
PORCUPINE QUILLS. A letter giving ſome account of the roots uſed by the Indians, in the neighbourhood of Hudſon's Bay, to dye porcupine quills - - *Forſter*		LXII 54	
PORES. The deſcription and uſe of the pores in the ſkin of the hands and feet - *Grew*		XIV 566	
—— Microſcopical obſervations on the pores *Leeuwenhoek*		XVII 949	III 685
PORISMS. Two general propoſitions of Pappus of Alexandria, taking in a great part of Euclid's poriſms, reſtored by - - *Simſon*		XXXII 330	VI 76
PORPHYRE. Directions for enquiries concerning ſtones, and other materials for the uſe of building, together with a ſuggeſtion for retrieving the art of hardening ſteel for cutting porphyre and other hard marbles - *Oldenburgh*		VIII 6010	
—— Letter concerning the porphyry pillars in Egypt *R. H.*		XIV 624	III 528

Potassium. On an easier mode of procuring Potassium than that which is now adopted. — Tennant, 1814 : 578.

		Tranſ.	Abridg.
Porpoise. An account of the diſſection of a porpoiſe, with ſome obſervations, omitted by Rondeletius	*Ray*	VI 2274	II 839
—— Of a venomous ſcratch with the tooth of a porpoiſe, its ſymptoms and cure	*Liſter*	XIX 726	— 824
Portland, Isle of. An account of the damage which happened in the Iſle of Portland, Feb. 3, 1695-6 -	*Southwell*	— 660	III 649
Port-Royal. Obſervations on the eclipſe of the moon, June 18, 1722, and the longitude of Port-Royal in Jamaica determined thereby	*Halley*	XXXII 235	VI 190
Posture Master. Of the poſture maſter	*Anon.*	XX 262	III 297
Pot-Ash. An account of the preparation and uſes of the various kinds of pot-aſhes	*Mitchell*	XLV 541	X 777
—— —— An account of a new and cheap method of preparing pot-aſh, with obſervations	*Percival*	LXX 345	
Pottery. An account of a Roman pottery near Leeds, in Yorkſhire -	*Thoreſby*	XIX 319	III 418
Pouhon-Water. An Experimental inquiry into the nature of the mineral elaſtic ſpirit or air, contained in Spa water, as well as into the mephitic qualities of this ſpirit	*Brownrigg*	LV 218	
Continued - -	*Brownrigg*	LXIV 357	
Powder. A deſcription of the uſes of a certain powder for yielding very cloſe and ſmooth metal, and of eaſy carriage, &c. for caſting of guns	*Anon.*	VIII 6040	II 557
—— Part of a letter, giving an account of ſeveral magnetical experiments, and of one who pretended to cure or cauſe diſeaſes at a diſtance, by applying a ſympathetic powder to the urine	*Leeuwenhoek*	XIX 512	III 685
—— The effects of Dampier's powder in curing the bite of a mad dog -	*Fuller*	XL 272	IX 224
Another caſe drawn up	*Hartley and Sandy*	— 274	— —
—— A report of the Committee appointed by the Royal Society to conſider of a method for ſecuring the powder magazines at Purfleet	*Committee of the Royal Socetiy*	LXIII 42	
Mr. Wilſon's diſſent to part of the preceding report -	*Committee of the Royal Society*	— 48	
Anſwer of the Committee to the objections		— 66	
Power. Short and eaſy methods for finding the			

	Tranf.	Abridg.
quantity and weight of water contained in a full pipe of any given height and diameter of bore; and confequently to find what degree of power would be required to work a common pump, or any other hydraulic engine, when the diameter of the pump-bore, and the height to which the water is to be raifed therein, are given - - *Ferguson*	LV 61	
PRECIOUS STONES. Some remarks on the precious ftone called the turquoife *Mortimer*	XLIV 429	X 633
—— —— Some obfervations upon gems or precious ftones; more particularly fuch as the ancients ufed to engrave upon *Dingley*	— 502	— 610
PRECIPICES OR CLIFFS. Extract of a letter containing obfervations on the precipices and cliffs on the north-eaft coaft of Norfolk *Arderon*	— 275	— 589
PRESERVATION OF BODIES. See *Death.*		
PRESSURE. Some experiments and obfervations on the force of the preffure of the water at great depths - - *Anon.*	XVII 504	I 521
PRICKLEBACK. Abftract of a letter concerning fome obfervations made on the banfticle or prickleback, and alfo on fifh in general *Arderon*	XLIV 424	XI 872
PRICKLY PEAR. The effects of the opuntia, or prickly pear, and of the indigo plant in colouring the juices of living animals *Baker*	L 296	
PRINTING. That Cofterus firft invented printing 1430 - - *Ellis*	XXIII 1416	V 2 11
—— Some obfervations concerning the invention and progrefs of printing to 1465 - *Anon.*	— 1507	— - 12
—— An effay on the invention of printing, by John Bagford; with an account of his collections for the fame - *Wanley*	XXV 2397	— - 18
—— An account of Mr. Le Blon's principles of printing in imitation of paintings, and of weaving of tapeftry in the fame manner as brocades - - *Mortimer*	XXXVII 101	VI 469
—— The defcription of an antique metal ftamp, in the collection of the Duke of Richmond, being one of the inftances how near the Romans had arrived to the art of printing; with fome remarks - - *Mortimer*	XL 388	IX 407
PRISM. An account of rings, confifting of all the prifmatic colours, made by electrical explofions on the furface of pieces of metal *Prieftley*	LVIII 68	

—— An

PRO

	Transf.	Abridg.
PRISM. An account of two giants causeways, or groups of prismatic basaltine columns, and other volcanic concretions in the Venetian State in Italy; with some remarks on the characters of those and other similar bodies, and on the physical geography of the countries in which they are found — *Strange*	LXV 5	
—— Account of a new instrument for measuring small angles called the prismatic micrometer *Maskelyne*	LXVII 799	
PROBLEM. See *Mathematics*		
PROBOSCIS. Microscopical observations on the proboscis of fleas — *Leeuwenhoek*	XXV 2305	V 2 267
PROJECTILES. A discourse concerning gravity and its properties, wherein the descent of heavy bodies, and the motion of projects, is briefly, but fully handled; together with the solution of a problem of great use in gunnery *Halley*	XVI 3	I 472
—— Some propositions on the parabolic motion of projectiles written in 1710 — *Taylor*	XXXI 151	VI 299
—— The motion of projectiles near the earth's surface considered, independent of the properties of the conic-sections — *Simpson*	XLV 137	X 196
PROPAGATION. Letter concerning the seeds of plants, with observations on the manner of the propagation of plants and animals *Leeuwenhoek*	XVII 700	III 685
—— Some microscopical observations and curious remarks on the vegetation and exceeding quick propagation of moldiness on the substance of a melon — — *Bradley*	XIX 490	IV 2 308
—— A letter concerning the propagation of misleto *Barrel*	XXXIV 215	VI 2 348
PROPORTION. An account of the several species of infinite quantity, and of the proportions they bear one to the other — *Halley*	XVII 556	I 102
—— An account of the proportion of the English and French measures and weights from the standard of the same, kept at the Royal Society *Anon.*	XLII 185	IX 489
—— Experiments and observations on the agreement between the specific gravities of the several metals, and their colours, when united to glass, as well as those of their other preparations *Delaval*	LV 10	
—— Observations for settling the proportion which the decrease of heat bears to the height of situation — *Heberden*	LV 126

	Tranſ.	Abridg.
Proportion. The general mathematical laws which regulate and extend proportion univerſally, as a method of comparing magnitudes of any kind together, in all the poſſible degrees of increaſe and decreaſe - - *Glenie*	LXVII 450	
Providence. An argument for Divine Providence, taken from the conſtant regularity obſerved in the births of both ſexes - *Arbuthnott*	XXVII 186	V 2 240
Prusa. An account of the city of Pruſa, in Bythinia *Smith*	XIV 431	III 473
Ptarmigan. Obſervations on the lagopus, or ptarmigan - - *Barrington*	LXIII 224	
Pudenda. A letter concerning the præter-natural ſtructure of the pudenda in a woman *Bennet*	XXXIII 142	VII 551
Puerpera. An account of an hydrops ovarii, with a new and exact figure of the glandulæ renales, and of the uterus in a puerpera *Douglas*	XXV 2317	V 294
Pullies. An account of two experiments of the friction of pullies - *Deſaguliers*	XXXVII 394	VI 322
—— A deſcription of a new tackle or combination of pullies - - *Smeaton*	XLVII 494	
Pulmonary Vein. A letter, giving an account of a polypus reſembling a branch of the pulmonary vein, coughed up by an aſtmatic perſon - - *Nicholls*	XXXVII 123	VII 504
Pulp. Inſtances ſhewing the correſpondence of the pith and timber, with the ſeed of the plant, as alſo of the bark, or ſap in the bark, with the pulp of the fruit, or ſome encompaſſing coat or cod containing the ſeed - *Beal*	IV 919	II 710
Pulse. Caſes of the remarkable effects of bliſters in leſſening the quickneſs of the pulſe in coughs, attended with an infarction of the lungs and fever - - *Whytt*	L 569	
Pumice stone. Microſcopical obſervations on the pumice ſtone - *Leeuwenhoek*	XXIV 2158	V 2 267
—— —— A letter relating to a ſurpriſing ſhoal of pumice ſtones, found floating on the ſea *Dove*	XXXV 446	
Pump. A draught and deſcription of a uſeful and cheap pump, contrived by Mr. Conyers, a trial of which was made at the repairing of the new canal of Fleet River, in London, and elſewhere *Conyers*	XII 888	I 545
—— Short and eaſy methods for finding the quantity		

and

Prostate gland. An account of a small lobe of the human prostate gland, which has not before been taken notice of by Anatomists. Home. 1806: 195.

Proteus anguinus. A historical and anatomical description of a doubtful amphibious animal of Germany, called, by Laurenti, Proteus anguinus. Schreibers. 1801: 241.

Prussiate. On the nature of the salts termed triple Prussiates, and on acids formed by the union of certain bodies with the elements of the Prussic acid. Porrett. 1814: 527.

Further analytical experiments relative to the constitution of the Prussic, of the ferruretted chyazic and of the sulphuretted chyazic acids and to that of their salts; together with the application of the atomic theory to the analyses of these bodies. Porrett. 1815: 220.

Pus. Observations and experiments on Pus. – – – – –Pearson. 1810: 294.

	Transf.	Abridg.
and weight of water contained in a full pipe of any given height and diameter of bore; and consequently to find what degree of power would be required to work a common pump or any other hydraulic engine, when the diameter of the pump-bore, and the height to which the water is to be raised, are given *Ferguson*	LV 61	
PUNIC. An attempt to explain a Punic inscription lately discovered in the island of Malta *Swinton*	LIII 274	
—— Observations on an inedited coin, adorned with two Punic characters on the reverse *Swinton*	LVIII 265	
PUNCTURE. An account of a suppression of urine cured by a puncture made in the bladder through the anus - *Robert Hamilton*	LXVI 578	
PUPPY. Account of a puppy in the womb that received no nourishment by the mouth *Brady*	XXIV 2176	V 34
PURGING MEDICINES. A solution of the problem for determining the doses of purging and emetick medicines - *Cockburn*	— 2119	— 273
—— —— The practice of purging and vomiting medicines, according to Dr. Cockburn's solution of his problem; with tables, shewing their doses in particular ages and constitutions *Cockburn*	XXVI 46	— 397
PURGING WATERS. An account of a new purging spring at Dulwich, in Surry *Marlyn*	XLI 835	VIII 653
—— An examination of the strength of several of the principal purging waters, especially that of Jessop's Wells - - *Hales*	XLVI 446	X 574
—— An account of the salt purging water of Pitkeathly, in the county of Perth, in Scotland *Monro*	LXII 15	
—— See *the particular Waters in their Places*		
PURPLE. Observations on the limax non cochleata purpuram ferens, the naked snail producing purple - - *Peyssonel*	L 585	
PURPLE FISH. Observations on the purple fish *Cole*	XV 1278	II 823
PUTRIFACTION. Instances, hints, and applications relating to a main point solicited in the preface to this fourth volume, concerning the use may be made of vaults, deep wells, and cold conservatories, to find out the cause, or to pro		

	Transf.	Abridg.
mote the generation of salt, minerals, metals, crystal, gems, stones of divers kinds, and helps to conserve long, or to hasten putrifaction, fertility of any kind of land &c. *Beale*	IV 1135	
PUTRIFACTION. An account of some substances resisting putrifaction - *Pringle*	XLVI 480	XI 1365
A continuation *Pringle*	— 525	— 1369
Further experiments - *Pringle*	— 550	— 1373
—— Some experiments on putrifaction *Crell*	LXI 332	
—— See *Antiseptic*, *Marshes*		
PUTRID DISORDER. Journal of the weather at Senegambia, during the prevalence of a very fatal putrid disorder; with remarks on that country *Schotte*	LXX 478	
PYRAMID. Account of a pyramidal appearance in the heavens, observed near Upminster, in Essex *Derham*	XXV 2411	IV 2 133
PYRITES. Of the nature of earthquakes; more particularly of the origin of the matter of them from the pyrites alone - *Lyster*	XIV 512	II 428
—— Observations concerning the spontaneous firing of the pyrites - *Lyster*	— 515	
—— Observations concerning thunder and lightening being from the pyrites - *Lyster*	— 517	— 182
PYRMONT WATERS. A short account of the nature and virtues of the Pyrmont waters; with some observations upon their chalybeate quality *Slare*	XXX 564	IV 2 201
PYROMETER. Description of a new pyrometer, with a table of experiments made therewith *Smeaton*	XLVIII 598	
PYROMETRY. An essay on pyrometry, and areometry, and on physical measures in general *De Luc*	LXVIII 419	
PYRORGANUM. A letter which gives a description of the figures of his electrical pyrorganum	XLIV 497	

4 Pyrites. An analysis of the magnetical Pyrites, with remarks on some of the other Sulphurets of Iron. Hatchett 1804: 315.

+Quadrant. Project for a new division of the Quadrant. Hutton 74:21.

Q

	Trans.	Abridg.
QUAB. A letter concerning an extraordinary fish called in Russia, quab, and concerning the stones called crabs eyes - *Baker*	XLV 174	X 876
QUADRABLE. Letter concerning the spaces in the cycloid, which are perfectly quadrable *Wallis*	XIX 111	I 116
QUADRANT. The description of a new quadrant for taking altitudes without an horizon, either at sea or land - *Elton*	XXXVII 273	
—— A spirit level to be fixed to a quadrant for taking a meridional altitude at sea when the horizon is not visible - - *Hadley*	XXXVIII 167	VIII 357
—— An account of Mr. Thomas Godfrey's improvement of Davis's quadrant, transferred to the mariner's-bow - *Logan*	— 441	
—— A description of a water level to be fixed to Davis's quadrant, whereby an observation may be taken at sea in thick and hazy weather, without seeing the horizon - *Leigh*	XL 413	— 366 — 360
—— A description of an astronomical mural quadrant freed from many of the inconveniences it has hitherto laboured under - *Gersten*	XLIV 507	X 143
—— A recommendation of Hadley's quadrant for surveying, especially the surveying of harbours, together with a particular application of it in some cases of pilotage - *Michell*	LV 70	
—— A letter describing some additions and alterations made to Hadley's quadrant, to render it more serviceable at sea - *Dollond*	LXII 95	
—— Remarks on the Hadley's quadrant, tending principally to remove the difficulties which have hitherto attended the use of the back-observation, and to obviate the errors that might arise from a want of parallelism in the two surfaces of the index glass *Maskelyne*	— 99	
—— See *Level*		
QUADRATRIX. The construction and properties of a new quadratrix to the hyperbola *Perks*	XXV 2253	IV 66

	Trans.	Abridg.
Quadratic. Universal solution of quadratic and biquadratic equations, viz. analytical, geometrical, and mechanical - *Colson*	XXV 2353	IV 66
Quadrature. Answer to the animadversions of Mr. Huygens upon Dr. Gregory's book, De vera circuli & hyperbolæ quadratura, as published in the Journal des Scavans *Gregory*	III 732	
—— Some consideration upon M. Huygens' letter, printed in vindication of his examen of the book, entitled vera circuli & hyperbolæ quadratura - - *Gregory*	— 882	
—— An addition to the scheme of quadratures *Craig*	XIX 373	I 407
—— Of the logarithmic curve - *Craig*	XX 373	— 56
—— Letter concerning the quadrature of the parts of the lunula of Hippocrates Chius, performed by Mr. John Perks, with the further improvements of the same, by Dr. David Gregory and John Caswell - *Wallis*	XXI 411	I 27
—— A specimen of the general method of determining the quadrature of figures *Craig*	XXIII 1346	IV 26
—— A ready description and quadrature of a curve of the third order, resembling that commonly called the foliate - *De Moivre*	XXIX 329	— 24
—— A demonstration of the 11th proposition of Sir Isaac Newton's treatise of quadratures *Robins*	XXXIV 230	VI 60
—— The general quadrature of trinomial hyperbolic curves - - *Klingerstein*	XXXVII 45	— 82
Quadrupeds. An account of the quadrupeds in the Philippine Islands - *Camel*	XXV 2197	
—— An account of a quadruped brought from Bengal *Parsons*	XLIII 465	XI 899
—— Divers means for preserving from corruption dead birds, intended to be sent to remote countries, so that they may arrive there in good condition; some of the same means may be employed for preserving quadrupeds, reptiles, fishes, and insects - *Reaumer*	XLV 309	
—— Account of several quadrupeds from Hudson's Bay - - *Forster*	LXII 370	
Quantity. An account of the several species of infinite quantity, and of the proportions they bear one to the other - *Halley*	XVII 556	I 102
—— An essay on quantity; occasioned by reading a		

treatise,

+ Quadrature. Dr. Halley's quadrature of the Circle improved - - - - Hellins 1794: 217.

++ Quantities. On the necessary truths of certain conclusions obtained by means of imaginary quantities. Woodhouse. 1801: 89.

Memoire sur les quantités imaginaires. Buée. 1806: 23.

+ Quicksilver. Experiments relating to the expansion of Mercury. Cavallo. 71: 520.

Experiments for ascertaining the point of mercurial congelation. Hutchins. 73: *303.

Observations on Mr Hutchins's experiments for determining the degree of cold at which Quicksilver freezes. — — — — Cavendish — 303.

History of the congelation of Quicksilver — — — — — Blagden — 329.

Experiments on the congelation of Quicksilver in England — — Walker 79: 199.

On a new fulminating Mercury. — — — — — — Howard 1800: 204.

On the action of Platina and Mercury upon each other — — Chenevix 1805: 104.

	Tranſ.	Abridg.
treatiſe, in which ſimple and compound ratios are applied to virtue and merit *Reid*	XLV 505	X 22
QUARIES. Account of ſtone quaries and talc rocks in Hungary - *Oldenburg and Brown*	V 1044	II 339
—— An extract of a letter concerning a quary of marble in the county of Farmanagh in Ireland - - *Nevill*	XXVIII 278	
QUASSI ROOT. Letter on the good effects of the quaſſi root in fevers at Antigua *Farley*	LVIII 80	
QUESNEL, ELIZABETH. See *Bones*		
QUICK LIME. A chymical experiment of the effects of quick lime upon alcaline ſal volatile *Schloſſer*	XLIX 222	
QUICKSILVER. Obſervations concerning quickſilver found at the roots of plants *Septalius*	II 493	— 425
—— A relation concerning the quickſilver mines of Friuli; confirming, as well the account given on that ſubject, vol. I, p. 21, as enlarging the ſame, with ſome additions - *Brown*	IV 1080	— 579
—— An attempt to render the cauſe of that odd phænomenon of the quickſilver remaining ſuſpended far above the uſual height in the Torricellian experiment - *Hugens*	VII 5027	— 23
—— Of the incaleſcence of quickſilver with gold *R. B.*	X 515	— 580
—— An account of ſome new experiments relating to the action of glaſs tubes upon water and quickſilver - - *Jurin*	XXX 1083	IV 428
—— A deſcription of an engine to raiſe water by help of quickſilver, invented by Haſkins, and improved by - - *Deſaguliers*	XXXII 5	VI 352
—— Experiments on quickſilver *Boerhaave*	XXXVIII 145	VIII 709
—— Experiments on quickſilver *Boerhaave*	XXXIX 343	— 717
More experiments - - *Boerhaave*	— 368	— 725
—— Part of a letter concerning the light cauſed by quickſilver ſhaken in a glaſs tube, proceeding from electricity - *Trembley*	XLIV 58	X 321
—— An account of the ſucceſs of ſome attempts to freeze quickſilver, at Albany Fort, in Hudſon's-Bay, in the year 1775, with obſervations on the dipping-needle - *Hutchins*	LXVI 174	
QUILLS. A letter giving ſome account of the root uſed by the Indians, in the neighbourhood of Hudſon's Bay, to dye porcupine quills *Forſter*	LXII 54	
QUINARIUS. Explication of a moſt remarkable mo-		

	Tranſ.	Abridg.
nogram on the reverſe of a very antient quinarius, never before publiſhed or explained *Swinton*	LXIV 318	
QUINSY. An account of a ſtone bred at the root of the tongue, and cauſing a quinſy *Bonavert*	XX 440	III 156

R.

RABBIT. Inveſtigation of the ſpecific characters which diſtinguſh the rabbit from the hare *Barrington*	LXII 4	
RAIN. A particular account of the origin of fountains, and to ſhew that the rain and ſnow waters are ſufficient to make fountains and rivers run perpetually - *Anon.*	X 447	II 329
— Obſervations concerning ſome little animals obſerved in rain, well, ſea, and ſnow water, where pepper has lain infuſed - *Leeuwenhoek*	XII 821	III 683
With the manner of obſerving them *Leeuwenhoek*	— 844	— —
— Obſervations on rain water *Leeuwenhoek*	XXIII 1152	
— An attempt to ſolve the phænomenon of the riſe of vapours, formation of clouds, and deſcent of rain - - *Deſaguliers*	XXXVI 6	VI 2 61
+ — The fall of, in various places. See *Meteorological Obſervations*		
RAINBOWS. An account of two rainbows, unuſually poſited, lately ſeen in France *Journal des Scavans*	I 219	II 188
— Some optical aſſertions concerning the rainbow from Leige - - *Linus*	X 386	— 194
— An account of the appearance of an extraordinary iris ſeen at Cheſter, Aug. 6, 1697 *Halley*	XX 193	— 188
— A geometrical diſſertation on the rainbow, ſhewing the means of obtaining the diameter of each bow, the ratio of refraction being given, with the ſolution of the reverſe problem, or that of finding the ratio of the refraction, the diameter of the bow being given - *Halley*	XXII 714	— 195
— A letter giving an account of a lunar rainbow ſeen in Derbyſhire, 1710-11 *Thoreſby*	XXVII 320	IV 2 131

6 — An

— Account of several Lunar Iris Tunstall 73:100.

+ Rain. Account of a new kind of Rain. Gioeni. 72:1st app. 1.

+ Rainbow. An account of two Rainbows, seen at the same time. Sturges. 1793: 1.

	Tranſ.	Abridg.
Rainbow. An account of two mock ſuns, and an arc of a rainbow inverted with an halo, and its brighteſt arc, ſeen on Sunday and Monday, Oct. 22, and 23, 1721, at Lyndon, in Rutland - - *Whiſton*	XXXI 212	VI 2 76
—— An account of a rainbow ſeen on the ground *Langwith*	— 229	— - 80
—— Extracts of ſeveral letters concerning the appearance of ſeveral arches of colours contiguous to the inner edge of the common rainbow at Petworth - - *Langwith*	XXXII 241	VI 122
Another letter with ſome other reflections on the ſame ſubject - *Pemberton*	— 245	— 123
—— A deſcription of an extraordinary rainbow obſerved July 15, 1748 - *Daval*	XLVI 193	X 481
—— An account of an inverted iris, obſerved on the graſs in September, and another in October. 1751 - - *Webb*	XLVII 248	
Obſervations on an evening, or rather nocturnal ſolar iris, June 5, 1757 - *Edwards*	L 293	
Ram. Part of a letter containing ſome microſcopical obſervations upon the animalcula in ſemine of young rams - *Leeuwenhoek*	XXVII 316	V 2 267
Rana Piscatrix. See *Frog-Fiſh*		
Rarefaction. An account of an experiment of ſhooting by the rarefaction of the air *Papin*	XVI 21	I 496
Rareties. Account of the chamber of rareties at Bohn - - *Ellis*	XXIII 1416	V 2 134
Rat. Examination of the teſticles of a rat *Leeuwenhoek*	XVII 593	III 685
—— Obſervations in the diſſection of a rat *R. W.*	— 594	
Rathbone-Place Water. Experiments on Rathbone-Place waters - - *Cavendiſh*	LVII 92	
Ratio. An eſſay on quantity, occaſioned by reading a treatiſe, in which ſimple and compound ratio's are applied to virtue and merit *Reid*	XLV 505	X 22
Rattle Snakes. The way of killing rattle ſnakes *Taylor*	I 43	II 373
A note touching this relation *Anon.*	— 76	— 811
—— —— The anatomy of a rattle-ſnake diſſected at the repoſitory of the Royal Society *Tyſon*	XIII 25	— 797
—— —— An account of the rattle-ſnake *Dudley*	XXXII 292	VII 410
Some obſervations upon vipers on occaſion of the above relation - *Sprengell*	— 296	— 409

	Transf.	Abridg.
RATTLE-SNAKE. An account of some experiments on the effects of the poison of the rattle-snake *Hall*	XXXV 309	VII 412
—— —— The anatomy of the poisonous apparatus of a rattle snake, with an account of the quick effects of its poison - *Ranby*	— 377	— 416
—— —— Conjectures on the charming or fascinating power attributed to the rattle-snake, grounded on credible accounts, experiments, and observations - *Sloane*	XXXVIII 321	IX 55
—— —— A letter concerning a cluster of small teeth observed at the root of each fang, or great tooth, in the head of a rattle-snake, upon dissecting it - *Bartram*	XLI 358	— 60
—— —— A letter containing an account of what he felt after being bit by a rattle-snake *Breintal*	XLIV 147	— 856
—— —— An account of the successful application of salt to wounds made by the bite of rattle-snakes - - *Gale*	LV 244	
RAY, JOHN. A letter to Mr. Ray concerning some particulars that might be added to the ornithology - - *Lister*	XV 1159	II 849 — 853
—— A letter giving an account of what manuscripts were left by Mr. John Ray *Dale*	XXV 2282	V 184
RAYS. (Natural Philosophy) A method by which a glass of a small plano-convex-sphere may be made to refract the rays of light to a focus of a far greater distance than is usual *Hook*	I 202	I 193
—— A new way of orthographically delineating, by parallel rays, the postures and actions of an human body, exactly observing the symmetry and proportion of the parts *Saint Clare*	VIII 6079	— 599
—— The effects of the different refractions of the rays in telescopical glasses - *Anon*	— 6086	— 156
—— Hopes of perfecting telescopes by reflections, rather than refractions - *Newton*	— 6091	— 158
RAZORS. Letter on the edge of razors *Leeuwenhoek*	XXII 899	V 2 266
—— Observations upon the edge of razors *Leeuwenhoek*	XXVI 493	— - 267
Second letter on the same *Leeuwenhoek*	— —	— - —
RECEIVER. Phænomena afforded by shell fishes in an exhausted receiver - *Boyle*	V 2023	I 304
—— A letter concerning a new contrivance of applying receivers to retorts in distillation *Langrish*	XLIII 254	XI 1225
RECTUM. An account of what was observed upon opening the corpse of a person who had taken several ounces of crude mercury internally;		

and

† Rattlesnake. The case of a man, who died in consequence of the bite of a Rattlesnake, with an account of the effects produced by the poison. Home. 1810: 75.

	Tranf.	Abridg.
and of a p'um ftone lodged in the coats of the rectum - - *Madden*	XXXIX 291	IX 152
Reculver. Obfervations on the foffils of Reculver Cliffe, with a note by the publifher, H. Sloane *Gray*	XXII 762	IV 461
Red Colour. Two letters giving an account of a red colour produced by mixture of a fulphureous fpirit with a volatile alcali - *Gibbons*	XIX 542	III 367
—— A further account of the bones of animals being made red by aliment only - *Belchier*	XXXIX 299	IX 105
—— Obfervations and experiments with madder root, which has the faculty of tinging the bones of living animals of a red colour *Du Monceau*	XLI 390	— 103
Red Sea. A letter accompanying a new chart of the Red Sea, with two draughts of the roads of Mocha and Judda, and feveral obfervations made during a voyage on that fea *Newland*	LXII 77	
Redi. Extract of a letter concerning Signor Redi's manufcripts - - *Anon.*	XXI 42	II 789
Reeks, Nicholas. Cafe of Nicholas Reeks, who was born with his feet turned inwards, which came to rights after being fome time ufed to fet crofs legged - - *Milner*	XLVI 239	XI 1113
		II 595
Refining. Experiments of refining gold with antimony - - *Goddard*	XII 953	— 597 — 598
—— The art of refining - *Merrit*	— 1046	— 591
Reflecting Telescopes. See *Telefcopes*		
Refraction. A method by which a glafs of a fmall plano convex fphere, may be made to refract the rays of light to a focus of a far greater diftance than is ufual - *Hook*	I 202	I 193
—— The effects of the different refractions of the rays in telefcopical glaffes - *Anon.*	VIII 6086	— 156
Hopes of perfecting telefcopes by reflections rather than refractions - *Newton*	— 6091	— 158
—— Extract of two letters concerning an inftrument to fhew the moon's true place to a minute or two; alfo the writer's defign of correcting the hitherto affigned motions of the fun; the other touching the neceffity of making new folar numbers, together with an expedient of making trial whether the refraction in Signor Caffini's table be juft - *Flamftead*	IX 219	— 162
—— An experiment of the refraction of air made at the command of the Royal Society *Lowthorp*	XXI 339	I 228

	Trans.	Abridg.
REFRACTION. A geometrical dissertation on the rainbow, shewing the means of obtaining the diameter of each bow, the ratio of refraction being given, with the solution of the reverse problem *Halley*	XXII 714	II 195
—— A description of the apparatus for making experiments on the refractions of fluids, with a table of the specific gravities, angles of observations, and ratio of refractions of several fluids *Hauksbee*	XXVII 204	IV 2 182
—— Some allowances to be made in astronomical observations, for the refraction of the air, with an accurate table of refractions *Halley*	XXXI 169	VI 167
—— An account of the double refractions in crystals *Beccaria*	LII 486	
—— Concise rules for computing the effects of refraction and parallax in varying the apparent distance of the moon from the sun or a star; also an easy rule of approximation for computing the distance of the moon from a star, the longitude and latitude of both being given, with demonstrations of the same - *Maskelyne*	LIV 263	
+ —— See *Air*, *Crystal*, *Telescopes*		
REFRACTIONS OF FLUIDS. See *Fluids*		
REGIMEN. Part of a letter on the antiseptical regimen of the natives of Russia - *Guthrie*	LXVIII 622	
REINS. An observation of the immoderate and fatal use of crab-stones, and such like absorbent earths, from whence have proceeded stones in the stomach and reins - *Breynius*	XLI 557	IX 171
REMEDIES. Of the diseases incident to, and remedies of, Northern countries - *Lloyd*	XXI 310-311	III 606
REPTILES. Divers means for preserving from corruption dead birds, intended to be sent to remote countries, so that they may arrive there in good condition; some of the same means may be employed for preserving quadrupeds, reptiles, fishes, and insects *Reaumur*	XLV 309	
REPULSIVE. Some electrical experiments, chiefly regarding the repulsive force of electrical bodies - - - *Whale*	XLI 98	VIII 406
RESIN. An account of the quantity of resin in the cortex eleutheriæ - *Brown*	XXXII 81	VII 738
RESISTANCE. Experiments relating to the resistance of fluids - - *Desaguliers*	XXXI 142	VI 299
—— Experiments to determine the law of the resistance of bodies on the surface of the water *Hée*	XLIX 1	
—— Experiments upon the resistance of the air Edgworth	73: 136	

+ Refraction. Investigation of a method of allowing for refraction in astronomical observations. Smeaton 77: 334.
Account of a singular instance of atmospherical refraction. Latham. 1798: 357.
Observations upon an unusual horizontal refraction of the air. Vince. 1799: 13.
On double images caused by atmospherical refraction. Wollaston. 1800: 239.
Observations on the quantity of horizontal refraction. ——— 1803: 1.
Observations on atmospherical refraction as it affects astronomical observations. Groombridge 1810: 190.
Some further observations on atmospherical refraction ——— 1814: 337.
On the communication of the structure of doubly refracting crystals to glass, muriate of soda, fluor spar, and other substances, by mechanical compression and dilatation. — Brewster. 1816: 156.
On the laws of polarisation and double refraction in regularly crystallized bodies. ——— 1818: 199.

Relistian Tin Mine. Account of the Relistian Tin Mine. Carne. 1807: 293.

+ Respiration. Observations on – – – – – – – – – – Priestley. 80: 106.

On the changes produced in Atmospheric Air, and Oxygen Gas by respiration. Allen & Pepys. 1808: 249.

On respiration. – – – – – – – – – – – ———— 1809: 404.

On the structure of the organs of respiration in animals which appear to hold an intermediate place between those of the class pisces and the class vermes, and in two genera of the last mentioned class. Home. 1815: 256.

		Tranſ.	Abridg.
Respiration. New pneumatical experiments about	*Boyle*	V 2011	II 215
—— Experiments concerning reſpiration upon very high mountains -	*Boyl.*	— 2038	
—— Account of an unſucceſsful attempt to prevent the neceſſity of reſpiration by the production or growth of animals in our vacuum	*Boyle*	— 2040	
—— Of the power of aſſuefaction to enable animals to hold out in air, by rarefaction made unfit for reſpiration - -	*Boyle*	— 2045	
—— Experiments ſhewing that air unfit for it may retain its wonted preſſure -	*Boyle*	— 2046	
—— An experiment of a ſurpriſing change of colour, from a pale tranſparent or clear liquor, to a very blue ceruleous one, and that in an inſtant, by the admiſſion of air only, applied to illuſtrate ſome changes of colour, and other effects on the blood of reſpiring animals	*Slare*	XVII 898	
—— A diſcourſe concerning ſome influence of reſpiration on the motion of the heart, hitherto unobſerved - -	*Drake*	XXIII 1217	V 253
—— Experiments on the perforation of the thorax, and its effects on reſpiration	*Houſton*	XXXIX 230	IX 138
—— Some experiments relating to reſpiration	*Haller*	XLVI 325	XI 965
—— Obſervations on reſpirations, and the uſe of the blood - -	*Prieſtley*	LXVI 226	
—— See *Lungs*			
Rest. An experimental examination of the quantity and proportion of mechanic power, neceſſary to be employed in giving different degrees of velocity to heavy bodies from a ſtate of reſt	*Smeaton*	— 450	
Retorts. A letter concerning a new contrivance of applying receivers to retorts in diſtillation	*Langriſh*	XLIII 254	— 1225
Reversions. Obſervations on the proper methods of calculating the values of reverſions dependent on ſurvivorſhips - -	*Price*	LX 268	
Rey. An account of a ſtrange ſort of rey growing ſometimes in certain parts of France	*Journal des Scavans*	XI 758	II 625
Rheum Palmatum. See *Rhubarb*			
Rheumatism. An account of the probable cauſes of the pain in rheumatiſms; as alſo of the cure of a total ſuppreſſion of urine, not cauſed by the ſtone, by the uſe of acids	*Baynard*	XIX 19	III 265

	Trans.	Abridg.
(The figure of a Rhinoceros with a double horn. Sloane	XLVI 118	XI 910
RHINOCEROS. A letter containing the natural hiftory of the rhinoceros - *Parfon*	XLII 523	IX 93
—— A letter on the double horns of the rhinoceros *Parfons*	LVI 32	
RHINOCEROS BEZOAR. A letter concerning the pietra di mombazza, or the rhinoceros bezoar *Sloane*	XLVI 118	XI 910
RHUBARB. An account of the rheum palmatum, or rhubarb plant, raifed at Edinburgh *Hope*	LV 290	
RICHMAN. Anfwer to Dr. Lining's query relating to the death of Profeffor Richman *W. Watfon*	XLVIII 765	
An account of the death of Mr. George William Richman, occafioned, by an electrical ftroke collected from thunder, tranflated from the Dutch - - *Anon.*	XLIX 61	
RIDING. An account of the death of Dr. Greene by a hurt in riding out - *Cameron*	XLIV 609	XI 1112
RIGHT-ASCENSION. Defcription of a method of meafuring differences of right-afcenfion and declination, with Dollond's micrometer, together with other new applications of the fame *Mafkelyne*	LXI 536	
RIGHT LINES. Propofitions felected from a paper on the divifion of right lines and folids *Glenie*	LXVI 73	
RINGS. An account of rings confifting of all the prifmatic colours made by electrical explofions on the furface of pieces of metal *Prieftley*	LVIII 68	
RISINGHAM. Vide *Infcription*		
RIVERS. (In general) A particular account of the origin of fountains, and to fhew that the rain and fnow waters are fufficient to make fountains run perpetually - - *Anon*	X 447	II 329
—— An attempt to account for the rifing and falling of the water of fome ponds near the fea, or ebbing or flowing rivers; where the water is loweft in the pond, at the time of high water in the fea or river; and the water is the higheft in the pond, at the time of low water in the fea or river; as alfo for the increafing or decreafing of the water of fuch pools or brooks as are higheft in the dry feafons, and loweft in the rainy feafons; with an experiment to illuftrate the folution of the phænomena *Defaguliers*	XXXIII 132	VI 2 165
—— An account of the ufe of furze in fencing the banks of rivers - - *Wark*	LII 1	
—— Treatife on rivers and canals *Mann*	LXIX 555	

Bell. 1793: 3.
Thomas. 1801: 145.

	Transf.	Abridg.
RIVERS (Particular) Relation of the effects of a violent storm at Acomack in America, Oct. 19, 1693, on the rivers of that country *Scarburgh*	XIX 659	III 667
—— A relation of the bad condition of the mountains about the Tungarouse and Batavian rivers, having their source from thence, occasioned by the earthquake between the 4th and 5th of Jan. 1699, drawn up from the account given by Tommagan Porbo-Nata (who had been there) - - *Anon.*	XXII 595	II 419
—— Part of a letter concerning the stocking the river Mene with oysters - *Rowland*	XXXI 250	VII 420
—— An account of the river Niagara, taken at Albany, Oct. 10, 1721 - *Barassar*	XXXII 69	VI 2 173
—— Account of the rise of some of the most considerable rivers of Europe - *Scheuchzer*	XXXV 577	VI 2 174
—— An account of the sinking of a river near Pontypool, in Monmouthshire, Jan. 1, 1756 *Matthews*	XLIX 547	
RIZZETTI. Experiment made in August, 1728, before the Royal Society, upon occasion of Signor Rizzetti's opticks, with an account of that book - - *Desaguliers*	XXXV 607	VI 110
ROCHESTER. Vide *Inscription*		
ROCKS. A way to break easily and speedily the hardest rocks - - *Du Son*	I 82	II 367
—— Advertisement from Scotland, concerning the surface of the earth, stones, rocks, &c. *Beal*	X 337	— 368
—— A lettter concerning a new method of cleaving rocks - - *Beaumont*	XV 854	
—— Extract of a letter from Calcutta concerning a burning rock,* and a burning well *Wood*	LII 415	
ROCK CRYSTAL. An observation of optick glasses made of rock-crystal - - *Anon.*	I 362	I 195
ROCK PLANT. Two letters concerning rock plants and their growth - *Beaumont*	XI 724	— 519
—— —— A further account of some rock-plants growing in the lead mines of Mendip Hills *Beaumont*	XIII 276	II 503
ROCKETS. Observations on the heights to which rockets ascend - - *Robins*	XLVI 131	X 201
—— Some experiments in order to discover the height to which rockets may be made to ascend, and to what distance their light may be seen *Ellicott*	— 578	— 202
ROMAN, JANE. An improvement on the practice		

of

	Trans.	Abridg.
of tapping, whereby that operation, instead of a relief for symptoms, becomes an absolute cure for an ascites, exemplified in the case of Jane Roman - - *Warwick*	XLIII 12	XI 1030
A method of conveying liquors into the abdomen during the operation of tapping *Hales*	— 20	
ROMANSH LANGUAGE. An account of the Romansh language - - *Planta*	LXVI 129	
ROME. Account of a way of restoring the salubrity of the country about Rome - *Donius*	V 2017	
—— Miscellaneous observations made about Rome, Naples, and some other countries, in 1683 and 1684 - - *Robinson*	XXIX 473	V 2 142
—— Account of an extraordinary heat observed at Rome in the summer, 1768 - *Byres*	LVIII 337	
ROME. See *Altar*, *Antiquities*, *Camp*, *Chyrograph*, *Coins*, *Colonies*, *Delgovitia*, *Eagle*, *Hypocaustum*, *Inscriptions*, *Legions*, *Measures*, *Money*, *Pavement*, *Pottery*, *Printing*, *Shield*, *Sweating-room*, *Tessera*, *Town*, *Urns*		
RONDELETIUS. An account of the dissection of a porpoise, with some observations omitted by Rondeletius - *Ray*	VI 2274	II 839
ROOMS. A proposal for warming rooms by the steam of boiling water, conveyed in pipes along the walls - - *Cook*	XLIII 370	XI 1391
—— Experiments and observations in an heated-room *Blagden*	LXV 111	
Dobson	— 463	
Blagden	— 484	
ROOTS (Mathematics.) Of the number of roots in several equations, their power and use *Halley*	XVI 387	I 68
—— A new and accurate method of finding the roots of equations of every kind without previous reduction - - *Halley*	XVIII 136	— 81
—— A method of raising an infinite multinomial to any given power, or extracting any given root of the same - *De Moivre*	XIX 619	— 90
—— A method of extracting the root of an infinite equation - - *De Moivre*	XX 190	— 95
—— An attempt towards the improvement of the method of approximating, in the extension of the roots of equations in numbers *Taylor*	XXX 610	IV 80
—— A letter concerning equations with impossible roots - - *Mac Laurin*	XXXIV 104	VI 19

—— A

+ Roots (Mathematics) A new method of finding the equal roots of an equation, by division. Hellins. 72: 417.

L Roots of plants. On the origin and formation of Roots. Knight. 1809: 169.
on the causes which influence the direction of the growth of roots. Knight. 1811. 209

Rowley - rag - stone. Analysis of — Withering 72: 327.

	Transf.	Abridg.
ROOTS. A method of determining the number of impossible roots in affected equations *Campbell*	XXXV 515	VI 9
—— Directions for making a machine for finding the roots of equations universally, with the manner of using it - *Rowning*	LX 240	
—— See *Equations*		
ROOTS OF PLANTS. Observations concerning quicksilver found at the roots of plants *Septalius*	II 493	II 425
—— Two observations, the one concerning the effects of a poisonous root, the other concerning the virtues of the leaves of hemlock *Ray*	XIX 364	
—— Observations on the roots of vegetables *Leeuwenhoek*	— 790	III 685
—— A letter giving some account of the roots used by the Indians, in the neighbourhood of Hudson's Bay, to dye porcupine quills *Forster*	LXII 54	
ROSA MALLAS. The manner of making styrax liquida, alias rosa mallas - - *Petiver*	XXVI 44	V 417
ROSETUM. An answer to Mr. Hobbes's rosetum geometricum - - - *Wallis*	VI 2202	I 247
ROSIN. The way of making pitch, tar, rosin, and turpentine near Marseilles - *Bent*	XX 291	
ROTATION. A new theory of the rotatory motion of bodies affected by forces disturbing such motion *Landen*	LXVII 266	*See Motion—(Mechanics)*
ROTHERTON. Vide *Salt*		
ROUEN. See *Fever*		
ROUND WORM. Lumbricus teres, or some anatomical observations on the round worm bred in human bodies - *Tyson*	XIII 154	III 130
ROY. See *Barometer*		
RUBIES. Some observations on rubies made in Ceilan *Strachan*	XXIII 1248	V 2 181
RUDSTONE. See *Antiquities*		
RUMINATING MAN. An account of a ruminating man, lately living at Bristol - *Slare*	XVII 525	III 110
RUMSEY. See *Figures, Inscription*		
RUNIC CHARACTER. An explanation of the Runic characters of Helsingland - *Celsius*	XL 7	IX 438
RUPTURE. Account of an unusual rupture of the mesentery - - *Swammerdam*	X 273	III 118
—— An account of what appeared most remarkable on opening the body of Anne Edwards, who died Jan. 5, 1729-30, having a large umbilical rupture - - *Ranby*	XXXVII 221	VII 516

	Transf.	Abridg.
RUPTURE. Of an inguinal rupture, with a pin in the appendix cœci, incrusted with stone *Amyand*	XXXIX 329	IV 24
—— An account of a rupture in the ileum, occasioned by a bruise without any wound *Wolfius*	XL 61	IX 160
—— Of a bubonocele, or rupture in the groin, and the operation made upon it *Amyand*	— 361	— 161
—— Account of a rupture of the navel *Taube*	XLIII 50	XI 1027
—— Letter concerning the dissection of a rupture *Le Cat*	XLVII 341	
—— See *Hernia*		
RUSMA. Concerning Rusma and Alcanna *Phil. Soc. Oxford*	XX 295	II 458
RUSSIA. Proposals for the improvement of the history of Russia, by publishing from time to time, separate pieces, to serve for a collection of all sorts of memoirs relating to the transactions and state of that nation *Muller*	XXXVIII 136	IX 399
—— Letter concerning the Russia castor *Mounsey*	XLVI 217	XI 925
—— Part of a letter on the antiseptic regimen of the natives of Russia *Guthrie*	LXVIII 622	
RYE. An odd effect of thunder and lightning upon wheat and rye in the granaries at Dantzick *Kirkby*	VIII 6092	II 174
—— An account of the disease, called ergot in French, from its supposed cause, viz. vitiated rye *Tissot*	LV 106	

S.

	Transf.	Abridg.
SACCUS. An uncommon dropsy from the want of a kidney; and a large saccus that contained the water *Glass*	XLIV 337	XI 1027
SAFFRON. An account of the culture or planting and ordering of saffron *Howard*	XII 945	II 635
—— A botanical description of the flower and seed-vessels of the plant, called crocus autumnalis sativus, that produces the true English saffron, with a figure *Douglass*	XXXII 441	VI 2 309
—— An account of the culture and management of saffron in England *Douglass*	XXXV 566	— 311
SAINT ALBAN's. See *Bones*		
SAINT EDMUND's BURY. Some account of a body lately

St. Michael's Island. A narrative of the eruption of a volcano in the sea off the island of St Michael.
Tilloch. 1812: 152.

4 Salt. An analysis of several varieties of British and foreign Salt, (Muriate of Soda) with a view to explain their fitness for different economical purposes.
Henry. 1810: 89.

	Tranſ.	Abridg.
lately found in uncommon preſervation, under the ruins of the abbey, at St. Edmund's Bury, Suffolk, with ſome reflections upon the ſubject *Collignon*	LXII 465	II 816
SALAMANDERS. A letter rectifying the miſtake of ſalamanders living in fire *Steno*	I 377	
SALEP. A letter containing a new manner of preparing ſalep - - *Moult*	LIX 1	
SALIVA. Obſervations on the ſalival duct *Bartholini*	XIV 749	III 58
—— An account of the external maxillar, and other ſalivary glands; alſo of the inſertions of all the lymphaticks (as well above as below the ſubclavians) into the veins; which glands and inſertions have not hitherto been mentioned, or not truly deſcribed by any author *Hale*	XXXI 5	VII 459
—— Obſervations on uncommon coloured ſaliva *Huxham*	XXXIII 63	— 583
SAL AMMONIAC. Method of making ſal ammoniac in Egypt - - *Haſſelquiſt*	LI 504	
SALT. The whole proceſs uſed in France for making ſea-ſalt by the ſun - *Anon.*	IV 1025	II 363
—— Some enquiries and ſuggeſtions concerning ſalt for domeſtic uſes; and concerning ſheep, to preſerve them, and to improve the race of ſheep for hardneſs, and for the fineſt drapery *Beal*	IX 48	II 364
—— A continuation of the diſcourſe concerning vitriol, ſhewing, that vitriol is uſually produced by ſulphur, acting on, and coagulating with a metal; and then making out, that allum is likewiſe the reſult of the ſaid ſulphur; as alſo evincing that vitriol, ſulphur, and allum, do agree in the ſaline principles; and, laſtly, declaring the nature of the ſalt in brimſtone, and whence it is derived *Anon.*	— 66	— 544
—— Microſcopical obſervations of the figure of ſugar and ſalt, and the probable cauſe of the difference of their taſte - *Leeuwenhoek*	X 380	III 683
—— An extract of a letter concerning the ſalts of wine and vinegar - - *Leeuwenhoek*	XV 963	— 685
—— An abſtract of a letter concerning the various figures of the ſalts contained in ſeveral ſubſtances - - *Leeuwenhoek*	— 1073	— —

	Transf.	Abridg.
SALT. Microſcopic obſervations on the figures of ſeveral ſalt particles, &c. *Leeuwenhoek*	XVII 949	III 685
—— Letter concerning the figures of the ſalts of cryſtal - - *Leeuwenhoek*	XX IV 1906	V 2 267
—— An extract of a letter containing microſcopical obſervations on the ſalts of pearls, oyſter-ſhells, &c. - - *Leeuwenhoek*	XXV 2416	- - -
SALTS (Chemiſtry.) An account of an odd ſalt ex-extracted out of a metallic ſubſtance *Lana*	VI 3060	III 325
—— The principles and cauſes of the volatilization of ſalt of tartar, and other fixed ſalts *Von der Becke*	VIII 5185	— 320
—— A way of extracting a volatile ſalt and ſpirit out of vegetables; intimated in vol. viii. p. 7002 *Coxe*	IX 4	— 326
—— A diſcourſe, denying the præ-exiſtence of alcalizate or fixed ſalts in any ſubject, before it were expoſed to the action of the fire; to which is added, a confirmation of an aſſertion, tion, delivered in vol. ix. p. 4, 5, and 6, viz. that alcalizate or fixed ſalts, extracted out of the aſhes of vegetables, do not differ from each other; the ſame being affirmed of volatil ſalts and vinous ſpirits - *Coxe*	IX 50	— 328
—— A continuation of a diſcourſe, begun in vol. ix. p. 150, touching the identity of all volatile ſalts, and vinous ſpirits; together with two ſurpriſing experiments concerning vegetable ſalts, perfectly reſembling the ſhape of the plants, whence they had been obtained *Coxe*	— 169	— 333
—— Remarks concerning factitious ſalts *F. Redi*	XX 281	— 339
—— The exact quantity of acid ſalts contained in acid ſpirits - - *Geoffrey*	XXII 530	
—— Part of a letter concerning the vitrified ſalts of calcined hay - *Leeuwenhoek*	XXIV 1856	V 2 267
—— An account of a large quantity of alcalious ſalt produced by burning rotten wood *Robie*	XXXI 121	VII 727
—— Obſervations and experiments on the ſal catharticum amarum, commonly called the Epſom ſalt - - - *Brown*	XXXII 348	
Further obſervations - *Brown*	— 372	VII 732
—— Extract of a letter concerning Mr. Seignette's		

ſal

Salts (Chemistry)

Specific gravities and attractive powers of various saline substances. R. Kirwan. 71: 7. 72: 179.

Conclusion of the experiments and observations concerning the attractive powers of the Mineral Acids. —— 73: 15.

Sur la maniere de preparer, avec le moins de perte possible, le Sel fusible d'Urine blanc, et pur, et l'Acide phosphorique parfaitement transparent. Duc de Chaulnes —— 288

On super-acid and subacid Salts. Wollaston. 1808: 96.

On a saline substance from Mount Vesuvius. Smithson 1813: 256.

On the action of Acids on the Salts usually called hyperoxymuriates, and on the gases produced from them. Davy. 1815: 214.

Further analytical experiments relative to the constitution of the Prussic, of the ferruretted Chyazic and of the sulphuretted Chyazic Acids, and to that of their Salts; together with the application of the atomic theory to the analyses of those bodies. —— Porrett 1815: 220.

Saltpetre. Observations respecting the natural production of Saltpetre on the walls of subterraneous and other buildings. Kidd, 1814: 508.

	Tranſ.	Abridg.
ſal polychreſtus Rupellenſis, and ſome other chemical ſalts - - *Geoffroy*	XXXIX 37	IX 393
SALT (Chemiſtry.) Experiments on applying the Rev. Dr. Hale's method of diſtilling ſalt water to the ſteam engine - - *Fitzgerald*	L 53	
—— An account of ſome neutral ſalts made with vegetable acids, and with the ſalt of amber; which ſhews that vegetable acids differ from one another; and that the ſalt of amber is an acid of a particular kind, and not the ſame with that of ſea ſalt, or of vitriol, as alledged by many chemical authors *Monro*	LVII 479	
—— A diſcovery of an indiſſoluble ſalt, ariſing from hempſeed, put into water till it becomes putrid *Ellis*	LIX 138	
—— Experiments and obſervations on various phænomena attending the ſolution of ſalts *R. Watſon*	LX 325	
—— An eaſy method to diſtill freſh water from ſalt water at ſea - - *Newland*	LXII 90	
—— Actual fire in detonation, produced by the contact of tin-foil, with the ſalt compoſed of copper and the nitrous acid *Higgins*	LXIII 137	
—— A letter relating to ſome ſpecimens of native ſalts, collected by Dr. Brownrigg, and ſhewed at a meeting of the Royal Society, June 27, 1774 - *Brownrigg*	LXIV 481	
SALT (Uſe of, in Medicine) Account of an experiment, by which it appears that ſalt of ſteel does not enter to the lacteal veſſels; with remarks - - - *Wright*	L 594	
—— An account of the ſucceſsful application of ſalt to wounds, made by the bite of a rattle ſnake *Gale*	LV 244	
—— An account of the ſalt purging water of Pitkeathly, in the county of Perth, in Scotland *Monro*	LXII 15	
—— See *Acid*, *Alkali*, *Sea-Water*, *Water*		
SALTPETRE Of the way uſed in the Mogul's dominions to make ſaltpetre, extracted from Thevenot's voyages - *Oldenburg* See Nitre	I 103	II 559
SALT SPRINGS AND MINES. Of the richeſt ſalt ſprings in Germany - *Anon.*	— 126	III 351
—— An account of an odd ſpring in Weſtphalia, to-		

gether

	Transf.	Abridg.
gether with an information touching salt-springs, and the straining of salt water *Anon.*	I 127	II 305
SALT SPRINGS AND MINES. Some enquiries concerning the salt springs, and the way of salt-making, at Nantwich, in Cheshire *Jackson*	IV 1060	— 352
—— An appendix to the discourses concerning the salt work - - *Jackson*	— 1077	— —
—— An account of a salt-spring in Somersetshire *Highmore*	— 1128	— 351
—— Instances, hints, and applications, relating to a main point, solicited in the preface to the fourth volume; concerning the use may be made of vaults, deep wells, and cold conservatories, to find out the cause, or to promote the generation of salt, &c. - *Beal*	— 1135	II 728
—— A relation concerning the sal-gemmæ mines in Poland - - *Anon.*	V 1099	— 524
—— Discovery of a rock of natural, at Rotherton in Cheshire - - *Martindale*	— 2015	— 523
—— An account of the salt waters of Droytwich in Worcestershire - *Rastell*	XII 1059	— 365
—— Observations on the sand found in the brine of the salt works in Staffordshire *Plott*	XIII 96	— 360
—— Observations of the Midland salt-springs of Worcestershire, Staffordshire, and Cheshire, of the crude salt which grows from the stone powder dejected by the said brines in boiling; of the specific difference between sea salt and common salt - - *Lister*	XIV 489	— 361
—— An account of a salt spring on the banks of the river Weare, or Ware, in the Bishoprick of Durham - - *Todd*	— 726	— 351
—— An account of the imperial salt works of Soowar, in Upper Hungary - *Bruckman*	XXXVI 260	VI 2 233
—— Part of a letter concerning the salt mines near Cracau, and various other notices *Mounsey*	XLVI 217	XI 925
—— Some account of a salt found on the pic of Teneriffe - - *Heberden*	LV 57	
—— An account of a pure native crystallized natron, or fossil alkaline salt, which is found in the country of Tripoli in Barbary *Monro*	LXI 567	
SALVADORA. The establishment of a new genus of plants, called salvadora, with its description *Garcin*	XLVI 47	X 699

	Tranſ.	Abridg.
SALUBRITY. Account of the air extracted from different kinds of waters, with thoughts on the ſalubrity of the air at different places *Fontana*	LXIX 432	
—— On the degree of ſalubrity of the common airs at ſea, compared with that of the ſea-ſhore, and that of places far removed from the ſea - - *Ingenhouze*	LXX 354	
SAMNITE. Some obſervations upon a Samnite Etruſcan coin, never before fully explained *Swinton*	LI 853	
—— An attempt to elucidate two Samnite coins, never before fully explained *Swinton*	LIX 432	
SAND. A curious and exact relation of a ſand flood, which has lately overwhelmed a great tract of land in the county of Suffolk, together with an account of the check, in part, given to it *Wright*	III 722	II 455
—— An ingenious propoſal for a new ſet of maps of countries, together with tables of ſands and clays, ſuch chiefly as are found in the north part of England - *Liſter*	XIV 739	— 450
—— Some experiments on a black ſhining ſand brought from Virginia, ſuppoſed to contain iron - - *Moulin*	XVII 624	
—— Part of a letter concerning the figures of ſand *Leeuwenhoek*	XXIV 1537	V 2 266
—— Part of a letter concerning the manuring of land in Devonſhire by ſea ſand *Bury*	XXVI 142	IV 2 301
—— An abſtract of a letter concerning experiments made on the Indian magnetick ſand *Muſchenbroek*	XXXVIII 297	VIII 737
—— Obſervations on ſand iron *Ellicot*	LIII 48	
SANTERINI. An account of a new iſland raiſed near Santerini, in the Archipelago *Sherard*	XXVI 67	V 2 196
—— A relation of a new iſland thrown up near the Iſland of Santerini - *Bourguignon*	— 200	— - 197
—— A relation of a new iſland, which was raiſed up from the bottom of the ſea, on the 23d of May 1707, in the bay of Santerini, in the Archipelago - - *Goree*	XXVII 353	
SAP. An experiment on Aloe Americana ſerrati-folia weighed, ſeeming to impart a circulation of the ſap in plants - *Merrel*	II 455	II 645
—— Experiments concerning the motion of the ſap in trees - *Willoughby and Wray*	IV 963	— 682

		Transf.	Abridg.
SAP. Observations, directions, and inquiries concerning the motion of sap in trees in pursuance of what was begun there in 1668, and the spring after — *Tonge and Willoughby*		V 1165	— 683
—— Some observations concerning the variety of the running of sap, compared with a weather glass in April, 1670 — *Tonge*		V 2070	— 684
—— Particulars about retarding the ascent of sap, with other queries relating to that subject *Tonge*		— 2072	I 681
Farther enquiries concerning the running of sap in trees, the keeping of such sap, and brewing with it — — *Tonge*		— 2074	II —
—— Extracts of divers letters touching some inquiries and experiments touching the motion of sap in trees; and relating to the question of the circulation of the same — *Lister*		VI 2119	— 686 — 689 — 752
A letter relating to some particulars in Mr. Lyster's communication — *Willoughby*		— 2125	— 685
Extract of a letter, both in relation to the further discovery of the motion of juices in vegetables, and removing the difference noted in Mr. Willoughby's letter *Anon.*		— 2126	— 686 — 688
—— Microscopical observations about the sap of plants — — — — *Leeuwenhoek*		X 380	III 683
—— A letter concerning the tubes, or canals, that convey the yellow sap in the herb called Chelidonium Majus, or Celandine *Leeuwenhoek*		XXIV 1730	V 2 267
—— Observations and experiments relating to the motion of sap in vegetables *Bradley*		XXIX 486	IV 2 302
—— An account of some new experiments, relating to different, and sometimes contrary, motion, of the sap in plants and trees *Fairchild*		XXXIII 127	VI 2 352
SASSAFRAS. An account of some oil of sassafras crystallized — — *Maud*		XL 378	IX 394
SATURN. Of an observation, not long since made in England on Saturn — *Ball*		I 152	I 365
—— A late observation upon Saturn, June 29, 1666, *Hook*		— 246	— —
—— An observation of Saturn made at Paris, Aug. 17, 1668 — *Hugens and Picart*		IV 900	— —
—— The appearance of, in 1670 — *Hevelius*		V 2089	— —
—— Observations of a late appearance of Saturn, Sept. 11 and 12, 1671 — *Hevelius*		VI 3032	— 366
—— Observations touching some late appearances of Saturn — — *Flamstead*		— 3034	— —

4 Sap. Account of some experiments on the ascent of the sap ~~in~~ trees. Knight. 1801: 333.
descent of the sap in trees. —— 1803: 277.
Experiments and observations on the motion of the sap in trees. —— 1804: 183.
Concerning the state in which the true sap of trees is deposited during winter - - - - - - - - - - - - - - —— 1805: 88.

Sarcocele. Description of a species of Sarcocele of a most astonishing size in a black man in the Island of Senegal, with some account of its being an endemial disease in the country of Galam. Schotte 73: 85.

+ Saturn. Determination of the heliocentric longitude of its descending Node. Bugge. 77:37.

Account of the discovery of a Sixth and Seventh Satellite of the Planet Saturn, with ~~the~~ remarks on the construction of its Ring, its Atmosphere, its Rotation on an Axis, and its spheroidical figure - - - - - - - - - - Herschel 80:1.

On the Satellites of the planet Saturn, and the rotation of its ring on an axis. Herschel —427.

On the ring of Saturn, and the rotation of the fifth Satellite upon its axis ——1792: 1.

Observations of a quintuple belt on the planet Saturn - - - - - ——1794: 28.

On the rotation of the planet Saturn on its axis - - - - - - ——48.

Observations of the singular figure of the planet Saturn - - - - ——1805: 272

Observations and remarks on the figure, the climate, and the atmosphere of Saturn, and its ring. ——1806: 455.

Account of a new irregularity lately perceived in the apparent figure of the Planet Saturn. ——1808: 145

	Tranſ.	Abridg.
Saturn. A remarkable obſervation on Saturn *Caſſini*	XI 689	I 367
—— A theory of the irregularities that may be occaſioned in the annual motion of the earth by the actions of Jupiter and Saturn *Walmeſley*	XLIX 737	
—— (Appulſes) Of the moon to Saturn, and the fixed ſtars, obſervable in the year 1671, foretold, and computed to the meridian and latitude of London - - *Flamſtead*	V 2029	— 453
—— (Belt) Obſervation on two belts of Saturn in 1766 - - - *M. Meſſier*	LIX 454	
—— A belt on the diſc of Saturn deſcribed *M. Meſſier*	LXVI 543	
—— (Conjunction) An account of three late conjunctions of Saturn and Jupiter, within the ſpace of ſeven months; together with an account of what other conjunctions of them have happened for more than 100 years laſt paſt, beginning at 1563; and a table computed, whereby to make an eſtimate of what other conjunctions have happened for the time paſt, or what will happen for the time to come *Flamſtead*	XIII 244	— 389
—— A ſhort account of the three great conjunctions of Saturn, Jupiter, and Mars, at Dantzick in 1682 and 1683 - *Hevelius*	— 325	— 395
—— (Occultation of) Obſervations concerning Saturn obſcured by the moon, June 1, 1671 *Hevelius*	VI 3027	— 347
—— Obſervation on the occultation of Saturn by the moon, Feb. 7, 1678 - *Bullialdus*	XII 969	— 353
—— An account of an occultation of Saturn by the moon, March 19, 1687 obſerved at Totteridge, near London, latitude 51° 39′ - *Haines*	XVI 268	— 365
—— (Ring of) Appearance of his ring in 1670 *Hugens and Hook*	V 2093	— 366
—— Obſervations concerning Saturn's ring, made at Paris - - - *Anon.*	VI 3024	— —
—— Letter on the foregoing obſervations on Saturn's ring - - *Hugens*	— 3026	— —
—— Of the diſappearing of Saturn's ring in 1743 and 1744 - - *Heinſius*	XLII 692	VIII 228
—— The diſparition of Saturn ring in 1773 *Varelaz*	LXIV 112	
—— (Satellites) A diſcovery of two new planets about Saturn, made at Paris - - *Caſſini*	VIII 5178	I 367
—— Some new obſervations concerning the two planets about Saturn, formerly diſcovered by him - - - *Caſſini*	XII 831	— 368

	Tranſ.	Abridg.
SATURN (Satellites.) A correction of the theory of the motion of the fourth ſatellite of Saturn *Halley*	XIII 82	I 370
—— An account of two new ſatellites of Saturn, lately diſcovered at Paris - *Caſſini*	XVI 79	— 369
—— Corrections of the theory of the five ſatellites of Saturn, with tables of the motions of thoſe ſatellites, adapted to the meridian of London, and the Julian account - *Caſſini*	— 299	— 376
—— A rectification of the motions of the five ſatellites of Saturn; with ſome accurate obſervations of them - - *Pound*	XXX 768	IV 320
—— Corrected tables of the motion of the five ſatellites of Saturn *Caſſini and Pound*	— 776	— 323
—— Obſervations on the ſatellites of Jupiter and Saturn - - *Hadley*	XXXII 385	VI 221
SAVERY. Letter concerning a paper of Servington Savery, relating to his invention of a new micrometer by means of divided object-glaſſes, or divided object-ſpeculum - *Short*	XLVIII 165	
SAUNDERSON. See *Equations*		
SAXON. Vide *Coins*		
SCALE. A ſcale of the gradation of heat *Anon.*	XXII 824	IV 2 1
SCALE OF MUSIC. A letter of the various genera and ſpecies of muſic among the antients, with ſome obſervations concerning their ſcale *Pepuſch*	XLIV 266	X 261
SCALES OF THE MOUTH. Letters concerning ſcales within the mouth, and the ſcaly child that was ſhewn - - - *Leeuwenhoek*	XIV 586	III 684
SCALES OF FISH. Of the phænomena of a ſcale fiſh in an exhauſted receiver - *Boyle*	V 2024	
—— An abſtract of a letter concerning the ſcales of eels - - *Leeuwenhoek*	XV 883	— —
—— Microſcopical obſervations on the ſcales of fiſh, &c. - - *Leeuwenhoek*	XVII 949	— 685
SCALLOP. The anatomy of the ſcallop *Liſter*	XIX 567	II 829
SCAPULA. Part of a letter concerning the coming off of the ſcapula and head of the os humeri, upon a mortification - *Derante*	XXXII 15	VII 676
SCARABÆUS GALEATUS PULSATOR. An account of the ſcarabæus pulſator, or the death-watch *Stackhouſe*	XXXIII 159	— 407
SCARBOROUGH SPAW. Some conſiderations relating to Dr. Wittie's defence of Scarborough Spaw, with a brief account of a leſs conſiderable ſalt-ſpring in Somerſetſhire, and of a medical ſpring		

+ Schehallien. Account of a lithological survey of Schehallien, made in order to determine the specific gravity of the rocks which compose that mountain. Playfair. 1811:347.

Scoria from Ironworks, which resemble the vitrified filaments described by Sir Wm Hamilton (in his account of the eruption of Vesuvius) Mora. 72:50.

	Transf.	Abridg.
in Dorsetshire - - *Highmore*	IV 1128	II 333
SCHEHALLIEN. An account of observations made on the mountain Schehallien for finding its attraction - - *Maskelyne*	LXV 500	
—— An account of the calculations made from the survey and measures taken at Schehallien, in order to ascertain the mean density of the earth *Hutton*	LXVIII 689	
SCILLY. An advertisement necessary for all Lizard and Scilly navigators, bound up the channel of England, laid down too far northerly *Anon.*	XXII 725	I 585
SCIRRHOUS TUMOUR. A relation of a scirrhous tumour included in a cystis, &c. *Russel*	XXVIII 276	V 220
—— An observation on a schirrus of the cerebellum *Haller*	XLIII 100	
—— A letter concerning a scirrhous tumour of the uterus - - *Templeman*	XLIV 285	XI 1021
SCIURUS VOLANS. De sciuro volante, sive muro Pontico aut Scythico Gesneri, & vespertilione admirabili Bontii, dissertatio - *Sloan*	XXXVIII 32	IX 76
SCOLOPENDRA MARINA. Account of a not yet described scolopendra marina - *Molyneux*	XIX 405	II 833
—— —— A supplement to the account of a scolopendra marina - - *Molyneux*	XXI 127	— 836
SCOTLAND. Advertisements occasioned by the remarks printed in N° 14, upon frosts in some parts of Scotland, differing in their anniversary seasons and force from our ordinary frosts in England; of black winds and tempests; of the warm and fertilizing temperature and steams of the earth, stones, rocks, springs, waters (some, in some places, more than others in other places) of petrifying and metallizing waters; with some hints for the horticulture of Scotland - - *Beal*	X 357	II 151 396 741 744 749
—— Several observations in the north islands of Scotland - - *Martin*	XIX 727	III 543
—— An account of some stones and plants lately found in Scotland - *Sibbald*	XXII 693	
—— Letter concerning a second volume of his Prodromus historiæ naturalis Scotiæ *Sibbald*	XXV 2314	V 25
—— Extracts of letters containing observations in natural history and antiquities in his travels through Wales and Scotland - *Lhwyd*	XXVIII 93	V 2 123
—— An account of a production of nature at Dun-		

	Transf.	Abridg.
bar in Scotland, like that of the Giants Causeway in Ireland - *Bishop of Offory*	LII 98	
An account of some productions of nature in Scotland resembling the Giants Causeway in Ireland - *Mendez da Costa*	— 103	
—— Vide *Antiquities, Natural History*		
SCRATCH. Of a venomous scratch with the tooth of a porpoise, its symptoms and cure *Lister*	XIX 726	II 842
SCULPTURE. A relation of the conference held at Paris, in the Academy Royal, for the improvement of the art of painting and sculpture *Journal des Scavans*	IV 953	I 603
—— An account of several Roman sepulchral inscriptions and figures in bas relief, discovered in 1755 at Bonn, in Lower Germany *Strange*	LIX 195	
SCURVY. A relation of some strange and wonderful effects of the scurvy, which happened at Paris in the year 1699 - *Poupart*	XXVI 223	V [359]
—— Observations on the scurvy - *Mertens*	LXVIII 661	
SCURVY-GRASS. Query concerning the scurvy-grass of Greenland, proposed to such as use the Greenland trade - *Nicholson*	XLI 317	VIII 765
SEA. Some considerations touching a letter in the Journal des Scavans concerning ways of sounding the depth of the sea without a line, and fetching up water from the bottom of it *Oldenburg*	I 228	II 364
—— Observations made in mines, and at sea, occasioning a conjecture about the origin of wind *Colepresse*	II 481	— 105
—— Animadversions upon Dr. Wallis's hypothesis about the flux and reflux of the *Childrey*	V 2061	— 279
Answer to the above - *Wallis*	— 2068	— 283
—— An estimate of the quantity of vapour raised out of the sea by the warmth of the sun; derived from an experiment shewn before the Royal Society - - *Halley*	XVI 366	
—— An account of the circulation of the watry vapours of the sea, and of the cause of springs *Halley*	XVII 468	— 126
—— A letter concerning the luminous appearance observable in the wake of ships in the Indian seas - - *Bourzes*	XXVIII 230	V 2 213
—— A short account of the cause of the saltness of the ocean, and of the several lakes that emit		

Screw. New method of applying the screw. G: Hunter. 71: 58.

Sea. Observations on the temperature of the ocean and atmosphere, and on the density of sea-water, made during a voyage to Ceylon.

Davy. 1817: 275.

	Tranſ.	Abridg.
no rivers; with a propoſal, by help thereof, to diſcover the age of the world *Halley*	XXIX 296	— - 216
SEA. The art of living under water; or, a diſcourſe concerning the means of furniſhing air at the bottom of the ſea, in any ordinary depths *Halley*	— 492	IV 2 188
— An attempt to account for the riſing and falling of the water of ſome ponds near the ſea, or ebbing and flowing rivers; where the water is loweſt in the pond at the time of high water in the ſea or river, and the water is higheſt in the pond at the time of low water in the ſea or river; as alſo for the encreaſing or decreaſing of the water of ſuch pools or brooks as are higheſt in the dry ſeaſons, and loweſt in the rainy ſeaſons; with an experiment to illuſtrate the ſolution of theſe phænomena - - *Deſaguliers*	XXXIII 132	VI 2 165
— A letter relating to a ſurpriſing ſhoal of pumice ſtones found floating on the ſea *Dov.*	XXXV 446	
— An account of an extraordinary fire-ball burſting at ſea - - *Chalmers*	XLVI 366	X 480
— An account of an unuſual agitation of the ſea at Ildfarcombe in Devonſhire, Feb. 27, 1756 *Prince*	XLIX 642	
— An account of the agitation of the ſea at Antigua, Nov. 1, 1755 - *Affleck*	— 668	
— Extract of a letter relating to an extraordinary agitation of the ſea at Barbadoes, March 31, 1761, and an epidemical diſorder in that iſland - - *Maſon*	LII 477	
— Experiments to prove that the luminouſneſs of the ſea ariſes from the putrefaction of its animal ſubſtances - *Canton*	LIX 446	
— An account of the reſult of ſome attempts made to aſcertain the temperature of the ſea in great depths, near the coaſts of Lapland and Norway; as alſo ſome anecdotes collected in the former *Douglas*	LX 39	
— Obſervations on the milky appearance of ſome ſpots of water in the ſea - *Newland*	LXII 93	
— Of the ſtilling of waves by means of oil *Franklin, Brownrigg, and Fariſh*	LXIV 445	
— On the degree of ſalubrity of the common air at ſea, compared with that of the ſea ſhore, and that of places far removed from the ſea *Ingenhouze*	LXX 354	

	Transf.	Abridg.
SEA. See *Navigation, Tides*		
SEA ANIMALS. An account of the sea polypus *Baker*	L 777	
——— ——— Observations upon the sea scolopendre, or sea millepes - *Peyssonel*	LI 35	
——— Sea-Leach. See *Hirundinella marina*		
SEA-CHART. Letter concerning the collection of secants, and the true division of the meridians in the sea-chart - - *Wallis*	XV 1193	I 527
SEA-PLANT. A description of a curious sea plant, frutex marinus flabelliformis cortice verrucoso obductus. Doodii. Raii Hist. tom. III, p. 7 et Synopf. edit. 3, p. 32. Coralloïdes granulosa alba, J. B. tom. III. p. 809. Erica marina alba frutescens. Mus. Pet. 50. Keratophyton flabelliforme, cortice verrucoso obductum. Raii Syn. edit. 3, p. 32 *Sloane*	XLIV 51	X 706
SEA-SAND. The improvement of Cornwall by sea-sand - - -	X 293	II 729
——— ——— Part of a letter concerning the manuring of land in Devonshire by sea-sand *Bury*	XXVI 142	IV 2 301
SEA WATER. Way of making it sweet *Hauton*	V 2048	II 297
Circumstances relating to the precedent invention - - *Hauton*	— 2049	
——— A table shewing to what degree air is compressible in sea water, from the depth of one foot, to 1947 feet, useful to divers *Anon.*	VI 2192	— 201
A supplement - - *Anon.*	— 2239	— 202
——— ——— Observations concerning some little animals observed in rain, well, sea, and snow water; as also in water where pepper had lain infused - - *Leeuwenhoek*	XII 821	III 683
With the manner of observing them *Leeuwenhoek*	— 844	— —
——— ——— Some experiments about freezing, and the difference betwixt common fresh water ice, and that of the sea water; also a probable conjecture about the original of the nitre of Ægypt *Lister*	XV 836	II 164
——— ——— A true method of nature of distilling sweet and fresh water from the sea water, by the breath of sea plants growing in it *Lister*	XIV 489	— 297
——— ——— An account of R. Boyle's way of examining		

Sea Cov. see Cov.

Sea Otter. A description of the anatomy of the Sea Otter. Home. 1796: 385.

	Trans.	Abridg.
mining water as to freshness and saltness; to be subjoined as an appendix to his printed letter about sweetned sea water *Boyle*	XVII 627	— 298
SEA WATER. An account of Mr. Appleby's process to make sea water fresh; with some experitherewith - - *W. Watson*	XLVIII 69	
—— —— An account of the distilling water fresh from sea water by wood ashes *Chapman*	L 635	
—— —— Case of a young lady who drank sea water for an inflammation and tumour in the upper lip - - *Lavington*	LV 6	
—— —— Experiments on water obtained from the melted ice of sea water, to ascertain whether it be fresh or not; and to determine its specific gravity with respect to other water; also experiments to find the degree of cold in which sea water begins to freeze - *Nairne*	LXVI 249	
SEA. (Instruments used at) Patterns of the tables proposed to be made for observing the tides promised in the foregoing transactions *Moray*	I 311	II 365
With other enquiries touching the sea *Boyle*	— 315	— 297
—— Observations about load-stones and sea-compasses *Oldenburg*	II 423	I 584
Answer to some magnetical enquiries proposed in the above observations - *Sellers*	— 478	II 601
—— An account of a machine for measuring any depth at the sea with great expedition and certainty - *Hales and Desaguliers*	XXXV 559	VI 2 163
—— A proposal of a method for finding the longitude at sea, within a degree, or twenty leagues; with an account of the progress he hath made therein, by a continued series of accurate observations of the moon - *Halley*	XXXVII 185	VI 401
—— A description of a water-level to be fixed to Davis's quadrant, whereby an observation may be taken at sea, in thick and hazy weather without seeing the horizon - *Leigh*	XL 413	VIII 360
—— The description and use of an apparatus, added as an improvement of Davis's quadrant, consisting of a mercurial level, for taking the co-altitude of sun, or star at sea, without the usual assistance of the sensible horizon which frequently is obscured - *Leigh*	— 417	— 362
—— A true copy of a paper found in the hand-writing of Sir Isaac Newton, among the papers of the late Dr. Halley, describing an instrument		

for

	Tranſ.	Abridg.
for obſerving the moon's diſtance from the fixed ſtars at ſea - - - *Anon.*	XLII 155	VIII 129
SEA. (Inſtruments uſed at) A machine for ſounding the ſea at any depth or in any part, invented by Mr. William Cock in the year 1738 *Anon.*	XLIV 146	X 261
—— An account of the bucket ſea-gage to find the different degrees of coolneſs and ſaltneſs of the ſea - - *Hales*	XLVII 214	
—— Some experiments upon a machine for meaſuring the way of a ſhip at ſea - *Smeaton*	XLVIII 532	
—— A letter containing the reſult of obſervations of the diſtance of the moon from the ſun and fixed ſtars, made in a voyage from England to the iſland of St. Helena, in order to determine the longitude of the ſhip, from time to time; together with the whole proceſs of computation uſed on this occaſion - *Maſkelyne*	LII 558	
—— Letter giving an account of obſervations at ſea for finding out the longitude by the moon *Horſely*	LIV 329	
SEAMEN Directions for ſeamen bound for far voyages - - *Royal Society*	I 140	III 631
An appendix to the directions *Royal Societ*	— 147	
—— A liſt of all the ſeamen and watermen of every denomination in Ireland in 1697 *South*	XXII 519	— 666
SECANTS. An eaſy demonſtration of the analogy of the logarithmic tangents to the meridian line, or ſum of the ſecants, with various methods for computing the ſame to the utmoſt exactneſs *Halley*	XIX 202	I 577
—— Letter containing an explanation of the late Dr. Halley's demonſtration of the analogy of the logarithmic tangents to the meridian line, or the ſum of the ſecants - *Robertſon*	XLVI 559	X 256
SECRETIONS. Letter concerning ſecretions in an animal body - *Morland*	XXIII 1291	
SEED (In general.) Inſtances ſhewing the correſpondence of the pith and timber, with the ſeed of the plant; as alſo of the bark, or ſap in the bark, with the pulp of the fruit, or ſome encompaſſing coat or cod containing the ſeed - - *Beal*	IV 919	II 710
—— Letter concerning the ſeed of plants *Joſephus de Aromatoriis*	XVIII 150	
—— Obſervations upon the ſeeds of plants *Leeuwenhoek*	XXXI 200	VI 2 234

+ Secretions. Hints on the subject of animal secretions. Home. 1809: 385.

Sedative salt. see Borax.

	Transf.	Abridg.
SEEDS. A method of raising some exotick seeds which have been judged almost impossible to be raised in England - - *Miller*	XXXV 485	VI 2 353
—— Some experiments concerning the impregnation of the seeds of plants - *Logan*	XXXIX 192	VIII 804
—— The discovery of a perfect plant in semine *Baker*	XLI 448	— 806
—— A letter concerning the wonderful increase of seed of plants, *e. g.* of the upright willow *Hobson*	XLII 320	— 824
—— Some observations relating to vegetable seeds *Parsons*	XLIII 184	X 750
—— Observations upon the minuteness of some seeds of plants - - *Baker*	XLVI 336	
—— An account of some experiments relating to the preservation of seeds - *Ellis*	LI 206	
—— A letter on the success of some experiments for preserving acorns for a whole year without planting them, so as to be in a state fit for vegetation, with a view to bring over some of the most valuable seeds from the East-Indies, to plant for the benefit of our American colonies *Ellis*	LVIII 75	
SEEDS (particular.) An extract of a letter concerning the propagation of elms by seed *Bulkley*	XVII 971	II 667
—— Microscopical observations on eels, mites, the seeds of figs, strawberries, &c. *Leeuwenhoek*	XIX 269	III 685
—— Letter concerning the seeds of oranges *Leeuwenhoek*	XXIII 1461	V 2 266
—— Observations on the seed vessels and seeds of polypodyum - - - *Leeuwenhoek*	XXIV 1868	— — 267
—— Microscopical observations on the seeds of several East-India plants - - *Leeuwenhoek*	XXV 2205	— — —
—— A letter concerning the seed of fern *Miles*	XLI 770	VIII 809
—— A letter concerning the vegetation of melon seed 42 years old - - *Trievald*	XLII 115	— 824
—— A letter concerning the seeds of mushrooms *Pickering*	— 593	— 812
Watson	— 599	— 815
—— Letter concerning the vegetation of melon seed 33 years old - - *Gale*	XLIII 265	X 761
—— A letter concerning the manner of seeding mosses; and in particular of the hypnum terrestre trichoides luteo virescens vulgare majus capitulis erectis, Raii Synops: ed. 3, p. 84 *Hill*	XLIV 60	— 758

	Transf.	Abridg.
SEEDS. The substance of some experiments of planting the seeds of moss - *Bonnet*	XLV 156	X 795
SEMBRADOR. Description of the Spanish Sembrador or new engine for ploughing, and equal sowing all sorts of grain, and, harrowing at once, by which a great quantity of seed-corn is saved, and a rich increase yearly gained *Lucatelo and Evelyn*	V 1056	
SEMEN. Animalculæ observed in femine humano *Leeuwenhoek*	XII 1040	
Answered by - *Oldenburg*	— 1043	
Answered by - *Leeuwenhoek*	— 1044	
With extracts from other letters *Leeuwenhoek*	— 1045	
—— Microscopical examination of the testicles of a rat, and the seed of muscles, oysters, &c. *Leeuwenhoek*	XVII 593	III 685
—— Answer to the objections made to his opinions concerning the animalculæ in femine masculino *Leeuwenhoek*	XXI 270	— 686
Further observations on the animalculæ in femine masculino - *Leeuwenhoek*	XXII 739	
—— Several microscopical observations and experiments concerning the animalculæ in femine masculino of cocks and spiders *Leeuwenhoek*	XXIII 1137	V 2 264
—— Part of a letter containing some microscopical observations upon the animalculæ in femine of young rams - *Leeuwenhoek*	XXVII 316	— - 267
—— A letter containing observations upon the seminal vessels, muscular fibres, and blood of whales - - *Leeuwenhoek*	— 438	— - —
—— Observationes de viis seminis - *Haller*	XLVI 340	XI 109
SENEGAMBIA. Remarks on the country of Senegambia - - *Schott*	LXX 478	
SENSE. A further account concerning the existence of veins in all kinds of plants, together with a discovery of the membranous substance of those veins, and of some acts in plants resembling those of sense; and also of the agreement of the venal juice in vegetables, with the blood of animals, &c. - *Lister*	VII 5131	II 693
SEPULCHRE. The verbal process upon the discovery of an antient sepulchre, in the village of Cocherel, upon the river Eure, in France *Anon.*	XVI 221	III 443
——. A copy of an antient chirograph, or convey-		

	Transf.	Abridg.
ance of part of a ſepulchre cut in marble, lately brought from Rome, with ſome obſervations upon it - *R. Gale*	XXXIX 211	IX 433
SEPULCHRAL INSCRIPTIONS. An attempt to explain two Roman inſcriptions, cut upon two altars, which were dug up ſome time ſince at Bath *Ward*	XLIV 285	XI 1021
—— An account of ſeveral Roman ſepulchral inſcriptions and figures in bas relief, diſcovered in 1755, at Bohn, in Lower Germany *Strange*	LIX 195	
SEPULCHRAL MONUMENTS. Vide *Antiquities*		
SERAPIS. An account of the temple of Serapis at Pozzuoli, in Naples - *Nixon*	L 166	
SERIES. A ſolution of the 15th general problem propoſed by Mr. de. Moivre, in his treatiſe De Menſura Sortis - *Bernoulli*	XXIX 133	V 2 255
Another general ſolution of the preceding problem, with the aſſiſtance of combinations and infinite ſeries - *De Moivre*	— 145	— - 266
—— A treatiſe of infinite ſeries - *Monmort*	XXX 633	IV 90
Appendix, in which the matter is treated in a different manner - *Taylor*	— 676	— 130
An addition *Taylor*	— 683	— 135
—— Of the fluents of multinomials and ſeries affected by radical ſigns which do not begin to converge till after the ſecond term *Simpſon*	XLV 328	X 1
—— An invention of a general method for determining the ſum of every 2d, 3d, 4th, or 5th, &c. term of a ſeries, taken in order, the ſum of the whole being known - *Simpſon*	L 757	
—— A new method of computing the ſums of certain ſeries - - *Landen*	LI 553	
—— A new and general method of finding ſimple and quickly converging ſeries; by which the proportion of a diameter of a circle to its circumference may eaſily be computed to a great number of places of figures - *Hutton*	LXVI 476	
—— A method of finding the value of an infinite ſeries of decreaſing quantities of a certain form, when it converges too ſlowly to be ſummed in the common way, by the mere computation and addition or ſubſtraction of ſome of its initial terms - *Maſeres*	LXVII 187	
—— A method of finding by the help of Sir Iſaac		

	Tranf.	Abridg.
Newton's binomial theorem, a near value of the very flowly converging infinite series $x + \frac{xx}{2} + \frac{x^3}{3} + \frac{x^4}{4} + \frac{x^5}{5}$, &c. when x is very nearly equal to 1 — *Maseres*	LXVIII 895	
SERIES. Of cubic equations and infinite series *Hutton*	LXX 387	
SERPENT. Of the nature of a certain stone found in the Indies, in the head of a serpent *Vernati*	I 102	II 814
—— Observations touching the bodies of snakes and vipers - - - *Oldenburg*	— 138	— 811
—— A relation of the symptoms that attended the death of Mr. R. Burdett, an English merchant at Aleppo, who was killed by the bite of a serpent - - *Goodyear*	XX 351	— 813
—— An account of the serpents in the Island of Ceilan - - - *Strachan*	XXIII 1094	V 2 179
—— Account of serpents at the Philippines *Camelli*	XXV 2266	V 183
—— Letter from Bombay, giving an account of a porcupine swallowed by a snake *Anon.*	XLIII 271	XI 855
—— A letter concerning the property of water efts, in slipping off their skins as serpents do *Baker*	XLIV 529	— 857
SERPENT STONE. A letter containing accounts of the pretended serpent stone, called Pietra de Cobra de Cabelos - - *Sloane*	XLVI 118	— 910
SERUM. An observation of a white liquor, resembling milk, which appeared instead of serum, separated from the blood after it had stood some time - - *Stuart*	XXXIX 289	IX 193
SEX. Observations of a difference of sex in missleto *Barrel*	XXXV 547	VI 2 251
—— Account of a monstrous foetus without any marks of sex - *Baster*	XLVI 479	XI 1208
SHARK. An account of the blue shark, together with a drawing of the same *W. Watson, jun.*	LXVIII 789	
SHEEP. Method to prevent the rot in sheep *Boyle*	VIII 7002	
—— Some inquiries and suggestions concerning salt for domestic uses; and concerning sheep, to preserve them, and to improve the race of sheep for hardiness, and for the finest drapery *Beal*	IX 48	II 912
—— An account of a lamb suckled by a wether sheep for several months after the death of the ewe - - - *Kirke*	XVIII 263	— 869
Second letter on the same *Kirke*	— 264

+Series. A new method of investigating the sums of infinite series. Vince. {72: 389. 81: 295.

On the summation of Series, whose general term is a determinate function of z the distance from the first term of the Series. Waring 74: 385.

Supplement to the third part of the paper on the summation of infinite Series. Vince 75: 32.

On infinite Series — — — — — — — — — — - - - Waring 76: 81. 81: 146.

Maniere elementaire d'obtenir les suites par lesquelles s'expriment les Quantités exponentielles et les fonctions trigonometriques des Arcs circulaires. L'Huilier. 1796: 142.

A new method of computing the value of a slowly converging Series, of which all the terms are affirmative. Hellins 1798: 183.

An easy method of obtaining the sums of many slowly converging series, which arise in taking the fluents of binomial surds. —— —— 527.

The application of a method of Differences to the species of Series, whose sums are obtained by Mr Landen, by the help of impossible quantities. Gompertz. 1806: 147.

An investigation of the general term of an important series in the inverse method of finite differences Brinkley. 1807: 114.

* Observations on the means of distinguishing those Serpents which are venomous, from those which are not so - - - - - - - Gray. 79: 21.

Observations on the orifices found in certain poisonous snakes, situated between the nostril and the eye. Russell.

with some remarks on the structure of those orifices, and the description of a bag connected with the eye, met with in the same snakes. Home. 1804: 70.

Observations intended to show that the progressive motion of snakes is partly performed by means of the ribs. — Home. 1812: 163.

On the structure of the poisonous fangs of serpents — Smith 1818: 471.

Shadows. An account of some experiments upon coloured Shadows. Thompson. 1794: 107.

\# Shark. On the mode of breeding of the oviviviparous Shark. Home. 1810: 205.

+ Sheep. On a new variety in the breeds of Sheep. D.
Humphreys. 1813: 88.

	Trans.	Abridg.
SHEEP. Letter concerning the worms in sheep's livers *Leeuwenhoek*	XXII 509	III 688
—— Part of a letter concerning worms observed in sheep's livers and pasture grounds *Leeuwenhoek*	XXIV 1522	V 2 266
—— A letter concerning worms in the heads of sheep *Thorpe*	— 1800	V 16
—— Of hydatides inclosed with a stony crust in the kidney of a sheep - *Cowper*	XXV 2304	— 54
—— Observations upon a fœtus, and the parts of generation of a sheep - *Leeuwenhoek*	XXXII 151	VII 445
—— Extract of a letter concerning a wether giving suck to a lamb; and of a monstrous lamb *Doddrige*	XLV 502	IX 1218
—— Some account of a sheep having a monstrous horn growing from his throat *Parsons*	XLIX 183	
SHELL. Observations upon shells found upon inland mountains - - *Septalius*	II 493	II 425
—— Observations concerning the odd turn of some shell-snales - - *Anon.*	IV 1011	— 822
—— Phænomena afforded by shell-fishes in an exhausted receiver - *Boyle*	V 2023	I 304
—— An abstract of a letter, giving an account of a shell found in one of the kidneys of a woman *Peirce*	XV 1018	III 162
—— Some notes on Dr. Swammerdam's book of insects, and on that of Steno concerning petrified shells - - *Lister*	VI 2219	II 765
—— Observations upon Steno's book of petrified shells *Lister*	— 2281	— 425
—— Three queries relating to shells proposed by S. Dale, and answered by - *Lister*	XVII 641	III 312
—— The description of certain shells found in the East-Indies - *Witzen and Lister*	— 870	II 826 — 831
—— An account of several shells observed in Scotland *Sibbald*	XIX 321	— 325 III 685
—— A catalogue of shells, &c. gathered at the island of Ascension, with plants observed thereon *Cunningham*	XXI 295	II 252
—— Letter concerning Broughton, in Lincolnshire, with observations on the shell-fish observed in the quaries about that place *De la Pryme*	XXII 677	— 428
—— Account of beds of oyster-shells found near Reading, Berkshire - - *Brewer*	— 844	
—— A description of some shells found on the Molucca Islands - - *Petiver*	— 927	IV 2 285

	Tranſ.	Abridg.
SHELL. A letter concerning Harwich Cliff, and the foſſil ſhells found there - *Dale*	XXIV 1568	IV 2 264
—— An account of animals and ſhells ſent from Carolina - - *Petiver*	— 1952	— - 325
—— A catalogue of foſſils, ſhells, metals, minerals, &c. which J. J. Scheuchzer, of Zurich, ſent to J. Petiver *Anon*	— 2042	— - 286
—— A catalogue of the minerals, petrified ſhells, and other foſſils ſent from C. M. Spener, of Berlin to J. Petiver	— 2082	— - —
—— A letter containing a relation of river, and other ſhells, digged up, together with various vegetable bodies, in a bituminous marſhy earth, near, Mear's Aſhby, in Northamptonſhire - - *Morton*	XXV 2210	— - 181
—— An account of ſome turbinated, bivalve, and univalve ſhells from the Philippines *Camelli*	— 2397	V 2 18
—— An account of petrified ſhells by Corn. le Bruyn, illuſtrated by - - *Klein*	XLI 568	VII 735
—— Obſervations on the hardneſs of ſhells *Collinſon*	XLIII 37	XI 861
—— A letter concerning the manuring of land with foſſil ſhells - - *Pickering*	— 191	X 796
—— A letter containing ſome obſervations upon certain ſhell-fiſh lodged in a large ſtone brought from Mahon harbour, by Mr. Samuel More *Parſons*	XLV 44	XI 862
—— Letter concerning the ſhells of crabs *Parſons*	XLVII 439	
SHELL-LAC. An account of an experiment touching the freezing of common water tinged with a liquid ſaid to be extracted from ſhell-lac *Haukſbee*	XXVI 304	VI 2 182
SHELTON. Obſervations on a clock of Mr. John Shelton, made at St. Helena *Maſkelyne*	LII 434	
SHIELD. Letter concerning a Roman ſhield *Thoreſby*	XX 205	
SHINING. Obſervations about ſhining worms in oyſters - - *Anon.*	I 203	III 826
—— Some obſervations about ſhining fleſh *Boyle*	VII 5108	— 641
—— Two inſtances of ſomething remarkable in ſhining fleſh - - - *Beal*	XI 599	— 644
—— An account of four ſorts of factitious ſhining ſubſtances - - *Oldenburg*	XII 867	— 345
SHIPS. A letter about preſerving ſhips from being worm-eaten - *Journal des Scavans*	I 190	I 596

SHIPS.

+ Shells. Account of some minute British Shells, either not duly observed, or totally unnoticed by Authors — — Lightfoot 76:160.
Experiments and observations on Shell and Bone — Hatchett 1799:315.

Ships. A disquisition on the stability of ships. Atwood 1798: 201.

On a new principle of constructing His Majesty's ships of war. Seppings 1814: 285.

Remarks on the employment of oblique riders, and on other alterations in the construction of ships. Being the substance of a report presented to the board of admiralty, with additional demonstrations and illustrations. Young 1814: 303.

De la structure des vaisseaux Anglais considérée dans ses derniers perfectionnements. Dupin. 1817: 86.

On the great strength given to ships of war by the application of diagonal braces. Seppings. 18[illegible].

	Tranſ.	Abridg.
Ships. An account of the advantage of Virginia for building ſhips - - *Anon.*	VIII 6015	III 255
—— A new way, by an Engliſh manufacture, to preſerve the hulls of ſhips from the worm, &c. better for ſailing, and more cheap and durable, than any ſheathing or graving hitherto uſed - - *Bulteel*	— 6192	I 596
—— An account of the manner of bending planks in his Majeſty's yards at Deptford, &c. by a ſand heat invented by Captain Cumberland - - - *Cay*	XXXII 75	VI 467
—— An account of a new machine called the marine ſurveyor, contrived for the menſuration of the way of a ſhip in the ſea, more correctly than by the log, or any other method hitherto uſed for that purpoſe, together with ſeveral teſtimonials ſetting forth the uſefulneſs of this invention - - *Saumarez*	XXXIII 411	VI 444
—— A further account of a new machine called the marine ſurveyor, deſigned for the menſuration of the way of a ſhip at ſea, more certainly than by the log, at preſent in uſe, or any other method hitherto invented for that purpoſe *De Saumarez*	XXXVI 45	— 456
—— An account of the horn of a fiſh ſtruck ſeveral inches into the ſide of a ſhip *Mortimer*	XLI 861	IX 72
—— Method of preventing ſhips from leaking, whoſe bottoms are eaten by the worms *Cook*	XLIII 370	XI 1391
—— An account of the great benefit of ventilators, in many inſtances, in preſerving the health and lives of people in ſlave and other tranſport ſhips - - *Hales*	XLIV 332	
—— Obſervations on the utility of ventilators in a ſhip - - *Hales*	XLVII 211	
—— Some experiment upon a machine for meaſuring the way of a ſhip at ſea - *Smeaton*	XLVIII 532	
—— An account of an extraordinary operation in the dock yard at Portſmouth *Robertſon*	L 288	
—— Some ſuggeſtions concerning the preventing the miſchiefs which happen to ſhips, and their maſts, by lightning - *W. Watſon*	LII 629	
—— An account of the effects of lightning on three ſhips in the Eaſt-Indies, Aug. 1, 1750 *Veicht*	LIV 284	
—— An account of the appearance of lightening on		

a con-

		Trans.	Abridg.
a conductor, fixed from the summit of the main mast of a ship down to the water	*Winn*	LX 188	
—— An account of a method for the safe removal of ships that have been driven on shore and damaged in their bottoms, to places (however distant) for repairing them	*Barnard*	LXX 100	
SHOE. See *Antiquities*			
SHOOTING. An account of an experiment of shooting by the rarefaction of the air -	*Papin*	XVI 21	I 496
—— Observations on the death of a dog on firing a volley of small shot -	*Clarke*	XIX 779	III 650
—— A brief narrative of the shooting of Dr. Robert Fielding; with a musket ball, and its strange manner of coming out of his head, where it had lain near 30 years, written by himself	*Fielding*	XXVI 317	V 205
—— Case of a lad shot through the lungs, drawn up by N. Peters - -	*Hallett*	XLIII 151	XI 966
SHORT-HAND. The elements of a short-hand	*Jeake*	XLV 345	XI 1381
—— —— A letter containing some remarks on Mr. Jeake's plan for short-hand	*Byrom*	— 388	— 1384
SHOULDER. The description of an instrument for reducing a dislocated shoulder	*Freke*	XLII 556	IX 264
—— An account of a case in which the upper head of the os humeri was sawed off, a large portion of the bone afterwards exfoliated, and yet the entire motion of the limb was preserved	*White*	LVI 39	
—— An extraordinary case of three pins swallowed by a girl, and discharged at the shoulder	*Lysons*	LIX 9	
SHROPSHIRE. See *Coins*			
SHUTTLE. Account of a shuttle-spire taken out of the bladder of a boy -	*Arderon*	XLIII 194	XI 951
SHWAN-PAN. An account of new invented arithmetical instruments, called a swhan-pan, or Chinese account table -	*Smethurst*	XLVI 22	X 13
SIBERIA. An account of some observations and experiments made in Siberia, extracted from the preface to the Flora Siberica, sive historia plantarum Siberiæ cum tabulis ære incisis auct. D. Gmelin - -	*Fothergil*	XLV 248	XI 1333
—— Account of the iron ore lately found in Siberia	*Pallas*	LXVI 523	

See Floating bodies.

Shipwreck. An account of the remarkable effects of a Shipwreck on the Mariners. Currie. 1792:199.

See Blindness, Cataract

& Sight. Case of a young gentleman, who recovered his sight when seven years of age, after having been deprived of it by cataracts, before he was a year old. Ware. 1801:382.

An account of two children born with Cataracts in their eyes, to show that their sight was obscured in very different degrees; with experiments to determine the proportional knowledge of objects acquired by them immediately after the cataracts were removed. Home. 1807:83.

Observations relative to the near and distant sight of different persons Ware. 1813:31.

An appendix to Mr Ware's paper on Vision — Blagdon. 1813:[illegible]

	Trans.	Abridg.
Sidon. A dissertation upon the Phoenician numeral characters antiently used at Sidon *Swinton*	L 791	
Sieve. Κοσκινον Ερατοσθενους or the sieve of Eratosthenes, being an account of his method of finding all the prime numbers - *Horseley*	LXII 327	
Sight. A letter concerning an optical experiment conducive to a decayed sight *Anon.*	III 727	III 41
With another confirming the former, and adding some other observations about sight *Anon.*	— 729	II 684
And a note relating to the same *Anon.*	— 765	
And another note about the same empty tubes *Anon.*	— 802	
An extraordinary case of a partial sight of objects. Under	XXXIII 147	VII 490.
—— The use of telescopic sights in astronomical observations - - *Hevelius*	IX 27	I 221
—— Extracts from Mr. Gascoigne's and Mr. Crabtrie's letters, proving Mr. Gascoigne to be the inventor of the telescopic sights of mathematical instruments, and not the French *Derham*	XXX 603	IV 345
—— Observations on some deceptions of sight through compound microscopes *Gmelin*	XLIII 382	X 761
—— An account of a remarkable imperfection of sight - - - *Scott*	LXVIII 611	
—— See *Microscope*, *Telescope*		
Silchester. A description of the town of Silchester in its present state - - *Ward*	XLV 603	XI 1267
Silk. Observations made on the ordering of silk-worms - - *Digges*	I 26	II 756
—— Account of a book on the designed progress to be made in the breeding of silk-worms, and the making of silk in France - *Oldenburg*	— 87	
—— A letter concerning an unusual way of propagating mulberry trees in Virginia, for the better improvement of the silk work; together with some particulars tending to the good of that plantation - *Moray*	I 201	— 653
—— Of the nature of silk as it is made in Piedmont *Aglionby*	XXI 183	— 757
—— A letter giving several experiments and observations on the production of silk worms, and of their silk in England, as made last summer *Barham*	XXX 1036	V 19
Silk-Pod. An account of a particular species of cocoon, or silk-pod, from America *Pullein*	LI 54	

Astronomy

	Tranf.	Abridg.
SILK-REEL. A new improved filk-reel *Pullein*		
SILVER. A way of guilding gold upon filver *Southwell*	XX 296	III 657
—— Obfervations on the diffolution of filver *Leeuwenhoek*	XXIII 1430	V 2 266
—— Obfervations on ftaining the fingers with a folution of filver in aqua fortis *Leeuwenhoek*	XXIV 1794	— - 267
—— Part of a letter concerning the particles of filver diffolved in aqua fortis - *Leeuwenhoek*	XXV 2425	— - —
—— A letter containing fome microfcopical obfervations upon the chryftalized particles of filver diffolved in aqua fortis - *Leeuwenhoek*	XXVII 20	— - —
SIMPSON, MATTHEW. See *Stone*		
SINAI. A letter containing an account of his journey from Cairo, in Egypt, to the Written Mountains in the Defart of Sinai *Montagu*	LVI 40	
SINGING. An account of one who had no ear to mufic, naturally finging feveral tunes in a delirium *Doddridge*	XLIV 596	XI 1084
SINKING. An account of the fubfiding or finking down of a hill near Clogher, in Ireland *Bifhop of Clogher*	XXVIII 267	IV 2 250
—— Account of a very uncommon finking of the earth near Folkeftone in Kent *Sachetti*	XXIX 469	— - 248
—— An account of the finking of three oaks into the ground at Manington, in Norfolk *Neve*	XXX 766	— - 252
—— An uncommon finking of the ground at Lymne in Kent - - *Anon.*	XXXV 551	VI 2 203
—— A narrative of an extraordinary finking down and fliding away of fome ground at Pardices near Auvergne - *Anon.*	XLI 272	VIII 704
—— An account of the finking down of a piece of ground at Horfeford, in Norfolk *Arderon*	XLIII 527	X 587
SINUOUS ULCERS. An account of the cure of two finuous ulcers poffeffing the fpace of the whole arm, with the extraordinary fupply of a callus, which fully anfwers the purpofes of the os humeri, loft in time of cure *Fawler*	XXV 2466	V 388
SIPHON. A letter concerning the Wurtemberg engine *Davis*	XV 846	I 537
—— The defcription of a fiphon, performing the fame things with the Sipho Wurtemburgicus *Papin*	— 847	— 538
—— Letter concerning the Sipho Wurtemburgicus *Reifelius*	— 1272	— 539
SIRIUS. Some remarks on a late effay of Mr. Caffini,		

wherein

4 Silver. Account of the discovery of Silver in Herland Copper mine. Hitchins. 1801: 159.

Skeleton. An [illegible] fossil human Skeleton from Guadaloupe

König. [illegible]

	Transf.	Abridg.
wherein he proposes to find by observation the parallax and magnitude of Sirius *Halley*	XXXI 1	VI 163
SIRIUS. A proposal for discovering the annual parallax of Sirius - *Maskelyne*	LI 889	
SITUATION. Observations for settling the proportion, which the decrease of heat bears to the height of situation *Thomas Heberden*	LV 126	
SIZE. On the degree of heat which coagulates the blood, the limph, and the serum of the blood, with an enquiry into the causes of the inflammatory crust, or size, as it is called *Hewson*	LX 384	
SKELETON. An account of an extraordinary human skeleton, whose vertebræ of the back, the ribs, and several bones down to the os sacrum, were all firmly united into one solid bone, without jointing or cartilage *Connor*	XIX 21	III 292
———— An account of the skeleton of an elephant lately dug up at Tonna - *Tentzelius*	— 757	II 438
———— An account of the impression of the almost entire skeleton of a large animal, in a very hard stone, found at Elston, near Newark, Nottinghamshire *Stukeley*	XXX 963	IV 2 272
———— An account of part of two human skeletons petrified - - *Scheuchzer*	XXXIV 38	IV 2 205
———— An account of an human skeleton of an extraordinary size, found in a repository at Repton, in Derbyshire, together with some examples of long life - - *Degg*	XXXV 363	VII 4 29
———— An account of an extraordinary skeleton *Bishop of Corke*	XLI 810	IX 245
Another account - *Copping*	— 816	— 247
Another account - *Shadwell*	— 820	— —
———— Letter giving an account of a fossil skeleton of a man found near Bakewell, in Derbyshire *Gale*	XLIII 266	X 793
SKIN. The description and use of the pores in the skin of the hands and feet - *Grew*	XIV 566	III 9
———— Of the scalyness of the skin *Leeuwenhoek*	XVII 646	— 684
———— An extract of a letter on the little scales found on the cuticula - *Leeuwenhoek*	— 838	— 685
———— Microscopical observations on the skin of the hand, &c. - *Leeuwenhoek*	— 949	— —
———— Some remarks upon the disposition of the parts and microscopical observations upon the contexture of the skin of elephants *Leeuwenhoek*	XXVII 518	
———— An abstract from the minutes of the Royal

	Tranſ.	Abridg.
Society, containing an uncommon caſe of a diſtempered ſkin - *Machin*	XXXVII 299	IX 105
SKIN. Account of a remarkable diſeaſe of the ſkin *Vater*	XXXIX 199	— 117
—— A letter concerning the property of water efts in ſlipping of their ſkins as ſerpents do *Baker*	XLIV 529	XI 857
—— An account of an extraordinary diſeaſe of the ſkin, and its cure, accompanied with a letter of the Abbé Nollet - *Cruſio*	XLVIII 579	
—— A ſupplement to the account of a diſtempered ſkin, publiſhed in vol. xxxvii. p. 299, of the Philoſophical Tranſactions *Baker*	XLIX 21	
—— Extract of a letter concerning the cuticular glove *Gooch*	LIX 281	
SKINS (Buck and Doe) The method the Indians, in Virginia and Carolina, uſe to dreſs buck and doe ſkins - - *Southwell*	XVII 533	II 825
SKULL. An extract concerning a deformed human ſkull - - *Dupre*	XXI 138	III 295
—— A letter, ſerving to accompany the pictures of the extraordinary foſſil ſkull of an ox, with the core of the horns - - *Klein*	XXXVII 427	VII 4 101
SKY. Account of a luminous appearance in the ſky, ſeen at London, March 13, 1734-5 *Bevis*	XLI 347	VIII 670
SLATE. Account of Iriſh ſlate *Phil. Soc. at Oxford*	XX 271	II 462
—— Some conſiderations touching the variety of ſlate, together with a computation of the charges in general for covering houſes therewith - - *Colepreſs*	IV 1009	I 588
SLEEP. An account of a perſon who took a great quantity of opium without cauſing ſleep *Anon.*	XXII 999	V [357]
—— A relation of an extraordinary ſleepy perſon at Tinſbury, near Bath - *Oliver*	XXIV 2177	V [353]
SLIME. The anatomy of the ſlime, within the guts, and the uſe thereof - *Leeuwenhoek*	XIV 586	III 684
—— Letter giving an account of a viſcous ſlime, or Byſſus, left after a flood in the territory of the Landgrave of Thurlingue, with obſervations thereupon by Mr. Watſon *Boſe*	XLVIII 358	
SLOES. An account of the miſchiefs enſuing the ſwallowing of the ſtones of bullace and ſloes *Derham*	XXIX 484	V 267
SLOW-WORM. Of the long continuance of one alive in a vacuum made in the pneumatick engine *Boyle*	V 2049	III 147

+ Small-Pox.

Account of a Child who had the Small-Pox in the womb. Wright. 71: 372.

		Transf.	Abridg.
SMALL-POX. The case of a woman big with child, who recovered of the small-pox, and was afterwards delivered of a dead child full of the pustules of that distemper *Derham*		XXVIII 165	V 313
—— —— An account of a remarkable instance of the infection of the small-pox *Jurin*		XXXII 191	VII 621
—— —— Part of two letters concerning a method of procuring the small-pox, used in South-Wales *Williams*		— 262	— 618
Another letter upon the same subject *Williams*		— 264	— 619
Another from Haverford-West *Wright*		— 267	— 620
—— —— A short account of the anomalous epidemic small-pox, at Plymouth, beginning in August, 1724, and continuing to June, 1725 *Huxham*		XXXIII 379	— 623
—— —— A letter giving an account of the condition of the town of Hastings, after it had been visited by the small-pox *Frewen*		XXXVII 108	— 632
—— —— A letter concerning a person who made bloody urine in the small-pox, and recovered *Dodd*		XLII 559	IX 211
—— —— A letter concerning the use of the Peruvian bark in the small-pox *Wilmot*		XLIV 583	XI 1035
—— —— Case of a lady who was delivered of a child, which had the small-pox appeared in a day or two after its birth *Mortimer*		XLVI 233	— 1041
Some account of the fœtus in utero, differently affected with the small-pox *William Watson*		— 235	— 1042
—— —— A letter of the use of the bark in the small-pox *Bayly*		XLVII 27	
—— —— Account of a woman who had the small-pox during pregnancy, and who seemed to have communicated the same disease to the fœtus *John Hunter*		LXX 128	
—— —— See *Inoculation*			
SMALT. Letter concerning cobalt, and the preparations of smalt and arsenic *Krieg*		XXIV 1754	V 420
SMELTS. An account of the degenerating of smelts *Dudley*		XXXII 231	VI 2 379
SMOAK. An account of an engine that consumes smoak, shewn lately at St. Germain's fair in Paris *Justell*		XVI 78	III 638
—— An account of a case of a young man stupified by the smoak of sea coal *Frewen*		LII 454	
SMYRNA. Observations in travels from Venice, through Istria, Dalmatia, Greece, and the

	Tranf.	Abridg.
Archipelago, to Smyrna - *Vernon*	XI 575	
SNAILS. Extract of a letter concerning the firft part of his tables of fnails, together with fome queries relating to thofe infects, and the tables themfelves - - *Lifter*	IX 96	II 112
—— Obfervations concerning the eggs of fnails, &c. *Leeuwenhoek*	XIX 790	III 685
—— Obfervations on the limax non cochleata purpuram ferens, the naked fnail, producing purple *Peyffonel*	L 585	
—— A letter concerning the revivifcence of fome fnails preferved many years in Mr. Simon's cabinet - - *Macbride and Simon*	LXIV 432	
SNAKE. See *Rattle-Snake. Serpent.*		
SNIPE. An account of a new-difcovered fpecies of fnipe or tringa - - *Edwards*	L 255	
SNOW. A way of preferving ice and fnow by chaff *Ball*	I 139	— 240
—— Obfervations touching the nature of fnow *Grew*	VIII 5193	II 148
—— A particular account of the origin of fountains, and to fhew that the rain and fnow waters are fufficient to make fountains and rivers run perpetually - - - *Anon.*	X 447	— 329
—— Obfervations concerning fome little animals obferved in rain, well, fea, and fnow water; as alfo in waters where pepper had lain infufed *Leeuwenhoek*	XII 821	III 683
With the manner of obferving them *Leeuwenhoek*	— 844	— —
—— Account of a red fnow at Genoa *Anon*	— 976	II 148
—— Part of a letter, giving an account of a woman who had lain fix days covered with fnow, without receiving any nourifhment, &c. *Bowdick*	XXVI 265	V [358]
—— Obfervations on the figures of fnow *Langwith*	XXXII 298	VI 2 59
—— A relation of obfervations concerning the falling dew, made at Middleburg, in Zeeland, by Leonard Storke, in the night between the 25th and 26th of July, 1741, with figures of the flocks of fnow obferved at the fame place, Jan. 1742 - - - *Anon.*	XLII 112	VIII 502
—— An account of a method of obferving the wonderful configurations of the fmalleft fhining particles of fnow, with feveral figures of them *Nettis*	XLIX 644	

+ Soil. Appearance of the soil at the opening of a Well in Lincolnshire. Englefield. 71: 345.

Solids. On the attraction of such solids as are terminated in planes; and of solids of greatest attraction. Knight. 1812: 247.

	Tranſ.	Abridg.
SNOW. An account of what happened at Bergemoletto, by the tumbling down of vaſt heaps of ſnow from the mountains there, in March 19, 1755, and ſeveral perſons taken out alive after being buried under the ſnow to April 24, *Bruni*	XLIX 796	
—— A letter containing an experiment to aſcertain to what quantity of water a fall of ſnow is equal - - *Brice*	LVI 224	
SOAL-FISH. Obſervations on the food of the ſoal-fiſh *Collinſon*	XLIII 37	XI 861
SOAP. An account of a ſtrange kind of earth taken up near Smyrna, of which is made ſoap, with the method of making it - *Smith*	XIX 228	II 457
—— (Uſed as a medicine) Method of making ſoap lees and hard ſoap for medicinal uſes *Geoffroy*	XLII 71	IX 368
—— A letter concerning the relief he found in the ſtone from the uſe of Alicant ſoap and lime water - - *Lucas*	XLIV 463	XI 1000
—— An account of the virtues of ſoap in diſſolving the ſtone, in the caſe of the Rev. Mathew Simſon - - - *Pringle*	L 221	
—— Obſervations on the lithontriptic virtue of ſoap *Whytt*	— 386	
—— See *Stone*		
SOCIAL WAR. Elucidation of an Etruſcan coin, of Poeſtrum in Lucania, emitted from the mint there about the time of the Social War *Swinton*	LVIII 246	
SOIL. Remarks upon the nature of the ſoil of Naples, and its neighbourhood - *Hamilton*	LXI 1 — 48	
SOLANUM LETHALE. A brief botanical and medical hiſtory of the ſolanum lethale, bella donna, or deadly night ſhade - *W. Watſon*	L 62	
SOLIDS. The dimenſion of the ſolids generated by the converſion of Hippocrates' Lunula, and of its parts about ſeveral axes, with the ſurfaces generated by that converſion *De Moivre*	XXII 624	I 29
—— A vindication of his problem for finding the ſolid of leaſt reſiſtance - *Facius*	XXVIII 172	
—— A caution to be uſed in examining the ſpecific gravity of ſolids by weighing them in water *Jurin*	XXXI 223	VI 327
—— A letter concerning the ſections of a ſolid hitherto not conſidered by geometers *Brakenridge*	LI 446	
—— Propoſitions ſelected from a paper on the diviſion		

ſion

	Transf.	Abridg.
sion of right lines, surfaces, and solids *Glenie*	LXVI 73	
SOLUTION. A letter on the solubility of iron in simple water by the intervention of fixed air *Lane*	LIX 216	
SOLWAY MOSS. An account of the irruption of Solway Moss on December 16, 1772 *Walker*	LXII 123	
SOMERSETSHIRE. Promiscuous observations made in Somersetshire - *Beale*	I 323 — 359	II 332, 423, 837
—— Vide *Antiquities*		
SOMERSHAM-WATER. A letter giving an account of the Somersham water, in the county of Huntingdon - - *Layard*	LVI 10	
Experiments on Somersham water *Morris*	— 22	
SORBUS PYRIFORMIS. Account of the sorbus pyriformis - - *Pitt*	XII 978	— 652
SOREA. An account of the sad mischief befallen the inhabitants of Sorea, near unto the Molucco's, by subterraneous fire, for which they were forced to leave their country - *Witzen*	XIX 49	— 391
SOUNDS. An introductory essay to the doctrine of sounds, containing some proposals for the improvement of acousticks *Narcissus Bishop of Ferns and Leighlin*	XIV 472	I 508
—— Some experiments and observations concerning sounds - - *Walker*	XX 433	— 506
—— An experiment upon the propagation of sound in condensed air; together with a repetition of the same in the open field *Haukshee*	XXIV 1902	IV 2 181
An experiment touching the diminution of sound in air rarefied - *Haukshee*	— 1904	
—— Experiments and observations on the motion of sound - - *Derham*	XXVI 2	
—— Letter on the nature and properties of sound *Grandi*	— 270	IV 414
—— An account of an experiment, shewing that actual sound is not to be transmitted through a vacuum - - *Haukshee*	— 367	IV 2 182
—— An account of an experiment, touching the propagation of sound, passing from the sonorous body into the common air, in one direction only - *Haukshee*	— 369	— — —
—— An experiment touching the propagation of sound through water - *Haukshee*	— 371	— — —
—— Enquiry concerning the respective velocities of electricity and sound - *W. Watson*	XLV 49	X 347

Solstice (Winter) Observations of the winter Solstice of 1812, with the mural circle at Greenwich. — — — — — Pond. 1813: 123.

Sound. Outlines of experiments and inquiries respecting Sound and light. Young. 1800: 106.

Spar. On the multiplication of images and the colours which accompany them in some specimens of calcareous spar. — Brewster. 1815: 270

Spectra (Ocular). New experiments on the ocular spectra of light and colors. Darwin. 76: 313.

	Trans.	Abridg.
Sound. Upon the sounds and hearing of fishes by Jac. Theod. Klein, or some account of a treatise intitled, An enquiry into the reasons why the author of an epistle, concerning the hearing of fishes, endeavours to prove they are all mute and deaf - - *Brocklesby*	XLV 233	XI 883
Sowing. See *Sembrador*		
Space. An account of the repetition of an experiment of the late Dr. Hooke's, concerning two liquors, which, when mixed together, will possess less space, than when separate; with another experiment confirming the same *Hauksbee*	XXVII 325	IV 2 182
Spa-Waters. An examen of the chalybeat, or Spa-waters, called by the Germans acid, or sowe brunns, or fountains; but proved to be of a contrary nature, that is, alkalis *Slare*	XXVIII 247	— - 198
—— An enquiry into the mineral elastic spirit in Spaw-water - - *Brownrigg*	LV 218	
Continued - - *Brownrigg*	LXIV 357	
Spain. Letters concerning some remarkable plants and insects observed in Spain - *Breynius*	XXIV 2045	V 10
—— Some observations on the country of Spain *Brice*	LVI 229	
Spar. An enquriy into the original state and properties of spar and sparry productions, particularly the spars or crystals found in the Cornish mines, called the Cornish diamonds *Borlase*	XLVI 250	X 642
—— An attempt to account for the formation of spars and harder crystals - *King*	LVII 58	
—— A letter containing some observations on a singular sparry incrustation found in Somersetshire - - *King*	LXIII 241	
Spawn. Letter concerning the spawn of cod fish, *Leeuwenhoek*	XXII 821	V 2 266
Specific Gravity. See *Gravity*		
Speculum. Experiments about making a concave speculum, nearly of a parabolick figure *Gray*	XIX 787	I 214
—— A new method of improving and perfecting catadioptrical telescopes, by forming the speculum of glass instead of metal *Smith*	XLI 326	VIII 113
—— See *Glasses, Telescope*		
Speech. Letter to Mr. Boyle concerning an essay of teaching a person deaf and dumb to speak and understand a language, with the success of it *Wallis*	V 1087	III 388

	Tranſ.	Abridg.
Reflections on Dr. Wallis's letter *Holder*	*Supp. Tranſ.*	*July*, 1670
SPEECH. An account of a young lady, born deaf and dumb, taught to ſpeak *Ellis*	XXIII 1416	V 2 134
—— An account of two deaf perſons, who can ſpeak and underſtand one another by the motion of their lips *Waller*	XXV 2468	— 219
—— A relation of a deaf and dumb perſon, who recovered his hearing and ſpeech after a violent fever; with ſome other medicinal and chirurgical obſervations *Martin*	— 2469	V [357]
—— An account of Margaret Cutting, who ſpeaks readily and intelligibly though ſhe has loſt her tongue *Boddington and Baker*	XLII 143	
—— The caſe of Henry Axford, who acquired the uſe of his tongue, after having been four years dumb, by means of a frightful dream *Squire*	XLV 148	XI 958
—— Account of the organs of ſpeech of the Orang-Outang *Camper*	LXIX 139	
—— See *Deaf*, *Dumb*		
SPELTER. A letter concerning ſpelter, melting iron with pit coal *Maſon*	XLIV 370	X 671
SPERMA-CETI. An account of ſuch whales as have the ſperma-ceti in them *Norwood*	II 565	II 844
—— Account of the ſperma-ceti of Bermudas *Stafford*	III 792	— 845
SPERMATIC VESSELS. An account of ſome uncommon anaſtomoſes of the ſpermatic veſſels in a woman *Mortimer*	XXXVI 373	VII 553
SPHERE. A method by which a glaſs of a ſmall plano-convex ſphere may be made to refract the rays of light to a focus of a far greater diſtance than is uſual *Hook*	I 202	I 193
—— The conſtruction and uſe of ſpherical maps, or ſuch as are delineated upon portions of a ſpherical ſurface *Colſon*	XXXIX 204	VIII 354
—— A letter concerning the true delineation of the aſteriſms in the antient ſphere *Latham*	XLI 730	— 218
—— A rule for finding the meridional parts to any ſpheroid with the ſame exactneſs as in a ſphere *Mac Laurin*	— 808	— 110
—— Some conjectures concerning the poſition of the antient ſphere *Latham*	XLII 221	— 216
—— Theory of the parallaxes of altitude for the ſphere *Mallet*	LVI 244	
—— A general inveſtigation of the nature of a curve, formed by the ſhadow of a prolate ſpheroid,		

4 Sphere. Demonstration of a theorem, by which such portions of the solidity of a sphere are assigned as admit an algebraic expression. Woodhouse. 1801: 153.

Spheroids. On the grounds of the method which Laplace has given in the second chapter of the third book of his Mecanique celeste for computing the attractions of Spheroids of every description — — Ivory 1812. 1.

On the attractions of an extensive class of Spheroids. — — 46.

Spikenard. See Nardus indica.

	Tranſ.	Abridg.
upon a plane ſtanding at right angles to the axis of the ſhadow - - *Witchell*	LVII 28	
SPHERE. ~~A method of working the object glaſſes of refracting teleſcopes truly ſpherical~~ *~~Short~~*	~~LIX 507~~	
SPHONDYLIUM VULGARE HIRSUTUM. A letter concerning a miſtake of Profeſſor Gmelin, concerning the ſphondylium vulgare hirſutum of Caſpar Bauhin - - *Miller*	XLVIII 153	
SPIDERS. Account of ſtrange ſpiders-webbs in the Bermudas - - *Stafford*	III 792	III 561
—— Obſervations concerning the darting of ſpiders *Anon.*	IV 1011	II 794
—— A confirmation of what was printed in N° 50, about the manner of ſpiders projecting their threads - - *Wray*	V 2103	— 795
—— —— —— *Liſter*	— 2104	— 796
—— A ſet of curious inquiries about ſpiders, and a table of the ſeveral ſorts of them to be found in England, amounting to, at leaſt, 33 *Liſter*	VI 2170	— 793
—— Letter on the projection of the threads of ſpiders *Liſter*	XIV 592	— 796
—— Letter concerning ſpiders, their way of killing their prey, ſpinning their webbs, generation, &c. - - *Leeuwenhoek*	XXII 867	V 2 266
—— Several microſcopical obſervations and experiments concerning the animalculæ in ſemine maſculino of cocks and ſpiders *Leeuwenhoek*	XXIII 1137	— - 264
—— A diſcourſe upon the uſefulneſs of the ſilk of ſpiders - - *Bon*	XXVII 2	V 21
—— An account of ſome ſpiders from the Philippines *Camelli*	— 310	— 183
—— Part of a letter concerning the venom of ſpiders *Robie*	XXXIII 67	VII 408
SPINE. An account of a preter natural tumor on the loins of an infant, attended with a cloven ſpine - - - *Rutty*	XXXI 98	VI 676
—— An obſervation of a ſpina bifida, commonly ſo termed - - - *Aylett*	XLIII 10	XI 1093
—— Some obſervations on the ſpina ventoſa *Amyand*	XLIV 193	— 1094
SPIRIT. A way of extracting a volatile ſalt and ſpirit out of vegetables, intimated in vol. viii. p. 7002 *Coxe*	IX 4	III 326
—— A continuation of a diſcourſe, begun in vol. ix.		

		Tranſ.	Abridg.
touching the identity of all volatile ſalts and vinous ſpirits; together with two ſurpriſing experiments concerning vegetable ſalts, perfectly reſembling the ſhape of thoſe plants from whence they had been obtained	*Coxe*	IX 169	III 333
SPIRIT. An account of an experiment touching the proportions of the aſcent of ſpirit of wine between two glaſs planes, whoſe ſurfaces were placed at certain different diſtances from each other	*Haukſbee*	XXVIII 151	IV 2 183
Account of ſome farther experiments	*Haukſbee*	— 153	— —
Farther account	*Haukſbee*	— 155	— —
—— An account of a ſpiritus vini æthereus, together with ſeveral experiments tried therewith	*Frobenius*	XXXVI 283	VII 744
—— An experiment concerning the ſpirit of coals	*Clayton*	XLI 59	IX 395
—— Abſtract of the original papers communicated to the Royal Society, concerning his ſpiritus vini æthereus, collected by C. Mortimer	*Frobenius*	XLI 864	— 379
—— An experimental enquiry into the mineral elaſtic ſpirit, or air contained in Spa-water, as well as into the mephitic qualities of this ſpirit	*Brownrigg*	LV 218	
—— A continuation of an experimental enquiry concerning the nature of the mineral elaſtic ſpirit or air contained in the Pouhon water, and other acidulæ	*Brownrigg*	LXIV 357	
SPIRIT LEVEL. A ſpirit level to be fixed to a quadrant for taking a meridional altitude at ſea, when the horizon is not viſible	*Hadley*	XXXVIII 167	VIII 357
SPITTLE. Microſcopical obſervations concerning blood, milk, bones, the brain, ſpittle, cuticula, &c.	*Leeuwenhoek*	IX 121	III 683
SPLEEN. The texture of the ſpleen, &c.	*Malpighi*	VI 2149	— 84
—— Some remarkable obſervations on a diſeaſed ſpleen	*Grew*	XVII 543	— 85
—— Microſcopical obſervations on the ſtructure of the ſpleen	*Leeuwenhoek*	XXV 2305	V 2 267
—— Obſervations on the glands in the human ſpleen	*Douglaſs*	XXIX 499	V 256
—— An account of the extirpation of part of the ſpleen of a man	*Ferguſon*	XL 425	IX 149
~~An account of a monſtrous~~ human fœtus, having ~~neither head, heart,~~ lungs, ſtomach, ſpleen,			

Spirituous liquors. Report on the best method of proportioning the excise upon spirituous liquors. Blagden. 80:321. 1792:425.

Tables for reducing the quantities by weight, in any mixture of pure Spirit and Water, to those by measure; and for determining the proportion, by measure, of each of the two substances in such mixtures. Gilpin 1794:275.

Experiments to ascertain the state in which Spirit exists in fermented liquors; with a table exhibiting the relative proportion of pure alcohol contained in several kinds of wine and some other liquors. — — — Brande. 1811:337.

Additional remarks on the state in which Alcohol exists in fermented liquors. Brande. 1813. 82.

4 Spleen. On the structure and uses of the Spleen. — — — — Home. 1808: 45.
Further experiments on the Spleen — — — — — — — — — — — — 133.

Spring. Indications of Spring . . . . Marsham. 79: 154.

	Transf.	Abridg.
~~pancreas, liver, nor kid~~neys - *Le Cat*	LVII 1	
SPONGE. Microscopical observations on sponges, &c. *Leeuwenhoek*	XXIV 2158	V 2 267
—— Observations upon the worms that form sponges *Peyssonel*	L 590	
—— On the nature and formation of sponges *Ellis*	LV 280	
—— An account of some very perfect and uncommon specimens of sponges from the coast of Italy *Strange*	LX 179	
SPOTS. An account of a negro-boy that is dappeled in several parts of his body with white spots *Byrd*	XIX 781	II 8
—— See *Jupiter*, *Sun*		
SPOUT. Letter concerning a spout of water that happened at Topsham, on the river between the sea and Exeter - - *Mayne*	— 28	— 104
—— An account of a water-spout observed in the Downs - - *Gordon*	XXII 805	IV 2 103
—— Letter concerning some water-spouts he observed in the Mediterranean - *Stuart*	XXIII 1077	— - —
—— Letter concerning a water-spout observed by him in Yorkshire - *De la Pryme*	— 1248	— - 106
—— Letter concerning a spout lately observed by him at Hatfield - *De la Pryme*	— 1331	— - 107
—— Part of a letter, giving a relation of a wonderful fall of water from a spout upon the Moors in Lancashire - *Richardson*	XXX 1097	— - 108
—— The description of a water-spout *Harris*	XXXVIII 75	VIII 655
—— An extraordinary meteor seen in the county of Rutland, resembling a water-spout *Barker*	XLVI 248	X 479
—— An account of a water-spout raised off the land in Deeping-Fen, Lincolnshire *Ray*	XLVII 477	
SPRING. An account of an ebbing and flowing spring in Westphalia, together with an information touching salt-springs, and the straining of salt-water - - *Anon.*	I 127	II 305
—— Of a remarkable spring about Paderborn, in Germany - - *Anon.*	— 133	— 331
—— Of some other not common springs at Basil, and in Alsatia - - *Anon.*	— 134	— 332
—— An account of a medical spring in Dorsetshire *Highmore*	IV 1128	— 333
—— Reflections relating to mineral springs considered, in vol. iv. 1050, with an account of some such		

springs

		Transf.	Abridg.
springs in England and other places, specifying how terrestrial steams may be the generative cause of minerals and metals, and of all the peculiarities of springs - *Beale*		V 1154	II 332
SPRINGS. Advertisements relating to springs, water, &c. - - - *Anon.*		X 357	— 396
—— An account of a medicinal spring on the banks of the river Weare, or Ware, in the bishoprick of Durham - *Toda*		XIV 726	— 333
—— An account of the circulation of the watry vapours of the sea, and of the cause of springs *Halley*		XVII 468	— 126
—— Letter concerning a medicated spring in Glamorganshire - *Aubry*		XIX 727	— 333
—— Conjectures upon the nature of intermitting and reciprocating springs - *Atwell*		XXXVII 301	VI 2 177
—— An account of a new purging spring discovered at Dulwich, in Surrey - *Martin*		XLI 835	VIII 653
—— Experiments by way of analysis upon the water of the Dead Sea, upon the hot springs near Tiberiades, and upon Hammon Pharoah waters *Perry*		XLII 48	— 643
—— Letter concerning the actions of springs *Jurin*		XLIII 46	X 160
—— See *Mineral Springs in their Places*			
SQUARE. The method of squaring any kinds of curves, or reducing them to more simple ones *De Moivre*		XXIII 1113	IV 15
SQUILLA AQUÆ DULCIS. Part of a letter concerning the squilla aquæ dulcis *Richardson*		XXXVIII 331	IX 54
SQUINTING. A new case in squinting *Darwin*		LXVIII 86	
SQUIRREL. A letter containing some remarks relating to Mr. Ray's description of the flying squirrel of America - - *Dale*		XXXIX 384	— 78
STAG. Extract of a letter concerning an extraordinary large horn, of the stag kind, taken out of the sea on the coast of Lancashire *Hopkins*		XXXVII 257	VII 449
—— A letter containing the description of a sort of stag in Virginia - - *Dale*		XXXIX 384	IX 84
STAKE. An extraordinary cure of a horse that was staked into his stomach - *Wallis*		XIX 118	
STALACTITES. Account of a beautiful stalactites, now in the Museum of the Royal Society *Huxham*		XLIII 207	X 627
STAMP. The description of an antique metal stamp in the collection of the Duke of Richmond,			

being

+ Springs. Account of an artificial spring of water. Darwin. 75: 1.

Squalus maximus. An anatomical account of the Squalus maximus (of Linnaeus), which in the structure of its stomach forms an intermediate link in the gradation of animals between the whale tribe and cartilaginous fishes. Home. 1809: 206.

Additions to an account of the anatomy of the Squalus maximus, contained in a former paper; with observations on the structure of the branchial artery. — 1813: 227.

Stapes. see Hearing, organ of.

	Tranf.	Abridg.
being one of the instances how near the Romans had arrived to the art of printing; with some remarks. *Mortimer*	XL 388	IX 417
STARS, FIXED. Some more accurate observations about Jupiter's transits near fixed stars, useful for determining the inclination of that planet to the ecliptic - - *Flamstead*	VIII 6033	I 401
—— New observations made after a new and accurate way, of the farthest elongations of the Medicean stars from the center of Jupiter; together with some uncommon ones concerning the diameters of the planets, and their distances from fixed stars, as also of the parallax of Mars, in opposition to the sun and in perigee, &c. - - *Flamstead*	— 6094	
—— The longitudes, latitudes, right ascensions, and declinations of the chiefest fixed stars according to the observations of the ancients *Bernard*	XIV 567	
—— A proposal concerning the parallax of the fixed stars, in reference to the earths annual orb *Wallis*	XVII 844	
—— Concerning the distance of the fixed stars *Roberts*	XVIII 101	I 233
—— An instrument for seeing the sun, moon, or stars, pass the meridian of any place; useful for setting watches in all parts of the world with the greatest exactness, to correct sun-dials, to assist in the discovery of the longitude of places - - - *Derham*	XXIV 1578	IV 464
—— An account of several nebulæ or lucid spots, like clouds, lately discovered in the fixed stars by help of the telescope - *Halley*	XXIX 390	— 225
—— Considerations on the change of the latitude of some of the principal fixed stars *Halley*	XXX 736	— 227
—— Of the infinity of the sphere of fixed stars *Halley*	XXXI 22	VI 147
—— Of the number, order, and light of the fixed stars *Halley*	— 24	— 148
—— A letter giving an account of a new discovered motion of the fixed stars *Bradley*	XXXV 637	
—— Observations of the appearances among the fixed stars, called Nebulous stars, owing to the motion of the earth, and the motion of light compounded together *Derham*	XXXVIII 70	VIII 132
—— The description and use of an apparatus added as an improvement to Davis's quadrant, con-		

	Tranſ.	Abridg.
ſiſting of a mercurial level, for taking the co-altitude of ſun or ſtar at ſea, without the uſual aſſiſtance of the ſenſible horizon, which frequently is obſcured - *Leigh*	XL 417	VIII 362
STARS. (Fixed) A letter concerning an apparent motion obſerved in ſome of the fixed ſtars, owing to a nutation of the earth's axis *Bradley*	XLV 1	X 32
—— Remarks on the mutations of the ſtars *Barker*	LI 498	
—— A letter containing the reſults of obſervations of the diſtance of the moon from the ſun and fixed ſtars, made in a voyage from England to the iſland of St Helena, in order to determine the longitude of the ſhip from time to time, together with the whole proceſs of computation uſed on the occaſion - *Maſkelyne*	LII 558	
—— Conciſe rules for computing the effects of refraction and parallax in varying the apparent diſtance of the moon from the ſun or a ſtar; alſo an eaſy rule of approximation for computing the diſtance of the moon from a ſtar, the longitude and latitude of both being given; with demonſtrations of the ſame *Maſkelyne*	LIV 263	
—— An inquiry into the probable parallax and magnitude of the fixed ſtars, from the quantity of light which they afford us, and the particular circumſtances of their ſituation *Michell*	LVII 234	
STARS. (Particular) Obſervations of the ſtar, called Nebuloſa, in the girdle of Andromeda, and of the wondrous ſtar in the neck of the Whale *Bullialdus*	II 459	I 251
—— Obſervations on the new ſtar near the beak of the Swan, and the other in the neck of the Whale - - - *Hevelius*	V 2023	— 304
—— Account of a new one diſcovered in the conſtellation of the Swan in 1670 - *Hevelius*	— 2087	— 248
—— Account from Paris of the earlier diſcovery of the ſame ſtar - *Oldenburg*	— 2092	— —
—— Further obſervations of the new ſtar, near the beak of the Swan - - *Hevelius*	VI 2197	— 250
Another account from the Journal des Scavans	— 2198	— 247
—— Obſervations concerning three new ſtars, one in the Whale's neck, the other two near the head and in the breaſt of the Swan *Hevelius*	XII 853	
—— Letter concerning drawing the meridian line		

by

Stars (Double) discovered in 1779. Nath. Pigott. 71: 84.

Catalogue of double Stars. — — — — Herschel — 72: 112. 75: 40.

Account of the changes that have happened, during the last 25 years, in the relative situation of double stars, with an investigation of the cause to which they are owing. Herschel. 1803: 339. 1804: 353.

+ Stars (Fixed) On their parallax. — — Herschel — — 72: 82.

An account of several changes that have happened among the fixed Stars since the time of Mr Flamstead. Herschel 73: 247.

On the means of discovering the distance, magnitude &c. of the fixed stars, in consequence of the diminution of the velocity of their light &c. Michell 74: 35.

On a method of describing the relative positions and magnitudes of the fixed stars. Wollaston — 181.

On the method of observing the changes that happen to the fixed Stars, to which is added a catalogue of comparative brightness, for ascertaining the permanency of the lustre of Stars. Herschel. 1796: 166.

Remarks tending to establish the rotatory motion of the stars on their axes, to which is added a second catalogue of the comparative brightness of the stars — — — — — — — — 452.

A third catalogue of the comparative brightness of the stars; with an introductory account of an index to Mr. Flamsteeds observations of the fixed stars contained in the second volume of the Historia coelestis. — 1797: 293.

A fourth catalogue of the comparative brightness of the Stars — 1799: 121.

On the declination of some of the principal fixed stars. — — — — Pond. 1806: 420.

turn over

Stars (variable) see Algol

Observations of a new variable star — — — — — — — — E. Pigott 75: 127.

Goodricke — 153.

Observations on, and discovery of, the period of the variation of the light of the Star marked δ by Bayer, near the head of Cepheus ——— 76: 48.

Observations and remarks on those Stars which the Astronomers of the last Century suspected to be changeable. E. Pigott — 189.

On the disappearance of the 55th Herculis — — — — — — — Herschel 1792: 26.

On the periodical star α Herculis — — — — — — — — ——— 1796: 452.

On the periodical changes of brightness of two fixed stars. E. Pigott. 1797: 133.

An investigation of all the changes of the variable star in Sobiesky's shield, from five year's observations, exhibiting its proportional illuminated parts, and its irregularities of rotation; with conjectures respecting unenlightened heavenly bodies. ——— 1805: 131.

On the parallax of the fixed stars. Pond. 1817: 158.

Appendix to the above paper. — — 173.

On the same subject. — — 358.

Do. Brinkley. 1818: 275.

On the different methods of constructing a catalogue of fixed stars.

On the parallax of the fixed stars in right ascension — Pond. — 405.

— 481.

Astronomical observations and experiments, selected for the purpose of ascertaining the relative distances of clusters of stars, and of investigating how far the power of our telescopes may be expected to reach into space, when directed to ambiguous celestial objects. Herschel — 429

	Transf.	Abridg.
by the pole ftar, and finding the hour by the fame - - - *Gray*	XXII 815	IV 462
STAR. An account of the variations of appearance of a new ftar in the neck of the Swan *Kirchius*	XXIX 226	— 222
—— A fhort hiftory of the feveral new ftars that have appeared within thefe 150 years; with an account of the return of that in collo cygni, and of its continuance obferved in 1715 *Halley*	— 354	— 224
—— The declinations of fome fouthern ftars of the firft and fecond magnitude, June 1738, and the way of finding the hour of the night at fea from looking at the fouthern crofs *La Condamine*	XLVI 139	X 53
—— Aftronomical obfervation on the periodical ftar in Collo Ceti - - *Herfchel*	LXX 338 1792 24	
STAR. (Appulfes) Obfervable appulfes of the moon to the fixed ftars in the year 1671, foretold, and computed for the meridian and latitude of of London - - *Flamftead*	V 2029	I 453
—— Letter concerning the appulfes of the moon for 1673, and the other planets to the fixed ftars, together with an obfervation of the planet Mars - *Flamftead*	VII 5118	— 424
—— The appulfes of the moon and other planets to the fixed ftars predicted for 1674 *Flamftead*	VIII 6162	
—— On the method of determining the places of the planets, by obferving their near appulfes to the fixed ftars - *Halley*	XXXI 209	VI 170
—— A new method of calculating the eclipfes, particularly of the earth, and of any appulfes of the moon to planets and fixed ftars *Gerften*	XLIII 22	X 55
STAR. (Occultation) Obfervations on a total eclipfe of the moon, Jan. 11, 1675, with the occultations of certain fixed ftars *Hevelius*	X 289	I 310
—— An account of an occultation of a fixed ftar by the moon, Feb. 29 - *Caffini*	XI 564	— 349
—— An occultation of Mars and certain fixed ftars obferved at Dantzick, Sept. 1, 1676 *Hevelius*	— 721	— 350
—— Obfervations on the occultation of fixed ftars in 1683, at Dantzick - *Hevelius*	XIII 331	
—— Obfervations of an occultation of a fixed ftar in Gemini by the body of Jupiter, Jan. 11, and of a very clofe tranfit of Mars below the		

	Tranſ.	Abridg.
northernmoſt ſtar in the ſcorpion's forehead, Feb. 5, 1717 - - - *Anon.*	XXX 546	IV 304
STAR. (Occultation) Propoſal of obſervations of occultations of the fixed ſtars by the moon, made at Paris, to determine the exact difference of longitude betwixt London, Paris, and Greenwich - *Maſkelyne and De Lalande*	LII 607	
—— Occultations of fixed ſtars by the moon obſerved at Greenwich, 1769 - *Maſkelyne*	LIX 399	
STAR. (Meteor) A method for determining the geographical longitude of places from the appearance of the common meteors, called falling ſtars - - - *Lynn*	XXXV 351	VI 400
—— See *particular Stars, and Stars in particular Conſtellations, in their Places*		
STAR FISH. Thoughts about the ſtellar fiſh, deſcribed in vol. v, 1153 - *Willoughby*	V 1201	
—— An account of the ſtellar fiſh, formerly deſcribed p. 1153, with the addition of ſome other curioſities - - *Willoughby*	VI 2221	II 832
—— An account of an echinus, or ſtar-fiſh, with a jointed ſtem, taken on the coaſt of Barbadoes, which explains to what kind of animals thoſe foſſils belong, called ſtar ſtones, aſteriæ, and aſtropodia, which have been found in many parts of this kingdom *Mendes da Coſta*	LII 357	
STARRY ANNISEED TREE. An account of a new ſpecies of illicium Linnæi, or ſtarry anniſeed tree, lately diſcovered in Weſt Florida *Ellis*	LX 524	
STAR-STONES. A letter containing obſervations on the aſtroites, or ſtar-ſtones *Liſter*	X 274	— 503
—— See *Aſtroites*		
STATICS. An account of ſome new ſtatical experiments - - *Deſaguliers*	XL 62	VIII 278
—— Extracts from two letters of Dr. John Lining, of Charles-Town, South Carolina, giving an account of ſtatical experiments made on himſelf for one whole year, accompanied with meteorological obſervations, and ſix general tables *Lining*	XLII 491	IX 276
—— Letter ſerving to accompany ſome additions to his ſtatical experiments - *Lining*	XLIII 318	XI 1350
STATICS. (Vegetable) Account of Mr. Hale's vegetable ſtatics - *Deſaguliers*	XXXIV 264 XXXV 323	VI 2 158

	Trans.	Abridg.
Station. See *Rome*		
Statues. Method of caſting ſtatues in metal; together with an invention for making ſuch caſt ſtatues, of an extraordinary thinneſs, beyond any thing hitherto known or practiſed *Valvaſor*	XVI 259	I 599
—— Extracts of two letters from Rome concerning ſome antient ſtatues, pictures, and other curioſities, found in a ſubterraneous town lately diſcovered near Naples - *Paderni*	XLI 484	IX 440
Extract of another on the ſame ſubject *Knapton*	— 489	— 442
Extract of another letter on the ſame ſubject *Criſpe*	— 493	— 444
—— See *Herculaneum*		
Steam. How terreſtrial ſteams may be the generative cauſe of both minerals and metals, and of all the peculiarities of ſprings - *Beale*	V 1154	II 833
—— Of the uſe of the air to elevate the ſteams of bodies - - - - *Boyle*	— 2048	— 297
—— Advertiſements occaſioned by the remarks, printed in vol. X. p. 307, of the warm and fertilizing temperature and ſteams of the earth *Beal*	X 357	
Steam Engine. The beſt proportions for ſteam engine cylinders of a given content, conſidered *Blake*	XLVI 197	
—— Further experiments for encreaſing the quantity of ſteam in a fire engine *Fitzgerald*	L 370	
—— See *Engine, Fire Engine, Fountains*		
Steatomatous Tumour. Account of an extraordinary ſteatomatous tumour, in the abdomen of a woman - - *Hanly*	LXI 131	
Steel. A ſuggeſtion for retrieving the art of hardening and tempering ſteel for cutting porphyre, and other hard marbles - *Anon.*	VIII 6010	— 599
—— The manner of making ſteel, and its temper; with a gueſs at the way the antients uſed to ſteel their picks, for the cutting and hewing of porphyry - - *Liſter*	XVII 865	— 560
—— A Memoir on the lacrymæ Bataviæ, or glaſs drops, the tempering of ſteel, and efferveſcence accounted for by the ſame principle *Le Cat*	XLVI 175	X 560
—— An account of an experiment, by which it appears that ſalt of ſteel does not enter into the lacteal veſſels; with remarks *Wright*	L 594	

On welding cast steel. Frankland 1795: 296.

Mmm 2 STEEL-

Experiments and observations to investigate the nature of a kind of steel, manufactured at Bombay, and there called Wootz. Pearson —— 322.

Experiments on Wootz. Mushet 1805: 163.

Entry	Author	Trans.	Abridg.
STEEL YARD BALANCE SWING. Description and uses of the steel yard balance swing	*Sheldrake*	XLII 20	IX 499
STELLAR FISH. See *Star Fish*			
STENO. Some notes on Dr. Swammerdam's book of insects, and on that of Steno, concerning petrified shells - -	*Lister*	VI 2219	I 216
STEVIN. An explanation of an obscure passage in Albert Gerard's commentary upon S. Stevin's works - -	*Simpson*	XLVIII 368	
STOCK. Some communications on the descent of sap	*Reed*	VI 2128	II 687
Some considerations on Mr. Reed's letter, shewing in what sense the sap may be said to descend and to circulate in plants, and the graft, to communicate with the stock	*Beal*	— 2144	— 690
STOMACH. Observations of a large bed of glands observed in the stomach of a pike	*Musgrave*	XIV 699	III 93
—— An extraordinary cure of a horse that was staked into his stomach -	*Wallis*	XIX 118	
—— Cure of a person who swallowed a knife which lay in his stomach a year and 7 months, and then worked out at an aposthem on his breast	*Sloane*	— 180	
—— Of the motion of the stomach observed in a dog	*Pitt*	XX 278	II 91
—— A letter concerning two cases of wounds in the stomach - -	*Field*	XXXII 78	VII 508
—— A letter concerning an impostumation in the stomach - -	*Atkinson*	— 80	— 507
—— A preter-natural perforation found in the upper part of the stomach, with the symptoms it produced - -	*Rawlinson*	XXXV 361	— —
—— Letter relating to the villi of the stomach of oxen, and the expansion of the cuticle through the ductus alimentalis -	*Price*	— 532	VI 441
—— A case of a stricture in the middle of the stomach in a girl, dividing it into two bags	*Amyand*	XXXVII 258	VII 508
—— An observation of the immoderate and fatal use of crab-stones, and such-like absorbent earths, and from whence have proceeded stones in the stomach and reins -	*Breynius*	XLI 557	IX 171
—— The case of Mr. Smith, surgeon, at Sudbury, in Suffolk; the coats of whose stomach were changed into an almost cartilegenous substance	*Murdock*	XLVI 39	

see Camel.

& Stomach. Observations on the structure of the different cavities, which constitute the stomach of the Whale, compared with those of ruminating animals, with a view to ascertain the situation of the digestive organ. Home. 1807:93.

Some account of the stomachs of different animals, which do not ruminate, compared with the more complex stomachs of those which do. ——— —139.

Experiments and observations on the influence of the nerves of the 8th pair on the secretions of the stomach. Brodie. 1814:102.

Observations on the gastric glands of the human stomach, and the contraction which takes place in that viscus. — Home. 1817:347.

		Tranf.	Abridg.
Stomach. Account of a young lady who had an extraordinary impoftume formed in her ftomach	*Layard*	XLVI 406	XI 1023
—— An account of a monftrous human fœtus, having neither head, heart, lungs, ftomach, fpleen, pancreas, liver, nor kidneys	*Le Cat*	LVII 1	
—— On the digeftion of the ftomach after death,	*Hunter*	LXII 447	
Stone. (Natural hiftory) Of a place in England, where, without petrifying water, wood is turned into ftone -	*Boyle*	I 101	II 325
—— Of the nature of a certain ftone, found in the Indies, in the head of a ferpent	*Vernati*	— 102	— 814
—— A relation of worms that eat out ftones	*De la Voye*	— 321	— 787
—— A Defcription of a Swedifh ftone, which affords fulphur, vitriol, allum, and minium	*Talbot*	— 375	— 501
—— Inftances, hints, and applications relating to ftones of divers kinds, &c. -	*Beale*	IV 1135	— 148
—— Account of fome ftone-quaries in Hungary	*Brown*	V 1044	— 339
—— Account of a ftone quary near Maeftricht	*Anon.*	— 2051	— 463
—— A defcription of certain ftones figured like plants, and, by fome obferving men, efteemed to be plants petrified -	*Lifter*	VIII 6181	— 493
—— Advertifements relating to ftones, rocks, &c.	*Beal*	X 357	— 396
—— A letter concerning fome formed ftones found at Hunton, in Kent -	*Hatley*	XIV 463	— 426
—— A refraction of the 7th and laft paragraph of Mr. W. Molyneaux's letter, vol. XIV. p. 552, concerning Lough-Neagh ftone, and its non-application to the magnet upon calcination	*Molyneux*	— 820	— 323
—— An account of an extraordinary tincture given to a ftone - -	*Reifel*	XVI 22	I 604
—— An account of the making pitch, tar, and oil out of a blackifh ftone in Shropfhire	*Ele*	XIX 544	
—— Letter concerning feveral figured ftones lately found by him - -	*Lhwyd*	XX 279	II 511
—— Account of a figured ftone found in Wales; with a note on it by Hans Sloane	*Llwyd*	XXI 187	— —
—— An account of fome ftones and plants lately found in Scotland -	*Sibbald*	XXII 693	
—— Account of the quarry at Maeftricht	*Ellis*	XXIII 1416	V 2 134

	Tranſ.	Abridg.
STONE. Microſcopical obſervations on the pumice ſtone, coral, ſpunges, &c. *Leeuwenhoek*	XXIV 2158	VI 2 267
—— A deſcription of the ſeveral ſtrata of earth, ſtones, coals, &c. found in a coal pit, at the weſt end of Dudley, Staffordſhire; to which is added a table of the ſpecifick gravity of each ſtratum - *Fettiplace and Haukſbee*	XXVII 541	IV 2 182
—— An account of the impreſſion of the almoſt entire ſkeleton of a large animal in a very hard ſtone found at Elſton, near Newark, Nottinghamſhire - - *Stukely*	XXX 963	— - 272
—— An account of the filtring ſtone of Mexico, and compared with other ſtones, by which it is ſhewn that it is of little or no uſe in purifying the waters which have paſſed through it *Vaters*	XXXIX 106	VIII 728
—— Remarks on ſtones of a regular figure found near Bagneres, in Gaſcony *Monteſquieu*	XLIII 26	X 788
—— An enquiry concerning the ſtone oſteacolla *Beurerus*	— 373	— 602
—— An account of perfect minute cryſtal ſtones *Parſons*	— 468	— 612
—— A letter concerning an extraordinary fiſh, called in Ruſſia, quab, and concerning the ſtones called crabs eyes - *Baker*	XLV 174	XI 876
—— Letter concerning a flat ſpheroidal ſtone, having lines regularly croſſing it - *Platt*	XLVI 534	X 638
—— A deſcription and figures of a ſmall flat ſpheroidal ſtone, having lines formed upon it *Mortimer*	— 602	— 639
—— An account of the impreſſion on a ſtone dug up in the iſland of Antigua - *Byam*	XLIX 295	
—— A letter concerning the ſtones found in Antigua *Pond*	— 297	
—— Remarks on the ſtones in the county of Naſſau, and the territories of Treves and Colen, reſembling thoſe of the Giants Cauſeway, in Ireland - - *Trembly*	— 581	
—— An account of a large ſtone near Cape-Town, with a letter from Sir William Hamilton, on having ſeen ſome pieces of the ſaid ſtone *Anderſon*	LXVIII 102	
STONE. (Diſorder ſo called) Account of a great number of ſtones found in one bladder *Goodrick*	II 482	III 149
—— An account of a ſtone cut out from under the tongue of a man - *Liſter*	VII 4062	— 155

STONE,

+ Particulars of the discovery of some very singular balls of Stone, found in the works of the Huddersfield Canal. Outram. 1796: 350.

Experiments and observations on certain stony and metalline substances, which at different times are said to have fallen on the earth; also on various kinds of native Iron. Howard. 1802: 168.

An account of some stones said to have fallen on the earth in France, and of a lump of native Iron, said to have fallen in India. Greville. 1803: 200.

	Tranſ.	Abridg.
Stone. (Diſorder) An account of a ſtone found in the bladder of a dog, and of another faſtened to the back-bone of a horſe *Giornale de Letterati*	VII 4094	III 164
—— Two obſervations about ſtones, one found in the bladder of a dog, the other faſtened to the back-bone of a horſe *Giornale de Letterati*	— 4094	— —
—— A relation of an human body opened at Dantzick, and of 38 ſtones found in the bladder thereof - - *Kirkby*	VIII 6155	— 149
—— An obſervation concerning ſome ſtones of a perfect gold-colour found in animals *Johnſtons*	IX 9	— 166
—— An account of ſeveral human calculus's of an unuſual bigneſs - *Garden*	XII 843	— 150
—— Anatomical obſervations of an abceſs in the liver, a great number of ſtones in the gall bag and bilious veſſels, an unuſual conformation of the emulgents and pelves, a ſtrange conſtruction of both kidneys, and a great dilatation of the vena cava - *Tyſon*	— 1035	— 81
—— An abſtract of a treatiſe on the calculus, in anſwer to ſeveral queries propoſed by Sir John Hoſkyns - - *Slare*	XIV 523	— 178
With a poſtſcript concerning two human calculi of unuſual form and bigneſs *Slare*	— 534	
—— An account of a ſtone grown to an iron bodkin in the bladder of a boy - *Liſter*	XV 882	— 162
—— An abſtract of a letter giving an account of ſtones voided by ſiege *Threapland*	— 961	— 160
—— The deſcription of a ſtone of the bladder *Anon.*	— 1015	— 150
—— Account of ſtones voided per penem *Cole*	— 1162	— 151
—— Deſcription of a large ſtone voided by urine *Anon.*	— 1269	— —
—— An account of the caſe of Margaret Lower from the year 1681 - - *Konig*	XVI 94	— 170
An examen of the ſtones ſent from Berne *Slare*	— 140	
Further trial of them by chymical diſtillations *Slare*	— 145	— 177
—— Account of a ſtone of an extraordinary bigneſs, ſpontaneouſly voided though the urethra of a woman at Dublin - *Mullineux*	XVII 817	— 151 — 182
—— An uncommon obſervation of a ſtone found in the kidneys - - *Wittie*	XVIII 30	— 151
—— An account of a ſtone of a prodigious ſize ex-		

	Tranſ.	Abridg.
tracted by ſection out of a woman's bladder, who is living - *Wood*	XVIII 103	III 185
STONE. (Diſorder) Of a ſtone found in the gall bladder of a woman - - *J. T.*	— 111	— 159
—— An account of two large ſtones which lodged in the meatus urinarius for twenty years paſt, and were from thence cut out *Bernard*	XIX 250	— 153
—— An account of a ſtone of the bladder which weighed 51 ounces, or three pounds three ounces, and a ſtone out of the bladder which adhered to it - - *Preſton*	— 310	— 154
—— An account of a gentleman's being cut for the ſtone in the kidney, with a brief inquiry into the antiquity and practice of nephrotomy *Anon.*	— 333	— 188
—— Some additional remarks on the extracting the ſtone out of the bladder of thoſe of the female ſex - *Molyneux*	XX 11	— 184
—— Letter concerning ſeveral ſtones voided by a boy - - *Sibbald*	— 264	— 154
—— An account of a ſtone bred at the root of the tongue, and cauſing a quinſey - *Bonavert*	— 440	— 156
—— An account of a ſtone found in the ſtomach of a lady on diſſection, another in the left kidney, and ſome ſmaller ones in the gall bladder *Clerk*	XXI 95	— 159
—— Part of a letter giving an account of the new way of cutting for the ſtone by the Hermit, with his opinion of it - *Buſſiere*	— 100	— 185
—— Account of a diſeaſe occaſioned by ſwallowing pebble ſtones; with remarks by Hans Sloane *Holt*	— 190	— 92
—— Letter concerning a ſtone cut from a child, having a flint within it - *Garden*	XXII 689	— 164
—— Letter concerning a ſtone cut out of the bladder, having hair on it - *Wallace*	— 688	— 155 — 164
—— A further account of the perſon mentioned to have ſwallowed ſtones - *Holt*	— 992	V 260
—— Account of a ball extracted from a perſon who had ſuffered by it 30 years, in which was a plumb-ſtone - *Young*	XXIII 1279	— 261
Some inſtances of other perſons who were hurt by ſwallowing plumb-ſtones *Sloane*	— 1283	— 264
—— An account of very large ſtones voided per urethram - - *Lhwyd*	XXIV 1804	— 288
—— Two extraordinary caſes of a large ſtone in the urethra, brought on by a venereal infection,		

and

	Tranf.	Abridg.
and a child born with a remarkable tumour on the loins - - *Huxham*	XXV 257	VII 536
Stone (Diforder.) A letter concerning the jaundice, occafioned by a ftone obftructing the ductus communis bilarius, which was afterwards voided by ftool - - *Margram*	— 2233	V 279
—— Of hydatides inclofed with a ftony cruft in the kidney of a fheep - *Cowper*	— 2304	— 54
—— An abftract out of a letter concerning ftones voided by ftool; with an anfwer to it by Dr. Cole - - *Holbrooke*	XXVII 28	— 265
—— A letter concerning large ftones voided per urethram - - *Thorefby*	— 536	— 288
—— An account of a new method of cutting for the ftone - *Douglas*	XXXII 83	VII 527
—— Obfervations upon diffecting the body of a perfon troubled with the ftone *Williams*	— 326	— 530
—— An account of the cutting of a man who died of the ftone in the kidnies - *Hardifway*	— 327	— —
—— A letter concerning ftones voided per anum *Martineau*	— 433	— 520
—— Remarkable obfervations on the diffection of a body of one who died of the ftone *Vater*	XXXIV 102	— 531
—— An account of a large ftone voided through the urinary paffages of a woman *Beard*	— 211	— 534
—— An account of a ftone taken out of a horfe, at Bofton, in New-England, 1724 *Dudley*	— 261	— 440
—— An account of feveral ftones found in the kidneys of a perfon - - *Dobyns*	XXXV 452	— 532
—— An account of a ftone in the bladder breaking fpontaneoufly, and paffing off through the urethra - - *Heifter*	XXXVII 13	— 534
—— Of an inguinal rupture, with a pin in the appendix cœci, incrufted with ftone *Amyand*	XXXIX 329	IX 153
—— A defcription of a very extraordinary ftone or calculus taken out of the bladder of a man after death - . *Caumont*	XL 369	— 172
Another account of the fame cafe *Zollman*	— 371	— 173
Anfwer to the Marq. de Caumont's account *Sloane*	— 374	— 174
—— An account of the cafe of a calculus making its way through an old cicatrix in the perinæum *Hartley*	XLI 349	— 176
—— An account of a ftone or calculus making its way out through the fcrotum - *Sloane*	— 351	— —
—— Cafe of an extraordinary ftone voided by the anus - - *Mackarnefs*	— 500	— 170

	Tranſ.	Abridg.
Stone (Diſorder.) An obſervation of the immoderate and fatal uſe of crab ſtones, and ſuch like abſorbent earths, from whence have proceeded ſtones in the ſtomach and reins *Brevnius*	XLI 557	IX 171
—— An account of ſome remarkable ſtones taken out of the kidney's of Mrs. Felles after her deceaſe - - *Sherwood*	— 610	— 502
—— An account of ſeveral ſtones found in bags formed by a protuſion of the coats of the bladder, as appeared on opening the body of Mr. Gardiner - - *Nourſe*	XLII 11	— 176
—— An account of the caſe of William Payne, with what appeared upon examining his kidney and bladder - - *Bell*	— 54	— 177
—— An account of a large ſtone voided by a woman with her urine - - *Revilas*	— 365	— 179
—— An account of an extraordinary calculus taken out of the body of a boy *Huxham*	XLIII 207	XI 976
—— Letter concerning a large ſtone found in the ſtomach of a horſe – *W. Watſon*	— 268	— 904
—— An account of a very large ſtone found in the colon of a horſe; and of ſeveral ſtones which were taken from the inteſtines of a mare; with ſome experiments and obſervations thereupon *Bailey*	XLIV 296	— 905
—— A letter concerning a ſtone taken out of the bladder of a dog, with a piece of dog graſs in its center - - *Fiage*	— 335	— 909
—— An account of a lady at Cottered, Hertfordſhire, who had a ſtone under her tongue *Freeman*	XLVI 5	— 959
—— Concerning a boy who had a calculus formed between the glans and the præputium *Clarke*	— 45	— 1004
—— An account of a very large human calculus *Heberden*	— 596	— 1005
—— Caſe of a piece of a bone, together with a ſtone in the bladder, ſucceſsfully extracted *Warner*	XLVII 475	
—— Relation of a large calculus found in a mare *W. Watſon*	XLVIII 800	
—— An account of two extraordinary caſes of gall ſtones - - *Johnſtone*	L 543	
—— A remarkable inſtance of four rough ſtones that were diſcovered in an human urinary bladder, contrary to the received opinion; and		

ſuc-

Stone. Experiments on human Calculi. Lane. 81: 223.

On Gouty and urinary concretions. Wollaston. 1797: 386.

Experiments and observations, tending to show the composition and properties of urinary concretions. Pearson. 1798: 15.

A letter on the differences in the structure of Calculi, which arise from their being formed in different parts of the urinary passages; and on effects that are produced on them, by the internal use of solvent medicines. Brande. 1808: 223.

Some observations on Mr. Brande's paper on Calculi. Home. —— 244.

An account of a Calculus from the human bladder of uncommon magnitude. Earle. 1809: 303.

Observations on the effects of magnesia, in preventing an increased formation of uric acid; with some remarks on the composition of the urine. Brande. 1810: 136.

On Cystic oxide, a new species of Urinary Calculus. Wollaston. —— 223.

Additional observations on the effects of Magnesia in preventing an increased formation of Uric Acid; with remarks on the influence of Acids upon the composition of Urine. Brande. 1813: 213.

	Tran.	Abridg.
ſucceſsfully extracted by the lateral method of cutting for the ſtone - *Warner*	L 579	
STONE (Diſorder.) An account of two ſtones of remarkable ſhapes and ſizes, which, for the ſpace of ſix years, were firmly lodged in the urethra of a young man, and ſucceſsfully cut out from thence - - *Warner*	LI 304	
—— An account of a ſtony concretion taken from the colon of a horſe - *Baker*	— 694	
—— The caſe of a patient, who voided a large ſtone through the perinæum from the urethra *Frewen*	LII 258	
—— Caſe of a man who had ſix ſtones taken out of the gall bladder - *Geach*	LIII 231	
—— An account of a hernia of the urinary bladder including a ſtone - *Pott*	LIV 61	
—— An account of a ſtone voided, without help, from the bladder of a woman - *Heberden*	LV 128	
—— The caſe of a patient voiding ſtones through a fiſtulous ſore in the loins, without any concomitant diſcharge of the urine of the ſame paſſage - - *Simmons*	LXIV 108	
STONE. (Remedies for the) An account of the acemella and its ſtone-diſſolving faculty *Hotton*	XXII 760	
—— A propoſal to bring ſmall paſſable ſtones with eaſe out of the bladder - *Hales*	XLIII 502	XI 990
—— The effects of the lixivium ſaponis, taken inwardly by a man aged 75 years, who had the ſtone, and in whoſe bladder, after his deceaſe, were found two hundred and fourteen ſtones *Cheſelden*	XXIV 36	— 992
—— A letter concerning the relief found in the ſtone from the uſe of Alicant ſoap and lime water - - *Lucas*	— 463	— 1000
—— The caſe of Horace Walpole, Eſq. drawn by himſelf - - *Walpole*	XLVII 43	
A ſequel to the caſe of Horace Walpole, Eſq. *Walpole*	— 472	
Caſe of the late Horace, Lord Walpole, being a ſequel to his own account at vol. XLVII, p. 43, and 472 - *Pringle*	L 205	
Obſervations on the caſe - *Whytt*	— 209	
—— An account of the virtues of ſoap in diſſolving the ſtone in the caſe of the Rev. Mr. Mathew Simpſon - - *Pringle*	— 221	
—— Poſtſcript to obſervations on Lord Walpole's caſe, with obſervations on the Lithontriptic virtue		

	Transf.	Abridg.
of the Carlsbad waters, lime-water, and soap *Whytt*	L 386	
STONE. (Operation for the) A description of a catheter made to remedy the inconveniencies which occasioned the leaving off the high operation for the stone - *Cleland*	XLI 844	IX 179
—— Remarks on the operation of cutting for the stone - - *Le Cat*	XLIII 391	XI 976
—— A remarkable case of a person cut for the stone in the new way, commonly called the lateral; by William Cheselden, Esq; *Reid*	XLIV 33	— 991
—— An observation of an operation made by the high apparatus according to M. le Cat's method, in the year 1743, from Philip Henry Zollman - - *Le Cat*	— 175	— 995
—— Part of a letter concerning the extracting a large stone by an aperture in the urethra *Howell*	— 215	— 999
—— Extract of a letter enclosing a proposal for entirely removing the only real defect in the lateral operation for the stone *Mudge*	XLVI 24	— 1002
—— The operation of lithotomy on women *Le Cat*	— 97	— 975
STONES. (Precious) Some observations upon gems, or precious stones; more particularly such as the ancients used to engrave upon *Dingley*	XLIV 502	X 610
—— Observations upon some gems similar to the tourmalin - - *Wilson*	LII 443	
STOOL. A letter concerning hydatitides voided by stool *Musgrave*	XXIV 1797	V 281
—— A letter concerning the jaundice occasioned by a stone obstructing the ductus communis bilarius, which was afterwards voided by stool *Musgrave*	XXV 2233	— 279
STORM. Extract of a letter, giving an account of an unusual storm of hail, which fell at Lisle, in Flanders, May 25, 1686	XVII 858	II 145
—— An account of a great hail storm at Hitchen, in Hertfordshire, May 4, 1697 *Tailor*	XIX 577	— 147
—— A relation of a great hail storm, in Herefordshire, June 6, 1697	— 579	— 148
Of the same storm in Monmouthshire *Lhwyd*	— —	
—— Relation of the effects of a violent storm at Acomack, in America, Oct. 19, 1693, on the rivers of that country - *Scarburgh*	— 659	— 104
—— Part of a letter concerning a strange effect of the		

		Tranſ.	Abridg.
late great ſtorm in Suſſex, 1703	*Fuller*	XXIV 1530	
STORM. A letter containing obſervations concerning the late ſtorm at Upminſter -	*Derham*	— —	IV 2 109
—— Part of a letter concerning the late great ſtorm obſerved at Delft -	*Leeuwenhoek*	— 1535	
Further account of the ſaid ſtorm	*Leeuwenhoek*	— 1544	
—— An experiment to ſhew the cauſe of the deſcent of the mercury in the barometer in a ſtorm	*Haukſbee*	— 1629	— - 181
—— Part of a letter, giving an account of a ſtorm of thunder and lightning that happened at Ipſwich, July 16, 1708 -	*Bridgman*	XXVI 137	— 2 128
The effects of the above ſtorm at Colcheſter	*Nelſon*	— 140	
—— Part of a letter concerning a ſtorm of thunder, lightning, and rain, at Leeds, in Yorkſhire, Auguſt 5, 1708 -	*Thoreſby*	— 289	V 2 40
—— A letter giving an account of a ſtorm of thunder and lightning which happened near Leeds, in Yorkſhire - -	*Thoreſby*	XXVII 320	IV 2 131
—— A letter giving an account of the damage done by a ſtorm of hail which happened near Rotheram, in Yorkſhire -	*Thoreſby*	— 514	— - 109
—— A relation of the effects of a ſtorm of thunder and lightning at Sampford Courtney, in Devonſhire, on Oct. 7, 1711	*Chamberlayne*	— 528	
—— A letter concerning the ſtorm, Jan. 8th, 1734-5, at Darlington -	*Forth*	XXXIX 285	
—— A letter concerning the ſtorm of thunder which happened June 12, 1748	*Miles*	XLV 383	X 475
—— An account of a ſtorm of thunder and lightning near Ludgvan, in Cornwall, Dec. 20, 1752	*Borlaſe*	XLVIII 86	
—— An account of the effects of a ſtorm of thunder and lightning in the pariſhes of Looe and Lanreath, in Cornwall, June 27, 1756	*Dyer*	L 104	
Letter on the ſame ſubject	*Miller*	— 107	
—— An account of the effects of a ſtorm at Wigton, in Cumberland -	*Thomlinſon*	— 194	
—— An account of an extraordinary ſtorm of hail in Virginia, July 9, 1758 -	*Fauquier*	— 746	
—— An account of a ſtor mof thunder and lightning at Norwich, July 13, 1758	*Cooper*	LI 38	
—— An account of the effects of a ſtorm of thunder			

and

	Tranſ.	Abridg.
and lightning at Rickmanſworth, in Hertford-ſhire, July 16, 1759 - *Whitfield*	LI 28a	
STORM. An account of two thunder ſtorms, on July 28, 1761, at Ludgvan church, the other Jan. 11, 1762, at Breag - *Borlaſe*	LII 507	
—— Account of the effects of a ſtorm of thunder and lightning on Pembroke college, Oxford, Jan 3, 1765 - *Griffith*	LV 273	
—— Obſervations upon a thunder ſtorm *Bergman*	LVII 97	
—— A letter deſcribing a remarkable ſtorm at Buckland Brewer, Devon, March 2, 1769 *Paxton*	LIX 79	
—— An account of a remarkable thunder ſtorm, Feb. 18, 1770, at St. Keverne, in Cornwall *Williams*	LXI 71	
—— Extract of a letter concerning a thunder and lightning ſtorm, by which Mr. Heartly, of Harrowgate, was killed, Sept. 29, 1772 *Kirkſhaw*	LXIII 177	
—— Account of the effects of a thunder ſtorm on the 15th of March, 1733, upon the houſe of Lord Tylney, at Naples *Sir William Hamilton*	— 324	
—— See *Hail*, *Lightning*, *Rain*, *Thunder*		
STOVE. An account of a lately invented ſtove for preſerving plants in the green-houſe in winter, publiſhed at the end of the Calendarium Hortenſe - - *Cullum*	XVIII 191	II 750
—— The manner in which the Chineſe heat their rooms - - - - *De Viſme*	LXI 59	
An account of the kang, or Chineſe ſtove *Gramont*	— 61	
STRAIGHT'S-MOUTH. A conjecture about an under current at the Straight's-Mouth	XIV 564	
—— —— Of the currents at the Straight's Mouth	XXXIII 191	VI 2 171
STRALSUND. See *Thunder*		
STRATA. An account of the ſtrata met with in digging for marle, and of horns found under ground in Ireland - - *Kelly*	XXXIV 122	— — 224
—— A deſcription of a petrified ſtratum formed from the waters of Matlock, Derbyſhire *Dobſon*	LXIV 124	
STRAWBERRIES. Microſcopical obſervations on the ſeeds of figs, ſtrawberries, &c. *Leeuwenhoek*	XIX 269	III 685
STRING. Concerning the motion of ſtretched ſtring *Taylor*	XXVIII 26	IV 391
STUPEFACTION. An account of a caſe of a young man ſtupified by the ſmoke of ſea-coal *Frewen*	LII 454	
STYLE. Letter judging of the age of the MSS of		

+ Strata. Account of the Strata observed in sinking for water at Boston in Lincolnshire. Limbird 77:50.

Some account of the Strata in the North of Ireland and Western Islands of Scotland. Mills. 80:73.

Steam. See Well.

Strength of materials. Account of experiments made on the strength of materials. — Rennie. 1818:118.

Strontionite. Account of a mineral Substance, called Strontionite. Schmeisser. 1794:418.

	Tranſ.	Abridg.
learned authors, painters, muſicians, &c. by the *Wanley*	XXIV 1998	V 2 1
Style. (Aſtronomy) Two letters concerning the alteration (ſuggeſted) of the Julian account for the Gregorian - - *Wallis*	XXI 343	III 406
—— The report made by Lord Treaſurer Burleigh to the Lords of the Council of a conſultation had, and the examination of the plain and brief diſcourſe by John Dee, for reforming the calendar - - *Anon.*	— 355	I 404
Reflections upon the foregoing paper *Greaves*	— 356	— 405
—— The concluſion of the Proteſtant empire Sept. 23, 1699, concerning the calendar *Houghton*	XXII 459	III 408
—— Remarks upon the ſolar and lunar years, the cycle of 19 years, commonly called the Golden Number, the Epact, and a method of finding the time of Eaſter, as it is now obſerved in moſt parts of Europe *Earl of Macclesfield*	XLVI 417	X 131
Styptic. Notice of an admirable liquor, inſtantly ſtopping the blood of arteries pricked or cut, without any ſuppuration, or without leaving any ſcar or cicatrice - *Denys*	VIII 6039	III 252
Experiments made with the liquor at London	— 6052	— 253
At Paris - - - *Anon.*	— 6054	— 291
An addition to the experiments *Anon.*	— 6074	— 254
Experiments in St. Thomas's Hoſpital *Anon.*	— 6078	— —
Further ſucceſs in the fleet - *Anon.*	— 6115	— 255
—— An account of ſome experiments lately made on dogs, and of the effects of Mr. John Colbatch's ſtyptics on human bodies, by *W. Cooper*	XVIII 42	— —
—— Some obſervations upon Dr. Eaton's ſtyptic *Sprengell*	XXXIII 108	VII 563
—— Remarks on the uſe of the ſtyptic, purchaſed by his moſt Chriſtian Majeſty *Faget*	XLVII 560	
—— See *Agaric, Lycoperdon*		
Styrax Liquida. The manner of making ſtyrax liquida, alias, roſa mallas - *Petiver*	XXVI 44	V 417
Submarines. A deſcription of ſome coralls, and other curious ſubmarines, lately ſent from the Phillippine iſles, by G. I. Gamel *Petiver*	XXIII 1419	V 2 286
Substances. An account of two uncommon mineral ſubſtances in ſome coal and iron mines in England - - *Jeſſop*	VIII 6179	II 458

Substances.

	Tranſ.	Abridg.
SUBSTANCES. Concerning the various figures of the ſalts contained in the ſeveral ſubſtances *Leeuwenhoek*	XV 1073	III 685
—— Letter concerning a ſubſtance coughed up reſembling the veſſels of the lungs *Buſſiere*	XXII 545	— 68
—— Caſe of a gentlewoman who voided with her urine hairy cruſtaceous ſubſtances; with Sir H. Sloane's anſwer, containing ſeveral obſervations of extraordinary ſubſtances voided by the urinary paſſages *Powel and Sloane*	XLI 699	IX 180
—— Caſe of hair voided by urine *Knight*	— 705	— 183
—— A ſummary of ſome late obſervations upon the generation, compoſition and decompoſition of animal and vegetable ſubſtances *Needham*	XLV 615	X 797
—— An account of a curious fleſhy coral-like ſubſtance, with ſome obſervations on it by Mr. John Ellis - *Schloſſer*	XLIX 449	
—— A deſcription of three ſubſtances mentioned by the Arabian phyſicians, in a paper ſent from Aleppo, and tranſlated from the Arabian by *J. Channing*	LVII 21	
—— A ſhort narrative of the ſtructure and effect of parabolick burning ſpeculums, made by the late Mr. Hoeſen, of Dreſden; and an account of experiments made with them on the fuſion of different ſubſtances - *Wolfe*	LIX 4	
—— Experiments on ignited bodies *Roebuck*	LXVI 509	
—— Experiments on ignited ſubſtances *Whitehurſt*	— 575	
—— Experiments on ſome mineral ſubſtances *Wolfe*	LXIX 11	
SUBTERRANEOUS FIRE. A ſpecies of ſubteraneous fire obſerved in Kent - *Neſbitt*	XXXV 307	VI 2 199
SUBTERRANEOUS STEAMS. Some obſervations on ſubterraneous ſteams - *Robinſon*	XV 922	II 349
SUBTERRANEOUS TREE. Obſervations concerning ſubterraneous trees in Dagenham, and other marſhes bordering upon the river Thames, in the county of Eſſex - *Derham*	XXVII 478	IV 2 219
SUCK. Relation concerning an aged woman of 60 years, giving ſuck to her grand child *Anon.*	IX 100	III 80
—— Account of a woman 68 years of age, who gave ſuck to two of her grand children *Stack*	XLI 140	IX 206
—— An account of a man who gave ſuck to a child *Robt. Biſhop of Corke*	— 810	— 208
SUGAR. Microſcopical obſervations on the figure of ſugar and ſalt, and the probable cauſe of the difference of their taſte *Leeuwenhoek*	X 380	III 683

SUGAR.

Sulphate of Ammoniac. Experiments and observations on its Decomposition. Hatchett. 1796: 313. ~~285~~

Sulphate of Magnesia. On the manufacture of the sulphate of Magnesia at Monte della Guardia, near Genoa. Holland. 1816: 294

	Tranſ.	Abridg.
Sugar. An account of a ſort of ſugar made of the juice of maple in Canada - *Anon.*	XV 988	II 668
—— Microſcopical obſervations on the particles of chryſtalized ſugar - *Leeuwenhoek*	XXVI 444	V 2 388
—— Obſervations upon the nature and properties of ſugar - - - *Slare*	XXVIII 273	V 353
—— An account of the method of making ſugar from the juice of the maple-tree in New England *Dudley*	XXXI 27	VI 2 379
—— Account of the method of cultivating the ſugar cane - - *Cazaud*	LXIX 207	
—— Knowledge neceſſary to judge of any kind of ſugar Mills - - ~~Mill.~~	LXX 318	
Sulphur. A deſcription of a Swediſh ſtone which affords ſulphur, vitriol, allum, and minium *Talbot*	I 375	II 531
—— Some obſervations and experiments about vitriol, tending to find out the nature of that ſubſtance, and to give further light in the inquiry after the principles and properties of other minerals *Anon.*	IX 41	
—— A continuation of a diſcourſe concerning vitriol. ſhewing, that vitriol is uſually produced by ſulphur, acting on, and coagulating with, a metal; and then making out, that allum is likewiſe the reſult of the ſaid ſulphur; as alſo evincing, that vitriol, ſulphur, and allum, do agree in the ſaline principle; and laſtly declaring the nature of the ſalt in brimſtone, and whence it is derived - *Anon.*	IX 66	— 544
—— Two letters giving an account of a red colour produced by mixture of a ſulphureous ſpirit with a volatile alcali - *Gibbons*	XIX 542	III 367
—— A relation of a ſtone quarry at Pyrmont, from which a ſulphurous ſmoke iſſues like that from the cave at Naples, called the Grotto of Dogs, deſcribed by Miſſon, and others - *Seip*	XL 266	VIII 659
—— A letter concerning a ball of ſulphur ſuppoſed to to be generated in the air *Cook*	— 427	— 522
—— An account of two caves, one of ice, the other throwing out noxious exhalations *Belius*	XLI 41	— 662
—— An eaſy method of procuring the volatile acid of ſulphur - *Seehl*	XLIII 1	XI 1226
—— Thoughts on the different impregnations of mineral waters; more particularly concerning the exiſtence of ſulphur in ſome of them *Rutty*	LI 275	
—— An account of the ſulphureous mineral waters		

O o o of

Experiments on Sulphur — Davy 1810: 231

On some combinations of Phosphorus and Sulphur and on some other subjects of chemical inquiry — Davy. 1812: 405.

		Transf.	Abridg.
of Castle-Leod and Fairburn, in the county of Ross, and of the salt purging waters of Pitkeathly, in the county of Perth, in Scotland *Monro*		LXII 15	
SUMMER. An inquiry into the causes of a dry and wet summer — *Anon.*		XLI 519	VIII 482
SUN. (In general) A method for finding the number of the Julian period for any year assigned, the number of the cycle of the sun, the cycle of the moon, and of the indictions for the same year, being given together, with a demonstration of that method — *Collin*		II 568	III 399
—— A certain phænomenon seen in Prussia, about the sun, a little before his setting, and the moon's conjunction, and the sun's eclipse, (which was not seen by him) *Hevelius*		IX 26	
—— A letter for correcting the hitherto assigned motions of the sun — *Flamstead*		— 219	I 162
—— Concerning the apparent magnitude of the sun and moon, or the apparent distance of two stars, when nigh the horizon, and when higher elevated — *Molyneux*		XVI 314	I 221
The sentiments of Dr. Wallis on the aforesaid appearances — *Wallis*		— 323	— 225
—— A discourse concerning a method of discovering the true moment of the sun's ingress into the tropical signs — *Halley*		XIX 12	— 266
—— Observations on the meridian height of the sun, to investigate the elevation of the pole at Lisbon *Carbone*		XXXIV 95	
—— An observation of an uncommon gleam of light proceeding from the sun *Collinson*		XLIV 456	X 481
—— Part of a letter concerning the gradual approach of the earth to the sun — *Euler*		XLVI 203	— 141
SUN. (Attraction of the) An estimate of the quantity of vapour raised out of the sea by the warmth of the sun, derived from an experiment shewn before the Royal Society — *Halley*		XVI 366	II 108
—— A resolution of a general proposition for determining the horary alteration of the position of the terrestial equator, from the attraction of the sun and moon, with some remarks on the solutions given by other authors to that difficult and important problem — *Simpson*		L 416	
—— On the precession of the equinoxes produced by the sun's attraction — *Milner*		LXIX 505	
SUN. (Conjunction with) An astronomical disserta-			

tion

Sulphurets. Description of a triple Sulphuret, of Lead, Antimony and Copper, from Cornwall; with some observations upon the various modes of attraction, which influence the formation of mineral substances, and upon the different kinds of Sulphuret of Copper. Bournon. 1804:30.

Analysis of a triple Sulphuret, of Lead, Antimony and Copper, from Cornwall. Hatchett. — 63.

On the composition of the compound Sulphuret from Huel Boys, and an account of its crystals. Smithson. 1808:55.

Experiments on the Alcohol of Sulphur or Sulphuret of Carbon. Berzelius and Marcet. 1813:200.

Sun. On the nature and construction of the Sun and fixed stars. Herschel. 1795:46.

Some remarks on the stability of the light of our Sun. ——— 1796:166.

An inquiry into the method of viewing the Sun advantageously, with Telescopes of large apertures and high magnifying powers. ——— 1800:255.

Observations tending to investigate the nature of the Sun, in order to find the causes or symptoms of its variable emission of light and heat; with remarks on the use that may possibly be drawn from Solar observations. ——— 1801:265, 354.

On the direction and the velocity of the motion of the Sun, and solar system. ——— 1805:233.

On the quantity and velocity of the Solar motion. ——— 1806:205.

	Tranſ.	Abridg.
tion on the viſible conjunction of the inferior planets with the ſun - *Halley*	XVII 511	
SUN. (Diſtance from the earth) A computation of the diſtance of the ſun from the earth *Horſley*	LVII 179	I 427
— On the computation of the ſun's diſtance from the earth, by the theory of gravity *Horſley*	LIX 153	
SUN. (Eclipſes of the ſun) Obſervations of the eclipſe of the ſun June 22, 1666, at London *Willoughby, Pope, Hook, and Philips*	I 295	I 280
Madrid - *Earl of Sandwich*	— 296	— 281
Paris - - *Payen*	— —	— —
— Calculation of the ſolar eclipſe, July 2, 1666 *Hevelius*	— 369	— 282
The reaſons why, in this eclipſe, the diameter of the moon did increaſe about the end *Auzout*	— 373	— 217
— Obſervations of the ſolar eclipſe of the ſun, June 1, 1676 - *Smethwick*	XI 637	I 284
Colſon	— —	
— Obſervations on the eclipſe of the ſun, June 23, 1675, at Dantzick - *Hevelius*	— 660	— 284
— Obſervations on the eclipſe of the ſun, June 11, 1676, in England		— 285
Flamſtead, Townley, and Halton	— 662	— 287
Paris - - *Caſſini*	— 664	— —
Dantzick - - *Hevelius*	— 666	— 288
— An obſervation on the ſolar eclipſe of June 11, 1676, at Avignon - *Gallet*	XII 1020	— 289
— Obſervation on an eclipſe of the ſun at Greenwich, July 2, 1684 *Flamſtead*	XIV 691	— 291
Paris - *Bullialdus and Caſſini*	— 693	— 292
Calculation of the ſame eclipſe, according to the Philolaic tables - *Flamſtead*	— —	
— Obſervations of the ſolar eclipſe, July 2, 1685, at Oxford - *Bernard*	— 747	— 294
Liſbon - - - - *Jacobs*	— 749	— 296
Dublin - *Aſh and Molyneux*	— —	
Tredagh - *Oſburn*	— —	
— Some obſervations on the eclipſe of the ſun, May 1, 1687, made at various places and ſent to the Royal Society	XVI 370	— 296
— Obſervations on the eclipſe of the ſun, July 12, 1684, at Bologna - *Gulielmini*	XVII 858	— 295
— Obſervations on the eclipſe of the ſun, Sept. 13, 1699, at Oxford - *Gregory*	XXI 330	
— Of the eclipſe of the ſun, Sept. 13, 1699, at Nuremberg - *Wurzelbaur*	XXII 619	— 297

	Tranſ.	Abridg.
SUN (Eclipſes.) June 12, 1694, and Nov. 27, 1703. obſerved at Cambridge, four miles from Boſton, in New England - *Brattle*	XXIV 1630	— 247 — 249
—— May 12, 1706, obſerved at Greenwich *Flamſtead*	XXV 2237	— —
Canterbury - - *Gray*	— 2238	— 250
Horton, near Bradford, Yorkſhire *Sharp*	— 2239	— 251
Bern, in Switzerland - *Stannyan*	— 2240	— —
Geneva - - *Duillier*	— 2241	— 252
Marſeilles - - *Chazelles*	— 2244	— 253
Zurich - - *Scheuchzer*	— 2246	— 254
—— A letter giving his obſervations on the eclipſe of the ſun, Sept. 3, 1708, at Upminſter *Derham*	XXVI 308	— 255
—— Obſervations of the late total eclipſe of the ſun, on the 22d of April, 1715, with an account of what has been tranſmitted from abroad concerning the ſame - *Halley*	XXIX 245	— —
More accounts of the above from abroad *Anon.*	— 314	— 267
—— Obſervations on the eclipſe of the ſun, Feb. 19, 1718, at Berlin - - *Kirch*	XXX 820	— 268
At Nurenberg - - *Wurtzelbaur*	— —	— —
—— An obſervation of an eclipſe of the ſun, Nov. 27, 1722, at Greenwich - *Halley*	XXXII 197	VI 171
London - - *Graham*	— 198	— —
At Wakefield - - *Hawkins*	— 199	— —
—— Part of a letter concerning the eclipſe of the ſun, November 27, 1722 - *Robie*	XXXIII 67	— 172
—— Obſervations on the eclipſe of the ſun, Sept. 23, 1726, at Padua - - *Polenus*	XXXIV 157	— 173
—— An obſervation of a ſolar eclipſe made at Liſbon, Sept. 25, 1726 - *Carbone*	XXXV 335	— 174
—— An account of the eclipſe of the ſun, July 15, 1730, N. S. at Wirtemberg - *Weidler*	XXXVI 394	— 182
—— Obſervation of an eclipſe of the ſun, June 14, 1730, at Padua - *Polenus*	— 396	— 183
—— An obſervation of an eclipſe of the ſun, July 15, 1730, made at Pekin *Kegler and Pereyra*	XXXVII 179	— —
—— Obſervation on the ſolar eclipſe, Nov. 27, 1722 *Robie*	— 273	
—— An obſervation of the eclipſe of the ſun on May 2, 1733, at London *Graham*	XXXVIII 113	VIII 135
An account of the ſame eclipſe at Norton-Court, and Otterden-Place *Wheler*	— 114	— 136
Of the ſame eclipſe at Yeovil in Somerſetſhire *Milner*	— 116	— 137
—— Obſervation of a total eclipſe of the ſun, made		

		Tranſ.	Abridg.
at Gothoburg, in Sweden, May 2, 1733, in latitude 57° 40 54″ -	*Vaſſenius*	XXXVIII 134	VIII 137
SUN (Eclipſes.) An account of the eclipſe of the ſun obſerved May 2, 1733, at Wirtemberg	*Weidler*	— 332	— 138
—— Obſervation on the ſolar eclipſe, Sept. 23, 1736, at London - -	*Bevis*	XL 98	— 139
—— Obſervation on an eclipſe of the ſun, Feb. 18, 1736-7, at Philadelphia	*Kearſley*	— 121	
—— A collection of the obſervations of the ſolar eclipſe, Feb. 18, 1736-7, Fleet-Street	*Graham*	— 175	— —
Greenwich - -	*Bevis*	— 176	
Edinburgh -	*Mac Laurin*	— 177	— 140
Edinburgh - -	*Clerk*	— 195	— 149
Cambridge -	*Kettering and Maſon*	— 197	
Bologna - - -	*Anon.*	— 199	— 151
Rome - - -	*Revillas*	— 200	— 152
Wirtemberg - -	*Weidler*	— 201	— —
—— A collection of the obſervations of the eclipſe of the ſun, Aug. 4, 1738			
London - -	*Graham and Short*	XLI 91	— 153
Upſal - -	*Celſius*	— 92	— 154
Wirtemberg - -	*Weidler*	— —	
Bononia -	*Manfredius*	— 94	
—— Obſervations on the eclipſe of the ſun, Aug. 4, 1739, at Witenberg -	*Weidler*	— 226	— 113
—— Obſervation of an eclipſe of the ſun, Dec. 19, 1739 - -	*Short*	— 633	— 172
—— The ſun's eclipſe of July 14, 1748, obſerved at Marlborough Houſe, with a twelve-foot refracting teleſcope, fixed as a finder to the tube of the great twelve-foot reflector	*Bevis*	XLV 521	X 68
—— An obſervation of the eclipſe of the ſun at Berlin, July 14, 1748 -	*Greſchow*	— 524	— 483
—— An eclipſe of the ſun, July 14, 1748, obſerved by the Earl of Morton, Mr. le Monnier, and Mr. James Short		— 582	— 69
—— July 14, 1748, made at Madrid	*Ulloa*	XLVI 10	— 77
—— Obſerved at Rome, Jan. 8, 1750	*Maire*	XLVI 322	— 78
—— Obſerved at Berlin Jan. 8, 1750	*Griſcow and Kies*	— 339	— —
—— A deſcription of a piece of mechaniſm, contrived by James Ferguſon, for exhibiting the time, duration, and quantity of ſolar eclipſes in all places of the earth -	*Ferguſon*	XLVIII 520	
—— An obſervation of an eclipſe of the ſun made at Liſbon, Oct. 26, 1753	*Chevalier*	XLVIII 546	

	Transf.	Abridg.
Sun (Eclipses.) An account of the eclipse of the sun, Oct. 16, 1762 - - *Dunn*	LII 644	
—— An account of the eclipse of the sun, April 1, 1764 - - *Ferguson*	LIII 240	
—— Observations on an eclipse of the sun, Oct. 17, 1762, at Ghyrotty, in the East Indies *Hirst*	LIII 259	
—— Observation of the eclipse of the sun, April 1, 1764, London - - *Short*	LIV 107	
Bevis	— 105	
Liverpool - *Ferguson*	— 108	
Brompton Park - *Dunn*	— 114	
Greenwich - - *Bliss*	— 141	
Shirburn Castle - - *Anon.*	— 144	
Oxford - - *Hornsby*	— 145	
Thorley Hall - *Raper*	— 150	
Chatham - - *Murray*	— 171	
—— Observations on the eclipse of the sun, April 1, 1764, at Schwetzing - *Mayer*	— 169	
—— An observation of an eclipse of the sun, April 1, 1764, in the Roman college, by the Jesuits	— 254	
—— Observations on the eclipse of the sun on the 16th August, 1765, made at Colombes, near Paris - - *Messier*	LVI 1	
—— Observation of the eclipse of the sun of August 16, 1765, made at Leyden *Lulof*	— 30	
—— Observations on the eclipse of the sun of August 5, 1766, made at Colombes *Messier*	— 259	
—— A letter containing the observations of the eclipse of the sun of August 16, 1765, and of the 5th of August, 1766, made at Calais, together with some remarks on the first of these eclipses - - *Prince de Croy*	— 262	
—— An observation of the eclipse of the sun at the island of Newfoundland, August 5, 1766 *Cook*	LVII 215	
—— Observations on the sun's eclipse 16th of August, 1765, at Caen in Normandy *Pigott*	— 402	
—— Observations of an eclipse of the sun at Greenwich, 1769 - *Maskelyne*	LVIII 364	
—— At Oxford - - *Hornsby*	LIX 172	
—— At Shirburn Castle *Lord and Lady Macclesfield*	— —	
—— A letter containing observations on the eclipse the sun, June 4, 1769, at Spital-square *Canton*	— 192	
—— Observation of the eclipse of the sun, June 4, 1769, at Kew - - *Bevis*	— 189	

+ Sun (Eclipses). Result of Calculations of the Observations made at various places of the Eclipse of the Sun, June 3. 1788. Piazzi. 79:55.

Account of some particulars observed during the late Eclipse of the Sun. Herschel. 1794:39.

Observation of the great Eclipse of the Sun of Sept. 5, 1793. Schroeter — 262

On the solar eclipse which is said to have been predicted by Thales. — — — Baily. 1811:220

		Tranſ.	Abridg.
SUN (Eclipſes.) At the North Cape	*Bayly*	— 268	
—— At Hawkhill	*Alemore and Luid*	— 342	
—— At Kirknewton	*Bryce*	— 349	
—— Obſervations on the eclipſe of the ſun made at the iſland of Hammerfoſt, for the Royal Society	*Dixon*	— 259	
—— Obſervations of a ſolar eclipſe, June 4, 1760, at Aiſthorpe, near Leeds, Yorkſhire	*Smeaton*	— 286	
—— Obſervations on the eclipſe of the ſun made at Gibraltar	*Jardine*	LIX 347	
—— Obſervations on the eclipſe of the ſun, June 4, 1769, in the morning	*Wollaſton*	— 407	
—— Extract of a letter incloſing ſome account of a ſolar eclipſe obſerved at the iſland of Otaheite, by Captain Wallis, July 25, 1767	*Wallis*	LXII 33	
—— Obſervations on the ſolar eclipſe which happened June 24, 1778	*Wales*	LXVIII 1013	
—— An eclipſe of the ſun, June 24, 1778, obſerved at Leiceſter	*Ludlam*	— 1019	
—— Obſervations on the eclipſe of the ſun taken the 24th of June, 1778, on board the Eſpagne, in the paſſage from the Azores	*Ulloa*	LXIX 105	
—— Vide *Halo, Parelia*			
SUN. (Heat of the) A diſcourſe concerning the proportional heat of the ſun in all latitudes, with the method of collecting the ſame	*Halley*	XVII 878	II 165
—— Account of an experiment made with a thermometer, whoſe bulb was painted black, and expoſed to the direct rays of the ſun	*Richard Watſon*	LXIII 40	
SUN. (Horizontal) Some thoughts concerning the ſun and moon, when near the horizon, appearing larger than when nearer the zenith	*Logan*	XXXIX 404	VIII 377
—— The deſcription and uſe of an apparatus, added as an improvement to Davis's quadrant, conſiſting of a mercurial level, for taking the co altitude of ſun or ſtar at ſea, without the uſual aſſiſtance of the ſenſible horizon, which is often obſcured	*Leigh*	XL 417	— 362
—— An attempt to aſſign the cauſe why the ſun and moon appear to the naked eye larger when they are near the horizon; with an account of ſeveral natural phænomena, relative to this ſubject	*Dunn*	LII 462	
SUN (As applied for determining the longitude.) An inſtrument for ſeeing the ſun, moon, or ſtars			

	Trans.	Abridg.
pass the meridian of any place, useful for setting watches in all parts of the world with the greatest exactness, to correct sun-dials, to assist in the discovery of the longitudes of places *Derham*	XXIV 1578	IV 464
SUN (As applied for determining the longitude.) A letter containing the results of observations of the distance of the moon from the sun and fixed stars, made in a voyage from England to the island of St. Helena, in order to determine the longitude of the ship from time to time; together with the whole process of computation used on this occasion - *Maskelyne*	LII 558	
—— Track of his Majesty's armed brig Lion, from England to Davis's Streights, and Labradore with observations for determining the longitude by sun and moon, and error of common reckoning; also the variation of the compass and dip of the needle, as observed during the said voyage in 1776 - *Pickersgill*	LXVIII 1057	
SUN. (parallax) Of the correspondency to be procured for finding out the true distance of the sun and moon from the earth, by the parallax, observed under (or near) the same meridian *Oldenburg*	I 151	I 300
—— A particular method by which the parallax of the sun, or its distance from the earth, may be ascertained by the assistance of the transit of Venus over the sun - *Halley*	XXIX 454	IV 214
—— An account of the sun's distance from the earth deduced from Mr. Short's observations relating to the horizontal parallax of the sun *Davat*	LIII 1	
—— Second paper concerning the parallax of the sun determined from the observations of the late transit of Venus - *Short*	— 300	
—— A discourse on the parallax of the sun *Hornsby*	— 467	
—— Concise rules for computing the effects of refraction and parallax in varying the apparent distance of the moon from the sun or a star; also an easy rule of approximation for computing the distance of the moon from a star, the longitudes and latitudes of both being given, with demonstrations of the same *Maskelyne*	LIV 263	
—— Supplement to Mr. Pingré's memoir on the parallax of the sun; deduced from his observations on the transit of Venus, vol. LII, p. 371 *Pingré*	— 152	

The parallax of the sun determined from the observations on the internal contact of Venus with the sun's limb, in the late transit. Short 52: 611.

	Trans.	Abridg.
SUN (Parallax.) An essay on the connection between the parallaxes of the sun and moon, their densities, and their disturbing forces on the ocean *Murdock*	LVIII 24	
—— A determination of the solar parallax attempted, by a peculiar method, from the observations of the last transit of Venus, in a letter to James Short - *Planman*	— 107	
—— The quantity of the sun's parallax as deduced from the transit of Venus, June 3, 1769 *Hornsby*	LXI 574	
—— A deduction of the sun's parallax from the comparison of the several observations of the late transit of Venus, made in Europe, with those made in George island in the South Seas, by Mr. Lexell - - *Euler*	LXII 69	
SUN (Spots in the) Accounts of some spots of the sun, observed at Paris, Aug. 1671 *Cassini*	VI 2238	
—— New observations of spots in the sun, made at Paris, Aug. 11, 12, and 13, 1671 *Cassini*	— 2250	
—— Observations of some of the spots in the sun, renewed after they had passed over the upper hemisphere of the sun - - *Hook*	— 2295	I 227
—— Observations on the spots of the sun *Cassini*	— 3020	— 275
—— Letter concerning the spots of the sun returned Nov. 1, 1671 - *Fogelius*	— 3033	— 277
—— Observations concerning the spots in the sun appearing in July and August, 1676 *Flamstead and Halley*	XI 687	— 278
—— Observations on a spot lately seen in the sun *Cassini*	— 689	— 279
—— An account of a spot seen in the sun from April 25, to May 8, 1684 with the line of its course predicted if it makes a second return *Flamstead*	XIV 535	— —
—— Two letters concerning the spots of the sun observed in June, 1703 *Grey*	XXIII 1502	IV 229
—— Some observations on the spots of the sun *Derham*	— 1504	— 230
—— Observations made on the spots upon the body of the sun in the months of May, June, and July, 1704 *Stannyan*	XXIV 1756	— 232
—— Observations upon the spots that have been upon the sun from the year 1703 to 1711; with a letter of Mr. Crabtree in the year 1640 upon the same subject - *Derham*	XXVII 270	— 235
Further account - *Derham*	— 278	— 240

		Tranſ.	Abridg.
Sun. (Spots in the) An attempt to determine the height of the ſun's atmoſphere from the height of the ſolar ſpots above the ſun's ſurface	*Horſley*	LVII 398	
—— Obſervations on the ſolar ſpots	*Wilſon*	LXIV 1	
—— Sketches of the ſolar ſpots	*Marſhall*	— 194	
Sun. (Solar tables) Some conſiderations on a late treatiſe, intitled, A new ſet of logarithmic ſolar tables, &c. intended for a more commodious method of finding the latitude at ſea by two obſervations of the ſun	*Pemberton*	LI 910	
~~**Sun.** (Tranſit of Mercury) An account of the appearance of Mercury, paſſing over the ſun's diſk on the 29th of October, 1723, determining the mean motion, and fixing the nodes of that planet's orb~~	~~*Halley*~~	~~XXXIII 228~~ (see Mercury)	~~VI 253~~
~~—— An obſervation of the paſſage of Mercury over the ſun, Oct. 31, 1738~~	~~*Huxham*~~	~~XLI 640~~	~~IX 164~~
~~—— The differences of longitude between the Royal Obſervatories of Greenwich and Paris, determined by the obſervations of the tranſits of Mercury over the ſun in 1723, 1736, 1743, 1753~~	~~*Short*~~	~~LIII 158~~ (see Longitude)	
~~—— Obſervations on the tranſit of Mercury over the diſk of the ſun~~	~~*Mohr*~~	~~LXI 433~~ (see Mercury)	
~~**Sun.** (Tranſit of Venus) Diſſertation on the next tranſit of Venus over the ſun~~	~~*Boſcovich*~~	~~LI 865~~	
~~—— The obſervations on the internal contact of Venus with the ſun's limb, in the late tranſit, made in different parts of Europe, compared with the time of the ſame contact, obſerved at the Cape of Good Hope, and the parallax of the ſun thence determined~~	~~*Short*~~	~~LII 611~~ (see Venus and Parallax	p. 478)
~~—— Obſervations on the tranſit of Venus over the diſk of the ſun~~	~~*Mohr*~~	~~LXI 433~~	
—— See *Venus*			
Sun-Dials. ~~Vide *Dials*~~ A new method of constructing sun-dials for any given latitude, without the assistance of dialling scales or logarithmic calculations.	Ferguson	57: 389	
Sun Fish. A paper concerning the mola ſolis, or ſun-fiſh, and a glue made of it	*Barlow*	LXI 343	IX 73
Sun-Plant. Of the culture and uſes of the ſon or ſun plant of Hindoſtan, with the account of the manner of manufacturing the Hindoſtan paper	*Ironſide*	LXIV 99	
Suratte. Inquiries for Suratte, and other parts of the Eaſt-Indies	*Royal Society*	II 415	III 632
Surd Roots. A diſcourſe concerning the methods of approximation in the extraction of ſurd roots	*Wallis*	XIX 2	I 98

Sun (Spots in the) Answer to the objections stated by M. De la Lande against the Solar Spots being excavations in the luminous matter of the Sun. Wilson. 73:144.

+ Survivorships. On the probabilities of Survivorships between two persons of any given ages, and the method of determining the values of reversions depending on these survivorships. Morgan. 78:331.

On the method of determining, from the real probabilities of life, the value of a contingent reversion, in which three lives are involved in the survivorship. Morgan. 79:40.
81:246.
1794:223.
1800:22

	Transf.	Abridg.
SURFACE. An experiment touching the weighing of bodies of the same species, but of very unequal surfaces, in common air *Haukfbee*	XXVI 306	IV 2 181
—— Propositions selected from a paper on the division of right lines, surfaces, and solids *Glenie*	LXVI 73	
SURGERY. Two chirurgical cases *Amyand*	XXVI 170	V 204 — 389
—— Various observations in a journey through Italy, begun 1703 - *Breynius*	XXVII 447	V 2 136
—— Remarks on a collection of ancient chirurgical writers in the Grand Duke's library *Schelhammer*	— 459	
—— An account of two remarkable cases in surgery *Steigertball*	XXXI 79	VII 665
—— An extraordinary case in surgery, of tumours *Atkinson*	XXXIII 340	— 666
—— Three extraordinary cases in surgery *Sheerman*	XLI 138	IX 253
—— A description of a machine for dressing and curing unweildy patients - *Le Cat*	XLII 364	— 272
—— Extract of a letter relating to two remarkable cases in surgery - *Huxham*	LII 515	
SURVEYING. A demonstration of an error committed by common surveyors, in comparing of surveys taken at long intervals of time, arising from the variation of the magnetic needle *Molyneux*	XIX 625	I 125
—— A new plotting table, for taking plans and maps in surveying, invented in 1721 *Beighton*	XLI 747	VIII 228
—— A recommendation of Hadley's quadrant for surveying, especially of harbours, together with a particular application of it in some cases of pilotage - - *Michell*	LV 70	
SURVIVORSHIP. A letter concerning the value of an annuity for life, and the probability of survivorship - - *Dodson*	XLVIII 487	
—— Observations on the proper methods of calculating the values of reversions dependent on survivorships - - *Price*	LX 268	
—— See *Annuities*, *Mortality*		
SUSSEX. See *Antiquities*		
SWALLOWS. Letter concerning the migration of swallows - - *Klein*	LI 459	
—— Remarks on swallows on the Rhine *Collinson*	LIII 101	
—— Of the house-swallow, swift, and sand-martin *White*	LXV 258	

	Transf.	Abridg.
SWALLOWS. Of the torpidity of fwallows and martins *Cornifh*	LXV 343	
SWAMMERDAM. Notes upon his book of infects *Lifter*	VI 2281	
SWAN. Remarks about the new ftar, near the beak of the Swan - *Hevelius*	V 2023	
—— A new ftar difcovered in the conftellation of the Swan in 1670 - *Hevelius*	— 2087	I 248
—— Account from Paris of the earlier difcovery of the fame ftar - - *Oldenburg*	— 2092	— 248
SWEAT. Microfcopical obfervations concerning fweat, *Leeuwenhoek*	IX 128	
—— An extract of a letter containing microfcopical obfervations on fweat, &c. *Leeuwenhoek*	XVII 949	III 685
SWEATING-ROOM. A defcription of a Roman fudatory, or hypocauftum, found at Wroxeter, in Shropfhire, 1701 - *Lifter*	XXV 2225	
Another letter - *Harwood*	— 2228	
Two letters relating to Wroxeter, and the hypocaufta of the ancients *Baxter*	— —	
—— An account of an extraordinary cure by fweating in hot turff; with a defcription of the Indian hot-houfes - *Dudley*	XXXIII 129	VII 669
—— An account of the remains of a Roman hypocauftum, or fweating-room, difcovered under ground at Lincoln, in 1739 *Sympfon*	XLI 855	IX 455
SWEDEN. See *Coins*		
—— A fhort account of fome Swedifh minerals, fent to Mr. James Petiver - *Angeftein*	XXVIII 222	IV 2 286
SWEETS. Obfervations on the clafs of fweet taftes, made by comparing the taftes of fweet plants with M. L' Emery's chymical analyfis of them, in his treatife of drugs - *Floyer*	XXIII 1160	V 406
SWELLING. An obfervation concerning a very odd kind of dropfy, or fwelling, in one of the ovaries of a woman - *Sloane*	XXI 150	III 207
SWIFT. Of houfe-fwallows, fwifts, and fand-martins - - - *White*	LXV 258	
SWIMMING. Confiderations on the fwimming bladders in fifhes - *Ray*	X 349	II 846
SWORD. Cafe of a man wounded in the left eye by a fmall fword - *Geach*	LIII 234	
SYCAMORE. Obfervations on fome fycamore trees *Willoughby*	V 1201	
—— Account of the bleeding of *Lifter*	— 2067	II 686
SYLLEY. An account of the great alterations which		

the

[S]wallows. Some account of the nests of the Java swallow, and of the glands that secrete the mucus of which they are composed.

Home. 1817: 332.

[S]ydneia. see Minerals.

	Transf.	Abridg.

SYL TAB

the islands of Sylley have undergone since the times of the antients, who mention them as to their number, extent, and position *Borlase* XLVIII 55

SYMPATHY. Of one who pretended to cure, or cause diseases, at a distance, by applying a sympathetic powder to the urine *Leeuwenhoek* XIX 512 III 685

SYRINGING. An account of what happened on syringing warm water into the thorax of a bitch *Musgrave* XX 181 — 78

SYRUP. Account of Mr. Alexander Orm's pectoral syrup, sent in a letter from Calcutta, 1733 *Anon.* XLI 769 IX 371

T.

Tabasheer. Account of — — — Russel LC: 273.
An account of some chemical experiments on Tabasheer — Macie 81: 368.

TABERG. An account of a mountain of iron ore at Taberg in Sweden *Ascanius* XLIX 30

TABLES. Patterns of the tables proposed to be made for observing of tides *Moray* I 311 II 365

—— With other inquiries touching the sea *Boyle* — 315 — 297

—— A description of a mathematical historical table *Megerlin* XI 667

—— An ingenious proposal for a new sort of maps of countries, together with tables of sands and clays, such chiefly as are found in the north parts of England *Lister* XIV 739 — 450

—— An estimate of the degrees of the mortality of mankind, drawn from various tables of the births and funerals at the city of Breslaw, with an attempt to ascertain the price of annuities upon lives *Halley* XVII 596

—— Emendations and notes upon the antient astronomical observations of Albatenius, with the restoration of his luni-solar tables *Halley* — 913 III 522

—— A table of the washes in Lincolnshire *Merret* XIX 392 II 267

—— A new method for making logarithms, and finding the number corresponding to a logarithm given, with tables *Long* XXIX 52 IV 160

—— The barometrical method of measuring the

height

	Trans.	Abridg.
height of mountains, with two new tables, shewing the height of the atmosphere at given altitudes of Mercury - *Scheuchzer*	XXXV 537	VI 2 30
TABLES. Calculations and tables relating to the attractive virtue of load-stones - *Anon.*	XXXVI 245	— 304
—— Thermometrical tables and observations *Stedman*	XLVII 4	
—— A view of the relation between Dr. Halley's tables, and the notions of Mr. de Buffon, for establishing a rule for the probable duration of the life of man - - *Kerseboom*	XLVIII 239	
—— Elements of new tables of the motions of Jupiter's satellites - *Dunthorne*	LII 105	
—— A comparative table of the corresponding observations of the first satellite of Jupiter, made in the principal observatories *Wargentin*	LXVII 162	
TACKLE. A description of a new tackle, or combination of pullies - - *Smeaton*	XLVII 494	
TADMOR. An extract of the Journals of two several voyages of the English merchants, of the factory of Aleppo, to Tadmor, antiently called Palmyra - - - *Anon.*	XIX 129	III 489 — 492
TADPOLES. Some observations made on the spawn of frogs, and the production of tadpoles therein *Waller*	XVII 523	II 818
—— Letter concerning the circulation and stagnation of the blood in tadpoles *Leeuwenhoek*	XXII 447	III 685
TAIACU. *Seu Aper Mexicanus Moschiferus*, or the anatomy of the Mexico musk hog *Tyson*	XIII 359	II 873
TALC. Account of stone quarries and talc rocks in Hungary - *Oldenburg and Brown*	V 1044	
TANGENTS. A breviat concerning Dr. Wallis's two methods of tangents - *Wallis*	VII 4010	I 116
—— Short and easy method of drawing tangents to all geometrical curves, without any labour of calculations - - *Slusius*	— 5143	— 18
—— Easy way of demonstrating his method of drawing tangents to all sorts of curves, without any labour of calculation - *Slusius*	VIII 6059	— 21
—— An easy demonstration of the analogy of the logarithmick tangents to the meridian line, or sum of the secants, with various methods for computing the same to the utmost exactness *Halley*	XIX 202	— 577
—— Of the tangents of curves, deduced immediately		

from

Tadpoles. On the formation of fat in the intestine of the Tadpole, and on the use of the yolk in the formation of the embryo in the egg. — — — — — Home. 1816: 301.

+ Tangents. On a new property of the Tangents of the three angles of a plane triangle. Garrard. 1808:120.

On a new property of the Tangents of three arches trisecting the circumference of a circle. Maskelyne. —— 122.

+ Tanning. Experiments to determine the quantity of Tanning principle and gallic acid contained in the bark of various trees. Biggin. 1799:259.

An account of some experiments and observations on the constituent parts of certain astringent vegetables, and on their operation in Tanning. Davy. 1803:233.

On an artificial substance which possesses the principal characteristic properties of Tannin. Hatchett. 1805:211 & 285
1806:109.

		Trans.	Abridg.
from the theory of maxima and minima *Ditton*		XXIII 1333	IV 7
TANGENTS. Letter containing an explanation of the late Dr. Halley's demonstration of the analogy of the logarithmic tangents to the meridian line, or sum of the secants *Robertson*		XLVI 539	X 256
TANGIER. A catalogue of plants growing within the fortifications of Tangier in 1673 *Spottswood*		XIX 239	II 752
TANNING. An improved method of tanning leather *Macbride*		LXVIII 111	
TAPESTRY. An account of weaving tapestry in the same manner as brocades *Martine*		XXXVII 101	VI 469
TAPPING. A remarkable case of a gentlewoman who died of an hydrops ovarii, in the 33d year of her age, after having been tapped 57 times *Belchier*		— 279	VII 544
——— The case of Mr. Cox, surgeon at Peterborough, who fell into a pestilential fever upon tapping a corpse dead of an hydropsy *Cox*		XLI 168	IX 212
——— Ascites, cured by - *Banyer*		XLII 628	— 151
——— An improvement on the practice of tapping, whereby that operation, instead of a relief for symptoms, becomes an absolute cure for an ascites, exemplified in the case of Jane Roman *Warwick*		XLIII 12	XI 1030
——— A method of conveying liquors into the abdomen during the operation of tapping *Hales*		— 20	
——— See *Dropsy*			
TAR. An account of making pitch, tar, and oil, out of a blackish stone in Shropshire *Ele*		XIX 544	
——— The way of making pitch, tar, rosin and turpentine, near Marseilles *Bent*		XX 291	
TARANTULA. An inquiry concerning tarantula's *Lister*		VI 3002	II 912
——— Observations made of persons pretending to be stung with tarantula's - *Cornelio*		VII 4066	III 285
——— Some account of the tarantula *Cirillo*		LX 233	
TARTARY. A voyage of the Emperor of China into Eastern Tartary, 1682 - *Anon*		XVI 39	— 632
——— A voyage of the Emperor of China into the Western Tartary, 1683 - *Anon.*		— 52	— —
An explanation necessary to justify the geography supposed in these letters *Anon.*		— 62	— —
——— An account of a large and curious map of the Great Tartary - - *Witsen*		XVII 492	
TASTE. Microscopical observations about the texture

	Trans.	Abridg.
of the blood, the ſap of ſome plants, the figure of ſugar and ſalt, and the probable cauſe of the difference of their taſtes — *Leeuwenhoek*	X 380	III 683
TASTE. Letter concerning the different taſtes of waters — *Leeuwenhoek*	XXII 899	V 2 266
—— Obſervations on the claſs of ſweet taſtes, made by comparing the taſtes of ſweet plants, with Mr. L'Emery's chymical analyſis of them, in his treatiſe of drugs - *Floyer*	XXIII 1160	V 406
—— An account of ſome trials to cure the ill taſte of milk, which is occaſioned by the food of cows, either from turnips, cabbages, or autumnal leaves, &c. alſo to ſweeten ſtinking water - - *Hales*	XLIX 339	
TAURUS. An account of an occultation of the ſtar ζ Tauri, by the moon, obſerved at Leiceſter — *Ludlam*	LX 355	
—— Occultation of α or of γ Tauri and other ſtars by the moon - - *Lexel*	LXV 280	
TEA. An account of a voyage to Chuſan, in China, with a deſcription of the Iſland, of the ſeveral ſorts of tea, of the fiſhing, agriculture of the Chineſe, &c. with ſeveral obſervations not hitherto taken notice of — *Cunningham*	XXIII 1201	V 2 171
TEARS. Microſcopical obſervations concerning ſweat, fat, tears, &c. - *Leeuwenhoek*	IX 128	
TEETH. Two caſes of perſons cutting teeth in their old age - - *Colepreſſe*	I 380	III 297
—— Microſcopical obſervations of the ſtructure of teeth, and other bones — *Leeuwenhoek*	XII 1002	— 684
—— Microſcopical obſervations about animals in the ſcurff of the teeth, the ſubſtance called worms in the noſe, &c. — *Leeuwenhoek*	XIV 568	— —
—— Concerning animalcules found in teeth — *Leeuwenhoek*	XVII 646	— —
—— Of a venomous ſcratch with the tooth of a porpus, its ſymptoms, and cure — *Liſter*	XIX 726	II 842
—— Obſervations on teeth — *Leeuwenhoek*	— 790	III 685
—— Letter concerning worms pretended to be taken from the teeth - *Leeuwenhoek*	XXII 635	— 686
—— Part of a letter concerning a perſon who had a new ſet of teeth after 80 years of age; with ſome obſervations upon the virtues and properties of ſugar - *Slare*	XXVIII 273	V [353]
—— A letter giving an account of ſome large teeth		

+ Teeth. Description of the teeth of the Anarrhichas Lupus Linn. and of Chaetodon nigricans Linn. with an attempt to prove that the teeth of cartilaginous fishes are perpetually renewed — — — — — — André. 74:274

Some observations on the structure of the teeth of graminivorous quadrupeds, particularly those of the Elephant and Sus aethiopicus. Home. 1799:237

Observations on the structure, and mode of growth, of the grinding teeth of the Wild Boar; and Animal incognitum. —— 1801:319.

TEE

		Tranf.	Abridg.
Fossil — lately dug up in the north of Ireland *Nevile*		XXIX 367	IV 2 236
Remarks on the above *Molyneux*		— 370	— - 237
TEETH. An account of elephants teeth and bones found under ground - *Sloane* (*Fossil*)		XXXV 457	VI 2 205
Part 2 - - *Sloane*		— 497	— - 211
—— A letter concerning a cluster of small teeth observed at the root of each fang, or great tooth, in the head of a rattle snake, upon dissecting it *Bartram*		XLI 358	IX 60
—— Letter concerning an extraordinary large fossil tooth of an elephant - *Baker* (*Fossil*)		XLIII 331	X 599
—— An account of some very large fossil teeth found in North America - *Collinson* (*Fossil*)		LVII 464	
Sequel to the account *Collinson*		— 468	
—— A dissertation on the bones and teeth of elephants, and other beasts, found in North America, and other northern regions, by which it appears they are the bones of indigenous beasts *Raspe* (*Fossil*)		LIX 126	
TELESCOPES. Judgment touching the apertures of object glasses, and their proportions, in respect to the several lengths of telescopes, together with a table thereof - *Auzout*		I 55	I 191
—— Of M. Hevelius's promise of imparting to the world his invention of making optick glasses; and of the hopes given by Mr. Hugens, of Zulichem, to perform something of the like nature; as also of the expectations conceived of some ingenious persons in England to improve telescopes *Hevelius, Hugens, and Du Sons*		— 98	— 193
—— Instance to Mr. Hook, for communicating a contrivance of making, with a glass of a sphere of 20 or 40 feet diameter, a telescope, drawing several hundred feet, and of his offer of recompensing that secret with another teaching to measure, with a telescope, the distances of objects from the earth - *Auzout*		— 123	
—— A method by which a glass of a small planoconvex sphere, may be made to refract the rays of light to a focus of a far greater distance than is usual - - *Hook*		— 202	— —
—— Method of polishing telescopic glasses by a turn-lathe, and the making of an extraordinary burning glass at Milan - *Anon.*		LII 795	— 194
—— An account of a new catadioptrical telescope invented by Mr. Newton - *Newton*		V 4004	I 197
Further suggestions about his reflecting telescope;

	Tranſ.	Abridg.
ſcope; together with his table of apertures and charges for the ſeveral lengths of that inſtrument - - *Newton*	— 4032	— 200
Anſwer to ſome objections made by an ingenious French philoſopher, to the new reflecting teleſcope - *Newton*	— 4034	— 201
Some conſiderations upon part of a letter of M de Berce, concerning the catadioptrical teleſcope, pretended to be improved and refined by M. Caſſegrain - *Newton*	— 4056	— 204
TELESCOPES. The effects of the different refractions of the rays in teleſcopical glaſſes *Anon.*	VIII 6086	— 156
—— Hopes of perfecting teleſcopes by reflections rather than refractions - - *Newton*	— 6087	— 158
—— The uſe of teleſcopic ſights in aſtronomical obſervations - *Hevelius*	IX 27	— 221
—— A ſure and eaſy way to make all ſorts of great teleſcopical glaſſes, with a generous offer of furniſhing induſtrious aſtronomers with them *Borelli*	XI 691	— 195
—— Letter about the price of his teleſcopes *Borelli*	XII 1005	— 195
—— The deſcription of an aerial teleſcope *Hugens*	XIV 668	
—— A dioptrick problem, why four convex-glaſſes in a teleſcope ſhew objects erect. *Molyneux*	XVI 169	— 189
—— Extracts from Mr. Gaſcoigne's and Mr. Crabtree's letters, proving Mr. Gaſcoigne to have been the inventor of the teleſcopick ſights of mathematical inſtruments, and not the French *Derham*	XXX 603	IV 345
—— A way for myopes to uſe teleſcopes without eye glaſſes, an object glaſs becoming as uſeful to them, and ſometimes more, than a combination of glaſſes - *Deſaguliers*	— 1017	— 188
—— Some remarks upon the method of obſerving the differences of right aſcenſion and declination, by croſs hairs in a teleſcope *Halley*	XXXI 113	VI 165
—— An account of a catadioptrick teleſcope made by John Hadley, Eſq. with the deſcription of a machine, contrived by him, for applying it to uſe - - - *Hadley*	XXXII 303	
—— A letter concerning obſervations made with Mr. Hadley's reflecting teleſcope *Pound*	— 382	VI 221
—— Obſervations on the ſatellites of Jupiter and Saturn, made with the ſame teleſcope *Hadley*	— 385	— —
—— A new method of improving and perfecting catadioptrical teleſcopes by forming the ſpeculums of glaſs inſtead of metal - *Smith*	XLI 326	VIII 113

TELE-

+ Telescopes.

A paper to obviate some doubts concerning the great magnifying powers used. Herschel. 72:173.

Description of a new system of wires in the focus of a telescope, for observing the comparative Right Ascensions and declinations of coelestial objects. Wollaston 75:346.

Description of a fortyfeet reflecting Telescope. Herschel. 1795:347.

On the power of penetrating into space by Telescopes, with a comparative determination of the extent of that power in natural vision, and in telescopes of various sizes and constructions. ——— 1800:49.

Experiments for ascertaining how far Telescopes will enable us to determine very small angles, and to distinguish the real from the spurious diameters of celestial and terrestrial objects: with an application of the result of these experiments to a series of observations on the nature and magnitude of Mr. Harding's lately discovered star. ——— 1805:31.

On the light of the Cassegrainian Telescope compared with that of the Gregorian. — — — Kater. 1813:206.

Further experiments on the light of the Cassegrainian Telescope compared with that of the Gregorian. ——— 1814:231.

++ Temperature of the Earth. Observations on the temp. of the earth below the surface in different climates. J. Hunter. 78:53

Observations on the temperature of the ocean and atmosphere, and on the density of sea-water made during a voyage to Ceylon. Davy. 181[illegible]:27[illegible]

	Tranſ.	Abridg.
TELESCOPES. The deſcription and uſes of an equatorial teleſcope - *Short*	XLVI 241	X 154
—— Letter concerning an improvement of refracting teleſcopes by increaſing the number of eye-glaſſes to enlarge the field of view *Dollond*	XLVIII 103	
—— Letters relating to a theorem of Mr. Euler, for correcting the aberrations in the object glaſſes of refracting teleſcopes *Short, Euler, and Dollond*	— 287	
—— An account of ſome new experiments concerning the different refrangibility of light by water, and different kinds of glaſs; and of a method thence deduced, of correcting the errors ariſing from the different refrangibility of light in the object-glaſſes of refracting teleſcopes *Dollond*	L 73	
—— An account of an improvement made by Mr. Dollond in his new teleſcopes, by compoſing his object-glaſs of two convex lenſes of crown glaſs, and one concave lens of white flint *Dollond*	LV 54	
—— A method of working the object glaſſes of refracting teleſcopes truly ſpherical *Short*	LIX 507	
—— Deſcription and uſe of a new conſtructed equatorial teleſcope, or portable obſervatory *Nairne*	LXI 107	
—— An improvement propoſed in the croſs wires of teleſcopes - *Wilſon*	LXIV 105	
—— Directions for making the beſt compoſition for the metals of reflecting teleſcopes; together with a deſcription of the proceſs for grinding, poliſhing, and giving the great ſpeculum the true parabolic curve - *Mudge*	LXVII 296	
—— Account of an iconantidiptic teleſcope *Jeaurat*	LXIX 130	
TEMPERATURE OF THE EARTH. Advertiſements of the warm and fertilizing temperature of the earth, ſtones, rocks, &c. - *Beal*	X 357	II 741
TEMPERS. An eſſay tending to make a probable conjecture of tempers by the modulations of the voice in ordinary diſcourſe - *Ent*	XII 1010	III 61
TEMPESTS. Advertiſements of black winds, tempeſts, &c. - - *Beal*	X 357	
TEMPLE. An explanation of the figures of a Pagan temple, and unknown characters at Cannara, in Salſet - - *Stuart*	XXVI 372	V 260
—— Part of a letter concerning the remains of an antient temple in Ireland, and of a ſtone hatchet of the antient Iriſh *Biſhop of Cork*	XLII 581	IX 457
TENDON. An account of ſtitching the great tendon		

See Eye-glasses, Object-glasses, Hair

	Tranſ.	Abridg.
between the calf of the leg and heel, with its union and cure, after an entire diviſion of it, with remarks - *Cowper*	XXI 153	III 498
TENDON. An account of the caſe of the firſt joint of the thumb torn off, with the flexor tendon in its whole extent torn out - *Home*	L 617	
—— Caſe of William Carey, aged 19, whoſe tendons and muſcles were turned into bones *Henry*	LI 89	
Further account - *Henry*	— 92	
TENERIFFE. An account of a journey from the port of Oratava, in the iſland of Teneriffe, to the top of the pike in that iſland, in Aug. 1715, with obſervations thereon by *Edens*	XXIX 317	V 2 148
—— Obſervations made in going up the Pic of Teneriffe - - *Heberden*	XLVII 353	
—— Some account of a ſalt found on the Pic of Teneriffe - - *Heberden*	LV 57	
TERCERA. Part of a letter concerning a new Iſland lately raiſed out of the ſea near Tercera *Forſter*	XXXII 100	VI 2 203
TERNATA. An account of the upper part of the burning mountain in the iſle of Ternata, according to the view taken thereof *Witzen*	XIX 42	II 392
TERRELLA. A letter about the load-ſtone, where chiefly the ſuggeſtion of Gilbert, touching the circumvolution of a globous magnet, called terrella, and the variation of the variation is examined - - *Petit*	II 527	— 607
TESSELLATED WORK. Part of a letter concerning an antient teſſellated or Moſaick work at Leiceſter - - *Carte*	XXVII 324	
TESSERA. A brief account of a Roman teſſera *Ward*	XLV 224	XI 1321
TESTICLE. Teſtis examinatus, formerly printed at Florence, by Vauclius Dathirius Bonglarus, now reprinted, becauſe the ſubject is under a ſeverer examination among the curious anatomiſts both here, in France, and Holland *Bonglarus*	III 843	III 191
—— Anatomical obſervations in the body of a woman about 50 years of age, who died hydropical in her left teſticle - *Sampſon*	XII 1000	— 206 — 218
—— An account of the forming of a fœtus in the teſticle - - *Maurice*	XIII 285	— 212
—— Examination of the teſticle of a rat, and the ſeed of muſcles, oyſters, &c. *Leeuwenhoek*	XVII 593	— 685
TESTIMONY. A calculation upon the credibility of human teſtimony - - *Anon.*	XXI 359	— 662

Toils of plants. See motion.

Teredines. Description of a rare species of worm shells, discovered at an island lying off the north west coast of the island of Sumatra. Griffiths. 1806:269.

Observations on the shell of the sea worm found on the coast of Sumatra, proving it to belong to a species of Teredo; with an account of the anatomy of the Teredo navalis. Home. — 276.

Termites. Account of the Termites of the hot climates. Smeathman. 71: 139.

Terra Ponderosa. Experiments and observations on — Withering. 74: 293.

Test liquor. On a new method of preparing a test liquor to shew the presence of Acids and Alcalies in chemical mixtures. Watt 74: 419.

	Tranſ.	Abridg.
Tetanus. Obſervations upon the effects of electricity applied to a tetanus, or muſcular rigidity of four months continuance *W. Watſon*	LIII 10	
Thales. Letter concerning the year of the eclipſe foretold by Thales - *Coſtard*	XLVIII 17	
—— An account of the eclipſe predicted by Thales *Stukeley*	— 221	
Thermometer. An account of ſeveral experiments made to examine the nature of the expanſion and contraction of fluids by heat and cold, in order to aſcertain the diviſions of the thermometer, and to make that inſtrument in all places, without adjuſting by a ſtandard *Halley*	XVII 650	II 33
—— Obſervations on the thermometer and magnetic needle, in his voyage to the Cape of Good Hope, 1700, - - *Cunningham*	XXII 577	
—— Account of a new thermometer depending on the variation of the ſpring of the air by heat and cold - - *Geoffroy*	— 962	
—— An account of an experiment made to aſcertain the proportion of the expanſion of the liquor in the thermometer, with regard to the degrees of heat - - *Taylor*	XXXII 291	VI 2 49
—— A meteorological, barometrical, thermometrical, epidemical, and magnetical diary, kept at Utrecht, 1729 *Van Muſchenbroek*	XXXVII 357	VII 4 71
		— - 86
1730 and 1731 *Van Muſchenbroek*	— 408	— - 90
—— Extract of a letter concerning the conſtruction of a quickſilver thermometer, and his obſervations on the eclipſes of Jupiter's ſatellites, in the years 1731 and 1732 *Deliſle*	XXXIX 221	VIII 467
—— Deſcription of the thermometer *Pickering*	XLIII 5	
—— A letter concerning the difference of the degrees of cold, marked by a thermometer kept within doors, or without in the open air, Dec. 1, 2, 3, 1747 - - *Miles*	XLIV 613	X 433
—— A diſcourſe concerning the uſefulneſs of thermometers in chymical experiments, and concerning the principles on which the thermometers now in uſe have been conſtructed; together with the deſcription and uſes of a metalline thermometer, newly invented *C. Mortimer*	— 672	— 435
—— A letter concerning a metalline thermometer, in the Muſeum of the Gentlemens' Society, at Spalding - - *Johnſon*	XLV 128	— 426
—— A letter concerning thermometers, and ſome		

obſervations

	Tranſ.	Abridg.
obſervations of the weather - *Miles*	XLVI 1	X 447
—— A letter of the near agreement of thermometers in London and at Tooting *Miles*	XLVI 208	— 471
THERMOMETER. Tables and obſervations *Stedman*	XLVII 4	
—— Thermometrical obſervations made by M. Demidoff, at Solikamſky, on the borders of Siberia, lat. 59°, in 1751, by a thermometer adapted to M. de L'Iſle's ſcale, which, in this extract, are reduced, likewiſe to thoſe of Fahrenheit, and M. Reaumur *E. of Macclesfield*	XLVIII 108	
—— A compariſon of different thermometrical obſervations in Siberia - *W. Watſon*	— 108	
—— An account of the ſtate of the thermometers, on the 8th and 9th of February, 1755 *Miles*	XLIX 43	
—— An account of the ſtate of the thermometer at the Hague, Jan. 9, 1757 *Trembly*	L 148	
—— A deſcription of ſome thermometers for particular uſes - - *Cavendiſh*	— 300	
—— Thermometrical account of the weather in Maryland for four years, 1753 to 1757 *Brooke*	LI 58 70	
—— A deſcription of a metalline thermometer *Fitzgerald*	— 823	
—— A deſcription of a new thermometer and barometer - - *Fitzgerald*	LII 146	
—— Thermometrical obſervations at Derby *Whitehurſt*	LVII 265	
—— Obſervations on the barometer, thermometer, and rain, at Plymouth, 1767 *Farr*	LVIII 136	
—— Account of an experiment made with a thermometer, whoſe bulb was painted black, and expoſed to the direct rays of the ſun *R. Watſon*	LXIII 40	
—— Extract of a regiſter of the barometer, thermometer, and rain, at Lyndon, in Rutland, 1772 *Barker*	— 221	
—— Extract of a regiſter of the barometer, thermometer, and rain in Lyndon, in Rutland, 1773 *Barker*	LXIV 202	
—— Extract of a regiſter of the barometer, thermometer, and rain, at Lyndon, in Rutland, 1774 *Barker*	LXV 199	
—— An account of ſome thermometrical obſervations at Allahabad, in the Eaſt Indies, in latitude 25° 30′ N. during the year 1767, and alſo during a voyage from Madraſs to England, in the year 1774 - *Sir Robert Barker*	— 202	

+ Thermometer. Description of a thermometrical barometer. Cavallo. 71: 524.
Account of an improved Thermometer. – – – – – Six. 72: 72.
An attempt to make a Thermometer for measuring the higher degrees of heat – – – – – – Wedgwood 305.
An attempt to compare and connect the Thermometer for strong fire with the common Mercurial Ones – – ——— 74: 358.
Additional observations on making a Thermometer for measuring the higher degrees of heat – – – ——— 76: 390

+ Thibet. Some account of the vegetable and mineral productions of Boutan and Thibet. Saunders. 79: 79.

	Transf.	Abridg.
THERMOMETER. Extract of a register of the barometer, thermometer, and rain, at Lyndon, in Rutland, 1775 - - *Barker*	LXVI 370	
—— Extract of a register of the barometer, thermometer, and rain, at Lyndon in Rutland, 1776 *Barker*	LXVII 350	
—— The report of the Committee appointed by the Royal Society to consider of the best method of adjusting the fixed points of thermometers, and of the precautions necessary to be used in making experiments with those instruments *Committee of the Royal Society*	— 816	
—— Abstract of a register of the barometer, thermometer, and rain at Lyndon, in Rutland, 1777 *Barker*	LXVIII 554	
—— A register of the barometer, thermometer, and rain at Lyndon, in Rutland 1778 *Barker*	LXIX 547	
—— Register of the barometer, thermometer, and rain, at Lyndon, in Rutland, 1779 *Barker*	LXX 474	
—— Thermometrical experiments and observations *Cavallo*	— 587	
—— See *Heights, Meteorological Observations*		
THERMOSCOPE. Some observations concerning the baroscope and thermoscope *Wallis & Beale*	IV 1113	II 32
THIBET. An account of the kingdom of Thibet *Stewart*	LXVII 465	
THIGH. A letter concerning a woman of 62 years of age, that lost her leg, and greatest part of her thigh, by a gangrene *Calep*	XXVI 41	V 389
—— Observations on a fracture in the upper part of the thigh bone - *Douglas*	XXIX 499	— 388
—— The case of Grace Lowdell, aged about 60 years, who had an extraordinary tumour on her thigh - - *Chandler*	XLI 365	IX 236
—— The description and draught of a machine for reducing the fracture of the thigh *Ettrick*	— 562	— 254
—— An account of a large piece of the thigh-bone which was taken out, and its place supplied by a callus - - *Richardson*	— 761	
THIGH. See *Aneurism, Luxation*		
THORACICUS DUCTUS. A new discovery of the communication of the ductus thoracicus with the emulgent vein - *Pecquet*	II 461	III 258
—— —— Annotations upon a discovery pretended to have been made by M. Pecquet of a communication between the ductus thoracicus and the vena cava - *Needham*	VII 5007	— 259

THORACIC

	Trans.	Abridg.
THORACIC DUCT. Account of an offification of the thoracic duct - - *Chefton*	LXX 323	
Chefton	— 578	
THORAX. An account of what happened on fyringing warm water into the thorax of a bitch *Mufgrave*	XX 181	III 78
—— Letter concerning a child who had its inteftines, mefentery, &c. in the cavity of the thorax *Holt*	XXII 992	V 269
—— An account of a præter-natural bony fubftance found in the cavity of the thorax *Rutty*	XXXIV 152	VII 505
THROAT. Some obfervations concerning the virtue of the jelly of the black currants, in curing inflammations in the throat *Baker*	XLI 655	VIII 838
—— Some account of a fheep having a monftrous horn growing from his throat *Parfons*	XLIX 183	
—— An account of the cafe of a man who died of the effects of the fire at Eddyftone light-houfe by melted lead running down his throat *Spry*	— 477	
Another account - *Huxham*	— 483	
THUMB. An account of the cafe of the firft joint of the thumb torn off, with the flexor tendon in its whole extent torn out - *Home*	L 617	
THUNDER. A relation of an accident by thunder and lightning at Oxford, May 10, 1666 *Wallis*	I 222	
—— A relation of the fad effects of thunder and lightning in Hampfhire, Jan. 24, 1665-6 *Neale*	— 247	II 172
—— Odd effects of a dreadful thunder-clap at Stralfund, in Pomerania, June 1670 *Anon.*	V 2084	— —
—— An odd effect of thunder and lightning upon wheat and rye in the granaries at Dantzick *Kirkby*	VIII 6092	— 174
—— Letter containing particulars of a philofophical nature viz. a narrative of the ftrange effects of thunder upon a magnetic card *Anon.*	XI 647	— 180
—— Obfervation concerning thunder and lightning being from the pyrites - *Lifter*	XIV 517	— 182
—— A relation of the effect of a thunder clap on the compafs of a fhip on the coaft of New-England, July 24, 1681 - *Oldenburg*	— 520	
A letter concerning former relations *Sir R. S.*	— 521	

	Tranſ.	Abridg.
Thunder. Some remarkable effects of a great ſtorm of thunder and lightning at Portſmouth, Oct. 23, 1685 - - - *Anon.*	XV 1212	II 174
—— The relation of a ſtorm of thunder, lightning, and hail, at Oundle, in Northamptonſhire *W. R.*	XVII 710	
—— An account of the effects of a very extraordinary thunder near Aberdeen in Scotland *Garden*	XIX 311	715 —
—— Letter concerning the generation of hail, of thunder, and lightning, and the effects thereof *Wallis*	— 653	— 183
—— Some additions to his letter about thunder and lightning - - *Wallis*	— 729	— —
—— A true and exact relation of the diſmal and ſurpriſing effects of a terrible and unuſual clap of thunder and lightning that fell upon the Trumbull galley, Nov. 26, 1696 *Mawgridge*	— 782	— 176
—— Letter concerning the effects of thunder and lightning at Everdon, in Northamtonſhire, (wherein divers perſons were killed) July 27, 1691 - - - *Wallis*	XX 5	— 177
—— An account of a young man ſlain with thunder and lightning, Dec 22, 1698 *Thoreſby*	XXI 51	— 179
—— Of an accident by thunder and lightning, at Leeds, April 27, 1700 *Thoreſby*	XXII 507	
—— A relation of the ſtrange effects of thunder and lightning which happened in the county of Down, in Ireland, Aug. 9, 1707 *Molyneux*	XXVI 36	IV 2 126
—— Part of a letter giving an account of a ſtorm of thunder and lightning that happened at Ipſwich, July 16, 1708 - *Bridgman*	— 137	— - 128
The effects of the above ſtorm at Colcheſter *Nelſon*	— 140	
—— Part of a letter concerning a ſtorm of thunder, and lightning, and rain, at Leeds, in Yorkſhire, Auguſt 5, 1701 - *Thoreſby*	— 289	V 2 40
—— A letter giving an account of a ſtorm of thunder, and lightning, which happened near Leeds, in Yorkſhire - *Thoreſby*	XXVII 320	IV 2 131
—— A relation of the effects of a ſtorm of thunder and lightning at Sampford Courtney, in Devonſhire, on Oct. 7, 1711 *Chamberlayne*	— 528	
—— An account of what happened from thunder in Carmarthenſhire, Dec 6, 1729 *Davies*	XXXVI 444	VI 2 74
—— An extract of a letter concerning the crooked and angular darts of lightning in thunder ſtorms - - *Logan*	XXXIX 240	VIII 507

		Tranf.	Abridg.
THUNDER. An account of two oak trees ftruck by thunder	*Clark*	XLI 235	VIII 507
—— A letter concerning the ftorm of thunder which happened June 12, 1748	*Miles*	XLV 383	X 475
—— Letter concerning the caufe of thunder	*Eeles*	XLVII 524	
—— Letter concerning the electrical experiments made in England under thunder clouds	*W. Watfon*	— 567	
—— An account of a ftorm of thunder and lightning near Ludgvan, in Cornwall, Dec. 20, 1752	*Borlafe*	XLVIII 86	
—— Electrical experiments, with an attempt to account for their feveral phænomena; together with fome obfervations on thunder clouds	*Canton*	— 350	
—— An account of the death of Mr. George William Richman, occafioned by an electrical ftroke collected from thunder, tranflated from the Dutch	*Anon.*	XLIX 61	
—— An account of the effects of a ftorm of thunder and lightning in the parifhes of Looe and Lanreath, in Cornwall, June 27, 1756	*Dyer*	L 104	
Letter on the fame fubject	*Miles*	— 107	
—— An account of a ftorm of thunder and lightning at Norwich, July 13, 1758	*Cooper*	LI 38	
—— An account of the effects of a ftorm of thunder and lightning at Rickmanfworth, in Hertfordfhire, July 16, 1759	*Whitfield*	— 282	
—— Of two thunder ftorms in Cornwall, one broke over Ludgvan church, the other at Breag, Jan. 11, 1762	*Borlafe*	LII 507	
—— Obfervations in electricity, and on a thunder ftörm	*Bergman*	LIII 97	
—— Account of the effects of a ftorm of thunder and lightning on Pembroke college, Oxford, June 3, 1765	*Griffith*	LV 273	
—— An account of a remarkable thunder ftorm, Feb. 18, 1770, at St. Keverne, in Cornwall	*Williams*	LXI 71	
—— Extract of a letter concerning a thunder and lightning ftorm by which Mr. Heartly, of Harrowgate, was killed, Sept. 29, 1772	*Kirkfhaw*	LXIII 177	
—— Account of the effects of a thunder ftorm on the 15th of March, 1773, upon the houfe of Lord Tylney, at Naples	*Sir William Hamilton*	— 324	
—— See *Lightning*			

THYME.

	Transf.	Abridg.
THYME. Dissertation on the camphire of Thyme *Neumann*	XXXVIII 202	IX 382
TIBER. See *Antiquities*		
TIBERIADES. Experiments by way of analysis upon the water of the dead sea, upon the Hot springs, near Tiberiades, and upon Hammon Pharoan water - *Perry*	XLII 48	VIII 643
TICUNAS. Experiments made on a great number of living animals with the poison of lamas and of ticunas - - *Herissant*	XLVII 75	
—— An account of the American poison ticunas - - *Fontana*	LXX 163	
—— Translation of Fontana's account of the American poison, called ticunas (Appendix)	LXX ix	
TIDES. A relation of some extraordinary tides in the West Isles of Scotland - *Moray*	I 53	II 291
—— An essay exhibiting the hypothesis about the flux and reflux of the sea *Wallis*	— 263	— 268
An appendix by way of answer to some objections made to the precedent discourse *Wallis*	— 281	
—— Some inquiries and directions concerning tides, proposed by Dr. Wallis, for the proving or disproving his lately published discourse concerning them - - *Wallis*	— 297	— 365
Considerations and inquiries concerning tides, likewise for a further search into Dr. Wallis's newly published hypothesis *Moray*	— 298	— 260
—— Patterns of the tables proposed to be made for observing of tides, promised in the next foregoing transactions - *Moray*	— 311	— 365
Other inquiries touching the sea *Boyle*	— 315	— 297
—— An account of several engagements for observing of tides - - *Oldenburg*	— 378	— 365
—— An account of the course of tides at Bermudas *Norwood*	II 565	— 268
—— An account of some observations made at and near Plymouth, 1697, by way of an answer to some of the queries concerning tides, in vol. I. 298, 311 - *Colepresse*	III 632	— 264
—— A letter concerning the variety of annual high tides, as to several places; with respect to his own hypothesis vol. I. p. 263 *Wallis*	— 652	— 278
The true time of the tides *Philips*	— 656	— 261
—— A letter concerning the present declination of

TID

		Transf.	Abridg.
the magnetic needle and the tides	D. B.	III 726	II 607
TIDES. Letter concerning the tides at the Bermudas	Stafford	— 792	— 268
—— Observations made in the Stony road, near Bristol in answer to some queries concerning the tides	Shtumy	— 813	— 265
—— Animadversions upon Dr. Wallis's hypothesis about the flux and reflux of the sea	Childrey	V 2061	— 279
Dr. Wallis's answer to the above	Wallis	— 2068	— 283
—— Letter concerning the flux of the Euripus	Babin	VI 2153	— 289
—— An account of the current of the tides about the Orcades	Anon.	VIII 6139	— 290
—— A correct tide table, shewing the exact times of high water at London Bridge, to every day in 1683	Flamstead	XIII 10	— 365
Account of the foregoing tables	Flamstead	— 12	— 263
—— A tide table of high water at London Bridge, in 1684, with directions for the use of it	Flamstead	XIV 458	— 365
—— Account of the tide on the coast of Guinea	Heathcott	— 578	— 268
—— An account of the course of the tides, at Tonqueen, with the theory of them at the bar of Tonqueen	Halley	— 677	— 292
—— Tide table of the times of high water at London Bridge, for 1685, with directions	Flamstead	— 821	— 365
—— Tide table of high water at London Bridge for 1686	Flamstead	XV 1226	— —
—— An account of the course of the tides at Dublin	Molyneux	XVI 192	— 263
Remark	Oldenburg	— 193	
—— Table of the high water on the coasts of France, upon the day of the new and full moon, taken from the French almanac, called La connoissance des temps, for 1687		— 220	— 267
—— Table of high water at London Bridge, for 1687	Flamstead	— 232	
—— Table of high water at London Bridge, for 1688	Flamstead	— 428	
—— An extract of a letter giving an account of an experiment made in the Bay of Biscay, of sinking a bottle close corked under various depths of water, and of Lay Well, which ebbs and flows	Oliver	XVII 908	— 305

		Trans.	Abridg.
Tides. An account of the tides in the Adriatic	*Strange*	LXVII 144	
Tiger-cat see Cat.			
Timber. Instances shewing the correspondence of the pith and timber, with the seed of the plant; as also of the bark, or sap in the bark, with the pulp of the fruit, or some encompassing coat or cod containing the seed -	*Beal*	IV 919	II 710
—— A discourse concerning the most seasonable time of felling of timber; written by the advice of S. Pepys - -	*Plott*	XVII 455	I 589
—— Letter concerning the difference of timber growing in different countries, and felled at different seasons of the year	*Leeuwenhoek*	XVIII 224	— 592
Time. Letter concerning a movement that measures time after a particular manner, with an account of the reasons of the said motion	*Wheeler*	XIV 647	— 468
—— A letter wherein he asserts his right to the curious and useful invention of making clocks to keep time with the sun's apparent motion	*Williamson*	XXX 1080	IV 394
—— Some remarks upon the equation of time, and the manner of computing it	*Maskelyne*	LIV 336	
—— Short and easy methods for finding the quantity of time contained in any given number of mean lunations, and the number of new lunations in any given quantity of time	*Ferguson*	LV 61	
—— A determination of the exact moments of time when the planet Venus was at external and internal contact with the sun's limb in the transits, of June 6, 1761, and June 3, 1769	*Dunn*	LX 65	
—— A new method of finding time by equal altitudes	*Aubert*	LXVI 92	
Tin. An account of some mineral observations touching the mines of Cornwall and Devon; wherein is described the art of training a load, the art and manner of digging the ore, and the way of dressing and blowing tin	*Anon.*	VI 2096	II 365
—— A relation of the tin-mines, and working of tin in the county of Cornwall	*Merrit*	XII 949	— 572
—— The method of making tin plates, extracted from the memoirs of the Academy of Sciences for 1725 - -	*Rutty*	XXXV 630	VI 2 240
—— Account of native tin found in Cornwall	*Borlase*	LVI 35	

Tides. Some account of the Tides at Naples. - - - - - - - - 1793:168.

Timber. Upon the extent of the expansion and contraction of timber in different directions relative to the position of the medulla of the tree. - - — Knight. 1817:269.

Toad-stone. Analysis of — Withering 72:333.

	Tranſ.	Abridg.
TIN. A letter containing a ſupplement to the account of the diſcovery of native tin *Mendes da Coſta*	LVI 305	
—— Letters giving an account of a ſpecimen of native tin found in Cornwall *Borlaſe and Roſewarne*	LIX 47	
TIN-FOIL. Actual fire and detonation, produced by the contact of tin-foil, with the ſalt compoſed of copper and the nitrous acid *Higgins*	LXIII 137	
TINCTURE. An account of an extraordinary tincture given to a ſtone - *Reiſel*	XVI 22	I 604
—— Several experiments about giving variety of tincture to water, &c. - *Southwell*	XX 87	III 656
TITHIMALUS HYBERNICUS. Letter concerning the effects of mackenboy or tithimalus hibernicus *Aſhe*	— 293	II 644
TOBACCO. Manner of planting and ordering tobacco in Virginia - *Glover*	XI 623	III 566
—— Obſervations on the planting and culture of tobacco in Zeylan - *Strachan*	XXIII 1164	IV 2 312
—— A letter concerning tobacco aſhes *Leeuwenhoek*	XXIV 1740	V 2 267
TOES. An account of one who had hairy excreſcencies, or extraordinary large nails, on his fingers and toes - - *Locke*	XIX 694	III 13
TOKAY. An account of the tokay, and other wines in Hungary - *Douglaſs*	LXIII 292	
TOMINEIUS. The deſcription of the American tomineius, or humming bird *Grew*	XVII 760	II 854
TONES. An explanation of the modes or tones in the antient Grecian muſic - *Styles*	LI 695	
TONGUE. Some diſcoveries concerning the tongue *Malpighi*	II 491	III 58
—— An account of a ſtone cut out from under the tongue of a man - *Liſter*	VII 4062	— 155
—— Letter concerning worms found under the tongue, and other parts of the body *Dent*	XVIII 219	— 137
Letter concerning the ſame operation *Lewis*	— 222	— —
—— An account of the tongue of a paſtinaca marina, frequent in the ſeas about Jamaica, and lately dug up in Maryland and England *Sloane*	XIX 694	
—— An account of a ſtone bred at the root of the tongue, and cauſing a quinſy *Bonavert*	XX 440	— 156
—— A letter concerning the whiteneſs on the tongue in fevers - - *Leeuwenhoek*	XXV 2456	V 2 267
—— Microſcopical obſervations upon the tongue *Leeuwenhoek*	XXVI 111	— - —

	Transf.	Abridg.
TONGUE. A letter containing observations upon the white matter on the tongue of feverish persons *Leeuwenhoek*	XXVI 210	V 2 267
—— A description of that curious natural machine, the wood peckers tongue - *Waller*	XXIX 509	V 55
—— A physiological account of the case of Margaret Cutting, who speaks distinctly, though she has lost the apex and body of her tongue *Parsons*	XLIV 621	XI 956
—— The case of Henry Axford, who recovered the use of his tongue, after having been four years dumb, by means of a frightful dream *Squire*	XLV 148	— 958
—— An account of a very learned divine who was born with two tongues - *Mortimer*	— 232	— 959
TOP. An account of an horizontal top invented by Mr. Serson - - *Short*	XLVII 352	
TORPEDO. Of the electric property of the torpedo *Walsh*	LXIII 461	
—— Anatomical observations on the torpedo *Hunter*	— 481	
—— Of torpedos found on the coast of England *Walsh*	LXIV 464	
—— Extract of a letter containing some experiments on the torpedo, made at Leghorn, Jan. 1, 1773 - - *Ingenhouse*	LXV 1	
—— An account of some attempts to imitate the effects of the torpedo by electricity *Cavendish*	LXVI 196	
TORQUES. A letter concerning a golden torques found in England - - *Mostyn*	XLII 416	IX 24
TORRICELLIAN EXPERIMENT. An attempt to render the cause of that odd phænomenon of the quicksilver remaining suspended far above the the usual height, in the torricellian experiment *Hugens*	VII 5027	II 23
—— —— See *Barometer*		
TORTOISES. Anatomical observations about the structure of the lungs of frogs, tortoises, &c. and perfecter animals - - *Malpighi*	VI 2149	— 653
—— Observations on the weight of a land tortoise, when he went into the ground in autumn, and when he came out in spring, for several years *Ent*	XVII 533	— 825
—— An anatomical description of the heart of land tortoises from America - *Bussire*	XXVII 170	V 74
—— An account of two new tortoises *Pennant*	LXI 266	

TOUCH.

+Tongue. Observations on the structure of the Tongue, illustrated by cases in which a portion of that organ has been removed by ligature. Home. 1803:205.

Torpedo. Some observations and experiments made on the Torpedo of the Cape of Good Hope in the year 1812. Todd. 1816:120.

An account of some experiments on the Torpedo electricus, at La Rochelle. —— 1817:32.

	Transf.	Abridg.
TOUCH. Observations on the effects of touch and friction - - *Oldenburg*	I 206	III 10
TOURMALIN. Experiments on tourmalin *Wilson*	LI 308	
—— On the electrical nature of the tourmalin *Bergman*	LVI 236	
TOWER. Vide *Antiquities*		
TOWN. Letter concerning the vestigia of a Roman town near Leeds, in Yorkshire *Thoresby*	XXIII 1285	V 2 37
—— Observations on the expectations of lives, the increase of mankind, the influence of great towns on population, and particularly the state of London with respect to healthfulness and number of inhabitants - *Price*	LIX 89	
TOXICODENDRON. Two letters concerning the toxicodendron (a native tree of Carolina) *Abbé Mazeas & Miller*	XLIX 157	
—— A letter attempting to ascertain the tree that yields the common varnish used in China and Japan; to promote its propagation in our American colonies, and to set right some mistakes of botanists - - *Ellis*	XLIX 866	
—— Remarks on Mr. John Ellis's letter on the toxicodendron - - *Miller*	L 430	
Answer to the remarks - *Ellis*	— 441	
TRADE WINDS. Concerning the cause of the general trade winds - - *Hadley*	XXXIX 58	VIII 500
See *Tropick*		
TRADESCANT. Some account of the remains of John Tradescant's garden at Lambeth *William Watson*	XLVI 160	X 740
—— A letter upon the early cultivation of botany in England; and some particulars about John Tradescant, a great promoter of that science, as well as natural history, in the last century, and gardener to King Charles I. *Ducarel*	LXIII 79	
TRANSFUSION OF BLOOD. See *Blood*		
TRANSITS. Some more accurate observations about Jupiter's transits near fixed stars; useful for determining the inclination of that planet to the ecliptic - - *Flamstead*	VIII 6033	I 381
—— Dissertation on the next transit of Venus under the sun - - *Boscovich*	LI 865	
—— See *Sun, Moon, Venus*		
TRANSPLANTING. Some communications on the season for transplanting vegetables *Reed*	VI 2128	II 655
—— Some considerations on the best season for transplanting - *Beal*	— 2144	——

	Tranſ.	Abridg.
TRANSYLVANIA. Inquiries to be made in Hungary and Tranſylvania - *Royal Society*	II 467	III 631
—— Directions and inquiries with their anſwers concerning the mines, minerals, baths, &c. of *Oldenburg and Brown*	V 1189	II 523
TRAVELS. Obſervations in travels from Venice through Iſtria, Dalmatia, Greece, and the Archipelago, to Smyrna - *Vernon*	XI 573	
—— A letter containing an account of his journey from Cairo, in Egypt, to the Written Mountains, in the Deſart of Sinai - *Montagu*	LVI 40	
—— An account of three journies from the Cape Town, into the ſouthern parts of Africa; undertaken for the diſcovery of new plants, towards the improvement of the Royal Botanical Gardens at Kew - *Maſon*	LXVI 268	
TREES. Experiments concerning the motion of the ſap in trees - *Willoughby and Ray*	IV 963	— 682
—— Obſervations, directions, and inquiries concerning the motion of ſap in trees, in purſuance of what was begun therein about the latter end of 1668, and the next ſpring *Tonge & Willoughby*	V 1165	— 683
—— Experiments concerning the bleeding of *Liſter*	— 2069	
—— How to multiply crab-ſtools, and propagate trees by layers - *Tonge*	— 2074	— 752
—— Some communications concerning the deſcent of ſap, and the ſeaſon of tranſplanting *Reed*	VI 2128	— 655
—— Some conſiderations of what choice of apples for the delicacy of the liquors in peculiar ſeaſons; and for eaſy and ſpeedy propagation: pears for ſome lands proper; their choice for manifold uſes; eſpecially for pleaſant, or for laſting liquor: and how to be planted and ordered to the beſt advantage *Beal*	— 2144	— —
—— A way of making all ſorts of plants, trees, fruits, and legums, grow to an extraordinary bigneſs - - *Anon.*	X 356	— 749
—— On the texture of trees, with notes thereon *Leeuwenhoek*	XI 653	— 873
—— A diſcourſe concerning the effects of the great froſt on trees and other plants in 1683, drawn from the anſwers to ſome queries ſent into divers countries by R. Plott, and from ſeveral obſervations made at Oxford by J. Bobart *Anon.*	XIV 766	— 155 — 751
—— Curious obſervations and experiments on the growth of trees - *Brotherton*	XVI 507	— 707

+ Trees. Some account of the annual growth of trees. — — . Barker. 78: 410.
Observations on the grafting of trees — — — — — — Knight 1795: 290.
On the inverted action of the alburnous vessels of trees. — ——— 1806: 293
On the parts of trees primarily impaired by age — — — — ——— 1810: 178.

	Tranf.	Abridg.
Trees. An extract of a letter on the bark of trees *Leeuwenhoek*	XVII 838	III 685
—— ~~A defcription of the~~ pimienta, ~~or Jamaica pepper tree~~ - - ~~*Sloane*~~	~~XVII 462~~	~~II 663~~
—— Relation of fubterraneous Youle, in Yorkfhire *Richardfon*	XIX 726	— 842
—— Letter concerning trees found under ground in Hatfield Chace - *De la Pryme*	XXII 980	IV 2 212
—— Letter concerning fubterraneous trees, &c. *De la Pryme*	XXIII 1073	— - 218
—— ~~An account of the~~ poifon wood tree ~~in New England~~ - - ~~*Dudley*~~	~~XXXI 145~~	~~VI 2 307~~
~~*Sherard*~~	~~— 147~~	~~— 2 308~~
—— Account of letters found in the middle of a beach-tree - - *Klein*	XLI 231	VIII 845
—— An account of two oak trees ftruck by thunder *Clark*	— 235	— 847
—— The effects which the farina of the bloffoms of different forts of apple trees had on the fruit of a neighbouring tree - *Cook*	XLIII 525	X 751
—— An account of the Bifhop of London's garden at Fulham, with a catalogue of the exotic trees remaining in it, June 25, 1751 *W. Watfon*	XLVII 241	
—— An account of fome trees difcovered under ground at Mount's Bay in Cornwall *Borlafe*	L 51	
—— Obfervations on the growth of trees *Marfham*	LI 7 1797: 128	
—— A letter on the trees which are fuppofed to be indigenous in Great Britain *Barrington*	LIX 23	
—— On the ufefulnefs of wafhing and rubbing the ftems of trees, to promote their annual increafe *Marfham*	LXVII 12 LXXI 449	
—— ~~Defcription and ufe of the~~ cabbage-bark tree ~~of Jamaica~~ - - ~~*Wright*~~	~~— 507~~	
—— See *Black-Poplar*, *Sycamore*, *Walnut*, &c. in their Places		
—— See *Sap*, *Vegetation*, *Graft*.		
Treves. Remarks on the ftones in the county of Naffau, and the territories of Treves and Colen refembling thofe of the Giants Caufway in Ireland - - *Trembly*	XLIX 581	
Triangles. Of triangles defcribed in circles and about them - - *Stedman*	LXV 296	
Trigonometry. Spherical trigonometry reduced to plane - - *Blake*	XLVII 441	
—— Abridged - - *Murdoch*	L 538	
—— Calculations in fpherical trigonometry abridged *Lyons*	LXV 470	

Trigonometrical survey, in the years 1791—1794. Williams 1795: 414.
1795 and 1796. 1797: 432.
1797, 1798 and 1799. Mudge 1800: 539.

	Transf.	Abridg.
TRIPOLI. An account of some observations relating to the production of the terra tripolitana or tripoli — — *Hubner*	LI 186	
Remarks on Mr. Hubner's paper on tripoli *Da Costa*	— 192	
TRIPOS. Some account of a curious tripos and inscription found near Turin, serving to discover the true situation of the antient city Industria *Baker*	XLIII 540	XI 1240
TRITURE. Observations on these three chymical operations, digestion, fermentation, and triture or grinding, (hitherto, in the author's opinion, not sufficiently regarded) by which many things of admirable use may be performed *Langelot*	VII 5052	III 315
TROCART. A new trocart for the puncture in the hydrocephalus, and for other evacuations which are necessary to be made at different times *Le Cat*	XLVII 267	
TROPICK. The breath of the sea plants probably the material cause of the trade or tropick winds *Lister*	XIV 489	II 129
—— An historical account of the trade winds, and monsoons, observable in the seas, between and near the tropicks, with an attempt to assign the physical cause of the said winds *Halley*	XVI 153	— 153
TROUT. Of the gillaroo trout — *Barrington*	LXIV 116	
Account of the stomach of the gillaroo trout *Henry Watson*	— 121	
—— Observations on the gillaroo trout, commonly called in Ireland the gizzard trout *John Hunter*	— 310	
TROY. Short and easy methods for finding the number of Troy pounds contained in any given number of averdupoise pounds, and vice versa *Ferguson*	LV 61	
TRUFFLES. An account of the tubera terræ, or truffles, found at Rushton in Northamptonshire; with some remarks thereon *Robinson*	XVII 824	— 624
TRUMPET. An account of the speaking trumpet as it hath been contrived and published by Sir S. Moreland, together with its uses both by sea and land — — *Moreland*	VI 3056	
—— Letter of his improvement of Sir S. Moreland's speaking trumpet, &c. — *Conyers*	XII 1027	I 505
—— A discourse concerning the musical notes of the		

trumpet,

Trinidad, Island. Account of a bituminous lake or plain there. Anderson. 79:65.

	Tranſ.	Abridg.
trump:t, and trumpet-marine, and of the defects of the ſame - - *Roberts*	XVII 559	I 607
TUBA EUSTACHIANA. A method propoſed to reſtore the hearing when injured from an obſtruction of the tuba euſtachiana *Wathen*	XLIV 213	
TUBES. An experiment, ſhewing that the ſeemingly ſpontaneous aſcenſion of water in ſmall tubes open at both ends, is the ſame in vacuo as in the open air - - *Haukſbee*	XXV 2223	IV 2 181
—— An account of ſome experiments, with an enquiry into the cauſe of the aſcent and ſuſpenſion of water in capillary tubes *Jurin*	XXX 739	IV 423
—— An account of ſome new experiments relating to the action of glaſs-tubes upon water and quickſilver - - *Jurin*	— 1083	— 428
—— Two letters concerning the rotatory motion of glaſs tubes about their axes, when placed in a certain manner before the fire - *Wheler*	XLIII 341	X 551
—— An account of experiments relating to odours paſſing through electrified globes and tubes *Winkler*	XLVII 231	
An account of the reſult of ſome experiments made here with globes and tubes, tranſmitted by Mr. Winkler to verify the facts above mentioned - - *W. Watſon*	— 236	
TULIPS. Microſcopical obſervations on tulips, &c. *Leeuwenhoek*	XVII 949	III 685
—— A letter giving an account of tulips, and other ſuch bulbous plants, flowering much ſooner when their bulbs are placed upon bottles filled with water, than when planted in the ground *Triewald*	XXXVII 79	VI 2 255
An account of the ſame experiment tried the next year by - - *Miller*	— 81	— 355
TULL. Account of Mr. Tull's method of caſtrating fiſh - - *Watſon*	XLVIII 870	
TUMOUR. The hiſtory of a tumour in the lower part of the belly - - *Giles*	XX 420	
—— An account of a very large tumour in the fore part of the neck - - *Douglas*	XXV 2214	V 213
—— An obſervation of a tumour on the neck full of hydatides, cured by - *Hewnden*	— 2344	— 216
—— An account of an extraordinary tumour or wen lately cut off the cheek of a perſon in Scotland *Bower*	XXX 713	— 217
—— An account of a præter-natural tumour on the		

loins

	Transf.	Abridg.
loins of an infant, attended with a cloven spine *Rutty*	XXXI 98	VII 676
—— An extraordinary case in surgery of a tumour *Atkinson*	XXXIII 340	— 666
—— Extract of two uncommon cases of tumours in the abdomen, from a Latin tract published at Strasburg, anno 1728, entitled Boecleri, &c. ad exteros medicos epistola - *Rutty*	XXXV 562	— 522
—— Two extraordinary cases, one of a large stone in the urethra, occasioned by a venereal infection, the other of a child born with a remarkable tumour on the loins - *Huxham*	XXXVI 257	— 536 — 560
—— An account of a large glandular tumour in the pelvis; and of the pernicious effects of crude mercury given inwardly to the patient *Cantwell*	XL 139	IX 184
—— An account of an extraordinary tumour in the knee of a person whose leg was taken off *Pierce*	XLI 56	— 271
—— The case of Grace Lowdell, aged about 60 years, who had an extraordinary tumour on her thigh - - *Chandler*	— 365	— 236
—— An account of tumours which rendered the bones soft - - *Pott*	— 616	— 247
—— A letter concerning a child born with an extraordinary tumour near the anus, containing some rudiments of an embryo in it *Huxham*	XLV 325	XI 1020
—— A letter containing the description of a new invented instrument for the extirpation of tumours out of the reach of the surgeon's fingers *Le Cat*	XLVI 72	— 1084
—— The case of an extraordinary tumour growing on the inside of the bladder successfully extirpated - - *Warner*	— 414	— 1006
—— An account of some extraordinary tumours upon the head of a labouring man - *Parsons*	L 350	
—— Case of a young lady who drank sea water for an inflammation and tumour in the upper lip *Lavington*	LV 6	
—— Account of an extraordinary steatomatous tumour, in the abdomen of a woman *Hanly*	LXI 131	
TUMULI. Extract of a letter concerning some tumuli at Danes Graves, near Kilham, Yorkshire *Knowlton*	XLIV 101	
TUNQUINESE MEDICINE. The effects of the tunquinese medicine - *Reid*	XLIII 212	— 1044

+ Turkey. Account of the Turkey. Pennant. 71:67.

		Tranſ.	Abridg.
Tunis. A letter containing a geographical deſcription and map of the kingdom of Tunis, with a poſtſcript relating to the cure of intermittent fevers in thoſe parts -	*Shaw*	XXXVI 177	VI 423
Turkeys. An account of two young turkeys joined together by their breaſts -	*Floyer*	XXI 434	II 898
—— An account of a bird, ſuppoſed to have been bred between a turkey and a pheaſant	*Edwards*	LI 833	
Turky. Inquiries for Turky -	*Mr. H.*	I 360	III 631
—— Some communications out of Turky	*Anon.*	VIII 6017	— 605
Turnips. An abſtract of a letter concerning the making of turnip bread, in Eſſex	*Dale*	XVII 971	II 667
—— Some inſtances of the very great and ſpeedy vegetation of turnips -	*Deſaguliers*	XXX 974	IV 2 311
—— An account of ſome trials to cure the ill taſte of milk, which is occaſioned by the food of cows, either from turnips, cabbages, or autumnal leaves, &c. alſo to ſweeten ſtinking water - -	*Hales*	XLIX 339	
Turning. The principal properties of the engine for turning ovals in wood or metal, and of the inſtrument for drawing ovals upon paper demonſtrated - -	*Ludlam*	LXX 378	
Turn-Lathe. Letters about the method of poliſhing teleſcope glaſſes by a turn-lathe, and alſo of the making of an extraordinary burning-glaſs at Milan - -	*Anon.*	III 795	I 194
Turpentine. The way of making pitch, tar, roſin, and turpentine near Marſeilles	*Bent*	XX 291	
Turquoise. Some remarks on the precious ſtone called the turquoiſe -	*Mortimer*	XLIV 429	X 633
Tycho Brahe. Letter concernining the remains of the obſervatory of the famous Tycho Brahe	*Gourdon*	XXII 691	I 216
Tyrol. Remarkable obſervations in a journey over the Tyrol Alps, with a catalogue of the plants obſerved - -	*Ehrhart*	XLI 547	IX 462 VIII 768
Tyrone. Vide *Antiquities*			

U.

	Transf.	Abridg.
ULCER. An account of an ulcer in the right groin emitting the fœces of the inteſtines *Earnſhaw*	XV 1204	III 119
— An account of a fœtus voided by the ulcered navel of a negro, at Nevis - *Brodie*	XIX 580	— 219
— An account of the diſſection of a perſon who died of an ulcer in the right kidney *Douglas*	XXVII 32	V 257
— Concerning the bones of a fœtus being diſcharged through an ulcer near the navel *Drake*	XLV 121	XI 1019
UNICORN FISH. An account of a narhual or unicorn fiſh, lately taken in the river Oſt, in the Dutchy of Bremen, 1736 - *Steigertahl*	— 147	— 71
A deſcription of the ſame fiſh - *Hampe*	— 149	— 72
URCHIN. An obſervation upon the motion of the hearts of two urchins, after their being cut out *Templer*	VIII 6016	III 69
URETERS. An anatomical obſervation of four ureters in an infant - - *Tyſon*	XII 1039	— 146
— An account of two large ſtones, which, for twenty years paſt, lodged in the meatus urinarius, and were thence cut out - *Bernard*	XIX 250	— 153
— Two caſes of inſects voided by the urinary paſſage - - *Turner*	XXXIII 410	VII 539
— A letter concerning the foramen ovale being found open in the hearts of adults, and of the figure of the canal of the urethra *Le Cat*	XLI 681	IX 134 — 186
— Caſe of Hannah Hitchcock, one of whoſe ureters was grown up - *Huxham*	XLIII 207	XI 1007
— An account of ſeveral caſes of hernias, and diſorders of the urethra - *Le Cat*	XLVII 324	
— A deſcription of the lymphatics of the urethra and neck of the bladder - *H. Watſon*	LIX 392	

Ulmin. On the substance from the Elm tree, called Ulmin. Smithson. 1813:64

+Urine. Letter concerning some peculiarities in the Urine of the Camel
(and of the Cow, Horse and Ass) - - - - - - - - - Hatchett. 1806. 372
Remarks on the composition of the Urine - - - - - - - Brande. 1810: 136.
Remarks on the influence of Acids upon the composition of the Urine 1813. 213.
On the urinary organs and secretions of some of the Amphibia - - - - Davy. 1818: 303.

Uric acid. see Stone. [handwritten]

	Transf.	Abridg.
URINE. Account of a bullet voided by urine *Fairfax*	III 803	III 160
—— Two experiments made for finding another passage of the - - *Hauton*	V 2049	— 147
—— Relation of a worm voided by urine *Ent*	XII 1009	— 135
—— The cure of a total suppression of urine, not caused by the stone, by the use of acids *Baynard*	XIX 19	— 148
—— Part of a letter giving an account of several magnetical experiments, and of one who pretended to cure or cause diseases at a distance, by applying a sympathetic powder to the urine *Leeuwenhoek*	— 512	— 685
—— A relation of a person who voided many hydatides in her urine - *Davies*	XXII 897	V 2 283
—— Letter concerning a bunch of hair voided by urine - - *Yonge*	XXVI 414	V 284
Observations upon the hair *Leeuwenhoek*	— 416	— —
Account of several solid bodies voided by urine *Yonge*	— 420	— 286
—— A remarkable comformation of the urinary parts *Bugden*	XXXVI 138	VII 540
—— A case of an extraordinary cause of a suppression of urine in a woman - - *Amyand*	XXXVII 258	— 540
—— Case of a gentlewoman who voided with her urine hairy crustaceous substances, with Sir H. Sloane's answer, containing several observations of extraordinary substances voided by the urinary passages - - *Powell*	XLI 699	IX 180 — 182
—— Case of hair voided by urine *Knight*	— 705	— 183
—— A case of a very long suppression of urine *Dawson*	LI 215	
—— An account of a hernia of the urinary bladder including a stone. - - *Pott*	LIV 61	
—— An account of a suppression of urine cured by a puncture made in the bladder through the anus *Robert Hamilton*	LXVI 578	
URNS. An extract of a letter giving an account of a large number of urns dug up at North Elmham in Norfolk - - *Neve*	XXVIII 257	V 2 97
URTICA MARINA. An account of the urtica marina *Gaertner*	LII 75	
USNEA. An historical memoir concerning a genus of plants called lichen by Micheli, Haller, and Linnæus and comprehended by Dillenius under the terms usnea, coralloides, and lichnoides;

	Tranſ.	Abridg.
tending principally to illuſtrate their ſeveral uſes - - *W. Watſon*	L 652	
UTERUS. An account of the diſſection of a bitch, whoſe cornua uteri being filled with the bones and fleſh of a former conception, had, after a ſecond conception, the ova affixed to ſeveral parts of the abdomen - -	XIII 183	II 904
—— Account of a fœtus lying without the uterus in the belly - - *Savard*	XIX 314	III 214
—— An account of an hydrops ovarii, with a new and exact figure of the glandulæ renales, and of the uterus in a puerpera *Douglas*	XXV 2317	V 294
—— An account of balls of hair taken from the uterus and ovaria of ſeveral women *Yonge*	— 2387	
—— An account of ſeveral extra-uterine fœtus	XXVI 424	— 306
Yonge	— 432	— 199
—— Letter concerning the bones of a dead fœtus taken out of the uterus of a cow *Sherman*	— 450	— 54
—— Account of an extra-uterine fœtus taken out of a woman, after death, that had continued five years and a half in the body *Houſton*	XXXII 387	VII 555
—— An account of an extra-uterine conception *Myddleton*	XLIII 336	XI 1010
—— A letter concerning a ſchirrous tumour of the uterus - - *Templeman*	XLIV 285	—102
—— Some account of the fœtus in utero being differently affected by the ſmall-pox *W. Watſon*	XLVI 235	— 1042
—— Deſcription of a double uterus and vagina *Purcell*	LXIV 474	
UVEA. Extract of a letter containing the particulars of the cure of a wound in the cornea, and of a laceration of the uvea, in the eye of a woman - - *Aery*	XLV 411	— 954

VACUUM.

s. On the passage of the ovum from the ovarium to the
terus in women. — Home. 1817: 23
mal conformation of the uterine system in women; and on some
hysiological conclusions to be derived from it. — Granville 1818: 3.

V.

	Trans.	Abridg.
VACUUM. Of the long continuance of a leach alive in the vacuum made in the pneumatic engine *Boyle*	V 2049	III 147
—— Experiments about the motion of pendulums in a vacuum - - *Derham*	XXIV 1785	IV 2 168
—— An account of an experiment to try the quality of air produced from gunpowder, fired in vacuo Boyliano - - *Hauksbee*	— 1806	— - 172
—— Experiments on the production and propagation of the light from the phoſphorus in vacuo *Hauksbee*	— 1865	— - 181
—— Experiments on the reſilition of bodies in common air, in vacuo, and in air condenſed *Hauksbee*	— 1946	— - —
—— Several experiments on the attrition of bodies in vacuo - - *Hauksbee*	— 2165	— - 180
—— An experiment ſhewing that the ſeemingly ſpontaneous aſcenſion of water in ſmall tubes open at both ends is the ſame in vacuo as in the open air - - *Hauksbee*	XXV 2223	— - 181
—— An account of an experiment ſhewing that actual ſound is not to be tranſmitted through a vacuum - - *Hauksbee*	XXVI 367	
—— An account of an experiment touching the propagation of ſound paſſing from the ſonorous body into the common air in one direction only *Hauksbee*	— 369	
—— An account of an experiment touching propagation of ſound through water *Hauksbee*	— 371	
—— An account of an experiment, ſhewing that an object may become viſible through ſuch an opake body as pitch in the dark, while it is under the circumſtances of attrition and a vacuum - - *Hauksbee*	— 391	— - 182
—— An account of an experiment to prove an interſperſed vacuum; or to ſhow that all places are not equally full - *Deſaguliers*	XXX 717	— - 173
—— An account of an experiment to ſhew by a new proof, that bodies of the ſame bulk do not contain equal quantities of matter, and, therefore that there is an interſperſed vacuum *Deſaguliers*	XXXI 81	VI 2 157

	Transf.	Abridg.
VACUUM. Experiments and observations of the freezing of water in vacuo - *Fahrenheit*	XXXIII 78	V 2 51
—— An account of the phænomena of electricity in vacuo - - *W. Watson*	XLVII 362	
VAGINA. An observation of hydatides voided per vaginam - *Watson*	XLI 711	IX 188
—— Description of a double uterus, and vagina *Purcell*	LXIV 474	
VALUE. Rules for correcting the usual methods of computing amounts and present values, by compound as well as simple interest; and of stating interest accounts - *Watkins*	XXIX 111	V 2 243
VAPOUR. An estimate of the quantity of vapour raised out of the sea by the warmth of the sun; derived from an experiment shewn before the Royal Society - *Halley*	XVI 366	II 108
—— An account of the circulation of the watry vapours of the sea, and the cause of springs *Halley*	XVII 468	—— 126
—— An account of the evaporation of water, as it was experimented in Gresham College, in 1693, with some observations thereon *Halley*	XVIII 183	—— 110
—— An attempt to solve the phænomenon of the rise of vapours, formation of clouds, and descent of rain - - *Desaguliers*	XXXVI 6	VI 2 61
—— An experiment to shew that some damps in mines may be occasioned only by the burning of candles, under ground, without the addition of any noxious vapour, even when the bottom of the pit has a communication with the outward air, unless the outward air be forcibly driven in at the said communication or pipe *Desaguliers*	XXXIX 281	
—— Some conjectures concerning the rise of vapours *Desaguliers*	XLII 140	VII 437
—— Letters concerning the cause of the ascent of vapour and exhalation, and those of winds; and of the general phænomena of the weather and barometer - *Eeles*	XLIX 124	
Remarks on the opinion of Henry Eeles concerning the ascent of vapours *Darwin*	L 240	
—— An account of some new experiments in electricity containing an enquiry whether vapour be a conductor of electricity, &c. *Henley*	LXIV 389	
VARNISH. The way of making several China varnishes, sent from the Jesuits in China to the great Duke of Tuscany - *Shexara*	XXII 525	I 602
—— An account of the strange effects of the Indian varnish - - *Del Papa*	—— 947	V 417

Variation of the Needle. see Magnets. p. 294.

+ Values. On the method of correspondent Values - - - - - - Waring. 79: 166.

	Transf.	Abridg.
VARNISH. Two letters on the texicodendron. *Abbé Mazeas and Miller*	XLIX 157	
—— A letter attempting to ascertain the tree that yields the common varnish used in China and Japan; to promote its propagation in our American colonies; and to set right some mistakes botanists appear to have entertained concerning it - - *Ellis*	— 866	
Remarks on Mr. J. Ellis's Letter on the texicodendron - - *Miller*	L 430	
Answer to the Remarks - *Ellis*	— 441	
VAULTS. Hints of the use to be made of vaults, &c. *Beale*	IV 1035	
VEGETABLES. Observations concerning cochineels, accompanied with some suggestions for finding out and preparing such like substances out of other vegetables - *Anon.*	III 796	I 212 II 655 — 687 — 690
—— Some communications on the season for transplanting vegetables - *Reed*	VI 2128	— 775 — 653
—— Some considerations on the best season for transplantation - *Beal*	— 2144	— 655 — 690
—— A considerable account touching vegetable excrescencies - - *Lister*	— 2254	— 768
Another letter enlarging his communications on vegetable excrescencies *Lister*	— 2284	— 770
Some additions - *Lister*	— 3002	— 771
—— Observations on the anatomy of the trunks of vegetables, &c. - *Anon.*	X 533	
—— An account of the nature and differences of the juices, more particularly of our English vegetable - - *Lister*	XIX 365	— 696
—— Observations on the roots of vegetables *Leeuwenhoek*	— 790	III 685
—— Some observations concerning some wonderful contrivances of nature in a family of plants in Jamaica, to perfect the individuum, and propagate the species, with several instances analogous to them in European vegetables *Sloane*	XXI 113	II 669
—— The anatomical preparation of vegetables *Seba*	XXXVI 441	IV 2 338
—— Part of a Letter concerning the electricity of vegetables - - *Browning*	XLIV 373	X 342
—— Account of vegetable balls which grow in a lake near the Humber in Yorkshire *Dixon*	XLVII 498	
With remarks - *W. Watson*		

	Transf.	Abridg.
VEGETABLES. A letter on the ſexes of plants and impregnation of vegetables *Styles*	LV 258	
—— On the nature of gorgonia, that it is a real marine animal, and not of a mixed nature between animal and vegetable *Ellis*	LXI 1	
—— Experiments on animals and vegetables, with reſpect to the power of producing heat *John Hunter*	LXV 446	
—— Of the heat of animals and vegetables *John Hunter*	LXVIII 7	
VEGETABLES. (Chymical preparations from) A way of extracting a volatil ſalt and ſpirit out of vegetables; intimated in vol. viii. p. 7002 *Coxe*	IX 4	III 326
—— A continuation of a diſcourſe begun in vol. IX. p. 4, touching the identity of all volatil ſalts and vinous ſpirits, together with two ſurpriſing experiments concerning vegetable ſalts perfectly reſembling the ſhape of the plants whence they had been obtained - - *Coxe*	— 169	— 333
VEGETABLE LAMB. An account of the Scythian vegetable lamb, called borametz *Breynius*	XXXIII 353	VI 2 317
VEGETATION. Queries concerning vegetation, eſpecially the motion of the juices of vegetables *Anon.*	III 797	II 752
—— Some communications relating to the queries about vegetation - *Beal*	— 853	— 676
A continuation of the anſwers *Tonge*	— 877	— 677
Additional anſwers to queries *Tonge*	— 880	— 676
Promiſcuous additions to what was formerly publiſhed in N° 43 and 44 - *Tonge*	IV 913	— 678
Inſtances ſhewing the correſpondence of the pith and timber, with the ſeed of the plant; as alſo of the bark or ſap in the bark with the pulp of the fruit of ſome encompaſſing coat or cod, containing the ſeed - *Beale*	— 919	— 710
—— Experiments concerning the motion of the ſap in trees - *Willoughby and Wray*	— 963	— 682
—— Hints tending to encreaſe the fertility of any kind of land, &c. - *Beal*	— 1135	— 728
—— Extract of divers letters, touching ſome enquiries and experiments; touching the motion of ſap in trees, and relating to the queſtion of the circulation of the ſame *Liſter*	VI 2119	— 686
A letter relating to ſome particulars in Mr. Liſter's communications *Willoughby*	— 2125	— 685
Extract of a letter both in relation to the fur-		

ther

+Vegetables. Some further considerations on the influence of the vegetable
kingdom on the animal creation. Ingen-housz 72:426.
Observations on the irritability of vegetables. - - - J. E. Smith 78:158.

Vegetation. On the direction of the radicle and germen during the vegetatin of seeds. Knight. 1806: 99.

On the action of detached leaves of plants. —— 1806: 269.

	Tranſ.	Abridg.
ther diſcovery of the motion of juices in vegetables, and removing the difference noted in Mr. Willoughby's letter *Anon.*	VI 2126	II 688
VEGETATION. Some communications on the deſcent of ſap - - - *Reed*	— 2128	
Some conſiderations on Mr. Reed's letter ſhewing in what ſenſe the ſap may be ſaid to deſcend, and to circulate the plants; and the graft to communicate with the ſtock *Beal*	— 2144	II 653 — 690
—— Some thoughts and experiments concerning vegetation - - *Woodward*	XXI.193	— 713
—— Some obſervations concerning vegetation *De la Pryme*	XXIII.1214	IV 2 310
—— Obſervations and experiments relating to the motion of ſap in vegetables *Bradley*	XXIX.486	V 267
—— Some microſcopical obſervations, and curious remarks on the vegetation, and exceeding quick propagation of moldineſs, on the ſubſtance of a melon - *Bradley*	— 490	IV 2 308
—— Some inſtances of the very great and ſpeedy vegetation of turnips - *Deſaguliers*	XXX.974	— - 311
—— Obſervations on ſome plants in New England, with remarkable inſtances of the nature and power of vegetation - *Dudley*	XXXIII.194	VI 2 342
——Letter concerning the vegetation of melon ſeed 33 years old - - *Gale*	XLIII 265	X 761
✝—— New obſervations upon vegetation *Muſtel*	LXIII 126	
VEINS. Anatomical obſervations of milk found in the veins inſtead of blood *Boyle*	I 100	III 239
A farther account of obſervations about white blood - - *Lower*	— 117	— —
—— A new diſcovery of the communications of the ductus thoracicus, with the emulgent vein *Pecquet*	II 461	— 258
—— Some experiments of injecting liquors into the veins of animals - - *Fracaſſati*	— 490	— 232
—— Some new experiments of injecting medicated liquor into the veins, together with the conſiderable cures performed thereby *Fabritius*	— 564	— 234
—— Some anatomical inventions and obſervations, particularly about the origin of the injection into the veins - - *Clarck*	III 672	— 290
—— An ingenious account of veins obſerved in plants analogous to human veins *Liſter*	VI 3052	I 691
—— Annotations upon a diſcovery pretended to have been made by M. Pecquet of a communicaiton		

		Transf.	Abridg.
between the ductus thoracicus and the inferior vena cava - - *Needham*		VII 5007	III 259
VEINS. A further account concerning the existence of veins, in all kinds of plants, together with a discovery of the membranous substances of those veins, and of some acts in plants resembling those of sense, and also the agreement of the venal juice in vegetables with the blood of animals, &c. - - *Lister*		— 5131	II 693
——— A note upon Mr. Lister's observations concerning the veins of plants - *Wallis*		VIII 6060	— 696
Remarks on Mr. Wallis's observations *Lister*			
——— Anatomical observations of an abcess of the liver; a great number of stones in the gall bag and bilious vessels; an unusual conformation of the emulgents and pelvis; a strange conjunction of both kidnies and a great dilatation of the vena cava - *Tyson*		XII 1035	III 81
——— Letter concerning powdered blue passing the lacteal veins - - *Lister*		XXII.819	V 259
——— An account of a polypus taken out of the vena pulmonalis, and of the structure of that vessel *Cowper*		— 797	— 221
——— An account of divers schemes of arteries and veins, dissected from adult human bodies by J. Evelyn, to which are subjoined a description of the extremities of those vessels, and the manner the blood is seen by the microscope, to pass from the arteries to veins in quadrupeds when living, with some chirurgical observations and figures after the life *Cowper*		XXIII 1177	— 335
——— An account of the veins and arteries of leaves *Nicholls*		XXXVI 371	VI 2 340
See *particular Veins in their Places*			
VELOCITY. Remarks upon a supposed demonstration, that the moving forces of the same body, are not as the velocities, but as the squares of the velocities - - *Eames*		XXXIV 188	VI 289
——— Remarks upon some experiments in hydraulics, which seem to prove that the forces of equal moving bodies are as the squares of their velocities - - *Eames*		XXXV 343	— 292
——— A letter occasioned by the present controversy among mathematicians, concerning the proportion of velocity and force in bodies in motion - - *Samuel Clarke*		— 381	— 294

	Transf.	Abridg.
VELOCITY. A letter containing a new manner of measuring the velocity of wind *Brice*	LVI 224	
—— An experimental examination of the quantity and proportion of mechanic power, necessary to be employed in giving different degrees of velocity to heavy bodies from a state of rest *Smeaton*	LXVI 450	
—— The force of fired gunpowder, and the initial velocities of cannon balls, determined by experiments; from which also is deduced, the relation of the initial velocity to the weight of the shot and the quantity of the powder *Hutton*	LXVIII 50	
VENEREAL DISEASE. Two extraordinary cases of a large stone in the urethra brought on by a venereal infection, and of a child born with a remarkable tumour on the loins *Huxham*	XXVI 257	VII 536
—— —— An attempt to prove the antiquity of the venereal disease, long before the discovery of the West Indies - *Becket*	XXX 839	IV 329
—— —— A letter concerning the antiquity of the venereal disease - - *Becket*	XXXI 47	VII 652
—— —— A letter to Dr. Halley, in answer to some objections made to the history of the antiquity of the venereal disease - *Becket*	— 108	— 663
—— —— An extraordinary venereal case *Huxham*	XLI 667	IX 214
—— —— An extract from the books of the town council of Edinburgh relating to a disease there supposed to be venereal in the year 1497 *Macky*	XLII 420	— 213
VENOM. Of a venomous scratch with the tooth of a porpus, its symptoms and cure *Lister*	XIX 726	II 842
VENTILATORS. An account of the great benefit of ventilators in many instances, in preserving the health and lives of people in slave and other transport ships - *Hales*	XLV 410	X 634
—— Observations on the utility of ventilators in a ship - - *Ellis*	XLVII 211	
—— An attempt to improve the manner of working the ventilators by the help of the fire-engine *Fitzgerald*	L 727	
VENTRICLE. An account of the left ventricle of the heart of an amazing magnitude *Douglass*	XXIX 326	V 231
VENUS. An account of several spots lately discovered in the planet Venus, at Bononia, extracted from the Journal des Scavans - *Cassini*	II 615	I 425

	Tranf.	Abridg.
VENUS. Conjunction of the moon and Venus, on the 11th of October, 1670 - *Hevelius*	V 2023	I 347
—— An account of the caufe of the late remarkable appearance of the planet Venus, feen this fummer for many days together in the day-time *Halley*	XXIX 466	IV 300
—— An account of an occultation of Venus by the moon, Sept. 19, 1729, at Berlin *Kirchius*	XXXVI 256	VI 352
—— An account of Mercury eclipfed by Venus obferved at Greenwich, May 17, 1737 *Bevis*	XL 394	VIII 207
—— Tranfit of Mercury over Venus, May 17, 1737, at Greenwich	XLI 630	
—— An obfervation of the planet Venus (with regard to her having a fatellite) made at funrife, Oct. 23, 1740 - *Short*	— 646	— 208
—— The phænomena of Venus, reprefented in an orrery, made by Mr. James Fergufon, agreeable to the obfervations of Seignior Bianchini	XLIV 127	X 95
—— Obfervation of the occultation of Venus by the moon, April 16, 1751 - *Bradley*	XLVI 201	
—— An occultation of the planet Venus by the moon, in the day time obferved at London, April 16, 1751 - - *Bevis*	XLVII 159	
—— Differtations on the next tranfit of Venus over the fun - - *Bofcovich*	LI 865	
—— Obfervations on the tranfit of Venus over the fun, on the 6th of June, 1761, taken at Greenwich - - *Blifs*	LII 173	
At Savile-Houfe, London - *Short*	— 178	
In Spital-fquare, London - *Canton*	— 182	
With a preceding account of the method taken for verifying the time of that phænomenon; and certain reafons for an atmofphere about Venus, made at Chelfea - *Dunn*	— 184	
—— In the ifland of St. Helena *Mafkelyne*	— 196	
At Lefkeard - *Heydon*	— 202	
—— Obfervations on the tranfit of Venus over the fun, on June 3, 1761, at Stockholm *Wargentin*	— 208	
	— 213	
Further in Sweden - *Wargentin*	— 216	
At Paris - - *De la Lande*	— 221	
In and near Paris - *Ferner*	— 226	
At Conftantinople - - *Porter*		
At Upfal in Sweden - *Bergman*	— 227	
At Cafeneburg in Sweden - *Wargentin*	— 231	
At Greenwich and Shirburn Caftle *Blifs*	— 232	
At Madrid - - *Eximenus*	— 251	

VENUS.

		Tranſ.	Abridg.
Venus. At Tobolſk in Siberia, by Abbé Chappe	*De la Lande*	— 254	
At Leyden - -	*Lulofs*	— 255	
At the Iſland of Rodrigues	*Pingré*	— 371	
At the Cape of Good Hope	*Maſon & Dixon*	— 378	
At Madraſs	*Hirſt*	— 396	
At Bologna - -	*Zanotti*	— 399	
At Calcutta in Bengal, communicated from the Court of directors of the Eaſt India Company	*Magee*	— 582	
—— The obſervations on the internal contact of Venus with the ſun's limb, in the late tranſit, made in the different parts of Europe, compared with the time of the ſame contact obſerved at the Cape of Good Hope, and the parallax of the ſun thence determined	*Short*	— 611	
—— A delineation of the tranſit of Venus, expected in 1769 - -	*Ferguſon*	LIII 30	
—— A letter from Sweden relating to the late tranſit of Venus, containing the obſervations made at Cajaneburg - -	*Wargentin*	— 59	
—— An account of the tranſit of Venus, at Schwezinga - -	*Mayer*	LIV 163	
—— Obſervations on the tranſit of Venus at St. John's in Newfoundland -	*Winthrop*	— 277	
—— Account of improvements to be made by obſervations of the tranſit of Venus in 1769	*Hornſby*	LV 326	
—— The tranſit of Venus over the ſun's diſc, obſerved June 6, 1761, at Upſal	*Mallet*	LVI 72	
—— Obſervations on the tranſit of Venus, over the ſun; and the eclipſe of the ſun, on June 3, 1769 - -	*Maſkelyne*	LVIII 355	
At the Middle Temple, London	*Horsfall*	LIX 170	
At Shirburn Caſtle, and Oxford	*Hornſby*	— 172	
At Oxford - -	*Horſley*	— 183	
At Kew - -	*Bevis*	— 189	
At Spital-ſquare -	*Canton*	— 192	
At Leiceſter - -	*Ludlam*	— 236	
Near Quebec	*Holland and St. Germain*	— 247	
At Hammerſoſt for the Royal Society	*Dixon*	— 253	
At the North Cape -	*Bayly*	— 266	
At the Iſle Coudre near Quebec	*Wright*	— 273	
At Grypſwald - -	*Mayer*	— 284	
At Norriton in Philadelphia	*Smith, Lukins, and Sellers*	— 289	
In Sweden - -	*Wargentin*	— 327	
At Glaſgow - -	*Wilſon*	— 333	

		Trans.	Abridg.
VENUS. At Hawkhill near Edinburgh, to which are added, some remarks by the Astronomer Royal, and further particulars relative to the observations communicated in other letters	*Lina*	— 339	
At Gibraltar - -	*Jardine*	— 347	
At Cambridge in New England	*Winthrop*	— 351	
—— At Paris and other places extracted from the letters of M de la Lande, and from a letter from Mr. Messier - -		— 374	
—— Transit observed June 3, 1769, with a Cassegrain reflector of J. Short, having a metal speculum of two feet focal length, and magnifying about 110 times -	*Aubert*	— 378	
At Stockholm - -	*Ferner*	— 404	
At East Dereham in Norfolk	*Wollaston*	— 407	
At Lewestown in Pennsylvania	*Biddle & Bayley*	— 414	
At the Round Tower, in Windsor Castle	*Harris*	— 422	
In Maryland - -	*Leeds*	— 444	
At Prince of Wales's Fort, Hudson's Bay	*Wales and Dymond*	— 480	
Account of several phænomena observed during the ingress of Venus into the solar disc	*Hirst*	— 228	
—— A determination of the exact movements of time when the planet Venus was at external and internal contact with the sun's limb, in the transits of June 6, 1761, and June 3, 1769	*Dunn*	LX 65	
—— Observations made at Dinapoor on the planet Venus, when passing over the sun's disk, with three different quadrants, and a two foot reflecting telescope - -	*Degloss*	— 239	
—— Observations on the late transit of Venus at Caen, in Normandy -	*Pigott*	— 257	
—— Phases of the transit of Venus, supposed to be retarded by the aberration of light	*Winthrop*	— 358	
—— Observations on the transit of Venus at Geneva	*Mallet*	— 363	
At Cavan, in Ireland -	*Mason*	— 488	
At Cape François - -	*Pingré*	— 497	
—— On the effect of the aberration of light, on the time of a transit of Venus over the sun	*Price*	— 536	
—— A short account of the observations of the late transit of Venus, made at St. Joseph's, in California - - -	*Doz*	— 549	
—— Short account of the late Abbe's Chappe's observations of the transit of Venus in California	*Bourriot*	— 551	
—— Transitus Veneris in ejus exitu e disco solis Jun. 4. 1769 observatus	Mohr	61: 433	

VENUS.

Venus. Astronomical observations made with a view to determine the heliocentric longitude of its nodes, the annual motion of the nodes, and the greatest inclination of its orbit — — — — — — — — — — — Bugge 80:21.

Observations on the athmospheres of Venus and the Moon, their respective densities, perpendicular heights, and the twilight occasioned by them. Schroeter 1792:309.

Observations on the Planet Venus. — — — — — — — Herschel 1793:201.

New observations in further proof of the mountainous inequalities, rotation, atmosphere and twilight of the planet Venus — — — — Schroeter 1795:117.

Vermes. An account of the circulation of the blood in the class Vermes, and the principle explained in which it differs from that in the higher animals. Home 1817:1.

Ver[illegible] See Ova.

4 On the nature of the intervertebral substance in Fish and Quadrupeds. Home. 1809:177.

A chemical analysis of the fluid contained in the intervertebral cavity of the Squalus maximus. Brande — 184.

	Transf.	Abridg.
VENUS. A deduction of the quantity of the sun's parallax from the comparison of the several observations of the late transit of Venus, made in Europe, with those made in George Island, in the South Seas, by Mr. Lexell *Euler, Junior*	LXII 69	
VENUS, (Statue of) An account of the discovery of an antient statue of Venus, at Rome *Mackinlay*	LII 44	
VERDIGRIS. Sequel to the case of Mr. Butler of Moscow, who was strangely affected by mixing verdigris and false leaf gold with aqua fortis *Baker*	LIV 15	
VERTEBRÆ. An observation of an infant, where the brain was depressed into the hollow of the vertebræ of the neck - *Tyson*	XIX 533	III 26
VESSELS. ~~Letter touching the true use of the lymphatick vessels~~ (lymphatic) ~~*De Bills*~~	~~III 791~~	~~— 262~~
—— Anatomical observations of an abcess in the liver; a great number of stones in the gall bag and bilious vessels; an unusual conformation of the emulgents and pelvis; a strange conjunction of both kidnies, and a great dilatation of the vena cava - *Tyson*	XII 1035	— 81
—— Letter concerning a substance coughed up resembling the vessels of the lungs *Bussiere*	XXII 545	— 68
—— ~~Observations on the seed vessels, and seeds of polypodium~~ (seeds) - ~~*Leeuwenhoek*~~	~~XXIV 1868~~	~~V 2 26~~
—— An account of some uncommon anastomoses of the spermatic vessels in a woman *Mortimer*	XXXVI 373	VII 553
—— ~~Observations on the origin and use of the lymphatic vessels of animals, being an extract from the Gulstonian Lectures~~ (lymphatic) ~~*Akenside*~~	~~L 322~~	
—— Account of an experiment, by which it appears that salt of steel does not enter into the lacteal vessels, with remarks - *Wright*	L 594	
VESSELS IN WOOD. Account of the appearance of several woods and their vessels *Leeuwenhoek*	XIII 197	— 684
VESUVIUS. A relation of the raining of ashes, in the Archipelago, upon the eruption of Mount Vesuvius, some years ago - *Robinson*	I 377	II 143
—— Of the burning and eruption of Mount Vesuvius, 1707 - - *Valetta*	XXVIII 22	IV 2 207
—— Extract of a letter giving several curious observations and remarks on the eruptions of fire and smoak, from Mount Vesuvius *Berkeley*	XXX 708	— - 209
—— An account of an extraordinary eruption of		

	Tranſ.	Abridg.
Mount Veſuvius in March, 1730, extracted from the meteorological diary of that year at Naples - - *Cyrellus*	XXXVII 336	VI 2 199
—— An account of the eruption of Veſuvius, May, 1737 - - *Prince of Caſſano*	XLI 237	VIII 670
Another account from an Engliſh gentleman *Anon.*	— 252	— 677
—— An account of the eruption of Mount Veſuvius in 1751 - - *Supple*	XLVII 315	
—— An account of the eruption of Mount Veſuvius in 1751, in a letter to Sir Mathew Fetherſtonhaugh - - - *Anon.*	— 409	
—— A letter concerning the late eruption of Mount Veſuvius - - *Parker*	— 474	
—— An extract of the ſubſtance of three letters concerning the late eruption of Mount Veſuvius *Jamineau*	XLIX 24	
—— Some account of an eruption of Mount Veſuvius, March 24, 1758 - *Paderni*	L 622	
—— An account of an eruption of Mount Veſuvius, Dec. 23, 1760 - *Styles*	LII 39	
Another account of the ſame eruption *Styles*	— 41	
—— An extract of a letter concerning the late eruption of Mount Veſuvius, dated at Rome, 9th of January, 1761, and the diſcovery of an antient ſtatue of Venus, at Rome *Mackinlay*	— 44	
—— Two letters giving an account of the late eruption of Mount Veſuvius, Nov. 17, 1764 *Hamilton*	LVII 192	
—— An account of the eruption of Mount Veſuvius in 1767 - - *Hamilton*	LVIII 1	
—— A letter containing ſome farther particulars on Mount Veſuvius, and other volcanos in the neighbourhood - *Hamilton*	LIX 18	
—— Obſervations on the heat of the ground on Mount Veſuvius - *Howard*	LXI 53	
—— An account of an eruption of Mount Veſuvius in Aug. 1779 - *Hamilton*	LXX 42	
VETTER. Some remarkable obſervations on the Lake Vetter - - *Hearne*	XXIV 1938	
VETURIAN. Remarks upon a Denarius of the Veturian family, with an Etruſcan inſcription on the reverſe - - *Swinton*	LVIII 253	
VIGILIÆ FLORUM. See *Plant*		
VILLA LUDOVISIA. See *Bones*		
VILLETTE. See *Burning-Glaſs*		
VINADIO. An account of the hot baths of Vinadio, in the Province of Coni, in Piedmont *Bruni*	LI 839	

+ Vesuvius. Some particulars of the present state of Mount Vesuvius. Hamilton. 76:365.
An account of the late eruption of Mount Vesuvius. ——— 1795:73.

		Tranf.	Abridg.
VINEGAR. The way of making it in France	*Anon.*	V 2002	
—— Obfervations on the mouths of the eels in vinegar, and alfo a ftrange aquatic animal	*Baker*	XLII 416	IX 38
VINES. A way of making vines grow to advantage, all over the roof of a houfe -	*Templer*	VIII 6016	II 656
VIPERS. An obfervation touching the bodies of fnakes and vipers -	*Oldenburg*	I 138	— 811
—— Some obfervations on vipers -	*Redi*	I 160	
—— The phænomena afforded by them, included in an exhaufted receiver -	*Boyle*	V 2012	
—— Experiments made upon vipers at Florence	*Platt*	VII 5060	——
—— A difcourfe of the viper, and fome other poifons, wrote by Sir Theodore de Mayerne, after difcourfing with Mr. Pontæus	*Mayerne*	XVIII 162	— 814
—— Some obfervations upon vipers	*Sprengell*	XXXII 296	VII 409
—— A letter containing fome obfervations on a man and woman bit by vipers -	*Atwell*	XXXIX 394	IX 63
—— Letter concerning the viper catchers, and the efficacy of oil of olives in curing the bite of vipers -	*Williams*	XL 26	— 66
—— Two letters concerning the efficacy of oil of olives in curing the bite of vipers	*Dufay*	— 444	— 68
—— A letter on the coluber ceraftes, or horned viper of Egypt - -	*Ellis*	LVI 287	
VIRGINIA. A letter concerning an unufual way of propagating mulberry trees in Virginia, for the better improvement of the filk work, together with fome particulars tending to the good of that plantation -	*Moray*	I 201	II 653
—— Inquiries for Virginia, and the Bermudas	*Royal Society*	II 420	III 631
—— An account of the advantage of Virginia for building fhips - - -		VIII 6015	II 566
—— An account of Virginia, its fituation, temperature, productions, inhabitants, and their manner of planting and ordering tobacco, &c.	*Glover*	XI 623	III 566
—— Extract of four letters relating to the natural productions of Virginia -	*Banifter*	XVII 667	II 822
With an additional note	*Anon.*	— 691	
—— A letter giving an account of feveral obfervables in Virginia, and in his voyage thither, more particularly concerning the air	*Clayton*	— 781	III 575
Second letter of farther obfervations on Virginia	*Clayton*	— 790	

		Transf.	Abridg.
Virginia. A continuation of the account of Virginia	*Clayton*	XVII 941	III 581
—— A letter giving a farther account of the soil, and other observables of Virginia	*Clayton*	— 978	— 589
—— A continuation of an account of Virginia	*Clayton*	XVIII 121	— 592
—— Answer to several queries of Dr. Grew's, in 1687, relating to Virginia	*Clayton*	XLI 143	IX 465
Viscous Slime. Letter giving an account of a viscous slime left after a flood in the territory of the Landgrave of Thuringue, with observations thereupon by Mr. Watson -	*Bose*	XLVIII 358	
Vision. A new discovery touching vision	*Mariotte*	III 668	
An answer - -	*Peequet*	— 669	
—— Answer to Mr. Peequet, concerning the opinion that the choroeides is the principal organ of - -	*Mariotte*	V 1203	
—— A continuation of a discourse about vision, with an examination of some late objections against it - -	*Briggs*	XIII 171	
—— Two remarkable cases relating to vision	*Briggs*	XIV 559 n. 159.	III 38
—— Letter concerning a contumacious jaundice, accompanied with a very odd case in vision	*Dale*	XVIII 158	— 286
—— See *Opticks*			
Vitriol. Of the mineral of Liege, yielding both brimstone and vitriol, and the way of extracting them out of it used at Liege	*Anon.*	I 45	II 530
—— Account of a pond, in Somersetshire, to which pigeons resort but cattle will not drink at it	*Anon.*	— 323	— 332
Further account of the (pond) vitriolate water, with some particulars touching water	*Anon.*	— 359	— —
—— A description of a Swedish stone, which affords sulphur, vitriol, allum, and minium	*Talbot*	— 375	— 531
—— Some observations and experiments about vitriol, tending to prove the nature of that substance, and to give further light in the inquiry after the principles and properties of other minerals - - -		IX 41	— 451
—— A continuation of the discourse concerning vitriol, shewing, that vitriol is usually produced by sulphur, acting on, and coagulating with a metal; and then making out, that allum is likewise the result of the said sulphur; as also			

+ Vision. Investigation of the cause of that Indistinctness of Vision which has been ascribed to the smallness of the Optic Pencils — — — Herschel 76:500.
An attempt to explain a difficulty in the theory of Vision, depending on the different refrangibility of light — — — — — — — Maskelyne 79:256.
— — — — — — — — Young. 1793:169.
ons on Vision. — — — — — — Hosack 1794:196.
tions and experiments on vision. — — — Wells. 1811:378.

	Trans.	Abridg.
evincing that vitriol, sulphur, and allum do agree in saline principles, and lastly declaring the nature of the salt in brimstone, and whence it is derived - - *Anon.*	IX 66	II 544
— An account of the increase of weight in oil of vitriol, exposed to the air - *Gould*	XIV 496	— 534
— Of the origin of white vitriol and the figure of its chrystals, not yet accounted for *Lister*	XXI 331	— 537
VITRUM ANTIMONII CERATUM. Observations on the effects of the - *Geoffroy*	XLVII 273	
VITULUS MARINUS. Some account of the phoca, vitulus marinus, or sea calf, shewed in London 1743 - - *Parsons*	XLII 383	IX 74
VITUS's DANCE. An account of the cure of St. Vitus's Dance by electricity *A. Fothergill*	LXIX 1	
VIVIPAROUS. An account of a kind of fly at this viviparous - - *Lister*	VI 2170	II 787
— Account of a fly that is viviparous *Lister*	XIV 592	— —
— A letter concerning the minute eels in paste being viviparous - *Sherwood*	XLIV 67	XI 799
VOICE. An essay tending to make a probable conjecture of tempers by the modulation of the voice in ordinary discourse - *Ent*	XII 1010	III 61
VOLATILE SALT. See *Salt*		
VOLCANO. An account of the upper part of the burning mountains in the isle of Ternata according to the view taken thereof *Witzen*	XIX 42	II 392
— A farther relation of the horrible burning of some mountains of the Molucco islands *Witzen*	— 529	— 394
— An account of a very odd eruption of fire out of a spot in the earth near Fierenzola in Italy *St. Clair*	XX 378	— 385
— A letter containing some farther particulars on Mount Vesuvius, and other volcanos in the neighbourhood - *Hamilton*	LIX 18	
— An account of two Giants Causeways or Group of prismatic basaltine columns, and other curious volcanic concretions, in the Venetian states in Italy, with some remarks on the characters of these and other similar bodies, and on the physical geography of the countries in which they are found - - *Strange*	LXV 5	—
— An account of a Volcanic hill near Inverness *West*	XVII 385	
— A letter giving an account of certain traces of		

		Trans.	Abridg.
volcanos on the banks of the Rhine +	Sir *W. Hamilton*	LXVIII 1	
—— See *Ætna*, *Vesuvius*, Morne Garou			
Volga. A specimen of the natural history of the Volga - -	*Forster*	LVII 312	
—— Some account of a new map of the river Volga	*Forster*	LVIII 214	
Voltaic apparatus. See Galvanism.			
Voluntaries. See *Music*			
Vomit. Extract of a letter containing some relations concerning odd worms vomited by children	*Lister*	X 391	III 135
Vomiting Medicines. The practice of purging and vomiting medicines, according to Dr. Cockburn's solution of his problem; with tables shewing their doses in particular ages and constitutions -	*Cockburn*	XXVI 46	V 397
Vortices. A physico-mathematical demonstration of the impossibility and insufficiency of vortices	*Sigorgne*	XLI 409	VIII 378
Voyages. Directions for seamen bound for far voyages - -	*Royal Society*	I 140	III 631
—— An appendix to the directions	*Anon.*	— 147	II 257
—— Observations made by a curious and learned person sailing from England to the Caribee Islands - -	*Stubbes*	II 493	III 546
An enlargement of the observations	*Stubbes*	III 699	— 551
The remainder of the observations in the same voyage - - -	*Stubbes*	— 717	— 557
—— Narrative of a voyage from Spain to Mexico, and of the minerals of that kingdom	*Anon.*	— 817	II 588
—— An account of a passage by sea to the East Indies	*Smithson*	IV 1003	III 416
—— A narrative of some observations made upon several voyages to find a way for sailing about the north to the East Indies, and for returning the same way from thence hither; together with instructions given by the Dutch East-India Company for the discovery of Jesso, near Japan; to which is added a relation of sailing through the northern America to the East-Indies -	*Van Nierop*	IX 197	— 505
—— A relation of a voyage from Aleppo to Palmyra in Syria - -	*Halifax*	XIX 83	— 489
—— An extract of the journals of two several voyages of the English merchants of the factory of Aleppo, to Tadmor, anciently called Palmyra.		— 129	— 492

Volcano. Some account of Volcanic appearances in the North of Ireland and Western Islands of Scotland. Mills. 80:73.

A narrative of the eruption of a Volcano in the Sea of the island of St. Michael. — — — — Tillard. 1812:152.

On a Saline substance from Mount Vesuvius. — — Smithson. 1813:256.

	Transf.	Abridg.
Voyages. Journal of a voyage from London to Constantinople, 1668 - *Smith*	XIX 597	
—— An account of a voyage to Chusan in China, with a description of the island, of the several sorts of tea, of the fishing, agriculture of the Chinese, &c. with several observations not hitherto taken notice of *Cunningham*	XXIII 1201	V 2 171
—— Journal of a voyage made by order of the Royal Society to Churchill River on the North West Coast of Hudson Bay; of thirteen months residence in that country; and of the voyage back to England, in 1768, 1769 *Wales*	LX 100	
—— Two letters of a voyage to Bengal, with observations made there - *Rose*	— 444	
—— Remarks and observations made on board the ship Kelsall, on a voyage to Judda and Mocha, in 1769 - - *Newland*	LXII 79	
—— The method taken for preserving the health of the crew of his Majesty's ship the Resolution during her late voyage round the world *Cook*	LXVI 402	
—— Journal of a voyage to the East-Indies, in the ship Grenville, Burnet Abercrombie Captain, in the year 1775 - - *Dalrymple*	LXVIII 389	
—— Tract of his Majesty's armed brig Lion from England to Davis's Streights and Labrador, with observations for determining the longitude by sun and moon, and error of common reckoning; also the variation of the compass and dip of the needle as observed during the said voyage in 1776 - *Pickersgill*	— 1057	
Vulture. An account of a prodigiously large feather of the bird cuntur, brought from Chili, and supposed to be a kind of vulture *Sloane*	XVIII 61	II 860

W.

Subject	Author	Trans.	Abridg.
Wales. A letter containing several observations in natural history made in his travels through Wales - -	*Lhwyd*	XXVII 462	V 34 V 2 117
With a further account of birds mentioned in it - - -	*Lhwyd*	— 466	V 34
Farther observations -	*Lhwyd*	— 467	V 2 118
—— A letter giving a further account of what he met with remarkable in natural history and antiquities in his travels through Wales	*Lhwyd*	— 500	— - 120
—— Extracts of letters containing observations in natural history and antiquities in his travels through Wales and Scotland	*Lhwyd*	XXVIII 93	— - —
Wall. Vide *Figures*			
Walling. Vide *Antiquities*			
Walnuts. Enquiries relating to the bleeding of walnut trees - -	*Tonge*	V 1196	II 676 — 684
—— Observations on -	*Willoughby*	— 1201	
—— A description of a new kind of walnut trees discovered by - -	*Reneaume*	XXII 908	IV 2 323
Walpole, Horace. See *Stone*			
Warming Rooms. A proposal for warming rooms by the steam of boiling water conveyed in pipes along the walls -	*Cook*	XLIII 370	XI 1391
Washes. A table of the washes in Lincolnshire	*Merret*	XIX 392	II 267
Wasps. Observations about wasps, and the difference of their sexes -	*Derham*	XXXIII 53	VII 404
—— An account of some very curious wasps nests made of clay in Pennsylvania	*Bartram*	XLIII 363	XI 847
—— A description of the great black wasp from Pennsylvania - -	*Bartram*	XLVI 278	— 848
—— Two letters from Cambridge in New England,			

concern-

+ Watches. Investigations, founded on the theory of motion, for determining the times of vibration of watch balances. Atwood 1794:119.

Entry	Author	Tranſ.	Abridg.
concerning two ſmall ſpecies of waſps	*Harriſon*	XLVII 184	
WASPS. Some obſervations upon an American waſp's neſt - - -	*Mauduit*	XLIX 205	
—— Obſervations on the yellowiſh waſp of Pennſylvania - -	*Collinſon*	LIII 37	
—— An account of a ſingular ſpecies of waſp	*Felton*	LIV 53	
WATCHES. A narrative concerning the ſucceſs of pendulum watches at ſea for the longitudes	*Holmes*	I 13	I 555
—— Inſtructions concerning the uſe of pendulum-watches, for finding the longitude at ſea; together with a method of a journal for ſuch watches - -	*Hugens*	IV 937	— 547
—— An extract concerning very exact and portative watches - -	*Hugens*	X 272	— 465
—— Extract of a letter concerning the principle of exactneſs in the portable watches of his invention - -	*Leibnitz*	— 285	I 466
—— An inſtrument for ſeeing the ſun, moon, or ſtars paſs the meridian of any place, uſeful for ſetting watches in all parts of the world with the greateſt exactneſs, to correct ſun dials, to aſſiſt in the diſcovery of the longitudes of places	*Derham*	XXIV 1578	IV 464
—— Account of advantages of a newly invented machine much varied in its effects, and very uſeful for determining the perfect proportion between different moveables acting by levers and wheel and pinion	*Le Cerf*	LXVIII 950	
WATERS. (Agitation of various) Twenty ſeven letters giving an account of an extraordinary and ſurpriſing agitation of the waters, Nov. 1, 1755, though without any perceptible motion of the earth, having been obſerved in various parts of this iſland, both maritime and inland on the ſame day, and chiefly about the time, that the more violent commotions of both earth and waters, ſo very extenſively affected many very diſtant parts of the globe; in many letters tranſmitted to the Society; in which are ſpecified the times and places when and where they happened		XLIX 351	
Portſmouth - -	*Robertſon*	— 551	
Suſſex and Surry - -	*Webb*	— 353	
Guildford - -	*Ades*	— 357	

		Transf.	Abridg.
WATERS. (Agitation of various) Petworth	*Hodgson*	XLIX 358	
Cranbrook - -	*Tempest*	— 360	
Chevening - -	*Pringle*	— —	
Rotherith - -	*Mills*	— 361	
Peerless Poole, London -	*Birch*	— 362	
Rochford, Essex - -	*Thomlinson*	— 364	
Reading - -	*Philips*	— 365	
Reading - - -	*Blair*	— 367	
Sherburn Castle, Oxfordshire -	*Parker*	— 368	
Devonshire, Cornwall, Plymouth, Mount's bay, Penzance, &c. -	*Huxham*	— 371	
Mount's bay - -	*Borlase*	— 373	
Swanzey - -	*Blair*	— 379	
Norwich - -	*Arderon*	— 380	
Yarmouth - -	*Barber*	— —	
Hawkeshead, Cumberland -	*Harrison*	— 381	
Durham - -	*Cowper*	— 385	
Edinburgh - -	*Stevenson*	— 387	
Luss in Scotland -	*Colquhoun*	— 389	
Kinsale - -	*Nicola*	— 393	
Toplitz, Bohemia -	*Staplin*	— 395	
Hague - -	*De Hondt*	— 396	
Leyden - -	*Allmand*	— 397	
—— An extract of a letter, with an account of an extraordinary agitation of the water in a small lake at Closeburn, in the shire of Dumfries, Feb. 1, 1756 - -	*Kilpatrick*	— 521	
—— Extract of a letter concerning an extraordinary motion in the waters in the lake Ontario in North America	*Belcher*	— 544	
—— An account of the agitation of the waters on the 1st of November, 1755, in Scotland and Hamburgh	*Pringle*	— 550	
—— Extract of a letter relating to the agitation of the waters observed at Dartmouth, Nov. 1, 1755 - -	*Holdsworth*	— 643	
—— An account of the agitation of the sea at Antigua Nov. 1, 1755 -	*Affleck*	— 668	
—— An account of the extraordinary agitation of the waters, in several ponds in Hertfordshire, Nov. 1, 1755 -	*Rutherford*	— 684	
—— Some account of the extraordinary agitation of the waters in Mount's bay, and other places, on the 31st of March, 1761	*Borlase*	LII 418	
WATER. (Chemistry) Way of examining waters as			

+ Water (Chemistry) Experiments relating to the seeming conversion of water into air. Priestley 73: 414.

Thoughts on the constituent parts of water — — — — — Watt 74: 329, 354.

Experiments and observations relating to water — — — Priestley 75: 279.

the composition of water —— 78: 147. 79: 7.

Additional experiments and observations relating to the decomposition of water — — — — — — — Priestley, Withering, Keir — 313.

	Tranf.	Abridg.
to frefhnefs and faltnefs - *Boyle*	XVII 627	II 298
WATER. (Chemiftry) Several experiments about giving variety of tinctures to water, &c. *Southwell*	XX 87	III 656
—— An account of the filtring ftone of Mexico, and compared with other ftones, by which it is fhewn that it is of little or no ufe in purifying the waters which have paffed through it *Vaterus*	XXXIX 106	VIII 728
—— An account of fome trials to keep water and fifh fweet with lime-water - *Hales*	XLVIII 826	
—— An account of fome trials to fweeten ftinking water - - *Hales*	XLIX 339	
—— A letter on the folubility of iron in fimple water by the intervention of fixed air *Lane*	LIX 216	
—— The defcription of an apparatus for impregnating water with fixed air, and of the manner of conducting that procefs - *Nooth*	LXV 59	
WATER, LIME. See *Lime*		
WATER. (Gravity) An invention for eftimating the weight of water in water, with ordinary balances and weights - *Boyle*	IV 1001	I 520
—— A new experiment concerning an effect of the varying weight of the Atmofphere upon fome bodies in the water - *Boyle*	VII 5156	II 204
—— Some experiments and obfervations on the force of the preffure of the water at great depths *Anon.*	XVII 504	I 521
—— An extract of a letter giving an account of an experiment made in the bay of Bifcay of the preffure of water at various depths on a bottle clofe corked, and of Lay Well which ebbs and flows - - *Oliver*	XVII 908	— —
—— An account of an experiment touching the proportion of the weight of air, to the weight of a like bulk of water, without knowing the quantity of either - *Haukfbee*	XXV 2221	IV 2 180
—— An account of fome experiments in relation to the weight of common water under different circumftances - - *Haukfbee*	XXVI 221	
—— An account of an experiment touching the different denfities of common water from the greateft degrees of heat in our climate, to the freezing point, obferved by a thermometer *Haukfbee*	— 267	VI 2 181

	Tranſ.	Abridg.
WATER. (Gravity) An account of ſome experiments in relation tothe weight of common water under different circumſtances - *Haukſbee*	XXVI 269	IV 2 181
—— An experiment touching the weighing of bodies of the ſame ſpecies, but very unequal ſurfaces in common water, being of an equal weight in common air - - *Haukſbee*	— 306	— - 181
—— The ſpecific gravity of ſeveral metalline cubes, in compariſon with their like bulks of water *Haukſbee*	XXVIII 521	
—— A caution to be uſed in examining the ſpecific gravity of ſolids by weighing them in water *Jurin*	XXXI 223	VI 327
—— A courſe of experiments to aſcertain the ſpecific buoyancy of cork in different waters, the reſpective weights and buoyancy of ſalt water, and freſh water, and for determining the exact weight of human and other bodies in fluids - - *Wilkinſon*	LV 95	
WATER. (Hydraulics) A way of producing wind, by the fall of water *Pope*	I 21	I 498
—— Undertaking for raiſing of water *Moreland*	IX 25	— 537
—— A new way of raiſing water *Papin*	XV 1093	— 539
—— Letter concerning Dr. Papin's way of raiſing water - - - *Vincent*	— 1238	— —
—— Letter concerning Dr. Papin's new water engine - - *Tenon*	— 1254	— —
—— A full deſcription, with the uſe, of a new contrivance for raiſing water - *Papin*	— 1274	— 450
—— Anſwer to ſeveral objections made by Mr. Nuis againſt his engine for raiſing water by the rarefaction of the air - *Papin*	XVI 263	— 542
—— An account of the motion of running water *Jurin*	XXX 748	IV 435
—— A deſcription of an engine to raiſe water by help of quickſilver, invented by Haſkins, and improved by Deſaguliers - *Anon.*	XXXII 5	VI 352
—— A defence of the diſſertation on the motion of running water againſt the animadverſions of P. A. Michelotti - *Jurin*	— 179	— 431
—— An account of ſeveral experiments concerning the running of water in pipes, as it is retarded by friction and intermixed air, with a deſcription of a new machine, whereby pipes may be cleared of air, as the water runs along, without ſtand-pipes, or the help of any hand *Deſaguliers*	XXXIV 77	— 347

		Trans.	Abridg.
WATER (Hydraulics) A description of the water-works at London Bridge -	*Beighton*	XXXVII 5	VI 3 58
—— An account of a new engine for raising water by horses - - -	*Churchman*	XXXVIII 402	VIII 322
—— Of the measure and motion of running waters	*Jurin*	XLI 5	— 282
With the conclusion -	*Jurin*	— 65	
—— A narrative of a new invention of expanding fluids by their being conveyed into certain ignited vessels, where they are immediately rarified into an elastic impelling force sufficient to give motion to hydraulo-pneumatical and other engines for raising of water and other uses, &c.	*Payne*	XLI 821	VIII 638
—— Part of a letter containing a description of a water-wheel for mills, invented by Mr. Philip Williams - -	*Arderon*	XLIV 1	X 247
—— A description of a clepsydra, or water clock	*Hamilton*	— 171	— 428
—— An experimental enquiry, concerning the natural powers of water and wind to turn mills, and other machines depending on a circular motion - -	*Smeaton*	LI 100	
—— Problems concerning the fall of water under bridges, applied to the fall under London and Westminster Bridges -	*Robertson*	L 492	
—— Short and easy methods for finding the quantity and weight of water contained in a full pipe of any given height and diameter of bore, and consequently to find what degree of power would be required to work a common pump, or any other hydraulic engine, when the diameter of the pump bore, and the height to which the water is to be raised, are given	*Ferguson*	LV 61	
—— A memoir concerning the most advantageous construction of water-wheels, &c.	*Mallet*	LVII 372	
—— An account of a machine for raising water, executed at Oulton in Cheshire, in 1772	*Whitehurst*	LXV 277	
WATER. (Medicine) An account of what happened on syringing warm water into the thorax of a bitch - -	*Musgrave*	XX 181	III 78
—— The art of living under water; or a discourse concerning the means of furnishing air at the bottom of the sea in any ordinary depths	*Halley*	XXIX 492	IV 2 188

	Tranſ.	Abridg.
WATER (Medicine) An addition to the deſcription of the art of living under water - *Rogers*	XXXI 177	VI 350
—— Of the uſe of cold water in fevers *Cyrillus*	XXXVI 142	VII 635
—— Relation of a girl three years old, who remained a quarter of an hour under water without drowning - - *Green*	XLI 166	IX 241
—— Caſe of a large quantity of matter or water contained in cyſtis or bags adhering to the peritoneum, and not communicating with the cavity of the abdomen - *Graham*	— 708	— 187
—— A letter concerning a man who lived eighteen years on water - *Campbell*	XLII 240	— 238
—— An account of an extraordinary cyſtis in the liver, full of water - *Jernegan*	XLIII 305	XI 971
—— A propoſal for warming rooms by the ſteam of boiling water conveyed in pipes along the walls - - - *Cook*	— 370	— 1391
—— Account of the airs extracted from different kinds of waters, with thoughts on the ſalubrity of the air at different places *Fontana*	LXIX 432	
WATERS (Mineral.) Account of a pond in Somerſhire to which pigeons reſort, but cattle will not drink at it - *Anon.*	I 332	II 332
Further account of the (pond) vitriolate water, with ſome particulars touching waters *Anon.*	— 359	— —
—— An account of ſome ſanative-waters in Herefordſhire - - - *Beale*	— 358	——
—— An anſwer to the hydrologia chymica of Mr. W. Simpſon - *Wittie*	IV 999	
The anſwer enlarged - *Wittie*	— 1038	
—— Some reflections made on the enlarged account of Dr. Wittie's anſwer to hydrologia chymica, chiefly concerning the cauſe of the ſudden loſs of the virtues of mineral waters *Foot*	— 1050	— 365
—— Some conſiderations relating to Dr. Wittie's defence of Scarborough Spaw, with an account of a ſalt ſpring in Somerſetſhire, and of a medical ſpring in Dorſetſhire *Highmore*	— 1128	
—— Diſcourſe relating to the notes of Dr. Foot in vol. IV. 1050, and of Dr. Highmore in vol. IV. 1128, concerning mineral waters, and extracts made out of them - *Wittie*	V 1074	
—— Advertiſements concerning ſprings, waters, petrifying and metallizing waters, &c. *Beal*	X 357	
—— Some queries whereby to examine mineral waters - - - *Petty*	XIV 802	— —

Water (Medicine) Experiments and observations on the influence of immersion in fresh and salt water, hot and cold, on the powers of the living body. Currie. 1792: 199.

	Transf.	Abridg.
WATER (Mineral) Two letters concerning some mineral waters - - *Cay*	XX 365	
—— Observations on rain-water - *Leeuwenhoek*	XXIII 1152	
—— A short account of the nature and virtues of the Pyrmont waters, with some observations on their chalybeate qualities *Slare*	XXX 564	IV 2 201
—— An historico-physical observation on the brass waters of Nisol commonly called cement-watszer, changing iron to brass *Belius*	XL 351	VIII 645
—— An examination of the Chiltenham mineral water, which may serve as a method in general for examining mineral waters *Seckenburg*	XLI 830	— 650
—— Experiments by way of analysis upon the water of the Dead Sea, upon the hot spring near Tiberiades, and upon Hamman Pharoan water - - - *Perry*	XLII 48	— 643
—— An account of the Carlsbad mineral waters in Bohemia - - *Milles*	L 25	
—— Thoughts on the different impregnations of mineral waters; more particularly concerning the existence of sulphur in some of them *Rutty*	LI 275	
—— Extract of an essay entituled, On the uses of a knowledge of mineral exhalations when applied to discover the principles and properties of mineral waters, the nature of burning fountains, and of those poisonous lakes which the antients called Averni *Brownrigg*	LV 236	
—— Experiments on Rathbone-Place water *Cavendish*	LVII 92	
—— An account of the sulphureous mineral waters of Castle-Loed and Fairburn in the county of Ross, and of the salt purging water of Pitkeathly in the county of Perth, in Scotland *Monro*	LXII 15	
—— Continuation of an experimental inquiry concerning the nature of the mineral elastic spirit or, air contained in the Pouhon water, and other acidulæ - - *Brownrigg*	LXIV 357	
—— See *Baths*, *Birch*, *Sea*, *Spout*		
WATER. (Natural history) Of a place in England, where, without petrifying water, wood is turned into stone - *Boyle*	I 101	II 325
—— The causes of mineral springs further inquired into and the strange and secret changes of liquors, examined - - *Beale*	IV 1131	— 712
—— A particular account of the origin of fountains,		

WAT

	Tranf.	Abridg.
and to shew that the rain and snow waters are sufficient to make fountains and rivers run perpetually - - *Anon.*	X 447	II 329
WATER (Natural history) Observations concerning some little animals observed in rain, well, sea, and snow water; as also in water where pepper had lain infused - *Leeuwenhoek*	XII 821	III 683
With the manner of observing them *Leeuwenhoek*	— 844	— —
—— Experiments and observations about the natron of Egypt, and the Nitrian water *Leigh*	XIV 609	II 525
—— Several observations and experiments on the animalcula in pepper water *Sir Edmund King*	XVII 861	III 654
—— The history of the generation of an insect by him called the Wolf; with observations on insects bred in rain water, in apples, cheese, &c. - - *Leeuwenhoek*	XVIII 194	— 685
—— Some microscopical observations of vast numbers of animalcula seen in water *Harris*	XIX 254	— 652
—— An account of an extraordinary eruption of water, in June, 1686, in Yorkshire *R. P.*	XX 382	II 328
—— Observations on some animalcula in water *Leeuwenhoek*	XXIII 1430	V 2 266
—— Part of a letter giving a farther account of an eruption of waters in Craven *Thoresby*	XXV 2236	IV 2 192
—— A picture and description of a water insect not before described - *Klein*	XL 150	IX 6
A description of the same sort of insect found in Kent - - *Brown*	— 153	— 7
With an addition - *Mortimer*	— —	
—— Observations on the mouths of eels in vinegar, and also a strange aquatic animal *Baker*	XLII 416	— 38
—— Observations upon several species of small water insects of the polypus kind - *Trembley*	XLIV 627	XI 807
—— An account of some remarkable insects of the polype kind found in the water near Brussels in Flanders - - *Bredy*	XLIX 248	
WATERS. (Natural philosophy) Some trials about the air usually harboured and concealed in the pores of water - - *Boyle*	V 2018	
—— Some experiments about freezing, and the difference betwixt common fresh water ice, and that of the sea water *Lister*	XV 836	II 164
—— An account of the evaporation of Water as it was experimented in Gresham College in

		Tranſ.	Abridg.
1693, with ſome obſervations thereon	*Halley*	XVIII 183	II 110
WATERS (Natural Philoſophy) Microſcopical obſervations and experiments - -		XIX 280	
—— Letter concerning the different taſtes of waters	*Leeuwenhoek*	XXII 899	V 2 266
—— Letter concerning making water ſubſervient to the viewing both near and diſtant objects, with the deſcription of a natural reflecting microſcope - - - - - -	*Gray*	XVIII 539	I 195
Farther account of his water microſcope	*Gray*	XIX 353	— 209
—— An experiment ſhewing that the ſeemingly ſpontaneous aſcenſion of water in ſmall tubes, open at both ends, is the ſame in vacuo as in the open air - -	*Haukſbee*	XXV 2223	V 279
—— Several experiments touching the ſeeming ſpontaneous aſcent water -	*Haukſbee*	XXVI 258	IV 2 181
Continuation - -	*Haukſbee*	— 265	
—— An experiment touching the freezing of common water, and water purged of air	*Haukſbee*	— 302	— - 182
—— An account of an experiment touching the freezing of common water tinged with a liquid ſaid to be extracted from ſhell-lac	*Haukſbee*	— 304	— - 182
—— An account of ſome experiments touching the keeping of fiſhes in water under different circumſtances - -	*Haukſbee*	XXVII 431	IV 2 182
—— Part of a letter concerning the aſcent of water between two glaſs planes -	*Taylor*	— 538	IV 423
	Haukſbee	— 539	IV 2 182
—— An account of ſome experiments, with an enquiry into the cauſe of the aſcent and ſuſpenſion of water in capillary tubes	*Jurin*	XXX 739	IV 423
—— An account of ſome new experiments relating to the action of glaſs tubes upon water and quickſilver - -	*Jurin*	— 1083	— 428
—— Experiments and obſervations of the freezing of water in vacuo -	*Fahrenheit*	XXXIII 78	VI 2 51
—— A letter concerning the electricity of water	*Gray*	XXXVII 227	— - 22
—— An experiment to prove that water when agitated by fire is infinitely more elaſtic than air in the ſame circumſtances -	*Clayton*	XLI 162	VIII 466
—— A diſſertation on the nature of evaporation, and ſeveral phænomena of air, water, and boiling liquors - -	*Hamilton*	I 146	
—— Experiments to prove that water is not incompreſſible - -	*Canton*	LII 640	

	Transf.	Abridg.
WATER. (Natural Philosophy) Experiments and observations on the compressibility of water, and some other fluids — *Canton*	LIV 261	
—— The supposed effect of boiling upon water, in disposing it to freeze more readily, ascertained by experiments — *Black*	LXV 124	
—— On the variation of the temperature of boiling water — — *Shuckburgh*	LXIX 362	
WAX. An advertisement of a way of making more lively counterfeits of nature in wax, than are extant in painting; and of a new kind of maps in low relievo, both practised in France *Anon.*	I 99	I 193
—— Extract of two letters concerning the effects of a cane of black sealing-wax, and a cane of brimstone, in electrical experiments *Miles*	XLIV 27	X 317
—— Observations on the Abbe Mazeas's letter on the Count de Caylus's method of imitating the ancient painting in burnt wax *Parsons*	XLIX 655	
WEATHER. See *Barometer, Meteorological Observations, Thermometer*		
WEATHER CORD. See *Hygrometer*		
WEAVERS. Account of the weavers alarm, vulgo larum — — — *Arderon*	XLIII 555	XI 1392
WEAVING. An account of Mr. Le Blon's principles of printing in imitation of painting, and of weaving of tapestry in the same manner as brocades — *Mortimer*	XXXVII 101	VI 469
WEDGE. An account of an experiment concerning the angle required to suspend a drop of oil of oranges, at certain stations, between two glass planes, placed in the form of a wedge *Hauksbee*	XXVII 473	IV 2 182
WEED. An account of a new dye from the berries of a weed in South Carolina *Lind*	LIII 238	
WEIGHTS. An invention for estimating the weight of water in water with ordinary balances and weights — — *Boyle*	IV 1001	I 520
—— Of the weight of a cubic foot of divers grain — — *Anon.*	XV 926	— 522
Further list of specific gravities of bodies *Anon.*	— 927	— 523
—— An account of some experiments in relation to the weight of common water under different circumstances — *Hauksbee*	XXVI 221

+ An account of a vegetable Wax from Brazil. Brande. 1811: 261

+ Weight. An account of some experiments on the loss of weight in Bodies on being melted or heated Fordyce 75: 361

	Trans.	Abridg.
WEIGHTS. An account of some experiments in relation to the weight of common water under different circumstances - *Haukshee*	— 269	IV 2 181
—— Experiments touching the time required in the descent of different bodies of different magnitudes and weights in common air from a certain height - - *Haukshee*	XXVII 196	— - 182
—— An account of an experiment explaining a mechanic paradox, viz. that two bodies of equal weight suspended on a certain balance, do not lose their equilibrium, by being removed one farther from, the other nearer to, the center - - *Desaguliers*	XXXVII 125	VI 310
—— A letter of weighing the strength of electrical effluvia - - *Ellicot*	XLIV 96	X 324
—— A course of experiments to ascertain the respective weights and buoyancy of salt-water and fresh water, and for determining the exact weight of human and other bodies in fluids - - - *Wilkinson*	LV 95	
WEIGHTS AND MEASURES. An experiment to compare Paris weights as they are now used with the English weights - *Desaguliers*	XXXI 112	VII 4 46
—— An account of the analogy betwixt English weights and measures of capacity *Barlow*	XLI 457	IX 488
—— An account of the proportion of the English and French measures and weights from the standard of the same kind at the Royal Society - - - *Anon.*	XLII 185	— 489
—— An account of a comparison lately made by some gentlemen of the Royal Society of the standard of a yard, and the several weights lately made for their use; with the original standards of measures and weights in the Exchequer, and some others kept for public use at Guildhall, Founders Hall, the Tower, &c. - - *Graham*	— 541	— 491
—— A state of the English weights and measures of capacity, as they appear from the laws as well ancient as modern; with some considerations thereon; being an attempt to prove that the present avoirdupoise weight is the legal and ancient standard for the weights and measures of this kingdom *Reynardson*	XLVI 54	XI 1356

	Trans.	Abridg.
WEIGHTS AND MEASURES. Short and easy methods for finding the number of Troy pounds contained in any given number of avoirdupoise pounds, and vice versa *Ferguson*	LV 61	
~~WEIGHTS. Remarks upon two Etruscan weights or coins never before published *Swinton*~~ (See Coins)	~~LXI 82~~	
—— An inquiry to shew what was the ancient English weight and measure according to the laws or statutes prior to the reign of Henry the Seventh *Norris*	LXV 48	
WEIGHTS. See *Coins*, *Measures*		
WEIGHT. Extract of a letter concerning two men of an extraordinary bulk and weight *Knowlton*	XLIV 100	XI 1245
WELL. The description of a well and earth in Lancashire, taking fire by a candle approached to it *Shirley*	II 482	III 149
—— An account of wells, both salt and sweet, digged near the sea at Bermudas *Norwood*	— 565	II 298
—— Instances, hints, and applications, relating to a main point, solicited in the preface to this fourth volume, concerning the use may be made of vaults, deep wells, and cold conservatories, to find out the cause, or to promote the generation of salt, minerals, metals, crystals, gems, stones of divers kinds, &c. *Beale*	IV 1135	
—— Observations concerning some little animals observed in rain, well, sea, and snow-water; as also in water where pepper had lain infused *Leeuwenboek*	XII 821	III 683
With the manner of observing them *Leeuwenboek*	— 844	— —
—— A letter from the king's officers at Sheerness giving an account of what they met with in opening an ancient well near Queensborough, in Kent, Jan. 8, 1729 *Collison*	XXXVI 191	IV 2 244
—— An observation of an extraordinary damp in a well in the isle of Wight *Cooke*	XL 379	VIII 658
—— A letter concerning a burning well at Brosely *Mason*	XLIV 370	X 586
—— An account of a new medicinal well, lately discovered near Moffat in Annandale, in the county of Dumfries *Walker*	L 117	
—— Extract of a letter from Calcutta, concerning a burning rock, and a burning well *Wood*	LII 415	

—— Descriptions of the King's Wells at Sheerness, Languard-Fort, and Harwich. Page. 74: 6.

Observations on the heat of Wells and Springs in the Island of Jamaica. J. Hunter. 78: 53.

An account of the means employed to obtain an overflowing Well. Vulliamy. 1797: 325.

4 Weights and measures. An account of some endeavours to ascertain a standard of weights & measure. Shuckburgh 1798:133.

Well. On an ebbing and flowing stream discovered by boring in the harbour of Bridlington. — Storer. 1815:54.

+ Whales. Observations on the structure and oeconomy of Whales. Hunter. 77: 371.
Some particulars in the anatomy of a Whale. Abernethy. 1796: 27.

		Trans.	Abridg.
Wen. An account of an extraordinary tumour or wen lately cut off the cheek of a person in Scotland - -	*Bower*	XXX 713	V 217
Wereedale. A letter concerning a subterraneous cavern in Weredale -	*Durant*	XLIV 221	X 588
Westashton Well Water. An examination of Westashton well water	*Hankewitz*	XLI 828	VIII 649
Westminster Bridge. Problems concerning the fall of water under bridges, applied to the falls under London and Westminster Bridges	*Robertson*	L 492	
Whale. (Astronomy) Remarks about the new star in the neck of the -	*Hevelius*	V 2023	
Whale. (Fish and fishing) Of the new American whale fishing about the Bermudas	*Anon.*	I 11	II 844
—— A further relation of the whale fishing about the Bermudas, and on the coast of New-England, and New Netherland	*Anon.*	— 132	
—— An account of the whale fishing at Bermudas, and of such whales as have the sperma-ceti in them - - -	*Norwood*	II 565	— 268
—— A letter concerning the whales at Bermudas and sperma-ceti - -	*Stafford*	III 792	— —
—— A letter concerning the flesh of whales, crystaline humour of the eye of whales, fish and other creatures, and of the use of the eye-lids	*Leeuwenhoek*	XXIV 1723	V 2 267
—— A letter containing observation upon the seminal vessels, muscular fibres, and blood of whales - -	*Leeuwenhoek*	XXVII 438	V 2 267
—— Of ambergris found in whales	*Boylston*	XXXIII 193	VII 423
—— An essay upon the natural history of whales, with a particular account of the ambergris found in the sperma ceti-whale	*Dudley*	— 256	— 424
—— An account of a machine for killing of whales	*Bond*	XLVII 429	
—— Vide *Cachalot*			
Wheat. An odd effect of thunder and lightning upon wheat and rye in the granaries at Dantzick - -	*Kirkby*	VIII 692	II 174
—— Letter about the grains resembling wheat which fell lately in Wiltshire -	*Cole*	XVI 281	
—— An account of some experiments by Mr. Miller of Cambridge, on the sowing of wheat	*William Watson*	LVIII 203	
—— A discourse proving from experiments, that the			

	Trans.	Abridg.
larger the wheels of a coach, &c. are, the more easily they may be drawn over a stone, or such like obstacle that lies in the way *Anon.*	XV 856	I 503
WHEEL. Account of the advantages of a newly invented machine much varied in its effects, and very useful for determining the perfect proportion between different moveables acting by levers and wheel and pinion - *Le Cerf*	LXVIII 950	
—— A memoir concerning the most advantageous construction of water-wheels, &c. *Mallet*	LVII 372	
WHELP. An account of an animal, resembling a whelp, voided per anum by a male greyhound *Halley*	XIX 316	II 904
WHITENESS. A letter concerning the whiteness on the tongue in fevers - *Leeuwenhoek*	XXV 2456	V 2 267
WHIRLWIND. Account of a whirlwind in Northamptonshire - - *Anon.*	XVIII 192	II 104
—— Account of a whirlwind which happened at Cerne Abbas in Dorsetshire, Oct. 30, 1731. *Derby*	XLI 229	VIII 499
—— An account of a meteor seen in New England, May 10, 1760, and of a whirlwind felt in that country, July 10, 1760 *Winthorp*	LII 6	
WIDGELL HALL. See *Figures*		
WILLIAMS. See *Water-Wheel*		
WILLOW. Observations on insects lodging themselves in old willows - *King*	V 2098	II 772
———————— *Willoughby*	— 2100	
—— Letter concerning excrescences growing on willow leaves - *Leeuwenhoek*	XXII 786	V 2 266
—— An account of the success of the bark of the willow in the cure of agues - *Stone*	LIII 195	
See Harmattan WIND. A way of producing wind by the fall of water - - *Pope*	I 21	I 498
—— Observations made in mines, and at sea, occasioning a conjecture about the origin of wind *Colepresse*	II 481	II 105
—— Extract of several letters from Edinburg, giving an account of an obelisk thrown down by a violent wind, of an extraordinary lake in Lord Lovat's lands in Scotland, of Lake Ness, and of a petryfying rivulet - *Makenzy*	X 307	— 104
—— Advertisements concerning black-winds and tempests - - *Beal*	— 357	
—— The breath of the sea plants probably the mate-		

rial

		Tranſ.	Abridg.
rial cauſe of the trade or tropick winds	*Liſter*	XIV 489	II 129
WIND. A letter concerning the uſe which may be made of the following hiſtory of the weather	*Plot*	XV 930	— 46
Obſervations of the wind, weath r, and height of Mercury in the barometer, at Oxford	*Plot*	— 932	
— Extract of a letter concerning the cauſes of ſeveral winds	*Garden*	— 1148	— 129
— An hiſtorical account of the trade winds, and monſoons, obſervable in the ſeas between and near the tropicks, with an attempt to aſſign the phyſical cauſe of the ſaid winds	*Halley*	XVI 153	— 153
— Part of a letter accompanying his obſervations of the height of the Mercury in the barometer, rains, winds, &c. for the year 1698	*Derham*	XXI 45	— 73
— Obſervations of the weather made in a voyage to China, 1700	*Cunningham*	XXIV 1639	
A regiſter of the wind and wea her at China, with the obſervations of the mercurial barometer at Chuſan from Nov. 1700, to Jan. 1702	*Cunningham*	— 1648	IV 2 26
— A proſpect of the weather, winds, and height of the Mercury in the barometer on the firſt day of the month, and of the whole rain in every month in 1703, and beginning of 1704, at Townley in Lancaſhire	*Townley*		
And at Upminſter	*Derham*	— 1877	
— Tables of the barometrical altitudes at Zurich in Switzerland, in the year 1708, by Scheuhzer, and at Upminſter in England, by Derham, as alſo the rain at Piſa in Italy in 1707, and 1708, by Tilli, and at Zurich in 1708, and at Upminſter in all that time: with remarks on the ſame table, as alſo on the winds, heats, and cold, and divers other matters occurring in thoſe three different parts of Europe	*Derham*	XXVI 342	
— An account of an extraordinary ſtream of wind which ſhot through part of the pariſhes of Termonomumgam and Urney, in the county of Tyrone, Oct. 11, 1752	*Henry*	XLVIII 1	
— Letters concerning the cauſe of the aſcent of vapour and exhalation, and thoſe of winds; and of the general phænomena of the weather and barometer	*Eeles*	XLIX 124	

		Transf.	Abridg.
WIND.	An experimental enquiry concerning the natural powers of water and wind to turn mills and other machines depending on a circular motion — *Smeaton*	LI 100	
——	A letter containing a new manner of measuring the velocity of wind - *Brice*	LVI 224	
——	Observations on the state of air, winds, weather, &c. made at Prince of Wales's Fort on the north-west coast of Hudson's Bay in 1768, and 1769 - *Dymond and Wales*	LX 137	
WIND GAGE.	Description and use of a portable wind gage - *Lind*	LXV 353	
WIND MACHINE.	Observations on Mr. Sutton's invention to extract foul and stinking air out of ships, with critical remarks upon the use of wind sails - *W. Watson*	XLII 62	VIII 630
——	Of the degrees and quantities of wind requisite to move the heavier kinds of wind machines. *Stedman*	LXVII 493	
WINDPIPE.	An account of grass found in the wind pipes of some animals - *Anon.*	I. 100	II 869
——	An account of a polypus coughed up by the windpipe - *Saunder*	XXXIV 262	VII 503
——	An account of some peculiar advantages in the structure of the aspera arteria, or windpipes of several birds, and in the land tortoise *Parsons*	LVI 204	
WINDOWS.	A dissertation on the antiquity of glass in windows - *Nixon*	L 601	
——	See *Glass*		
WINDSOR LOAM.	A letter concerning Windsor loam *Hill*	XLIV 458	X 605
WINE.	Of the globules in the blood and in the dregs of wine *Leeuwenhoek*	XXXII 436	VII 562
——	An account of the Tokay and other wines in Hungary - *Douglas*	LXIII 292	
WINTER.	Account of damage done in his garden by the preceding winter - *Evelyn*	XIV 559	II 153
——	An account of the lately invented stove for preserving plants in the green-house in winter *Cullum*	XVIII 191	—— 750
WIRE.	An account of the effect of electricity in shortening of wires - *Nairne*	LXX 334	
WOLF.	The history of the generations of an insect by him called the wolf; with some observations on insects bred in rain water, in apples, cheese, &c. - *Leeuwenhoek*	XVIII 194	III 685

+Wire. An Account of Wire being shortened by lightning. Nairne. 73: 223.

A [illegible] method of drawing extremely fine Wires. Wollaston. 1813: 114.

Observations tending to show that the Wolf, Jackal and Dog, are all of the same species. Hunter 77: 253. 79: 160.

		Trans.	Abridg.
Wolf. An anatomical description of worms found in the kidneys of wolves -	*Klein*	XXXVI 269	VII 456
Woman. An account of a woman who had a double matrix - -	*Vassal*	IV 969	III 205
—— A letter concerning a woman of 62 years of age, that lost her leg and greatest part of her thigh by a gangrene -	*Calep*	XXVI 41	V 389
—— A letter containing the case of a woman who had her menses regularly to 70 years of age	*Yonge*	XXVIII 236	— 360
—— An account of what appeared on opening the big-bellyed woman near Haman in Shropshire, who was supposed to have continued many years with child -	*Hollings*	XXIX 452	— 293
—— An account of an extrauterine foetus taken out of a woman that had continued five years and a half in the body -	*Houstoun*	XXXII 387	VII 355
—— On the preternatural structure of the genital parts of a woman -	*Huxham*	— 408	— 546
History of the same woman	*Oliver*	— 413	— 548
—— A letter concerning the preternatural structure of the pudenda in a woman	*Bennet*	XXXIII 142	— 551
—— Two newly discovered arteries in women going to the Ovaria -	*Kanby*	XXXIV 159	— 541
—— Account of a woman 63 years of age, who gave suck to two of her grand children	*Stack*	XLI 140	IX 206
—— Case of one who had a foetus in her abdomen nine years - -	*Bromfield*	— 697	
—— An abstract of the remarkable case of a woman from whom a foetus was extracted that had been lodged in one of the fallopian tubes 13 years	*Mounsey*	XLV 131	XI 1032
—— Extract of a letter containing the particulars of the cure of a wound in the cornea, and of a laceration of the uvea in the eye of a woman	*Acry*	— 411	— 954
—— Account of the remarkable alteration in the colour of a negro woman	*Bate*	LI 759	
—— Account of an extraordinary steatomatous tumour in the abdomen of a woman	*Hanly*	LXI 131	
Womb. Letter concerning the structure of the womb	*Malpighius*	XIV 630	III 197
—— An account of an uncommon case of a dropsy between the coats of the womb	*Anon.*	XVIII 20	— 205
—— Account of a puppy in the womb that received no nourishment by the mouth	*Brady*	XXIV 2076	V 310

		Trans.	Abridg.
WOMB. Account of a child's crying in the womb	*Derham*	XXVI 485	
————————		— 487	V 310
—— An account of a large bony substance found in the womb, 1733 -	*Hody*	XXXIX 189	IX 191
—— Letter concerning the extirpation of an excrescence from the womb -	*Burton*	XLVI 520	XI 1022
WOOD. Of a place in England, where, without petrifying water, wood is turned into stone	*Boyle*	I 101	II 325
—— Of the abundance of, found under ground in Lincolnshire -	*Anon*	V 2050	— 423
—— An account of the appearance of several woods and their vessels -	*Leeuwenhoek*	XIII 197	III 684
—— An extract of a letter containing several observations on the texture of the bones of animals compared with that of wood	*Leeuwenhoek*	XVII 838	— 685
—— Observations upon the vessels in several sorts of wood - -	*Leeuwenhoek*	XXXI 134	VI 2 336
—— An account of the poison wood tree in New England - -	*Dudley*	— 145	— - 307
————————	*Sherard*	— 147	— - 308
—— An account of a capricorn beetle found alive in a cavity within a sound piece of wood	*Mortimer*	XLI 861	IX 11
—— A short description of some high mountains on which are a great quantity of fossil wood	*Hollman*	LI 506	
—— The principal properties of the engine for turning ovals in wood or metals, and of the instruments for drawing ovals upon paper, demonstrated - -	*Ludlam*	LXX 378	
WOOD-PECKERS. A description of that curious natural machine, the wood-pecker's tongue	*Waller*	XXIX 509	V 55
WOOLLEN MANUFACTURE. An account of a balance of a new construction supposed to be of use in the woollen manufacture -	*Ludlam*	LV 205	
WORCESTER. See *Figures*			
WORMS. Observations about shining worms in oysters - -	*Auzout*	I 203	III 826
—— A relation of worms that eat out stones	*De la Voye*	— 321	II 787
—— Observations on several sorts of worms found in the guts - -	*Lister*	VIII 6060	III 119

Wombat. An account of some peculiarities in the anatomical structure of the Wombat. Home. 1808: 304.

Wootz. see Steel.

		Transf.	Abridg.
Worms. Extract of a letter concerning odd worms vomited by children	Lister	X 391	III 135
—— Relation of a worm voided by urine	Ent	XII 1009	— 135
—— Microscopical observations about animals in the scurff of the teeth, the substance called worms in the nose, the cuticula of scales	Leeuwenhoek	XIV 568	— 684
—— A letter giving an account of the Connough worm	Molyneux	XV 876	II 758
—— Lumbricus hydropicus, or an essay to prove that hydatides often met with in morbid animal bodies, are a species of worms or imperfect animals	Tyson	XVII 506	III 133
—— Letter concerning worms found in the tongue and other parts of the body, with the manner of extracting them	Dent	XVIII 219	— 137
Another letter confirming the same operation	Lewis	— 222	— —
—— Part of a letter from Fort St. George, in the East Indies, giving an account of the long worm which is troublesome to the inhabitants of those parts	Lister	XIX 417	— 138
—— Letter concerning the worms in sheeps livers	Leeuwenhoek	XXII 509	— 688
—— Letter concerning worms pretended to be taken from the teeth	Leeuwenhoek	— 635	— 686
—— Observations concerning the worms of human bodies	Bonomi	XXIII 1296	V 199
—— Part of a letter concerning worms observed in sheeps livers, and pasture grounds	Leeuwenhoek	XXIV 1522	V 2 226
—— A letter concerning worms in the heads of sheep	Thorpe	— 1890	V 16
—— An anatomical description of worms found in the kidneys of wolves	Klein	XXXVI 269	VII 456
—— A dissertation on the worms which destroy the piles on the coast of Holland and Zealand	Basler	XLI 276	IX 12
Part of a letter concerning some worms whose parts live after they have been cut asunder	Lord	XLII 522	— 117
—— A letter with some microscopical observations on the farina of the red lily, and of worms discovered in smutty corn	Needham	— 634	VIII 816
—— An account of worms in animal bodies	Nicholls	XLIX 246	
—— Case of a boy troubled with convulsive fits cured by the discharge of worms	Oram	L 518	

Another

		Transf.	Abridg.
Another account *Gozz*	L 521		
More observations *Wal.*	— 836		
WORMS. Observations on various sorts of worms as well human as from horses *Limbourg*	LVI 126		
WOUND. Account of a child born with a large wound in the breast supposed to proceed from the force of imagination *Cyprianus*	XIX 291	III 222	
—— A brief narrative of the shot of Dr Robert Fielding with a musket ball, and its strange manner of coming out of his head, where it had lain near thirty years, written by himself *Fielding*	XXVI 317	V 205	
—— An account of part of the colon hanging out of a wound for 14 years *Vater*	XXXI 89	VII 515	
—— An essay upon the use of the bile in the animal oeconomy found on an observation of a wound in the gall bladder *Stuart*	XXXVI 341	— 572	
—— Some observations on wounds in the guts *Amyand*	XXXIX 329	VIII 131	
—— An account of a wound which the late Lord Carpenter received at Brihuega, whereby a bullet remained near his gullet for a year wanting a few days *Carpenter*	XL 316		
—— The cure of a wound in the cornea of the eye cured by *Thomas Baker*	XLI 133	IX 121	
—— A remarkable cure of a wound of the head complicated with a large fracture and depression of the skull, the dura mater and brain wounded and lacerated *Cagua*	— 495	— 118	
—— Extract of a letter concerning the particulars of the cure of a wound in the cornea, and of a laceration of the uvea in the eye of a woman *Aery*	XLV 411	XI 954	
—— Case of a man wounded in the left eye by a small sword *Geach*	LIII 234		
—— An account of the successful application of sal. to wounds made by the bite of rattle snakes *Gale*	LV 244		
—— An extraordinary cure of wounded intestines *Nourse*	LXVI 426		
WRITINGS. Copy of a letter concerning the books and antient writings dug out of the ruins of an edifice near the site of the old city of Herculaneum, to Monsignor Cerati of Pisa; with a translation by Mr. Locke *Anon.*	XLIX 112		
—— Extract of a letter concerning a supposed connection between the hieroglyphical writing of antient Egypt, and the characteristic writing which

+ York. Latitude and Longitude of York - - - - - - E. Pigott 76:409

		Transf.	Abridg.
is in use at this day among the Chinese	*Morton*	LIX 489	
WRITING. The elements of a short hand	*Jeake*	XLV 345	XI 1381
Remarks on Mr. Jeake's plan for short-hand	*Byrom*	— 388	— 1384
WRITTEN MOUNTAINS. A letter containing an account of his journey from Cairo in Egypt to the Written Mountains, in the Desart of Sinai	*Montagu*	LVI 40	
WROXETER. Two letters relating to Wroxeter in Shropshire - -	*Baxter*	XXV 2228	
WIRTEMBERG ENGINE. See *Syphon*			

X.

		Transf.	Abridg.
XENOPHON. Letter concerning an eclipse mentioned by Xenophon -	*Costard*	XLVIII 155	

Y.

		Transf.	Abridg.
YARD. An account of a comparison lately made by some gentlemen of the Royal Society of the standard of a yard, and the several weights lately made for their use; with the original standards of measures and weights in the Exchequer, and some others kept for public use, at Guildhall, Founders-hall, the Tower, &c.	*Graham*	XLII 541	IX 491
—— A problem for finding the year of the Julian period by a new and very easy method	*De Billy*	I 324	III 398
YEW TREE. A letter concerning the farina foecundans of the yew tree -	*Badcock*	XLIV 189	X 757
YORK. Vide *Antiquities*, *Bas-Relief*			
YOUNES EBN. Translation of a passage in, with some remarks thereon -	*Costard*	LXVII 231	

Z.

	Tranſ.	Abridg.
ZANGARI AND BANDI, COUNTESS CORNELIA. An extract of an Italian treatiſe, written by Joſeph Bianchini upon the death of the Counteſs Cornelia Zangari and Bandi of Ceſena *Rolli*	XLIII 447	XI 1068
ZENITH. Some thoughts concerning the ſun and moon, when near the horizon appearing larger than when in the zenith *Logan*	XXXIX 404	VIII 377
ZETLAND. Two letters concerning the Iſlands of Zetland - - *Preſton*	XLIII 57	XI 1328
ZINC. On the uſe of an amalgam of zinc for the purpoſe of electrical excitation *Higgins*	LXVIII 861	
ZIRCHNITZER SEA. An account concerning an uncommon lake, called the Zirchnitzer ſea in Carniola - - *Brown*	IV 1083	II 306
—— Some queries and anſwers concerning a ſtrange lake in Carniola, called the Zirchnits ſea *Brown*	IX 194	— 306
—— A full and accurate deſcription of the wonderful Lake of Zirknitz in Carniola *Valvaſor*	XVI 411	— 307
ZODIAC. The obſervations of the ancients concerning the obliquity of the Zodiac *Bernard*	XIV 721	I 260
—— A letter containing a ſketch of the ſigns of the zodiac, found in a Pagoda, near Cape Camorin in India - - *Call*	LXII 353	
ZOOPHYTES. A diſſertation on zoophytes *Baſter*	LII 108	
—— Letter on the animal nature of the genus of zoophites called Corallina *Ellis*	LVII 404	
ZOOPHYTON. A letter concerning a zoophyton ſomewhat reſembling the flower of the marygold - - *Hughes*	XLII 590	XI 111

B L

Zeolite. On the composition of Zeolite. Smithson. 1811: 171.

+ Zoophytes. Chemical experiments on Zoophytes. Hatchett. 1800: 327.

www.ingramcontent.com/pod-product-compliance
Lightning Source LLC
Chambersburg PA
CBHW081836230426
43669CB00018B/2727